Of Gods and Monsters

"To a new world of Gods and Monsters!"

— Ernest Thesiger, *Bride of Frankenstein*

Of Gods and Monsters

A Critical Guide
to Universal Studios'
Science Fiction, Horror
and Mystery Films, 1929–1939

by JOHN T. SOISTER

McFarland & Company, Inc., Publishers
Jefferson, North Carolina, and London

British Library Cataloguing-in-Publication data are available

Library of Congress Cataloguing-in-Publication Data

Soister, John T., 1950–
Of gods and monsters : a critical guide to Universal Studios'
science fiction, horror and mystery films, 1929–1939 /
by John T. Soister
p.   cm.
Includes bibliographical references and index.
ISBN 0-7864-0454-X (case binding : 50# alkaline paper) ∞
1. Universal Pictures Company — Catalogs.
2. Horror films — Catalogs.
3. Science fiction films — Catalogs.
4. Detective and mystery films — Catalogs.
I. Title.
PN1999.U57S65   1999
016.79143'615 — DC21   98-38144   CIP

Manufactured in the United States of America

McFarland & Company, Inc., Publishers
Box 611, Jefferson, North Carolina 28640

This book is dedicated to my wonderful wife, Nancy,
who may not understand why I care so much for these old films,
but will never (I hope) wonder why I am so much in love with her;

and to my children, Katelyn, Jake, and Jeremy,
who have learned from their Dad
that Karloff's Monster was nothing more than an overgrown child,
and vice versa.

TABLE OF CONTENTS

THE FILMS

Acknowledgments

I want to give credit here to those poor devils who encouraged me, aided and abetted me, loaned me stuff, gave me information or advice, and lifted me up when I was down. These are the people who made this book possible.

Many thanks and a tip of my Sunday hat to my buddy, John Duvoli, who started me writing again, and to the lovely Linda — Mrs. Duvoli — who has put up with both of us over the years. (To my sister, Cheryl; my brother, Bill; my Mom, my Dad, and my Grandmother — who have put up with me since my birth — there aren't thanks enough.) Thanks to Greg Luce (of Sinister Cinema) and George Stover (of Baltimore's Cinemacabre Video); without them, I couldn't have run tapes backwards and forwards in order to discover that Lester Matthews wore a rug or that Paul is dead. Thanks to Gary Don Rhodes for cheerfully sharing information on *Postal Inspector*, and to Madeline F. Matz of the Library of Congress for facts on a half-dozen obscurities. A bow from the waist to Richard Koszarski of the American Museum of the Moving Image for furnishing some superlative graphics and for unearthing some reel treasures for me. To Kaye MacCrae, Lynanne Rollins, Chris Shannon, and Ed Stratmann of Rochester, New York's, George Eastman House, *gracias* for your help with this project. *Danke schön* to Justin Faber, Jim Coughlin, Randy Miller, and veteran film writer Dick Bojarski for sharing resources and enthusiasm.

No one is allowed to author a book on horror or science fiction films nowadays without consulting either or both of the masters, Greg Mank and Tom Weaver — I think it's a law — so *grazie tanto* to them and to John Brunas and to Michael Brunas (and thanks for the kind words, Mike). My appreciation, too, for David Skal's devotion to *Dracula* and for James Curtis' study of James Whale. Many important and sometimes obscure points on Universal Pictures were discovered in I.G. Edmonds' *Big U: Universal in the Silent Days*, Clive Hirschhorn's *The Universal Story*, and Michael Fitzgerald's *Universal Pictures*, splendid works all, which should be in every genre fan's library; thank you, gentlemen. To Howard Mandelbaum of PhotoFest, Claire at Eddie Brandt's, Buddy Barnett of Cinema Collectors, producer Radley Metzger, and Jerry Ohlinger, *obrigado*.

Merci bien aussi to Ron Borst and John Parnum; that this tome contains some real photographic gems is due to their lifelong devotion to the genre.

To film historian Kevin Charbeneau, who has allowed us all a deeper look into the Paul

ix

Leni canon, I owe you one. I'm also in the debt of Conrad Veidt's number one fan and biographer, J.C. Allen, whose *Conrad Veidt: From Caligari to Casablanca* ought to be sitting, well-thumbed, on everyone's shelf.

A kowtow to Richard Finegan; his knowledge of the studio and the time frame is matched only by his willingness to share the wealth.

Producer Richard Gordon is as much a Curator-at-Large of Film History as he is a part of it, and the essay on *The Cat Creeps* is in every way far richer for his support material and his insights.

Filmmaker and film historian Robert G. Dickson has (among many other accomplishments) co-authored with Spaniard Juan B. Heinink an indispensable work on the Spanish versions of thirties' Hollywood pictures, *Cita en Hollywood*. Bob responded both graciously and generously to the requests for help from a total stranger — the cosmically rare advert from *La voluntad del muerto* is here because of his efforts — and I cannot express how moved I am by his acts of kindness.

Thanks to Calvin and Forry, who have made my childhood last a lifetime.

Dozo to my professional colleague Barry Palmer, without whose kindness and technical assistance I would have been the monkey at the typewriter, and this book might still be a mass of typo-ridden foolscap.

To Blackie Seymour, whom I have known a lot of years: many, many thanks. The lion's share of the posters and ads in this volume are from Blackie's Pentagram Library. The library is the Universal mother-lode and is available to anyone looking to record Uncle Carl's little eccentricities, Junior's preoccupations, or the studio's output. If the author now warming up in the on-deck circle, preparing to chronicle *any* of the Universal product, will take a word of advice: get to know His Blackness — he's unique, he's user-friendly, and he's a prince.

Many of these offbeat theories and hypotheses of mine stem from the innumerable conversations, BS sessions, arguments, and reminiscences I've had with buddies and fellow buffs over the years. The "monster movies" which set us apart from other kids in our old neighborhoods have, through time, fostered a close-knit, ever-growing coterie of friends who recognize the gift of imagination that was needed to make films such as these and who possess the gift of imagination necessary to appreciate them.

PREFACE

When *Universal Horrors* hit the streets several years ago, the consensus was that *the* book on everyone's favorite studio had finally been written. Michael Brunas, John Brunas, and Tom Weaver received zillions of well-earned plaudits, and deservedly so; they filled a long-standing need with a magnificent work. Snatching my children's milk money, I quickly bought and devoured the book, from cover to cover, in a single sitting. The *vox populi* had been right on the button: the boys *had* received manna from above and had passed it on to legions of horror fans, each eager and grateful for a taste.

When I was given a copy of Greg Mank's *It's Alive* some 10 years ago, I thought I had died and gone to heaven. The wealth of detail, combined with the author's clever insights and excellent narrative style — it just didn't get any better than this. During the time that has passed since *It's Alive* came my way, Greg has authored several more books on the genre (*Hollywood Cauldron* and *Karloff and Lugosi*, to name but two), and each has managed to equal if not outperform its predecessor in terms of pure information and stylistic charm.

A new kid hit the genre block in perfect sync with the arrival of the new decade, and David Skal set the horror movie world on its ear with *Hollywood Gothic*, a work of enormous scope and precision. Following Skal's masterpiece, Lugosi's *Dracula* was viewed amid layers of newfound respectability (which it may or may not have deserved); nevertheless, no one can deny that the first of the Universal chillers is best served by the audience's being aware of the property's long and convoluted journey to the screen. Two other books have followed the Dracula chronicle — *The Monster Show* and *Dark Carnival*, the latter a critical biography of Tod Browning — and both have solidly supported the author's staking (sorry) the gothic territory.

The emergence of this new breed of genre historians and critics is a two-edged sword. On the one hand, these men are owed an enormous debt of gratitude; not since Carlos Clarens' *An Illustrated History of the Horror Film* opened the eyes of the more mainstream crowd almost three decades ago have dedicated and talented fellow-fans moved horror/science fiction film criticism to such levels of excellence and respectability. Because of them, we avid readers have come to expect more, to *demand* more from our literary "arm" than we've settled for in the past. The gauntlet has been thrown, and it remains every writer's challenge to approach these new standards. This, my friends, is a very tough row to hoe.

The sharper edge of that sword has been

the perceived superfluity of any further discussion on the subject. Why, I've been asked, would I waste any of my remaining years covering films on which every other hack has dulled his pencils, and which have already been given the "definitive" treatment by the heavy hitters listed above? Because, I've answered, I'm entitled to my opinion.

Opinion is what this book is all about.

I'm not an itinerant film historian. My proclivity to pursue tenuous leads or to trace a rumor to its source has taken a different bent in recent years. I've come to feel that the most in-depth, impeccably documented account of anything and everything will always fall short of absolute certainty; it is as impossible for a historian to view *all* the pertinent evidence or to collect *all* the relevant statements as it is for that historian to be perfectly unbiased. The material he chooses for inclusion, the order in which he presents it, even his choice of the words to be used in his writing the account — all conspire to tip the scales of impartiality out of balance, if only slightly. The true historian can never really say, "I'm finished here"; he always lives with the hope (and the fear) of new discoveries. As I hold that the last word on anything can never be uttered, a purely historical approach is not what I attempt.

Nor am I an interviewer. Thank God that Tom Weaver has devoted much of his professional life to tracking down and pegging the survivors of various genre eras for us. With each passing year, the number of people who actually *made* these grand old movies grows smaller, so Tom's gift to fandom is virtually inestimable. (In fact, I'm awestruck that some of these old-timers can still recall the most inconsequential details after a half-century or so; I'm usually hard pressed to remember where I put the car keys twenty minutes ago.) I've spoken with a couple of my favorites over the years, but in most instances, the only recourse I would have to the precious memories of the Golden or Silver Age horror superstars remains Tom's interviews (which we've all read and enjoyed), or a ouija board.

If anything, I am a commentator. The approach I've taken in this book is culled from the "So what do *you* think?" school of film discussion. Apart from viewing the films themselves, the most fun to be had within our genre has always been the (usually) good-natured arguments over a movie's merits, an actor's performance, an appealing/appalling special effect, and the like. I grew up loaded for bear with opinions on the classics, the crud, and everything in between, and I suspect that readers of this book did, too.

Film historian and memorabilia mogul Ron Borst feels it was our love for "monster movies" — drawn from the vintage stuff on TV, the '50s/'60s theatrical releases by Hammer, Universal, and AIP (among others), and *Famous Monsters (of Filmland)*, *Castle of Frankenstein*, and their imitators — that forged scores of long-distance friendships which have endured, to date, for over thirty years. Many of us, including Gary Svehla, Mark Frank, John Duvoli, Dave Szurek, Alex Soma, Tom Reamy, *moi*, and dozens of others, started fanzines of our own, not only out of a driving need to have our say about this most fascinating of movie types, but also to touch base with other, similarly oriented life-forms. I'm sure that some of us evolved into super-jocks or BMOC, but the lion's share of horror fans of our vintage were more on the outside than the in-, and we found a good measure of acceptance and joy in each other's fanzine articles, LoCs (letters of comment), and company.

This book deals with the studio's horror/science fiction/twisted mystery output during the first decade blessed by sound. If you already own *Universal Horrors*, you'll find a second look at the films discussed therein. (The sole exception is *Night Life of the Gods*; I have never in my life seen it and can add nothing to the excellent package the other three authors have put together.) In addition to those mainstays, I've included coverage of the balance of the original TV *Shock Theater* parcel (which were non-supernatural mysteries usually offering a quirk of some kind), an accounting of the *Crime Club* series, several pre–*Dracula* genre outings, and a couple of borderline undertakings by the old masters.

The appendices add some shorter items of tangential interest.

The essays appearing herein represent a good deal of original research, the careful weighing of available options, and many frustrating attempts at reconciling the sometimes wildly disparate accounts found in the body of current published film history. They include a wealth of opinion — my own, that of numerous scholars, critics, and historians, perhaps yours — as well as logical analysis, conjecture, hypothesis, and hearsay. Some chapters are significantly lighter-hearted than others. As several movies deal with real-life Weighty Issues, I tried to approach those issues, if not the pictures themselves, with the respect they deserve. Admittedly, there are more than a few duds considered in these pages, but these are offset either by a genuine diamond or by other, semi-precious shivers. At any rate, my thoughts reflect a love of the subject, a devotion to the genre, and a grateful admiration for the studio under discussion.

Where the most familiar of the titles are concerned, I don't go in much for lengthy synopses. The presumption is that we've already committed *Frankenstein* and *Dracula* to memory, and that highlights or quieter moments of pictures like *Murders in the Rue Morgue* and *The Black Cat* can be retrieved from long-term memory by a few choice paragraphs. I spend a bit of time on *The Old Dark House* for a number of reasons, not the least of which is that, until not so long ago, the film hovered on the fringes of availability and remained elusive for many fans. Essays on the more workaday offerings will rehash story details if I'm trying to make a point, seldom-seen pictures like *Secret of the Blue Room* generally receive a more comprehensive summary, and obscurities like *Remember Last Night?*, *Postal Inspector*, and *The Man Who Cried Wolf* get the royal treatment, plotwise. Most of the plums are available on MCA pre-records, and everyone's time would be better spent watching the movie than reading it. Still, there should be enough information herein for even the rawest recruit to get into the swing of things.

One final distinction begs to be drawn. I *love* these films; for me, they are the one part of Toyland's borders which *can* be crossed, again and again. As old as they are, they belong to my youth, for it was during my youth that I first fell under their spell. The Frankenstein Monster, the Wolf Man, Dracula, the Mummy, and all the rest were childhood friends who supplanted my earliest favorites (Huey, Dewie and Louie), and who shared cherished places in my imagination with Wild Bill Hickok (and Jingles), Roy Rogers, Bat Masterson, and the Range Rider. As I grew older, they vied with the New York Yankees, rock and roll, and girls for my fickle attention. They are immortal and so have stayed fresh and dependable and timeless while I and my fellow baby-boomers have become older and less spry. They remain untarnished but bear that proud patina of respectability which comes with acceptance and with love.

That's not to say that I like all these films. Some of them — the monsterless mysteries or the *Crime Club* entries, for example — I actively resented as a kid. It was only as I grew and as my "horizons" widened that I could come to accept them for the hybrids that they are. Yet despite my mellowing, there are a few pictures which I actively dislike. If the boys at *Universal Horrors* ever nailed one right on the head, it was with their assessment of *Life Returns*. No mad scientist's cockamamie process in the world can return to me the hour I wasted on it, and I'll go to my final reward resenting Robert Cornish, Eugen Frenke, and this miserable little movie.

Whether I felt all warm and mushy or not, I tried to see the "beauty" in each picture, to appreciate the director's vision, to experience the thrill or feel the excitement for which the first-run audience had paid good money. Like our dear old monsters' capacity to frighten, many of the subtler aspects of the decidedly lesser features have dissipated over the years, and (in some instances) their dated materials and more rudimentary techniques can become something of an obstacle to one's enjoyment of the moment. Let me apologize now for having only my own sensibilities, which began to develop some two decades after the last of the pictures in this volume hit the screen upon which to draw in my appraisals. I may not like a few of these films individually (any more than I cared for Mickey Gubitosi in the latter *Our Gang* shorts), but just as I still adore the *Little Rascals* as a timeless ensemble and as a concept, so do I love the body of the genre work which Universal Studios presented to a changing world during the 1930s.

So, whether you absolutely despise my all-time favorite, or I have trashed the film you've chosen to be buried with, at least let's enjoy hashing out our differences, swapping our various opinions, and quibbling about all those minutiae which are either beyond belief or beneath consideration. These old movies are still a cherished cache of riches, and maybe this book will help uncover a nugget or two of pure gold that we've hereto overlooked.

John T. Soister
Orwigsburg, Pennsylvania
Summer 1998

INTRODUCTION:
IN THE BEGINNING THERE WAS CARL

If asked to give a one word description of Carl Laemmle, the founding father of the Universal Film Manufacturing Company, a good number of savvy film buffs would probably respond with "imp." The diminutive mogul, affectionately dubbed "Uncle Carl" by most of his employees (he *was* Uncle Carl to the rest of them), governed his "Universal City" with a twinkle in his eye and a healthy supply of strategically placed signs ("Keep smiling!" — Carl Laemmle).

"Imp," however, was more than just a facile tag for the studio chief; it was also the initials of Universal's corporate predecessor, the Independent Motion Picture Company, founded by Laemmle in 1909 as a counter-measure to Thomas Edison's Motion Picture Patents Company, which had legally enjoined all of the country's independent film exhibitors from buying or selling films from exchanges not registered with the MPPC (or the "Trust," as it was later known). In addition to controlling distribution of existing product, Edison also required licensing fees and rental charges from film producers using cameras and projection equipment constructed according to his patented designs.

Names apart, IMP turned out to be a deadly serious venture on the part of the German émigré. If he or the other courageous entrepreneurs who banded with him had failed to overthrow the Trust, the growing motion picture industry would have become little more than Edison's toy, with the added danger that artistic freedom would have taken a very distant second to the patents-holder's avarice or caprice. Federal suits initiated in April 1912 finally saw the dissolution of both the Motion Picture Patents Company and the General Film Company, which had acted as the "enforcing arm" of the Trust in its many brushes with independent filmmakers.

Laemmle's newly victorious team soon had problems of its own: too many cooks. Uncle Carl and Robert H. Cochrane (representing IMP) and their many partners* found their corporate elbows becoming chafed from constantly rubbing each other the wrong way.

*Per I.G. Edmonds (Big U: Universal in the Silent Days): Pat Powers and the Powers Company, David Horsley of Nestor, Charles Jourjon of Eclair, Fred Balshofer, Adam Kessel, and Charles Bauman of the New York Motion Picture Company, Mark Dintenfass of the Champion Company, William Swanson of Rex Pictures, and William Steiner of Yankee.

"It took a million years to make this picture…" and we're still waiting. *Mystery of Life* was among the pipe dreams Universal announced but never made. PENTAGRAM LIBRARY.

Almost from the moment the first signature was affixed to the declaration of incorporation on June 2, 1912, the Universal Film Manufacturing Company was a hotbed of accusations, counteraccusations, threats, fights, and ultimatums. Laemmle sought reconstruction, and in October of that same year, Universal reemerged with the tiny titan as the undisputed CEO, and Bob Cochrane as its president. Meanwhile IMP, which remained a decidedly minor entity unto itself, would continue to provide films for release under its own or someone else's banner for another five years.

The IMP and Universal output had to be, well, *universal* if it was to attract picture-goers from all walks of life, and so there was a fair sprinkling of genre material among the more mundane offerings. Early packages consisted of split-reels and one- or two-reel shorts, and were seldom longer than four reels *in toto*. (Clive Hirschhorn reports that a week's worth of Universal product, permitting a daily change in program, could be had for as little as $105.) Most of the more fantastic themes had low comic overtones. Still, out of the sea of spoofs and pastiches, apart from the numerous short chillers concerned with hypnosis, came a couple of offerings worth a closer look.

In 1913, Universal and Bison Pictures joined forces to produce *The Werewolf*, a two-reeler that is generally acknowledged as the film in which lycanthropy made its screen debut. Taken together with *The White Wolf* (wrought by Universal and Nestor pictures, another former partner, the following year), the movies were grounded in Native American mythology rather than in the European legends which would become so prevalent decades later. More pertinent than the pair of films' sharing the honors as the first cinematic combination of American Indian folklore and werewolfery is the fact that, to date, they represent the only mixture of the two popular themes. (*Death Curse of Tartu*, a 1966 effort produced by another independent, Falcon Pictures, dealt with the vengeful spirit of a Seminole medicine man who took the shape of a husky Indian brave, a snake, an alligator, and a shark during the course of the action, but the wolf was conspicuously absent from the assemblage of were-animals, presumably owing to the paucity of wolves in the Everglades.) With the dawn of the Teutonic Age of Silent Horror just around the corner, it's a pity that no more creative effort was expended on depicting the frissons that lay closer to home. Universal's classic horrors of the thirties would all involve bogeys who committed their various misdeeds thousands of cinematic miles from the Land of the Free and the Home of the Brave.

The year 1916 saw Stuart Paton's ambitious, $500,000 adaptation of Jules Verne's *20,000 Leagues Under the Sea*. The film, which incorporated elements both from the title work and from the author's *Mysterious Island*, made a pile at the box office, and a "photoplay" edition, courtesy of New York's premier reprint publishers, Grosset and Dunlap, dropped a bundle into Uncle Carl's lap. Imagine an advertising scheme that the public would pay for, would bring into their homes, and would peruse again and again! Hardcover novelizations of original screenplays soon came to supplement reprints of source literature, in the hope that reading the book beforehand would whet a person's appetite for the film, and that poring over the pages after having viewed the picture might lead the reader back into the theater a second time.

Also released in 1916 (by the soon-to-disappear Ocean Pictures), was *Life Without Soul*, the first full-length screen version of *Frankenstein*. Impressive in scope and provocative in its advertising — "A photoplay embracing a theme never before attempted in cinematography, and stupendous in its execution" — the film nevertheless did little business, either when it opened (suffering from poor distribution) or when it was re-released only months later, following a good bit of reediting by Raven Pictures, itself on the skids. The financial possibilities of a similar film, bolstered by an effective advertising campaign and comprehensive distribution, may have insinuated itself into the collective Laemmle unconsciousness. Who knows?

Less impressive financially and historically, but still amusing when viewed in retrospect, are some rather lightweight IMP efforts (the most potent of which is the 17-minute farce *The Haunted House*) nestled among such future blockbuster titles as *The Mummy* (three different one- and two-reelers in 1911 alone), *Notre Dame de Paris* (the first feature length version to hit the screen, courtesy of Pathé), H. Rider Haggard's *She* (at 30 minutes, and with James Cruze), and *Dr. Jekyll and Mr. Hyde* (at 15 and also with Cruze). Except for the Haggard adventure, Universal would get around to cashing in on everything listed, with a respectable enough 1913 version of the Robert Louis Stevenson tale which boasted Uncle Carl's presence as producer as well as president and two outright smashes in the sagas of Lon Chaney's Quasimodo (in 1923) and Karloff's Im-ho-tep nine years later.

Horror fans during the early twenties frequently had to look to studios other than Universal in order to find movies to their liking. Although *Hunchback of Notre Dame* was rightly celebrated for its scope and grandeur, it was much more a costume romance than a tale of terror. Chaney's pathetic bell-ringer may have been nothing to look at (or everything to look at, if you were into grotesque deformity), but as his white hat was clearly visible to those who had eyes to see, there was no element of danger or uncertainty to spice things up.

Earlier in '23, Universal had starred Lon Chaney as Wilse Dilling in Lambert Hillyer's rendition of *The Shock*. The Master of Makeup started the film as both a crook and a cripple, but made it through to the end enjoying health in body and soul and getting the girl to boot. Albeit a treat for the swelling legions of Chaney fans, it was not a horror film. Neither was that same year's *Legally Dead*, a crime exposé wherein the hero (Milton Sills) infiltrates a prison to interview prisoners on the capricious practice of capital punishment; later, he is arrested for murder and is executed. Despite his being pronounced (you got it) legally dead, a good shot of adrenaline revives him for a happy ending. Something of a precursor to *Life Returns*, *Legally Dead* and its all-too-marginal science fiction overtones left genre fans colder than Mr. Sills.

In 1929, the Fox Film Corporation released *Behind That Curtain*, a Charlie Chan mystery featuring Warner Baxter, Gilbert Emery, and Boris Karloff. Five years earlier, Universal had unveiled the similarly titled *Behind the Curtain*, a story of murder and (fake) spiritualism, and featuring no one of note whatsoever. While in 1924 Germany offered Robert Weine's *Orlacs Hände* and Paul Leni's *Das Wachsfigurenkabinett*, Universal City's only other shot at attracting the horror buff that year was the dangerously named *Excitement*, a comedy-melodrama starring Laura LaPlante and filled with ersatz Egyptian sarcophagi and bogus mummies.

And so 1924 came and went. Much more to the morbid tastes of genre buffs was Rupert Julian's *The Phantom of the Opera* (1925), in which Mr. Chaney combined his love of the bizarre with his talent for disguise, and created a character whose warring emotions and physical repugnance remain unequaled to this day. In spite of inexplicable and repeated interference of comic relief[*] in the film and the hash made of attempts at reissuing it as a part-sound hybrid at the close of the decade, *Phantom* was a resounding success (although not quite in the same financial league as *Hunchback* had been), and Chaney's Erik became *the* horror icon of the twenties.

While *The Phantom of the Opera* had been a patchwork quilt of disparate directorial styles, differing interpretations, and Uncle Carl's meddling, it exhibited to some degree the stylistic palette that had made its genre forebears so memorable. The several thrillers which followed *Phantom* reflected even more the striking visual qualities of Expressionism, and it is important to understand the influence the movement had on Universal, which was surely the most Germanic of studios when under con-

---

[*]*Although a lifelong fan of silent comedy, I have yet to meet a single person who professes the slightest admiration for the work of Snitz Edwards, an extremely minor comedian. Mr. Edwards' presence in* The Phantom of the Opera *is a horror in itself.*

"The PHANTOM of the OPERA"
A Universal Production

Powerless to resist, Christine is led by 'The Phantom' into the house on the underground lake.

In this lobby card for *Phantom of the Opera*, the head bogey's face is obscured to keep suspense alive, a practice the studio would continue well into the sound era. *AUTHOR'S COLLECTION.*

trol of the Laemmles, if we are to appreciate the trend-setting flavor of the studio's later classic horrors. Expressionism sought to visualize and concretize one's inner feelings through the use of stylization, easily recognizable character types, and symbols. Hence, the eternal struggle of good vs. evil within man took on a life unto itself. All sorts of representations of duality — life and death, beauty and deformity, lucidity and madness, the sacred and the profane — were given human (or near-human) shape.

As all of these contrasting pairs had roiled beneath the human surface since the advent of the earliest man, they were intimately tied with man's questions about the meaning of life and the possibility of life after death. Organized religion claimed that divine revelation, the

communication between God and man, held the answers to these questions, and most creeds claimed a share in the Ur-experiences in which the creation first beheld the Creator. Ethnic and national folk history likewise attempted to explain whence and whither man. *Die Niebelungen*, for example, became the Teutonic groundwork for the story of life and the source of most of Germany's subsequent mythic drama.

Together with the pervasive influence of such geniuses of contemporary stagecraft as Max Reinhardt and Leopold Jessner, Expressionism led to the most strikingly visual period to date of German cinema and theater. The years 1919–1923 are still held as the high-water mark of that nation's Expressionistic bent, and such earth-shakers as *Das Kabinett*

Lobby card for 1927's part-chiller, part-comedy *The Cat and the Canary*. RONALD V. BORST/HOLLYWOOD *MOVIE POSTERS*.

des Dr. Caligari (1919), *Der Golem* and *Genuine* (both 1920), *Der Müde Tod* (1921), and 1922's *Nosferatu — Eine Symphonie des Grauens* became the archetypes after which subsequent pictures were modeled. Universal and other studios borrowed stylistically from the German technique for their own late silent and early sound pictures, when not importing outright the German technicians to do the stylizing for them. Performances notwithstanding, Karl Freund's knack for lighting and frame composition captured art director Charles D. Hall's expansive ruins for all time, thus giving Tod Browning's lethargic *Dracula* whatever atmospheric oomph it did have, and ditto a thousand times over for Robert Florey's kinky and contorted *Murders in the Rue Morgue*.

The only semi-genre outing Universal made in 1926 was *The Mystery Club*, a big budgeted melodrama which outlined a series of crimes proven ultimately to be bogus, but 1927 brought a couple of real gems. Unable to beg, borrow or steal Chaney — now under exclusive contract to MGM (and so, too expensive, it being accepted that the accountants at Universal had trouble conceiving the lofty figures their counterparts at MGM dealt with on a daily basis)— the movers and shakers in the San Fernando Valley turned to two sources of inspiration which they knew wouldn't let them down: Broadway and Victor Hugo.

The storyline of John Willard's *The Cat and the Canary* had had a thick layer of dust on it when the play had opened to critical indifference but popular approval back in 1922. As chills and chuckles had always been kissing cousins, the day after someone had first shivered at the goings-on in a haunted house, someone else was busy spoofing them. Harold Lloyd and Buster Keaton had already staked their claims to the territory with *Haunted Spooks*, 1920, and *The Haunted House*, 1921, respectively, and scarcely a week would pass without some comedian or other killing two reels with predictably frenetic antics among the low-budget interiors of a decrepit old mansion. Nevertheless, his particular mix of grasping relatives, secret passages, and things that go bump in the night made Mr. Willard a nice piece of change.

Visions of some of that money heading his way prompted Laemmle to buy the rights to the play and to act as producer for the filming. The playwright had no complaint with the respectful treatment his masterwork received; imported *Shreckmeister* Paul Leni had reached deep into his Expressionistic bag of tricks and had painted a fascinating mélange of light and shadow on the celluloid canvas. Leni's film afforded Willard's popular claptrap a profoundly macabre dignity, something the confines of the theater and the constraints of the then relatively primitive stagecraft had been unable to do, from the moment the breathtaking titles filled the screen. Albeit a comedy in the main, the 1927 *The Cat and the Canary* produced more than its fair share of thrills and remains the definitive example of the silent comedy-melodrama subgenre for most knowledgeable viewers.

Interestingly, most of the features produced by Universal during the twenties were classified by budget within corporate confines and were released under certain quasi-coded "tags" which identified both the monetary investment in the film as well as the expected level of return. The films fell into one of five basic categories: Super Jewel (the most extravagant), Jewel, Bluebird, Butterfly, and Red Feather. *The Cat and the Canary* was a Jewel, as was *The Phantom of the Opera*. Quasimodo, that lucky bugger, received the red carpet treatment, as he got to scamper about in Super Jewel splendor. In all three cases, the money really showed on the screen.

Later in 1927, Universal plunged back into the musty collected works of verbose French novelist Victor Hugo, and, hoping for a property which would satisfy the audience's taste for spectacle à la 1923's *The Hunchback of Notre Dame*, recalled Paul Leni and asked him to work his magic once again on *The Man Who Laughs*. Both Hugo novels had been historical romances centered around gargoyles with noble instincts and hearts of gold, and both film versions were sumptuous feasts for the eye. Both novels had been filmed time and again,* in varying lengths and with markedly less success than the Laemmle productions, and *Hunchback* would go on to numerous subsequent interpretations. *The Man Who Laughs* reunited Leni with Conrad Veidt, who had worked with the director in *Prinz Kuckuck* (1919) and *Lady Hamilton* (1922), and had appeared in the Ivan the Terrible episode of *Das Wachsfigurenkabinett*, and their combined artistry was appreciated by critics and ticket-buyers alike. Filmed as a silent, the film was held up for months in order to add a musical track and sound effects, finally seeing a carbon arc in November 1928. The delay swelled audience interest. Veidt's character, Gwynplaine, whose mouth was carved into a permanent smile by the demented and sadistic king, couldn't help but appear to laugh; the multitudes of female fans who filled the theaters couldn't help but weep, and their sympathetic tears spelled fiscal relief for Uncle Carl and the promise of additional work at Universal for Messrs. Leni and Veidt.

It is sad that so many pictures made during the 1928–1930 "interim" period have totally disappeared. Released during that brief span

---

Quasimodo made his cinematic debut in a ten-minute French one-reeler entitled Esmeralda *(Gaumont, 1906). Between that incarnation and Chaney's definitive silent treatment, the bell-ringer scurried through a half-dozen treatments here and abroad; in 1922, in fact, the British put Sybil Thorndike and Basil Conway through their paces in* another version entitled Esmeralda. *Gwynplaine hadn't quite so substantial a track record, but his sardonic phiz had been filmed twice before Leni took his turn:* L'Homme Qui Rit, *a 1909 French short subject, and Austria's* Das Grinsende Gesicht *in 1921.*

Unlike its mid–1940s "remake" with Boris Karloff and Susanna Foster, the 1930 version of *The Climax* was devoid of horrific content. PENTAGRAM LIBRARY.

when the studios finally realized that the silent era was moribund but few theaters (either independent or company-owned) had yet completely retooled to handle the embryonic sound technology, most of these pictures were regarded by their own creators as neither fish nor fowl, so little money was spent on either publicity or distribution. Fewer than usual prints were struck, and this shortage of product, coupled with more liberal rental guidelines extended to theater owners, led to a cavalier attitude with respect not only to the picture's worth at the box office, but also to its value in the long run.

Censorship was imposed on state or local levels, and it was not unusual for each theater owner to clip out sections of a film which he found personally offensive. The reinsertion of this footage before the print was returned to the exchange was often left to chance, and some projectionists gave away to interested filmgoers (or to children) the clips they found on the projection booth floor. Making things worse, rather than storing prints of late silents or early part-sound features with an eye to re-release, the studios frequently saw to it that positives were cut up for leader or junked for their silver content, while negatives were allowed to lie fallow and decompose in some forgotten vault far off the beaten track.

Opposite: Shot before *The Cat and the Canary* but held up for postproduction sound upgrades, *The Man Who Laughs* reunited Paul Leni with Conrad Veidt. Note the 1920s version of the Universal globe logo. RONALD V BORST/HOLLYWOOD MOVIE POSTERS.

Herald for *The Charlatan*, a picture that is today among those essentially impossible to see. PENTAGRAM LIBRARY.

The handwriting *had* been on the wall for a while, and many prestige pictures like *The Man Who Laughs* received whatever technical upgrading was possible before economic constraints demanded their being released. Other films, usually blatant B's or slapdash remakes, were hustled into the showplace with only the bare minimum of post-production support and were quickly forgotten by the studios which had made them.

The Last Warning, *The Last Performance*, and *The Charlatan* are absent nowadays from the Universal vaults, and each has an availability index of near-zero. A chance remark made to film historian Richard Koszarski led to my being able to track down the "*Last*" features to their lairs, and long-time Universal buff Richard Finegan made possible the comprehensive look at *The Charlatan* which follows shortly. Ironically, had it not been for the

efforts of private collectors, viewed as criminals and pirates by Universal and other studios in bygone days, these pictures would have vanished utterly from the face of the earth.

The Cat Creeps (1930) and its Spanish-release version, *La voluntad del muerto*, are nowhere to be found (yet). That they have received even a modicum of their due is possible only through the courtesy of the several institutions and individuals who have supplanted the studios in taking responsibility for the preservation of the American film heritage. Nothing much has been written to date on these early hybrids, so my extremely rudimentary remarks may have to suffice until the films themselves become readily accessible to public scrutiny and for public enjoyment, or until someone with more drive, greater opportunity and resources, and a more thorough grasp of the period takes the time to render them superfluous.

THE LAST WARNING (1929)

Carl Laemmle had come to America to seek his fortune before the new century had dawned, but his heart still held a place for Laupheim, and his business instincts led him constantly back to Europe. This proximity to the European market gave the wily Laemmle first dibs on most of the native artisans looking to come West to ply their Old World craftsmanship for New World money. Karl Freund, Edgar Ulmer, Joe May, Kurt Neumann, Robert and Kurt Siodma(r)k: all would journey from the Fatherland or its environs to the Land of Opportunity, and would leave their own particular stamp on the burgeoning genre of the American horror picture. One of the first to make the trip was the Stuttgart-born Paul Leni.

Barely in his thirties at the time of his migration, Leni brought a solid reputation with him to California. The young filmmaker had designed sets for theatrical genius Max Reinhardt and posters for the Expressionistic film school, had served as art director on any number of visually arresting productions (including two silent versions of the Abbé Prévost's sappy *Manon Lescaut*), and had scripted and directed respectable productions of his own. The most famous of these in the horror genre was the moody, episodic *Das Wachsfigurenkabinett* (*Waxworks*), which survived both the sea voyage and the distributor's tampering to win the admiration of American audiences.

Determined to exploit the young Leni's eye for the macabre, Uncle Carl bought the rights to the Broadway spook show *The Cat and the Canary* and assigned him to transfer it to the silver screen.

If there had ever been any suspicion in Laemmle's mind that the revenue generated by *The Phantom of the Opera* had been a freak accident, the sacks of gelt brought in by *Cat* dispelled it immediately. The premise of the play may have been hoary the day it opened, but the profit at the Universal box-office indicated that hoary was ho-kay, so long as it was dished up with style. In reviewing the film for *The New Republic* (October 26, 1927), Louise Bogan found that

> Paul Leni, a director imported by Universal Pictures, has done his best for *The Cat and the Canary*, a story full of complicated disappearances and such box-office horrors as long taloned hands appearing from wainscoting. He has invention — a turn for grim lighting and sinister composition not ineffective even when applied to this thin material — which should come through magnificently, given a picture of really terrifying implications.

As the émigré would scarcely live to see the autumn of 1929, that film of "really terrifying implications"—*Dracula*—came and went

15

Window card for *The Last Warning*. RONALD V. BORST/HOLLYWOOD MOVIE POSTERS.

Poster for Paul Leni's lost *The Chinese Parrot*, the first Charlie Chan film. AUTHOR'S COLLECTION.

without benefit of his genius. Between that picture and *The Cat and the Canary*, though, the expert Expressionist set his hand to *The Chinese Parrot*, *The Man Who Laughs* (mentioned earlier), and *The Last Warning*.

Like *Cat*, *The Chinese Parrot* was designated as a Jewel. The first full length film to feature Earl Derr Biggers' Chinese sleuth, Charlie Chan, *Parrot* followed by a year Chan's first screen appearance ever, in *The House Without a Key*, a ten-chapter serial Pathé had released in 1926. The Universal offering saw Chan portrayed by Kamiyama Sojin, an emaciated Japanese eccentric who even then had a cult following; a handful of critics and most of the paying public had sworn that Sojin had been the real *Thief of Baghdad*, easily stealing the picture from nominal star Douglas Fairbanks. Based on one of the least impressive of the Biggers novels, the picture had Charlie proffer the solution to a jewel theft and kidnapping in part because a parrot — which had witnessed the villainy firsthand — spilled the beans to him in Chinese! Among the cast members in what was most likely a tepidly scripted adventure were George Kuwa, who had created the role of the Honolulu-based policeman for the screen in the Pathé serial; the lovely Anna May Wong; and ex–Keystone Kops Slim Summerville and Edgar Kennedy.

Dismissing the Chan mystery because of the ludicrousness of its denouement, though, ignores its most potent attractions: its Jewel status, indicating that some serious money (serious for Universal, at any rate) had been allotted the movie, and its having Paul Leni at the helm. Respect for his Expressionistic eye (along with *Waxworks*) having preceded him to America, the startling visuals of *Cat* cemented the expectations of the movie-going populace. On the basis of the German import and that one "domestic" picture (the release of *The Man Who Laughs* would be held up for a year and a half, pending post-production tinkering and technical improvements necessitated by the advent of sound), there was already a critical awareness of the trademark "Leni touch." As Miss Bogan went on to describe to readership of *The New Republic*, Leni's "talent, more discreet and less violent than Murnau's, is yet one that can save sets from their three-walled monotony, switch them into impressive design, give them tenseness and angularity."

Although a world-class set designer in his own right, Leni left the creative end to Charles D. Hall and his colleagues. *The Chinese Parrot* was also designed by Hall, and again, the young visionary director milked the sets for all they were worth. Despite the less than arresting nature of the plot, *Parrot* won decent reviews. As had been the case with *Cat*, the Chan feature received most of its kudos for its artistic style and not for its literary substance. In its January 2, 1928, number, *Variety*'s anonymous critic noted that:

> In his present offering, Mr. Leni once more proves that with individual treatment an only fair-to-middling story can be made into a film that is at once original and imaginative... The production progresses in a straightforward and natural manner. By an ingenious use of shadows, lights and photographic angles, Mr. Leni has created the eerie atmosphere necessary in a house where sudden death and sinister happenings occur.... Mr. Leni is a master of camera technique.

Chan fans are doubly inconsolable when it comes to *The Chinese Parrot*. First of all, speculating on the undoubtedly brazen antics of Sojin as Charlie Chan as Ah Kim (the Chinese cook) remains an awfully poor substitute for viewing the crafty sleuth snatch another one. (The above-cited reviewer asserts that "The acting honors must be bestowed on K. Sojin as Charlie Chan, an Oriental detective.") Secondly, although the film was remade with Warner Oland as *Charlie Chan's Courage* in 1934, that version has vanished as well. On another level, the loss of any segment of Leni's American canon is very much to be deplored.

By the time *The Last Warning* went into production in August 1928, the motion picture industry was in mid-crisis. Al Jolson's nasal voice had turned the world on its ear, and sound was king. Jolie's brash and inimitable style had sent studios scrambling to withdraw and reconfigure expensive pictures already in release, to alter footage sitting in the can, and to revamp plans for all future product; every major save Universal was going into hock to wire its theaters for sound. With Junior, who was already production head although barely out of his teens, Uncle Carl drew up plans to weather the talkie tempest. Such silent war-horses, as *The Phantom of the Opera* were reissued in "partial sound" versions, and prestige pictures underwent reconstructive surgery before release, but most films shot during the changeover period were to have dialogue sequences (narrative titles were usually retained), sound effects, and a dedicated musical score. *The Last Warning* was no exception.

From late 1928 to early 1930, many features had been shot both in silent format and with either sound on film or "synchronized" soundtracks on oversized records which accompanied the 35mm prints from theater to theater. The latter obviously was a stopgap measure, but it was effective and especially appreciated by many smaller, independent movie houses that were slow to rewire for sound, the procedure being time-consuming and expensive. Special machines, capable of playing the sound disks from the inside out, were on loan from Vitaphone or similar outfits, and they allowed these theaters to go head to head with their larger, studio-owned competitors. Even before *Dracula* was released, every theater with any business sense at all had converted to sound, so most of the 35mm nitrate positives went out from the studio with an audio track; nevertheless, until mid–1932, sound disks for more important features were made available to any last holdouts who had supported Universal during that most unwieldy turn of the decade.

The print of *The Last Warning* that I viewed prior to writing this chapter may be one of only several in America. Part of Rochester, New York's, George Eastman House collection, it comes from the Cinémathèque Française and is slightly edited, completely silent, and cursed with French intertitles so that one has no idea whether the original English titles

Even the 1934 remake of *The Chinese Parrot*, titled *Charlie Chan's Courage*, has disappeared. PENTAGRAM LIBRARY.

were rendered literally or idiomatically into French, or even if they were all used. At least one title is inserted into the action in the wrong spot, and the names of the characters range from approximations (Arthur McHugh became Mac Hugh, Brady to Brody) to pieces of whimsy (Gene to "Birds," Sammy to "Buddy"). A copy of Alfred Cohn's second whack at a continuity script, very generously provided by film historian Kevin Charbeneau, set the record straight as to some of the characters' identities (the cast is less populous in the script than in the film itself), but the titles proposed in this early draft don't even approximate their Cinémathèque Française counterparts, leaving us still somewhat in the dark as to what was actually used in the release print.

The recorded sound effects include numerous cries, screams, and whimpers (viewing totally silent footage, I was struck how frequently most of the cast members launched into an open-mouthed assault on the audience), and the talkie segments are limited to the opening twelve minutes ("All talk," complained *Variety*), the closing nine, and "a four minute interlude of sides." There's no way of determining the aggregate of sound footage (including the effects, which *Variety* noted as "multiple, continuous and in detail to the extent of reproducing a kiss"), but it's a safe bet that it accounted for barely a third of the film's running time, which was itself rather lengthy for the period at 87 minutes.

The Last Warning is very much more a horror picture than *The House of Fear*, its remake of a decade later. With a grotesque phantom and any number of ghostly sightings in addition to the ubiquitous spirit messages and threats, the film stacks the deck and shows its clutching hand at every opportunity. For example, on the day it is reopened for rehearsal, the Woodford Theater resembles nothing less than the fearsome face of Moloch, his mouth agape as if to swallow whole those foolhardy enough to enter; the concept is similar in intent to the worker-devouring machine-cum-ogre in *Metropolis*. Nothing remotely like this anthropomorphic vision greeted audiences sitting through Joe May's 1939 version.

Leni opens *The Last Warning* with an extended, kaleidoscopic montage of Broadway theater marquees, leggy chorines, and bright lights, out of which emerges a police car and an escort of cops on motorcycles. The police are waved into the Woodford Theater by the frantic doorman, and an early example of deep focus allows us to peer over the shoulders of audience members as a fabulously bearded man announces to the house, "John Woodford is dead!" Through the stunned crowd two detectives climb onto the stage.

One of the detectives (Fred Kelsey, wearing his trademark derby and mustache) is brought to the stage mantelpiece, where he is informed that "In plain sight, the moment he [Woodford] grabbed the candlestick, he fell over!" The detectives (Tom O'Brien is Kelsey's partner) move to Woodford's dressing room, where the actor's cadaver and the doctor who just happened to be in the house when the fabled call went out await their arrival. As the doctor (Charles K. French) tells his tale, a flashback shows Woodford being backed at swordpoint to the mantelpiece; the dragoon-costumed actor reaches above and behind himself, ostensibly to grab a candlestick and fight off his adversary. The moment contact is made, Woodford grimaces, shrieks, and clutches at his chest. The stage lights flicker and die, and the actor is seen motionless on the stage floor when the lights come up again moments later. A cut to the theater floor has the camera looking almost directly *up* at the tiers of boxes and allows a peculiar vantage point as, to a man, the occupants of the boxes stand and stick their heads out for a better look.

Ingenue Doris Terry (Laura La Plante) lets out a bit of a scream of her own, and the audience leaps to its collective feet. The curtain is wrung down, and the prompter moves out onto the stage apron as it falls. (So does the camera, managing to duck under the descending curtain at an incredibly low level.) The plea for medical assistance is made, the doctor is seen elbowing his way through the milling crowd, and the flashback ends.

The phone is used to summon the coroner, and Detective Kelsey moves into the back-

A posed shot that does not appear in *The Last Warning*. Here the body of John Woodford lies on the dressing room floor while (in foreground, left to right) Mike Brody (Bert Roach), Robert Bunce (Mack Swain) and comic relief stagehand Tommy (Slim Summerville) react. PHOTOFEST.

stage corridors to grill the actors. A metal door slides back to admit the Bunces: the old and crotchety Josiah (Burr McIntosh) and his younger brother, the corpulent Robert (Mack Swain). The brothers are co-owners of the Woodford Theater. The doctor is dismissed for the nonce, and much of the company — including director Richard Quayle (John Boles), Miss Terry, and Irish stage manager Mike Brody (Bert Roach) — mills around under Kelsey's scrutiny. Brody reluctantly admits to having overheard an earlier argument between Woodford and Quayle, and that statement sends Kelsey's partner into the ingenue's dressing room. The room is awash with floral bouquets, and O'Brien notes that the most opulent offerings bear the calling cards of John Woodford

(D'Arcy Corrigan) and Harvey Carleton (Roy D'Arcy), the play's secondary lead. A small bunch of tiny roses is found on the floor by the actress's chaise lounge, and one of the tiny buds has been tucked into the framed photo of Quayle, which reposes alone by the makeup mirror.

Returning to the scene of the interrogations, the crafty detective holds the flower next to its twin, which the actress has carefully arranged in her neckline. The number of men vying for the attentions of the blond beauty has been reduced by one, and both Doris and Quayle are aware of the official's suspicions. Everyone scats to prepare for the arrival of the coroner, and Leni has cinematographer Hal Mohr hold on the door to the dressing room for ten long seconds, an eternity in which there is no movement whatsoever. The forceful entrance of said coroner breaks this spell, but it only takes him a moment to ascertain that the room holds no cadaver, and his indignant announcement sends the police into a whirlwind of action. Miss Terry runs from the background toward the camera, letting loose with another healthy-looking scream, and the scene fades.

A cut brings us to an exterior view of the New York City corner occupied by the Woodford Theater. One by one, newspapers arise from below the frame line (and from behind each other), heralding the frustrating tack the investigation takes: *Stage Star Slain!* yells the first banner. *Woodford's Body Still Missing*, proclaims the *Brooklyn Daily Eagle*, as editions of *The New York Times* and the *Herald Tribune* appear to advise *Woodford Mystery Unsolved*, *Absolve Cast in Woodford Murder*, *Theatrical Murder Baffles Police*, and *Murder Victim's Body Stolen!* At the end of the sequence, the screen is completely covered by the various papers, an effect more startling and powerful than the more customary succession of banner headlines. (The scene made an impression on the anonymous, second-string movie reviewer of the real-life *New York Times*, who reported, "One of the imaginative stretches in this film is where the director deals with the newspaper headlines of the murder. This, Mr. Leni had accomplished so that it reminds one of a street dripping with ink." Nevertheless, the reviewer couldn't resist sniffing, "It matters not to Mr. Leni, however, whether the newspapers would ever use the headlines he puts under the familiar mastheads of New York publications.") A subsequent headline in the *Evening World* announces that *Lovers Separate Over Woodford Murder* and reveals that *Mystery Envelopes Doris Terry's Sudden Departure for Europe; Quayle Refuses to Be Interviewed!*

Time passes, and the exterior of the theater has taken on an ominous appearance (see drawing). As we watch, the building's "right eye" opens, and a cut to the inside of the structure reveals that a shade has been raised to allow the light in; the old building is to be let once again. Gene (Torben Meyer), the comic

relief factotum, throws open curtains, doors, and the skylight of the theater; sunlight pours into the musty auditorium. A title announces that "Three years have passed... [Five years in the U.S. copyright registration submission] ...The Woodford Theater, house of mystery, reopens its doors." This little scene, together with the footage that follows, gives the interested viewer probably the most extensive look at Universal's great "Phantom stage" that any film would allow, and that includes both versions of *Phantom of the Opera*, and 1939's *The House of Fear*.

In rapid succession, back from wherever, come Mike Brody and comic relief stagehands Tommy (Slim Summerville) and Sammy (Bud Phelps); the fact that the perennially frightened Gene was once Woodford's secretary comes out. The four comics head up to the green room, where the cast of *The Snare* is slowly gathering at the invitation of a new impresario.

Downstairs, Miss Barbara (Carrie Daumery), an elderly character actress who had also been present when Woodford was murdered, gingerly enters the building. (Barbara's subsequent introductory title is handled with easy grace in the French translation: "notre ancienne grande coquette.") The camera focuses on a busy little spider and his web in extreme closeup, and on the actress *through* the gossamer web. A gratuitous wide-mouthed shriek later, Miss Barbara has managed to become almost completely covered with webbing. Her slow climb up the stairs to the green room allows Leni and Mohr a splendid point of view shot — the camera becomes the actress — of the four cowering men on the other side of the sticky, silky lacework.

No more than a minute after Quayle arrives, Arthur McHugh (Montagu Love) strides into the green room and announces that he has leased the theater with the intention of reopening with *The Snare*, the same play (and same cast!) that had shut the doors on the night of John Woodford's death. Quayle initially refuses: despite the dead-end police investigation, he has always borne the brunt of everyone's suspicions. When Doris Terry saunters through the door, the tension in the room

Miss Barbara (Carrie Daumery) in her encounter with the spider web in *The Last Warning*. PHOTOFEST.

becomes palpable. A cut to the hallway shows a pair of very shapely, silk-stockinged legs, and the camera appears to have a difficult time leaving leg-level in order to note Robert Bunce's appreciative reaction. The legs belong to Evelyn Hendon (Margaret Livingston), who has been sent to the theater by her agent in order to take over the role of Anne. The elder Bunce, vulture-like with peaked white hair and a beakish nose that has to be seen to be believed, pauses to chastise his younger brother for his attention to the lovely woman before approaching McHugh over a disturbing telegram. We read it as McHugh does:

> Don't attempt to open my theater.
> First warning.
>   (signed) John Woodford

Thoughtful but unmoved by the warning, McHugh confronts both Quayle and Doris and threatens point-blank to inform the police of their refusal to go along before the couple change their minds about participating. McHugh then calls in the rest of the company, and Gene runs to fetch the scripts. A handwritten note reading "Don't disturb the sleep of the dead!" is found in the drawer, and this is enough cause for another display from Woodford's former aide. Not to be outdone, Mike, Tommy, and Sammy hurry in and announce that they have just seen the ghost of Woodford! Everyone reacts, there are several gaping maws (insert screams here), and the door to the green room slowly opens. Thankfully, it is only Harvey Carleton, come in answer to his invitation. "*There* was your

A little bit of Gene (Torben Meyer) and some Expressionistic touches go a long way — just ask Doris Terry (Laura La Plante). *PHOTOFEST*.

phantom, Mike!" thunders McHugh, but the chubby stage manager shakes this off: "It's dangerous," he quivers, "to reopen this theater!"

Advised that he'll be playing the part that Woodford had enacted on the night of his death, Carleton shrugs and accepts his script with a smile. The smile quickly fades, however (and there's another round of apparent screams), when the cast sees "This is the dead man's role! (signed) John Woodford" scrawled across the actor's sides. Making matters worse, a dusty chest which had housed the scripts shoots a drawer out onto the floor. "It's Woodford's hand!" screeches Barbara, and McHugh,

about up to here with temperamental furniture and creaking doors, heaves the chest to the floor. Worse still, smoke begins to pour into the room from under the now locked door. More screams. In an eye-opening display of strength, McHugh punches a hole in the door, but through that same hole a hideous apparition is seen. Bravely, the impresario reaches out and manages to unlock the door from the outside.

Barbara is carried down to the stage area, and all the women are revived. The source of the smoke (and the apparition) is revealed to be Tommy, who's wearing a gas-mask to protect

New man Jeffries (Francisco Maran) is caught up in the spirit of the moment, along with Richard Quayle (John Boles), Doris (Laura La Plante), Robert Bunce (Mack Swain) and the lovely Evelyn Hendon (Margaret Livingston). PHOTOFEST.

himself while fumigating. The rehearsal starts, but Barbara is so beside herself that she doesn't notice sinking into the stage's cellar when a trapdoor elevator is accidentally activated. She does notice another spider — perhaps bigger than the first — as it climbs its own thread back up into the flies. The camera follows the tiny creature as it alights on a wooden staircase, which hangs precariously above the cast. The imperceptible additional weight causes one of the supporting ropes to give way, and only Quayle's quick action prevents Doris Terry from joining John Woodford in the bosom of Abraham.

Evelyn walks the shaken Doris to her dressing room, as Mr. Jeffries (Francisco Maran), the new actor hired to take over Harvey Carleton's old part, arrives to run through his lines. Doris

sends Evelyn back onstage, where she greets a jovial Robert Bunce; rehearsal starts again. Back in her dressing room, the spent Doris senses she is not alone, but sees nothing. Behind the walls of the room lurks a grotesquely deformed figure, dusted with cobwebs and clad in what seem to be floor-length robes. Through a secret door, a misshapen hand reaches in; Doris turns, and the hand withdraws. The camera tracks over to the wall, sliding into soft-focus as it does, and an eye — bloodshot and angled *sideways*— peers through a jagged hole.

Unable to shake the feeling of unease, Doris leaves the room and rejoins the troupe. Behind her, the phantom's arm snatches the actress's purse, sachet, and lace handkerchief from her makeup table. (The arm we see both here and earlier is blatantly fake, a small hook attached to the inside palm of the hand. The prop "grasps" each item without clenching its fingers, and no attempt is made to disguise this. Perhaps footage giving the rationale to this conspicuous device was missing from the print, but I still can't even remotely fathom why such an artifice would be useful or necessary to the killer.)

From her blocked position at stage left, Doris watches as Jeffries backs Carleton up to the mantelpiece with his imaginary saber. Mohr's camera is now behind the fireplace, and the ersatz Woodford reaches back for the fateful candlestick; the lights drop dramatically and the candlestick almost glows in contrast. Before Harvey's hand can make contact, director Quayle stops the action and makes some recommendations. Again the men set to it, but this time, the camera assumes Doris' point of view, and the actress sees both Carleton and a ghostly Woodford backing towards certain doom. A quick cut as the living actor reaches again for the prop, and the camera spies the phantom quickly descending a stage ladder from the flies. The caped figure madly pulls the switches on the master control panel and Carleton's eyes widen as his hand hits the candlestick. He screams — a quick shot of Doris' eyes as they widen in horror — then the lights fail totally as Harvey Carleton pitches forward onto his face.

From the audience, McHugh warns everyone to stay put. Moving the beam of his flashlight out from under his own face (a splendidly eerie shot) to the stage proper, he pins down Evelyn, Jeffries, Quayle, and Doris with his light (another nod to *Metropolis*, wherein Rotwang had transfixed Maria with the beam of his own torch), and catches the burly younger Bunce stumbling blindly about the stage. A pan over to the control board reveals Tommy and Mike, each armed with a flashlight, working feverishly to restore the house lights. "Someone's cut the power," yells Tommy. When the lights come up, Barbara is perched atop a high flat, and young Bunce is caught bearing the unmistakable imprint of Evelyn's lips on one of his fleshy cheeks; Carleton is nowhere to be found.

Barbara screams yet again: "Carleton has disappeared, just like Woodford!" When calmed down sufficiently, the elderly actress puts McHugh on to something when she claims to sense the odor of death about the theater. There *is* an odor, and it's traced to Doris' sachet, which is lying on the stage floor. Near tears, the blond ingenue denies the perfume is hers — her sachet is back in her dressing room. As Quayle takes her in his arms, Doris glances up to one of the theater boxes where she sees (as does the viewer) the ghastly figure of John Woodford. She screams, but the figure drops to the floor of the box, virtually disappearing, before anyone else onstage can see it. McHugh orders everyone save Quayle and the stagehands out of the building, growling, "We're going to search the theater."

Nothing much is found, save a pair of grizzled dummies which give Tommy a scare, but an unearthly cry is heard. (No doubt one of the missing sound effects; a shot of two hands, desperately trying to claw their way through or out of something, is superimposed over the ring of frightened men.) Determined to get to the bottom of this, McHugh demolishes the wooden barrier to John Woodford's dressing room with a fire ax, and he and Quayle enter the locked room together. As the lights flicker again, McHugh watches Quayle pocket something he has discovered within the room (it is Doris' little purse) and finds a lace handkerchief and vial of scent himself.

The cry and the clawing noise begin again, the superimposed hands return to the screen, and both men move to the dressing room wall. A lever is found behind on of the hanging pictures; when pulled, a hidden door swings open. Backing away from the aperture, the men wait; again, Leni and Mohr allow some serious time to pass without movement of any kind. Finally, a hand becomes visible, and Harvey Carleton, shaken and bloodied, pulls himself erect. The actor can only mumble that he has no idea how he got into the passage before collapsing once more. McHugh and Quayle bravely head into the tunnel.

Some footage is missing from the print at this point. Following an unsettling shot of twin

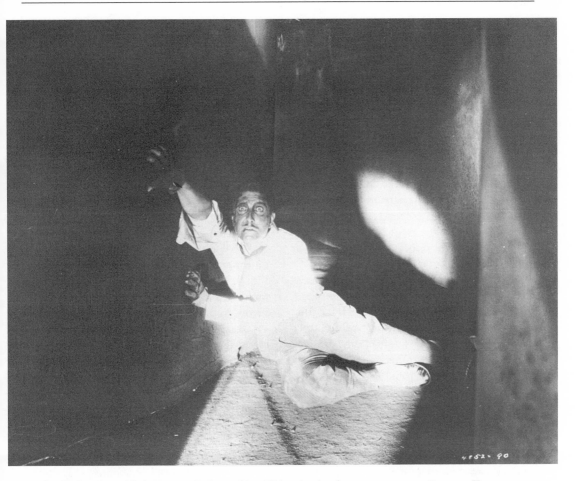

Bloodied and terrified, Harvey Carleton (Roy D'Arcy) exits the secret passage. *Richard Koszarski.*

lights moving toward the camera, we see that a trapdoor in the tunnel floor has been opened, and that McHugh is *climbing up* from below. In the 1939 remake, Woodford's body is found within the walls of the tunnel; nothing in the balance of the print or in the continuity script indicates a similar discovery here.

The men open another door, situated at the far end of the passageway and find themselves in Doris Terry's dressing room, along with Doris herself! Quayle pretends to have discovered Doris' handbag on the spot, but McHugh is having none of it. The hankie the actress takes from her purse is the twin of the one McHugh had found in Woodford's dressing room, and neither the ingenue's insistence that she knew nothing of the secret passage nor her lover's declaration that he will take over

"the dead man's role" in order to prove the pair's innocence seems to cut much ice with the glowering impresario. Oblivious to the young couple's dazed reaction, McHugh phones the police department, and arranges to have a squad of plainclothesmen and uniforms present at the reopening of *The Snare*, as he swears that the opening performance of the play will prove to be the end of the line for the phantom of the Woodford Theater.

The next morning, another note: "If you open my theater, you will not have more than one performance. Last warning!"

As at the start of the film, a montage of cars, pedestrians, street lamps, marquees, and first-nighters announces the gala return of play and players to Broadway. As the overture begins, the camera irises in on the solitary figure of McHugh from its vantage point in the flies. A cut has the detective watching an ominous movement beneath the canvas cover of the stage floor culminate at the base of a prop grandfather clock. A superimposed gong strikes, and, in an extreme long shot, the curtain rises. At first we watch the action from the wings, just over McHugh's shoulder; then we become McHugh — another POV shot — as one of the many disguised policemen alerts us that "The wire comes out from the clock. Keep your eye on the clock." The cop moves, and the scene continues until a second undercover man takes the place of the first: "400 volts... The wire runs under the floor covering and ends at the candlestick."

In a clever move, this second man moves behind one of the flats and peers through a horizontal crack between panels to watch the proceedings; the camera joins him, and we share the narrow vista. The fateful scene is soon being played out. True to his word, it is Quayle who is being prodded back towards the candlestick. The plucky juvenile reaches his hand back, and, an instant before he touches the metal prop, McHugh lurches onstage, madly blowing his whistle. Quayle lunges headfirst onto the stage floor, Doris lets out a scream, and — via a fascinating long shot from the rear of the auditorium — we watch all of the flats whisked up and away from the stage in the twinkling of an eye.

Before anyone else can move, McHugh races to center stage and tears open the door to the grandfather clock. Caught in the act is the phantom. The cops motion him out of the clock, but the killer drops beneath the stage in the trapdoor elevator and shoots in the shoulder the detective who follows him below. Pandemonium reigns as the audience mills toward the exits and the frustrated police take axes to the now-locked trap. A detective and a uniform cautiously invade the below-stage warrens, but the killer uses the darkness to his advantage and wings both men.

Time is running out, however. The phantom scampers madly out from under the stage and scales the tiers of boxes in his effort to escape. McHugh makes everyone's job that much harder when he barks, "Don't shoot. I want him alive!" and the chase becomes a merry one. As the masked man climbs up into the backstage flies, a shout rings out: "Mike Brody!" The title card and the shout are Robert Bunce's, and the hefty young theater owner points the frantic figure out to the circling cops just as a body comes hurtling down from above. It is the dummy of John Woodford that Doris Terry saw earlier.

Leaping onto a rope, the phantom swings out over the heads of the stagebound police and away from those who have followed him aloft. More than any other time in the film, Leni has Hal Mohr's camera jumping through hoops. One moment we are above the fugitive, watching, as he does, the floor sway back and forth far beneath him. The next moment we are below him, gazing dizzily as he swings and gyrates against the lines and angles of the theater ceiling. Most impressively, we *become* the phantom, swinging madly to and fro in breathtaking POV shots that were achieved by mounting the camera on a trapeze-like contraption. The wild roller-coaster ride is finally brought to an end when a stagehand undoes the rope in question and lowers the cloaked figure into the waiting arms of the police.

As young Bunce had shouted, it is indeed Mike Brody beneath the ghastly mask. Mike wastes no time in evening the score: the brains behind Woodford's murder and the subsequent "haunting" of the theater is none other than Robert Bunce! Brody swears that he thought Bunce had only wanted him to scare Woodford, but that the voltage of the rig was set too high; he had never intended to kill the actor. Bunce, it seems, had wanted to sell the theater outright rather than lease it (as his brother had), and the ghostly occurrences were meant to dissuade anyone from renting the property. Adding insult to the corpulent Bunce's injuries, the lovely Evelyn collaborates everything while producing her own detective's badge for inspection.

The heavies are taken away, there's some comic by-play between Doris and Quayle which culminates in a Hollywood kiss, and the Black Maria pulls off into the twin of the montage that opened the picture.

The flies have flown, and Mike Brody stands exposed as the phantom. *RONALD V. BORST/HOLLYWOOD MOVIE POSTERS.*

Top billed Laura La Plante doesn't have as much to do here as she had in *The Cat and the Canary*; a teenage beauty contest winner before making her motion picture debut at the age of 15, the lovely blonde spends most of her time onscreen reacting to assorted assaults, visions, and set-ups. Still, her presence in both the first and the last of Paul Leni's American quartet somehow legitimized them as major efforts, as the actress seldom appeared in anything other than Jewels. While Miss La Plante graced many a silent Universal feature during the twenties (between them, she and Priscilla Deane starred in 50-odd productions for the company), her output fell off dramatically following the advent of sound. This was in no way due to any vocal shortcomings (in his *Classics*

of the Silent Screen, Joe Franklin purred that "Her voice … was in fact the sort of voice I had imagined while watching her silents"); the actress decided to curtail her career in order to spend more quality time with her family and to pursue other interests.

Although his name appears second on the cast list, Montagu Love walks off with *The Last Warning*. The husky British expatriate was cast against type here; along with the Beerys (Noah and Wallace), Warner Oland, and Jean Hersholt (in his pre–Doctor Christian days), Love had usually been considered the *crème de la crème* of American silent screen heavies. His Arthur McHugh is a no-nonsense type, as adept at reading a facial tic as at driving his fist through an office door. He may be taken aback

As was customary, a smiling Paul Leni (seated at center) poses with his production unit. Hal Mohr sits under his camera. *RICHARD KOSZARSKI*.

at odd moments by the strange occurrences at the theater, but he's never seriously deterred from mounting his revival of *The Snare* or from getting his man. Come the talkies, the popular actor would be in constant demand and would spend a good bit of time at Warner Brothers, where such mega-action pictures as *Gunga Din* and *The Adventures of Robin Hood* would be all the more exciting for his presence. The haunted theater opus was his first picture for the House That Carl Built; he would return the following year for *The Cat Creeps*, the sound remake of Paul Leni's first Universal triumph. 1942's *Sherlock Holmes and the Voice of Terror* marked the immortal detective's first adventure at the studio and Montagu Love's last. One of a select group of truly memorable cads, Love died in 1943, with a handful of pictures bearing his

unmistakable stamp awaiting posthumous release.

Beautiful Margaret Livingston would be back, legs and all, for another Universal Jewel a couple of months later, when George Melford's *The Charlatan* saw release. Like Laura La Plante, Miss Livingston had debuted in motion pictures while still in her teens (her first Universal film, 1924's *Butterfly*, saw her supporting her blond *Warning* co-star), but spent most of her two-decade career as a free agent. Within a year of her working with Paul Leni, the lovely ingenue was featured in the 1930 RKO remake of George M. Cohan's spooky *Seven Keys to Baldpate*. Surviving her undeniably prolific Hollywood career by some 50 years, Livingston died in 1985.

John Boles is most familiar to genre fans

A trade ad, the typesetter of which must soon have received his own last warning from the "Leammles." KEVIN CHARBENEAU.

as Victor Moritz, the most forgettable character in the unforgettable *Frankenstein*. The
handsome Boles does a decent enough job in
the first part of *The Last Warning* (a contemporary review admitted that he and the others
"do their best to help out the weird activities"),
but is reduced to little more than biting his lip,
shooting sidelong glances, and googling his
eyes once the theater reopens for business.
Sadly, the discrepancy as to his screen name
(Quaile in the Cohn continuity, Quayle in the
film — at least per Fred Kelsey's handwriting)
is the most interesting facet to the character.
Boles' talents as a song-and-dance man would
come to the fore along with the surfeit of "All
talking! All singing! All dancing!" musicals
which the early thirties would offer sound-
hungry audiences.

For genre aficionados who have come to
know Bert Roach only as the highly epicene
(and embarrassing) Paul in Robert Florey's
Murders in the Rue Morgue, the chubby thesp's
turn as the button man in *Warning* may come
as a surprise. Perhaps in response to Paul Leni's
direction, or perhaps because the film is populated by so many other comic types, Roach
manages to avoid playing for cheap laughs and
creates a credible stage manager in Mike Brody
(Brady). D'Arcy Corrigan, who also surfaced
in the Florey flop (in a bit as the morgue
keeper), is likewise commendable in his brief
footage as the doomed Woodford. It's a shock
to see Mack Swain, a perennial foil for Charlie
Chaplin and countless other silent clowns,
cleaned up and well dressed; the hefty Swain is
better at fleshing out Robert Bunce than one
might think. George (Slim) Summerville is as
lugubrious as ever, and as I really can't think
of anything good to say about his diminutive
side-kick, Bud Phelps, I'll let it go at that.

Reviews of *The Last Warning* were almost
uniformly good (but not great), with remarks
about Paul Leni's mastery of the lights and the
lens rising to the top. The *New York Times*, for
example, allowed how "One can admire parts
of Mr. Leni's work without being wrought up
about the murder or who did it." And again,
"It is quite evident that [Leni] revels in some
dissolves and camera angles, but other scenes

don't appear to interest him nearly as much."
Apparently, the anonymous critic expected
even the more mundane bits of exposition or
the intrusive stretches of comic relief to be
couched in the same arresting style that Leni
reserved for the quasi-supernatural vignettes
or for the action scenes.

Displaying the penury of praise which
would earmark its opinion of horror films
during the ensuing decades, *Variety* damned
The Last Warning with a so-so review. As "Sid"
put it:

> Picture has spots where it grips and misses,
> but no doubt of there being too much of it.
> …Plenty of hoke and a wild imagination,
> but probably okay for moderate grosses,
> because there are enough screams to stim-
> ulate the average film mob into sticking
> through it plus the La Plante name to draw
> in those localities where she's strong.
> …Leni should learn that dialog must have
> pace. He probably won't make the same
> error again, but it's a glaring fault here….
> Its production and camera work should
> count, with numerous trick lens effects
> mostly used at the opening and close.

A wonderful film that easily holds one's
attention even in total silence, *The Last Warning* deserves to be released on tape as part of
the current MCA series. Ed Stratmann, the assistant curator of the George Eastman House,
opines that the question of legal title to the
film, as well as the perennial shortage of funds,
mitigates against any such move in the near
future. If the film hasn't already fallen into the
public domain, the legal issue might well be the
greater of the two stumbling blocks. Should
that prove surmountable, an effort should be
made to raise the necessary monies in order to
clean the extant materials, to research and
replace the original titles, and at the very least,
to reintroduce a scored silent version of Paul
Leni's final American triumph to countless fans
for whom it would mean Christmas whenever
it appeared.

The Last Warning

Released January 6, 1929; 87 minutes/
8 reels

Cast: Laura La Plante (Doris Terry); Montagu Love (Arthur McHugh); John Boles (Richard Quayle); Roy D'Arcy (Harvey Carleton); Burr McIntosh (Josiah Bunce); Mack Swain (Robert Bunce); Margaret Livingston (Evelyn Hendon); Carrie Daumery (Miss Barbara); Bert Roach (Mike Brody); Slim Summerville (Tommy); Bud Phelps (Sammy); Torben Meyer (Gene); D'Arcy Corrigan (John Woodford); Charles K. French (Doctor); Francisco Maran (Jeffries); Ella McKenzie (Ann); Fred Kelsey, Tom O'Brien (Detectives); Harry Northrup (Coroner)

Credits: Presented by Carl Laemmle; Supervised by Carl Laemmle, Jr.; Director— Paul Leni; Story Supervisor—Edward Montagne; Based on the play *The Last Warning: A Melodrama in Three Acts* by Thomas F. Fallon, and the novel *House of Fear* by Wadsworth Camp; Scenario—Alfred A. Cohn; Dialogue and Titles—Tom Reed; Adaptation—Alfred A. Cohn, Robert F. Hill, J.G. Hawks; Photographer—Hal Mohr, ASC; Art Director— Charles D. Hall; Film Editor—Robert Carlisle; Musical Score—Joseph Cherniavsky

Released both with talking sequences, sound effects, and a music score (Movietone), and as a silent feature with musical cue sheets for orchestral/piano accompaniment.

THE CHARLATAN (1929)

Clowns, whiteface, the twin masks of comedy and tragedy — all can be traced back to Thespis and company, who started the ball rolling with dramas involving Greek gods and manipulated mortals. It would take a book-length treatise to cover the subsequent historical development and the psychological milieu of the clown, highlighting the Italian Renaissance and the birth of the European circus tradition, but for our purposes, we need only look at the cinema in its silent days. As early as 1900, clowns made it onto film; Edison's *The Clown and the Alchemist* took fewer than 50 feet to demonstrate the latest tricks the motion picture camera could play on the descendants of Harlequin.

The genre had a couple of notable run-ins with clowns, and who else but Lon Chaney was responsible for them? Within the space of four years, Chaney filmed adaptations of two Broadway shows: Leonid Andreyev's *He Who Gets Slapped* (1924) and David Belasco and Tom Cushing's *Laugh, Clown, Laugh* (1928; taken, in turn, from Gausto Martino's Italian drama *Ridi Pagliacci*, itself derived from Ruggiero Leoncavallo's opera.) Both pictures were MGM successes, neither was helmed by Tod (as in clod) Browning, and each dealt with the comic figure's personal angst. In the former, a cuckolded husband runs off to join the circus,

becoming He Who Gets Slapped, a clown with an immense talent and a masochistic streak. In the latter, the clown is already unlucky in love; his laughter and merry Punchinello hijinks are shams, held firmly in place to disguise his broken heart. *Laugh, Clown, Laugh* was unique in its day, as the studio offered theater managers their choice of denouements: tragic (ending with Lon's noble self-sacrifice) or happy (wherein it was suggested that the plucky performer would surmount all those broken bones and rise again to the *huzzahs* of his grateful public).

The Charlatan was ostensibly based on the eponymous Broadway play by Ernest Pascal and Leonard Praskins, but it — like its slicker MGM cousins — owed more than a passing nod to Signore Leoncavallo, the Commedia dell'Arte, and a shopping list of tired bromides, ranging from "He who laughs last, etc." to "What goes around, comes around." The Universal melodrama pulled something of a dramatic reversal, however, as its protagonist initially runs away *from* being a circus clown to settle into a weightier and more serious profession: crystal gazer. Still, despite the changes in costume and deportment, despite a shift in goal and modus operandi, despite the necessary retooling of accouterments and props, our hero has merely moved from the garish

34

exuberance of the Big Top to the quirky confines of life's sideshow.

More comprehensive thoughts on magic and the like can be found in the essay on *The Last Performance*; as Count Merlin (the eponymous charlatan) is more properly a seer than a magician (though he does perform the odd card trick and illusion), we should examine this wrinkle briefly before moving on.

The several decades which preceded and followed the turn of the century saw a tremendous interest in spiritualism, a quasi-religious movement wherein a person's faith in the afterlife was buoyed up by tangible evidence such as seances, automatic writing and spirit photography. One of the most acclaimed proponents of spiritualism (a term he despised; he much preferred "psychic religion") was Sir Arthur Conan Doyle, the literary sire to Sherlock Holmes and a bulwark of Victorian eccentricity. Conan Doyle was extremely vocal in his praise of the superhuman efforts expended by such mediumistic personalities as Eusapia Palladino, the Fox sisters, and the Davenport brothers, and lost a good part of his reputation when these and others were exposed as frauds through the efforts of Harry Houdini and his outraged colleagues. While the "psychic religion" gradually lost its hold on all save the most obtuse, the movies' interest in the dramatic end of other-worldly communication never waned.

Seances and spiritualism were common themes in the early silent days, with much of the pertinent output coming from France (primarily from Georges Méliès). Few of the short films treated the topic with respect, as Pathé and French Gaumont (and Carl Laemmle's IMP) found the duplicitous aspects of a seance of greater cinematic interest than its supposed results. In 1919, Bernard Veiller's stage melodrama *The Thirteenth Chair* was adapted to the screen for the first time, starring Creighton Hale, who would later leave his mark on the field of comedy spookers with such prestige efforts *as The Cat and the Canary* (1927) and *Seven Footprints to Satan* (1929). A somber tale of mediums and murder, *Chair* left its lesser competitors in the dust and set the wheels in motion for more sophisticated views of adult themes. The 1929 MGM remake paired Tod Browning with Bela Lugosi for a historic and enjoyable (if slow motion) stroll through the venerable plot.

More germane to the matter at hand than spiritualism is clairvoyance, that pseudo-supernatural attribute in psychically "sensitive" persons which allows them a glimpse of planes not evident to ordinary man. As some sort of spiritual ties provide the rationale for this ability, at least in the motion picture world, the presumption is for a relationship between mediums and seers. Some four years before he had highlighted both Margaret Wycherly's brogue and Bela Lugosi's unique intonations in *Chair*, Tod Browning had set his hand (literally; he wrote the original story) to carnivals and clairvoyants in *The Mystic* (1925, also MGM). Having cut his teeth on carny life and having mastered the intricacies of being a woman's director during his years at Universal (see the notes on *Dracula*, following), Browning set down a story about the criminal practices of a gang of Hungarian gypsies, which was centered around hotcha fortune-teller, Zara (Aileen Pringle). The film's underlying similarities to *The Unholy Three* didn't escape the notice of the critics, and while it made money, *The Mystic* couldn't hold the earlier film's coat at the box-office.

Fast forward to 1929 again, and Harry Cohn's new Columbia Studios was gearing up for more of the same. This time around, the title was *The Faker*, and the chief practitioner of things preternatural was Warner Oland. Phony seances gave way to genuine falling in love, and once again, the ne'er-do-wells who sought to profit by exploiting the spiritual naïveté of the great (albeit rich) unwashed were brought to justice. Both *The Mystic* and *The Faker* had their respective cads at home at the floating table; *The Charlatan* eschewed more substantial spiritualistic furniture for the crystal ball and the low-overhead field of palmreading.

Although both the part-sound and silent versions of *The Charlatan* have made it through the years, I was able to screen only the latter.

Unlike the silent print of *The Last Warning* which suffered the slings and arrows of editing and title translation, and that of *The Last Performance*, which was nearly halved in its abridgment, *The Charlatan* is virtually complete. The film's status as a Jewel is as plain as the nose on the live action swami who prognosticates under the main titles. The narrative intertitles are displayed over a hand-drawn tableau of a mystic at work.

> TITLE: A glimpse of the past, a glance into a roseate future; old wrongs righted and new hopes builded [sic]. All is possible.
> TITLE: That is why a certain address on Roxbury Drive holds an unfailing fascination for ladies of fashion.

One need only see the sign adorning that Roxbury Drive address to understand why some might find it fascinating:

> Count Merlin
> Master of Occult Sciences
> By appointment only

A closeup of Count Merlin (Holmes Herbert), gazing deeply into his crystal, fades to a long shot of the seer and a customer at a small table. Opulent drapes hang everywhere, and the couple are flanked by a pair of flaming braziers. This is the mystic's holy of holies.

Out in the "waiting room," easily a half-dozen other well-heeled women cool those heels while a beautiful young servant, clad fetchingly as a harem girl, totes refreshments to them. Two male servants — one a dwarf, both outfitted in turbans and Indian attire — espy two new arrivals, and the taller servant, Rasha, goes to welcome them. The older of the two women, Mrs. Deering (Rose Tapely), has Rasha announce the younger woman's arrival to the Count. "Mrs. Deering is here, Sahib. She brings the one for whom you have waited." Merlin, himself turbaned and splendidly bearded, seems pleased: "Send her in and see that I am not disturbed. I will see no one else today."

The one for whom he has waited (Margaret Livingston) doesn't so much walk as saunter into the room, and she loftily challenges the Count to call her by name. When he refers to her as Florence Talbot, she pooh-poohs the news: "That isn't clever; my friend told your attendant my name. When Merlin addresses her as Florence *Dwight*, however, and reveals that the man she loves "has never really loved [her]," her attention perks up. Mrs. Talbot sits for a consultation, and the crystal ball provides the flashback so necessary at this time.

The ball shows a younger Florence Talbot: she is a trapeze artist in a circus and the wife of Peter Dwight, one of the Big Top's featured clowns. Taking their bows together, the couple repairs to their tented private quarters, where Peter nuzzles his little daughter, Ann, and Florence is slipped a note — "I have everything in readiness for tonight. Love, Dick" — by her dresser. While the husband heads off to change into his street clothes, mother and daughter pile into a touring car with the homebreaker. The ringmaster breaks the news to the bewildered clown ("You must have been blind not to have seen this coming!"), who thunders: "I haven't been blind! But I didn't think she'd take Ann. I swear I'll spend my life to get my baby back!"

The flashback ends; Count Merlin sits exhausted at the crystal, and Florence, having dropped some bills onto the table, stumbles back out through the parted curtains. Aghast, she tells Mrs. Deering, "He's a fiend. He told me things no one possibly could know!" Inside the crystal chamber, Merlin admits to Rasha: "As false and treacherous as ever. She's treating Talbot as she treated me." Master and servant move to an inner room, where the seer doffs his costume and removes his beard and make-up. Count Merlin is Peter Dwight, and his plans are simple: "She'll pay, but first I want my daughter!"

> TITLE: No occult power was necessary to divine the undercurrent of restlessness in the fashionable Talbot home.

Walking a half-mile or so through a cavernous foyer, the Talbot butler admits Doctor and Mrs. Paynter (Philo McCullough and

Florence Dwight's smile is less genuine than her husband's, and his is painted on. A moment of harmony, early in *The Charlatan*. PHOTOFEST.

Anita Garvin) to the fashionable home alluded to in the title. Dick Talbot (Rockliffe Fellowes) promises to keep Mrs. Paynter entertained — there's a bridge game in progress — while the doctor sees to Florence. Mrs. Talbot "has another one of her headaches," Dick explains, and Dr. Paynter's "usual sugar-coated pills" will probably do the trick again. There's more here than meets the eye, however; once the physician has entered Florence's bedroom, the truth comes out. "If you loved me, you'd take me away at once," the beautiful woman sobs. Begging a bit more time in which to settle his affairs, the medico gets down to some high-level osculation, and only his keen hearing allows him to break from the clenches and grab Florence's wrist in the accepted pulse-taking

fashion as the clearly suspicious Mrs. Paynter enters the room without knocking.

All three head downstairs, where the bridge game has come to a screeching halt due to Mrs. Deering's preferring to discuss Count Merlin rather than play cards. Hubby Frank (Crauford Kent), who happens to be the district attorney, would like nothing better than to run the occult master and his gang out of town. When Florence's daughter, Ann (Dorothy Gould), asks whether Merlin can't be brought to perform in the Talbot mansion, Frank sees his chance: "How about it, Talbot? Let's show this bird up!"

Title: There were many fates of interest to Count Merlin at the Talbot home.

Apparently, the invitation had been extended and accepted. As the Count busily reads Mrs. Deering's palm in the extravagant surroundings of the Talbot drawing room, other of the usual guests mill about and observe. When the D.A. sits for a reading, though, he's taken aback:

> MERLIN: Here is the skeptic — a combative force, with which it is difficult to cope.
> FRANK: How do you know I'm a skeptic?
> MERLIN: I'll quote the words you spoke when it was proposed to bring me here.

And so he does. Holding Deering's left palm flush against his forehead, Merlin intones: "Sooner or later, my office will get the goods on that bird and run him out of town." Still, the D.A. is having none of it and seems more belligerent than ever, until the mystic warns him: "I told Mrs. Deering of *her* first love affair. Shall I tell her of yours?" Deering bails out, and Ann takes the seat.

The rest of the company strolls off into other parts of the house as Merlin takes the young girl's hands in his own and proceeds to speak from his heart: "My child, your future holds nothing but love and happiness ... You have the devotion of a boy whose love has endured since your first school days — and another love, denied since your babyhood, has come back to watch over you." Ann is puzzled at first, but then breaks into a lovely smile, as does the ecstatic charlatan. "The folks are waiting at your disappearing cabinet," she tells him. "Perhaps we'd better join them." They do.

The disappearing cabinet is just what it sounds like: a phone booth-sized box on casters, replete with a velvet curtain (interestingly ornamented with a Star of David in front). The onlookers look on as Merlin has his Indian servants spin the box before drawing the curtain. A mystical flourish later, the curtain is opened, and the lovely young harem girl has magically appeared. The curtain is closed once more, another flourish, and the girl has vanished, presumably whence she came originally. District

Attorney Deering knows better: "There's nothing to it. The girl is your accomplice." Merlin shrugs: "I assure you, anyone will do. Whom do you suggest?" When Ann opines that they should draw lots to decide the next assistant, the Count whips out a handy deck, and — after each of the women has selected a card fair and square — has a duplicate of Florence's card rise untouched from a goblet held by Frank Deering. Before the plucky Mrs. Talbot can enter the cabinet, though, the butler arrives to announce that dinner is imminent and that everyone ought to dress. "Let's postpone the excitement until after dinner," Florence advises, and everyone departs.

A cut to the bedroom level sees Dr. Paynter sneaking into Florence Talbot's boudoir. Merlin's dwarf has seen the whole thing and tells his master, who (temporarily free of greasepaint and crepe hair) plants himself on the verandah outside the scene of the assignation and eavesdrops. Florence is adamant that she and the doctor make their move that very night. "I'm desperate, Walter," she cries out. "I won't be discarded!" Reluctantly, Paynter nods in agreement and has scarcely left when Merlin enters through the French doors. It takes only a moment for Florence to recognize the man she abandoned well over a decade earlier, and she laughs at his demand that his daughter be made aware of what has happened. Nonetheless, when she threatens to call the police, the furious Peter/Merlin counters, "Why the police? Call your guest, the district attorney. You can tell him about me, while I discuss your recent visitor with your husband." Florence is uncharacteristically silent, and her ex-husband makes things clear: "Before you leave all this, I want my daughter to know the truth!"

A cut shows deviltry in progress. In extreme closeup, a pair of pliers affixes a thin nail to the inside wall of the disappearing cabinet, and a drop of liquid is then applied to the point. Cut to a long shot: the drapes that conceal the entire cabinet from view are billowing, as if disturbed from within. Ann's boyfriend, Jerry Starke (Fred MacKaye) happens onto the scene while these wheels are in motion and rushes up to snatch open the curtains. No one's there, but through the French doors, he apparently catches sight of someone against the lightning flashes of the storm that has arisen.

Fade to the drawing room. The guests begin to assemble and down the stairs — arm in arm! — come Florence and Mrs. Paynter. Florence reaches back furtively to slip a note to Dr. Paynter, who is walking just behind her, and this is seen by Peter, once again done up in his Count Merlin regalia. Merlin, though, is also spotted — by Ann — as he grabs Florence's arm and whispers through clenched teeth at her ("Remember, I've waited too long to take any chances now!"). As seer and hostess enter the drawing room, Dr. Paynter steps out and catches a glimpse of the note he was handed: "Everything is in readiness, dear. Just a few more hours and then — life together. F." Dick Talbot comes out to retrieve the doctor, who quickly shoves the paper back into his pocket. "Dinner is served."

After dinner, the company reconvenes to watch Florence take her spin in the disappearing cabinet. With a bow and a wave, she gamely climbs aboard, pausing to shake Merlin's hand and inform him, "I believe I know enough of your magic to perform this trick to perfection." The curtain is drawn, we see the accommodating woman trigger the secret door within the box, and Count Merlin gestures magically. As expected, Florence has vanished. No way, however, can he bring her back; the curtain is drawn and opened three times before the concerned crowd runs to examine the trick box. The back door is released, and Florence Talbot drops motionless into the arms of Count Merlin. Followed by Doctor Paynter, Dick carries his wife up to the nearest bedroom. With a strange look on his face, Dick turns to the physician: "You'll be able to fix things up, Doc — the usual sugar-coated pills." Dick rejoins the group downstairs as Paynter, in the course of an incredibly cursory examination, comes upon a bloody scratch on the woman's exposed shoulder. He, too, moves downstairs where he announces Florence Talbot's death. "She died from a powerful poison," he advises

everyone, "inoculated into her shoulder by a sharp-pointed instrument."

Deering takes charge, forbids anyone to leave the house, and orders the police be called and the cabinet be examined; Jerry finds the nail sticking though the back door. After Dr. Paynter runs a couple of tests on the "sharp-pointed instrument" in Dick's office, he announces: "The needle was dipped into a poison similar to Curare, the South American virus which has instant fatal reactions." When asked, Merlin admits a familiarity with South American poisons, and things get bleaker when Ann comes forward and spills the beans about the Count's pre-dinner threats to her mother. Deering dismisses the house guests and closets himself with Merlin and his servants in order to do some questioning. The "questioning" amounts only to an invitation to confess. In a well-choreographed move, the dwarf snaps off the lights, the girl opens the French doors to the outside, and Rasha and Merlin gag Deering and carry him off into the night.

As the occasional cut shows the police hurtling towards the mansion during the storm, Merlin and company lug Deering into their rooms, where he's tied to a chair while the charlatan makes himself up in the D.A.'s spitting image. Borrowing the bound man's pince-nez, Merlin heads back down to Dick Talbot's office and takes over the investigation. "Detain everyone in the hall," he barks at the newly arrived cops. "Have the men round up that magician and his gang. And bring that scoundrel's cabinet in here!" Merlin douses the lights in Talbot's office, and with the able assistance of "Captain Dodds from headquarters," begins to study the case by the illumination from the fireplace and the odd lightning bolt from the raging storm. The first one called in by the ersatz D.A. is Dick Talbot: "I realize how upset you are," Dick is told, "but I need you here in the room."

Comfortably seated behind Talbot's desk, Merlin has Dodds next summon Doctor Paynter, who admits that both he and his wife ("She was my nurse, before I married her") are *also* familiar with deadly poisons. Dodds is then ordered to "Send in the maid, and have Mrs.

Paynter wait in the hall until I call." The maid is asked, pointblank, to finger the man she had frequently escorted to Mrs. Talbot's room. She indicates Dr. Paynter and is excused before Merlin lets it drop that the physician has had a secret love affair with Mrs. Talbot and then *really* lowers the boom: "She wanted you to take her away tonight — but that did not suit your plans!" Dodds has to drag the irate widower from Paynter's throat. Physically spent, Talbot withdraws from the office and climbs the stairs, headed for his room.

Mrs. Paynter is brought in, but is unmoved by any news of her husband's indiscretions with Florence Talbot. "You knew they intended to elope tonight," the disguised Merlin sneers, and *this* hits home. Upstairs, Dick Talbot is clubbed into unconsciousness as he enters his room, and an oddly manicured hand retrieves a paper from his pocket. Meanwhile, neither Paynter nor his wife will admit to anything more serious than infidelity and anger; "He hasn't nerve enough," the glowering woman smirks. Outside, a cop on watch grabs Jerry Starke, who is bundled up against the weather and on his way off the property. When confronted in the office by the outraged would-be Deering ("Why did you attempt to leave the house against my orders?"), Starke says nothing. Ann runs in a moment later; her father has disappeared. Jerry and Ann pause to comfort each other, while Merlin steps to the French doors, whence he receives the paper Rasha had taken from Dick Talbot's pocket: it is the note Florence had slipped to Doctor Paynter earlier!

All of a sudden, doors fly open with the pace of a French bedroom farce. In wobbles Dick, supported by Captain Dodds. Through the outside doors barrels a uniformed policeman, carrying the sodden and struggling dwarf. Another cop barges in from the foyer, one arm around Rasha and the other around the harem girl. After an awkward pause, Merlin stands and raises himself to his full height. "I now ask your cooperation and fairness, while I unmask the real murderer." The camera jumps from face to face, from cop to suspect and back again, before settling in again on Merlin. Slowly, Merlin takes off his pince-nez

and removes his crepe goatee and mustache. No one quite knows what the hell is going on — except for Dick. Merlin turns to the widower and demands, "Richard Talbot — Who am I?" Shocked and disbelieving, the man can only mutter, "Peter Dwight."

His Deering guise removed and his Merlin persona abandoned, Peter Dwight motions for the lights to be turned on. Indicating Talbot, Peter looks at Ann and admits, "Fifteen years ago this man stole my wife and baby from me." He hands Dick the note that Rasha had purloined. "Today I learned the woman planned to leave him as she left me — with another man!" Peter appeals to Jerry Franke: "Jerry, you're trying to protect Talbot for Ann's sake. *I* am her father; tell what you know." The young man mulls this over for a moment, and then allows he saw Talbot "meddling with the back of the cabinet." Peter is triumphant: "Jealousy got the better of you, Talbot. *You* killed your wife!" Wrapping things up neatly, Talbot confesses: "Yes, I killed her — killed her with poison I got from her lover's bag!"

Ann, of course, finds consolation with Jerry and also on the shoulder of her natural father. As Dick is led away in cuffs, Frank Deering is rescued from the bowels of the disappearing cabinet — where he has heard everything. Nonplused, the only thing the district attorney can say is "I'll thank you for my glasses." The film wraps as Mrs. Deering instructs a reporter, "Don't forget to say that my husband, Mr. Deering, conducted the investigation in his usual brilliant manner."

Simply put, *The Charlatan* is lots of fun. The trappings of magic and mysticism go a long way to dress up a *very '20s* tale of sin begetting sin and the inevitability of justice. The story might have had a contemporary ring to it when it premiered on the Great White Way back in 1922, but by the advent of sound, it smacked more of a vintage morality play in glad rags than an adult drama set in the present day. Robert N. Lee should have nudged his adaptation toward the up-and-coming decade and spared us stuff like the lines he forces Florence to mouth as she introduces Ann to Count

His wife's betrayal has caused Peter Dwight (right) to become Count Merlin. Her subsequent murder will force him to assume the identity of district attorney Deering (the real article is at left behind the pince-nez and beard) in order to solve the mystery and clear his name(s). PHOTOFEST.

Merlin: "My daughter isn't the usual flapper; you can't fill her mind with nonsense." Still, almost 70 years after its first run, the *au courant* fashions are as picturesque as the Indian frippery, and one is left with a vista nearly as timeless as the Germania of the Frankenstein features.

A bit old-fashioned, too, is the totally happy ending: the unfaithful wife and mother has met a well-merited fate; the pseudo-father, himself a home wrecker, proves himself weaker than the natural father by succumbing first to sins of the flesh and then to the temptation to murder. God knows he deserves whatever punishment he gets. Even the pompous and short-sighted district attorney is handled with poetic justice; rendered as impotent physically as he

is intellectually, he's reduced to being a lump on the side of the proceedings. When his bout of "questioning" Merlin takes a turn toward the easy way out...

> DEERING: You may as well confess. Every bit of evidence points to you.
> MERLIN: That is true. But if you were competent, you'd realize someone has planned it that way.

...the charlatan realizes his only hope lies in his ability to metamorphose once again and fend for himself.

As we shall see also with regard to *The Last Performance*, the picture's title can refer to any of the principals. Despite her ties to the

The disappearing cabinet, the vehicle in the assassination of Florence and the largest bit of balderdash in the film. *PHOTOFEST.*

"fashionable world," Florence leaps from fidelity to betrayal with the verve she once displayed as Queen of the High Wire. Her marital loyalties run parallel to her passions; when the latter subside, the former are switched, and she needs to be "taken away" once again, so that she can begin her acrobatics anew. Dr. Paynter cheats on his missus and his Hippocratic oath through medical ministering that is widely recognized as ersatz — sugar-coated pills and all that — and he uses his status as physician merely to gain entrance to women's bedrooms. At this juncture, Mrs. Paynter is no longer wife or nurse.

At first Jerry Starke — the name suggests simplicity; his actions, complicity — keeps silent (a move which would definitely result in the arrest of an innocent man, should the D.A. not be forcibly removed) out of misplaced loyalty. He is no less a sham than any of the others for his choosing to ingratiate himself with Ann's family by escaping an awkward situation rather than to act with integrity. Frank Deering's professional ability is all bluster, and Mrs. Deering is not really what she seems to be either, if only because no one could really be *that* gullible. Merlin says as much at the demonstration in the Talbot home: "Your palm reveals that you are a good woman — really too good to be true." Even Ann, whose ultimately groundless accusations stem from words she does not comprehend, actions she misunderstands, and circumstances of which she is completely unaware, can be said to be displaying passions which are no more an authentic part of her real personality than the fake beard is part of her father's.

Dwight's Count Merlin is an amalgam of every level of the art of snookery known in 1929. He looks freely into the past, can foretell the future, reads virtue and vice in an outstretched palm as easily as others read the newspaper, and does parlor tricks in his spare time. Rumor even has it that he is a medium; at least Mrs. Deering moans that "If I weren't the wife of the District Attorney, I'd have him at my home for a seance." And while in the guise of Frank Deering, Merlin refers to himself as a magician, further compounding the

confusion. The only item missing from the picture's mystical agenda is hypnosis, which, ironically, was the silent cinema's most popular conduit to heavy melodrama.

While this potpourri is probably no less than could be expected for the time, it actually undermines the identity of the title character and assaults the integrity of the plot. The seer's shingle trumpets him as "Master of the Occult Sciences," yet his schlepping that massive disappearing cabinet over to the Talbot's manse marks him as yet another stage conjurer — and a not terribly mystifying one at that, for as the box is wheeled about on its casters, we note that it's deep enough to conceal not only Florence Talbot but also a couple of Rockettes. Since the assembled witnesses to the fatal disappearance make a beeline for the *back* of the cabinet, apparently they have all noticed the same thing. More distressing is the magical rigamarole in which Merlin indulges when lots are chosen by potential volunteers. All the hoopla involving a card rising unaided from a long-stemmed goblet is picturesque but smacks of parlor magic and throws the whole process of selection into a dubious light.

The Charlatan marked Holmes Herbert's debut at Universal. Born in England as Edward Sanger, Herbert migrated in 1917 to the colonies, where he started a lengthy career of second list roles, pausing now and again (as he did here) to snag top billing. Later in 1929, he would show up in the Tod Browning remake of *The Thirteenth Chair*, and the ensuing decade would find him aghast yet again in George Seitz's reworking of same (reprising the role of Sir Roscoe Crosby), along with some 75 other features. He was a good guy in *The Invisible Man*, a bad guy in *The Black Doll*, and moved with ease from the reddest of herrings to the blackest of knaves.

Herbert's prim, angular features and thinning hair are so well disguised by the uncomplicated but effective makeup of Count Merlin that there might well be another man undertaking the role of the mystic. With *The Charlatan* — hardly the most subtle scenario to come down the '20s cinematic pike, and a product of the tail end of the silent era with its attendant techniques — the actor must have felt tempted to exaggerate the more ethnic or bizarre elements of the "Master of the Occult Sciences"; he opted to instead underplay, and the resultant portrait is free of the broad strokes a lesser artist would have used. Having survived total abandonment in his former life and having become inured to skepticism and ridicule in his present incarnation, the man is nobody's fool and has settled into a comfortable modus operandi. Like the blind Tiresias, condemned by the gods to speak the truth always despite the pain and anguish pure veracity may cause, Dwight/Merlin reveals his secrets to the consternation of the people who would mock him. Herbert perfectly conveys both the profound loss of Peter Dwight and the insightful talent of Count Merlin. That the one has largely caused the other is a plot contrivance traceable to the Pascal-Praskins original. That we can accept the film's message — that blindness to one's own personal misfortune can lead to one's ability to perceive clearly the trials of others — attests to the talent of Holmes Herbert.

Margaret Livingston's niche in the genre was mentioned in the previous chapter, but her turn as Florence Talbot here deserves comment. The body of Livingston's film work was done during the silent era (she made only a handful of talkies, before retiring from the screen in 1934), and the actress had parlayed her substantial beauty, along with a flexibility which allowed her to wed a film's tenor to a proportionate degree of subtlety or outrageousness, into a solid if not quite stellar career. *The Charlatan* requires her character to abandon *two* men within moments of screen time; the implication is that this is standard operating procedure for the lovely Florence and that she may decide upon yet another midstream change of stallion before her looks give up the ghost. Livingston conveys the desperate sexual needs of this woman without reducing her to being a nymph or a harlot. Florence is not admirable in the least — she is duplicitous, arrogant, and vengeful — but she can have her more attractive side, seen briefly in the sporting manner in which she enters the disappearing cabinet. We may not shed a tear over her

removal from the scene, but we can't help feeling that, somehow, she was as much a victim to forces beyond her control as Peter Dwight and Dick Talbot were victims of her caprice.

Rockliffe Fellowes' pasty features are unremarkable in both composition and expression, but the Canadian actor managed to be nearly ubiquitous during the mid to late twenties. Like Miss Livingston, Fellowes drew his last cinematic breath in 1934. Crauford (aka Craufurd) Kent and Philo McCullough were both the sort of chameleon-like character men whose presences were often noted by film fans even if their names were unknown. Neither is given much raw material with which to work here — Deering is little more than a buffoon, Paynter nothing less than a cad — but few of the dozens of features in which the men would appear in the coming decade would offer them as much screen time, or as clearly identifiable character types, as would *The Charlatan*.

It's a pity that Anita Garvin wasn't given more to do here, other than glare daggers. The lovely actress, a talented comedienne in her own right and a frequent foil for Laurel and Hardy, Charley Chase, et al.), was capable of bringing greater dimension to the role of Mrs. Paynter; would that J. G. Hawks' scenario had extended her the professional courtesy. On the other hand, Dorothy Gould hasn't much to do, either, but doesn't seem that she could handle more than the few peas on her plate, anyhow. Miss Gould, whose Ann Talbot bears an eerie resemblance to Ed Wood squeeze Dolores Fuller in spit-curls, seems to have vanished without benefit of a disappearing cabinet. Fred MacKaye is barely noticeable as Jerry Starke; the notes on *The Last Performance* include more, although not better, mention of the actor.

The Charlatan was the first genre product of the two Georges, Melford and Robinson, who would delight horror buffs with the Spanish version of *Dracula* and tantalize them with the promise of the still unrecovered *La voluntad del muerto*. Neither George made much effort to exploit the "It was a dark and stormy night" baloney which the screenplay had dictated to accompany Florence Talbot's murder;

perhaps the savvy technicians saw the device for the cliché it was, and conspired to give it no more than the wink it deserved. As Count Merlin is not a preternatural being, is not possessed of supernatural abilities, and cannot divine the future or read men's souls, he is spared the rigors of low-key lighting and rococo shadow-work. This willful departure from stylistic self-indulgence actually works for the good of the picture and signals the meticulous care with which both men approached their assignments.

Harrison's Reports (April 20, 1929) said, "Pretty good; nothing extraordinary. It is not, in fact, a much higher than program grade." *Variety* (April 17, 1929) commented as much upon the part-talkie formula as on the film itself when it advised:

> Technique is the one now pretty familiar, of using silent screen with titles to get over the planting of the story with all possible speed, and then going articulate when the climax approaches and holding dialog to the finish. It works well enough here.

Still, the show business bible found that the procedure didn't compensate for the old-fashioned plot and pronounced the hybrid "far from perfect." In the *New York Times* review, the nameless critic groused that "The real crime is the removal of the lovely Margaret Livingston from the scene so early in the story." He gets no argument from me.

One man's meat may be another man's poisoned needle, but I still vote "Aye!" for *The Charlatan*. Tough to find but worth every calorie expended to locate it, the film makes no pretense at being other than it is: a tale of revenge set among the trappings of unbridled lust and pseudo-mysticism. Its quirk factor is high enough to guarantee an interesting hour to mystery aficionados, and the chance to see genre favorite Holmes Herbert in the batter's box instead of in his usual spot in the on-deck circle shouldn't be bypassed.

The Charlatan

Released April 7, 1929 (as a silent), and 14 April, 1929 (as a part-talkie); 64 minutes (silent)/60 minutes (part sound)

Cast: Holmes Herbert (Peter Dwight/ Count Merlin); Margaret Livingston (Florence Talbot); Rockliffe Fellowes (Richard Talbot); Philo McCullough (Dr. Walter Paynter); Anita Garvin (Mrs. Paynter); Crauford Kent (Frank Deering); Rosa Tapley (Mrs. Deering); Fred MacKaye (Jerry Starke); Dorothy Gould (Ann Talbot); Wilson Benge (Butler)

Credits: Presented by Carl Laemmle; Director — George Melford; From the play *The Charlatan* by Ernest Pascal and Leonard Praskins; Adaptation — Robert N. Lee; Scenario — J.G. Hawks; Dialogue — Jacques Rollens, Tom Reed; Cinematographer — George Robinson, ASC; Titles — Tom Reed; Film Editor — Maurice Pivar, Robert Jahns; Costumes — Johanna Mathieson

THE LAST PERFORMANCE (1929)

By now, it should be obvious that the studio had made inroads into the realm of wonder and imagination almost from its inception. Much as the genre explosion that followed in the wake of *Dracula* and *Frankenstein* owed a tremendous debt to the Laemmles, so also did those Laemmles need to acknowledge the body of fantastic film that had preceded their corporate arrival. Hundreds of shorts dealing with devils and demons, witches and warlocks, myth and magic had already paved the way from France, England, and Italy (to say nothing of other venues in southern California) right to the almighty box office.

The earliest genre films were all studies in stage illusion, rendered by newly discovered camera snookery and reinforced by acres of painted cardboard. Georges Méliès, the venerable magus-cum-trick photographer, started a not long but awfully prolific and undeniably important career with his two-minute miracle, *Conjuring a Lady at Robert-Houdin's* (1896); the Father of Fantasy Film went on to create almost 500 more of the same. Still, it didn't take a year for Méliès to lose his monopoly in the field. Roy Kinnard (*Horror in Silent Films: A Filmography 1896–1929*) notes how the sixth such film ever made was the product of one George Albert Smith, also a professional magician. By the end of 1897, the movies had seen

treatises on mesmerism (*The Hypnotist at Work*), alchemy (*The Alchemist's Hallucination*), maverick science (*The X-Ray Fiend*), evil incarnate (*The Laboratory of Mephistopheles*), and the supernatural (Smith's *The Haunted Castle*). With that kind of starting lineup, could there be any doubt that magic and magicians would automatically go with the genre territory?

There was also the silent filmmakers' mad rush to immortalize rogue hypnotists. Usually framing devices to account for optical tricks or mildly risqué shenanigans, those hypnotists required little in the way of attention to detail; a pocket watch (easily supplanted by pre-Lugosi arm-waving) and a modicum of eye makeup were all that was needed to turn a disingenuous character actor into a rampaging mesmerist. In 1915, when feature-length offerings were becoming more commonplace, Svengali had his way with the eponymous heroine of Maurice Tourneur's *Trilby*. (Actor Wilton Lackeye was not the first Svengali to hit the screen, however. In 1908, scarcely a dozen years after George du Maurier had penned the story, the Danes had fashioned a short based on the characters.) Nevertheless, it was when Werner Kraus etched sideshow mesmerist Dr. Caligari in celluloid in 1919 that the sluice gates were opened, and the heretofore distinct types *seer*, *charlatan, hypnotist, magician, necromancer,* and *scoundrel* began to overlap, both in the public's eye and in the normally confused perceptions of the industry.

Magic and the genre began to walk hand in hand. If that oversized figure under the sheet wasn't empowered by electricity or the atom, potion or incantation filled the bill. The heavy's choice of garb — surgical smock or wizard's hat — tipped the viewer to gear up for either a transplantation of brains or a transmigration of souls. (The studio's *Black Friday* of 1940 would intimate that, like love and marriage, you couldn't have one without the other.) Genre buffs were enthralled by one man's drive to create life without reckoning upon God and were consumed by another man's need to destroy life which had been prolonged by diabolical means. Hence, the choices became life or death, creation or destruction, the chemist or the alchemist: it was the lady or the tiger, taken to the nth degree, and we settled for nothing less.

These latter paths, of course, led through rite and ritual to magic. Once the demons were loosed, only certain talismans, certain usually arcane formulae, could be counted on to drive those demons away. Garlic, the crucifix, silver bullets, wolfbane, the *crux ansata*: these symbols joined the forces of nature (especially sunlight, running water, and a good hot fire) in dispelling the powers of darkness and restoring normalcy. To the uninitiated, these appeared to be futile weapons wielded by elderly men in the most desperate of circumstances. The cognoscenti knew, however, that they were witnessing the mythic struggle of white magicians against hellish spawn (unless, of course, they were watching something by Monogram, in which case futile, elderly, and desperate were back in the running.)

The step from the occult arts to stage conjuring was not an altogether illogical one, and genre aficionados were no less captivated by tales of mad magicians or wily hypnotists than they were by stories more openly steeped in cosmic good vs. evil. The seekers of ultimate power have always found their polar opposites in the masters of illusion; for every Hjalmar Poelzig one encountered, there was a Chandu

the Magician. Both Paul Wegener, in MGM's *The Magician* (1926), and Gustav von Seyffertitz, Fox's choice for 1927's *The Wizard*, waded hip-deep in those murky, mystical waters which the God-fearing left alone. Across the metaphysical street, pulling rabbits out of top hats while still confounding the rabble, was Conrad Veidt's Erik the Great: Rabbi Löw, meet Harry Houdini.

Nevertheless, with the silent era having devoted countless shorts and features to magicians of one sort or another, it might seem that Universal's *The Last Performance* would have capped the twenties with a tale of magic and mystery to end all such tales. Sadly, stories like that of Erik Goff and his fall from power had been equally well handled (if not bettered) before Paul Fejos had tried his hand at James Ashmore Creelman's derivative screenplay. *Performance* does remain one of Conrad Veidt's most entertaining vehicles; as for mystery, however, nothing in the film could hope to match the circuitous path the film itself took. From our (disad)vantage point, some 70 years after published reviews marked the moody melodrama's late 1929 release, we can only guess at the whys and wherefores of the confused state of affairs which surrounded *The Last Performance* when it hit the screen.

Supposedly filmed both in part-sound (with music, sound effects, and talking sequences) and silent versions, *Performance* has apparently survived only as a silent cut-down, though we can still hope that there is a mint, full-length original kicking around out there in some garage in Bratislava. Whereas the feature had originally screened at a respectable 72 minutes in either format, the extant print is some 30 minutes shy when projected at silent speed. I was initially at a loss to determine just what the missing footage could have been, as the print I viewed had seemed complete, storywise.

When taken in conjunction with the brief historical overview of magic and such outlined above, a remark made *en passant* in a contemporary review gave me the answer. With both the film's production history and its original continuity as mysterious as any of Erik the

Trade ad for 1929's *The Last Performance*. PENTAGRAM LIBRARY.

A frame enlargement of one of Erik the Great's publicity pieces. *J. C. ALLEN.*

Great's box tricks, a little bit of deductive reasoning awaits us. Before any of that, however, let us consider *The Last Performance* as it stands in perhaps the only existing negative in the United States.

> TITLE: A tale of three passions: love, desire and hate
>
> TITLE: Concerning three humans: a youth, a girl and a man

Flanked by two cherubs, a sign invites all to enter the Budapest Casino, where Erik the Great, "Europe's Foremost Magician," is headlining. The poster also announces that Erik is "assisted by Julie Fergeron and Buffo Black," the "girl" and the "youth" of the drama.

With the outside long shot of the building, it's *déjà vu* all over again for the frequent Universal ticket-buyer. Standing in for the Budapest Casino is that very same street-corner theater set (sans its Moloch-like glass shot addition) that had represented the Woodford Theater in Paul Leni's *The Last Warning* some months earlier. (Both *Last* pictures were Jewels and, as such, would have been apportioned healthy chunks of the year's production budget. Viewing them back-to-back makes one realize the advantages Leni had had getting to some of the company's standing sets first.) The Magyar equivalent of Pops, the stage-doorman, is working up a lather, admitting everyone from well-wishers to photographers to theatrical types to florists. One of the latter arrives with a huge bouquet and a message: "Flowers for Julie Fergeron — from Erik the Great!"

As we watch the florist and his armful head into the elevator and onto the upper level of dressing rooms situated in the flies, we're treated, for the second time in 10 months, to an exhilarating and comprehensive tour of Universal's Phantom stage. A series of quick shots establishes backstage bustle, and then a man at a control board hefts a phone to summon Erik the Great.

The fire curtain, festooned with announcements and local ads, rises majestically as the house lights drop. The orchestra saws away at Erik's entrance music, and the magician

steps into the spotlight. As he hands his hat, cane, and cape to an assistant, his lean form is caught between the illuminated, scallop-shaped prompter's box and the concentrated beam of the baby spot; Erik is eerily aglow as the audience applauds.

A cut takes us back behind the curtain, which opens only a moment after two stagehands perform some last-second magic of their own. The camera is now ostensibly at the stage's back wall, giving the movie audience not only a vista of the entire performance area to either side of and behind Erik the Great, but a gander at the theater audience and the back wall behind them. If Paul Leni had had Hal Mohr insinuate his camera into every possible nook and cranny of the Phantom Stage, Paul Fejos had conspired with him to lay bare the extremities of the set once and for all. Erik turns his back on the audience and motions offstage right. The side curtains part, and a lovely, slender, and joyous Julie Fergeron (Mary Philbin) steps into view. His eyes not leaving his young protégée for even a moment, the magician makes a half-hearted gesture with his right hand.

Through the matching side-curtains at stage left peers Buffo (a pale and drawn Leslie Fenton). Erik brings the young girl to center stage with a nod and a smile, and, again without so much as glancing at him, summons Buffo to a twin of that position with a curt hand movement. In a long shot from the backstage wall, the magician and his two assistants bow to the theater audience as a half-dozen stagehands wheel a large box into their midst. They spin the box, showing all sides to the captivated audience, among whom the camera now sits. The graceful Julie climbs in, guided gently and lovingly by Erik, and from the flies come two ropes which, when attached, haul the box some 15 feet into the air above center-stage.

Mohr's camera cuts to reaction shots (an open-mouthed couple in the auditorium, a stagehand watching nervously from the wings, two military types with clipped mustaches and Rupert of Hentzau uniforms gaping stoically), a glimpse of the orchestra, and the sorcerer and

The lovely Julie will disappear from that little box, and the somber Erik just dares anyone to take a second look at the obviously ordinary platform upon which the box rests. PHOTOFEST.

his apprentice, jockeying for position. Buffo crosses the apron and ceremoniously hands a revolver to his master, who aims, pauses dramatically, and then fires! The box falls to pieces; the beautiful waif has vanished! We're treated to several more quick peeks backstage — a couple of chorus girls chatting in the wings, a property mistress helping Julie alight from the recesses of the magic box's wheeled platform — before we watch Erik acknowledge the enthusiastic applause of the mystified seatholders.

That wheeled platform business caused a bit of an imbroglio with a national fraternity of conjurers. During the first few decades of the century, magic was a *very* popular and profitable commodity. Spending an evening with Kellar, Blackstone, Houdini, Thurston, or any of the other internationally acclaimed master magicians was a most acceptable alternative to the opera or the theater, and its attendant secrets were jealously guarded. Real life prestidigitators were frantic over the possibility that their cinematic impersonators would reveal tricks of the trade in the course of unraveling the plot to ticket-buyers.

Universal's attempt to open *The Last Performance* painlessly was thwarted by the Society of American Magicians (S.A.M.), the oldest association of prestidigitators in the land, which had caught wind that James Ashmore Creelman's screenplay exposed several still potent and viable illusions. Fred Shepard [of the Society's "Exposure Committee"] made contact with executive management, and Robert Cochrane, the company's vice president and Uncle Carl's partner since day one, not only arranged for Shepard to scrutinize *Performance* in his own private projection room but also acted upon the dismayed magician's recommendations. In a letter to the Society's I.I. Altman (printed in the October 1929 number of *The Sphinx,** a trade magazine which published accounts of the goings-on of the S.A.M.), Cochrane acknowledged Universal's willingness to accede to the demands of the troubled miracle workers:

> My dear Mr. Altman: It is gratifying to find in your letter the same cooperative spirit that Mr. Shepard evidenced when he talked with Mr. Gulick [Paul Gulick, Universal's publicity director] as they were looking at *The Last Performance*. I gather from your letter that there is only one exposure which is particularly damaging, from the standpoint of the Society of Magicians [sic]. That is the one you ask us to change. I find that this change, referred to in your letter as item 1, can be made, and I have ordered the elimination made. The only difficulty that I cannot overcome, however, is the matter of the prints we serve with discs instead of carrying the sound on the film, as we do in the great majority of cases. It is impossible to re-make the disc record at this time. However, these serve accounts which are in very small towns, — towns so small that it is very improbable that any members of the Society of Magicians [sic] would ever play there. Sincerely yours (Signed) R.H. Cochrane, Vice-Pres.

The effect to which the S.A.M. had most passionately objected was Julie's disappearance from the box suspended above the stage. (Thankfully, compromises were reached, and the whole magical brouhaha had a happy ending.)

Alone in her dressing room, Julie is musing over a pair of photos of the magician; the inscriptions seem to give her pause: "Berlin, 1926 — Julie, My assistant, companion and dearest friend. Perhaps some day — you'll be

more? Erik" and, again: "Prague, 1929 — To Julie, my love, my bride to be! Erik!" The young woman seems uncomfortable with the way things have developed, but she's all smiles when the boss shows up to escort her home. Back at Budapest's imposing Hotel Royal, man and girl saunter through the ornate lobby, and a chaste continental kiss of Julie's hand is their only exchange of affection.

Erik's rooms are in perfect proportion to the cavernous reaches of the hotel's lobby, and they are bizarrely appointed; grotesque masks adorn the walls, and a hefty Chinese Buddha has staked claim to an incidental table. Doffing his overcoat and donning a dressing gown, the master magician nibbles a bit of dinner as he peruses a telegram just in from America:

> Erik Goff/Royal Hotel/Budapest
> When you are in Paris please grant interview my agent — stop — He will complete arrangements your American tour — stop — Regards Will Herman

Erik notes in his diary:

> America will be our honeymoonland — for Julie's eighteenth birthday is only two months away. I sometimes wonder if our love is only a dream. Her heart is that of a child, still unawakened.

While the love-smitten wizard is smiling longingly at a framed but uninscribed photograph of his intended, a man is seen busily climbing onto the penthouse level and entering the magician's rooms by the French doors. The doorman, a witness to the whole thing, runs into the lobby and alerts the desk clerk, who noisily summons the night staff. Before they can rush up to the penthouse, Erik has casually surprised the young man, and determining the motive for his "crime" to be hunger, has fixed a plate for him. Unflappable host watches uninvited guest, as Buffo and Julie, informed of the break-in by the desk clerk, pound on Erik's door.

**And reprinted here courtesy of Ed Thomas, associate librarian at the Herbert Downs Library of the S.A.M. Hall of Fame and Magic Museum, Inc.*

When a band of hotel staff shows up an instant later, they're greeted by the sight of Erik and Julie at table with a third man, while Buffo puffs on a cigarette by a credenza. Erik asks innocently: "Why all the excitement? I didn't ring." In a flash, the employees have scattered, and Erik turns back to the third man: "You are free to go—but next time you visit any-one, young man—use the door." The youth, speechless and ashamed, can't bring himself to accept the money Erik offers him. Julie begins to weep softly, and Erik, who can deny her nothing, promises his young love: "If it will please you, I'll make him Buffo's assistant." Volumes are exchanged in the looks which pass between the man, Mark Royce (Fred MacKaye), and Buffo; Mark's face mirrors the uncertainty of his standing, while Buffo's, framed by Hal Mohr's camera between the visage of Buddha and one of those wall-mounted grotesques, is itself an expressionless mask, obscured by clouds of cigarette smoke.

> TITLE: A few weeks later, in Paris—with Buffo's envy threatening to be a fourth and dangerous passion.

Buffing his nails determinedly, Buffo coldly watches as Mark is fitted for stage costumes and civilian clothing by a tailor in Erik's Parisian hotel suite. In the main dressing room before that night's performance, Julie affixes a bou-tonniere to the lapel of Erik's tailcoat and then does the same for the tuxedo-clad Mark. Onto the stage they all go where the camera takes its favored position behind the perform-ers and records the little troupe's working a minor miracle. A cut to the wings, after the show, finds Mark chatting with the young girl. He is clearly interested in her, but at this point, there is no evidence of her returning his feelings. Erik's sudden appearance causes no concern—after all, nothing wrong has been done—and the scene fades on the picture of complacency.

> TITLE: Time speeds quickly when its wings are charmed by youth and friend-ship.

Another glimpse of the diary: "Tonight I am to see the American agent about our trip. But until then only golden hours in Julie's company." Back at the theater (the Phantom stage again, pulling double duty), Julie and Mark talk openly, as Erik and the American agent negotiate in the dressing room. Round the corner comes Buffo, who stalks jealously up to his partners: "Again—hanging around Erik's door! The under-assistant is ambitious, it seems!" Such carryings-on garner a chuckle from Julie but a full-fledged icy glower from Erik, who has suddenly opened his door for the departing theatrical agent and is less than thrilled to find the bitchy Buffo holding court. A kiss of Julie's hand, though, and Erik's good humor returns: "Julie, we sail for America at once."

The title hangs in the air as a visual col-lage of nautical images (steamship ticket, smokestack, ship's wake) unfolds behind it; Erik's breathless announcement fades only with the appearance of the New York skyline. The arrival in America is heralded by a close-up of a steamer trunk, stenciled with the name "Erik" and dotted with exotic shipping labels. As the camera moves back, the trunk and many of its companions line the floor of the master suite of the New York hotel. The little troupe unpacks and hangs those startling masks in their accustomed positions.

One peek (a long shot) of the "New York" theater interior, and we recognize the Phan-tom stage, back for the third time in as many reels. As Buffo and Mark struggle with some large crates, Erik readies a small structure, made to resemble an oversized doll's house, for its "load." Up through the stage trap shoots Julie, whom the magician gingerly lifts and car-ries to the illusion, as a man might lovingly carry his new bride across the threshold. Care-fully deposited inside, Julie takes a few moments to make sure the false doors all open correctly. Meanwhile, the two male assistants have taken a break below stage, where Buffo lights a cigarette and taunts Mark with the "good" news: "Do you know that Julie is to be Mrs. Erik Goff in two weeks?"

Mark slowly nods, and neither he nor his

partner notice that the stage trap has descended behind them. Erik and Julie look down on them from the stage above, hearing their every word. The magician motions his young protégée to be silent, as Buffo begins to wave his arms dramatically: "Erik, the *fool*, thinks she really loves him — but I know better!" A cut shows the couple listening; only the slightest of glances at Julie indicates that Erik may believe what he hears. In the next breath, Mark stands up to the conniving Buffo: "You're just a jealous rat — I know your kind. You can't turn me against Erik!"

Mark stomps up the stairs from the storeroom; a moment later, Buffo slowly follows and starts to reassemble the doll's house for that night's show. Not revealing what he has heard, Erik calmly plucks the cigarette from his assistant's mouth and grinds it underfoot; the visual metaphor is anything but subtle. Mark walks into the frame, and Erik puts his arms around his and Julie's shoulders: "True friends are seldom found — I always want you with me." The pasty-faced Buffo cowers anxiously behind the slanted roof of the doll's house.

The setup for the fall begins with an entry from Erik's diary: "My great hour will soon be here, for tonight, I am giving a birthday banquet to Julie — to announce our engagement!" And out go the engraved invitations. While the hotel wait staff readies the formal dining room, Erik gives his dresser a chuckle as he pauses to kiss a photograph of Julie. Erik turns on the man and glowers angrily at him, but only for an instant; he and his servant break into a hearty laugh over the magician's helplessness in the face of love.

In the hotel garden, Mark and Julie sit together and resign themselves to the inevitable: "We both owe him so much, Mark — I'm afraid it has to be." Erik has approved the place settings and has the guests admitted, while Buffo, loath to participate in the celebration, wanders off to a side room and buffs his nails. Through the French doors, however, he spots Julie seated with her arm around Mark. Seeing Erik

approach to summon Julie to table, Buffo cannily draws the drapes, concealing the couple from sight. He grabs the startled magician by the arm: "Wait, Master — You must see *this* trick! It is a deception you will remember till your dying day!" Buffo backs to the door and opens the drapes with a flourish.

Fejos has Hal Mohr record the unveiling in a splendid long shot, rife with symbolism: dwarfed by the immense shadow of Erik on the wall behind (and between) them, Mark and Julie quickly rise from the bench, as if two children caught playing doctor. Mohr follows with a closeup of Erik, allowing us to register the abrupt shift from the magus' casual, disinterested glance to the moment when the bomb drops, when his eyes widen in understanding. Moving between the stunned magician and the surprised couple, Buffo gloats, "Master! Use your magic now!" And then, as Iago corrupted Othello's thoughts, Buffo counsels: "It doesn't pay to take a thief into confidence — Great Erik the Blind!"

Veidt's genius fills Erik's next closeup; although the illusionist's face is inscrutable, the audience is keenly aware of the emotions roiling beneath the surface. Again in the long shot, the menacing shadow grows smaller, as the dazed illusionist walks toward the couple. He takes each by the arm and walks them into the banquet room, where he seats them next to each other at the head of the table. Buffo uneasily takes his chair at the far end of the table whence, in the picture's first truly memorable bit of photographic artistry, the camera coasts the length of the table between the seated diners and the rows of candelabra before coming to rest at arm's distance from the smiling Erik and the miserable juveniles.* Erik is flawlessly magnanimous:

TITLE: My friends, I promised you a surprise concerning my Julie, this evening... Drink to her happiness and that of my assistant, Mark Royce — for they soon — shall wed!

Courtesy of the camera crane Paul Fejos and Hal Mohr had invented for the filming of special sequences in Universal's Broadway *(1929).*

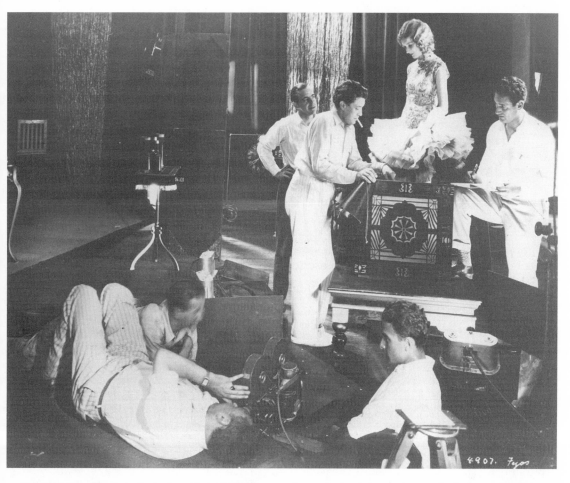

Paul Fejos (with cigarette) gives Mary Philbin some last-minute pointers on magical choreography. *Richard Koszarski.*

On their feet, glasses raised in toast, the guests form a human bower. (At this point, the print contains a jump-cut; as if in one of his magic tricks, Erik instantaneously vanishes from behind Mark and Julie. Finding him again, the camera follows his dejected figure as he descends the hotel's grand staircase; he has been devastated.) Meanwhile, Buffo beats a retreat to his rooms, intending to pack and make a run for it; a superimposed image of Erik haunts his thoughts until the scoundrel throws down his bag in impotent fury. Out in the garden, back on that infamous bench, Julie assures Mark that everything will be all right: "He understands — I know he will forgive us." Moments later, while making a brave face of it, Erik tells the couple just that. *Fade*

TITLE: ...And then Erik revived an old sword trick...

The three men are busy practicing the illusion, wherein a volunteer is placed in a box, the box is skewered with a dozen or so swords, and the plucky volunteer still escapes unharmed. Erik coaches Mark on the best way to flourish the sabers, while showing Buffo the workings of the secret door in the trunk.

TITLE: The play goes on —

The theater: a packed house. Behind the curtain, Mark and Buffo quarrel, nearly coming to blows. Before a half-dozen stage hands, Mark threatens, "Mention Julie's name again

Hal Mohr (pointing, at left) traces the path of the camera crane he invented with Paul Fejos (in shirt-sleeves at top center). Conrad Veidt seems taken by it all. *RICHARD KOSZARSKI*.

and I'll kill you!" Ever the conciliator, Erik moves between the two angry men, his face barely reflecting the glimmer of an idea.

The show starts. As he had in Budapest, Erik hands off his hat, cape and gloves to an assistant. This time, however, there are no sardonic smiles; the magician is obviously preoccupied. The trunk is wheeled onto center stage, and Erik grandly proclaims, "My assistant, Mark Royce, will perform an old sword trick of mine." Mark takes his bow, and with Buffo serving as the volunteer, he presents a sword to the audience with the flourishes he has been taught. Behind his back, Erik glares daggers at Buffo, who is terrified. Unmindful of the

tension between his partners, Mark all but forces the cowering Buffo into the trunk.

An armful of gleaming sabers is plunged into the trunk, which is then wheeled about so that all sides are visible to the captivated audience. Mark then plucks the swords one by one from their notches and hands them to Erik, who drives their sharpened points into the floorboards. An interesting low shot, virtually a throwaway, has Erik barely visible amidst a forest of quivering sabers. The audience reacts and then leaps to its feet when the last of the weapons withdrawn is covered with blood. Erik whips open the trunk and yanks Buffo's lifeless body into view; from offstage, Julie lets out with a healthy scream. Pandemonium reigns as the curtain is rung down and two of New York's finest are led backstage. With no hesitation whatsoever, the stage manager fingers Mark: "There's your man!"

As the bulls slap the cuffs on Mark, Julie goes to pieces; a closeup of Erik, though, catches the faintest of smiles playing on his lips. For once, he is unmoved by Julie's tearful display. Mark's shackled hands fade into a jail cell door being locked, and a headline explains, "Theatre Murder Trial Opens; Fervid Throng Packs Court Room as Accused Assistant Pleads Not Guilty." In an effective zoom shot, the front page photograph fills the screen and then segues imperceptibly into "live" action. We're in the Court of General Sessions of the State of New York.

Mark is brought to trial. As the stage manager takes the stand, flashbacks to the backstage argument between Mark and Buffo and the fatal sword trick itself are superimposed over his figure. When the ghostly recreation of Erik exposing Buffo's bloodied body to the audience plays across his testimony, the witness nearly works himself into a frenzy. Mark is hardly encouraged when he glimpses one of the prosecutors doodling a sketch of the electric chair.

Another headline indicates the trial has been in the public consciousness for some time: "Death Chair Looms for Royce; Testimony of Star Defense Witness Proves Boomerang." Again, the accompanying photo of a fetching but distraught Julie provides the metamorphosis back into the court room drama. The prosecutor is caught mid-summation, and a series of superimposed titles ("Outraged Society!" "Guilt Proven!" "Electric Chair!") pretty much shows which way the prevailing wind is blowing; the insert of the judge boning up on the death penalty procedure is totally unnecessary. In hysterics, Julie turns to her boss: "You've never failed me, Erik! For my sake, save him!"

Torn between his incredible love for her and his need to be avenged, Erik stands and asks to be heard. "Will Your Honor permit me to perform the sword trick as it was done that night on the stage?" His Honor will, but for some reason, Mark is dead set against Julie's taking Buffo's place in the reenactment. With a little prodding, the all but condemned man helps his darling into the trunk, whence she counsels him sweetly, "You can trust Erik, dear." In front of everyone, Julie pops the escape hatch, stands erect and watches intently as Mark first skewers the trunk and then removes the swords, handing them off to Erik. As the last blade is withdrawn, the feisty young woman reenters the box through the secret panel.

As he did on that fateful night, Erik handles the last sword with a flourish of his own; he slides it through his closed hand, drawing blood. After quickly opening the box, he raises himself to full height, with one hand ruddy and wet, the other holding a knife.

> TITLE: Only a magician's trick, Your Honor. The blood is *my* blood — the dagger was concealed up my sleeve. I killed Buffo Black, sir — and placed the guilt on Mark Royce!

Julie arises from the trunk, but Erik cannot bring himself to face her:

> TITLE: I thought if Mark were out of the way, Julie would come back to me — but they love each other, and I am old... There's nothing left in life for me — It was murder, Your Honor — and I will pay!

With that, the magician drives the dagger into his own stomach. Faltering, he manages a smile for his young protégée: "I've never failed you, Julie." He falls, and as the courtroom erupts into activity, Erik the Great acknowledges his audience: "That is all — ladies — and — gentlemen."

The four reels comprising what's left of Paul Fejos' *The Last Performance* are surprisingly complete, dramatically. There is virtually no element of the love quadrangle (Mark Royce's appearance on the scene finally giving Julie the means to escape being the apex of an

A symbolic publicity shot which hints at hypnotic control. The surviving footage shows Erik as putty in Julie's hands, rather than the reverse. *PHOTOFEST*.

uncomfortable triangle) left unseen, and the narrative is straightforward and uncomplicated as it stands. Almost totally missing from the print, however, is a subplot which fleshes out the "hold" Erik has on Buffo, casts at least a shadow of a doubt on the magus's relationship with Julie, and proffers another dimension to the power and personality of Erik the Great. At least 20 minutes of the lost footage was devoted to illustrating how Conrad Veidt's quirky character was not only a world-famous illusionist, but also a sinister hypnotist.

This "hypnotic evil genius" wrinkle can only have been lifted from *Svengali*, but to what extent (and why) is uncertain. Julie clearly isn't a Trilby figure (if anything, that honor must go to Buffo), and although undeniably the object of three men's passions, she initially resigns herself to a loveless marriage with an older man out of a sense of obligation, not because her brain has been rewired by the piercing glare of Veidt's heavily made-up eyes.

As depicted in the extant streamlined footage, Erik is basically a decent sort, definitely gaga about Julie and maybe a little moody, but also given to such acts of charity as hiring Mark and not above laughing at himself, as when caught in the act of smooching Julie's photo by his dresser. His also being an unscrupulous mesmerist just does not ring quite true. This was as much as admitted in the *New York Times'* review of the film, which refers to a scene no longer in evidence (at least in the print in question):

There are scenes backstage and others depicting Erik facing his audiences. During the course of one sequence, Erik is perceived on stage, hypnotizing a woman in a theatre box. But that has little to do with the tale, except to demonstrate Erik's malignant influence over certain persons.

With Erik the Great both an illusionist and a mesmerist, one would be left wondering to what extent the magus would have been the victim of circumstances, caught up in Julie and Mark's act of "betrayal," and to what degree he would have been the perpetrator. In fact, targeting those hypnotic big guns at Buffo might well have had an adverse effect on winning anyone any sympathy. An older man, enchanted by the charms of youth and beauty, might use decidedly questionable means to win a woman's love and still retain a modicum of the viewers' compassion. This long-distance torment of his chief male aide, however, is a sure-fire sympathy loser. There is obviously no love lost between the two men; the miracle is that Erik keeps Buffo on after Mark Royce has been hired. Either Buffo knows where the Goff skeletons are buried, or the magician has his nefarious uses for Buffo. Based on the film at hand, we are completely in the dark, but the smooth flow of the storyline validates the feeling that the hypnosis angle was a superfluous element from the beginning.

While Erik's courtroom turn is doubtless the "last performance" in question, the enigmatic title can refer to each of the principals in turn. For Buffo Black, Mark's compulsive hunger spells the beginning of the end. Already caught up in a tangle of jealousy and unrequited lust himself (the picture owes more than a passing nod to Leoncavallo's opera *Pagliacci*, and the name "Buffo" even suggests "buffoon"), the chief assistant finds that the pain he seeks to inflict on Erik ultimately rebounds and destroys them both. Given his post because of Julie's tenderness and Erik's love for her, Mark has been performing as the magician's second assistant and primary cuckold from the day he's garbed in new clothes. There's not the least suggestion that he and Julie have consummated their love (this being 1929), but Mark's acting

the role of the innocent comes to an end at the same fête at which Erik's dreams are forever shattered.

Julie's mask also slips in the penthouse garden on the night of her birthday banquet, but one is left with a couple of disturbing thoughts: To what extent has the ingenue consistently bent her employer's will to her own over the years they've been together? And, is her tearful manipulation of the love-struck Erik in the courtroom just another performance on her part? This was how the real-life conjurers and their friends read the film's denouement at a special, invitation-only screening that Universal had arranged for the Society of American Magicians prior to the picture's national release; as shown in this review from *The Sphinx* of December 1929:

> The story concerns itself with the murder of the magician's assistant during a presentation of the trunk and sword mystery and the subsequent trial of the murder. The illusion is again presented at the trial and the magician, *who is innocent of the crime* [emphasis added] insists upon his own guilt to save another assistant who is in love (as is the magician) with a third assistant, Julie, whose part is played by Mary Philbin.

If this admittedly unorthodox interpretation of the film's closing moments is valid to any degree at all, than Julie's last and most telling performance begins with her tears on the night Mark Royce is caught filling his pockets with fruit in Erik's rooms.

For Erik the Great, the evening of Buffo's murder must vie with the afternoon of his own suicide for the honor of the "last performance." As Lon Chaney had done as that *other* Erik, the mad magician seeks to force the heroine's hand by putting her lover in peril of his life. When that and all else fails, the two doomed Eriks can find peace only in death, and each film closes with its tragic anti-hero holding the mob aghast for a final dramatic moment. Both men prove triumphantly — the Phantom with his "hand grenade," the Magician with his dagger — that the hand is quicker than the eye

In a scene missing from the extant print, Erik responds to Julie's "betrayal" with an outburst of violence. Note blocking tape under Veidt's right foot. PHOTOFEST.

before they surrender to the inevitability of their fate.

Hence, we can see that *The Last Performance* operates on at least two levels. It is an obvious but clever reworking of themes, motifs, and personnel from *The Phantom of the Opera*: Against a background of baroque theater, surrounded by masks, music and murder, and within the very confines of his earlier misadventure, Erik once again loses Mary Philbin to a rival who is younger and handsomer, but far less worthy, than he. This may be further complicated by adding the familiar plot lines of *Pagliacci* alluded to above: The head of a wandering troupe is driven to murder through his own jealousy and the machinations of

another actor, who is also in love with the "heroine." The Svengali-like facets which have failed to resurface suggest yet another dimension to Paul Fejos' tale of jealousy and murder, but precisely how they fit in remains a puzzle.

A far greater mystery involves the year in which production is said to have started (1927) as opposed to the year in which the film was released (1929). The *American Film Institute Catalog* (1921–1930) avers that the film premiered in New York on November 2, 1927, yet also indicates that the national release was October 13, 1929. This would seem to imply that a silent version had made the rounds before being withdrawn, doctored, and re-released almost two years later. In a review dated

November 4, 1929, the *New York Times'* critic opined that "This production, *which was made some time ago* [emphasis added] by Dr. Paul Fejos at the Universal studio, was probably Conrad Veidt's last performance in Hollywood before returning to work in Germany."

If, as J.C. Allen maintains in his excellent biography, *Conrad Veidt: From Caligari to Casablanca*, "on February 10, 1929, Connie [Mr. Veidt], Felicitas [his wife] and Viola [their daughter] sailed for Europe," we are left with an awkward situation. As no sound prints of the title can be found, we cannot determine whether Veidt himself played any part in the recording session(s) necessary to transform a silent feature into a "part-talkie." Veidt departed America, Allen reports, because his "command of the English language was very limited at the time and he felt that his usefulness in Hollywood was at an end"; would he therefore have settled for recording his lines imperfectly? And if he had, what subsequently held up the film's release for another eight months?

Also of great interest is a comment made by David Skal in *Hollywood Gothic*. In recounting the measures which Lugosi took to assure himself the title role in the up-and-coming *Dracula*, Skal claims, "Lugosi went so far as to donate his services to Universal's foreign-language unit, dubbing Conrad Veidt's role in *The Last Performance* into Hungarian...." When taken with Richard Bojarski's insistence (in *The Films of Bela Lugosi*) that this came to pass in 1928, this is a real baffler. First of all, "dubbing" per se just wasn't technically feasible that first year after sound changed the face of the movie industry; it was all that technicians could do to keep pitch and volume constant while recording dialogue under optimum conditions. In fact, when 1925's *The Phantom of the Opera* was reissued as a "part-talkie" in February 1929, dubbing was still beyond the scope of the infant technology. Universal added a synchronized music track and some sound effects, but had to reshoot dialogue sequences between Mary Philbin and Norman Kerry. And, had it been even remotely practicable at the time, wouldn't the studio have had

someone dub in some lines for Chaney? A disclaimer would have been necessary, sure — but the film ended up being re-released with a disclaimer anyhow: "Lon Chaney's Portrayal of the Phantom Is Silent."

Second, there is no evidence whatsoever that foreign-language versions of the part-sound *The Last Performance* were even made. At this stage of the sound game, studios were hard-pressed to satisfy the various niches of the domestic market; as already related, just keeping the local movie palaces in product demanded silent, sound-on-film, and sound-on-disc variations on the theme. In 1929, overseas markets were forced to settle for silent features with intertitles that had been translated into the appropriate language. Only by 1930 had the insanity died down to the point that Spanish, French, German, and other versions began production.

Bela *had* served as interlocutor in prints of Paul Whiteman's musical biography, *The King of Jazz* (1930), set for Hungarian release. All that was required there, however, were inserts of the tuxedo-clad actor introducing the sundry personalities and musical numbers; these were cut into existing prints of the English-language musical. Hence, there really never was any true "Hungarian version" of *The King of Jazz*.

In his monumental work *Lugosi: His Life in Films, on Stage, and in the Hearts of Horror Lovers*, Gary Don Rhodes staggers the imagination by providing names and credits for *Last Performance*'s "Hungarian version," by alleging the existence of actual footage of the "dubbing session," and then by getting the movie's basic plot details wrong. Based on studio puff pieces and the Lugosi myth, one might almost as easily choose to believe that in his quest to ingratiate himself to the Laemmles and to whoever else would have had a say in the casting of *Dracula*, Bela had offered to voice Conrad Veidt's lines in his heavily accented English for the picture's *domestic* part-sound release. Veidt may well have been uncertain about his efficacy in any language other than his own, but we have documented proof that Lugosi did a damn fine job of spooking Broadway audiences night after night in a part he had initially delivered phonetically.

Two questions come to mind in response to all this fuss about the film's being originally released as a silent in 1927: Why is there no corroboration available in the form of newspaper or trade reviews? And, why is there no copyright notice for the earlier version on file at the Library of Congress? If the film had merited a New York premiere, the studio would doubtless have seen to its legal registration. Jolson's *The Jazz Singer* had opened scarcely two weeks earlier, so the gut-wrenching panic about talking pictures was still off in the distance; how could a prestige production just disappear from the scene?

Every last one of the reviews consulted in conjunction with this essay is dated 4 November 1929 or later, just after the film's "national" release, yet not one makes any mention at all of the picture's dedicated musical score, sound effects, or dialogue sequences. How could this be when literally every other part-talkie receiving a critique during this period had its sound elements scrutinized and evaluated? Does this indicate that the picture's aural dimensions were so unremarkable that they didn't deserve even a comment made in passing?* Or that, for some unfathomable reason, the film was never released in its part-talkie incarnation?

The smoking gun might well be the November 9, 1929, issue of *Motion Picture News*. The layout on page 37 highlights four one- and two-reelers, and as many features. Nestled among such titles as *Condemned* and *The Bride of the Desert* (both "All Dialogue") and *Come Across* ("Part Dialogue") is Fejos' *The Last Performance* ("Silent"). The review calls a spade a spade: "In the silent days this feature would have stood up anywhere and prove [sic] a real box-office attraction. In this day of sound pictures there isn't a chance for it except in silent houses. For those theatres it should prove a real money-getter."

Despite Robert Cochrane's concerns over sound discs and the transatlantic recording sessions mentioned in the endnote, it doesn't appear that *The Last Performance* ever did see the light of a carbon arc as a part-talkie. A possible scenario would be that test prints were struck, the Veidt transcriptions were found wanting, "dubbing" (with Lugosi or anyone else) was deemed unfeasible, and the film was re-released as a silent. And let's be honest: If the "parent" production was ultimately marketed nationwide as a silent remnant, would the Laemmles have gone to what were then incredible measures to synchronize a dubbed soundtrack for Hungary, the least of the European markets? If there was no English language

***

In a letter to me, Veidt biographer J.C. Allen maintained that the Universal brass instructed Fejos to "re-work the silent film and give it some talking sequences, since silent films were passé by [1928]. Fejos agreed to this and began the many necessary revisions. However, he soon realized that, in his attention to many small details, he had neglected to get his star, Veidt, to come to the studio and record all of his dialogue for the new talkie version."

A photograph from a German magazine of the period shows Veidt on the telephone surrounded by studio officials and sound engineers. Per Mr. Allen, "The caption doesn't give many details but it does give a date of March, 1929 and says that in early 1929, Veidt was asked by a Universal producer [Paul Kohner?] if he would agree to a special long distance telephone hook-up from Berlin to Hollywood, in which Veidt would speak his 'TLP's' character's lines from a script which had been mailed to him. Veidt agreed and gave the necessary remaining dialogue to the Universal sound engineers, who later took the recorded voice of Veidt and incorporated it into the newly revised soundtrack of the film."

As I subsequently suggested to Mr. Allen, the mystery remains unsolved. Why would one go to the trouble of speaking lines over a transatlantic phone line (which, in those days, virtually guaranteed lousy reception and aural distortion) when one could record the dialogue in Ufa's (or someone else's) state-of-the-art studio and send the recordings themselves back to Universal? (This photo might lend some credence to Gary Don Rhodes' insistence that Veidt had recorded a German track for the picture, if this didn't then open Pandora's box concerning the dubbing process for the rest of the cast.) And if Universal had gone to such incredible lengths to obtain Veidt's plummy tones, isn't it likely that the publicity department would have raised a commotion to be heard 'round the world, and that the contemporary reviews of the film would have at least mentioned the phone stunt, if not the dialogue itself?

dialogue version for this Jewel, there surely was no Hungarian talkie.

As for the cast, Mark Royce, the least of the principals, is done to a journeyman's turn by Fred MacKaye (aka McKaye), the least of the first-string actors. This was Fred's second shot at being Mary Philbin's sweetie within six months; the couple had interacted to widespread indifference in Universal's *Girl Overboard*, a part-talkie which had surfaced in July of 1929, only to sink from sight by the time *The Last Performance* was released nationally. Henceforth, MacKaye's career took as big a plunge as did the stock market, and only a handful of credits — mostly small supporting roles under Ken Maynard, followed by the most minute of bits at other studios — attest to the actor's dimming star. Here, he does nothing to separate Mark from the legions of other faceless juveniles thrust into narratives to get things moving. Why Julie would look twice at a drip like Mark Royce is a question only screenwriter James Ashmore Creelman could answer.

This was Mary Philbin's third and last career highlight of especial interest to the genre community, and the pert actress is incalculably better than she had been while trying to hold her own against Lon Chaney. Philbin had been either only 17 (or only 22, depending on which publicity puff one chooses to believe) when she had staggered her way through the immortal role of diva Christine Daae, but she had already had her feet more or less set in the cement of melodrama when she had starred (again opposite Norman Kerry, again under Rupert Julian's flamboyant vision) in Universal's *The Merry-Go-Round*, a 1923 romantic Viennese Super-Jewel. The tale of organ grinders, counts, puppeteers, and hunchbacks had been more notorious for its behind the scenes squabbling — Julian had been brought in to replace a profligate Erich von Stroheim — than notable for its artistic merit, but it made the young actress the studio's reigning queen of costume melodrama for several years.

Apart from *The Phantom of the Opera*, the most pertinent assignments which then came her way were *The Man Who Laughs* and, of course, *The Last Performance*, both with Conrad Veidt. Even in the heady broth of these latter two films, Philbin is so much more natural and assured, so much less stiff and affected, than she was in *Phantom* that we have no choice but to point the finger at Rupert Julian for having hidden the young woman's genuine talent under fright wigs, grimaces, and painfully old-fashioned posturing. Julie Fergeron is a charming little sprite (there's no doubt whatsoever of the power she has over Erik) and Philbin, who may have been pushing 30 in November 1929, is completely convincing as the teenage object of everyone's interest.

The erstwhile queen of melodrama retired from the screen in 1931, having finally appeared in a comedy (*The Shannons of Broadway* with James and Lucille Gleason) and having finally left Universal, for lesser pap like Beacon Productions' *After the Fog*. A genre goddess, and one of the first silent "scream queens," Mary Philbin died in 1993.

In many ways, Leslie Fenton's most memorable cinematic accomplishments occurred behind the camera. The British-born character artist had acted his way through a good number of silent and early sound efforts, including *Broadway* under Paul Fejos, and the 1933 British version of *F.P. 1 antwortet nicht* with Conrad Veidt, before assuming the director's mantle himself. Although Fenton picked up the reins with the sort of mellers and potboilers in which he had frequently appeared (like 1939's *Tell No Tales*, or 1941's *The Saint's Vacation*), he gradually settled into grade A horse operas. Among the last of the handful of oaters bearing the Fenton touch was Alan Ladd's first, the near-classic *Whispering Smith* (1948).

As an actor, Fenton was often cast as an Oriental, as in *Chinatown Squad*, because of the unusual stamp of his features, or as a heavy; evident in several of Buffo's blank stares and glances is the actor's ability to convey a dispassionate threat. With his (and, apparently, everyone else's) role rather drastically abridged in the print on hand, Fenton's Buffo is an enigma, as is that hypnotic spell under which Buffo is evidently ensconced. Having Erik the Great force Buffo to slay Mark, the magician's romantic rival, during the performance of the sword trick would have given some substance to the ploy. Having the dispatching take place *vice versa*, though, renders the whole plot twist meaningless and irrelevant. Still, Fenton admirably conveys Buffo's quasi–Jekyll & Hyde personality.

Conrad Veidt was born in either 1892 or 1893 in the village of Potsdam, near Berlin, and in his short lifetime (he died from an arterial blood clot in April of 1943), he achieved international renown as a superlative purveyor of cold-blooded villainy. Along with Paul Wegener, he became associated early on with Expressionistic demons, and his silent work included not one but several genuine genre milestones: 1919's *Das Kabinett des Dr. Caligari* and 1924's *Orlacs Hände*, both for Robert Weine; 1920's *Der Januskopf*, for F.W. Murnau; *Das Wachsfigurenkabinett* in 1924, for Paul Leni; and for Henrik Galeen in 1926, *Der Student von Prag*, which reunited him with Werner Krauss.

With the coming of sound, mainstream audiences regarded Veidt as one of cinema's quintessential Nazis (peaking as Major Strasser in Michael Curtiz's *Casablanca*), but horror, sci-fi, and fantasy fans continued to view his work in such pertinent fare as Leni's *The Man Who Laughs* and Alexander Korda's *The Thief of Bagdad* (1940) as *de rigueur*. In life the most affable of men, according to biographer J.C. Allen, Veidt was pretty much typed as a heavy by his gaunt and distinctive appearance. There is little doubt that had he been less scrupulous professionally, impressionists building reputations by aping Universal's Dracula along with sundry other icons would have been imitating Conrad Veidt's sonorous treatment instead of Bela Lugosi's.

Even without the footage devoted to his more sinister side, Veidt's Erik manages to squeeze off a look or two that freezes the marrow of Buffo's bones and disquiets the viewer. Clearly something of a patrician, couching even his acts of kindness in magisterial overtones, he is haughty and self-assured, yet easily swayed by Julie's slightest whim. Veidt's genius permits us to see not only Erik's steely resolve, but the uncertainty and despair that lie just under the surface. The conjurer wears his heart on his tuxedo sleeve; still, whether he acknowledges his doubts in the privacy of his diary or has them flung in his face by Buffo, he is too adept at playacting both as magician and as suitor to allow the truth to hit home until it is too late. The grotesque masks with which the illusionist decorates his keep are as excessive and unreal as his hopes. Even in the face of death, his instincts dictate his epitaph; for the man unable to divorce himself from pretense even for a moment, there can be no last performance.

Cinematographer Hal Mohr was a godsend to Universal and other of the majors, and his creativity and savvy boosted the entertainment value of many an otherwise mediocre picture. With Paul Fejos, the designer of the mobile camera crane that would forever change the face of cinematography, Mohr put visual pizzazz into a handful of memorable genre efforts, including MGM's tongue-in-cheek *The Monster* (1925, starring the Man of a Thousand Faces), Warner Brothers' moody *The Walking Dead* (1936, with Mr. Karloff), and Universal's 1943 Technicolor *Phantom of the Opera*, for which Mohr and W. Howard Greene copped the Oscar. A popular and prolific technician, Mohr was in constant demand virtually up to the end of his life in 1974, and over five dozen mainstream features such as *Captain Blood* (1935), *Destry Rides Again* (1939), and *The Wild One* (1954) guaranteed that his special talents would be appreciated by millions of moviegoers worldwide.

References to *Doctor* Fejos in contemporary reviews should be taken seriously, as the Hungarian emigrant had (among other things) worked his way through medical school back in the old country. Born in Budapest in 1897, Fejos journeyed to America in the early twenties and spent several years in bacteriological research in New York City. Late in the decade, germs gave way to the movie bug, and the doctor went west. Fortuitous circumstances soon found him helming *The Last Moment*, a visually innovative, stylistically Expressionistic, and totally lost psychological feature.

Conrad Veidt (left) has just learned how to cope with inadequate party lighting. Paul Fejos (middle) and Hal Mohr ready a closeup at the banquet scene. *RICHARD KOSZARSKI.*

This brought him to the attention of the Laemmles.

The director's first shot at Universal was *Lonesome* (1928), a romantic drama with Barbara Kent and Glenn Tryon, which garnered both critical acclaim and popular success. Next up was *Broadway*, Junior's "Million Dollar Musical," which reunited Fejos with star Tryon and introduced him to photographic genius Hal Mohr. The film contained a number of color sequences, was an absolute blockbuster, and cemented Fejos' brilliant future at Universal.

As production wrapped on *The Last Performance*, the rights to Erich Maria Remarque's anti-war novel *Im Westen nichts Neues* were acquired by the studio, and George Abbott sat down to adapt it for the screen as *All Quiet on the Western Front*. Although Fejos lobbied to direct the message-heavy melodrama, the plum assignment fell to Lewis Milestone. That was all she wrote for the temperamental Hungarian, who walked off *La Marseillaise* (completed as *Captain of the Guard* by John S. Robertson) and out of the Laemmle world forever. According to writer Bruce Frankel ("Double Vision: The Film Career of Paul Fejos" in *Natural History* magazine, November 1996), Fejos' film career lasted out the thirties and took him back to Europe, into Denmark, on to Siam, and into the wilds of Madagascar and Peru. His latter films were interesting marriages of cinema and anthropology, and his scientific background emerged once more. Spending the last 20-odd years of his life in New York (he died in 1963), Doctor Fejos' devotion to the study of anthropology built for him a second reputation for genius.

The Last Performance opened to mixed notices. The *New York Times* groused that "Some of the straight camera work is not up to scratch"(!), but allowed as how

> Dr. Fejos has handled his scenes with no small degree of imagination. They are not always as well photographed as one might hope for, but, due to the fantastic nature of the story, the occasional glimpses of the way in which the magician, Erik the Great, deceives the eyes of his audiences, Mr. Veidt's clever acting and Mary Philbin's captivating charm, this picture holds one's attention.

This was head and shoulders above the opinion of *Film Daily*, which not only got a good bit of the plot wrong, but also opined in its November 10, 1929, number, "Ordinary production with draggy story and a lot of morbid and depressing atmosphere. Lacks audience appeal."

When, apart from their historical or cultural value, the *remnants* of an early motion picture can still entertain and edify in their own right, you've got a winner on your hands that has withstood the test of time. The whole of *The Last Performance* is very much more than just the sum of its parts; it is a panorama of technical artistry and technique which not only more than compensates for the lack of sound, but actually obviates it. Although the surviving reels demonstrate fewer breathtaking camera effects than Leni's and Mohr's *The Last Warning*, the more mundane (if still offbeat) nature of the tragic fall of Erik the Great warrants a less over dramatic visual approach than the pseudo-supernatural goings-on at the Woodford Theater.

With the extant version available on videotape, fans of the principal players, of the technical geniuses who crafted the film, or of silent melodrama owe it to themselves to witness firsthand this fascinating entry in the Universal genre canon.

The Last Performance

Released October 13, 1929; 72 minutes/ 7 reels

Cast: Conrad Veidt (Erik Goff); Mary Philbin (Julie Fergeron); Leslie Fenton (Buffo Black); Fred Mackaye (Mark Royce); Gustav Partos (European Theater Manager); Eddie Boland (American Theater Manager); William H. Turner (Booking Agent); Anders Randolf (Judge); Sam De Grasse (District Attorney); George Irving (Defense Attorney)

Credits: Presented by Carl Laemmle; Supervised by Carl Laemmle, Jr; Director — Paul Fejos; Titles — Walter Anthony, Tom Reed; Story/Scenario — James Ashmore Creelman; Photography — Hal Mohr; Film Editor — Edward Cahn, Robert Carlisle, Robert Jahns. Reportedly released both with talking sequences, sound effects, and a music score (Movietone), and as a silent feature.

THE CAT CREEPS /
LA VOLUNTAD DEL MUERTO (1930)

When Forrest Gump's mama declared, "Life is like a box of chocolates," she might just as well have been speaking about the movies. You never know what you're going to end up with.

Take *Dracula*. Studio records indicate that principal photography started on 29 September 1930, and save for retakes and added scenes, wrapped on 15 November. The production was distributed both as a silent, despite its 1931 release date, and as a talkie. The latter version was offered in two distinct formats: with Movietone (optical) sound and with sound on discs. A partial adaptation of a Broadway hit and — hold on to your hats, now — objectively, a partial "remake" of the German "original," *Dracula*'s importance was such that a Spanish-language version, intended primarily for the profitable Mexican market and secondarily for Spain and the Americas, was shot simultaneously on the same sets. Some 65 years after the pair of films debuted in Hollywood and elsewhere, they remain the objects of criticism, study, and enjoyment.

Things worked out differently for *The Cat Creeps*. Available information, of which there is not much, tips the production's starting date at around July 8, 1930, with its submission for

copyright listed on October 23. Though released earlier than the vampire saga, *The Cat Creeps* was distributed in the two sound modes only; its silent version, 1927's *The Cat and the Canary*, was still on call for any theaters who might be looking for the theme, but who had not yet sprung for sound technology. Itself a virtual remake of that same Paul Leni original, which had been an adaptation of a Broadway hit, *The Cat Creeps* warranted a Spanish-language version which was also photographed on standing sets when the "real" company had gone home for the night. Some 65 years after these films hit the screens, neither is extant, and their absence demonstrates the cold-blooded indifference which the industry displayed towards its changeling children, born on the cusp of the new era.

Only the most fortuitous circumstances, of course, prevented that same black hole from enveloping *Drácula*. The Laemmles had agreed with *wunderkind* Paul Kohner that the *oro* in them thar *montañas* could be had by filming alternate versions of the studio's more popular films (usually those featuring offbeat or unlikely plots or recounting tales of passionate emotions) for the Spanish/Latino market. Neither Kohner nor Universal could

English and Spanish advertising for *The Cat Creeps/La voluntad del muerto*. RONALD V. BORST/HOLLYWOOD MOVIE POSTERS; ROBERT G. DICKSON.

Lupita Tovar's Anita is speechless, as is Andrés de Segurola's Attorney Crosby for other reasons, in *La voluntad del muerto*. RONALD V. BORST/HOLLYWOOD MOVIE POSTERS.

be really called a trendsetter here; virtually every big studio in Hollywood was cranking out foreign versions for export. Lucrative overseas markets had become so crucial that anyone with a dictionary and an ounce of schooling could find a job translating title cards. These outlets couldn't be written off just because the public insisted on going with the times and opting for sound. These pictures could be shot quickly, utilizing much of the same blocking on standing sets, and cheaply (there being no high-salaried contract players with whom to haggle, and virtually no overhead), and then distributed vigorously, albeit with far less expensive publicity campaigns, to audiences who walked through the theater doors already appreciative of the effort involved.

The major hurdles to be jumped came after the films had seen their initial release. Neither the comparatively primitive projection and storage capabilities in certain parts of Latin America nor the equatorial heat and humidity did much to help keep circulating prints in pristine shape. Whereas most stateside theater owners had begun to wean themselves of their annoying tendency to edit down the movies in their care, the Catholic Church in Mexico, Argentina, or Cuba didn't hesitate to order cuts for what it deemed moral or theological reasons. Apart from unstable nitrate film stock, the insular nature of foreign language features usually mitigated against their getting into the hands of preservationists, and very few titles survived long enough to experience transfer to safety film.

Nor was much thought given to releasing the Spanish renditions in mainstream, English-speaking communities, another factor that worked against their being seen, appreciated, or conserved. The original, glossy, "grown-up" Hollywood productions had already wended their profitable ways through big-city and small-town America, so there was little point in following them up with "second-string" efforts starring ethnic unknowns delivering incomprehensible dialogue. And *had* some enterprising executive voiced the feasibility of breaching the language barrier, he would have been chastised as a dreamer. At the time, the only means to affect the goofy idea would have been to have the foreign casts deliver their English lines phonetically (essentially necessitating that a *third* version be shot and obviating any need for a foreign cast in the first place), or to employ intertitle translations and thereby increase the running time by some 25 percent. (Sub-titles, per se, were the provenance of the effects photographer at this stage of the game and would remain prohibitively expensive for some time to come.) Since the Spanish language features were already substantially longer than their American partners, this would have been intolerable.

These factors, then, may serve to explain the disappearance of *La voluntad del muerto* and the piecemeal (until recently remedied) survival of George Melford's *Drácula*, but why and whither went *The Cat Creeps*? This was a major production from a major studio (a Jewel, in fact), targeted right at middle America and enjoying the fruits of the Universal publicity mill. What happened here? The seeds of the picture's fate can be found in excerpts from two contemporary reviews:

> Except for its speech, [*The Cat Creeps*] is not noticeably better or worse than its silent predecessor, and it has no new thrills for those already familiar with the awful happenings of a night in the mansion of the eccentric Cyril [sic] West.
> —*New York Times*, November 8, 1930

And

> Generally warmed over silents take a chance, a gamble not especially helped by a revival of a popular play type vogue that has gone cold. Both of these circumstances operate against the new release which thus has to make its way against a handicap.... The story ... now gets nothing from the sensational run of the stage play.
> —*Variety*, November 12, 1930

Rupert Julian's *Cat* was even then recognized for what it was: an all-too-quick second trip to the Willard well, taken before the studio relinquished the rights to the play and before the public found venues other than haunted houses on which to spend its money. The film appeared a bit too late to fend off this second trend, and despite a slate of excellent performers and decent notices (one can only wonder if Mr. Julian took any pride in his version being adjudged "not noticeably ... worse" than that of the brilliant Paul Leni), it was really just more of the same.

The Cat Creeps and *La voluntad del muerto* (literally, *The Dead Man's Will*) followed slavishly the plot lines of Willard's play and Leni's photoplay; there is nothing "lost" here, at least in terms of story. Twenty years after the death of Cyrus West, his six hopeful heirs gather at Glencliff Manor, the eccentric millionaire's home, to hear lawyer Crosby read the will at the stroke of midnight. The group is told that Annabelle West, a distant niece, is to inherit everything unless she is found to be of unsound mind; a sealed document naming the contingent heir will then be opened. People disappear, Crosby is murdered, and everyone but Annabelle and young Charlie Wilder behaves in a highly suspicious manner. As the greedy heirs presumptive circle in ever more closely for the financial kill, the Cat is let out of the bag (sorry), and the handsome and helpful Charlie is unmasked as the killer. The nod for second-place heavy goes to Hendricks, the keeper of the nearby asylum.

What has been lost, so far, is our opportunity to appraise and experience (à la *Drácula*) the recounting of a familiar tale in unfamiliar circumstances. The world may still need a good fifty-cent cigar more than another

Charlie Wilder (Neil Hamilton) and M'am Pleasant (Blanche Frederici) exchange meaningful glances.
RADLEY METZGER.

stilted demonstration of Rupert Julian's fondness for dramatic miscalculation, but the flamboyant director was blessed with a far more capable cast in *Cat* than he had been in 1925's *The Phantom of the Opera* (with the exception of Lon Chaney, of course), and if any crepe is to be hung, it should be in their memory.

Just about everyone in the cast, with the exception of the juveniles, Helen Twelvetrees and Raymond Hackett, is a familiar name to genre fans. Neil Hamilton, for example, hit Baby Boomers between the eyes in the mid-sixties when he and Alan Napier (and most of the show's guest villains) lent presence and an air of legitimacy to the screwy pop art of TV's *Batman*. Prior to stooging for Adam West as Commissioner Gordon, the stocky ex–leading man

had buoyed up a couple of classic 1930s Tarzan flicks (MGM's *Tarzan, the Ape Man* and *Tarzan and His Mate*, of 1932 and 1934) and was also the love interest in two of Warner Oland's adventures as the Malicious Mandarin in Paramount's *The Mysterious Doctor Fu Manchu* (1929) and *The Return of Doctor Fu Manchu* (1930).

Lilyan Tashman made only one other appearance in her short career which fell within genre boundaries — Paramount's *Murder by the Clock*, 1931 — but her ability to stir a man's blood while making him chuckle was without peer when injected into overly preposterous proceedings. In his landmark *Classics of the Horror Film*, William K. Everson praised her style while admitting that "The Tashman performance prevents [*Murder by the Clock*] from being taken too seriously...." Likewise, *Variety*'s "Rush" noted that, so far as *The Cat Creeps* went, "The comedy woman character that is the meat of the piece goes to Lilyan Tashman, who does her usual workmanlike job of it." Dead at 35 in 1934, the saucy and sparkling young woman will always merit a spot on the minor league rosters of genre immortals.

Angular Blanche Frederici, Tashman's co-star in both films, also made quite an impression on reviewer and historian alike. As *Variety* noted about *Cat*, "Prize part in the cast is that of the West Indian housekeeper with her spooky manner and voodoo suggestion and the character is played here for its full worth by Blanche Frederici, who stands out for balanced, effective playing." So also did Mr. Everson laud her performance in *Murder*: "Those who saw [*Murder by the Clock*] then remember it fondly ... even those who cannot recall the title have never forgotten the horn in the crypt, and the nocturnal prowlings of Blanche Frederici." Adding to the double-barreled impressions made above, the actress deserves mention for her bringing up the rear behind Myrna Loy and C. Henry Gordon in RKO's offbeat *Thirteen Women* (1932).

Jean Hersholt may be kindly Doctor Christian to all those middle-aged Goody Two-Shoes out there, but he's one of the powers behind such horrors as 1930's *Mamba*, 1932's *Mask of Fu Manchu*, and 1935's *Mark of the Vampire*, among others. Just prior to his Dr. Patterson role in the Willard remake, the Danish emigrant had starred as Kathryn Crawford's voice teacher in the emphatically non-horrific original version of *The Climax* (1930). Around and about since the mid-teens, Hersholt had been the heavy more often than the hero of the pictures in which he appeared. Here, even with his playing only one eccentric in a picture brimming with them, Hersholt merited special mention. As the *New York Times* averred in its review of *Cat*, "Mr. Hersholt is particularly effective in his brief appearance as the mysterious doctor who is called in to minister to the badly frightened heroine."

Montagu Love was one of the silent screen's great scoundrels (cf. *The Last Warning*, 1929), and his assumption of the role of Hendricks, the unhinged asylum keeper (George Siegemann in the 1927 production), spread a little more icing on that cake. Chubby Lawrence Grant had been before the eyes of mystery and horror fans since the original *The Great Impersonation* back in 1921. *Cat* separated the actor's credits in such fascinating whodunits as *The Canary Murder Case* and *Bulldog Drummond* (both 1929) from such bona fide chillers *as Daughter of the Dragon* (1931), 1935's *WereWolf of London*, and the 1941 *Dr. Jekyll and Mr. Hyde*. The British "secondary artist" had a more prolific career than any three leading men, and more's the pity that his turn as the notorious and ill-fated Attorney Crosby ("Lawrence Grant is splendid," crowed the *Times*) has been lost to this point.

Raymond Hackett's star seems to have been in the ascendancy only during this interim period between the death of silent films and the perfection of their noisy successors. I found no source crediting the handsome young actor with more than a half-dozen or so screen appearances. Universal's *Seed* (1931), a gabby domestic drama (Bette Davis was struck from *Frankenstein* for *this*?), was his last credit of note.

Ingenue Helen Twelvetrees (*not* a Native American), on the other hand, graced over 30 features during the 11 years covered by this volume. *The Cat Creeps* was Miss Twelvetrees' only real genre outing, although she had starred the year before in Fox's *The Ghost Talks*, a comedy-melodrama involving crooks and hotels (but not ghosts) and featuring black comic Stepin Fetchit as a character named Christopher Lee. The actress received good notices for her work in the Julian spooker, after which she settled in to a 10-year run of three-handkerchief women's pictures and a decade-long spate of lukewarm reviews. In his volume *Hollywood Players*, film historian William T. Leonard bemoans the fact that her "name has filtered down through recent generations as an analogy to monumentally poor acting," and maintains this was because "She was an integral part of that decade in which sob-stories

One hopes the lovely Helen Twelvetrees was given more to do than bat those beautiful eyes in *The Cat Creeps*. AUTHOR'S COLLECTION.

were very much in fashion." To each his Dulcinea.

Cinematographer Hal Mohr came to the production with a well-deserved reputation and a genre-oriented eye he had developed in working alongside such creative directors as Roland West and Paul Leni. Having manned, dismantled, and repaired every model of domestic movie camera made since 1915, Mohr was as much an inventor as he was an insightful technician. According to William Everson in *More Classics of the Horror Film*, Paul Kohner, who at the time was supervising *Cat*'s Spanish version after hours, worked arm-in-arm with Rupert Julian to dress down the sets and modify the (over)lighting of the

"parent" production after Junior found the rushes of *La voluntad* to be the more atmospheric. Though Julian rather surprisingly acceded without a tantrum, the bottom-line changes in lighting and lenses fell to Mohr, and it was his moody end-product which earned the few nods the movie received for physical power.

Photography is excellent throughout, with several interior shots that are highly important in maintaining the atmosphere of suspense and fear around which the play is built.

　　　　　　—*Exhibitor's Herald-World*,
　　　　　　November 15, 1930

Tension, anyone? Lupita Tovar keeps Paul Ellis (left) and Antonio Moreno at bosom's breadth. *BUDDY BARNETT/ CINEMA COLLECTORS.*

The Cat Creeps didn't knock any of the critics dead, an indication that the novelty of sound in and of itself had already worn off. More importantly, though, the dearth of praise for the technology signaled that the artistry of the silent era was still so deeply ingrained in the 1930 collective consciousness that the mere addition of the spoken word was no guarantee of approval or acceptance. If anything, contemporary reviewers felt that the dialogue worked *against* the pace of the film. As *Variety's* "Rush" stated,

> The start is particularly tedious. First 32 minutes are devoted to the actual mechanical planting of the story background and haunted house atmosphere and it is not until the entrance of the counterfeit insane asylum keeper ... that the hair raising episodes begin.... It is the necessity of developing the background in dialog instead of crisp titles that slows up the beginning.

This, at least, we can judge for ourselves.

Film producer Richard Gordon very graciously loaned me all that survives of the Leni remake: a cassette of the soundtrack of *The Cat Creeps*. Taken from a set of 16-inch sound discs, the track is useful primarily in pegging the film's primitive talkie qualities. As each disc runs about 10 minutes

Opposite: Hailed as "La novia de México"— Mexico's sweetheart — Lupita Tovar carried a candle as everyone south of the border carried a torch. *AUTHOR'S COLLECTION.*

Lupita Tovar, Antonio Moreno and Nicolás Ruiz will soon discover Paul Ellis under the cat disguise. Ruiz's comeuppance as the secondary villain will come moments later. RONALD V. BORST/HOLLYWOOD MOVIE POSTERS.

(the movie itself chugged along for some 71–72 minutes), and the changeover between discs is quite easy to note aurally, somewhere between 40 and 45 percent of the film was essentially silent; there's nothing to be heard on almost half the track save for the scratchiness one associates with old records. As if unused to the presence of microphones (and they were), many of the cast declaim their lines rather than deliver them conversationally. The picture's release during the transition from the silent days, when almost every feature worth its salt brought an orchestral or organ score to the theater along with its nitrate stock, to the sound era was also marked by a singular paucity of music. As were most films until sev-

eral years later, *The Cat Creeps* was sent out with musical accompaniment only under the opening and closing titles. Since these scored portions still retain their punch despite the lack of any dialogue, one has to shake one's head yet again at the naïveté and shortsightedness of most filmmakers regarding background music during the early sound period.

In the end, the film's proximity to the already near-classic *The Cat and the Canary*, the most popular work of the recently departed and sorely missed Paul Leni, relegated it to a place in one of that film's many shadows. All things considered, its progression from apathy to obscurity and thence into the void is not really difficult to understand.

Lupita Tovar may have won the part of "Anita" West in *La voluntad del muerto* based on a screen test for the same Paul Kohner she would soon marry, but the vivacious Mexican actress was talented and extremely capable all the same. Prior to *Muerto*, Tovar was basically an untried commodity having appeared only in Fox's *The Veiled Woman* (1929), a woman's melodrama which was produced in both silent and Movietone versions and which did nothing except generate weekly paychecks for any of its participants. The gulps, gasps, and histrionics which defined the part of the pert West heiress, however, and which Laura La Plante had made her own in the Leni photoplay (*Variety*, 1930: "Helen Twelvetrees gives the role merely youthful grace and the beauty that is hers"), were right up Tovar's alley. Judging by her not altogether dissimilar Eva in *Drácula*, and by her seductive and impassioned Niela in George Melford's *East of Borneo* (1931), the young beauty was remarkably adept at overcoming her natural reticence for the camera.

Playing cousin Pablo to Tovar's Anita was Antonio Moreno, the broodingly handsome Spaniard who was as savvy in Hollywood as Lupita was green, having debuted in *Voice of the Million* as long ago as 1912. Proficient in English to the point of being glib, Moreno moved effortlessly from studio to studio and from genre to genre in the course of a professional jaunt that lasted more than five decades. (To horror and science-fiction fans, Moreno will always be Carl Maia in Universal-International's *The Creature from the Black Lagoon*. To comedy buffs, he'll ever be the gypsy who snatched Mae Busch from Oliver Hardy in *The Bohemian Girl*. To aficionados of the silent era, he is for all time the store owner bewitched and ensnared by Clara Bow, the very incarnation of *It*.)

Still very much a romantic lead throughout the thirties, Moreno crossed paths with Lupita Tovar again in the Spanish version of Universal's *Storm Over the Andes* (1935). Miss Tovar's English-language woes would prevent her from assuming the leading role of Theresa in the domestic release (wherein Mona Barrie took the prize), but Moreno (essaying the part of Major *Tovar*) and her old flame from *Drácula*, Barry Norton, received checks from both productions due to their idiomatic talents. (When Phil Rosen helmed the 1931 Spanish version of Howard Hawks' *The Criminal Code* for Columbia, the cast list read like old home week from George Melford's *Drácula*: Carlos Villarias, Barry Norton, Manuel Arbó, José Soriano Vosca, along with María Calvo from *Voluntad*.)

For most of the remaining cast members, the six-week shoot at Universal City was typical of their Hollywood experience: chiefly inexpensive freelance piecework, shot at night, offering little chance for career advancement.* Pablo Álvarez — not to be confused with *Drácula*'s Pablo Álvarez Rubio — was a linguist proficient in seven languages and a wrestler ("El español incógnito" during his mat career in Cuba), as well as a part time actor in Hollywood and elsewhere. Lucio Villegas, who would grump his way through *La voluntad* as the ersatz doctor, spent a couple of weeks (along with future Doctor Seward, José Soriano Viosca) on *Oriente y occidente*. Loopy maidservant Mabel — the Hispanic equivalent to *The Cat Creeps*' peculiar Ma'm Pleasant — was played by Soledad Jiménez, who (with Mexican Van Helsing Eduardo Arozamena, went on to

---

Several foreign performers, however, were brought to Tinseltown under exclusive contract. Ernesto Vilches (the Spanish "Man of a Thousand Faces"), for example, had disembarked in southern California at Paramount's behest. Disagreements over compensation and billing and personality clashes soon caused a parting of the ways, and Vilches went out on his own. Genre buffs would most likely hold MGM's Wu Li Chang (1930; a sound remake of Chaney's 1927 hit Mr. Wu) and Cheri-Bibi (1931; the Gaston Leroux melodrama originally planned to follow the sound version of The Unholy Three) in high regard; both versiones españolas featured Vilches in the roles essayed by and intended for Chaney, Sr. In fact, the Spanish rendition of Cheri-Bibi was already in the can before John Gilbert took over for the deceased Chaney and The Phantom of Paris (the film's final title) went into production.

The Cat, aka Charlie Wilder, Paul Ellis, Manuel Granado, Benjamín Ingénito. *PENTAGRAM LIBRARY.*

sometime actor Aldo Franchetti. Music was the Spaniard's first love. A *basso cantante*, he had appeared in Puccini's *La Bohème* alongside his close friend Enrico Caruso when the century was young, and turned to the cinema only after the great tenor had died and the world of opera had thus lost its appeal for him.

Some of the Mexican and Spanish nationals made a nice living playing secondary roles in the dozens of popular comic shorts made for overseas distribution. *Voluntad*'s María Calvo (Susan) and Carmen Guarrero, the Lucía Weston of *Drácula*, pitched in to keep Charley Chase on pitch in *El alma de la fiesta* (loosely, *The Life of the Party*), a featurette comprised of Charley's popular two-reeler *Thundering Tenors* and three reels of Latin silliness. According to Florentino Hernández Girbal and Juan Heinink's updated *Los que pasaron por Hollywood*, Calvo had been performing in musical theater since the age of 11, and was tagged by virtually every major Tinseltown studio to enact old ladies and eccentrics. The lovely Carmencita also drew a check from Chase for *Girl Shock*, a 1930 comedy released only in English. Not to be outdone, Paul Ellis (born Benjamín Ingénito, aka Manuel Granado) supported the comic in *Monerías* (*Rough Seas*) and *La señorita de Chicago* (*The Pip from Pittsburgh*; I don't get it either).

Mr. Laurel and Mr. Hardy likewise hired Hispanic (and French and Italian and German) actors to populate the foreign versions of their wildly successful two- and three-reelers. *Pardon Us*, Stan and Ollie's first feature-length picture, along with its four European clones, was shot in 1930 and released in 1931; the

enliven *Resurrección* for Lupe Velez (but not for John Boles).

Andrés de Segurola (attorney Crosby) turned up in the occasional domestic release such as RKO's *We're Rich Again* (1934), but he could also draw upon his musical talents to help pay the rent when film roles were scarce. A cut to Universal's *Nice Girl?* (1941) allows us to hear Deanna Durbin's lovely soprano bestowing brief fame on "Perhaps," a love song de Segurola had co-written with Italian

A low shot of one of the splendidly atmospheric sets, if you can see beyond the cowering (left to right) Roberto Guzmán, Andrés de Segurola, María Calvo and Conchita Ballesteros. *BUDDY BARNETT/CINEMA COLLECTORS.*

terror of the prison and the story's chief heavy, the Tiger, was portrayed in the France-bound footage by a pre–*Frankenstein* Boris Karloff!

La voluntad del muerto was the product of essentially the same unit that was responsible for the later *Drácula*, and according to William Everson was "a far better film" than the Mexican vampire tale, at least in the opinion of Paul Kohner. The studio retained writer Baltasar Fernández Cué to adapt the script Gladys Lehman and William Hurlbut had fashioned from the Willard stage play, reworking it into colloquial Spanish. Cué, who also drew the odd check under the nom de plume Gabriel Argüelles, was responsible for Universal's entire catalogue of Spanish titles in 1930-1931, in addition to similar work at Warners and Fox. Returning to Spain when dubbing made his command of language superfluous, he sat out the Civil War in prison, where he had been tossed by Franco as a suspected informer and enemy of the people.

As he would for *Drácula*, dialogue director Enrique Tovar Ávalos tried to leach the more obvious regional vocal variances from the patchwork Spanish, Mexican, and Hispanic cast. Kohner's eye for dust and shadow was more quickly, and without a doubt more appreciatively, exploited by director George Melford and cinematographer George Robinson than by the autocratic Rupert Julian, and although one is forced to judge the effect by stills alone, the lighting and sets appear to be up to the exquisite Paul Leni/Hal Mohr standards of meticulously arranged, atmospheric decay.

Shot under the working title of *El gato y*

el canario, the film opened (as *La voluntad del muerto*) at the Balmori theater in Mexico City on November 20, 1930, some 10 days after *The Cat Creeps* took Hollywood by drizzle. Delayed by the vagaries of cargo transport via steamship, the Spanish premiere at Madrid's Callao theater took place on 9 December. Genre aficionados in Buenos Aires, however, had to wait until the following summer for the film. The attendant ballyhoo more than made up for the delay; the picture had built up such advance interest that — as *La Heredera de Mr. West* — it required two theaters (the Callao and the Versalles) to hold the crowds; both movie palaces were packed to the rafters for weeks following the 11 July 1931 premiere.

La voluntad del muerto clocked in at 87 minutes, a quarter hour longer than its American cousin, and it is unfortunately impossible to speculate on just what contributed to the longer running time; not even the sound discs seem to have survived the years. Still photographs are at a premium and publicity paper is all but nonexistent. It's as if time were conspiring with film history to render futile and frustrating any quest for ephemera from the picture, let alone the picture itself.

Possibly of greater interest for their inaccessibility than for their respective merits, *The Cat Creeps* and *La voluntad del muerto* occupy that same niche which until relatively recently shielded *The Old Dark House* from sight. We can only keep our fingers crossed that they'll eventually be recovered and hope that, when they do resurface, they'll be spared the condescending malarkey revisionist critics have been heaping on old films made for enjoyment rather than metaphysical debate.

The Cat Creeps

Released November 10, 1930; 71 minutes

Cast: Helen Twelvetrees (Annabelle West); Raymond Hackett (Paul); Neil Hamilton (Charlie Wilder); Lilyan Tashman (Cicily); Lawrence Grant (Crosby); Jean Hersholt (Dr. Patterson); Blanche Frederici (Ma'm Pleasant); Montagu Love (Hendricks); Theodore von Eltz (Harry Blythe); Elizabeth Patterson (Susan)

Credits: Presented by Carl Laemmle; Director — Rupert Julian; Based on the play *The Cat and the Canary* by John Willard; Continuity — Gladys Lehman; Dialogue — Gladys Lehman, William Hurlbut; Photography — Hal Mohr, Jerry Ash; Film Editor — Maurice Pivar; Recording Engineer — Edward Wetzel, C. Roy Hunter; Sets — Charles D. Hall; Make-up — Jack P. Pierce

La voluntad del muerto

Released November 20, 1930; 87 minutes

Cast: Lupita Tovar (Anita West); Antonio Moreno (Pablo); Paul Ellis (Carlos); María Calvo (Susan); Andrés de Segurola (Crosby); Soledad Jiménez (Mabel); Roberto Guzmán (Harry); Lucio Villegas (Doctor); Conchita Ballesteros (Cecilia); Nicolás Ruiz (Hendricks); Agostino Borgato (Guard); with Manuel Ballesteros, Pablo Álvarez

Credits: Presented by Carl Laemmle; Production Supervisor — Paul Kohner; Director — George Melford; Script — Gladys Lehman and William Hurlbut; Based on *The Cat and the Canary* by John Willard; Photography — George Robinson; Adaptation and Spanish Dialogue — Baltasar Fernández Cué; Dialogue Director — Enrique Tovar Avalos; Sets — Charles D. Hall; Makeup — Jack P. Pierce

DRACULA (1931)

The Journey of a Thousand Miles

Among the many fascinating cinematic odds and ends involving Bela Lugosi is a brief shipboard interview he gave in 1952. Returning to the United States from Great Britain, where he had starred in what can only be described as a disastrous run of his signature play, *Dracula*, before walking off with the amusing but altogether uneventful *Mother Riley Meets the Vampire*, a visibly tired Lugosi fielded a series of tepid questions concerning his future plans and his past triumphs for Jack Magadan of *Ship's Reporter*.

As the interview wound up, the question on everyone's mind was asked:

> Magadan: Doesn't Dracula ever end for you?
> Lugosi: No, no; Dracula never ends. I don't know whether I should call it a fortune or a curse, but it never ends.

While it is undoubtedly true that Dracula never did end for him, it is not a little ironic that Bela virtually had to claw his way through a crowd of competitors before, amid embarrassing circumstances, he was awarded the part which ultimately ruined his professional life.

Just about every recent serious appraisal of the horror cinema's golden years has taken the time to outline the list of contenders for the coveted title role in Universal's original *Dracula*. Tom Weaver has done it twice: once in *Universal Horrors* (which he co-authored with Michael and John Brunas), and briefly again in the later, equally requisite *Poverty Row Horrors*. David Skal took a bit more time to unwind the kinks (with some very impressive photographic relics) in his *Hollywood Gothic*.

Nevertheless, the hows and whys of the casting of the plum role — still a mite foggy despite numerous attempts at understanding the logic so peculiar to the Laemmles and to "the pets of their pets" — have to be the point of departure if one is to appreciate fully the subsequent ironies of the picture itself. The first authorized filming of *Dracula* (not having sought the permission of the Stoker estate, Murnau's *Nosferatu** of 1922 did not use the familiar nomenclature found in the novel) occurred within circumstances so unwieldy

---

*With Nosferatu, *F.W. Murnau was pulling his second scam in as many years. In 1920, he and the boys over at Decla-Bioscop had shot* Der Januskopf, *a lengthy rip-off of Stevenson's* Dr. Jekyll and Mr. Hyde. *Inasmuch as the American author had died in the South Seas in December 1894, Murnau probably needn't have troubled*

John Wray (b. 1890) would have made an aquiline but jowly lord of the undead. Thanks to his success in *All Quiet on the Western Front,* his name was bandied about first (but least) for the role of Dracula. *PENTAGRAM LIBRARY.*

Universal, among other studios, extended hesitant offers for rights to the novel via one set of agents and intermediaries, and made cautious overtures with regard to the Hamilton Deane–John Balderston drama through another. Studio readers delved through Stoker's masterwork in order to determine its feasibility as a film and to estimate audience reaction, while other researchers attended the play so as to cadge ideas meant to save money without skimping on impact. This *ballet comique* was performed against quite a dappled backdrop: the aged Florence Stoker's fears and suspicions; entrepreneur Horace Liveright's desperate attempts to retain some say in the proceedings after a series of poor decisions on his part had all but assured that he would not share in the filmed version's expected windfall; the precarious balance struck 'twixt Uncle Carl's distaste for horror themes and his son's eagerness to capitalize on a hot prospect; Bela Lugosi's cryptic mutterings about "the biggest studio" and attendant production values, a veritable procession of playwrights and novelists commissioned to sire a viable screen adaptation; and the stock market crash of 1929.

Predictably, the bottom line won out, and *Dracula* plunged in status from "Super Production" to an "A" picture for a studio whose ledgers usually reflected returns on quantity,

that, save for the then novelty of the theme and the potency of the product's name, which was still packing Broadway audiences in during preproduction, it's a wonder that the film made any impact at all.

himself with changing the dual protagonists' names to Dr. Warren and Mr. O'Connor or with fudging the identities of the supporting cast. When he got creative with Dracula, *however, he received the brunt of the wrath of the widow Stoker, who was then ensconced in the London suburbs, within comfortable suing distance of Germany. The ironic thing was that* Nosferatu, *vigorously pursued for the explicit purpose of its destruction and enacted by virtual unknowns, survived;* Der Januskopf, *conceived and executed amid no brouhaha whatsoever and featuring both Conrad Veidt (even then a star) and Bela Lugosi (soon to be something of one himself), disappeared into the abyss of time.*

rather than on quality; still, it was miles (and dollars) ahead of most of the non-genre product being lensed at Universal. Overseer of the $350,000-plus budget was Junior Laemmle, both Universal's top producer and Uncle Carl's only son, whose capacity for groveling had led to his renouncing his birth name, Julius, in order to cement his birthright (those 230 acres in the San Fernando Valley).

As budgeted monies decreased, out went any consideration the novel itself might have received as source material for the film. Although several of the studio readers had noted the lurid (and, for some, unacceptable) aspects of the novel, there was no doubt that Stoker's original tale contained many more sequences with purely cinematic potential than did the rather anemic adaptation to the proscenium arch. The success of the stage version, however, sounded the death knell for a more ambitious treatment. If theater-goers were willing to pay a healthy price for the live performance and were willing to travel some distance for the privilege, how many more "reasonably priced" tickets to the filmed *Dracula*— basically the same rendition as the Broadway hit — were just *begging* to be sold?

Ironically, some two years after the film's February 1931 debut, it was discovered that the novel had always been in the public domain in the United States, for Bram Stoker had neglected to observe the legal requirement of depositing two copies of his work with the U.S. copyright office. Universal or any other studio could have produced a less turgid, more faithful adaptation of *Dracula* in just about any medium at all, without negotiating with a soul. Some $20,000 spent needlessly for rights could have been utilized punching up existing scenes, augmenting the pathetically sparse special effects, or shooting an additional vignette or two from the novel.

Having purchased more rights than it actually needed, though, Universal became self-righteous and legalistic; other vampires might rise and fall, but none save the Voivode was a legally protected contractual entity. Dracula's presence would soon become all-pervasive, and no one dared ignore the copyright notice embroidered on the hem of his cloak. The determination to wring the last drop of monetary value from those superfluous rights would become most evident in the studio's later 15-year battle over the Count's essence with Bela Lugosi's survivors. In 1977, the California Supreme Court reversed a lower court's findings and maintained that, while the face that belonged to Universal's "classical" Dracula image was indeed Bela Lugosi's, the studio retained the right to market that image following the actor's death. The fiscal children of the successors to the Laemmle family had kept Lugosi's vampiric icon alive, while fighting successfully to keep dead and buried whatever rights the actor's children had claimed.

No one had dreamt that the ultimate bloodsuckers would be the lawyers when the search for Dracula was officially begun back in 1930. Although, as of October of 1927, Lugosi had been playing the eponymous character at New York City's Fulton Theater, his was not the first name bandied about by the Universal movers and shakers. That honor seems to have gone to John Wray, a newly celebrated character man who had displayed an impressive versatility in Universal's "Super Production" *All Quiet on the Western Front*, in which Wray's character, Himmelstoss, changed visibly in the course of the film from a nondescript postal worker to a brutal and sadistic soldier. While it may be said that such a range would help any potential Dracula affect his mood swings from gentility to sanguinity, no one could swear that Wray's admittedly top-notch performance wasn't just a fluke, and there was too much riding to allow a basically untried actor to shoulder the costly production himself. Wray's name vanished almost immediately from public view in conjunction with the up-and-coming vampire epic, although the actor went on to other studios for such genre goodies as 1932's *Doctor X* and Bob Hope's comedic reworking of *The Cat and the Canary* (1939).

It's hard to determine the precise order of the next round of hopefuls, but those under consideration included stage thespian William Courtenay; socially conscious movie character actor Paul Muni; the extremely busy but

Left: The profile of the young Ian Keith makes Universal's consideration of him quite understandable. *Right:* Joseph Schildkraut had signed with Uncle Carl in 1929 and, rumor had it, was in line for the role of the Count in the Tod Browning talkie. *Both PENTAGRAM LIBRARY.*

increasingly unreliable Ian Keith; and Joseph Schildkraut, whose good looks and leading-man status were briefly scrutinized in the unlikely event the studio decided not to succumb to more obvious casting traits. Courtenay's appeal was chiefly physical: The New York actor was tall and distinguished, was aristocratic in demeanor, and had swirled his black cloak magnificently during an extensive

national tour of *The Spider.* Neither his mien nor his mantle proved to be enough, and Courtenay likewise faded from the scene.

Paul Muni, also touted as a possibility, had received an Academy Award nomination for his film debut in 1928's *The Valiant.* In the course of a number of classic performances which spanned the thirties, he submitted to complex makeups (à la Lon Chaney) in order to create unforgettable characters. Muni became increasingly taken with historical fiction and biography as the decade progressed, though, and it is unlikely that, *Scarface* notwithstanding, he would have seriously considered a role so remorselessly one-sided, so blatantly melodramatic, so socially unredeeming, as Tod Browning's *Dracula*. Still, just announcing Muni's name was sound, publicity-wise, and made splendid press.

Ian Keith has suffered at the hands of Lugosiphiles who feel that he bears the stigma of being the one man who dared to stand in Bela's path toward immortality, not once, but twice! The earlier of the two competitions cannot be denied, although Ian Keith was but one of a handful of actors whom Universal was regarding with lust in its corporate eye.

Given recent developments, it is virtually certain that the second of the two "competitions," involving the 1948 *Abbott and Costello Meet Frankenstein*, was no more than a self-serving pipedream concocted by a peripheral but interested party. Much has been written (most of it unflattering) about the last of Lugosi's agents, Don Marlowe. Almost exclusively through his own testimony, Marlowe has gone down in genre history as the man who waved Bela's pitiful early contract in the faces of his pitiless later bosses in order to save the Hungarian's primal role (once again!) from the canny clutches of Keith.

Respected genre film writer Greg Mank discovered that Lugosi had put his John Hancock on a bona fide "U-I" contract almost two weeks before Marlowe supposedly flourished his documents and made his from-the-heart pitch. There is no evidence that Keith ever so much as acknowledged losing the part. For Ian Keith, 1948 wasn't the year of *Abbott and Costello Meet Frankenstein*, but of *Nightmare Alley*. Twentieth Century–Fox's unsettling classic had offered him "the role of a lifetime" as the alcoholic carny.

Chester Morris, Mr. Skal maintains, was actually approached (or, at least, his management team was) and point-blank offered the role. As the diminutive Morris was being groomed for romantic roles (his later *Boston*

Blackie series emphasized his attractively aggressive personality), his declining the honor can well be understood.

It is also part of legend that John Carradine turned down the role. Carradine, a favorite genre actors of most fans, swore for years that he had been offered the part of Frankenstein's Monster before Karloff but had refused, citing the fact that the part was a mute one. Although the actor would continue to appear in excruciatingly minor roles at Universal for some years after *Frankenstein* (a cult member in *The Black Cat*, a hunter in *Bride of Frankenstein*, etc.), he never tired later of claiming dibs on the Monster. Given Carradine's distinctive and mellifluous voice, his balking at non-speaking parts was understandable.

Why, though, would he turn down Dracula? While the 1931 film script may not have dripped with immortal dialogue, a number of individual lines did emerge as worthy of a unique and commanding delivery. If, indeed, Carradine did decline the opportunity to test for the part, the logic of such a move is lost to posterity. (In the mid-forties, the gaunt character man would enact what many fans consider the definitive Count, supplanting Lugosi's earlier interpretation.)

There would have been no need at all for a search, the story goes, had Uncle Carl's number one choice been available. Despite his long association with bizarre roles, though, and his essaying at least one classically grotesque portrayal, Laemmle's Gothic superstar announced that he was unavailable for the part. Fearing that his spoken English might prove unequal to the demands of sound movies, Conrad Veidt packed his bags and headed back to Germany.

David Skal rather tenuously argues that Conrad Veidt's being heralded by Uncle Carl as the bearer of Dracula's mantle was due, in part, to the executive's knowledge of the terminal nature of Chaney's illness. Even had he viewed the actor's Erik Goff in *The Last Performance* (1929) as "virtually a screen test for the role," Laemmle's hole card was trumped as Veidt's professionalism would not allow him to continue in English-language talking

Chester Morris could be much more dapper than the next man (especially when the next man was Tom Dugan). But ... Dracula? *PENTAGRAM LIBRARY.*

pictures when he felt less than perfectly comfortable. The repatriative move would permit the actor to master the techniques of sound movies while enabling him to perfect his English away from prying eyes and critical ears. Yet his portrayal of the eponymous *Rasputin* in a 1930 feature was his only truly worthwhile effort in a mere handful of German productions; all of his other thirties films were either in English or actually made in England. Veidt even opted for the lead in the English-language version of *F.P. 1 antwortet nicht* (1933; rather tersely titled *F.P. 1* in Great Britain), rather than work in the German original. The actor's subsequent return to the United States, motivated more by a loathing for Hitler and Nazism than by any career necessity, revealed an artist of extraordinary suavity, capable of subtle yet profound villainy.

The other member of Uncle Carl's proposed "winning team" was director Paul Leni, another German emigrant whose magnificent credentials extended back to the heyday of German Expressionism. Leni had helmed Veidt's silent triumph *The Man Who Laughs* for Laemmle and had piloted *Waxworks* (also with Veidt) for Germany's Neptun Films in 1924. If ever there were two men who together could have (in the words of Mr. Skal) "elevated *Dracula* to pantheon status," Paul Leni and Conrad Veidt were those men. Paul Leni died from blood poisoning in September 1929, just after the release of *The Last Warning*, which he had directed for Junior at Universal. By that time, Conrad Veidt had been back home for some seven months.

While Uncle Carl may have seen his dream team collapse before his eyes, Junior didn't pause to shed a tear; *his* first choices had always been those Metro moneymakers, Lon Chaney and Tod Browning.

Although Chaney was usually associated with complex, torturous makeups, many of his later portrayals (including Tiger Haynes in *Where East Is East*, Grumpy Anderson in *Thunder*, and Professor Echo in the sound remake of *The Unholy Three*) eschewed buckets of greasepaint and putty. Chaney's vampire (the "Man in the Beaver Hat" in MGM's *London After Midnight*, 1927) had given him the chance to spin a purely visual grotesque; the sound adaptation of *Dracula* might have moved him to adapt his awesome talent for pantomime in support of what he may have viewed as a more vocal challenge.

The versatile star would have been forced to pass on many of the makeup techniques he had successfully employed during the silent era; his most celebrated trio of goblins — Quasimodo, Erik, and that nameless, top-hatted vampire — all had been fitted with oral appliances which made speech impossible. And although Dracula may not have had the most

sides in the production, he did need to articulate a number of lines, both to get the ball rolling and to keep his hand in later. It's a safe bet that Chaney would have concocted a special makeup for Stoker's Voivode, and that he would not have indulged in the excesses which had been needed earlier as compensation for a totally silent milieu.

Chaney's dual role as Echo/Mrs. O'Grady in *The Unholy Three* proved that the actor's resilient voice would have added to his chameleon-like reputation. No one really can say whether Dracula's more familiar lines ("The blood is the life, Mr. Renfield," or "I never drink ... wine") would have retained the impact they received from Mr. Lugosi's peculiar cadences. Neither the eloquent William Courtenay nor the sonorous John Carradine was saddled with an accent, and the latter opted not to affect one in either *House of Frankenstein* or *House of Dracula*. With the Man of a Thousand Faces' all-consuming passion to *become* his film personalities (he admitted, more than once, that "between pictures, there *is* no Lon Chaney"), whatever vocal nuances he might have selected to complement his facial appearance would doubtless have been carefully researched and assiduously applied.

This last must be considered, as many Lugosiphiles aver that much of what little power the 1931 *Dracula* still retains is due to Bela's unique vocal "presence." The eccentricity of Bela's speeches was due not to any studied plan of action on the Hungarian actor's part, but to the fact that he was Bela Lugosi. The man could not speak in any other fashion. In *Dark Eyes of London*, he had to be dubbed by English actor O.B. Clarence (while, in effect, pantomiming the role of Dr. Dearborn), as he wasn't able to disguise his tones so as to convince the audience that he could fool the other cast members. In the 1935 *Mark of the Vampire*, Bela cut a far more imposing and frightening figure than he did in *Dracula*, yet he had nary a word to say until the gag ending. This fact does not, in any way, denigrate Lugosi's performance as the Vampire King; to this day, almost any popular imitation of the classical

Bela Lugosi, from a private shoot during the release of *The Thirteenth Chair*. The role he coveted was not yet within his grasp. *AUTHOR'S COLLECTION.*

image of Dracula includes an attempt at duplicating Bela Lugosi's distinctive voice.

Whether the fact that Carl Laemmle, *père*, had originally opted for Connie Veidt was due to the studio boss's artistic acumen, to some sort of Teutonic loyalty, to his being on the inside track concerning Chaney's throat condition, or to his knowing only too well that MGM wasn't about to loan out one of its top stars at terms Universal could afford is a mat-ter for discussion. There had been some trouble at MGM; the 1929 stock market disaster had affected the Metro cash flow, and there was talk of a buy-out. Rumors had Irving Thalberg and Louis Mayer at odds, with no guarantees as to which man would emerge victorious from the power struggle. Things quieted down, however, and new contract in hand, Chaney maintained his rightful place at the studio which had "more stars than there are in the heavens."

Although Universal had borrowed Chaney from MGM for its enormously popular *The Phantom of the Opera* back in 1925 (there had been no MGM, per se, in 1923, when Universal nabbed the silent star for *The Hunchback of Notre Dame*), the larger studio had balked at providing him for purposes of reshooting scenes for a sound reissue of *Phantom* at the close of the decade. Nonetheless, subject to certain contractual conditions, Chaney did have the right to freelance, so his longtime associate, Tod Browning, was brought over to Universal City in an attempt at sweetening the pot for *Dracula*.

For some time, Browning had been considered the perfect yin to Chaney's yang, as he had helmed the lion's share of the star's perverse yet wildly successful features. Recent reappraisal of Browning has led many to conclude that Chaney's undeniable talents shine through in these films *despite* their relatively pedestrian direction and not because of it. Most film scholars feel that, under the creative guidance of a Rex Ingram or a Paul Leni, Chaney's star would have ascended to even more dazzling heights.

It remains uncertain whether Browning was brought to Universal as a sop to attract Chaney or because Laemmle, knowing what he did, felt that, as the surviving member of the "Unholy Two," the director would add a touch of that special *frisson* for which his gallery of MGM grotesqueries had made him notorious. Between Conrad Veidt's flight from Hollywood and Lon Chaney's death from throat cancer, both Universal's private hopes and filmdom's public expectations were dashed on the rocks of destiny. Hence, the "search."

During all this brouhaha, Bela Lugosi had set out on his own campaign to prove his worth to the Universal brass. According to various accounts, the Hungarian had communicated with Florence Stoker for the express purpose of obtaining the rights to her husband's novel at a more reasonable rate than the widow had been demanding. In addition, Bela had let it slip that one of the majors —*the* major, as a matter of fact — was not only intrigued with the property, but had more than a passing interest in a certain eastern European stage actor who, in turn, had more than a casual familiarity with the intricacies of the title role.

Nor had Lugosi been averse to expressing in the trade press his own opinions regarding certain nuances of the role which might now be possible, given the more expansive parameters of motion picture film. He or his management saw to it that photographs from the stage play, as well as a number of atmospheric poses from a private publicity shoot, were made available to the fan magazines; these publications had wielded considerable influence during the movies' silent years and would continue to do so through the early fifties. Letter campaigns, instigated by magazine editors and carried out by multitudes of rabid movie fans, had been known to affect casting decisions. It was worth a shot.

Lugosi went all out in his efforts to have the Laemmles realize that he was, after all, the right man for the part. True, there appeared to be a sort of myopic rivalry growing between those who trod the boards and their cinematic counterparts, but that hadn't prevented William Courtenay from being scrutinized, had it? How much more logical to have someone who not only had extensive stage experience, but also had shown an affinity for film work, had already been acclaimed for his interpretation of the role, was letter-perfect in delivery, and was authentically Hungarian, to boot?

How could any reasonable person fail to come to the same conclusion?

Whether it took that long for Junior Laemmle to own up to being a reasonable person (Conrad Veidt having bailed out, Uncle Carl's heart was no longer in the production), or whether the "search" had truly exhausted every other contender, on September 20, 1930, Universal Pictures announced to the world that Bela Lugosi had won the part of Dracula.

Bela probably celebrated with a boilermaker and a choice Havana cigar.

He didn't know it, of course, but it was all downhill from there.

The Film

Over the years, gallons of ink have been spilt in the course of dissecting Universal's first major horror film. A summary of the collected opinions of published film critics, historians, scholars, and what-have-you would probably account for as many viewpoints as there are writers, and in that way lies madness. Instead, it seems both succinct and obvious to theorize that, based on an evaluation of the finished picture, the more vibrant and memorable material was derived from the novel, and the static and constrictive elements were lifted from the popular Deane-Balderston stage play.

Following the scene depicting the arrival of the *Vesta* (the *Demeter* in the novel) at Whitby, virtually every good commentary I've ever read about *Dracula* begins to shift gears, making apologies for the decidedly uncinematic quality of the Count's stay in England. Blame has traditionally been apportioned among the niggardly bean-counters who cut the operating budget, banking on a higher proportional return on a smaller investment; producer Junior Laemmle, who didn't fight for "First Class, All The Way," or, if he did, chose not to wage his battle in the public forum; and the director, Tod Browning, whose publicized penchant for the macabre was more than offset by his mediocre professional capabilities. It accomplishes nothing to point a finger at anyone some 65 years after the initial release. That the film suffers greatly after the second reel is fact; who was ultimately responsible is the stuff of which great debates are made.

The breathtaking glass shot that provides the audience with its initial view of Castle Dracula has lost none of its impact in the course of time and of repeated viewings. The transition to Charles D. Hall's sumptuous decay is flawless, and apart from some poor judgment (those absurd armadillos and the bugs emerging from pathetic miniature sarcophagi), the smoothly mobile camera notes all of the corruption which underlies Dracula's veneer, as it glides noiselessly through the castle's vaults.

Divorced from all sound, save for the occasional creak or scurry, the visual power of this introductory vignette is stunning. Reminiscent of the studies in light and shadow which permeated the classic German Expressionist horror films of the previous decade, Karl Freund's reverent treatment of the vampire's awakening and the subsequent encounter between predator and prey sets a tone which the nonstop chattering of later, expository scenes cannot hope to match. Lost in the requisite dialogue in the second half of the picture is the power of the silence of the tomb. The movie has no music apart from Universal's favorite *Swan Lake* excerpts under the main titles and the Wagnerian rumblings of a canned orchestra during the theatre scene; a nice touch, though, is having that scene peter out to the accompaniment of Schubert's *Unfinished Symphony*.

When Hamilton Deane had first adapted the Stoker novel for the English stage, he had necessarily narrowed its scope and condensed the action to fit comfortably within the confines of the proscenium arch. John L. Balderston, brought in by former publisher and future producer Horace Liveright to "adapt the adaptation" to make it palatable to Broadway audiences, for all practical purposes rewrote the play, omitting superfluous characters and virtually translating most of Deane's ungainly dialogue into readily understandable English. It was this "Deane-Balderston" version of the play (Balderston had initially demurred at placing his name on so tacky an enterprise, but later opted for co-author's credit) that opened in New York in 1927 and that later served as the basis for the Universal film.

Considering the radical surgery needed to transform the sprawling novel into the tight stage drama, it's small wonder that the plot lines of the screen version are so straightforward and simple: Dracula is an aristocratic vampire who is compelled by circumstances to seek fresh blood in foreign climes. Before he

Opposite: **One-sheet for** ***Dracula.*** RONALD V. BORST/HOLLYWOOD MOVIE POSTERS.

can do much more than scout the new neighborhood, however, his identity is discovered, and he is promptly and easily dispatched. This may be something of a *reductio ad absurdum*, but the brevity of the summation clearly points out that, per the treatment afforded him by Garrett Fort's derivative screenplay, Stoker's mighty Vampire King is little more than a pathetic loser.

Granted, despite a series of rousing adventures and that splendidly exciting climactic chase back to the very courtyard of his castle, the Count doesn't come out on top in the novel, either. The play, however, had stripped the character of his grandeur; it had robbed him of his history, his milieu, his roots. The Deane-Balderston Dracula is scarcely more than yet another swarthy foreign type, deemed irresistible by virginal young British girls and viewed with bewildered distaste by stalwart Englishmen. Doggedly following this depiction of the Count as continental lounge-lizard, the film's only concessions to the novel are its opening scenes; these remain the most evocative and the most memorable.

On his ancient battlegrounds, striding upon the blood-soaked earth which supported him in life and which constitutes his grave in life-in-death, Dracula reigns supreme. He climbs down walls (headfirst!), confounding efforts at pursuit. Wolves, rats, and other creatures of menace or pestilence act at his command, both to restrict the movements of his enemies and to facilitate his escape. Ancestral spirits, the shades of those who gave their lives to assure his continued dominion, the "many memories" of which Stoker's terrifying figure had spoken to an uncertain Jonathan Harker: These, too, contribute to the malevolent aura which surrounds the Count. Such are the experiences and qualities which are only hinted at during the film's Transylvania scenes, yet they help to create that profound sense of unease which permeates the film's first two reels, and which is so distressingly absent from the rest of the picture.

The essential lesson to be learned? Dracula is Lord in his native land; there, he is the demonic fiddler who plays the tune to which

the people must dance. Once removed from that venue, he has only his preternatural personal presence upon which to draw, but as is evident from the film (and from all the other Universal treatments), it is not enough. In Transylvania, Dracula is all-powerful. Away from his homeland, separated from his history, without the support of the intimidating influences of myth and legend, he is screwed (or, more properly, impaled).

Onscreen, Van Helsing carries the ball (Dracula having pretty much shot his expository wad back at the castle), and he takes up lots of footage talking about vampires and their powers. Edward Van Sloan does a decent job at blathering at the assembled forces of good, yet seems, at times, to be as unsure of himself as Harker is of him. Hampered by a pair of incredibly thick lenses, the actor frequently indulges in obvious stage mannerisms (stroking his chin, doing myopic double-takes), and takes forever unloading his explanatory dialogue. In the novel, Stoker made Van Helsing very nearly incomprehensible; as the Dutch paranormalist was intended to make things *clear* to his fellows and to the readership, this device was unintentionally comic and dramatically frustrating. Van Sloan's doctor may have no such vocabulary problems, but he still insists on dragging out the simplest of phrases. Many fans hold that this aggravating tendency was part of Tod Browning's overview, and they may be right. In the Browning-less sequel, *Dracula's Daughter* (1936), *Von* Helsing speaks at a calm but steady clip.

Hamilton Deane had pared down the list of *dramatis personae* in London, and John Balderston had done away with several more in New York, so the movie saw the heroine's coterie of admirers shrunken drastically to the short-tempered Jonathan Harker. For budgetary and dramatic reasons surnames were switched, Mina became Dr. Seward's daughter, and Renfield took Harker's place on the fateful trip to Transylvania. Admirers of the novel were not a little perplexed by the capricious treatment accorded familiar characters in the film, and more than one movie goer who had sat faithfully through the endlessly verbose

A quintessential image of Bela Lugosi. *Buddy Barnett/Cinema Collectors.*

play, must have wondered why Universal's movie didn't wrap with the same visual panache with which it had begun.

Herbert Bunston's Doctor Seward doesn't have much to do except throw up his hands from time to time, but in all fairness to Bunston, he did the best he could with a part which only charity could term two-dimensional. Frances Dade's Lucy is charming, savvy, and beautiful; possessed of a sense of humor and an appreciation of the ridiculous, her character out-nuances Mina, and the lovely actress easily dominates the few moments she shares with Helen Chandler. It's nearly unbelievable that someone didn't notice the disparity in the two women's personalities and performances, and suggest a switching of roles.

That never happened because, for reasons which remain unfathomable to modern audiences, Helen Chandler was at that time enjoying substantial popularity, due mainly to roles in such now-forgotten films as *A Rough*

Romance and *Mother's Boy*. Chandler was a fragile beauty whose delicate features added to her sense of vulnerability. (That may have been another reason why the Count chose her over her girlfriend; the vivacious Lucy may have given as well as she got! Catch the look of bewilderment on Lugosi's face while Dade recounts the toast to the dead.) What can't be denied, however, is that her range of emotion never seems to be equal to the challenge of the part. I can't remember where I read it first, but I agree that, in the course of Chandler's portrayal, it's tough to determine just when she begins acting spacey. Most of the actress's other movies were "women's pictures" and have not been resurrected via videotape due to their obscurity. In a nod to worthier opinions than mine, though, Leslie Halliwell felt that Chandler's "early retirement through personal problems robbed Hollywood of an interesting personality."

I seem to be in the minority here, but I've never been much disturbed by David Manners' truculent Jonathan Harker, owing chiefly to my laying the ultimate blame for the role's annoying side at the feet of Messrs. Deane, Balderston, and Fort. If anything, the Canadian actor can be adjudged guilty only of mouthing Harker's more petulant speeches with greater conviction than he does the insipid love business or his relatively few civil comments. As the young hero is the only remnant of the veritable crowd of heroine-worshippers that populated the pages of the novel, his constant kvetching can be excused in the light of compacted dialogue. The sheer amount of complaining he has to do, however, combined with his propensity to wear knickers, does leave the audience with the distressing picture of Mina's champion as a snotty little boy in short pants.

It's not the fault of the actor that Harker is dealing with a rival whom he can't defeat with his fists. Manners' attempts at displaying this frustration are always more than adequate, and he deserves a respite from the heat he has taken for some years now over his "interpretation." The shallowness of the character (along with many other of the less attractive elements

of the play) has been transferred faithfully to the film, and this accounts for the feeling one gets that Harker must be led along like a child, step by step, and that he can't be trusted out of the sight of the grown-ups, even for a moment. (This, sadly, proves to be true. Left alone with Mina on the veranda for five minutes, the nominal hero is very nearly overpowered and vampirized himself. And after he's been saved by a weary, crucifix-wielding Van Helsing, the bully-boy once again throws a tantrum and physically accosts the elderly doctor.)

The Jonathan Harker of the Universal epic is not the embodiment of saintly virtue, but is jealous, obstinate, easily angered, and disrespectful; he continually verges on refusing to cooperate with the others in their attempts to save the woman he loves and ultimately isn't worth a pitcher of warm spit in the undeniably tepid climax. Most of the film's numerous critics, however, seem to have forgotten that the many glaring defects are those of the character and not of the actor hired to impersonate him. Manners' crime is that he succeeds too well in portraying Jonathan Harker's seamier side.

Manners seems to have gotten bad press for all of his early Universal heroes, and this is difficult to understand. His turn as Frank Whemple in *The Mummy* (1932) is quite realistic; the young archaeologist is equal parts cynic, romantic, and genuinely nice guy. His falling in love at first sight is certainly not without precedent on the silver screen, and he surely can't be faulted for any of the protective measures he takes for the sake of Helen Grosvenor. As Peter Alison in *The Black Cat* (1934), Manners is finally married to the lady in distress, so he has, if anything, a more legitimate gripe about the pickle in which he and his love discover themselves. Apart from his climactic drilling of the benevolent yet raving Dr. Werdegast in what can only be termed a classic failure to communicate, Alison behaves rationally and realistically. It's difficult to fathom the criticism of Manners' involvement in both roles unless one carps about the grating nature of some of his dialogue.

The part of Renfield (first name unknown), the real estate agent–cum–insect-eating lunatic,

Lobby card showing Renfield in a quiet moment, the brides of Dracula scarcely believing their eyes. *AUTHOR'S COLLECTION.*

was won by diminutive Dwight Frye, a former stage actor who had been something of a minor league "Toast of Broadway" earlier in his career. Whether Universal's casting department had seen other Frye films (he had for example done a competent job as Casper Gutman's semi-psychotic enforcer in the Ricardo Cortez version of *The Maltese Falcon*), or whether he had actually tested for the part has never been made clear. What couldn't be clearer is Frye's inadequacy in the role.

From the moment he's espied being jostled aboard the Rumanian carriage, Frye's Renfield has milquetoast written all over him. Hardly seeming the sort to venture out alone on such an arduous trip, he is all but apologetic in explaining his business to the peasants

at the inn. At the castle, the prissy little man's every reaction is overdone, and he delivers many of his lines as if he were talking to a child. (Much of Frye's distinctly mannered behavior goes unnoticed during these early scenes as he's constantly being overshadowed by Lugosi's kabuki posturings and vocal acrobatics.) As poorly as his words and expressions meld, though, the several instances in which Frye is asked merely to sit still until things pick up again are downright embarrassing. Take a gander at the Harry Langdon imitation he tenders, right after Dracula has backed off at the sight of the dangling rosary, or home in on him during the first few moments of the film, while he's still minding his own business in the carriage. Gadzooks.

Sadly, for all this, the first part of the film contains his best work. His later efforts at portraying madness range from comical stabs at menace to a bitchiness worthy of Bette Davis. The character's cocky attitude and constant warnings about the coming of "the master" soon grow tiresome. The tedious nature of the dialogue is not Frye's fault, but his grating delivery very much is. The little actor also totally fails in his several attempts at depicting Renfield's being torn between the vestiges of his basic goodness and the adverse influences of Dracula. These lightning-fast mood shifts, intended to show the Count's pervasive mental control, are handled in so painfully amateurish a fashion as to render them unforgivably annoying. The most vivid memory I have of my first viewing of *Dracula*, on television's *Shock Theater* in the mid-fifties, is wanting to belt Frye right in the mouth after he had mucked his way through "Dracula? I never even *heard* the name before!" It augurs ill for a film when irritation with a secondary character is the most intense feeling a viewer has.

Fort also has the schizophrenic continually escaping from his cell (another element swiped directly from the play), but the action becomes ludicrous through repetition. Well done, though, and not just in comparison with the rest of his shtick, is Frye's enacting Renfield's murder at the hands of Dracula. For once, the pleading tone in his voice hits just the right note, and the lunatic's subsequent tumble down the massive staircase manages to elicit some degree of sympathetic reaction from the audience.

Frye's next shot at being a demented sidekick would see him better at it, partly for the experience garnered in *Dracula*. Fritz, in James Whale's *Frankenstein*, would be an uncomplicated assignment, requiring little in the way of complex behavior or sudden changes in personality; it lay well within the actor's range. As the sadistic hunchback, Frye would create an archetype which would influence similar roles, whether comic or serious, to the present day. As for his part in *Dracula*, however, Lillian Lugosi once opined to Greg Mank:

"Dwight Frye — he had to be the worst Renfield ever!"

An interesting postscript to the Renfield issue: Bela Lugosi had not been the only actor to lobby for the privilege of having his stage role captured on film. Equally single-minded in the task was Bernard Jukes, the English actor who had created the part of Renfield while a member of Hamilton Deane's company. Like his more successful co-star, Jukes planted notices of intent and availability in the trades and won quite a bit of support due to his admirable portrayal of the entomophagous loony.

Jukes circulated thousands of photographs of himself in character, both in person and via the mails, in an effort to bring anyone with any influence at all into his camp. So firmly associated with the part was he, having played Renfield over 4,000 times throughout England and with both major American companies, and having appeared with virtually every stage Dracula of note, that the actor didn't even bother identifying either himself or his persona in the massive publicity campaign. To this day, errant photographs of Jukes are mistaken for Universal "P" shots of Frye in character, and more than one has been published as such. There's irony in there somewhere. Jukes, who, in the words of David Skal, "was to Renfield what Yul Brynner was to the King of Siam," is finally enjoying a backhanded taste of the immortality which probably should have been his.

Tod Browning's name has come up once or twice so far, and the director has shouldered most of the blame for *Dracula*'s ultimate inadequacy. No matter why Browning was brought in to helm the film, he carried with him an enviable track record (all those profitable Chaney chillers over at MGM), as well as some less desirable baggage (his well-known alcoholism). Early in his career, he had done more than a bit of work for Uncle Carl, but while Lon Chaney was starring in *The Hunchback of Notre Dame* and *The Phantom of the Opera* at Universal, Browning was building a name for himself on the same lot as the regular director of... Priscilla Deane! Over two-thirds of the dozen-odd silent features guided by Browning for Universal during the twenties starred Priscilla Deane, including a pair which featured Chaney: 1919's *The Wicked Darling* and 1921's *Outside the Law*.

Dracula sailed through production with little difficulty, save for several cast members' taking exception to Bela Lugosi's aloofness, but the end product was quickly attacked for having failed miserably to live up to its potential. The film was accused of creeping along at a funereal pace (true of all except the first two reels, wherein only Lugosi moved at a funereal pace), and complaints about the excess of reaction shots and the excess of long shots vied for numerical supremacy. Comparing the dreary unspooling of the vampire yarn with just about any of the surviving features from the Chaney/Browning/MGM canon can only lead one to the inescapable conclusion that, for all intents and purposes, Chaney had ignored Browning's direction. In his *Lon Chaney: The Man Behind the Thousand Faces*, author Michael F. Blake maintains that "Browning probably did not direct Chaney in the true sense of the word; rather, it is likely the director let Lon play the scene according to his emotions, guiding him only if he felt Chaney was going off in the wrong direction in his performance."

It seems that Chaney had grown accustomed to being left to his own devices by almost everyone during the last decade of his career. In the eyes of the more "mainstream" movie fan, the two films with which the actor remains associated are, of course, *Hunchback* and *Phantom*, neither of which featured Browning's hand at the wheel. According to George Turner, in his fascinating introduction to the MagicImage filmbook on *The Hunchback of Notre Dame*, "Chaney was instrumental in bringing in Wallace Worsley, who had directed him in the Goldwyn production, *The Penalty*.... Worsley was aware of Chaney's directional ability and allowed him to direct some of his own scenes." Chaney's professional disagreements with Rupert Julian, the director of the 1925 *The Phantom of the Opera*, also led to the actor's weaving his own interpretation and arranging his own blocking; Chaney would

merely have a third party advise the director of his plans, and Julian was left to the task of synchronizing the movements of the remaining cast members with those of the titular star. Both *Hunchback* and *Phantom* enjoyed huge success at the box office, and neither film was criticized for having a lethargic pace.

For the greater part of his career as a featured or star performer, Lon Chaney was used to doing his own thing. Thanks to the man's undeniable talent and almost obsessive work ethic, this usually resulted in a solid framework around which the nominal director would fashion the balance of the movie.

This, clearly, was not the case in *Dracula*. Browning would not have tolerated such independence on the part of Bela Lugosi, who, despite a number of screen appearances (including a leading role in the director's *The Thirteenth Chair*), was not yet a formidable name or presence. That didn't stop Lugosi from trying to throw his weight around, however. Having made a nuisance of himself in the very act of winning the part, the actor immediately alienated makeup wizard Jack P. Pierce by insisting both on retaining only the minor cosmetic application the character had received in the stage production, and on applying the subtle makeup himself. Browning, who must have been grateful that, for once, his efforts might not be upstaged by a mobile mound of painted putty, did not go on record as opposing his vampire's self-concept, and Junior Laemmle, anxious only to get things going, wasn't about to hold up production in order to permit experimentation in an area which the reaction of the theater-goers showed to be of very little import in the first place.

Browning's established pacing was imposed on his cast, and the exigencies of primitive sound recording did nothing to add fluidity to the studied movements or lengthy speeches. It's necessary to remember, however, that Van Helsing's incessant expository passages were crucially important to audiences of the day. While the vampire mythos is as familiar today as the tradition of Santa Claus, moviegoers of the twenties and thirties had come to know the term "vampire" only in reference to a predatory woman of great beauty who left the sexually lifeless husks of her male victims lying in her wake. Every item of the supernatural bloodsucker's prowess was news to ticket-buyers, and Van Helsing's ritualistic recitations — along with the hero's pouty and naïve questions — were as necessary to advancing the plot for the uninitiated as they are tedious and overlong to viewers some 60 years later.

Still, the blocking reflects the boundaries of the stage and not the more liberal parameters of film. Characters seldom advance towards the all-seeing lens, moving far more frequently from left to right and back again, as if bound to imitate the two dimensions of the screen itself; when movement in depth is achieved, it is due to the camera's motion rather than to the performers'. In addition, these tedious processions are usually done at half-speed (or less), turning the most routine movement into an establishing shot and stripping the dramatic weight from many entrances and exits. There are some quite beautiful shots — and not only in the first two reels, when Karl Freund is given his lead. The tableau of Dracula awaiting Mina in the garden is almost breathtaking in its composition, and several of the stationary poses Lugosi strikes, apart from the ill-advised and poorly executed pin-spots to the eyes, make for fascinating portraits. Unfortunately, however, such moments are few and far between and belong more properly to the field of still photography than to cinema.

Browning's natural propensity to take things at an easy pace, combined with Lugosi's tendency to award Dracula's every glance, word and action with staggering portent, renders the vampire's presence more wearisome than weird. Apart from his two encounters with a crucifix (the first of which has the Voivode seeking refuge in his armpit) and the mirror sequence, Dracula's studied rhythms are slow to the point of stalling the action. Even the film's not quite thundering climax finds the vampire leisurely sauntering behind the entranced Mina. It is only following Renfield's murder that Dracula rather uneasily hefts the heroine (displaying a bit more strain than befits

a creature "as strong as twenty men"), and hies her double-time (all things being relative) to whatever safety lay behind the rusted and oversized portals of Carfax Abbey.

One of the very few times that Dracula reacts naturally is when he is confronted with that pesky little cigarette box by Van Helsing, and then he moves too quickly. For someone who has spent several lifetimes in a desolate pile of ruins away from mirrors and such, the Count is unbelievably quick at catching on to the Dutchman's little revelation. In the Spanish version of the film, Carlos Villarias indulges in full-fledged shtick when the box is shoved into his face. First he glances cannily sideways at Van Helsing, as if to get a clue from his nemesis's triumphant map as to what's going on. His eyes move slowly down to the box, and pause quizzically on the cigarettes themselves: Can "No fumo ... cigarillos" be running through his mind? Raising his eyes to the mirror, Villarias hesitates — remember: Drácula is looking at empty air here — before realizing that his cover has been blown. The Spanish vampire's face registers every emotion from disbelief at having been outsmarted so easily to anger at Van Helsing's effrontery, to bestial fury at his being revealed through such a mundane contrivance. Both Carlos and Bela do admirable jobs of recovering their composure after the destruction of the box[es], but the nod must go to the Iberian for the more logical behavior beforehand.

Bela's choreographed slow motion, doubtless enacted with Browning's official blessing, is matched instance for instance by his trademark manhandling of the English language. As tiresome as it is to wait for Dracula to lug Renfield's hat and coat all the way across that huge room and through a second doorway, it is doubly so to sit through hourlong recitations of such brief statements as "We will be leaving tomorrow evening." One comes away with the feeling that the drugged wine that the Count slips to the little estate agent wasn't *quite* so old at the beginning of the sentence.

More's the pity that there weren't some kind of truly special effects in evidence throughout the film. Visual effects genius John Fulton

So that's where the hat and coat went. *BUDDY BARNETT/CINEMA COLLECTORS.*

wouldn't show his face until 1932 (when he assisted Bela's Doctor Mirakle in *Murders in the Rue Morgue*), so bat transformations were out of the question. A shot or two of a German shepherd loping across the Seward lawn would have at least relieved the monot-ony of hearing about things a more ambitious production would have supplied (if only via stock footage). To be fair, the sequence wherein Dracula (in bat form) guides the carriage horses as they bring the terrified Renfield to the castle is extremely well done. Equally fair, however, is the observation that the effect *ought* to have been nothing more than a throwaway and not the visual highlight that it proves to be.

Rumor has it that Fulton was responsible for the wonderful glass shots used in the Transylvania scene, but no collaborative evidence seems to exist. The technician was an artist, first and foremost, and the excellent glass work reflects a master's touch, surely not unlike his own. With no credit seemingly given him anywhere, however, I am loath to jump to the otherwise logical conclusion.

Dracula is, if anything, a careless film. Continuity errors abound, making today's trend of goof-spotting a most rewarding pastime. At the outset of the picture, innkeeper Michael Visaroff's hefty pipe jumps back and forth between his hands as inserts alternate with medium long shots. The Count later wears a silk topper as he balefully stares up at the window of the beautiful Lucy. Within moments, he approaches her bedside (having tastefully metamorphosed offscreen, twice), blood in his eye, but no hat on his head. Unforgivably, the erros that plague the production begin with the title card, on which Uncle Carl is identified as the "Presient."

An undeniably important film historically, *Dracula* is miles from classic status. (William Everson relegated the film to almost afterthought mention in a vampire catch-all chapter in his marvelous *Classics of the Horror Film*.) It's difficult to appreciate the impact that the tepid thrills (decried as such in many contemporary reviews) may have had on the crowds at the picture's first run; more than enough theater seats were occupied to assure the picture's overwhelming profitability. Still, as was mentioned above, the novelty of the theme most likely accounted for much of its box-office success.

Lugosi's performance elicits both favorable and unfavorable emotional reactions from horror buffs to this day, although many of the popular actor's fans have come to prefer his later portrayal in *Abbott and Costello Meet Frankenstein*, or (blasphemy!) even his thinly disguised Count in Columbia's old-fashioned but effective *Return of the Vampire* (1944). Bela's greatest challenge as a character actor would lie some eight years in the future, with the role of Ygor, the twisted shepherd, in *Son of Frankenstein* (1939). Nonetheless, for generations of fans, his slow-moving, eccentric Count Dracula would remain the peak from which he would soon fall.

Scheduled to open on Friday, the thirteenth of February 1931, *Dracula* couldn't have possibly asked for a more propitious date. The universally recognized feast day of disaster and doom would have provided a tie-in made in heaven with Universal's cinematic celebration of death and horror. Alas! It was not to be. In a trade announcement made at the eleventh hour (February 7, to be exact), Tod Browning appealed to the exhibitors, and citing the attendant superstitions as being too much for him to bear, pleaded that they consent to change the opening day for *Dracula*. Some may have shaken their heads in wonder, but most people looked beyond the director's dramatic appeal in order to find his real motive. Opening the following day, February 14 — Valentine's Day — would brilliantly underscore the advertising campaign, which touted the film as "The strangest passion the world has ever known." Interestingly, Hamilton Deane had introduced the thirsty Count to London theater-goers at the Little Theatre on February 14, 1927; whether the date was chosen by accident or design is not known. At any rate, such a move would be a stroke of genius.

Genius, did we say? Tod Browning, master of the macabre, showman extraordinaire, moved *Dracula*'s debut *up* a day, to the more emotionally neutral February 12. The logic of a move to Valentine's Day is so compelling that most fans remain positive that that's when the film opened. While narrating the TV special, "Lugosi: The Forgotten King," even Forrest J Ackerman maintained that the picture, billed as a gothic romance, "premiered Valentine's Day in 1931." Once again, Browning had snatched defeat from the jaws of victory. How fitting that the next genre outing for the original Man with His Head up His Ass was MGM's *Freaks*.

Dracula

Released February 12, 1931; 78 minutes (later 75 min.)

Cast: Bela Lugosi (Count Dracula); Helen Chandler (Mina Seward); David Manners (Jonathan Harker); Edward Van Sloan (Prof. Van Helsing); Dwight Frye (Renfield); Herbert Bunston (Dr. Seward); Francis Dade (Lucy Weston); Charles Gerrard (Martin); Moon Carroll (Maid); Michael Visaroff (Innkeeper); Joan Standing (Briggs); Josephine Velez (Nurse); Wyndham Standing (Surgeon); Carla Laemmle (Reader on Coach); Dorothy Tree, Jeraldine Dvorak, Cornelia Thaw (Dracula's Brides); Daisy Belmore, Nicholas Bela, Donald Murphy (Coach Passengers); John George (Assistant to Van Helsing); Tod Browning (voice of Whitby Harbormaster)

Credits: Producer — Carl Laemmle, Jr.; Director — Tod Browning; Associate Producer — E.M. Asher; Screenplay — Garrett Fort; Based on the novel *Dracula* by Bram Stoker, and on the legitimate play of the same name by Hamilton Deane and John L. Balderston; Scenario Supervisor — Charles A. Logue; Continuity — Dudley Murphy; Photographer — Karl Freund; Art Director — Charles D. Hall; Musical Director — Heinz Roemheld; Casting — Phil Friedman; Film Editor — Milton Carruth; Supervising Film Editor — Maurice Pivar; Set Designers — Herman Rosse and John Hoffman; Set Decoration — Russell A. Gausman; Recording Supervisor — C. Roy Hunter; Photographic Effects — Frank J. Booth; Art Titles — Max Cohen; Research — Nan Grant; Assistant Director — Scott Beal; 2nd Assistant Director — Herman Schlom; Still Photographer — Roman Freulich; Script Girl — Aileen Webster; 2nd Unit Photography — Joseph Bretherton; Makeup — Jack P. Pierce; Costumes — Ed Ware and Vera West

DRÁCULA (1931)

A number of zealous horror fans have expended incredible effort in tracking down the steadily decreasing number of missing (and presumed dead) chiller features which have acquired semi-ethereal reputations due to their absence from the scene. Many of these rediscovered "classics" have experienced cool receptions, their almost mythical status punctured by modern critical insensitivities. This may be almost inevitable, given the inordinately ridiculous analytical depth to which many of today's film scholars aspire, but it is certainly not fair.

Michael Curtiz's two early Warners beauties, for example—*Doctor X* (1932) and *Mystery of the Wax Museum* (1933)—reemerged to white-hot enthusiasm, only to fall victim to huffy "reevaluations" by supercilious "experts" who scrubbed away the charming patina of age and naïveté to triumphantly reveal works foreign to modern sensibilities, understandably lacking in nineties technical artistry, and displaying old-fashioned virtues regarded

nowadays with superiority and contempt. For legions of fans, however, these restored pictures retain much of the magic conjured up over the years by tantalizing photographs and personal reminiscences. It was within this heady atmosphere that George Melford's Spanish interpretation of *Dracula* resurfaced a few years ago.*

Until its restoration, accomplished by combining footage held by the Library of Congress with scenes copied from the only other existing print, lodged within Castro's Cuba, the Spanish *Drácula* enjoyed a unique status among "lost" films: For all intents and purposes, it had traditionally been dismissed as a footnote to the Browning/Lugosi production. Seemingly only a handful of stills existed and cogent commentary had more or less been limited to mention in William Everson's second volume, *More Classics of the Horror Film*. Thankfully, the film's eagerly anticipated video release was preceded by Bill Littman's excellent essay "Drácula Español" in the massive anni-

---

And it fared no better than any of its colleagues for being compared with its "sister" production. Variety's "Archive Review" of October 5, 1992, lowered the boom, finding the Browning version — which that same paper had showered with indifference back in 1931— far superior. Proffering an almost unique opinion, reviewer Paul Lenti cited the Spanish film as "Far less ambitious technically" with "images [which] are more static with less tension" than its American counterpart. Lenti likewise averred that "The Browning version clocks in at a brisk 75 minutes [while] Melford's creeps along to 104 minutes [sic] with ponderous pauses and plodding dialog." While each is certainly entitled to his own opinion, the Variety critic pretty well capped it in his second sentence, wherein he labeled Melford's film a "curiosity."

More opulently dressed and more creatively lit than Tod Browning had ventured, the sets in the Spanish *Drácula* seemed to belong to the earlier proposed "Super Production." AUTHOR'S COLLECTION.

versary edition of the long-running fanzine *Midnight Marquee* (1988); by George Turner's article "The Two Faces of Dracula" in the May 1988 issue of *American Cinematographer* magazine; and by a chapter-length analysis in David Skal's *Hollywood Gothic*.

The restored *Drácula*, which is superior in almost every way to its American counterpart, hasn't been available long enough to receive exhaustive coverage, but it deserves the royal treatment. It's hard to believe that the Spanish version was shot on the same sets; more opulently dressed, more creatively lit, more effectively utilized, many of the standing sets seem not to belong to the concurrent "sister" production, but rather to the earlier, proposed "Super Production" which fell victim to budget cuts. Melford made good use of all of Charles D. Hall's Transylvanian interi-

ors, including some inexplicably ignored or cut by Browning.

Although some 24 minutes longer than the U.S. version, *Drácula* is more dynamic and thus belies the vintage the two films share. The only exceptions to the constant forward thrust are the two scenes wherein *el Conde* curiously invades Eva's bedroom twice within minutes (in both real and "reel" time), using virtually the same *modus operandi* and achieving virtually the same result. Apart from this bewildering repetition (which can't have been done merely to pad the 100+ minute running time), the picture unspools smoothly, and even with the lengthy explanations all Van Helsings are forced to provide, moves along at a good clip.

Melford and cinematographer George Robinson's joint work aids immeasurably here.

Spanish trade ad for *Drácula*. *JUAN B. HEININK AND ROBERT G. DICKSON, FROM THEIR BOOK* CITA EN HOLLY-
WOOD.

The Spanish cast does a great deal more than scurry sideways, crab-like; the constant use of movement toward or away from the lens gives a heightened sense of depth perception which the American version sorely lacks. This is not to say that the picture is totally free of long shots or tableaux, à la Browning and Freund; like their more famous counterparts, Melford and Robinson had also cut their teeth on silent film and had also employed contemporary techniques to mirror the visual style which would ultimately come to be known as the "'30s look." Compared with the American team's "flat" look and more stationary camera placements though, *Drácula* seems almost to be an exercise in early 3-D.

This dynamic is evident from the first: Browning's credits are displayed over the static image of a stylized bat, festooned with cobwebs. In contrast, Melford's cast and company are introduced over a live-action flickering candle (also festooned with cobwebs) which, with an eye to imagery and foreshadowing, is blown out mid-sequence. Both unfold over ominous strains from Tchaikovsky's *Swan Lake*, yet the "Spanish" reading of the music seems more symphonic and runs longer, extending into the carriage scene. Odd snatches of violoncello accompany *el Conde* as he emerges from his assorted boxes and these, in turn, are counterbalanced by the operatic creaking of vampiric doors, which groan as if with the weight of the ages as they open and close unassisted. The only musical shortcoming occurs at the concert hall where, following some impressive canned Wagner, Drácula et al. watch the curtain rise on a piece of grainy footage from the 1925 *The Phantom of the Opera*, and are aurally accosted by a classical track for which the adjectives "tinny" and "rinky-dink" may have been first coined.

Unlike the U.S. version, the Spanish title card features the Laemmle moniker only twice, but has Uncle Carl being given his titular due without orthographic mistake. A bit puzzling is the attribution credit, which highlights Bram Stoker's authorship while giving no recognition to the play by Deane and Balderston. It has been suggested that this sin of omission was committed because of the complexities of copyright and such, but with the foreign-language effort nearly a word-for-word transfer of the English script, it's difficult to understand why one film would have to post notice while the other would not.

As a result of budget limitations* (raw stock, salaries for cast and crew members, an array of properties for the sets, and a few opticals were the only approved expenditures over and above the sum alloted to the English production), both cast and audience were again denied a peek at the Voivode in wolf form, darting across the yard between abbey and sanitarium. The Spanish ticket-buyers, however, may have regarded the sight of the furious Dracula stomping out through the French doors as more dramatically satisfying than David Manners' lame recitation.

Castwise, the Latins outshine their American cousins almost to a person. Most affecting is probably Pablo Álvarez Rubio, whose memorable Renfield leaves the more stylized Dwight Frye in the maniacal dust. Shrieking hysterically with a fervor that would have done Fay Wray proud, the Spaniard still manages to imbue Renfield's quieter, more lucid moments with a genuine pathos, thus affording a profoundly clear view into his tormented soul. *Drácula* was the second of only two films the actor made in Tinseltown, the first being *Los que danzan*, the export edition of First National's *Those Who Dance* (1930). Despite profuse congratulations from the likes of Charlie Chaplin, Álvarez Rubio felt that the Spanish agenda in Hollywood was decaying, and he returned to Spain in short order. The erstwhile law student, poet, and sportswriter appeared in some four dozen Castilian features before passing away in his native Madrid in April 1983.

Eduardo Arozamena's Van Helsing seems warmer and more human than Edward Van

---

According to David Skal, Melford and Kohner brought the whole enchilada in for under $68,000. One can only wonder whether any of the Spanish cast were better compensated than Mr. Lugosi.

Sloan's coldly formidable doctor. One never doubts for a moment that Van Sloan's vampire fighter will triumph in the end; even in the confrontation scene in the library, where Dracula appears to have the upper hand, it's a virtual certainty that the ramrod-straight Dutchman will muster his resources and escape the Count's hypnotic influence. Peering owlishly from behind a set of the Coke-bottle lenses the Universal wardrobe department so freely dispensed, Arozamena's plump figure neither inspires nor displays the same confidence, yet the dramatic tension which exists between *el Profesor* and *el Conde* is all the more effective for this ambiguity. Only an awareness of then-contemporary theatrical conventions makes the Mexican Van Helsing's final victory a foregone conclusion.

Doing his best to fill David Manners' knickers is Argentine juvenile Barry Norton. Whereas most of his colleagues spoke only Spanish at the time *Drácula* was being shot, young Norton was functionally trilingual; besides English, he was proficient enough at French to win the romantic leads in the Gallic export versions of *Slightly Scarlet* and *The Benson Murder Case* over at Paramount. (He also copped the same parts in the Spanish-language renditions.) Before the movies had decided that chatter was essential, Norton's blond good looks had snagged him the high-visibility assignment as one of Gary Cooper's American buddies in the studio's *Legion of the Condemned* (1928). As for his English, Universal thought it good enough to award him a small part in the prestigious adaptation of Fanny Hurst's tearjerker *Imitation of Life* (1934), and Laurel and Hardy had originally tagged Norton for the romantic lead in their feature-length comedy, *Bonnie Scotland*. (Letter perfect in his dialogue, he was replaced by William Janney after getting a bit lost among Stan's and Ollie's improvisations.) Still, his Pablo Díaz was prominently featured in both the Spanish and American release versions of Jack Holt's 1935 testosterone celebration, *Storm Over the Andes*.

Lupita Tovar is in all ways a brighter, more attractive Eva (read: Mina) than the semi-comatose Helen Chandler. Both the heroine's normal *joie de vivre* and her later predatory stalking of her boyfriend are head and shoulders above the American actress's best efforts. A bit more Reubenesque in some scenes than in others (in an interview arranged to coincide with the video release of the restored *Drácula*, the actress confessed to chowing down constantly on chocolates sent her way by admiring crew members), the lovely Tovar's décolleté charms likewise indicated in a most pleasing fashion that her immortal soul wasn't the *only* thing on Juan Harker's mind. While Carmen Guerrero is also quite fetching, especially in her black two-piece lingerie, as the unlucky-in-love Lucía (Lucy), I still have to give Frances Dade the nod. It may be that her performance is all the more vivid because of the anemic Chandler, but the contrast between the two characters is more satisfying, dramatically, than the chemistry between the two señoritas who, for all their obvious appeal, are cut of the same cloth.

Manuel Arbó, a native of Madrid like Álvarez Rubio, brings asylum attendant Martín in from the Warner Bros. cartoon expanses inhabited by Charles Gerrard. More laconic than the rubber-faced Gerrard, and given more to alluding to Thomas Aquinas and less to wearing his peaked cap sideways, Arbó paints a picture of a working stiff who is not so much confounded by mysterious goings-on as inconvenienced by Renfield's talent for getting loose. (*Variety*'s "archive critic," Paul Lenti, already quoted above, reinforces my opinion of his tenuous grasp on reality when he pronounces that "the part of Martin has been expanded in the Spanish from that of a Cockney *skeptic* [emphasis added] to a genuine comic buffoon.")

Arbó had just appeared at Universal with Edward G. Robinson and Lupe Velez in *Oriente y occidente* (*East Is West*, with Barry Norton standing in for Lew Ayres) and would continue

Opposite: On the backlot, the cast of *Drácula* poses behind Paul Kohner. *From left to right*: José Soriano Vosca, Carlos Villarias, Carmen Guerrero, Lupita Tovar, Amelia Senisterra, Barry Norton, Eduardo Arozamena and Pablo Álvarez Rubio. **Author's Collection.**

The film all boils down to the monster and the girl: Carlos Villarias and Lupita Tovar. *LUPITA TOVAR.*

to make the rounds of the majors for the rest of the decade. He, rather than Sidney Toler, was the fifth actor to portray Charlie Chan when he took over for Warner Oland in *Eran trece*, the Spanish language version of Fox's 1931 *Charlie Chan Carries On*. Arbó's later career was more truly international, and among his Spanish films, *Tres eran tres* (*Three Were Three*, with Pablo Álvarez Rubio), may deserve special mention to genre fans. A comedy triptych, the picture follows the efforts of a group of penurious filmmakers as they seek to make and release three films: a gypsy adventure, a western, and a monster movie. This last episode would doubtless be most to our liking, as it highlights Señor Arbó, in full makeup, offering a comic take on Karloff's Frankenstein Monster.

I know this is heresy, but I've come to view Lugosi's 1931 Dracula as running in a dead heat with that of Carlos Villarias. Made to wear the Hungarian's soup and fish (and sporting his hair as well), the Spaniard was also privy to his colleague's blocking and interpretation; Villarias was the only cast member allowed to view Freund's and Browning's rushes. To his credit, Sr. "Villar" manages to avoid most of the excesses of the Lugosi portrayal. Nonetheless, both vampires are prone to mugging, and each has his own inimitable style. Lugosi's predatory grimace, seen at its zenith in Lucy's bedroom, could just as readily be mistaken for some gastrointestinal condition, while Villarias' tendency to google his eyes and flash his pearly whites at the slightest provocation quickly loses its edge. Neither display plays as

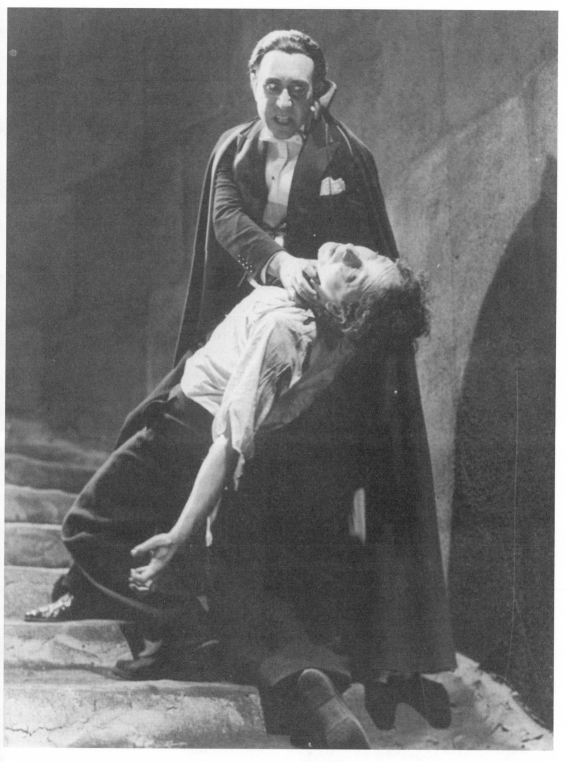

Instead of life, Renfield finds death at the hands of the Master. Van Helsing and his stake will finish the job. *Ronald V. Borst/Hollywood Movie Posters.*

effectively as it ought, but Bela's hardcore star-
ing, gaping, and leering seem more purposely
discourteous than menacing. The Spanish
Count, *al contrario*, shares Álvarez Rubio's
facility for depicting rather more natural expressions when he shows Drácula's "public"
face; less easy to take are the stormy glances *el
Conde* hurls this way and that when he thinks
no one is looking.

Born Carlos Villarias Llano in Córdoba,
Spain, in 1892, the actor enjoyed a long and
varied career in front of the lens. Some sources
have him appearing in First National's *Svengali*
in 1931; regardless, he went on to grace both
American films and their Spanish cousins until
late 1935, when he moved to Mexico. Editor
Juan Heinink (*Los que pasaron por Hollywood*)
lists over 100 titles Villarias had under his belt
by 1952, but it's doubtful that the actor, who
was thoroughly fluent in English by his mid-
twenties, ever again enjoyed anything like the
fame *Drácula* brought him.

George Melford ("Uncle" George to the
cast, according to Ms. Tovar) does an excep-
tional job at keeping the atmosphere roiling,
the lights ominous, and the action nonstop.
Even the infrequent talking heads seem more
animated, thanks to Melford's direction, Robinson's mobile camera, and the cast's admirable
tendency to make the dialogue sound like conversation and not oratory. An occasional stumble (the complex and unbelievable steps taken
by Drácula to avoid a cross concealed by Van
Helsing, for example) is more readily forgiven
amid the wealth of creativity generated on the
whole by the two Georges.

The two even looted Browning's outtakes
("unused negative," per David Skal) to plug
up some of the smaller holes in the narrative.
They also shot several sequences which Browning had lensed and abandoned, or thought
superfluous or inconsequential: Harker and
Van Helsing returning from the crypt wherein
they have put Lucía's wandering soul to rest,
an insert of the rising sun filtering through a
grate in the catacombs, Van Helsing's explanation that he cannot leave Carfax Abbey until
he has kept his promise to Renfield. This last
should have been given some serious thought

if the vampire mythos — still in the process of
gestation — was to survive its birth in one
piece. Both Renfields had been vampirized to
some extent at Castle Dracula (Frye by Lugosi,
Álvarez Rubio by the three brides), so neither
a broken neck nor (to use Bill Littman's excellent phrase) "an air-sucking drop" should
have caused more than a temporary setback to
the estate agent's subsequent adventures as a
vampire.

Melford, Robinson, and the Latins imbue
the story with a greater sense of impending
tragedy than does the American crew, and they
do this, quite simply, by having their characters visibly demonstrate their affection and love
for each other. From the moment Eva's health
and salvation are threatened, few of the cast
can refrain from touching, embracing, or otherwise physically supporting her. She is their
treasure, and they hold her tight, lest she be
stolen from them. With basic gestures such as
these, Melford's *dramatis personae* strike a
human chord that Browning's icy Dutchman
and stolid Brits avoid like the plague; Mina is
not so much a bundle of life and warmth and
dreams as an object of study to be held at arm's
length. Only self-styled master of the macabre
Tod Browning could remain oblivious to the
normal passions and emotions so desperately
important to a picture like *Dracula*.

Evincing a richness which the English
language version only approximates, *Drácula*
leaves one wishing that Melford had guided
both productions. (You have to wonder how
much more memorable the extant MGM Chaney
features would be had Browning been supplanted earlier as well.) And even the staunchest Lugosi fanatic has to admit to the dream of
Bela trotting his stuff under what evidently
were close to optimum circumstances. The
availability of both versions on videotape
allows the more curious to make their own
comparisons, but no matter which "interpretation" one prefers, Dracula proudly retains its
status as trend-setter. The Voivode opened the
creaky door to an incredible array of genre
offerings. Without his venerable presence, the
horror field as we know it might never have
come to pass.

Drácula

Released May 8, 1931; 102 minutes. Previewed at Universal City in January 1931. International premiere, Mexico City, 4 April 1931

Cast: Carlos Villar(ias) (El Conde Drácula); Lupita Tovar (Eva Seward); Barry Norton (Juan Harker); Eduardo Arozamena (Prof. Van Helsing); Pablo Álvarez Rubio (Renfield); José Soriano Viosca (Dr. Seward); Carmen Guerrero (Lucía); Manuel Arbó (Martín); Amelia Senisterra (Marta)

Credits: Producer — Carl Laemmle, Jr; Director — George Melford; Associate Producer — Paul Kohner; Based on the novel *Dracula* by Bram Stoker; Spanish Translation — B. Fernández Cué; Art Director — Charles D. Hall; Recording Supervisor — C. Roy Hunter; Photographer — George Robinson, ASC; Supervising Film Editor — Maurice Pivar; Film Editor — Arturo Tavares; Makeup — Jack P. Pierce

FRANKENSTEIN (1931)

The first "classic" horror film I ever *almost* saw on TV was James Whale's *Frankenstein*. All of seven years old when the film opened the *Shock Theater* series in the New York area, I remained on the edge of my seat until Colin Clive and Edward Van Sloan, hearing those shuffling footsteps, killed the lights; within moments, the laboratory door was nudged open, the gigantic black figure began to back into the room, and I was out of there. I spent a sleepless night gaping fearfully at my own bedroom door, knowing it would open at any moment and reveal the Frankenstein Monster, mystically transported across space and time to freeze the bone marrow of a terrified kid in a Brooklyn apartment. It wasn't until well over a year later that I could steel myself to confront the giant Karloff, and then I was supported by my father, whose presence gave me strength and whose leg pinned me to the couch.

The television debut of *Frankenstein* had to be a mirror image of the hurricane force with which the film had originally struck box offices some 25 years earlier. The movie first hit the big screen on November 21, 1931, some nine months after *Dracula* had sucked not only blood, but substantial amounts of hard cash from Depression-era moviegoers, and had changed forever the primary definition of the word "vampire." Had the Stoker-Browning-

Lugosi epic been anything other than the sensation that it was, the Laemmles might have looked elsewhere for inspiration. As always, the corporation was robbing Peter to pay Paul, and despite the vindication Junior must have felt while poring over his firstborn horror's healthy take, Universal's financial status was still less than secure. Another monstrous hit was needed — and fast!

From the moment the vampire picture's first disappointing reviews hit the papers; through the announcement of a follow-up property which would build on its predecessor's strengths and avoid its weaknesses; amid a peculiar series of reversals and recantations; to the final, unbelievable success of the finished product, *Frankenstein* was truly no less than the son of *Dracula*. The nine months between the appearance of the Golden Age of Horror's primogenitor and his worthy successor were really a gestation period which would lead to the emergence of other classic goblins and their assorted sons, daughters, and hangers-on.

For Universal, the really nice thing about *Frankenstein* was that its author had been dead since 1851, there were no distant relatives queuing up for a piece of the action, and the novel was undoubtedly in the public domain. True, the book was something of a snoozer, with its handful of bloodcurdling highlights nestled among the Creature's incessant metaphysical arguments and ponderously didactic rhetoric. This hadn't stood in the way of numerous stage adaptations, though, nor deterred Thomas Edison's film company from winnowing the wheat from the chaff as early as 1910. Plus, a good part of the projected audiences had at least heard of *Frankenstein*, and their tenuous grasp of the plot details would actually help to sell the title without having to deal with preconceived notions. On top of that, there was a play kicking around in London, and the rights to it could probably be had cheaply, thus insuring an unencumbered path to the film version (and probably a couple of good ideas to boot).

Hamilton Deane's troupe had been offering that play since late 1927, in repertory with Deane's own adaptation of *Dracula*, but the creative hand in question this time was not his, but Peggy Webling's. If truth be told, Webling's play was not terribly good; even given the long-winded, flowery material whence she had drawn her inspiration, her prose was as awkward and unlikely as Hamilton Deane's had been, before John Balderston had stepped in to tighten the actor-errant's *Dracula* and to put dialogue instead of declamation into his characters' mouths. Deane, in fact, had been begging Balderston for quite some time to rework Webling's play to make it more commercially viable. Failing that, the lanky actor had even tried rewriting it himself; *Frankenstein*'s subsequent move from the hinterlands to London's West End demonstrated that Deane's literary capabilities ran much more to dressing up someone else's fluff than to composing his own.

The evolution from play to screenplay is recounted definitively in David Skal's *The Monster Show*. Briefly, however, it went as follows: After Deane's own revision of Webling's *Frankenstein* opened in London's The Little Theatre in February 1930, Balderston had second thoughts about collaborating with the distaff playwright (he had signed an option to do so, some months earlier, but had allowed the option to expire without acting on it). If his experience with *Dracula* had taught him anything, it was that there was very little correlation between easy money and good taste.

Consequently, the erstwhile newspaperman swallowed his pride and, having first made sure that the ensuing American performance rights were safely tucked into his billfold, began to work in earnest alongside Webling for the express purpose of creating a more palatable monster.

While *Frankenstein*'s playwright and her redactor settled down to fight over scenes and hone phrases, the play itself closed after a brief run in the West End. Despite press puffery to the effect that it "out-Draculas *Dracula*," the more sophisticated playgoers in and around London had found *Frankenstein* somewhat less than irresistible. The vintage ham-fisted melodramatics in which Deane and co-star Henry Hallatt indulged (to revive audience members who might have succumbed to the stilted Deane-Webling prose) had failed to capture the magic of similar tactics the actor had first employed in his vampire entertainment. The die had been cast, however; if Frankenstein (Webling had the Creature share his creator's name so as to underscore the many ties which bound them to each other) would no longer cast a transplanted eye about an English theater, he nevertheless could almost envision a stage being readied for him on Broadway.

Horace Liveright likewise had a vision regarding *Frankenstein*, and both the Great White Way and Hollywood figured prominently therein. The haughty impresario probably regarded his presence in the negotiations as a foregone conclusion. After all, it had been under his auspices that Deane and Balderston had first joined forces back in 1927, and their resultant amalgam, *Dracula*, had been providing exultant theater owners with full houses ever since. Wasn't it just more of the same with this new collaboration?

Unfortunately for him, between the dismayed reactions of Miss Webling (whom Liveright had bullied in his attempt to come to terms), John Balderston's growing impatience with his constant creative interference, and the incipient overtures by Universal Pictures, it would prove to be just that — more of the same. Just as in *Dracula*'s circuitous path between theater and cinema, Liveright would be left out

The still photographer sometimes worked under less than optimal conditions. Here the prone Karloff is not fully made up, and in the recesses behind John Boles (left), a sharp print shows a "Positively No Smoking" sign. With torch is Colin Clive; at right is Edward Van Sloan. *JOHN PARNUM.*

in the cold. Although he had held an option on the performance rights for the revised *Frankenstein*, these were lost when the perennially underfunded impresario had failed to mount a timely production. This inability had rendered moot his 50 percent interest in the impending film option. Nor could Liveright expect either sympathy or an extension from the Universal brass; the spiteful payment terms he had earlier dictated in return for his quitclaim to *Dracula* had burned that bridge. Junior Laemmle, nobody's fool despite snickers about nepotism or lackluster capabilities, would never come to regard the ex-publisher as anything other than an ineffectual nuisance.

When Universal mailed the checks for the rights to film *Frankenstein*, none would have Horace Liveright's name on it. Nor would any Webling-Deane-Balderston play be opening soon in an American theater; Universal would risk no loss of audience share to a "rival" production, and had insisted upon total product exclusivity until some indeterminate future date. For the second time, in circumstances not unlike those of *Dracula*, Horace Liveright's hopelessly smarmy blustering had rendered him little more than a spectator to a box office bonanza. The painful irony was that, given the provincial nature of both of the source plays, neither film would probably have been made (at least, not under the conditions which ultimately led to its success) without the arrangements of the distraught producer.

The exclusivity proviso wasn't the only unusual feature of the option contract, however. Cash poor as always, Universal cast about wildly and then offered Webling and Balderston (Deane was never a part of the movie negotiations) $20,000 up front and 1 percent of all the gross earnings of *Frankenstein*. The evidence of their signatures implies that they were satisfied with the offer. The Universal team, likewise, must have come away pleased: If the film did little business, they'd gotten off cheaply; if it was a smash, Webling and her partner would deserve every dime they received.

Cut to 1952: Peggy Webling has gone to her reward some five years earlier, but her heirs and a crusty John Balderston, accompanied by any number of attorneys familiar with contractual law, approach Universal with an interesting claim. As the original Frankenstein concept (that recorded by Universal in 1931) had served as the basis for the seven subsequent film appearances of the Monster and Henry Frankenstein and various descendants, which had (more or less) faithfully preserved the mythos which Webling and Balderston had virtually created from elements taken from a rambling, public domain work, then Mr. Balderston and Miss Webling's estate should be entitled to 1 percent of the worldwide gross receipts of the entire *Frankenstein* series.

Ye Gods and Little Fishes! Amid much harrumphing and legalistic hair-splitting, the court battle raged for a year or so until the studio, in return for the plaintiffs' quitclaim to all rights involving their version of the Monster, the mythos, and every other damned thing connected with *Frankenstein*, agreed to settle. Rumor has it the parsimonious Universal had to part with more than $100,000 to be forever rid of the cantankerous Balderston and Peggy Webling's shade.

Still, on April 8, 1931, the date on which the Monster became the legal ward of Universal Studios, there wasn't the remotest inkling of the controversy that was to come. But there was more than enough unrelated controversy

stirring already. There was, for example, the little matter of Monsieur Florey.

Robert Florey was a well-known and well-liked man about Hollywood during the cusp between the '20s and the '30s. The French émigré had rubbed elbows with just about every film personality worth knowing during the latter years of the silent era, and had demonstrated his professional range through a series of impeccable performances as publicist, advance manager, technical advisor, and assistant director to any number of demanding world-class artists and technicians. The popular Florey had a number of directorial credits under his belt as well, having helmed several early talkies while under contract to Paramount, and gained renown as the guiding light behind the camera for some remarkable experimental films. His impressive credentials, together with his reputation for bringing order out of chaos (he had directed the madcap Marx Brothers in their first film, 1929's *The Cocoanuts*) soon brought him to the attention of Universal's Richard Schayer, the story department head.

Florey met over lunch with Schayer, who intrigued the tall Frenchman with an offer to work on a horror property — *The Invisible Man* and *Murders in the Rue Morgue* were the titles reportedly discussed — to be released in *Dracula*'s wake. While flattered by the offer and fascinated by the genre (as a teenager, he had worked in Paris's *Théàtre du Grand Guignol*), Florey insisted that *Frankenstein* was hands down the best choice for Universal's second horror epic. Advised by Schayer that his next step would be to sell the idea to Junior, Florey went to work on preparing a five-page outline, drawing heavily on *Grand Guignol* and German Expressionistic cinema, with a bit of Mary Shelley mixed in for flavor. The kernel of the deal was that the outline would be expanded into a complete script should the young production chief take a shine to it and agree to Florey's being named director.

Had the earnest Frenchman known that, per the peculiar arrangements outlined above, Junior was then awaiting the satisfactory conclusion to negotiations with Peggy Webling and

John Balderston, he might have saved the wear and tear on his writing hand. Of course, had he not composed the sample synopsis, *Frankenstein* might have been filmed without a couple of its most recognizable elements: the windmill and the business about the abnormal brain. For the record, however, Greg Mank in his production background essay for the *Frankenstein* volume of the MagicImage Universal Film Script series reveals that Florey's original script also contained several vignettes of gratuitous violence which would have defeated any attempts at creating sympathy for the Monster. Sympathy may have been the last thing on the French writer's mind, however; Mank maintains that, in Florey's treatment

> Frankenstein is simply a smug, bullying mad doctor, with little personality and no sympathy for his creation; the first time we see Monster and Monster-Maker together after the laboratory creation sequence, Frankenstein is torturing his creature with a whip and a hot poker! As for the Creature, he is simply a howling, hellish demon, totally devoid of the profound sympathy which later made Karloff's monster movie mythology.

The final screenplay would consist of Garrett Fort's and Francis Faragoh's combined reworking (with a liberal infusion of pathos) of an earlier Florey-Fort collaborative effort which had included a number of items from the Webling-Balderston overhaul of the original Peggy Webling play. The Brunases and Tom Weaver claim in *Universal Horrors* that the early Florey-Fort screenplay "outlines virtually every scene in the finished film, with some minor adjustments." If this be true, the omission of Robert Florey's credit as screenwriter from U.S. prints of the film and all domestic advertising (prints destined for overseas markets, along with their attendant publicity materials, were naturally prepared separately, and the Frenchman received his due therein) is a blatant injustice which some film historians have endeavored to explain away as a Writers' Guild decision, and which others have attributed to a bitchy and egotistical James Whale.

Wherever the blame may lay, it was this early screenplay which served as the basis for the now legendary test footage featuring a sullen and unenthusiastic Bela Lugosi. His ego fanned by countless letters from females seeking to discover Dracula's more intimate side, the handsome and eccentrically loquacious actor was furious that neither of these attributes would be in evidence in this follow-up exercise to his greatest success.

There must be a half-dozen different accounts of the test-reel fiasco, and no two agree on all of the details. The footage was shot on the standing *Dracula* sets on June 16 and 17, 1931, and both Edward Van Sloan and Dwight Frye were on hand to add their evolving Dr. Waldman and Fritz personas. (Contract players were assigned to go through the motions of the still uncast Henry Frankenstein and Victor Moritz.) Famed cinematographer Paul Ivano manned the camera, his good friend Robert Florey was behind it, and Junior Laemmle sat comfortably in his office, awaiting the results while making phone calls to bookies and girls.

Bela Lugosi's aloof temperament and inability to keep his mouth shut are already a matter of record, so their reemergence at this point in the narrative should come as no surprise. When apprised that he would head the cast of *Frankenstein*, the actor's first thought was that he would portray that tragic zealot, Doctor Henry Frankenstein. As the screenplay was set in some indeterminate region of central Europe, his pronounced accent would fit right in. All that juicy dialogue, some tangible dramatics, a love interest: What was there not to like about the picture? The first fly in the ointment came when Junior informed the Hungarian romantic that he was going to be the monster, and not the scientist. Florey was disconcerted by the announcement, but Lugosi was floored. Why would they even think of him for the monster? Dracula was not a monster; he was the very *human* epitome of evil: insinuating, seductive, and passionately irresistible.

Still, as portrayed in the novel, the monster didn't seem to be too bad: all that juicy dialogue, some tangible dramatics — there was still more than enough on the plate to satisfy one's professional appetite. Besides, the advance publicity featured an artist's rendition of an oversized yet not wholly unattractive creature terrorizing the countryside. Again, what was there not to like about the picture? Bela's copy of the screenplay for the test must have contained the straw that broke the camel's back. Gone was the juicy dialogue — *this* monster grunted and groaned as though suffering from dyspepsia and stumbled about the ruins of the Castle Dracula set (another insult!) as if constructed from nuts and bolts instead of flesh and blood. How much pure acting skill did it take to shuffle around and moan?

If Lugosi found any merit at all to the part of the monster as depicted in Florey and Garrett Fort's early treatment, it may have been the challenge it presented in the field of the cosmetic arts. Having designed and applied his own makeup in the course of dozens of demanding theatrical engagements, Bela may have taken some consolation in the thought that he could shape the monster's image — as he had done in *Dracula* — to conform both with his facial lines and his dramatic concept.

At this point in the saga, the details become more than ordinarily confusing.

Some accounts maintain that Bela was allowed to work up his physical appearance without any input at all from the fuming Jack P. Pierce. "Lugosi thought his ideas were better than anyone else's," Pierce once snapped, when asked about the *Frankenstein* test. "Lugosi looked like the Golem!" recalled the venerable Edward Van Sloan in an early sixties issue of *Famous Monsters*; subsequent remarks from the erstwhile Dr. Waldman failed to shed any light on whose facial design the actor had sported. Snippets from the contemporary trade press reveal how Bela's striated greasepaints tended to melt and meld under the klieg lights, making the supposed ogre look like "a clown instead of a menace." In almost any context, observations such as these make it appear that the blame for the failure of the "test Monster" to terrify lay solely on the Hungarian's shoulders.

Yet other versions of the situation place Lugosi squarely in Pierce's hands. Pierce was not an easy man to get along with, and his tight-lipped fits of pique had been witnessed at one time or another by most of the occupants of his chair. A good number of the genre actors and actresses who labored mightily to bring Universal's horror classics to the screen railed against the makeup king in interviews or their memoirs. Elsa Lanchester went on record more than once to denounce the diminutive Greek émigré as a veritable tyrant who regarded his tiny studio as his domain and who frequently spewed the barest of civil instructions through clenched teeth at anyone failing to observe his house rules.

With the test ordered even before the completion of the script, Pierce doubtless was not given a generous lead time and had to scramble to stay on schedule. Adding to the pressure he felt was the animosity he had for Lugosi; the actor had haughtily waved off Pierce's sketches and ideas for *Dracula*, and in doing so, had earned the autocratic technician's enmity. Inasmuch as Lugosi had no first-hand concepts to draw upon for the monster (as he had had for the vampire), he had little choice other than to entrust himself to Pierce's care. It may well be that striped applications of garishly colored paints and the unconscious recreation of the Golem image were the best that the harried makeup man could come up with in so short a time. I've always harbored a suspicion, though, that Bela Lugosi's appearance was Jack Pierce's revenge for *Dracula*. Having once experienced the Hungarian's professional pride, personal vanity, and short fuse, the wily Pierce provided the push over the edge when he crafted a guise which would evoke not the chills which the Universal brass demanded, but incongruous laughter which the patrician Lugosi so desperately feared.

Some have said that it was Junior's reaction to the test — he reportedly laughed out loud — that resulted in Bela's being removed from the picture. Others have insisted that it was Lugosi who called the shots, and who demanded that the studio look elsewhere to fill the demeaning role; he supposedly suggested that they might start among the rosters of extras. No matter who made the decision, Robert Florey must have been profoundly dismayed; not only did his monster walk, but the casting of his romantic leads was still in limbo and the clock was ticking. Whatever was he going to do?

He needn't have worried. Almost immediately relieved of all responsibilities regarding *Frankenstein*, Florey was advised that another subject would shortly be presented to him for approval. Stunned, the director ran to peruse his contract. *Nom de Dieu*! Whereas the document did indicate that he was to direct a feature for Universal, nowhere did it specify that the feature in question was to be *Frankenstein*. The guileless Frenchman had been the victim of the studio's cannily constructed duplicity; awaiting him would be *Murders in the Rue Morgue*, one of the selfsame titles Robert L. Schayer had proposed during their Musso and Frank luncheon months earlier. The memory of that meal must have stuck in Florey's craw for years to come.

As for the casting, all sorts of names had already been raised, discussed, and rejected. Leslie Howard and Bette Davis, for example, had been mentioned *en passant* whenever the leading roles of Henry Frankenstein and his Elizabeth were considered. (Supposedly, one look at her legs was all it took for Junior to nix the unconventionally attractive Davis for *Frankenstein*. Another anecdote relates how it was Uncle Carl who nixed *Frankenstein* for Davis, preferring to hold off showcasing her obvious talent until a more worthy vehicle emerged.) As stated above, *Dracula* alumni Edward Van Sloan and Dwight Frye were among the earliest of the *Frankenstein* cast to enter their names with the payroll office. Still, as the director would have the final say on the casting decisions, it made little sense to go any further before he had been selected. That choice wasn't long in coming.

Precise, supercilious, and aristocratic in mien if not by heritage (having been born in Dudley, a depressing industrial town plopped in the "Black Country" of the English Midlands), James Whale had managed to carve quite a reputation for himself, based almost

solely on his association with Robert C. Sherriff's angst-filled drama of the Great War, *Journey's End*. That epic's opening notices had found little fault with Whale's direction or with his sterling cast, which included a young Maurice Evans as Lieut. Raleigh, a young Laurence Olivier as the tormented Captain Stanhope, and, as Lieut. Osborne, George Zucco, who seemed to have been born at the age of 50. Nevertheless, the play itself had needed some tightening and a bit of professional luck before it moved to London's Savoy Theatre on January 21, 1929. Neither director nor playwright need have lost any sleep over reaction to their baby this time around; the critics vied to out-superlative each other, and empty seats at the Savoy gradually became an unknown commodity. Even the gamble on the new man had worked out; there had been a couple of tense moments when Olivier departed, having committed to *Beau Geste* at His Majesty's Theatre on 30 January, but the tightly wound Colin Clive had fit the tightly wound Captain Stanhope's boots perfectly.

With all due respect to the nightly receipts, it was the collective critical huzzah that made James Whale the pro tem darling of the English theatre. Creating an American company of *Journey's End* would give him the opportunity to add Broadway to his list of conquests, but both he and Sherriff were initially wary of the venture, lest the play prove too British for the Colonists to digest. It didn't take long for them to change their minds, however, or to assemble a cast-for-export. The new players may have had little time for frivolity as they steamed across the Atlantic on the *Aquitania*, but their endless shipboard rehearsals allowed them to memorize their lines while toning down their various British accents so as to be more comprehensible to the New York first-nighters. Such sacrifices were not in vain; within 72 hours, *Journey's End* would open at the Henry Miller Theater on 43rd Street, and Whale and Company would be showered with hosannas again. Like the West End, Broadway was theirs.

The immediate reaction to the international acclaim now accorded *Journey's End* was to arrange for the definitive motion picture version. Although Robert Sherriff no longer retained a financial interest in his brainchild, having sold his share in the property to self-styled impresario Maurice Browne for enough cash to pay for his transatlantic crossing on the *Aquitania*, he (and Whale and Browne) insisted that the movie be produced by a British company. While the screenplay for the impending English movie was being readied in New York, Whale flew out to California where, looking to gain some experience in the film industry, he signed on with Paramount, much as Robert Florey had done not long before. His mastery of the spoken word, and not the several insipid features with which he became involved, brought him to the attention of RKO's Howard Hughes, who was desperate for someone to supervise the filming of dialogue scenes for his already completed, but totally silent, *Hell's Angels*. Whale was his man, and the aviation epic, on the verge of obsolescence even before its release, was applauded for its exciting dogfights, its engaging banter, and its platinum blond heroine, Jean Harlow.

Journey's End would be shot in Hollywood, but would remain so British that the names of four participating English companies — Gainsborough, Welsh, Pearson and Tiffany — were displayed before the credits even started to roll. Heading the all–British cast and effectively repeating his original role of Stanhope was Colin Clive. As expected, the film was a smash.

Whale subsequently had to do some quick legal maneuvering in order to get out of his contract with England's Tiffany Pictures before he could accept an offer to direct Robert Emmet Sherwood's *Waterloo Bridge* for Universal. Mindful of the aggravation he had endured in order to wring acceptable vocals from Jean Harlow in *Hell's Angels*, Whale demurred from casting another glitzy beauty as Myra, the war drama's female lead, and instead chose Columbia contract player Mae Clarke for the role. Clarke was brilliant, *Waterloo Bridge* was a huge success, Whale was deemed a genius, and Junior gave his new Number-One Director *carte blanche* with

respect to the sundry projects on Universal's slate. Whale opted for *Frankenstein*.

Whale's selecting the horror fantasy reflected not so much a love for the macabre (although this aspect of his personality would soon become apparent) as his desire to escape the war movie rut into which he was in danger of falling. Poking about in the rubble left behind by the relieved Hungarian and the disbelieving Gaul, Whale began to fill in the open cast slots while peering critically at the screenplay which had led to Florey's downfall. The script, he determined, had to go; so did Leslie Howard. The captivating yet highly strung Colin Clive signed on as Henry Frankenstein. Whale asked that Universal borrow Mae Clarke once again (for Elizabeth) and also recalled gruff old Frederick Kerr, whose Major Wetherby had stolen every scene in which he had appeared in *Waterloo Bridge*, to flesh out the part of the old Baron. The featured casting was essentially completed when John Boles, hitherto a singularly bland song-and-dance man, was chosen as Victor Moritz, Frankenstein's dull but steadfast friend. The smaller parts would be filled from the list of contract players, but where did one turn in order to come up with a monster?

Boris Karloff never tired of chuckling about how he was summoned to Whale's table at the Universal commissary, where, while dressed in his best suit and feeling rather proud of his appearance, the bow-legged character man was invited by the most important director on the lot to test for a monster! Karloff's astonished reaction? "I said I'd be delighted." Whale had been taken with the actor's angular features, which had most recently been showcased in Howard Hawks' *The Criminal Code* for Columbia; the not unhandsome face did have "startling possibilities." The British actor's lanky frame posed no problem, there being dozens of ways to bulk up his physique artificially. But those sad, tormented eyes! Running out to buy a copy of Shelley's novel, Boris sat down with Jack Pierce, and...

Take two: Breathing easy following his release from the *Frankenstein* commitment, Bela Lugosi magnanimously offered to help

A marvelously composed still, with all angles and surfaces emanating from or leading to Karloff's monster—a visual metaphor of sorts for the public and critical reaction to the film. *BUDDY BARNETT/ CINEMA COLLECTORS.*

everyone out by keeping his eye open for a replacement. Coming upon the footloose Karloff somewhere in his travels, the big star advised the featured player to stop by the Universal casting office; an unusual role had just become available. "The part's nothing," Lugosi admitted candidly, "but it may make you a little money." Acting on the Hungarian's tip, the eager Karloff rushed over to the studio, somehow scrounged a meeting with James Whale, and the rest ... history!

I've never met anyone who believed for a

moment that Bela Lugosi ever looked further than the end of his ever-present cigar for a designated monster. For one thing, despite the success of *Dracula*, his name simply did not carry enough weight to sway the outcome of any casting decisions of consequence. And as the heights, lengths, and depths of desperation to which he had gone for the role of the Vampire King were still regarded as ludicrous by the studio bosses, any recommendation he might have made would have been painted with the same brush. The chief proponent of the Benevolent Bela scenario—his widow, Lillian Arch Lugosi Donlevy—died in 1981, and no one has stepped into that unlikely breach since then. Neither Arthur Lennig nor Robert Cremer, the Hungarian actor's chief biographers, even made mention of the unsubstantiated act of charity in their respective works, *The Count: The Life and Films of Bela "Dracula" Lugosi* and *Lugosi: The Man Behind the Cape*. Bela's altruistic bent seems little more than wishful thinking on the part of the actor's devoted widow.

With everyone from Karloff's daughter, Sara, to Whale's significant other, David Lewis, vouching for Boris's version of the tale, it seems a safe and logical position from which to proceed. Happy with Whale at the wheel and anxious to get things moving, yet twice-shy where the pivotal monster was concerned, Junior still wanted to see some test footage. Pulling an about-face, Jack Pierce spent countless hours on anatomical research, pencil sketches, and puttering with putty on the Karloff life-mask that he had fashioned; the rest of his waking hours were spent with Karloff himself. The makeup man was determined that no one would laugh condescendingly at *this* monster. It may well be that Pierce could also discern which way the wind was blowing. To date, he had crafted several fantastic makeups, ranging from Jacques Lerner in Fox's *The Monkey Talks* (1926) to Conrad Veidt's Gwynplaine in *The Man Who Laughs* (1928) to the sundry uglies in *The Last Warning* (1929) and both versions of *The Cat Creeps* (1930), but apart from those, he had spent most of his professional life powdering ingenues' noses and buoying up the

sagging jowls of aging leading men. With everyone gearing up to make *Frankenstein* even bigger and better than *Dracula*, it was apparent that monster movies were going to be the wave of the future. Job security beckoned; if Jack Pierce didn't get in on the ground floor, someone else would.

The slender English actor was as different from the lofty Hungarian star as night from day. Courteous, patient, willing to help, Karloff endured weeks of experimentation without complaint. In the course of the trials attempted and the errors committed within the cramped trailer, even James Whale had offered a suggestion, and Pierce was more than willing to comply. The director's "what if"—matching subcutaneous brow tendrils encircled by metal rings—proved to be difficult to justify scientifically, but the actor's respectful observation that the monster's eyes seemed too alert, too rational, merited action.

The Pierce-Karloff *Frankenstein* collaboration was an instant classic, and the resultant grotesque would thereafter be referred to as *the* Monster. Whale's feeling that the actor's facial angles could be satisfactorily exploited had been justified; the pounds of makeup which Jack Pierce applied to Karloff's face and head somehow left his eyes (despite their waxen coverings), mouth and cheekbones nearly naked to the camera. The Monster's every thought, every feeling, could be telegraphed via the subtlest of changes in expression. Karloff's remarkable talent, highlighted rather than hidden by the brilliant work of his cosmetic protégé, resulted in a test which knocked Junior on his ear and reinforced James Whale's faith in his own judgment. It was this filmed trial which finally clenched the role for Karloff. Whale's enthusiasm for the Briton notwithstanding, Junior had been getting antsy over the interminable makeup experiments and had seriously considered recalling Bela Lugosi, despite the Hungarian's low opinion of the screenplay and public disavowal of the role; after all, a contract was a contract.

Ironically, fewer details exist of Boris Karloff's successful audition footage than of the near-mythical Lugosi test. No record can be found to identify the cameraman, for example; it's doubtful whether Paul Ivano would have accepted the assignment following Robert Florey's removal from the project. Did the Monster play against other characters (such as Waldman or Fritz, as had Lugosi's Golem), or was he a solo act? Scads of fascinating questions beg to be asked, but no answers can be forthcoming; like Bela's first shot at the Monster, Boris's has disappeared.

The story behind the celebrated makeup wouldn't be told during the first run of *Frankenstein*, or even during the monumental release of *Bride of Frankenstein*. (Given the neurotic Whale's many petty jealousies, his imposing a gag order on his underlings to prevent the errant flow of publicity in any direction other than his own would not strain belief. Is it merely coincidental that photos of the "Whale variation" on the classic makeup still exist, while — intriguingly — no photographic evidence at all of the Lugosi construct seems to have survived the Brit's assumption of command?) Although enormously gratified by the public's positive reaction, Jack Pierce wouldn't spill the beans on the hows and whys of the timeless guise until the second sequel, *Son of Frankenstein* (1939), was ready to open. Cowboy heavy Glenn Strange, who would have the classic lines adapted to his own facial furrows by Pierce in both *House of Frankenstein* (1944) and *House of Dracula* (1945), admitted that he and his brother, Virgil, had been overwhelmed by their first glimpse of Karloff back in 1931. "Where in hell," the future Monster's naïve sibling had wondered, "did they ever find a guy who looked like that?"

According to Pierce's published accounts, he spent months poring over charts and texts concerned with everything from anatomy to surgery to electrodynamics. The diminutive Greek designed the makeup to suggest that Frankenstein, who was not a practicing surgeon, had chosen the simplest method to open a skull and had cut straight across the cranium. While I can't fault the statement's logic, I've always puzzled over how that type of incision would make the Monster's head *square*. The electrodes on the neck were a marvelous touch,

too, but I'm not buying that business about a five-pound steel spine ("the rod which conveys the current up to the Monster's brain"). With Universal's frugal bean-counters always bent on shaving pennies from proposed budgets, it was usually an uphill battle to assure that all the dramatically necessary props would make it to the screen; time and money would never be wasted on an unseen device built to lend support to a bit of spurious scientific claptrap which went unarticulated in the movie anyhow.

Pierce's ploy of shortening the sleeves of the Monster's jacket in order to make his arms look distended (this from research done on ancient burial customs, or some such) doesn't cut it either. Once one gets past the initial shock of seeing the days-old monstrosity wearing a *suit*, the next impression is that the jacket's sleeves are just too short. And as for those built-up boots; what plot-driven logic would possess Frankenstein to have his newborn shod in those clunky asphalt-spreaders when its feet — taken from the same array of cadavers which provided the other parts — must have been relatively normal originally? Shelley had had her scientist construct a larger-than-life man in order to make both the organic work and the requisite surgery easier; in the film, Henry produces a more or less normal-sized man, whom he inexplicably proceeds to make larger. Obviously, the supine and erect versions of the Monster were not meant to undergo microscopic comparison, or to withstand such minute scrutiny. So, too, the whole of the genius of Frankenstein's immortal Monster will always be greater than the sum (or the size) of its parts.

The first audience to witness Frankenstein was the trade press corps, which assembled in the Universal screening room early in November 1931 to determine whether the Laemmles had another offbeat hit on their hands. According to Greg Mank, it was Uncle Carl who initiated the outcry for deletions, additions, and retakes. The conservative CEO was upset by the Monster's inadvertent drowning of little Maria (about which the English director had been adamant, overruling the objections of

Karloff and others). In lieu of the controversial toss into the pond, the scene ended with the smiling Monster reaching out for the tike; when coupled with a later sequence, showing her stunned father carrying her lifeless body into town, the logical (but mistaken) conclusion drawn by most people was that an unspeakable act of brutality had taken place.

In a virtual segue from the recorded curtain speech delivered by Edward Van Sloan in prints struck for *Dracula*'s original release, a prologue was added to *Frankenstein*, wherein Van Sloan, standing in front of a similar curtain, warned ticket buyers that the film they were about to see was no walk in the park. Some additional changes came as a result of public outrage: Henry Frankenstein's remarks about knowing what it feels like to be God, for example, struck more than a few viewers as downright blasphemous. The remedy proved to be a well-positioned thunderclap that obscured any fragmentary sounds surviving the excision of the offending footage. Other changes, like the elimination of the closeup of the hypodermic needle wielded by Dr. Waldman, were later ordered by Joe Breen, who had come to take his responsibilities as avatar of the Production Code very, very seriously.

An abrupt refilming of the picture's finale, wherein a conventional happy ending replaced the morbid wrap-up originally consigned to Henry and Elizabeth, distressed Colin Clive to no end. Whether reshot due to Uncle Carl's demand for a respite from the movie's assorted horrors, or because a sequel could be more readily concocted if one of the necessary protagonists was still breathing, Whale took full and immediate credit for the decision. In a four-page article published in the *New York Times* some two weeks after the movie's Big Apple debut ("James Whale and Frankenstein," December 20, 1931), the egotistical Brit averred that "the semi-happy ending was added to remind the audience that after all it is only a tale that is told, and could easily be twisted any way *by the director*" (emphasis added).

Whale's enormous need for approval by the industry and admiration from the public was of no concern to the thousands of normally dispassionate New Yorkers who overwhelmed the Mayfair Theater (where the film had opened on December 4) in their attempts to be chilled by something other than the weather. Additional showings had to be arranged, house records were broken, and, as Roddy McDowall maintained in the excellent TV biography *Boris Karloff: The Gentle Monster*: "When *Frankenstein* was first released, it was as gigantic an onslaught as, like, *E.T.* [*sic*] Nothing had ever been seen like it."

Whale may have resented the newfound fame that the hitherto nobody Boris Karloff was enjoying, but he certainly wouldn't have let that stand in the way of his own limelight. It was *déjà vu* all over again, as the critics lavished praise on the director and his abnormal brainchild. Even Mordaunt Hall, the chronically underwhelmed *New York Times* first-string reviewer, had to admit, "It is far and away the most effective thing of its kind. Beside it, *Dracula* is tame."

Everyone and everything connected with *Frankenstein* was suddenly golden. Arthur Edeson's camerawork deservedly was singled out for praise; acting on Whale's insights, the genre veteran (he had already photographed Fairbanks' *The Thief of Baghdad*, Willis O'Brien's *The Lost World*, and Roland West's now-lost masterpiece *The Bat*) captured more than his fair share of atmospheric moments in the course of the 71-minute (later, 67-minute) running time. The Monster's memorable three-tiered introduction was as much due to Edeson's technical savvy as to Whale's vision. Art Director Charles D. Hall not only effectively redressed a good number of the *Dracula* sets, but also used his share of the overall budget (some $90,000 less than had been allotted for the vampire film) to create the Tyrolean set which would, as the saga continued, be identified as the villages of Goldstadt, Frankenstein, Vasaria, and Visaria.

Electrical whiz Kenneth Strickfaden fell heir to a good-sized wad of some $10,000 to whip up the whirring, sputtering, spark-producing, humming, buzzing, gosh-oh-golly impressive life-inducing machinery which would prove to be as immortal as the Monster himself. Not in evidence anywhere, but surely as unnecessary in this film as wings on a pig, was a musical score. It was his call all the way, and James Whale had enough faith in the cacophony of snarls, gasps, screams, baying hounds, creaking doors, and electrical sibilants to pass on orchestral accompaniment. Inasmuch as one of the many perceived weaknesses of *Dracula* had been its long, awkward moments of total silence, Whale's decision was all the more daring. That one never notices the absence of music throughout the picture's length is not a comment on its brevity, but a testimony to its capacity to enthrall.

As with its predecessor, *Frankenstein* suffered a few logical gaffes. When Victor Moritz first comes calling on the worried Elizabeth, the well-to-do young woman is comfortably ensconced in the plush living room of her own little mansion. Her mail is delivered here ("The first word in four months; it just came"), and she thanks Victor for coming and walks him to the door; the presumption of ownership is readily made. Later, during the wedding scene, the same opulent rooms double as the Frankenstein chateau — or else the garrulous Baron has an alarming way of making himself at home at his future daughter-in-law's, going so far as to import delicate family heirlooms, order the servants about, and promise the villagers a good drunk from the familiar reaches of the bay window.

Another slip-up occurs at Goldstadt Medical College as Dr. Waldman is busily pointing out the differences in convolutions and tissue condition which exist between two brains in conveniently labeled jars at his fingertips. The camera helpfully tracks from one specimen to the other, from the jar bearing the neatly typed notations "Cerebrum" and "Normal Brain," to its neighbor, which contains an "Abnormal Brain" (or "Dysfunctum Cerebrum") and likewise bears two neatly-typed notations, to prove it. Moments later, the lecture hall deserted, the inept Fritz has shuffled noiselessly up to the jars and is giving them the once-over. For the benefit of audience members who left their bifocals at home, the labels are now hand inscribed with thick underlined printing.

Inexplicably, the dwarf removes the lid from the jar and then walks *away* from his point of ingress. Startled by the sound of a gong(!), Fritz drops the jar and scrambles back for its undamaged partner. These labels have also been altered in the interim: not only has the Latin description changed (it's now grammatically incorrect), but the English tag bears the same childish, heavily underlined print that the first had. Back out the window goes Fritz. (An unworthy query, recorded here only because it has been argued fruitlessly for 60 years, concerns Henry Frankenstein's inability to take in such vital information scrawled in so noticeable a manner. Perhaps the offbeat but once-popular explanation for Sherlock Holmes's insisting that *Watson* read aloud any missives arriving at Baker Street — the hypothesis that the great consulting detective was a functional illiterate — might be considered here. Then again, perhaps Fritz, the sneaky little bastard, just tore off the labels.)

The other instance of decidedly peculiar behavior belongs to Doctor Waldman. It would seem that a total dissection would be performed most efficaciously when working from the extremities inward. The speedy removal of a towering, murderous fiend's arms might be the first and wisest step to take in rendering him harmless. Yet, working at his own leisurely pace (despite a diary entry attesting to the Monster's growing resistance to the anesthetic, the fussy medico takes the time to pen a few more thoughts), Waldman begins the crucial operation some 12 inches above the navel, without even removing the Monster's jacket. As a successful disassembly would have meant a distressingly brief and pointless film, there's never any doubt that the Monster will rise from the table over Waldman's dead body. Nonetheless, a more logical approach might have provided a tad more of both realism and suspense.

A couple of days after he had made the East Coast his easy and willing victim, Frankenstein's Monster worked his lumbering, inarticulate magic on the jaded Southern Californians. The December 6 premiere didn't look too promising at first; neither Mae Clarke nor Colin Clive attended, and the lowly Boris

Karloff wasn't even invited. By the time the cast list was flashed the second time, however, it was the Karloff name which drew the most comments and the Karloff performance which garnered the most praise. The last thing the know-it-alls at Universal had expected was that the journeyman actor's portrayal would steal the picture from such celebrated stars as Clarke and Clive. The *Motion Picture Herald* praised the characterization to the skies: "Because of his restraint, his intelligent simplicity of gesture, carriage, voice, and makeup," explained the dazzled writer, "Karloff has truly created a Frankenstein Monster."

Within days, the country was awash with waves of critical and popular acclaim for the picture, its director, and — as he was now perceived — its star, Boris Karloff. The superlative-drenched commentaries must have seemed a bit excessive to Bela Lugosi; those endless, unflattering comparisons with *Dracula* probably nettled a little, as well. To the end of his life, the temperamental Hungarian would publicly belittle the Frankenstein Monster as an unchallenging part which anyone might play. (The studio's neglecting to have Karloff attend the Santa Barbara premiere seems to indicate that a low opinion of the demands of the role was had by all, at first.) It's impossible to say, however, whether Lugosi privately accorded the responsibility for the Monster's tremendous impact to his newly minted rival's talents, to the monumental job Jack Pierce had done on the Briton's final makeup, or to the dogmatic but inspired direction of the increasingly eccentric James Whale. Bela Lugosi, Jr., revealed in *Boris Karloff: The Gentle Monster* that his dad had later expressed remorse at turning down the role, but didn't opine as to whether the feeling was due to the unfortunate turn his dad's career took or to the boost the role gave Karloff, who split with Lugosi what proved to be a very slender field and who came away with the better deal almost every time.

From the moment the title music blared over an interesting bit of artwork, reminiscent of that rendition of the Monster which had been circulating during the Lugosi promotion, and the credits rolled over a motif of swirling eyes, which obscured a featureless face (again, a possible remnant from the earlier campaign, wherein the huge monster's eyes had fired rays of some sort at the fleeing populace), the nightmarish Frankenstein Monster had the captivated public in the palm of his oversized, black-nailed hand. Within weeks as much of a horror icon as Dracula would ever be, the Monster slowly came to symbolize the appeal that the bogeys of make-believe had for children of all ages. Never a threat to those who understood, who saw beyond the façade, who could identify with the pain and the loneliness, the giant figure would be as welcome as Halloween itself.

Frankenstein

Released November 21, 1931; 67 minutes

Cast: Colin Clive (Henry Frankenstein); Mae Clarke (Elizabeth); John Boles (Victor Moritz); Boris Karloff (The Monster); Edward Van Sloan (Dr. Waldman); Frederick Kerr (Baron Frankenstein); Dwight Frye (Fritz); Lionel Belmore (Vogel); Marilyn Harris (Little Maria); Michael Mark (Ludwig); Arletta Duncan, Pauline Moore (Bridesmaids); Francis Ford (Hans); with Mary Sherman

Credits: Producer — Carl Laemmle, Jr.; Director — James Whale; Screenplay — Garrett Fort, Francis Edwards Faragoh, John Russell (uncredited), and Robert Florey (uncredited); Based on the composition by John L. Balderston; Adapted from the play by Peggy Webling; From the novel *Frankenstein; or, The Modern Prometheus* by Mary Wollstonecraft Shelley; Associate Producer — E.M. Asher; Scenario Editor — Richard Schayer; Continuity — Thomas Reed; Director of Photography — Arthur Edeson; Supervising Film Editor — Maurice Pivar; Film Editor — Clarence Kolster; Art Director — Charles D. Hall; Recording Supervisor — C. Roy Hunter; Set Designer — Herman Rosse; Technician — William Hedgcock; Makeup — Jack P. Pierce; Assistant Director — Joseph A. McDonough; Special Electrical Effects — Kenneth Strickfaden, Frank Graves and Raymond Lindsay; Technical Advisor — Dr. Cecil Reynolds; Music — David Broekman; Property Master — Eddie Keys

MURDERS IN
THE RUE MORGUE (1932)

Child that I still am, it's frequently difficult for me to appreciate the excitement that horror fans must have felt back in the 1930s. That incredible succession of movies, all enjoying their first runs supported by comprehensive advertising campaigns and dazzling publicity materials: those fantastic thirties lobby displays, replete with luscious (and nowadays stratospherically expensive and rare) posters, life-size standees and silken (okay, satin) banners which must have lured willing victims up to the box office with their mute but hypnotic siren's song. Way before television, people actually would read now and again, and specially appointed bookstore windows would capture the attention of passersby with piles of Grosset and Dunlap or A.L. Burt photoplay editions of the chiller playing down the street. Needless to say, scads of mouth-watering stills would complement the wildly colored dust jackets, and the overall effect would doubtless result in either a sale or an admission.

Wonderful little throwaway heralds would be available somewhere in those opulent theater lobbies. They were meant to plant that seed of "must-see" in your consciousness before the movie's trailer hit the screen, or reinforce it for you on your way home. Even the wildly juve-nile and sometimes dangerous street ballyhoo suggestions that the pressbook writers dreamed up in hallucinatory moments would occasionally cross the bridge to reality, and that kind of nonsense must have been *fun*.

Once in the theater, nestled in their seats (or scrunched down sideways, depending upon their tolerance for terror), the thirties Universal horror fans probably found it at least subconsciously reassuring that all of the ghoulies and long-legged beasties scaring their socks off were firmly bound to foreign climes. Most of the goings-on took place in Transylvania or the backwards regions of Central Europe. Egypt was a biggie, too, but not nearly as popular as England, which seemed to draw vampires and werewolves as a flame draws moths. While Warner Bros. had the temerity to set both of its big guns (*Doctor X* and *Mystery of the Wax Museum*) in New York, and RKO chose the same locale for the fabulous climax of its mind-blowing *King Kong*, the U.S.A. was virtually a no monster's land, so far as Universal's "Golden Age" product was concerned.

The lack of horrific activity in France is a little hard to understand, though. Couldn't France be considered the birthplace of the horror movie, given the dozens of macabre shorts written, produced, directed, photographed, and (for want of a better word) decorated by sci-fi pioneer filmmaker Georges Méliès? Hadn't the two great and greatly profitable Universal horror spectacles of the previous decade — *The Hunchback of Notre Dame* and *The Phantom of the Opera*— been set in Paris? Wasn't 1928's *The Man Who Laughs* a "French" money-maker for Universal? Didn't *Le Théâtre du Grand Guignol*, which had specialized in lurid melodrama with elements of classic terror and torture for almost 40 years, continue to enjoy international notoriety (and huge revenues)?

Why so few Gallic chillers? It wasn't a question of budget; there were all sorts of standing sets that could be pressed into service. Apart from the *Phantom* stage, the massive Notre Dame Cathedral and their environs, there were numerous backlot streets that could easily pass as French. Nor was it a question of that creaky old German Expressionistic influence hogging the production slate at this late date. It was, however, an issue of authorship. The lion's share of the films we would come to regard as Universal's classics of the 1930s had been penned (no matter where they'd been set) by British novelists such as Bram Stoker, Mary Shelley, the later J.B. Priestley and H.G. Wells, and even the immortal Charles Dickens. Their sundry ogres and goblins were apportioned carefully: The more articulate, more "civilized" villains operated hither and thither on English soil. The shaggier of the pack (vocal or not) were exiled to murky Germania.

Universal had already plundered Victor Hugo's dramatic storehouse, and Gaston Leroux's masterpiece had just been reissued (as a part-sound attraction) late in 1929. With genuine Gallic horror writers clearly unavailable, the Laemmles targeted the Americans they had under contract to concoct thrillers set in or around the City of Lights. The lesser of these American writers was one Lawrence G. Blochman, whose derivative "original" story would evolve into the studio's tepid period mystery *Secret of the Chateau*. The infinitely more renowned American writer was Edgar Allan Poe, who didn't hold a Universal contract, as he

had been dead for 80 years. You couldn't beat arrangements like those. Every one of Poe's offbeat short stories and poems was available gratis and was thus fair game; a glance at the collected genre titles from the cinema's silent days shows how widely this opinion was held.

It was Poe's *The Murders in the Rue Morgue* which had been offered (as an alternative to *The Invisible Man*) to Robert Florey in the wake of *Dracula*'s success. The work, together with the subsequent *The Mystery of Marie Roget* and *The Purloined Letter*, had introduced C. Auguste Dupin and the detective story to the world. Despite the opportunity to create an intriguing cross-genre hybrid, Florey initially passed on Poe and opted for Shelley. We can only wonder whether the Gaul's adaptation of *Murders* would have been substantially different had he taken the title on its own merits when it had first been offered, rather than as a "consolation prize" for the *Frankenstein* fiasco.

By 1932, most rational people would have hooted aloud at any cinematic plot twist wherein the killer would ultimately be revealed to be an ape; the premise deserved ridicule as being ludicrously primitive and dramatically embarrassing for the times. Hard-core monster fans might continue to believe that manacled monkeys and murky old mansions went arm in arm, but only the poorest of the independent studios would continue to propagate that myth. Even though Dian Fossey's groundbreaking behavioral discoveries lay decades in the future, the more sophisticated horror buffs (those viewers who might break down and *buy* a photoplay edition or two) had already bypassed the much-maligned gorilla as a source of cheap and obvious thrills. Spoiled by the more innovative offerings of the majors, the sharper viewers would much prefer the vast assortment of non-simian monstrosities which were then clogging the movie houses.

In light of this spontaneous "growthspurt" in taste and incredulity on the part of the public, one would think that any proposed treatment of the Poe piece would require some radical literary surgery. The wily detective

Papa Freund (with camera) and M. Florey (under camera) home in on Charlie Gemora (gorilla) and his lovely burden (Sidney Fox). *PENTAGRAM LIBRARY.*

could perhaps maneuver among the picturesque Parisian boulevards as he tracked to his lair the fiendish Rue Morgue murderer, who would be unmasked as a far more credible (but not necessarily less colorful) insane criminal mastermind. In place of that wildly risible ape, you could draw on opulent laboratories, wickedly eccentric hideouts, and deformed or demented assistants. These were elements of the formula which the studio had already exploited profitably and which would continue to flesh out the barest of its cinematic skeletons for years to come.

Radical surgery *was* performed by Monsieur Florey, but per the old joke, while the operation was successful, the patient had died. The surgeon skillfully reworked C. Auguste Dupin, the father of all consulting detectives, transforming him into *Pierre* Dupin, the most insipidly florid of lovers. The irresponsible seaman of the Poe original had been nipped and tucked into Bela Lugosi's Dr. Mirakle, the mother of all grandiloquent lunatic practitioners of ersatz science. Rather than chuck that formula for the cliché it was rapidly turning out to be, Florey treated it with a reverence more becoming an archbishop on Easter morning. The opulent laboratory and the wickedly eccentric hideout would check in for service but, because of the small (and, at first, rapidly dwindling) budget, would be combined into one garret-like super-haunt. Art director Charles D. Hall could have phoned in his designs for the digs; Mirakle hung his hat in the old watchtower set borrowed from *Frankenstein*. The deformed or demented assistant would in this instance be "Janos, the Black One," and would be played by the popular black actor Noble Johnson, in a makeup which would make him paler than Bela Lugosi. Most distressingly, in direct defiance of professional judgment and common sense, Erik the Ape would be reinstated to the vaunted position he had held in the novelette. So much screen time would be afforded the hirsute horror, in fact, that little Charles Gemora and his ape suit had to share the honors with footage of a chimpanzee from a local zoo.

If you've ever read the original story, you know what goes on. Once you get past Lugosi's Chico Marx wig and that riveting, solitary eyebrow of his (except for Ygor, Bela's experiences with bizarre makeups were singularly unfortunate), you'll find his over-the-top Doctor Mirakle to be among his most flamboyant and enjoyable portrayals. The actor's translation of Erik's gibberish keeps the lower life-forms in the know as to the Ape's throbbing libido, and his delivery of the hokey, rococo dialogue is priceless. From the viewpoint of the narrative, however, Mirakle is superfluous once Erik gets his mitts on the heroine's bonnet. His oily efforts at winning Camille's confidence are pathetically, laughably hopeless; is he really hoping to arouse the young girl's interest in the stubby Erik? Are we watching Edgar Allan Poe's *The Murders in the Rue Morgue*, or Henry Wadsworth Longfellow's *The Courtship of Miles Standish*?

Nor does Mirakle's big scene with the terrified "woman of the streets" (Arlene Francis) cut any logical mustard, especially considering where it ended up in the release print. The film was to have begun with the fateful knife-fight between the two apaches, followed by the woman's ghastly but mercifully brief experience on Mirakle's Saint Andrew's cross. Supposedly considered a downer from which subsequent events would never recover, the impressive but sadistic vignette was reedited into a later spot, following the introduction of human and near-human principals at the carnival. We are thus left with a scenario in which Erik sets his heart on Camille, the leering Mirakle clucks his approval, and then both monkey and master cruise the streets *anyhow* in search of babes.

Was it yet another form of punishment for Bela Lugosi, or was it Universal's typical poor judgment which led them to give the precious and diminutive Sidney Fox top billing in *Murders in the Rue Morgue*? In anticipation of, yet actually reversing, an oddball movie practice wherein the capable heroines of sundry '50s sci-fi programmers would bear some kind of ambisexual Christian name like Pat or Lee or Terry, the actress named Sidney enacts Camille L'Espanaye as the childlike, essentially helpless damsel-in-distress of decades past. The little actress may not have found artistic or personal fulfillment in dated pap like *Murders*, but it had to have been a step up from her involvement in such achingly base drivel as RKO's *Down to Their Last Yacht* (1934). She committed suicide in 1942.

Leon Ames, then operating under his real name of Leon Waycoff, later had the good sense to pass the entire venture off to the follies of youth. In character, however, he does what he can with impossible dialogue, improbable situations, and an unlikely plot which requires him to graduate from a state of adolescent

Worse than flies in the attic are gorillas on the roof. *JOHN PARNUM*.

near-imbecility to heroic overtures in an hour or so. (The most improbable of the situations shows the manly if baroquely romantic Pierre sharing digs with Bert Roach's Paul, an apparent homosexual. The prevailing cynical opinion is that the existence of a female love interest for Paul had to be concocted, if only to keep audiences from snickering about the two men.) Ames would go on to a long and prolific career that included three TV series, demonstrating over and again that, given a well-written part and decent direction, he could create realistic and memorable characters.

Murders in the Rue Morgue is a hard film to really *like*. (The *Motion Picture Herald*, mirroring its colleagues' sentiments, gave the pic-

ture the most tepid of strokes, pronouncing it "fairly effective.") One problem is that its horrors are not merely unpleasant, but bleak and nasty. While several other films considered '30s classics also deal with interspecies dating (Paramount's *Island of Lost Souls* jumps immediately to mind), they manage to avoid the interminable dreariness that pervades the Florey piece. Charles Laughton's Dr. Moreau, for example, is another misguided man of science who seeks to discover evolutionary links, no matter the means or consequences. Yet Philip Wylie and Waldemar Young do a top-notch job of wrestling a complex and near-sympathetic persona from H.G. Wells' more prosaic portrait, and Laughton aids immeasurably by going against personal type and underplaying for all he's worth in many of the expository scenes.

There is neither complexity nor sympathy in *Murders in the Rue Morgue*. From the reedited outset, Mirakle chews the canvas, only just stopping short of gnawing on Erik's bars. His sole obsession is that maddeningly elusive "pure blood," and woefully transparent is his every attempt to disguise his true purpose. You come away feeling that, even if Bela's character weren't out to disprove the biblical account of man's development, he would just as readily have his simian companion chase after Camille on some other spurious pretext.

Yet in Dr. Mirakle, not only is there no sign of divided loyalties, outside interests or human relationships, there is no possibility of them. Whereas even Colin Clive's tautly neurotic Frankenstein has his moments of peace with Elizabeth, and Laughton's Moreau reveals fascinating glimpses of yet other dreams through his calm ruminations with Parker, Mirakle plods mechanically along his straight and narrow course. The audience tires of the game very quickly and abandons him to his destiny. Bela's plot-driven singlemindedness results not so much in a classic portrait of pure malice, but rather in an unsophisticated sketch of malevolent tunnel-vision.

Neither Robert Florey's original treatment nor Tom Reed and Dale van Every's screenplay gives the viewer much chance to contrast the low-hanging tension and gloom with anything close to normalcy. An idyllic interlude, meant to provide just such a contrast, comes off as blatantly unreal as the baggy skins on Charlie Gemora. Whoever filled Pierre's mouth with such vapid and starchy nonsense (it wasn't Poe) palpably demonstrates a tin ear for dialogue; such rubbish is scarcely believable even when it's sung. The "humorous" bit where three foreigners squabble over the "language" heard at the time of the murder of Camille's mother is also a resounding dud. A disastrous holdover from Poe's original story, the vignette reads better than it plays, and it doesn't read terribly well to start with. It's just another painful spell of "comic relief" which has no more basis in

reality than the vision of Mirakle and Erik taking a friendly jaunt around the city in their carriage. For that matter, most of the supporting cast reacts far too broadly far too often, but perhaps this hokum demands comic-opera emoting and cardboard reality.

Maybe that's why I've never really enjoyed *Murders in the Rue Morgue*: it's just too relentless in its simple-minded absurdities for my tastes. When the romantic leads are as grotesquely fraudulent as the guy in the gorilla suit, I tend to get uninvolved pretty fast. I remain fascinated, though, by the stylized silent masterpieces of Robert Weine, Fritz Lang, F.W. Murnau, and others. How is it possible to be so taken with more technically primitive efforts, yet be so underwhelmed by a later and obvious homage? Maybe because *Caligari, Metropolis, Nosferatu,* and the rest were originals, stylistically years ahead of their time, and steeped in legend, national history, and humanity. They were not derivative throwbacks to an earlier era or to a base and naïve art-form.

I may be expecting too much of an old-fashioned hourlong programmer shot on a limited budget by a bitter and disgruntled director, but I'm not alone in thinking that *Murders in the Rue Morgue* is a '30s "classic" only by association.

Murders in the Rue Morgue

Released February 21, 1932; 62 minutes

Cast: Bela Lugosi (Dr. Mirakle); Sydney Fox (Camille L'Espanaye); Leon Waycoff (Pierre Dupin); Bert Roach (Paul); Betsy Ross Clarke (Mme. L'Espanaye); Brandon Hurst (Prefect of Police); D'Arcy Corrigan (Morgue Attendant); Noble Johnson (Janos, the Black One); Arlene Francis (Woman of the Streets); Edna Marion (Mignette); Charlotte Henry, Polly Ann Young (Girls); Herman Bing (Franz Odenheimer); Agostino Borgato (Alberto Montani); Harry Holman (Landlord); Torben Meyer (The Dane); John T. Murray, Christian Frank (Gendarmes); D. Vernon (Tenant); Michael Visaroff, Ted Billings (Men); Charles T. Millfield (Bearded Man at Sideshow); Monte Montague (Working Man/Gendarme); Charles

Gemora (Erik, the Ape); Joe Bonomo (Double for Gemora); Hamilton Green (Barker); Tempe Piggott (Crone)

Credits: Producer — Carl Laemmle, Jr.; Director — Robert Florey; Associate Producer — E.M. Asher; Screenplay — Tom Reed and Dale van Every; Based on *The Murders in the Rue Morgue* by Edgar Allan Poe; Adaptation by Robert Florey; Additional Dialogue — John Huston; Scenario Editor — Richard Schayer; Cinematographer — Karl Freund; Art Director — Charles D. Hall; Recording Supervisor — C. Roy Hunter; Film Editor — Milton Carruth; Supervising Film Editor — Maurice Pivar; Musical Director — Heinz Roemheld; Special Effects — John P. Fulton; Special Process — Frank Williams; Makeup — Jack P. Pierce; Set Designer — Herman Rosse; Assistant Directors — Scott Beal, Joseph McDonough, and Charles S. Gould; Technical Advisor — Howard Salemson

THE OLD DARK HOUSE (1932)

Producer's Note: Karloff, the mad butler in this production, is the same Karloff who created the part of the mechanical monster in *Frankenstein*. We explain this to settle all disputes in advance, even though such disputes are a tribute to his great versatility.

With Kino Video's release of *The Old Dark House*, the legions of fans of Whale, Karloff, Universal, and thirties horror in general fans who have been awaiting an "official pre-record" of the elusive film can finally begin to dispute characterization, intent, black comedy, and what-have-you. The film had been available via bootleg tape for some time through the network of passionate private collectors, without whom a great deal of otherwise "lost" material would truly be lost, but many buffs chose to pass on it, either in favor of something more trendy, blatant, or lurid, or because of facile critiques they might have read, which pictured the film as anything from a pathetic misfire to a veritable knee-slapper, as far from a horror picture as one could imagine. (In his James Whale biography, James Curtis describes the movie as "frequently hilarious.") The various respectful and intelligent reviews which have accompanied the film's sanctioned reappearance, however, together with such insightful essays as are found in Gary and Susan Svehla's

Boris Karloff, Brunas and Brunas and Weaver's *Universal Horrors* or Greg Mank's *Hollywood Cauldron*, will hopefully go a long way towards correcting any misunderstandings that may have arisen over the years.

That we still have the film at all is due to the tenacity of genre director Curtis Harrington, whose lengthy and determined search in the late 1960s unearthed a fine grain print moldering in one of Universal's vaults, when both uninterested studio executives and sketchy records had informed him otherwise. With funding from Eastman House of Rochester, New York, Harrington had a preservation negative struck and *The Old Dark House* displayed its peculiar charms once again.

The studio's blasé reaction, however, cannot be condemned without its day in court; as much as we'd all like to think that filmmakers work their wonders solely for the fun of it all, stockholders (whose money sets the magic machinery in motion in the first place) are usually rather insistent in their demands for returns on investments. Author J.B. Priestley had sold all pertinent rights to Columbia Pictures early on for the purpose of a remake, so 1932's *The Old Dark House* was no longer commercially viable to the original studio. In the course of gleaning the vaults, negatives and positives were liquidated in the transfer process without checking whether some archival material existed elsewhere. Why go to the trouble or expense of storing product which could not be legally exploited? That, somehow, a fine grain print did still exist was miraculous.

Haunted houses, the vast majority of which were old and dark, were always a favorite setting during the silent era and made the transition to sound with far greater ease than many aged juveniles or twittery-voiced ingenues. The rigors of copyright infringement held no fear for those poorly heeled but savvy moguls who had featured some musty old manor house as the premier horror in their films. Hence, most of the independent studios had met the sound age head on with moaning winds, creaky doors, and dank and desolate mansions of their own — usually replete with apes or related beasties. Among the proliferation of what would come to be regarded as classic horror pictures from the majors, the constant flow of goons and gorillas from the indies, and the requisite spoofs of same by the era's most popular comedians (e.g., *The Laurel-Hardy Murder Case*, 1930), by 1932 the only corner on the desolate old façade into which no one had yet ventured was the definitive treatment.

That same year saw Universal scratching about, looking for a suitable vehicle for its overnight sensation, Boris Karloff. The tremendous acclaim he had received as the sympathetic yet terrifying monster in *Frankenstein* had astonished the actor and the studio. The British star was seemingly everywhere at once; he loped across the screen in United Artists' *Tonight or Never* and *Scarface*, Columbia's *Behind the Mask*, Fox's *Business and Pleasure*, and Paramount's *The Miracle Man*, all within four months of *Frankenstein*'s release. Although the Laemmles had a contract (the actor had put his Boris Hancock on Universal's dotted line as soon as he could be corralled after the *Frankenstein* notices were out), the only offers they had extended so far were a cameo (as himself, surely something of an indication that he had finally arrived) in *The Cohens and Kellys in Hollywood* and the decent but not terribly suitable part as honest nightclub owner "Happy" MacDonald in *Night World*.

While Junior grumbled about the lack of a suitable horror part for his new star, what with *The Invisible Man*, touted earlier by Richard Schayer to Robert Florey, still a year or so from feasibility, James Whale sauntered in with a copy of an odd yet popular British novel, just brimming with offbeat types. J.B. Priestley's *Benighted*, maintained Whale, would make a fabulous film. It would also make an inexpensive film, requiring essentially just one set and a small cast of fascinating, quirky characters. No torch-bearing crowds here. What was even better, the story could easily be adapted to highlight the mute and brutish butler, Morgan, which would be a pip of a role for Boris Karloff.

How could Junior refuse his ace director? Counting on another Whale-Karloff blockbuster, Uncle Carl's pride and joy okayed the negotiations for rights with J.B. Priestley and entered *The Old Dark House* (the novel's American title) on the studio slate. It was felt that "benighted," a British term referring to involvement in physical or moral darkness — or to being overtaken by the night — would confuse potential ticket-buyers, who might expect a period piece set in Arthurian times. Nevertheless, Melvyn Douglas would toss off the word in one of the screenplay's few awkward lines.

Whale, meanwhile, had lost little time in assembling the staff technicians who had demonstrated their flair for gothic horror (and for putting up with his snits) during *Frankenstein*. Arthur Edeson's moody camera setups would once again caress the murky and mysterious nooks of Charles D. Hall's lavishly decrepit sets. Jack Pierce was anticipating not only the challenge of Morgan's appearance, but also the pleasure of Karloff's company. As Priestley's 1928 novel was far more contemporary than that period piece of Mary Shelley's, Whale asked that contemporary novelist and old friend Benn Levy be hired to pen the screenplay. No problem there, either. Levy had worked with Whale at Universal several years earlier, when he had successfully adapted Robert Sherwood's *Waterloo Bridge* to the screen.

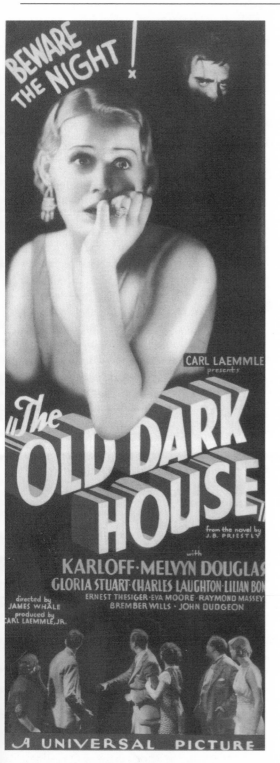

Insert for **The Old Dark House**. RONALD V. BORST/
HOLLYWOOD MOVIE POSTERS.

The next step was the casting, and Whale had some very specific requests in that department as well. With the story set somewhere in the crumbling Welsh mountains, it made little sense to populate the film with flat-voiced American contract players. There were scores of Brits to draw from in Southern California, and the cream of the English expatriates comprised the distinguished British Colony of Hollywood. The brightest of the Colony's stars were generally available on a trade basis, lesser luminaries could be obtained on a loan-out, and dozens of instantly recognizable freelancing character people were to be had on a moment's notice. With Karloff the film's only given, Whale began to marry actors with roles.

Charles Laughton was in town, waiting for the preproduction morass of *The Devil and the Deep* to subside over at Paramount. (By an interesting and suspicious coincidence, it was Benn Levy's knotty script problems with *The Devil* which were holding up the works.) Typically, the actor had been ordered from London to Hollywood on a "Hurry up!" basis and had since been sitting around for some weeks with his wife, lovely pixie Elsa Lanchester. Whale's call to some chums at Paramount cinched Laughton's being cast as the bluff, aptly named Sir William Porterhouse. Per his latest biographer, Simon Callow, Laughton "had no very warm feelings for any of the cast"; in his eyes, the virtually all–British-starring chiller was just a job to keep him busy while Paramount sorted out details with Mr. Levy.

Gloria Stuart's presence on the set was also due to an odd bit of Universal-Paramount synergy. Simultaneously clamoring for the beautiful actress's services, the two studios had agreed to abide by the toss of a coin from the lady's lovely fingers. To the actress's professed chagrin, Universal's luck held out, and the glorious Stuart signed on as Margaret Waverton, the "white flame" (Whale's phrase) which would capture the eye of the drunken Morgan.

Melvyn Douglas was the other American in the cast, called on to replace fellow Yank Russell Hopton as Roger Penderel. The actor brought to the role an easy affability and charm that few male stars could equal (certainly not

Hopton, a reputable "light leading man" who may have been considered a tad *too* light for the present company). Douglas would come to regard most of his juvenile parts, wherein he played amusing but world-weary sophisticates, as inconsequential and tedious. Speaking of these roles later in life, he admitted that "It's true they gave me a world-wide reputation I could trade on, but they also typed me as a one-dimensional non-serious actor." (Douglas would come to achieve the respect he had always craved — and two Academy Awards — in his advanced years.) Tedious or not, it's to the suave actor's credit that Penderel comes off as a straight shooter, even when exchanging unbelievably contrived declarations of love with ex–chorus girl Gladys Du Cane.

The whole screwy thing begins with a bang — a landslide, actually — somewhere in the anonymous Welsh countryside. The main titles are sparser than usual, and prominently misspell author Priestley's name. As he had with *Frankenstein*, Whale opted to pass on a musical score here, trusting that the myriad sound effects and varied vocal performances would provide a perfectly satisfactory underlying rhythm; they do. There's not more than a minute or two of music under the opening titles and the "dispute" notice, but Messrs. Brunas, Brunas, Weaver and Mank have, among them, given three composers (David Broekman, Heinz Roemheld, Bernhard Kaun) credit for the moody themes.

A top-notch miniature rock-fall almost gently pushes a splendid miniature canvas-topped convertible out of its path, and the old dark house, the exterior of which cannot possibly contain the four interior levels and sprawling floor plan throughout which we shall wander, comes into view. The car's passengers, the bickering Wavertons (young Raymond Massey is Miss Stuart's onscreen other half) and Roger Penderel, knock for shelter. A cynical thought strikes Penderel: "Wouldn't it be dramatic, supposing the people inside were dead, all stretched out with the lights quietly burning about them?" Benn Levy closely follows Priestley's clever narrative, lifting much of the dialogue almost verbatim from the novel.

The extent of R.C. Sherriff's contribution of "additional dialogue" is unclear.

Before anyone can respond, sounds of the massive door being unbolted are heard above the storm. In an intriguing variation of Whale and Edeson's first triple-tiered door-frame closeup of Karloff as the Frankenstein Monster, the technicians have Morgan open the door enough to reveal only half of his face, followed by three closeup reaction shots of the waterlogged travelers. (Later in the film, Morgan will receive a triple closeup of his own, moving from full-face, to the top half of his head, to his scarred and twisted nose and mouth.) The hulking giant's lips are seen to move, and some odd, almost whining noises issue forth. Morgan, it transpires, is mute; his strange moans, also heard after the drunken butler later shuts the door behind Margaret and closes in for the chase, are not Karloffian, but were looped in during post-production.

Other principals emerge. Parading down the stairs is Horace Femm (Ernest Thesiger), prim and fussy resident of the house (but not its master, as he is pointedly reminded). Male only by accident of birth, alternately bitchy and fawning, the epicene host, whose surname might well be shorthand for "feminine," manages to raise more hackles than hopes. Whale had imported the gaunt Thesiger, with whom he had worked in England during the twenties, on the feeling that, with only a modicum of guidance, the prissy actor could move Femm into line with the director's vision.

With his razor-sharp, beak-like profile and his white shock of hair an almost albino plumage, Femm is made to resemble an angry bird, pecking his way about his dark and foreboding cage. (Over a glass of his well-liked gin, in front of the roaring fireplace, Femm will later admit to the band of travelers that he is wanted by the police. "After all," he asks, "could you conceive of anybody living in a house like this if they didn't have to?") To reinforce Horace's appearance and attitude, Whale had Edeson vary slightly his camera angles on Thesiger during the actor's delivery of his lines; Femm's being espied at somewhat different angles each time the camera returns to him captures both his bird-like skittishness and his being out of sync with his surroundings. By words ("You will *have* to stay here; the misfortune is yours, not ours") and by actions (both his own and those of the camera) it becomes more than obvious that the house is not to his liking, either.

Louder (she's deaf), less tolerant (she's a fanatic), and more brashly masculine (she's a sexless spinster and the more dominant of the sibling "couple") than Horace is his sister, Rebecca (Eva Moore). Making her entrance with both lungs pumping at full capacity, the less feminine Femm barks orders in the face of which Horace is impotent: ("No beds! They can't have beds!" "As my sister *hints*, there are, I'm afraid, no beds"), issues edicts, and lords it over the towering Morgan, if only when he's sober. When not glaring disapprovingly at the source of the laughter that has invaded her home or stuffing her mouth at table with the grace of a starving longshoreman, Rebecca fills her quieter (but no less intense) moments by recounting the miserable history of the Femms and their decaying house. Great mention has been made of her powerful scene with Mrs. Waverton, wherein the gnomish old woman predicts the same decay for Margaret's delicate dress ("That's fine stuff, too, but it'll rot"), as well as for the distraught young woman's personal beauty ("That's finer stuff still, but it'll rot too in time").

As with Thesiger, Whale had enticed Eva Moore to take a voyage across the pond and to make her American film debut in *The Old Dark House*. The actress had been one of the belles of the English stage at the close of the earlier century and the onset of the current, and had gained a good bit of notoriety as the "lady friend" of Queen Victoria's son Edward. The 62-year-old Moore, an undoubtedly faded beauty (but nowhere near the frumpy hag Jack Pierce and his staff unleashed on the company), went on to grace a handful of forgettable films (her final major appearance was in *The Bandit of Sherwood Forest* in 1946) and enjoyed her last vicarious moments of fame as Jill Esmond's mum.

Dinner is interrupted by the intrusion of the aforementioned Sir William Porterhouse and his friend, Gladys Du Cane (the lovely and refreshingly unglamorous Lillian Bond). Gladys's impromptu *Ach der Lieber Augustin*, cheerfully vocalized while stomping about in Penderel's old shoes, infuses such life into the heretofore stuffy proceedings that she merits a particularly baleful glare from Rebecca and an admiring glance from Roger. The dinner is resumed, more unsavory potatoes and pickled onions are shared, and as Morgan heads for that fateful bottle in the kitchen, Horace and the little band make for the comfort of the fireplace.

At this point in the novel, the group begins a game of "Truth," wherein questions asked of individuals must be answered with complete honesty. The gist of the game survives in the film, and here we see J.B. Priestley's dramatic theme: It is darkness and uncertainty (and not light and security) that move people to confront their innermost selves. Because Benn Levy had pretty much pared away the more despondent edges of the source work, wherein the air of futility is much greater, and Penderel is killed in the act of stopping the maniacal act of arson, the various admissions indicate salvageable dilemmas. Porterhouse's driving ambition, for example, reflects his determination to get even with the haughty types whose arrogance drove his wife to an early grave. Gladys's company is poor consolation; as Penderel notes, "I think he's in love with that little dead wife still."

Penderel discovers aloud that he really has nothing worth living for; in the novel, the war and personal failures of one sort or another have left him an empty shell. Although set up maliciously by Sir William, Gladys charmingly confesses that Du Cane is only her stage name (she's really a Perkins), and that she's from a dismal little section of England. Penderel's rush to her defense ("I think I'm finding you a little bit offensive," he advises the bluff businessman) leads moments later to the two of them braving the storm and heading for the car, where the beginnings of romance and a welcome bottle of whiskey await.

The Wavertons, too, have undergone

Beauty and the butler: a splendid study of Karloff's makeup and Gloria Stuart's appeal. *BUDDY BARNETT/ CINEMA COLLECTORS.*

changes in the few hours they've spent in the old house; the snap and bite that had characterized their relationship back in the car have been replaced by soft words, smiles, and winks. Philip, who earlier spent every moment sparring verbally with his wife, fights madly to protect her from the drunkenly amorous Morgan. In turn, the shadows allow Margaret to view her husband in a different light; what she had regarded as a stubborn streak is now recognized as sensible behavior. Nor is she left with any doubt that her husband's way of handling things is the way a man ought to act.

With Penderel and Gladys comfortably closeted with their newly discovered feelings and that whiskey; with Sir William off to fasten Rebecca Femm's storm-battered windows; with Philip wandering in search of an oil lamp at the top of the house; and with Horace Femm firmly sequestered in his own room, Margaret

Waverton finds herself alone with Morgan, the brutish butler. This is the scene wherein Gloria Stuart is James Whale's "white flame," pursued round and about the dining room and up the stairs by Boris Karloff. Rushing in response to his wife's frantic screams, Waverton comes face to face with the Neanderthal-like servant. After flailing away uselessly with his fists, Philip heaves the heavy oil lamp into Morgan's face and sends the brute crashing down to the landing below.

Penderel, Gladys, and Porterhouse meet up in the foyer, and the young couple tell the Yorkshire squire of their love. (Per Elsa Lanchester, her husband's affected accent was Yorkshire; I've read Lancashire in several other places. Let's not have this break up an old friendship.) Meanwhile, the Wavertons have together gone to the locked room on the next landing, where they have an enlightened chat with Sir Roderick Femm, the 102-year-old patriarch of the dysfunctional clan. Whale's kinky humor reaches its zenith at this point as he helps Priestley's profound darkness affect its most unlikely change: The wizened figure in the four-poster is played by a woman! "Jimmy couldn't find an actor who looked old enough to suit him," David Lewis once stated to James Curtis, "so he finally used an old stage actress he knew called Elspeth Dudgeon. She looked a thousand." That "old" stage actress was the same age as Eva Moore, was also enjoying her film debut, and must have chortled along with Whale and Jack Pierce at fooling the ticket-buyers; the credits list at both ends of the film identify the dying old man as being enacted by a *John* Dudgeon.

This was Elspeth Dudgeon's moment to shine, and, replete with putty and wispy chin whiskers, shine she did. Just as her Sir Roderick asks no sympathy, nor does he offer any; listening to the ancient invalid's ramblings, the Wavertons discover that things can only get worse.

> MARGARET: Would you like to go to sleep now?
> RODERICK: No, not just yet. You see, it may be...
> PHILIP: It may be what?
> RODERICK: It may be dangerous.
> PHILIP: You mean Morgan?
> RODERICK: No, not Morgan. I mean from my eldest son (he points to the ceiling), Saul... Saul is the worst, you know. We have to watch him because you see he wants, he just wants to destroy, to kill... Poor Saul.

It's a quite good performance by Dudgeon. The actress must have had some feeling for the horror/mystery field, as she went on to offer support in *The Moonstone* (1934), played an unbilled cameo in *Bride of Frankenstein* (1935) as a favor to Whale, was the eponymous heavy in the bizarre and little known *Sh! The Octopus* (1937), and performed twice again with Charles Laughton, in *The Canterville Ghost* for MGM in 1944 and in *The*

Paradine Case for Alfred Hitchcock, four years later.

The last of Whale's "special imports" was Brember Wills, who would play Saul. Like Saul, Wills is something of a cipher. Elsa Lanchester referred to the diminutive Brit *en passant* when discussing the film in her early work, *Charles Laughton and I*, but gave no particulars. While the actor is listed in numerous reference works, the entries usually consist only of his dates (1883–1948) and the mention of his work in *The Old Dark House*. The most I've been able to discover is that Wills played the part of the Stage Manager (with Joseph Schildkraut) in British and Dominions Film Corporation's *Carnival* (1931), was the title character in the 1934 British Warner Bros. feature, *What Happened to Harkness?* (featuring longtime Laurel and Hardy foe, Jimmy Finlayson), and supported Helen Chandler (and the Vienna Boys Choir!) in Cine-Allianz's biography of Franz Schubert, *The Unfinished Symphony*, that same year. Whence came Brember Wills, and whither he went is a mystery, but his splendidly maniacal Saul Femm will always keep his name alive among genre fans.

Horace pops his head out the door to snitch on Morgan; the revived ogre has gone to let Saul out! Saul is forgotten for the nonce, however, as Morgan himself stumbles downstairs and lunges at Margaret. It takes the combined strength of the three men to subdue Morgan, and as Porterhouse and Philip wrestle the powerful servant into the kitchen, Penderel locks Margaret and Gladys in a handy closet. On the landing above, a hand tentatively reaches out along the banister; Saul has arrived. Short, graying, initially timid, the oldest of the Femm heirs begs Penderel for compassion. The wry and wicked look that passes over the little man's face when Penderel's back is turned, however, gives the lie to polite conversation. Within moments the two men are seated opposite each other, when Saul lays his cards on the table (along with the wicked-looking carving knife he's retrieved from the floor), and says, "You see, I am a clever man... That is why we understand one another and that is why you understood so quickly that I wanted to kill you."

Penderel ducks the knife thrown by the psychopathic Saul but is knocked down with a chair. The eldest Femm grabs a flaming brand from the fireplace, and, rushing up to the second floor landing, begins to set the drapes afire. His left arm useless, Penderel struggles with Saul and the two men fall through the railing and onto the floor below. Morgan has meanwhile crashed through the hallway door, and hearing a pounding at the cupboard, frees the terrified women. It is only when Margaret indicates the fallen Saul that the butler turns his attention away from her. Cradling the crumpled body in his massive arms as a mother might her injured child, Morgan carries Saul back up into the upper reaches of the house, totally oblivious to Porterhouse and Philip, who have just broken through their door and have rejoined the others.

The cinematic Penderel survives, and come "the cold clear light of morning," he proposes to his loving Perkins. The Wavertons leave to fetch an ambulance, Porterhouse stays on to keep an eye on his erstwhile companion and her injured friend, and Rebecca scowls a good riddance down from her window. The storm having passed, the birds are singing, and Horace Femm, clad ludicrously for the hour in winged collar and French cravat, merrily chirps "Good-bye! Good-bye! So happy to have met you" along with them.

The magic of *The Old Dark House* resides in the awesome interaction of its many components. None of its actors had ever appeared together in pictures, yet they play so well against each other here that they seem to belong to an established theatrical ensemble. John Boynton Priestley's source novel was not typical of his extensive body of work. A number of his books, the majority of which were concerned with English regional politics or social mores, had provided solid foundations for the ever-nationalistic British film industry, and one of his plays, *An Inspector Calls*, became a monumentally successful international hit with Alastair Sim. *Benighted* did, however, boast *dramatis personae* who moved, more or less uniformly, among the shadowy and symbolic reaches of the Femm mansion.

Whale seized upon Levy's splendid adaptation and moved his actors along and about the remote corners and landings of the old dark house as a master at multi-dimensional chess would control his pieces. Meticulously plotted by Whale and Arthur Edeson (King Gray and Jack Eagen did the actual camera work), the grand design allows each individual a solo moment or two in the spotlight. Then, as couples (spouses, siblings, lovers, masters and servants), the interaction moves on to another level; we watch relationships change or mature, due more to the characters' increased perception of themselves than to their uncomfortable surroundings. At moments when most of the company seeks comfort by the fireplace or mills about some other flickering mise-en-scène (even the electric light flickers in this place), Edeson's camera shifts to note every action and reaction, gesture and response, line and rejoinder.

The thrusts and parries do begin to resemble the various exchanges in a chess game, where positioning sometimes forces the engagement of pieces of disproportionate weight or importance. Yet the constantly moving, ubiquitous lens seems to capture all corners of the house and every nuance of its occupants — whether these last are huddled together for protection or separated by circumstance — despite the darkness and gloom. In wide shots, viewers may home in where they will; there are enough bits going on at any moment to hold one's attention. Whale and Edeson make certain through their selective focus that no one will lose track of relevant detail or lose sight of the film's cumulative power.

And although Ernest Thesiger ultimately snags the brass ring, *The Old Dark House* represents the closest thing to gothic repertory acting that the cinema has ever presented.

Karloff's Morgan is also a job extremely well done. Junior Laemmle had been a tad concerned at the butler's hovering on the periphery of the plot for a good piece of the picture, but Levy's tight screenplay (wherein Morgan's *absence* is frequently made to seem as menacing as his lumbering about in everyone's midst) and Karloff's sheer presence are more than enough to deal with such concerns until the forbidden liquor takes effect, and hell-bent-for-Margaret, the brutish manservant clearly takes his place in the forefront. The actor then pulls a marvelous about-face when it's drilled into him that Saul has been hurt. His eyes widen as the import of Margaret's words sinks in; he rushes to the little inert body with the frantic air of a mother bear searching for a lost cub and then totally breaks down, all desperate sobs and futile tears. Morgan's incredible transformation is not complete until, as Greg Mank perfectly recounts, he "picks up Saul and miserably minces up the steps, rocking him, his hips swaying effeminately." From the most nightmarish of Hydes to the most gushing of Jekylls within seconds, without (or despite) makeup, Boris Karloff vindicates his celebrity and gives the role (which a lesser man might have rendered one-dimensional) a masterful interpretation, displaying a nuance and an insight no one can dispute.

Amid inky blackness, hesitant light, and sardonic humor the Femms shape-shift in any number of fashions. Rebecca changes before our eyes from spiritual zealot to vain and faded *grande dame*. The normally indifferent camera distorts her features (as her ages-old mirror will distort Margaret Waverton's lovely face) even as her twisted passions color her recounting of the family history. Her brother's metamorphoses, however, are psychological rather than physical; ever the image of a wild bird, the drawn and easily intimidated Horace embodies the morbid qualities of the vulture, the ominous associations of the raven, and most incongruously, the lightweight tittering of a sparrow. Saul's quick-change from Milquetoast to maniac is the most obvious, of course, and the bedridden Sir Roderick's dual personality is the result of James Whale's having an unusual sense of humor and of Elspeth Dudgeon's being a good sport.

Once in a while, and particularly when dealing with material of such vintage as *The Old Dark House*, peculiar claims or heretofore unknown bits of information surface in the course of research. An intriguing footnote can be found at the end of director William Wyler's filmography in Ted Sennett's valuable volume, *Great Movie Directors*: "Uncredited: 1932: *The Old Dark House* (with James Whale; Univ)."

Such an entry can be mind-blowing in the light of the reputation for autonomy that James Whale had during life and the quasi-deification the director has received from genre fans after his death. The only corroboration of this claim that I'm aware of is in Brooks Bushnell's 1994 tome *Directors and Their Films: A Comprehensive Reference, 1895–1990*, and this, in itself, may speak volumes. Much more likely, though, is a mundane explanation such as the following.

That William Wyler was working on the Universal lot in 1932 is indisputable; he was, in fact, Junior's second cousin. Wyler had been directing "B" features (mostly western programmers) for Uncle Carl since 1926 and may have asked his well-placed relative for a chance to get involved with something a bit more substantial. It's not impossible to envision Junior asking Whale to let Wyler handle a couple of the more routine setups; phrased correctly, in fact, the request may have tickled the vain director's fancy. Whether there had been any understanding of cousin Willie's getting so much as an "uncredit" for his "help," though, may never be discovered.

This whole business of "uncredited" credits leaves a bad taste in my mouth. The concept includes such "uncredits" as the fully-costumed Eddie Parker taking the knocks for Boris Karloff in *Abbott and Costello Meet Dr. Jekyll and Mr. Hyde* (or any of the stuntpersons who doubled in that era before lengthy and all-inclusive end-credits). How about Robert Florey's notorious "uncredit" for Frankenstein? How many screenwriters or composers devoted untold hours to contributions which were bought and paid for, but went uncredited? Did they, like Marni Nixon, who warbled off-screen for decades while Audrey Hepburn and others lip-synched for the applause, find creditless consolation in a healthy paycheck? How does a researcher know which credits reflect genuine input and which are listed merely pro forma (like the vast majority of "supervisors") or per contract (like Natalie Kalmus, whose ubiquitous credit as "Technicolor Consultant" from 1933 on was due to her wedding ring)?

William Wyler went on to a long and distinguished career without depending on any such "uncredit" as *The Old Dark House*; the powerful John Barrymore drama *Counsellor at Law*, and the charming *The Good Fairy* (with Margaret Sullavan, whom he would later marry) would be two peacock feathers in his cap within three years of *House*'s release. Magnificent films, the respect of his peers, and three Academy Awards would await him in the future. The only grumbles to be heard would come from genre fans: The classic *Wuthering Heights* (1939) and *The Collector* (1965) would be his sole ventures even remotely near their turf.

A true monster movie, an excellent horror film, and a witty and ironic black comedy (although not, in my opinion, "frequently hilarious"), *The Old Dark House* is the ultimate fun park ride. Like the unfortunates who seek shelter, the viewer is caught up with resident goblins; swept along through bleak corridors and into funereal chambers; assaulted by maniacal laughter, creaking and splintering doors, and howling winds; menaced by rampaging ogres; and deposited, basically none the worse for wear, back in the sunshine at the movie's end. Whether (as per William K. Everson) the film "invariably disappoints on its first viewing," or the killer combination of Whale, Wales, and walls (that fabulous cast helps, too) is considered from the start to be the thrill of a lifetime, it's a hell of a ride.

The Old Dark House

Released October 20, 1932; 71 minutes

Cast: Boris Karloff (Morgan); Melvyn Douglas (Roger Penderel); Charles Laughton (Sir William Porterhouse); Gloria Stuart (Margaret Waverton); Raymond Massey (Philip Waverton); Ernest Thesiger (Horace Femm); Lillian Bond (Gladys DuCane/Perkins); Eva Moore (Rebecca Femm); Brember Wills (Saul Femm); Elspeth [John] Dudgeon (Sir Roderick Femm)

Credits: Producer — Carl Laemmle, Jr.; Director — James Whale; Screenplay — Benn W. Levy; Based on the novel *Benighted* by J.B. Priestley; Additional Dialogue — R.C. Sherriff; Director of Photography — Arthur Edeson; Film Editor — Clarence Kolster; Art Director — Charles D. Hall; Music — Bernard Kaun; Assistant Director — Joseph A. McDonough; Sound Recorder — William Hedgcock; Makeup — Jack P. Pierce

THE MUMMY (1932)

Among the Golden Age horrors viewed by younger genre fans, *The Mummy* is one of those most often dismissed as boring. Poetry's proper place, you see, is high-school English class, and if "lyrical" is used at all nowadays, it's thought to derive from "leer." Direct to video releases have portrayed mummies as rampaging killers, geared more toward tearing living flesh than searching among the female cast members to find the whisper of earlier soulmates. It's a shame, really. *The Mummy* offers so much more than masked psychotics, jumping up suddenly from below the frameline. Allowing oneself to get caught up in the storied atmosphere of the tale does take patience, but the rewards include a pervasively eerie romantic tragedy, a number of chilling sequences, and magnificent performances all around.

Early in 1932, Nina Wilcox Putnam and Universal's Richard Schayer concocted a fantastic story of forbidden love which had spanned millennia, only to reach its shattering conclusion in the exotic reaches of modern Egypt. Titled *Imhotep*, it was a natural. Scarcely a decade before, Howard Carter's sensational discovery of the tomb of Tutankhamen, an extremely minor pharaoh of the Eighteenth Dynasty, had primed the pump and much of the world had been in an Egyptian blather since.

Following the transfer of the treasures to the Egyptian Museum in Cairo, it was found that the most popular attraction of all was the shrunken body of the pharaoh. The wizened figure captured the imagination of the curious visitors, who gaped at the relics of the king's former splendor while shuddering at the relic the king himself had become. Tragic yet horrifying, both the vessel of ancient passions and the embodiment of inevitable death, always and in every way inscrutable, the mummy fascinated the crowds even as it repelled them. What a part for Karloff!

Boris Karloff's sudden and far-reaching popularity had stepped up demand for imaginative treatments from Universal's scenario department. *The Old Dark House* had been an excellent showcase for the actor's talent at pantomime, but the time had come to provide him with a fittingly macabre vehicle in which he would speak. The Englishman's voice, unheard in either of his turns for James Whale (and not heard by that many ticket buyers in the casually received *Night World*), was soft and could be coldly menacing, but for a pronounced lisp. John L. Balderston was brought in to tighten the original story and rephrase any of the lines which might make Karloff the Uncanny sound like Sylvester the Cat (no mean feat with all that talk of scrolls), and the script doctor was

Lobby card showing Karloff in the title role of *The Mummy*. AUTHOR'S COLLECTION.

simply too well-versed not to recognize *Imhotep*'s debt to another story and another author.

The combined efforts of Balderston, Schayer and Putnam gave rise to a work of stunning beauty and understated menace, with a stately narrative that balanced each quiet moment with a dollop of horror. The team had the supernatural lover rise from his coffin, physically metamorphose, and finally undergo true death because of a woman. He possessed otherworldly powers, such as incredible strength, telepathy, and irresistible hypnotic command. He enslaved menials, parried with canny nemeses, was foiled by the protective power of religious talismans, and sought to seduce the doe-eyed heroine away from her uncomprehending boyfriend. You could understand why John Balderston must have smiled so smugly at the assignment; he had worked on this story

before. And he realized that the name missing from the writing credits was Bram Stoker's, for *The Mummy* was essentially a remake of *Dracula*.

A wonderful miniature diorama of the Sphinx and the Great Pyramid of Giza drags our eyes to the main credits, and our ears are treated to yet another rendition of the *misterioso* theme from Tchaikovsky's *Swan Lake*. Following a cameo by the Scroll of Thoth (played by the Papyrus of Hunefer, a section of the *Book of the Dead*) and a few stock shots of the Valley of the Kings, we come upon a rough wooden sign: This is "Season 1921" for the British Museum Field Expedition. The digs, played in long shots by Red Rock Canyon, are under the supervision of Sir Joseph Whemple (Arthur Byron), a dedicated archaeologist who voices his beliefs sibilantly through whistling dentures, and who seems to be wearing someone else's hair. Sparring with him philosophically is young Ralph Norton (Bramwell Fletcher), and up against a dimly seen sarcophagus, working all the while, is Dr. Joseph Muller (Edward Van Sloan). Van Sloan's "entrance" is magnificent; it's only when he turns from the mummy to confront Whemple with a crucial discovery that his distinctive voice and familiar features are recognized by the audience.

The mummy is identified as Imhotep, High Priest of the Temple of the Sun at Karnak. Discovering that his cadaver lacks the usual embalmer's incision, the archaeologists conclude that Imhotep was buried alive. The absence of the usual protective invocations in his sarcophagus indicates that he was "sentenced to death, not only in this world, but in the next." Norton is much more intrigued by a small casket found with the mummy which carries a hefty curse: "Death, eternal punishment for anyone who opens this casket in the name of Amon Ra, the King of the Gods." Sir Joseph and his young colleague are all for prizing the box open then and there, but Dr. Muller is unwilling to offend the Egyptian gods and heads out under the "stars of Egypt" for a confab with Whemple.

This leaves the antsy Norton on his own and sets up one of four impossibly perfect revelation scenes in classic horror (the other three being Chaney's unmasking at the hands of Mary Philbin, Fay Wray's smashing Lionel Atwill's waxen face to bits in *Mystery of the Wax Museum* [1933], and 1931's unveiling of the Frankenstein Monster). Light years away from sudden movements and spastic violence, the silent synergy of Freund, Karloff, cinematographer Charles Stumar, and Jack Pierce sends a palpable chill down the spine. Cocksure and curious, Norton not only uncovers and translates the Scroll of Thoth, but also mouths the words. The incantation proves far more powerful than the cynical young man has dreamed ("surely a few thousand years in the earth would take the mumbo-jumbo off any old curse"), as even the faintest of audible breaths sets the restorative spell working. A cut from Norton's excited recitation brings a closeup of Imhotep to the screen. For long moments ... nothing. Then slowly, inexorably, the eyes of the mummy open — only the smallest fraction, but enough to catch light from the lamps. Again, a hold for a long moment; as those tiny intimations of life burn ever brighter, Imhotep's right arm painfully begins its passage from the spot where it has reposed for 3700 years.

For all his earlier (and subsequent) larger roles, Bramwell Fletcher never had a more memorable moment onscreen than his mad scene in *The Mummy*. Usually remembered more for being Diana Barrymore's husband than for any of his other achievements, the actor makes the impatient Norton likable, and his hysterics at the sight of the mobile mummy ("He went for a little walk") are powerful and totally convincing. The famous shot of Imhotep leaning over to retrieve his scroll, as recorded by the still cameraman and evident on one of the original lobby cards, is nowhere in the film. An insert of the bandaged and bejeweled hand (the scarab ring later serving to focus Imhotep's malevolent mesmeric powers) and those twin gauze tatters, trailing their master's feet from the room, are the only indications we have of what has transpired. Fletcher's masterful performance fills in the mind-blowing details.

A snatch of arabesque melody alerts us that we're still at the dig, but a rather polished-looking sign informs us that eleven years have passed. Professor Pearson (Leonard Mudie) and Sir Joseph's son, Frank (David Manners), are shutting down the unsuccessful seasonal expedition when the door opens and a tall, gaunt, withered figure intrudes. Ardath Bey (Karloff, of course) has a clue to the whereabouts of the tomb of the princess Anck-es-en-Amon, which, he avers, is "not one hundred yards from where we are."

Naturally he knows what he's talking about, and in two shakes, Pearson and Whemple are standing at the door to the intact tomb. A copy of *The Egyptian Mail* reveals the scope of the fabulous find, which is credited in part to "Ardath Bey, an Egyptian scholar." The tomb is transferred to the Cairo Museum.

Ardath Bey stares with puppy-like devotion at the glass case holding his princess's mummy, but it is her life image, on the cover of her sarcophagus, which sends us across the city to the beautiful and eerily similar face of Helen Grosvenor (Zita Johann). It devolves that Helen, part English and part Egyptian, is the latest reincarnation of Anck-es-en-Amon, and in short order Imhotep/Ardath Bey catches on to this fact.

Until MCA unveiled "restored" versions of the 1930s Universal horrors, most of the extant prints of war-horses like *Frankenstein* and *Dracula* had been incomplete; pre- and post-release snips had been made, ranging from the odd bit of sound (Renfield's neck being snapped by the Count) to lines (Henry Frankenstein's blasphemy) to pieces of scenes (the Monster and little Maria). Hopes that a complete *Bride of Frankenstein*, from which more than 15 minutes had been excised after its premiere, might follow suit were dashed by the appearance of a gorgeous, remastered edition of that film's traditional 75-minute version. In light of this, the odds of *The Mummy*'s original cut ever seeing the light of day are slim; entire scenes were trimmed, almost on a wholesale basis, even before the film was released.

The cuts were ordered by Junior, who felt that the pacing of the core story of the relationship between Imhotep and Helen/Anck-es-en-Amon was deliberate enough without dragging in extraneous elements. Gone were a number of period vignettes, illustrating previous incarnations of Imhotep's princess. While available stills indicate that each of the set pieces possessed a certain charm, they tended to defuse the narrative thrust and upset the balance of the love story. With her forbidden lover moldering in the grave, Anck-es-en-Amon was zipping through some pretty picturesque periods of history, struggling to right social and religious wrongs, and fending off the ardor of suitors far more insistent than Frank Whemple.

There's no denying that the extended panorama of Helen's previous, adventuresome "lives" would have made any real-life proponents of reincarnation positively delirious;

even in its truncated form, *The Mummy* managed to win the endorsement of the Rosicrucians, an esoteric religious association. Retaining the scenes, however, would have made the spiritual bond between Helen and Anck-es-en-Amon far less powerful and the princess's relationship with Imhotep would have come dangerously close to seeming just another affair in a long line of frothy and colorful trysts. Who could argue persuasively that Anck-es-en-Amon herself wasn't an incarnation of a personality from a yet earlier era? Viewed with this in mind, Junior's decision seems unimpeachable; both in terms of pacing and of drama, *The Mummy* benefits greatly from the pre-release paring.

Helen's entranced response to Ardath Bey's whispered invocations leads her to the Cairo Museum, where Frank Whemple is given his chance to put in his romantic oar. When the young woman recovers, back at the Whemple home, some clever dialogue:

> FRANK: You'll think me silly, but I rather fell in love with [Anck-es-en-Amon].
> HELEN: Do you have to open graves to find girls to fall in love with?

Miss Johann's refreshingly capable interpretation (her heroine will *not* be ordered about or spoken down to) gives the relationship between the juveniles a breath of realism amid all this mystical miasma.

An interesting error in applied logic occurs earlier in this scene. While still unconscious upon the divan, Helen murmurs a number of unfamiliar words, including the name Imhotep; Sir Joseph, his eyebrows arching nearly to his powdered hairline, unhesitatingly responds in that same unknown tongue. He tells the curious Frank, "It's the language of ancient Egypt, not heard on this earth for 2000 years, and the name of a man unspoken since before the siege of Troy."

While this is enormously impressive, how could anyone know what a language which has gone unvocalized for two millennia possibly sounds like? Phonograph records? The trans-

In the original cut, Anck-es-en-Amon (Zita Johann) zipped through quite a bit of history while Imhotep was moldering in the grave. *AUTHOR'S COLLECTION.*

literation and study of hieroglyphics may uncover their meaning, but they provide no clue to their pronunciation. While several other critiques have made a great deal of Imhotep's being resurrected by Norton's spoken *English* words, logically, he couldn't have done otherwise. Far from being ludicrous, the reading aloud of a translation of the spell implies that the tremendous power of Egypt's ancient gods has transcended time, culture, and language.

Equally preposterous is Sir Joseph's assumption that, throughout all of Egypt's history, there was only one man named Imhotep. As the Anck-es-en-Amon of this film is but one of a pair (or more), mightn't the possibility of several Imhoteps in the course of 2000 years likewise be considered? Then again, a 72-minute

running time doesn't allow time for wrong guesses or testing of hypotheses.

Ardath Bey shows up, ostensibly to pay his respects, but he senses the presence of the Scroll of Thoth, which he abandoned at the museum following a lethal altercation, and he literally lights up (via John P. Fulton's wizardry) when he comes upon Helen. His subsequent confrontation with Dr. Muller is almost a replay of the Van Helsing–Dracula drawing room scene, down to the doctor's producing some heady evidence as to the unwelcome intruder's real identity. If nothing else, Muller's impressive threat, "If I could get my hands on you, I'd break your dried flesh to pieces," shows he must know something of Ardath Bey's occult standing of which we are unaware. At least we hope he does; otherwise his snarling away while at mere arm's length from the mummy is just so much macho blathering.

Sir Joseph meets his fate through the mummy's ancient spells before he can burn the scroll; his Nubian servant (inexplicably allowed to stick around although everyone knows for whom he's working) rescues the papyrus from the fireplace. While awaiting the scroll, Ardath Bey summons Helen to his haunts, where the young woman experiences flashbacks to ancient Egypt; she is enthralled as she witnesses a more vigorous Imhotep relive the sacrilege which resulted in their current state of affairs. (It was at this point in the pre-release print that Helen watched the spirit of Anck-es-en-Amon dash through history.) Returning to her hotel and remembering only "a dream" and the fact that her dog, Wolfram, is dead, Helen more or less agrees to remain under the watchful care of the Mullers. When the next telepathic call comes, Helen steps over Frank's nearly lifeless body (another attempt at psychic murder, foiled by a protective talisman) and heads for the museum.

The heroine finds herself garbed in more familiar royal raiment with fetching new hair styling and slides easily into the persona of Anck-es-en-Amon. Ardath Bey promises only a few moments of horror before an "immortality of love," but his touch leaves a residue of death on the woman's arm, and the desire to live, fueled by two struggling souls within her, opens the woman's beautiful eyes to the truth. A revived Frank and Muller show up in the proscribed nick of time, but are rendered helpless by Imhotep's unholy magic. It is Anck-es-en-Amon's contrition before a statue of Isis which saves her body (if not her migrating soul) from the knife-wielding mummy. The goddess's arm, empowered by the pleas of her priestess, points the *crux ansata* at the terrified Imhotep, and there is a blinding flash of light. Before our eyes, Imhotep decays and falls literally to pieces, as Frank recalls the young woman he loves from the embrace of a time long since gone.

The Mummy was golden at the box office, attracting not only genre fans, spiritualists and believers in reincarnation, but any number of viewers who were drawn both by the grandeur of the love tale and by the novelty of a "horror picture" without explicit violence. While Imhotep is responsible for four deaths (the two museum guards, Sir Joseph, and Norton, at least indirectly), he is never depicted as laying so much as a finger on any of them. As Ardath Bey, his ancient spells are potent enough to deal with enemies whether close at hand or across town, yet his splaying the bars of the museum window gives graphic evidence that he's quite capable of handling himself should push come to shove. Perhaps it is not so much a question of his need to avoid physical contact as it is his fear of its consequences. Most telling is that one instance in which he forgets his "Eastern prejudice" and touches the arm of Anck-es-en-Amon; the moldy handprint causes the young princess to recoil in disgust and to shake free from whatever mental bonds Imhotep has contrived.

The Mummy was the first of only a handful of films which were directed by Karl Freund. The Czech-born "Papa" had had a sterling reputation as a world-class cinematographer when he arrived in the United States at the outset of the thirties. A master of light and shadow, Freund had photographed such fantasy and science fiction classics as UFA's 1920 *Der Golem* and Fritz Lang's monumental *Metropolis* (1926, along with Günther Rittau). It was his Expressionist eye that added visual depth to Tod Browning's otherwise pedestrian handling of *Dracula*, and his knack with hues and shades which provided virtually the only dimension to the cartoonish goings-on in Florey's *Murders in the Rue Morgue*.

For his first directorial assignment, Freund tried to do more than merely adapt his bag of Germanic tricks to an Egyptian motif. (Yet Willy Pogany's archaeologically perfect sets still managed to convey an air of mid-twenties UFA about them. The flashback footage involving Karloff's entombment and the slaves' and soldiers' executions also resembled the earlier German style, and was, in fact, briefly thought to have been lifted from some forgotten silent epic.) Freund's strengths as a director had their genesis in his photographic skills, and his own expertise with the camera, coupled with the talents of ace cinematographer Charles Stumar and optical magician John P. Fulton, resulted in nothing less than a sumptuously lyric, cinematic poem. If there was a downside to such meticulous attention to framing, lighting and composition, it was Freund's willingness to allow the story's sublime visual lines to dictate the picture's deliberate pace.

The makeup for Morgan the butler was a romp in the woods compared to Jack Pierce's designs for Imhotep and Ardath Bey. In their various discussions of *The Mummy*, critics tend to drop to their literary knees in admiration for the time-consuming, full-body job that Pierce applied to Boris Karloff, and well they might. A series of still-extant production stills (to be found in the MagicImage Filmbook on *The Mummy*) traces the fascinating but arduous process as it unfolded in the fall of 1932. Transforming the long-suffering Karloff into Imhotep took some eight hours of wrapping, dusting and baking; shooting on the movie's opening scene wouldn't wrap until 2:00AM. The product of Pierce's genius and Karloff's physiognomy may not have looked like any other mummy, before or since (Bramwell Fletcher even has a covering line to handle any cynical viewer who might have already taken a gander at King Tut's emaciated physique), but the sheer scope and ambition of such a job set new standards within the industry. Imhotep's disintegration during the movie's closing moments was accomplished by John Fulton's impeccable matte work, utilizing shots of progressively more desiccated treatments on a Karloff life-mask and bust.

Considering the views of the sarcophagus-bound mummy which survived the pre-release edit, we've got to wonder if more of that "little walk" wasn't filmed but left behind before the picture's premiere. Whether by accident or design, however, the audience's imagination is required to take over when eyes and lenses are denied a further glimpse of the spectacle; thankfully, the end result is most satisfactory.

Alongside its more opulent partner, Pierce's exquisite ultra-brittle look for Ardath

Bey usually gets short shrift, and this is a shame. The makeup itself is fairly simple, and Pierce needed only an hour and some conventional supplies to create the mummy's more youthful look. Because Karloff parades about in this guise for most of the film and initially appears merely quite elderly and frail, there's a tendency to dismiss the treatment as commonplace and to save one's admiration for the Imhotep scene. The point is that Ardath Bey can pass among mortal men because he is *not* a physically bizarre figure. Any inkling of a more "otherworldly" dimension to the skeletal Egyptian scholar is relegated to John P. Fulton's singular talents. Fulton optically augments several of Bey's closeups and, with the aid of Pierce's mastery, creates a withered yet plausible patrician while leaving no doubt— even to genre novices — that there is more to this man than meets the eye.

Ardath Bey is one of Boris Karloff's finest portrayals. Relying upon the subtle facial artistry he demonstrated to a startled world in *Frankenstein*, the actor conveys the mummy's singleminded determination to pick up exactly where he left off, some 37 centuries earlier. Karloff's eyes had always been his most notable feature, capable of speaking volumes even when obscured by waxen covers or subdued by brutish eyebrows. As ominous and magnificent an effect as it is, Fulton's spectral highlighting of those eyes is almost dramatically superfluous, as Boris's unenhanced gaze is more than sufficient to reveal the mummy's obsession with his princess and his willingness to destroy any who might try to thwart his plans again.

Striving to lower his voice it its most cavernous depths, the actor takes the somewhat stilted dialogue in stride. (Why is it that Hollywood screenwriters of yesteryear always felt that lines couched in the pluperfect subjunctive somehow conveyed foreign cultures or earlier eras?) Bey is vocally dispassionate — a little sarcastic, perhaps — with the trifling mortals with whom he is forced to deal. When he comes upon Helen, however, his voice nearly breaks as he realizes that he has found his Anck-es-en-Amon, and that she's very much alive already.

Karloff's mellifluous tones, every bit as distinctive and ripe for imitation as Lugosi's, work their magic and almost seduce the reincarnated princess back into his arms. As was mentioned above, the tragic irony is that the decaying residue from those arms breaks his carefully contrived spell and leads to Imhotep's being reunited, not with love, but with death. The moral has an almost O. Henry type twist: If to touch your beloved means death, what value has life in the first place?

Zita Johann might well have been selected for her unusual beauty as for her undeniable talent. With huge, expressive eyes dominating her face, her Helen Grosvenor stakes a far greater time staking her claims to maturity and independence than do any other contemporary genre ingenues. She's not about to go to her room or sit tight merely because someone in trousers tells her it's the appropriate thing to do. In this case, though, the cinematic apple didn't fall far from the tree; Johann was herself a strong-willed and opinionated woman who never hesitated to exercise her contractual options and passed on any number of movie roles which she felt were unsuitable, unchallenging, or demeaning. A Broadway "star" in her own right long before she was approached with the role of Helen, the actress, who died in 1994 at the venerable age of 90, would have considered it a sad commentary on celebrity had she known that her obituary would inevitably highlight her being "The Bride of the Mummy" some 60 years after the fact.

David Manners' Frank Whemple is by far the best of his genre juvenile performances. Like Karloff, he's burdened with a couple of lines which would fluster all but a consummate professional; like Karloff, he does admirably. Boyishly charming, he makes the idea of his being enamored with an ages-old princess seem like the most natural thing in the world. Frank is light-years away from Jonathan Harker, his counterpart in *Dracula*; rather than succumb to a lot of meaningless male posturing, young Whemple is quite willing to give Helen her due, and to settle for an equal share in their relationship. At first he does appear a bit chagrined by such untypical behavior in a woman, but it doesn't for a moment deter him from his purpose.

Dr. Muller would be the last of Edward Van Sloan's immortal heroic roles, but his trio of elderly professors would serve as models of integrity and determination for the actors who would follow in his footsteps. Van Sloan appeared only once more opposite Boris Karloff, in Columbia's *Before I Hang* (1940), but he did check in with his other erstwhile nemesis, Bela Lugosi, for Universal's *The Phantom Creeps* (1939). Apart from these ventures, Van Sloan turned up most often in tales of intrigue and murder, with an occasional return to the genre in which he first made so big an impression.

Despite indications to the contrary, that really is Arthur Byron's hair. A native of Brooklyn, New York, Byron was born into a theatrical family and spent the first three decades of this century treading the boards with the likes of Katherine Cornell, John Gielgud, and Ethel Barrymore. One source avers that during his stage career, the actor "portrayed three hundred different characters and gave some ten thousand performances." *The Mummy* seems to have marked the beginning of a rather prolific film career for the ex–Brooklynite, which ended only with his death on July 17, 1943.

As is evident in the opening moments of the film, Byron's Sir Joseph is very clearly a man of tremendous scientific curiosity; as with most movie scientists, he is willing to take any risk to further the cause of knowledge. ("Good Heavens!" he intones, having translated some hieroglyphs from that forbidden casket. "What a terrible curse!" In the next instant, he and Norton are ready to pounce, curse or no curse.) The events surrounding Imhotep's disappearance and Norton's madness and eventual death, however, seem to put a more human edge to the resolute archaeologist. As we are informed by Professor Pearson, "When the best excavator England has turned out, a man who loved Egypt, said he'd never come back ... that meant something."

Byron resists the temptation to reduce the

effects of a decade's fear and uncertainty to a bit of white in his hair. His older and wiser alter-ego is no less sharp than he had been at the dig ten years earlier, but he is far more open to Muller's occult insights and to the unsettling miasma he finds about himself. The final tragedy is the realization that the casket containing the Scroll of Thoth was Pandora's box, as Sir Joseph ultimately receives his due for the sacrilegious action he condoned many years before.

The Mummy shed all Helen Grosvenor's previous incarnations save one before the picture had its official premiere at New York's Mayfair Theater on January 6, 1933. Bolstered by the public's fascination both with things Egyptian and with Boris Karloff, the picture did tremendous business. Once inside the Mayfair, the viewer's fascination for that Karloff fellow quickly was complemented by his admiration for that Karloff fellow. The Briton's powerful performance, on which most reviews concentrated along with Zita Johann's characterization, demonstrated his great versatility far more than had the comparatively uncomplicated role of Morgan in *The Old Dark House*. Not only was his character unlike any that had been seen before, the movie itself was a radical departure from the rapidly burgeoning horror pictures that were then making the rounds. (The *New York Times'* original review admitted, "It begs description ... one of the most unusual talkies ever produced.")

The Mummy was somehow more than just another spook show. It was a tale of endless devotion, of a passion which defied death and embraced resurrection; it was also a story of epic tragedy, wherein even unbridled love was seen to have its limits, and where the object of adoration proved to be far less committed than the timeless lover had hoped. (Another sound reason for removing earlier reincarnations: Helen's desperate choice of life over love-in-death with Imhotep would have seemed far less monumental if yet *another* spin on life's merry-go-round were seen to be awaiting her a few years down the road.)

Even with its similarities to *Dracula* and its borrowing from the classic "boy meets girl; boy loses girl; boy wins girl" formula, *The Mummy* managed to transcend the more familiar aspects of both. There were no rough and tumble battles between life-forms; viewers anxious for a good choking or a couple of broken backs were bound to come away disappointed. Imhotep's strengths were more insidious. The ancient spells had proven their potency to the cynical Norton and would be the means by which the superannuated High Priest would manipulate this new generation to his own end. Scenes which had toyed with the audience's nerves in the vampire picture (the confrontation between Dracula and Van Helsing, or the demonstration of the protective power of the cross) wrought similar reactions when transferred and translated into the Egyptian milieu. The chief distinction between the two scenarios lay in motivation: Imhotep operated solely out of undying love, whereas with the screen *Dracula*'s substitution of Renfield for Harker in the Transylvanian "prologue," the Count's later attraction to Mina can only be described as capricious.

One of those films which can be either pilloried or praised according to one's mindset, *The Mummy* has always been considered the most sublime of Universal's original nightmares. For those viewers who gauge horror pictures in terms of their number of throttlings, then the studio's effort is tame indeed. Those who would prefer that the requisite murders be affected with flair and subtlety will regard the film as an early study in suggestion and restraint. Even the dog dies off-screen! I've always ranked his work in *The Mummy* among Boris Karloff's top three genre portrayals, along with his dazzling triple role of Gregor, Anton, and Gregor *as* Anton in Columbia's beautiful *The Black Room*, and (of course) his Monster. Imhotep's incredible devotion — having endured burial alive and entombment for almost four millennia, his first thought is to unearth and likewise resurrect Anck-es-en-Amon — is offset by the devastation of his final rejection by his princess. Like that "terrible curse" of Amon-Ra, *The Mummy* will always have portent and timelessness.

The Mummy

Released December 22, 1932; 72 minutes

Cast: Boris Karloff (Imhotep/Ardath Bey); Zita Johann (Helen Grosvenor/Anck-es-en-Amon); David Manners (Frank Whemple); Edward Van Sloan (Dr. Muller); Arthur Byron (Sir Joseph Whemple); Bramwell Fletcher (Ralph Norton); Noble Johnson (The Nubian); Kathryn Byron (Frau Muller); Leonard Mudie (Professor Pearson); James Crane (King Amenophis); Eddie Kane (Dr. LeBarron); Tony Marlow (Inspector); Pat Somerset (Dancing Partner); C. Montague Shaw, Leyland Hodgson (Dining Room Patrons); Gordon Elliott (Dance Extra); Henry Victor (Saxon Warrior); Arnold Grey (Knight) (cut from release print)

Credits: Producer — Carl Laemmle, Jr.; Director — Karl Freund; Associate Producer — Stanley Bergerman; Screenplay — John L. Balderston; From a story by Nina Wilcox Putnam and Richard Schayer; Photographer — Charles Stumar; Film Editor — Milton Carruth; Art Director — Willy Pogany; Music — James Dietrich; Special Effects — John P. Fulton; Makeup — Jack P. Pierce

SECRET OF THE BLUE ROOM (1933)

Not every chiller Universal produced in the early thirties was heir to the Laemmle largesse. *Dracula* and *Frankenstein* had led the pack in terms of dollars invested, but this was done with an eye to the future; the two trailblazers' standing sets would be utilized in a score of Universal features and would more than pay for themselves in leasing fees to the independents. *Murders in the Rue Morgue* enjoyed a doubling of its original budget because of *Frankenstein*'s success, and both *The Old Dark House* and *The Mummy* hovered around the $200,000 mark. Even with some impressive box-office returns, that kind of outlay was a little rich for the corporate blood; sooner or later, the partnership of creativity and cash-flow had to favor the former, or Universal would be up against it once again.

One solution was to seek out stories which could be had cheaply, which required little or nothing in the way of special effects, and which could be crafted without an awesome "Cast of Thousands!" With the right story, clever screenwriters, capable contract players, and a streetwise director who worked with one eye on the clock and the other on the budget, it should be possible to bring in a winner for a hundred grand.

Secret of the Blue Room came in under seventy.

The decision to shoot the Teutonic mystery on a beer and pretzel budget was purely economic: There just wasn't the cash to go around. *The Invisible Man* was still in production when *Blue Room* was released in July 1933, but the Wells epic had already been leaking money (mostly for script treatments) for some 18 months. That was bad enough in itself, but, taken together with the astronomical costs of John P. Fulton's optical gags, the payments to the various writers would help crown *The Invisible Man* as the most expensive horror/science-fiction project until 1939's *Son of Frankenstein*. And while, by year's end, the studio would have channeled some 33 features out into theaters, the largest yearly output since 1930, several of the mainstream pictures (notably *Counsellor at Law*, starring the erratic but still brilliant John Barrymore, and James Whale's *The Kiss Before the Mirror*) took more than their fair share of the yearly budget.

Junior undoubtedly felt that an all-star cast would compensate for any second-rate production values. For Robert von Helldorf, he lured Lionel Atwill over from First National, where the actor had proven himself to be a horror man of the first order by virtue of his Technicolor *Doctor X* (1932) and *Mystery of the Wax Museum* (earlier in '33). Gorgeous Gloria Stuart, who was then enjoying a spate of nonstop activity at the studio and would appear in her third James Whale prestige production before the year was out, was slotted as Irene von Helldorf, the love interest to the three juveniles.

At 44 years old, Paul Lukas was a little long in the tooth to be considered a "juvenile," but the fact that he exudes class and urbanity from his every pore makes his Captain Walter Brink a credible front-runner for Miss Stuart's affections; in fact, the lovely heiress tips her hand when she warbles, "You'll never know, dear, how much you mean to me" directly at him.

Closer to the heroine's vintage is Onslow Stevens' Frank Faber, a journalist excited by the prospect of "spending a night with a ghost," yet honest enough to be concerned as to whether "there's anything to it." Faber offers the right blend of maturity, ability, and virile good looks, and was probably pegged more times than not as "Mr. Right" by the match-makers in the audience. The only thing preventing Frank from carrying Irene off into the sunset, of course, is his being shot dead in the fourth reel.

Outclassed by his two rivals ("I haven't a glib tongue like Frank ... and don't wear a handsome uniform like Walter") is Tommy Brandt, played with nasal brashness by William Janney. The 24-year-old Janney wears his character's impetuousness like an overcoat; Tommy is still at an age where he thinks more with his loins than with his brains, and his reactions to situations unfolding around him are superficial and obvious. (During Irene's piano serenade, Tommy and Frank catch each other's eye; Onslow Stevens speaks volumes with a raised eyebrow, while Janney stops just short of sticking out his tongue.) Janney would later take his patented whiny delivery over to MGM where, among other of his accomplishments, he would more or less drag Laurel and Hardy's *Bonnie Scotland* to a screeching halt.

Castle Helldorf lay in some nebulous region of specter-heavy Germania, and the mysterious Blue Room is introduced during a conversational turn at Irene von Helldorf's birthday party. Some 20 years earlier, three people, including Irene's aunt, were murdered

in the Blue Room at precisely 1:00 AM on various nights. The killings were never solved, and the chamber has since been locked, with faithful old retainer Paul (Robert Barrat) the keeper of the key.

With three suitors to every available heiress, the locked room is the perfect tie-breaker. When Irene reveals that the quality she admires most in a man is courage, the impulsive Tommy is off to the Blue Room, maintaining that an overnight vigil there will prove his mettle. Being older, they should know better, but Frank and Walter also agree to take their turns in the accursed room. The night seemingly passes without incident, but when the door is unlocked in the morning, Tommy has vanished! As there is no *corpus delecti*, Robert argues against calling in the police.

After dinner, Frank informs Walter that they might have a chance of solving the riddle of Tommy's disappearance if they abide by the agreement to spend the night in the Blue Room. Packing a revolver, the game newspaperman heads up to confront his destiny; this time around, the door is left unlocked behind him. To while away the time and to signal that's he's still kicking to Walter and Irene, Frank pounds away at the spinet as the fatal hour approaches. The clock strikes one, a shot is heard, and the pair runs upstairs. It's "Good-night, Irene" for Frank, whose body is discovered at the keyboard. Walter notices that the late journalist hadn't even had a chance to fire his pistol in self defense. A heartbeat later, the service alarm in the butler's pantry flashes "Blue Room"! Hurrying back to the scene of the crime, Walter finds that Frank's gun is now missing, and that a cat is playing with the bell rope. How did the cat get into the locked room?

Police Commissioner Forster (the redoubtable Edward Arnold) shows up with retinue and immediately begins his investigation, but apart from uncovering some tawdry details about the help, he doesn't get very far. Robert is caught in a lie, however, and the arrival of the mysterious stranger, an unidentified man who has tried (more than once) to get his foot in the door during the first three reels, forces him to come clean. The stranger is his brother — Irene's real father, who deserted the girl and her mother two decades earlier. Robert, who has raised Irene as his own daughter, is to give the faithless man some money that very night. That explains a hell of a lot and puts the investigation at an impasse. Realizing that the next step is inevitable, Walter confides in Forster and then climbs the stairs to the Blue Room.

At one o'clock, another shot rings out — from a secret panel in the wall! Saved by his own ingenuity — a dummy's head has taken the bullet — Walter chases the assassin into the cavernous reaches below the castle. Punches are traded after the bullets run out, and it doesn't look good for the last of the foolhardy suitors. Forster and his men have followed Brink down into the depths, though, and nab the killer before he can notch his gun belt again. Gasps are heard all around: It's Tommy Brandt! Having discovered the hidden passageway leading from the Blue Room, the desperately smitten Tommy concocted a foolproof way to emerge victorious from the battle for Irene's hand: Eliminate the competition. As Tommy is led away in the arms of the police, Irene nestles comfortably into Walter's.

A ripping good yarn, *Secret of the Blue Room* shuffles all the usual "dark and stormy night" cards and deals a full house. Based on a short story by Erich Philippi, the film is an enjoyable (if not completely puzzling) mystery rather than a full-blown horror picture. Like homicidal gorillas, storm-tossed haunts would continue to bolster low-rent productions for years to come. The major studios, however, had come to regard James Whale's satirical *The Old Dark House* as the absolute last word in real estate–oriented shivers. Any spooky old dwellings to follow would have to be erected in the shadow of the Femm mansion, and the odds of weathering such scrutiny or surviving the comparison were slight. (*Blue Room*'s interior *was* the Femm mansion, albeit more comfortably appointed and lit by a surer hand at electricity than Morgan's.) The monster-mashes of the mid–1940s notwithstanding, it wouldn't be until the early sixties (with films

as disparate as Roger Corman's *House of Usher* and Robert Wise's *The Haunting*) that haunted houses would once again be unholy ends in themselves and not merely atmospheric icing on the cake.

Sixty-odd years after its initial release, *Secret of the Blue Room* is still batting about .500 in terms of hoodwinking alert viewers. The average might have been higher, only some of the hows and whys are never divulged, and the handful that are are slender. A disappearance from within a locked room may not lead inevitably to murder, but it does pretty much point to a secret passage. The improbable tack here is not the existence of the secret passage, but that the glandular Tommy would discover it while von Helldorf, who has inhabited the castle all his life, would remain clueless. In confessing his ill-thought-out plan to Irene at the film's closing moments, Tommy admits that he had discovered the passageway three weeks earlier. Just how he pulled that off is never spelled out.

Nor are the decades-old murders ever explained. The omission may well have been either an oversight or a charming and intentional little *frisson*; most probably, the constabulary some 20 years earlier was little more competent than Forster. For all his logical deductions and probing questions, the police detective sees his every lead run through his fingers like water through a sieve, and comes up empty. And although his plan ultimately leads to the capture of Tommy and the solution to the secret, the device on which the idea turns — a mannequin in Walter's image, wearing one of Walter's uniforms — stretches credibility more than the other myriad mysteries combined.

Either Erich Philippi's original story or William Hurlbut's adaptation of it for the screen borrows here and there from the Sherlock Holmes canon. That dummy in the chair — Where did it come from in so short a time? — is nearly as technically perfect as the Great Detective's French-sculpted bust in *The Adventure of the Empty House*. *The Hound of the Baskervilles* proffered the mysterious affair of the lights in the nighttime between servant and mystery man, and the nefarious goings-on at 1:00 AM can be traced to *The Adventure of Wisteria Lodge*. Forster's clever comment concerning Max's cigar ash sounds like an aside in one of Holmes's fabled published monographs. Locked-room mysteries predated even Conan Doyle; what would finally become a subgenre of the mystery field was created by Edgar Allan Poe in *Murders in the Rue Morgue*. Nevertheless, while the potpourri of something borrowed/something blue strikes any number of familiar chords, it still leads the willing viewer down the primrose path.

As with any good murder mystery, the red herrings swim in schools. Naturally, the most glaring has to be the "mysterious stranger," but his menacing moves toward Irene notwithstanding, anyone who can't even get *into* the joint on the up and up certainly isn't sufficiently established to be the heavy. Lionel Atwill can likewise be eliminated from contention, if only in light of his two previous spookers. Whodunit buffs worth their salt know enough to disregard the lies von Hellsdorf tells; a perfectly acceptable explanation will be forthcoming. Likewise, palpable attempts at creating confusion — like having the master of the house and the phantom gunman buy their caps and overcoats off the same rack — ought to be dismissed out of hand. Even the police can see that the butler didn't do it (Universal being the one studio where the butler *never* actually did it), and as Walter's nobility shines brightly in Irene's lovely eyes, the process of elimination has worked once again.

Everyone does a swell job of keeping things moving without sacrificing a nod to characterization. This holds even for Janney, although I still think his glares and grimaces give the show away before anything really happens. Russell Hopton had originally been set for the leading part of Roger Penderel in *The Old Dark House*; here, he's serviceable in the nothing part of Max. In many ways, Hopton's career ran parallel to that of Dwight Frye. Both actors had enjoyed early success as light romantic leads (with Frye receiving his kudos on Broadway), only to become typed as the decade progressed and the caliber and number

of the parts offered to them dwindled. Hopton's henchmen and sidekicks were, however, infinitely preferable to Frye's ghoulish hunchbacks.

Edward Arnold had been born Gunther Schneider, but he sounds no more like a local police commissioner than Lionel Atwill does a German *Landesgraf*. Even without a trilled "r," however, Arnold conveys a no-nonsense air of Teutonic officiousness; it's a shame his Forster can't manage to unearth a solution to the mystery while he's uncovering skeletons in the von Helldorf closet. No matter. Arnold's rich and varied career would present him with numerous opportunities at unraveling significantly more notorious crimes. Not long after *Blue Room*, the portly actor confounded audiences (in more ways than one) as the eponymous detective in *Meet Nero Wolfe* (Columbia, 1935).

At this point in their respective careers, Paul Lukas and Bela Lugosi were deadringers for each other, vocally. The former, however, would work like the devil on Americanizing his English, and as his distinctive pronunciation softened, would be offered peachy roles from the trees lining the mainstream. The latter, of course, steadfastly refused to approach the language in any other than his normal, deliberate stride and remained narrowly typed for the duration of his professional life. Lukas also had more artistic sense than his fellow countryman. Parlaying his continental charm into a mystique that was headily enjoyed by female ticketbuyers throughout the country, Lukas would move easily among such famed beauties as Carole Lombard and Gloria Stuart. Concurrently, Lugosi's encouraging an aura of mystery about himself may have piqued the interest of a fraction of the distaff viewers, but his few dealings with "love interest" would usually smack of necrophilia. Bela, unfortunately, moved easily only among the likes of Minerva Urecal and Angelo Rossitto.

Along with the stock footage and the story itself, director Kurt Neumann was also a product of Germany. With the passing of what Lotte Eisner called the "great period" of Expressionism in the late 1920s, the number of actors and technicians moving to Hollywood would be

From the Man who Knows the Secret of the Blue Room — *William Janney*

Some carefully composed glaring for a lobby card. RONALD V. BORST/HOLLYWOOD MOVIE POSTERS.

rivaled only by the wholesale flow of pioneer nuclear scientists fleeing the Third Reich a decade or so later. Neumann had been brought over by the Laemmles in 1925, but didn't helm an American film until Universal's *My Pal the King* (1932), with Tom Mix and Mickey Rooney. *Blue Room* would turn out to be Neumann's only genre contribution of the decade and his nationality probably played a major part in his getting the Philippi assignment in the first place. Most of his other work for Junior had him keeping company with either Rooney or Chester Morris.

Neumann does a nice job, working hand-in-hand with Charles Stumar's exquisite camerawork and milking the familiar sets of their still-potent scope and design. As Walter follows the phantom killer farther and farther into

the depths, for example, Neumann's practiced touch allows both men to duck and dodge on the same stretch of scenery—the Frankenstein watchtower staircase—three times running. In fact, the climactic chase on those catacomb stairs is a wonderful example of how skilled direction, precision camera movement, and superb lighting arrangements can heighten a scene's suspense while dropping the action virtually into the audience's lap, and all without blowing the "surprise" ending.

More noteworthy even than the action-packed wrap-up is Neumann and Stumar's insert of Frank Faber in the *Blue Room*. Not only is there nothing like the stylized vignette in the rest of the movie, the overall tone is virtually unique within the contemporary genre. Hammering away at the spinet, Frank is

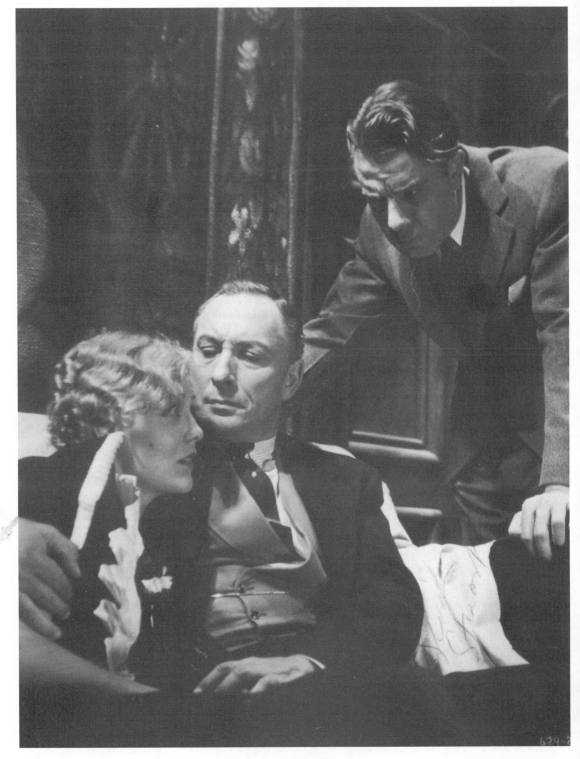

Irene is distraught, Robert von Helldorf is a bastion of strength and support, and Frank Faber is on his way to the keyboard in the Blue Room. *PENTAGRAM LIBRARY.*

ominously lit from below. He also appears to be lit from within, as he turns and tosses a drunken grimace right at the lens, cigarette dangling from his lips. Half Erik at the organ, half sodden cocktail lounge pianist, the least lucky of the three suitors is given one hell of a visual send-off before the clock on the wall strikes one.

Calvin Beck once said that, based on film titles, "secrets" were just "mysteries" without balls. Within the next ten years or so, *Secret of the Blue Room* would be remade twice, and neither of the successive versions would be as ballsy. With an excellent cast, sturdy direction, superlative cinematography, and everyone's favorite Tchaikovsky piece under the main and end titles, the original outing remains a full-bodied mystery. And that's the plain truth.

Secret of the Blue Room

Released July 23, 1933; 66 minutes

Cast: Lionel Atwill (Robert von Helldorf); Paul Lukas (Capt. Walter Brink); Gloria Stuart (Irene von Helldorf); Onslow Stevens (Frank Faber); Edward Arnold (Commissioner Forster); William Janney (Tommy Brandt); Robert Barrat (Paul); Russell Hopton (Max); Elizabeth Patterson (Mary); James Durkin (Kruger); Anders van Haden (The Stranger); Muriel Kirkland (Betty)

Credits: Producer — Carl Laemmle, Jr.; Director — Kurt Neumann; Screenplay — William Hurlbut; Based on the story by Erich Philippi; Photographer — Charles Stumar; Art Director — Stanley Fleischer; Film Editor — Philip Cahn; Music — Heinz Letton

THE INVISIBLE MAN (1933)

In the pre–DNA-awareness days of the *Shock Theater* era, the hallmark of science fiction films was chemical glassware. If you could find a rack of test tubes or a couple of retorts and beakers amid the chaos, you were obviously dealing with ersatz or quasi-science. Hence, despite their attendant physical grotesques, *Frankenstein*, *Dr. Jekyll and Mr. Hyde*, and *Island of Lost Souls* were science fiction movies. Supernatural beings didn't need microscopes or Bunsen burners to weave their spells, so *The Mummy* and *Dracula* were horror pictures, despite the presence of assorted physicians and archaeologists. Some films were harder to categorize, though, and others tried desperately to be something that they weren't. Even though Bela Lugosi's Dr. Mirakle harped on the link between stages of human development and waxed semi-coherently about the qualities of blood, *Murders in the Rue Morgue* has never seemed anything other than an embarrassingly old-hat monster movie.

There never has been any question, I think, about *The Invisible Man*. Apart from the requisite displays of unmistakably scientific stuff, the thrust of the whole picture is the tragic result of research gone awry. Even the most insistent of the science fiction purists can find little dramatic fault when an experiment of apparent and admitted value takes an unexpected and disastrous turn.

That all this happens in a setting which is, in its own way, as picturesque to American audiences as the Carpathian Mountains does nothing to lessen its science fiction basis. Heck, H.G. Wells would have had it no other way. Wells didn't live to see George Pal's splendid cinema adaptation of his Martian invasion epic, but had been actively involved in the London Films production of *Things to Come* (1936); along with Lajos Biro, he adapted his own novel, *The Shape of Things to Come*, for the screen. Despite (or perhaps because of) the weight of his well-known prose and his constant presence on the set, the film failed extravagantly with audiences who were looking for entertainment rather than eulogies. Wells was displeased with Alexander Korda and William Cameron Menzies' epic, feeling that his most crucial pronouncements had been sacrificed to such secondary factors as dramatic flow and pacing. Nor was the author thrilled by well-intentioned comparisons with the enormously popular *Metropolis*. He had hoped that his own vision of the future would provide viewers with both a portent and a realism that Fritz Lang's film — which he regarded as "hopelessly silly"— had not.

The Invisible Man, however, won both the

approval of its literary sire and the wide-eyed appreciation of critics and ticket-buyers alike. While R.C. Sherriff's screenplay may not have retained any of Well's views on world socialism, it was nevertheless deemed a faithful adaptation, and thus received the great man's blessing. One can only shudder at Wells' reaction had the film contained, as originally intended, the grimmer aspects of Philip Wylie's 1931 novel *The Murderer Invisible*, or any of the other outlandish situations through which Sherriff had waded in order to placate James Whale and to be true to himself.

Like most Brits, Whale was an admirer of Wells and was pleased at the thought of bringing this most personal of the author's imaginative works to the screen. He was not pleased, however, at the prospect of Boris Karloff's assuming the bandages and false nose of the tragic protagonist. More germane than even the director's resentment of the actor's sudden fame was the fact that *The Invisible Man* was not a horror picture, but a darkly comic scientific fantasy. There would be no lumbering brutes or insidiously supernatural creatures; only a very human, disturbed man caught up in his own wretched excesses. If there were no opulent character makeups, why would one seek out an actor whose fame was due primarily to putty and Fuller's earth? His Fu Manchu and Ardath Bey notwithstanding, how would Karloff, whom Whale viewed as a practitioner of essentially mute roles, fare in a part where his voice would be the ultimate measure of dramatic success or failure?

If all this seems like so much rationalization, you're right. "From the very start," averred Whale's lifelong friend and significant other, David Lewis, "Jimmy said that Claude Rains was the only man for the part." Like Karloff, Rains had decided at an early age that the actor's life was for him, and strove to overcome the lisp (another item shared with that most gentle of monsters) and Cockney accent with which he had been burdened since his childhood in the London slums. Unlike Karloff, Rains had set his eye on the British stage, feeling early in his career that the legitimate theater would offer the greatest challenge and also

provide the greatest reward. So poorly versed was he in the cinematic art that James Whale's first action upon awarding Rains the part of Jack Griffin was to send him out to watch as many movies as he could before filming commenced.

Unaccustomed to receiving any kind of flak at all from Junior, Whale was taken aback when the diminutive studio chief initially nixed the diminutive actor. Rains admitted to 5'8", was probably as much as two inches shorter, and used to "go to sleep praying that I'd awaken with a couple of inches added to my height." Despite his successes in the West End and on Broadway, Claude Rains was an unknown commodity in Hollywood, and there was simply too much at stake with an important project like *The Invisible Man* to allow anyone unknown to go unseen. Besides, didn't the actor make a complete muck-up of a screen test over at RKO for *A Bill of Divorcement*? Whale couldn't deny the screen-test fiasco, but insisted that Rains was the only invisible man for him. Unfortunately for Whale, Carl Laemmle Junior was holding out for Karloff. Fortunately for Whale, Carl Laemmle Senior held out *on* Karloff.

Following the *Frankenstein* bonanza, while the name Boris Karloff was tripping off the tongue of anyone who was anyone to do anything about it, Uncle Carl didn't let any of that San Fernando grass grow under his feet when it came to tying the actor's fortunes to those of Universal. Hefty salary increments were scheduled on a regular basis, and both labor and management professed to be happy with the contract. Around mid–1933, however, things began to get a bit tight. The studio had posted a loss in excess of $600,000 for the recently ended six-month period, and Uncle Carl was looking once again for ways to cut corners. Karloff was more than willing to forgo his expected raise from $750 to $1,000 per week if it was understood that, the next time a salary increase was due him, he would jump right to the then-scheduled amount of $1,250 per week. Laemmle agreed, but he tried the same baloney when that "next time" came around and found himself without one of his most bankable assets.

CARL LAEMMLE presents
H.G.WELLS'
FANTASTIC SENSATION
THE
INVISIBLE
MAN
with
GLORIA STUART-CLAUDE RAINS
Wm. HARRIGAN-DUDLEY DIGGES-UNA O'CONNOR
HENRY TRAVERS-FORRESTER HARVEY
Screenplay by R.C. SHERRIFF - Directed by JAMES WHALE, director of 'FRANKENSTEIN' - Produced by CARL LAEMMLE, Jr.
A UNIVERSAL PICTURE

For Whale, Uncle Carl's penury was a godsend. With Karloff off the scene, the director could go to work on Junior with a passion. Whether he was wooed by visions of another overnight sensation or was seduced by Whale's paean to the quality and dimension of Rains's voice, Junior okayed the stage star, and things started moving.

As *The Invisible Man* opens in the "typical" English village of Iping (Bramblehurst in the novel), Whale began once again to assemble his supporting cast from the usual suspects found on the fringe of Hollywood's British Colony. Homey, comfortable faces, already well-known to the mainstream movie crowd, Irishman Forrester Harvey and London-born Holmes Herbert would come to grow familiar to genre fans as well. Dudley Digges had forsaken the Abbey Theatre for Hollywood, and Whale's delight with Irish banshee Una O'Connor, who for most was an acquired taste, helped move the actress to the forefront of eccentric supporting roles. No one but no one could say "'Ere, now. Wot's all this?" like old E.E. Clive, who would be a welcome presence (usually as an overreaching petty official, a burgomaster, or a butler with pretensions to royalty) in over 80 films before his death in 1940.

From the film's opening moments, wherein his forlorn figure is seen stumbling along the countryside in the snow, Jack Griffin (Claude Rains) is totally alone in this world. His appearance in the doorway of the Lion's Head causes the locals to clam up and stare; even the player piano is rendered silent at the sight of the bandaged and goggled newcomer. From this point on in cinema history, the gods of mystery and imagination decreed that whenever a stranger would walk into a pub or tavern in a genre film, the customers would be required to cut short all conversation and glare rudely at the intruder.

Rains' marvelous voice betrays an imperious tone even at this early moment, but velvety pleas and steely threats will prove to be no match for the shrieking and caterwauling of Una O'Connor's hyper innkeeper, Jenny Hall. If Jack Griffin had hoped for the peace and quiet necessary for his crucial research at this

tavern, events occurring within the next few minutes (weeks, in reel time), set him straight. Driven to his limit with prying and screeching, Griffin roughs up the landlord (Harvey) and is badgered by the local constabulary; that tears it. In a series of wildly petulant moves, Griffin denudes his scalp, removes his glasses and nose, and unravels that curious gauze, revealing to the stunned townspeople (and to the astonished 1933 audiences) an apparently headless body!

With *The Invisible Man*, Universal's resident special effects wizard John P. Fulton finally came into his own; the techniques he created set the industry on its ear. Fulton was essentially an artist (capable of magnificent glasswork) who augmented his considerable talents through the mastery of the mechanics of the motion picture camera. Fully cognizant of the relatively new traveling matte process, he convinced Junior that he could indeed pull off the gags necessary for total belief in an invisible man. Although the property had been kicking around the studio for a while — Richard Schayer had "offered" it to Robert Florey some two years before it was actually filmed — it is doubtful that either Fulton or Universal studios would have been able to pay justice to the technical end much before mid–1933. Fulton was always tinkering, always experimenting; among other things, he had improved upon the Frank Williams Laboratory's original traveling matte technique. His speaking to Junior when he did indicates that it was only at that point that he felt confident that he could supplant the hoary, cruder means of showing movement of objects by unseen means that had been used in movies up to that time.

It remained for the brilliant technician to utilize his own methods whereby the possibilities inherent in the camera itself, together with some imaginative work in the photographic lab, would supplant wires and padded clothing to suggest a truly invisible man.

The concept of invisibility, of course, is a timeless "what if?" fantasy shared by just about all living, breathing human beings at some point in their existence. There is, unfortunately, a fly in the ointment and Wells, who was also a biologist, had to be more than casually aware of why an invisible man would be in no position to lord it over the rest of mankind.

If every part of his anatomy were transparent, Jack Griffin would be as blind as a bat. In order for him to insinuate himself into impregnable fortresses, secret council chambers, backstage at the follies, his optic nerves would have to receive impressions of those places from his retinas. If there is no image formed by the lens on the retina (because light simply passes through it, as it does with every other part of his unseen being), then there is no sight, and far from having the world grovel at his feet, the Invisible Man would have to feel his way from one adventure to the next.

Now Wells, who damn well knew this, too, wasn't about to let a little thing like light and retinas get in the way of a bloody good tale. Short of having Griffin maneuver among men on his hands and knees (visible retinas would be much less noticeable if not paraded about at normal eye-level), there was nothing to be done except to divert attention away from the sticky points with smoke and mirrors. It is for this reason (and for the picturesque images conjured up) that Griffin goes on about how he mustn't venture out within an hour or so of a meal, lest the undigested food give him away. (Wells and Sherriff both assiduously avoid the mention of invisible man droppings.) In a similar fashion, smoke, rain, fog, and dirt under the fingernails do what they can to keep all those maturing frog-dissectors in the audience from giving any thought to the business about the eyes.

For all this, Claude Rains' reading of his expository lines is as totally convincing as are John Fulton's complex effects. Before he falls victim to the mind-altering effects of monocane, the scientist desperately seeks to get away from prying eyes, to find the peace and quiet he needs to discover the means to rejoin society. After the drug has done its worst, though, he begins to move among men not as a member of society, but rather as (in his own mind) its new master. This is the tragic irony which the team of Rains, Whale, Fulton and Sherriff so successfully conveys in the movie. True, Whale's fabled black humor is nowhere more

in evidence than in his title character's fantastic physical displays of contempt for authority and society at large. But while the invisibility gags are mind-boggling exhibitions, eliciting wonder and amusement from the viewer, it is Griffin's inexorable descent into madness which adds the dimension of horror to *The Invisible Man*.

Whale at first moves back and forth between the increasingly unstable Griffin and the joint efforts of his honey, Flora Cranley (Gloria Stuart), and her father (Henry Travers) to find him. Allowing even the slowest ticket-buyer to catch on to the growing imagery of distance and separation, the device does have its drawback; it reveals the disparity in quality which exists among the various roles. While the part of Griffin is an actor's dream, running the emotional gamut from A to Z (and featuring a deathbed scene!), neither of the Cranley portraits offers its interpreter more than a one-dimensional opportunity. Whether the fault lies with Sherriff's need to concentrate primarily on extracting a viable personality for Griffin from the many sources he had thrown in his lap, or with Wells' original treatment, is a matter for individual opinion. Far from being dramatically well-rounded, Flora Cranley walks onto the scene wringing her hands, signs off at the climax while wringing her gloves, and unloads her lines in between in a weepy and breathless monotone. It is not Miss Stuart's finest hour, but she does the absolute best she can with what she has been given.

This is not to say that the lovely actress doesn't have a few moments in which she can take professional pride. Finally able to confront the fantastically arrayed Griffin, Flora demonstrates a concern which is as sincere as is her growing horror that her beloved Jack has, indeed, slipped a major cog. For Miss Stuart, this scene demands more compacted emotion, more pure dramatic realism than the sum total of her flashier role in *The Old Dark House*; more's the pity that the remainder of the part as written is so singularly tedious.

Henry Travers, who would play his most memorable part under Frank Capra's (ahem!) wing in *It's a Wonderful Life*, walks through the

Claude Rains, done up for a bit of John P. Fulton's magic. In the film, the lower part of Rains' face will simply not be there. *AUTHOR'S COLLECTION.*

picture as if he were under sedation; even when declaiming insistently that something must be done, he doesn't appear to have the heart to actually do it. His Dr. Cranley seems weary and resigned to failure, and we get the impression that, no matter when he shows up, we just missed witnessing his letting out a huge sigh of futility. Cranley's knowledge of monocane and its mind-altering propensities, however, is the only hope that Griffin has, and first-time viewers who expect a happy ending have nothing else on which to seize.

Doctor Kemp may be a less than capable colleague of Griffin's, but there is no doubt that he's a world-class snake; it's unfortunate that circumstances compel Griffin to impress the sniveler into service as a co-conspirator in his up-and-coming reign of invisible terror. It is to Kemp that Griffin confides about his specific needs if he is to remain unseen in all but the best of weather. It is from Kemp that the Invisible One experiences almost immediate and total betrayal. In fact, given the understanding that Dr. Cranley can help restore his former assistant to visibility and to lucidity, Kemp's calling in the police when he does effectively dooms Griffin long before the picture's climax.

As delineated in the screenplay (the character had a more redeeming side in the novel), William Harrigan's Dr. Kemp is as transparent as is Jack Griffin. His first step is to put the moves on Flora, whom he regards as fair game now that Jack isn't around. A poor scientist (Griffin's opinion) and a false friend (empirical evidence), the only aspect about Kemp which strikes a sincere note is his abject fear of the Invisible One. Unlike Griffin, whose violent actions are due to forces beyond his control, Kemp digs his own holes and richly deserves everything he gets at the hands of his erstwhile partner. While the part is not written with any greater complexity than those of the Cranleys, Kemp's singleminded villainy is very much necessary and appreciated. Had he kept his word to Jack, Cranley could have intervened, and the subsequent random acts of terrorism and murder might never have taken place. Kemp, and not Griffin, has to be seen as the true heavy of the piece.

According to Whale biographer James Curtis, Chester Morris originally signed to play Kemp, but proved recalcitrant when it came to sharing top billing with Rains, then a cinematic novice. Obviously not willing to have his plans screwed up when victory was within sight, Whale had Morris removed and brought in William Harrigan to essay the oily doctor. Harrigan may not have been much more than a designated hitter, but he does an admirable job of keeping the sympathy flowing towards an increasingly sociopathic Griffin. *The Invisible Man* would be the most notable of the actor's rather undistinguished film credits, but Harrigan's plummy tones do allow him to hold his own opposite Rains and that assorted band of scene stealers from the UK.

Appearing as an unnamed newspaperman in the second half of the picture, Dwight Frye makes a decent impression, standing erect and speaking in complete sentences. Genre fans are usually taken aback when they spot Frye acting very much against type, and his "cameo" gives us all a peek at the diminutive actor's more normal and pleasant side.

Following a montage of mayhem, including a splendid train wreck done in miniature, Griffin seeks refuge from another snowfall, and holes up in an old barn. Hearing "breathing" in the barn, the farmer runs to the police, who cordon off the wooden structure, and set it afire. When Griffin hies it into the open, his footprints (curiously, they are actually shoeprints) give him away, and he receives a well-placed bullet. In hospital, the misguided scientist dies, and the effects of the monocane die with him; John Fulton's parting nod is a breathtaking sequence wherein the incredibly young-looking Griffin (Rains was 43 at the time) gradually returns to visibility.

The Invisible Man introduced Claude Rains to a medium which he would come to master in later years. As the crises and emotions unveiled in the film are all staggeringly human, devoid of any supernatural powers or otherworldly considerations, the burden of evoking the audience's understanding and sympathy lies on the shoulders of the title character. Perhaps James Whale's insistence on

Although coerced into helping the Invisible Man, Kemp rather than Griffin must be seen as the heavy of the picture. *AUTHOR'S COLLECTION.*

going with the unknown Rains was yet another flash of brilliance that must be accorded the lanky director.

Boris Karloff might well have matched Rains' performance in terms of pathos, but even at this early date, his presence would have moved the audience to suspect that Jack Griffin was something other than human. There were no such viewer preconceptions about Rains, and the actor used his prodigious talent to create an image of Griffin as tragic victim, whose noble instincts were undermined both by the devastating side-effect of monocane and by the calculated betrayal of a colleague whom he could not ever begin to trust.

That *The Invisible Man* shows little signs of wear and tear after more than six decades is at least partly due to the fact that human nature changes little over the years, and that the sympathies of the audience will always be with the underdog, providing they can relate to him. If a grotesque character evokes sympathy, then the actor who portrays him, the author who creates him, and the director who guides him have all succeeded in making that grotesque immortal. One need only look at Boris Karloff's Monster or his Imhotep/Ardath Bey to understand. Despite their most appalling circumstances, both "horrors" share the common emotions of the audience: loneliness, love, fear, uncertainty, betrayal, anger, and sadness. To gauge the timelessness of Karloff's characters, one need only look at the lack of any such humanity evidenced by the various successors to either part.

Claude Rains' invisible man, while not technically a "grotesque," manages to run that requisite gamut of emotion, and succeeds in creating a three-dimensional personality with whose frustrations and torment the public can identify. Denied even the capacity to raise an eyebrow or furrow his brow, the soon-to-be-celebrated Rains makes his Griffin seem all too human even in his throes of madness and despair, largely by dint of his magnificent voice. Of the successors to this role, only Vincent Price is able to transcend the superficialities of bandages and dark glasses.

The credit for the film's classic status must

be shared by others as well. The darkly comic touches, those still-thrilling moments when a wildly exasperated Griffin throws caution and bandages to the wind and reveals to the incredulous bystanders the secret they've been dying to discover, reveal John P. Fulton's genius in a way that has never been more magnificently realized. As concocted by R.C. Sherriff (with plaudits and apologies to H.G. Wells), the moments of calm and lucidity, contrasted with the terrifying downward spiral into lunacy and self-destruction, reveal a schizophrenia that is far more frightening and real than the ever-popular and easily parodied *Dr. Jekyll and Mr. Hyde*. The delicate balance between comic invention and tragic denouement, and the fragile line between dramatic satiety and excess, represent yet another exercise in genius, outlined and polished by James Whale.

Sadly, Whale's erratic personality would follow Griffin's tragic lead, and his later years would be pocked with recurring paranoid outbursts. Those same, fragile human emotions which both separated his bizarre creations from other of the numerous "monsters" which prowled the night and earmarked them for immortality would lead the director to a premature and self-inflicted death.

The Invisible Man

Released November 13, 1933; 70 minutes

Cast: Claude Rains (Jack Griffin); Gloria Stuart (Flora Cranley); William Harrigan (Dr. Kemp); Henry Travers (Dr. Cranley); Una O'Connor (Jenny Hall); Forrester Harvey (Herbert Hall); Holmes Herbert (Chief of Police); E.E. Clive (P.C. Jaffers); Dudley Digges (Chief of Detectives); Harry Stubbs (Police Inspector Bird); Donald Stuart (Inspector Lane); Merle Tottenham (Milly); Walter Brennan (Man with Bicycle); Dwight Frye (Reporter); Jameson Thomas, Craufurd Kent (Doctors); John Peter Richmond (John Carradine) (Informer); John Merivale (Newsboy); Violet Kemble Cooper (Woman); Robert Brower (Farmer); Bob Reeves, Jack Richardson, Robert Adair (Officials); Monte Montague (Policeman); Ted Billings, D'Arcy Corrigan (Villagers)

Credits: Producer — Carl Laemmle, Jr.; Director — James Whale; Screenplay — R.C. Sherriff; Based on the novel *The Invisible Man* by H.G. Wells; Director of Photography — Arthur Edeson; Art Director — Charles D. Hall; Film Editor — Ted Kent; Special Effects Photography — John P. Fulton; Retake Photography and Miniatures — John J. Mescall; Music — W. Frank Harling; Makeup — Jack P. Pierce

THE BLACK CAT (1934)

The first of five Karloff-Lugosi teamings at Universal (excluding the pair's participation in *The Gift of Gab*, which amounted to little more than cameo appearances), 1934's *The Black Cat* is, in many ways, the best of the lot. It is undoubtedly the kinkiest.

At first, the front office regarded the situation as not so much kinky as galling. Boris Karloff had earlier won the right to work at other studios while affiliated with Universal, and he had been busy doing just that. He had jumped at the chance to work with John Ford over at RKO, garnering quite respectable notices as the demented Sanders in *The Lost Patrol*, and then had further impressed the demanding mainstream crowd with his splendid performance opposite wily old George Arliss in 20th Century–Fox's *The House of Rothschild*. If there was any consolation to be had, neither film was direct competition for Universal's popular horror product. With typical lack of insight, the Laemmles continued to type this most flexible of Hollywood's actors as a bogeyman; apart from inconsequential piffle like that bit in *The Gift of Gab* (1934), it wouldn't be until 1948 that Universal-International would feature the brilliant character man in a non-genre role (as Tishomingo, in *Tap Roots*).

Not that Karloff minded; the soft-spoken Briton was pleased as punch to be in demand, relishing any part for its dramatic challenge and financial opportunity. He had no problem with creating nightmares over at Uncle Carl's; his versatile talents would be employed in more diverse assignments elsewhere.

More objectively disturbing was the paucity of viable offerings being readied for him at Universal City. All sorts of titles were mentioned, considered, and dismissed for any of a variety of reasons. As insistent as Junior had been on a quick follow-up to *Frankenstein*, for example, he hadn't cared much for the assorted twists and turns the sequel's proposed treatment was taking. The enticing prospect of Karloff's heading up an underground civilization in *A Trip to Mars* was bandied about constantly, getting shuffled around among excellent but idiosyncratic writers and studio hacks and finally being rejected due to its expensive nature. Come what may, it was all the same to Boris Karloff.

Bela Lugosi, on the other hand, could not afford to be so cavalier. Given the kind of town that Hollywood has always been, the Hungarian's fiscal ineptitude was almost as legendary as his continental temperament. A very public bankruptcy late in 1932 had shown Bela to be in need of a second job, but his struggle with the language didn't increase his chances of getting one. The late Carroll Borland, who had gone on record just about everywhere as a life-long platonic Lugosi idolater, admitted to Greg Mank (in *Karloff and Lugosi: The Story of a Haunting Collaboration*) that Bela "had a great deal of difficulty with English." This observation is somewhat at odds with that of Lillian Lugosi Donlevy, who told Mr. Mank in no uncertain terms (in the same book) that "Bela knew the language very well. I venture to say that his vocabulary was larger than Karloff's!" One of these ladies must have been mistaken, but there is no question that Lugosi's pronounced accent stood in the way of his escaping typecasting as a heavy.

Bela's work away from Universal (unlike Karloff, he had not been offered a long-term contract after his initial success) was almost always in the horror/mystery genre; while this kind of thing did help fund soirees and meet the notes, it did nothing to break the stereotype which was growing stronger, picture by picture. The actor, though, could not afford to be choosy. Whereas his British rival enjoyed his tea-breaks at Warners, RKO, or Fox during the thirties, Bela was spending far too much time toiling before the cardboard sets of Mascot, World-Wide, or Principal. The money may have been just as green, but it was somehow less respectable for having come from Poverty Row. Still, until the death knell of horror films at the end of 1936, Lugosi was forced to make *all* the rounds, hitting the majors and the independents alike.

When a call came from Universal, Bela was more than merely willing; he was raring to go. The offer was for *The Black Cat* as part of a three-picture package with *Dracula's Daughter* and *The Suicide Club*. (The first would ultimately be made sans Lugosi and the second sans Universal.) A bit of shmoozing with the director had resulted in assurances that he, Bela Lugosi, would be *Black Cat*'s enigmatic but sympathetic hero! Touted as a further dramatic touch was his character's "all-consuming fear of cats," which was hopefully an opportunity for the artistic complexity Bela had always sought to display and not merely a mouthful of empty words to lend justification to the title. Responsible for Bela's enthusiasm was

Edgar G. Ulmer, an eccentric young Austrian who had arrived in Hollywood with a string of uneven accomplishments, a quirky personality, and an affinity for stretching a budget. Having served his lengthy apprenticeship under German Expressionistic masters Wegener, Murnau, et al., Ulmer had entered the Laemmle circle during the mid-twenties and had become something of a confidant to Junior. *The Black Cat* was Ulmer's chance to make his American directorial debut in one of the genres with which he would become associated throughout his life. Apparently, he relished the assignment but hated the script and so went to work on one of his own. The result is a fascinating duel between the obliquely mysterious forces of good (represented by Bela) and the straightforward, unapologetic powers of evil, embodied by Boris Karloff.

Karloff's Hjalmar Poelzig was based to no little extent on Alister Crowley, a Peck's Bad Boy from Hell whose notoriety had captivated Edgar Ulmer for years. Known as a self-styled Satanic high priest who published graphic accounts of his depravity as well as pieces of "exotica" (pornography) when not in the throes of frequent opium dreams, the British Crowley, who claimed also to be an adept at *magick* (i.e., the real thing), was very much more a sort of diabolical P.T. Barnum than the anti–Christ. Nevertheless, he made a very nice living, leading bizarre people in bizarre and degenerate games and espousing the kind of blasphemous folderol designed to outrage the moralistic tight-asses of his generation. Ulmer's ultimate insight into Crowley's ludicrously concocted persona is nowhere more evident than during the Black Mass scene, wherein Karloff, with crepe-hanging solemnity, intones such impressive incantations as *Magna est veritas, et pro evolebit* (The truth is great, and it will come to the fore) and *cum grano salis* (with a grain of salt).

At 65 minutes, *The Black Cat* would be the shortest of the classic horrors Universal had released to that time, but a heck of a lot — perhaps too much — transpires within that brief running time. Just about every word spoken drips with hidden meaning, and few looks are

"Enter freely, and of your own will" — maybe Karloff mouths some other lines at this point, but Bela doesn't look pleased at being on the receiving end. AUTHOR'S COLLECTION.

shot or exchanged which don't immediately cry out, *Significant*! (During his entrance, Bela scarcely squanders a smile before commencing to invest his soap-opera dialogue with meaningful pauses; his glances out the train window likewise reek of portent. Clearly, something monumental is coming down.) While one may give thanks for the relief from more obvious and simplistic options, the sheer number and weight of such devices soon becomes overwhelming. The array of vices paraded throughout the film is so comprehensive, it's a wonder that Universal's publicity department didn't come up with the tag line that "No matter your propensity, it's present with intensity!"

The lovely Jacqueline Wells (later Julie Bishop) is Joan Alison, wife of Peter Alison (David Manners) and the subsequent target of lust, obsession and violence. She and her husband are on their honeymoon, and the last thing they're looking to do is to get involved with anyone outside their circle of newlywed intimacy. In his third and last bout with the studio's premier bogeymen, Manners is outnumbered and out-acted by Boris and Bela, but gives his unexciting lines a decent reading. It's not his fault that his conventional and logical behavior is completely overwhelmed by the Brobdingnagian emotions flashing about him.

Bela underplays most of that opening scene, and Werdegast's aura of tragic mystery is all the more poignant for its less than Lugosian tone. His attempt at humor — how it's "better to be frightened than to be crushed" — strikes a realistic chord; the intruder senses the couple's disappointment at his presence, and is striving to lighten things up a bit. Less acceptable, and far too pat for a subtle characterization, is his stroking Joan's hair while she sleeps. If cinematic realism was truly called for, Peter would have punched the presumptuous doctor right in his long-suffering mouth. In Ulmer's original treatment, however, the new Mrs. Alison was to have been possessed in Marmaros by some sort of seductive feline spirit; with this in mind, the stroking could be taken as foreshadowing, for the time will come when Vitus conquers his ailurophobia. As Joan's *houri* manifestation never made it past the second wrap, the action has to serve as the smoking gun that sets up Lugosi's speech about the fate of the Werdegast females.

A number of touches in Ulmer's original treatment never made it to the release print. Joan's transformation was excised; a "comic" scene wherein Peter Alison displays the disrespect and petulance more proper to Jonathan Harker also ended up on the cutting room floor. Mercifully scrapped was footage revealing the seamier side of Vitus Werdegast; far from being the avuncular hero presented at the outset, he would regress to becoming the maddest of doctors and vie with Poelzig, not in order to save the heroine, but to deflower her! Both Carl Laemmles were distraught at the Austrian auteur's vision and demanded that he eliminate what they considered to be excessively deviant elements. To their and Lugosi's relief, Werdegast's nobility was restored, and a new scene of Poelzig's taking the psychiatrist on a guided tour of a stylized underground crypt took the place of much of the rest.

Karloff survived the reshoot with his character's sinister aberrations firmly in place. In fact, the new insert of the glass-encased cadavers made Poelzig seem even more perverse and *outré* than before. During this vignette Werdegast's phobia, which plays so crucial a part in the unraveling of the kinky plot, is first witnessed. Also evident here (whether by accident or design is left to one's imagination) is the visualization of the myth of a cat's nine lives. Moments after Vitus frantically skewers Poelzig's pet, the feline (or yet another black cat) is safely back in the satanist's arms. If the

unholy beasts are in some ways immortal, perhaps it does make sense to fear them.

This uneasy observation brings to mind a discussion my friends and I had more than once when we were kids. Why, we wondered, would Universal opt for a creatureless piece of weirdness like *The Black Cat*, when the studio had virtually cornered the market on the creation of new and instantly classic grotesques? Since the mid-twenties, Uncle Carl's stable of creative minds had given celluloid life to hunchbacks, phantoms, monsters, vampires, mummies, and invisible psychopaths, and, by the time Edgar Ulmer's showboat had hit the screens, there was also talk of werewolves lurking around every corner. Why would the Laemmles buck the trend they had created in favor of a tale of revenge couched in all-too-human terms? It took me a long time to arrive at the answer, and I never quite managed to convince most of my horror-loving friends.

The Universal forces, I would argue, didn't abandon their consistently effective introduction of monsters. Rather, under Edgar Ulmer's offbeat genius, they merely tempered the appearance of this latest product off the line, and actually indulged in a bit of subtlety. Forget those annoying critters petted by Karloff and dispatched by Lugosi. The monster of the piece was *The Black Cat*, and the black cat was Hjalmar Poelzig.

From the top of his feline haircut to the bottoms of his noiseless pads, the black-clad Poelzig prowls Marmaros through the night hours with the calm confidence of a cat patrolling his territory. Those formidable walls may still deny access to unwanted visitors and frustrate the escape of helpless visitors, but it is Poelzig's diabolical presence which delineates the lethal boundaries of Marmaros as surely as the spray of a predatory cat announces off-limits to possible intruders. Within his rival's territory and bound by convention and rationality (he is, as Poelzig ironically notes, "one of Hungary's greatest psychiatrists"), Werdegast is unable to deal with the engineer's pervasive aura. Hjalmar senses this and toys with the bitter Vitus as a cat plays with a mouse; can the symbolism of their chess game be any more obvious than when viewed in this light? Even Werdegast's mute henchman, Thamal (Harry Cording), a menacing, powerful bulldog of a man, is as powerless as his master within the shadow of the cat. The dog is reined in and given orders to heel which circumstances dictate must be obeyed.

In contrast to Werdegast's Lugosian intensity and vigor, Poelzig never raises his voice, allowing his threatening purr to overwhelm the noisier histrionics and revealing them for the useless blathering that they are. (Even Karloff's celebrated lisp lends a perpetual hiss to his character's pronouncements.) Nor does Poelzig feel constrained to loyalty or love; his casual but deadly solution to superficial relationships is, in effect, put on display for dramatic effect. The "crypt," wherein the body of Werdegast's lost wife (among others) pays silent tribute to Poelzig's many former "lives," is much more a trophy room than a mausoleum. Let the ailurophobic Vitus waste his weapons on the black tabby prancing about the floor; as the weirdly beautiful bodies attest, Poelzig has other of his nine lives remaining to him. Ironically, however, it will be the engineer's promiscuity — his habit of "catting around" — which ultimately leads to both his own destruction and to that of his coven.

Beholden only to dark forces far greater than his own, Poelzig shows no kinship to the demented fools who number his followers. Catlike in his autonomy, he leads them further into their degradation, which culminates in the "Black Mass" that triggers the film's wild conclusion. As the Latin doggerel sets the rhythm, Poelzig is at once very nearly the Devil himself *and* that most popular of familiars to the pathetic degenerates in his charge. His comeuppance at Vitus's hands gives new meaning to the old chestnut about skinning a cat; in the ensuing explosion, the Black Cat — along with his catnip, litter box, toys, and kittens — is blown directly to hell.

Imposing additional feline imagery on this already powerful portrait may have proven too much of a good thing, and for that reason, I don't mourn the scrapping of the earlier footage. Sure, Joan Alison's transmogrification

into a Cat-being would have reinforced Poelzig's metaphor, but it would also have worked to undermine the High Priest's unique status both in Marmaros and in what passed for life. Bela Lugosi was right-on in his aghast reaction to Werdegast's waffling emotions; switching motives midstream from *blood*lust to *breast*lust would have trivialized Vitus's original mission and made the unhinged medical man's climactic tussle with the lithe satanist little more than a catfight over the mouse.

Bela's character had to remain the voice of reason, at least for the lion's share of the picture. Werdegast's slipping to the other side of the screwy line too early (as per Ulmer's original shoot) would have undermined the doctor's professional and personal integrity. If the authority figure is thus revealed to be little more than an incompetent or a sham, the big denouement with its classic struggle between good and evil loses a lot of its symbolic steam. As the film now stands, the Alisons find themselves in a pickle due to Werdegast's profound respect for "the rules of the game." The psychiatrist appears impotent, however, in his attempts at dealing rationally with blasphemy and depravity.

It is only when he confronts his recently murdered child that the psychiatrist loses it all and enters the spirit of Marmaros. Suddenly on Poelzig's level, eye to cat's eye, the crazed Werdegast unleashes the dog; Thamal plays his part in the beginning of the end. That this spells a final end for the Black Cat reeks more of poetic justice than of Poe. In a powerful reversal of their roles to this point in the picture, Poelzig's latest, most savage action succeeds in transforming his old enemy into a cat. In his madness, Werdegast becomes a rogue lion who invades Poelzig's pride and causes the death of his devilish progeny. No trace of humanity remaining in the glint in his eye, Vitus the lion unsheaths his claws and shreds to pieces the erstwhile Master of Marmaros.

The Black Cat received a critical drubbing. It was way too offbeat for mainstream tastes and even dared to deviate from the more "conventional" species of creepers and crawlers that

Paul Panzer (third from left) and Michael Mark as cult members have Jacqueline Wells in their clutches while the paraphernalia are readied for the climactic Black Mass. *Buddy Barnett/Cinema Collectors.*

had lately packed the movie houses. Universal, however, happily acceded to the views of the ticket-buyers, whose personal quirks led them to provide Uncle Carl with some $140,000 in pure profit. Bela Lugosi probably felt vindicated, having at last proven himself capable of heroics. No one, of course, would give this a second thought, and "one of Hungary's greatest heavies" would be back on the darker side of the action almost immediately. Boris Karloff could likewise feel vindicated; he had essayed a remarkable portrait of undiluted menace and malice without Jack Pierce's customary excesses.

Although responsible for a spectacularly profitable genre masterpiece, Edgar Ulmer would find himself *persona non grata* at Universal for having disrupted the marriage of a minor Laemmle with a studio employee. Still, the Austrian director would go on to a career checkered with minor successes, but always encumbered by low budgets. His uniquely bizarre world view would find legions of proponents among fans of science fiction and film noir, but little in his personality would lend itself to conventional comedy.

Enjoyment of *The Black Cat* demands one's full attention; it's not enough to look up from the crossword upon hearing a growl, a snarl, or a Hungarian cadence. Edgar Ulmer's array of degenerate emotions is unveiled through visual innuendo (he was right in thinking that the Universal brass wouldn't catch the full spectrum of perversity evident in the mausoleum scene) and vocal inference, rather than with the ham-fisted blatancy that less sophisticated *frissons* deserved. Clever, subtle, and richly ironic, the picture is perhaps the first horror film for grown-ups that Universal produced in its "Golden Age."

The Black Cat

Released May 7, 1934; 65 minutes

Cast: Boris Karloff (Hjalmar Poelzig); Bela Lugosi (Dr. Vitus Werdegast); David Manners (Peter Alison); Jacqueline Wells (Joan Alison); Lucille Lund (Karen); Harry Cording (Thamal); Egon Brecher (The Majordomo); Albert Conti (The Lieutenant); Henry Armetta (The Sergeant); Anna Duncan (Maid); Andre Cheron (Train Conductor); Luis Alberni (Train Steward); George Davis (Bus Driver); Tony Marlow (Patrolman); Paul Weigel (Station Master); Peggy Terry, John Peter Richmond [John Carradine], Lois January, Symona Boniface, Paul Panzer, King Baggot, Virginia Ainsworth, Michael Mark (Cult Members)

Credits: Producer — Carl Laemmle, Jr.; Director — Edgar G. Ulmer; Screenplay — Peter Ruric; Based on a story by Peter Ruric and Edgar G. Ulmer, suggested by a tale by Edgar Allan Poe; Director of Photography — John J. Mescall; Supervisor — E.M. Asher; Art Director — Charles D. Hall; Assistant Directors — W.J. Reiter and Sam Weisenthal; Film Editor — Ray Curtiss; Musical Director — Heinz Roemheld; Special Photographic Effects — John P. Fulton; Makeup — Jack P. Pierce; Camera Operators — King Gray, John Martin; Continuity — Tom Kilpatrick; Script Clerk — Moree Herring

THE LOVE CAPTIVE (1934)

Another missing item from Universal's sound catalogue, *The Love Captive* merits inclusion in this book as that spiritual child of *Svengali* and *Cagliostro*: the tale of hypnosis and seduction. Notes on the ubiquity of mesmerism and the unfailing popularity of sagas of infidelity in the cinema are sprinkled throughout this volume, but I'll sum up succinctly. Just as most boys growing up in the fifties and sixties at some point sent in their allowance to buy a pair of X-ray glasses which would allow them to peruse the unadorned glories of the female form, so also did most of the many silent and early sound genre films concerned with hypnotism also involve the exploitation of women.

Villains lacking cash or sex appeal (or personal hygiene, like John Barrymore's *Svengali*) usually had to resort to some kind of mental control in order to win female attention. Since "getting girls" was the underlying *raison d'être* for most horror and science fiction movies, mesmerism filled the bill until cloning, alternate universes, parallel dimensions, and the like took over in recent years. Extending back to 1908 and 1910, respectively, Svengali and Count Cagliostro have always been the cinema's primo horny hypnotists. Conrad Veidt brought the latter to silent pre-eminence for Micco-Film in 1920, and Orson Welles lent his substantial presence to the role in Fox's *Black Magic* in 1947. Barrymore's 1931 rendition of Trilby's worst nightmare remains unsurpassed by any of the numerous versions which flanked it.

Per the essay on *The Last Performance*, Mr. Veidt's Erik the Great was also said to have been something of a practitioner of hypnosis, but the abridged nature of the extant print precludes our becoming fully aware of just how the obsessed magician put his talent into practice. Universal's timeless goblins, Dracula and Imhotep, were both well-versed in the mesmeric art, and neither hesitated for a moment to turn his baleful eye upon the object of his desire. Over at Fox, Edmund Lowe as Chandu the Magician was constantly (to borrow a phrase from Lee Falk) gesturing hypnotically, while undisputed king of the eye-wideners, Bela Lugosi as Roxor sloughed off his opponent's trademark hooey as "Hypnotism only!" If we also consider Doctor Mabuse's ongoing bouts of mesmerism, we find ourselves knee-deep in the stuff.

With *The Love Captive*, Universal tried to take a slightly different tack. Sure, the hypnosis shtick would still be wrought in conjunction with the sexual angle, but the narrative would be aimed at a more gentile unfolding; the target was the mainstream adult market and priorities

Lobby card for the lost 1934 film *The Love Captive*. PENTAGRAM LIBRARY.

had to be reordered. Infidelity? Of course. Murder? Naturally. Monsters? Not in your life.

In the film Dr. Alexis Collender (Nils Asther) is a present-day American hypnotist of questionable character who uses his power to influence Alice Trask (Gloria Stuart), his new office nurse, to break her engagement with Doctor Norman Ware (Paul Kelly) and live with him. Collender becomes prominent through the publicity given him by reporter Larry Chapman (Russ Brown), whom he has cured of severe hiccups through hypnotic methods. His turn of fortune makes it possible for him to move from his shabby quarters and set himself up in luxurious offices.

Ware, who is broken-hearted over the loss of Alice, works on convincing the County Medical Society to prefer charges against Col-

lender for unethical medical practices. He produces Mary Williams (Virginia Kami), Collender's former nurse (who has also been seduced and abandoned), to testify against him, but the woman once again falls under the hypnotist's power and retracts her statements. When told that the medical society is holding a meeting at the home of Robert Loft (Alan Dinehart), Collender intends to demonstrate the efficacy of hypnosis by performing an experiment in which a person will hypnotically be made unable to exert enough force to discharge a revolver with a hair trigger.

Refused admittance to the meeting, Collender wanders into the garden, where he encounters Loft's wife, Valerie (Renee Gadd). He immediately places her into a hypnotic state and wills that she give her affection only to him. He returns with her to the house, and Loft and

Ware realize that some strange influence has been exerted over Valerie. Collender returns home, where he determines to rid himself of Alice and take on Valerie. This decision is reinforced by the sudden appearance of Ware, who demands that Alice be released from her trance.

In the days that follow, Alice and Ware resume their engagement, but Valerie, still under Collender's influence, is restless and unhappy. When her husband discovers that she is the hypnotist's constant companion, he vows to kill the unscrupulous wretch. An opportunity presents itself when the medical board finally grants Collender a hearing and okays that risky revolver experiment; Loft offers himself as a subject. When the hypnotist declares, "You will try to shoot me, but will be unable to do so," Loft, who has been shamming his trancelike state, pulls the trigger. It is agreed that the fatal shot was fired while Loft was under the hypnotist's influence, and he is exonerated, having committed the perfect crime.

The studio synopsis seems to indicate that the theme was presented with greater decorum than the more blatantly genre efforts were wont to do. The *Motion Picture Herald* was right on target when it reported on June 16, 1934:

> Highly melodramatic material of the hypnotic eye variety, this production ... is considerably lacking in action and is the type of film in which women are much more apt to be interested. ... The romance of the young couple ... and the adjunctive second complication, whereby the hypnotist comes close to wrecking a happy marriage, indicate how thoroughly the film tends toward feminine appeal. ... The title itself, if too heavily emphasized, is apt to result in a rather complete lack of interest by the masculine portion of the patronage....

While the *Herald* was meant to give the skinny about new releases to theater owners and thus help them promote the pictures as effectively as possible, its opinions were not necessarily those of the trade or popular critics. Unfortunately, the mainstream press opted to pass on *The Love Captive*, not because it was a movie obviously geared towards women (nothing wrong with that), but because it was yet another hypnosis film! In this respect, *Harrison's Reports* of June 9, 1934, was typical:

> Just one of those things! Hypnotism is the means by which the producers sought to interest the picture-goer, and I have not yet seen a picture based on display of hypnotic powers to make any kind of sensation on the screen.

The same review deemed the picture

> not particularly edifying for adolescents. Children under twelve may not understand it but they will not enjoy it, and there is no good lesson that they can learn from it.... It is a picture for mature audiences, if they can stand it.

With the exhibitors down on the film because it fragmented their audiences, and the critics down on the film because it was neither exciting nor even terribly interesting, where could it go? No 1934-vintage parents in their right minds would have given Junior and Missy a quarter and a "God Bless" and sent them off to a movie about infidelity and promiscuity. (With virtually no genre elements in sight, and a title that promised the ultimate in *Yecch!*, the kids wouldn't have wanted to go anyhow.) Thanks to all the reviewers chalking it up as a snoozer (or worse, a woman's picture), Mom would have needed a mesmerist or a revolver herself to get the old man to take her to see *The Love Captive*. Besides, it should have been evident from the start that combining a treatise on the immoral uses of hypnotic power with a resolve to downplay any sensationalistic angles was a money-losing proposition.

And there were other problems, too. First of all, not everyone believes in hypnosis; for every articulate medico who maintains that smoking or overeating can be stopped by means of mental suggestion, there's another, equally convincing authority who dismisses the whole thing as faith healing or balderdash. The split is aggravated by advocates' opinion that one must be intelligent in order to be hypnotized, a view that makes the smug

That faraway look in Gloria Stuart's beautiful eyes is the product of Nils Asther's hypnotic suggestion. Paul Kelly appears duly concerned. *PENTAGRAM LIBRARY.*

pro-hypnosis crowd an elitist bunch. To the pooh-poohing, anti-mesmerism contingency, such an argument smacks of the Emperor's New Clothes: If you can't, for the life of you, believe in the procedure or accept its dubious claims, then there's something wrong with you.

Secondly, the only other apparent use for hypnosis (apart from its arguable medical value) is entertainment. Cabaret and nightclub hypnotists — frequently lumped together in the public's mind with psychics, magicians, and fire eaters — have acquired followings and fortunes by inducing members of their audiences to bray like jackasses or to hop about on one

foot whenever the band strikes up *The Star Spangled Banner*. And that's about it.

It's the nature of the beast: Mesmerism and sensationalism go hand in hand. To most rational people, hypnosis is either a miracle or bunk; either way, it cries out for exploitation, for flamboyance, for larger-than-life surroundings. In the nineties, our perceptions run to salvation ("Only *I* can stop you from taking another wedge of cheesecake!") or diversion ("When I clap my hands, you will awaken, remembering none of this"). Back in the thirties, before the birth of the computer age, the advent of instantaneous worldwide communication, and the dawning of the age of haute sophistication, hypnosis was entrenched in the pupilless eyes of a Svengali, in the pinspotted eyes of a Dracula, in the luminescent eyes of an Ardath Bey!

Hypnosis was the property of the movies, and a quick glance will indicate *which* movies. No one associated mesmerism with normal people, with everyday life, with mundane passions. Even a couple of years down the road, when James Whale would arrange for his cadre of dissipated millionaires to consult a hypnotist in the interest of dredging up forgotten information (q.v. 1935's *Remember Last Night?*), he had Gustav von Seyffertitz's Professor Jones drag in a whirling thingamajig (which might have been lifted from Whale's *Bride of Frankenstein* lab set) in order to do the deed. (Hell, one look at von Seyffertitz — even decked out in a conservative business suit — was enough to cinch the debate on the normalcy of hypnotists.)

The conclusion? A noble attempt at the dramatic unfolding of a tale of moral peril resulting from abusive mental control in conventional adult circumstances was predestined to failure. Mesmerism had been guilty by association with the unhinged, the uncanny, and the undead for so many years that Max Marcin's best shot at bringing his play to life on the screen was undeniably too little and too late. No one interested in a serious love story could believe for an instant in the hypnosis angle, while hardly anyone slavering at the mouth for twirling watches or googled eyes wanted to see such raw power frittered away on a couple of semi-bourgeois socialites. The film's disappearance, it seems, was preceded by the public's indifference to it.

For gorgeous Gloria Stuart, *The Love Captive* was a far cry from the glory days of James Whale, *The Old Dark House*, and *The Invisible Man*. Only *The Gift of Gab*, another of Universal's "lost" mid-thirties talkies, stood between her and a contract with Darryl F. Zanuck's 20th Century–Fox. Unfortunately for Miss Stuart, the pickings there were almost as slim as they had become at the House That Carl Built. The lovely actress closed out the decade at Fox, and then, following a few one-shots for

Columbia and the independents, wrapped her film career for the next fifty years with *She Wrote the Book* (for Universal!) in 1946. Nineteen-ninety-seven saw Ms. Stuart's triumphant return to the screen. Eighty-seven years young, she garnered an academy award nomination for best supporting actress for her role in James Cameron's epic, *Titanic*.

With the film currently unavailable, it's impossible to determine whether Paul Kelly played Dr. Norman Ware in *Captive* in the same irritating fashion he had displayed as Scoop Hanlon in 1938's *The Missing Guest*. Many found Kelly's brash personality accountable for his prolific film career; he appeared in over 90 pictures in the course of some 30-odd years. For others, the actor never amounted to more than the violent lout who had broken up musical comedy star Ray Raymond's home before kicking the man to death in the presence of Raymond's five-year-old daughter. Neither assessment is as facile as it appears. Raymond had often beaten his wife, actress Dorothy Mackaye, and may never even have been legally married to her, but in an interesting reversal of its collective behavior during Roscoe Arbuckle's trial, the Hollywood community backed Kelly and Dorothy, and both performers survived a brief bout in the Big House to prosper in their field.

Nils Asther was a Swedish import, and he gave the women something to look at while their dates were eyeing Loretta Young in *Laugh, Clown, Laugh*, Joan Crawford in *Our Dancing Daughters* (both 1928), and Greta Garbo in *The Single Standard* (1929). If you ignore *Captive* and an ill-advised appearance in 1949's *The Feathered Serpent*, Asther's big genre credit is the atmospheric *The Man in Half Moon Street* (1944). Alan Dinehart's face was (and still is) far more familiar than his name. Some readers of this book may be able to recall him in the relatively thankless role of Joseph Morton in Universal's 1939 *The House of Fear*, but no one should have a problem conjuring up visions of the actor's Paul Bavian (fraudulent seer and target of Ruth Rogen's impossibly powerful hands) in Carole Lombard's only genre offering, *Supernatural* (Paramount, 1933).

"You will try to shoot me, but you will be unable to do so," says hypnotist Nils Asther. "Bang," replies Alan Dinehart's trusty revolver, his trance being only an act. PENTAGRAM LIBRARY.

The Love Captive was based on *The Humbug*, a melodrama with a moderately profitable run during Broadway's 1929 season. In directing the film adaptation, *Humbug* playwright Max Marcin vowed to transfer every deathless nuance from the boards to the screen. It was supposedly the magic of the movies which had enticed the remarkably versatile Marcin to favor Hollywood with his presence and ability at the outset of the 1930s. He amassed credits on such films as Gary Cooper's *City Streets* (1931) and Cary Grant's *The Last Outpost* (1935) as writer, adapter, scenarist, dialogue director, and director.

It's impossible to see for ourselves whether cinematographer Gilbert Warrenton was as moodily effective under Marcin's direction as he had been under Paul Leni's for 1927's *The Cat and the Canary*. Then again, as Marcin and

Universal were apparently looking to set the offbeat theme in purposefully non-horrific surroundings, such a comparison would really be pointless. May it suffice to say that none of the contemporary reviews of *The Love Captive* I found singled out Warrenton's artistry for comment.

Shot as *Dangerous to Women* in 19 days in March of 1934 (with additional scenes done on April 21), *The Love Captive* came and went. The AFI catalog reveals that the studio had dickered unsuccessfully with Paramount and RKO for the loan of Randolph Scott and William Gargan. If the presence of either of the popular leading men, the latter of whom would soon become a Universal mainstay, might not have saved the film from its ultimate obscurity, it certainly couldn't have hurt its chances with the male portion of the audience.

Perhaps the notion of hypnotically bidding beautiful women to one's side had been the provenance of cloaked and swathed scoundrels for too long a time to permit a non-horrific or noncomedic treatment of the theme at that point. Perhaps Alexis Collender and his pocket watch would have met with greater success had they been featured regularly on the radio; as it stands, the whole idea certainly seems tailor-made for television soap operas. Whatever the case may be, in the interest of fairness, we must suspend judgment until that day when a print of Max Marcin's masterpiece is found, wedged under a porch in Upper Sandusky.

The Love Captive

Released May 21, 1934; 63 minutes

Cast: Gloria Stuart (Alice Trask); Nils Asther (Alexis Collender); Paul Kelly (Norman Ware); Alan Dinehart (Roger Loft); Renee Gadd (Valerie Loft); Russ Brown (Larry Chapman); Virginia Kami (Mary Williams); John Wray (Jules Glass); Ellalee Ruby (Annie Nolan[d]); Addison Richards (Doctor Collins); Robert Grieg (Butler); Demetrius Alexis (Doctor Freund); Samuel T. Godfrey (Doctor Blake); Alfred P. James (Janitor); Jane Meredith (Mrs. Forndyce); King Baggott (Cop); Patricia Caron (Dr. Ware's Nurse); Edith Arnold (Elinor); Gigi Parrish, Lois January (Girls); Dean Richmond Benton (Boy); Larry Steers (Guest); Vesey O'Davoren (Second Butler); Franklyn Ardell (Pete Nolan[d]); Ralph Remley (Roner); with Arnold Gray

Credits: Presented by Carl Laemmle; Executive Producer — Carl Laemmle, Jr.; Director — Max Marcin; Associate Producer — E.M. Asher; Associate Director — Edward D. Venturini; Assistant Directors — R.E. Taylor & Charles Gould; Continuity — Karen De Wolf; Based on the play *The Humbug* by Max Marcin; Cameraman — Gilbert Warrenton; Process Photography — John P. Fulton; Art Director — Harrison Wiley; Film Editor — Ted Kent; Supervising Editor — Maurice Pivar; Sound Supervisor — Gilbert Kurland; Make-Up — Jack P. Pierce; Production Manager — M.F. Murphy; Still Photography — David Farrell

SECRET OF THE CHATEAU (1934)

Movies like 1934's *Secret of the Chateau* tend to upset the genre fan's conditioned sensibilities. Made during the absolute peak of genre glory by the people who had offered shocks and chills as greatly desired alternatives to the pressures and disappointments of the Great Depression, *Secret* is a tepid effort at best. Is this a thirties Universal melodrama, or a poverty row potboiler? Where are the vibrant shades and shadows? The richly dramatic personalities? The opulent eccentricities? Where are the cribbed portions of Dracula's castle or Dr. Frankenstein's laboratory? Where are those measures from *Swan Lake*? Where's the menace? Where's the mystery? Where's the beef?

Most contemporary buffs had their major beef with the blah nature of the château's secret. Compared with the innovative grotesques which had been appearing frequently at neighborhood theaters everywhere, this tale of Gallic passion (for *books*, mind you, not even for you-know-what) couldn't have raised a hackle had it been injected intravenously. Granted, 1934 was hardly the most fertile of those lush years in that most astounding of decades for the beloved genre. Apart from the

May release of *The Black Cat* and later the extremely peripheral horror *The Man Who Reclaimed His Head*, which hit the screens on Christmas Eve, *Secret of the Chateau* was all she wrote for Universal that year.* Marketed as a legitimate thriller entry, the film offered precious little to recommend it.

More than a half-century later, and scratching as low as possible, we can at least take the following consolation. Since the tempest in this seedy little teapot concerns a hefty Gutenberg Bible, the statement "there is no little mention of the supernatural in this picture" has undeniable validity.

Skulking about Paris, ubiquitous and seemingly untouchable, is "Prahec," an evil genius of Moriarty-like reputation who has been accumulating rare volumes while dispatching all rival collectors for well over a decade. Prahec's nemesis is Chief Inspector Marotte of the Sûreté (Ferdinand Gottschalk), a man of dogged determination but not much else. Marotte has been trailing the arch-villain for ten years now and still hasn't the foggiest notion of what he looks like.

An eminent and extremely well-heeled

There was also Louis Friedlander's serial The Vanishing Shadow, *which managed to outshine either of these last two works, boasting a 12-week run. Of course, the creaky science-fiction chapterplay only tied up the projector for 14 to 16 minutes at a time.*

184

bibliophile, Le Duc de Poisse, has been murdered, so Marotte turns up at the auction of the nobleman's rare manuscripts and first editions, hoping to spot Prahec lurking amid the folios. As his wide-eyed scrutiny of the overdressed customers may serve to put a damper on sales, the *petit* detective is greeted by the celebrated rare book dealer Monsieur Fos (William Faversham) with all the enthusiasm of W.C. Fields at a temperance meeting. To make a long auction short, Marotte doesn't espy Prahec (then again, maybe he does; how would he know?), but he does notice Julie Varlaine (Claire Dodd), an erstwhile book thief (these are apparently a *centime* a dozen in Paris) and ex-jailbird. Julie's not a bad sort, really, but she's under the power of the shifty Lucien (the shifty Jack La Rue), who directs her to check out the *crème de la crème* of M. Le Duc's collection — an original Gutenberg Bible — which is closeted in the Château Aubazines.

Julie has already met one of Le Duc's heirs, a young chap named Paul (Clark Williams) who's a regular, down to earth sort of fellow; this we can tell at a glance, for he's the only man at the auction who's not wearing a cravat. As the song says, it only takes a moment, and Paul is half in love; he invites the young lady out to the château, ostensibly to look at his bibles. After giving the egotistical Marotte the slip and checking in with Lucien, Julie heads for the highlands, and courtesy of stock footage, we get a brief glimpse of an impressive manor house.

So much for appearances. The château is currently little more than a high-class flophouse, with people staying on for the most spurious of reasons, or even sneaking in to cadge a room on the sly. Not that there is any shortage of rooms; Paul allows as how there are 26 bedrooms, but only one bathroom — this oversight and the lack of electric light are chalked up to the late Le Duc's old-fashioned propensities. Inhabiting the manse as of late are Madame Rombiere (Helen Ware), Paul's aunt and heiress to half the book collection; Louis Bardou (DeWitt Jennings), the grumpy and imperious executor of the estate; Paul's

buddy, Armand (George E. Stone, in an extremely grating performance); Didi (Alice White), a shapely, semi-coherent blonde who will cheerfully shake the dust of the Château Aubazines from her high-heels if only someone will give her 2000 francs; and, of course, the servants. Chief among these last is Martin the butler (Osgood Perkins, who's the only cast member to take a whack at a French accent) and his nameless, morose wife (Cecile Elliott), who is also the cook.

The bible everyone's been lusting after has been locked in a trick cabinet (outfitted with a raucous burglar alarm) by the obnoxious Bardou. Neither the mysterious Prahec nor any of his competitors should so much as bother trying to break into the cabinet; there is, the notary-cum-executor announces proudly, but one key in the country, and he has got it. (Through the secret manipulations of most of the major characters, it will later be revealed that there are more keys circulating throughout the house than there are fleas on a sheepdog.) In addition, Bardou has had a counterfeit bible produced, and this will doubtless confound any thief who might have successfully breached the alarm. The real Gutenberg lies immediately below the fake and is concealed only by a hinged shelf; to the viewer, the protective niche seems about as undetectable as the "secret compartment" in a man's wallet. The fact that the lovely Julie can spot the facsimile book for what it is within six seconds doesn't seem to faze the glowing Bardou.

His late arrival forces Professor Raque ("He's a lovable old hunchback," smiles Julie) to miss out on all the exposition. Raque is given to understand that he will be able to buy the Gutenberg from Paul if he hangs around until morning, so he agrees to take one of those vacant rooms; he hasn't thought to bring pajamas or a toothbrush, but, hey, this *is* supposed to be France. Auntie Rombiere is upset by the idea of Paul's promise to sell — she maintains the bible will fetch a lot more than the Ministry of Art can afford to pay — and Bardou huffs and puffs over the notion of the heir actually thinking he has a right to any of the property he's inheriting. (The terms of M. Le Duc's will are

The overbearing Louis Bardou and his fake Gutenberg. Julie is incredulous, Paul is amused, and Armand seems fascinated by the fuzz atop Louis's dome. Pentagram Library.

peculiar. It seems that the executor can do whatever he pleases with the chattels until Paul steps in to claim them as his own, some five years down the line. At one point, Paul ungrammatically jokes, "I don't know whether I am the heir or getting it.")

The personable Paul tries his level best to win the lovely Julie's affection, but for the nonce the young lady's checkered past weighs heavily upon her ability to respond in kind. Nevertheless, with her blessing, Paul makes a sort of vow to abscond with the Gutenberg himself. His newly drafted long-range plans include selling the book to Raque, building a love nest with his lanky beauty, and devoting the rest of his life to perfecting the art of upside-down painting. (Don't ask.)

After a bit of comic byplay concerning that solitary bathroom and an example of far-

cical group choreography that would have done the Marx Brothers proud, a bell begins to ring. Yes, the château has an old tower, with an old bell, and an old legend, pithily recounted by old lady Rombiere: "Its ringing is always followed by a death!" Apparently none of the former doomed occupants of the house ever thought to remove the bell, but it's too late now. As best as they can, everybody settles in for the night. In the privacy of her room, Julie unpacks a rod and a flashlight from her overnight bag, but is interrupted by the sudden appearance of Lucien. *He* had rung the bell for a lark, and he's going to hang around to make sure that the young woman snatches the bible.

In rapid succession, the audience is treated to some atmospheric shadow-play (yes, there is a little, and one particularly lovely effect rendered by the moonlight through the latticework), a person or persons unknown, the now-open cabinet, the clanging alarm, a gunshot, and a scream. Daylight finds the pushy Bardou suitable only for pushing up daisies, and an armful of gendarmes combs the house and grounds. The ranking officer soon turns over the investigation to the newly arrived Marotte, whose first canny move is to inquire whether the murder weapon belongs to any of the assembled guests. He seems genuinely disappointed and not a little annoyed when no one 'fesses up. Herding everyone else into the breakfast room, Marotte detains Julie, who admits to having crafted a duplicate key from a wax impression. (So! In addition to her nightie and her toothbrush and her pistol and her torch, the devious young thing had a portable smelter stowed away in that remarkable valise of hers.)

Breakfast is but another brilliant ploy on the part of the famous policeman, who believes that innocent people chow down with vigor. Disconcerted at being unable to make an arrest based on the number of sausages consumed, Marotte launches into a series of offensive questions and is repaid with a number of inconclusive answers. For his next trick, the chief inspector then shows the fake bible to Professor Raque, who takes all of three seconds to blow the whistle. (Why would Bardou have gone to the trouble of having so obvious an imitation made?) The breakfast-room *mise-en-scène* is filled with sound and fury, but signifies zilch.

The day passes without further incident. But the night...

The bell sounds again; this time it's cranky, pig-headed Madame Rombiere who has shuffled off to Marseilles. As ignoring the advice of the resident authority is always tantamount to suicide in films like these, no one who bought a ticket to get in is surprised at the discovery of the old dear's artfully arranged cadaver. In an effort to forestall any more murders, Marotte ushers the crowd into the library. "I know who Prahec is," he lies. It soon becomes apparent to everyone that they're getting nowhere, but before they can actually

arrive, the bell rings again. Most of the men head north to the belfry; it is the beginning of the end of the affair.

Back in the library, Prahec reveals himself as the real bible has just been discovered inside a magnificent globe. Pontificating villainously — the only way he can be sure that Marotte will get all the details right — the master criminal is an inch from drilling the great detective when the bell sounds once more. Marotte leaps for the gun, a couple of bystanders belatedly lend a hand, and the legendary thief-murderer of Paris is unmasked. Prahec is Raque, who is Fos! (Remember Fos?)

Prahec is dragged off to the guillotine, Martin and the missus are looking at 30 years on Devil's Island (they were the fiend's accomplices and rung the bell from the kitchen, using a wire attached to the bell-rope), and Lucien will be away for a decade and a half. And Julie? Marriage with Paul: "It looks like life, Julie, for better or worse. I can't improve on that." His work here done, the magnanimous Marotte dons his hat and heads off to new adventure.

The word that springs to mind when considering *Secret of the Chateau* is "eclectic." Like a dish of chow mein, the movie is composed of a number of popular elements, each with its own flavor and appeal, which lose more than they gain by being mixed haphazardly. Skirting about the edges of numerous genres (farce, romantic comedy, whodunit, old dark house) without being rooted in any one of them deprives the film of a much-needed base. What the dish and the film both need is a dash of some recognizable spice. Like Didi's two overlong grunt and grab sessions with Bardou (she ends up with his toupee and his watch), *Chateau* gropes awkwardly, searching for a personality; like Marotte's eternal quest for Prahec, it fumbles around listlessly, looking for clues to its identity. Perhaps it was felt that the picture's grab-bag nature would attract a wider audience share than would any of its individual component parts. Much more likely, Albert DeMond and Harry Behn's disjointed screenplay was just the inevitable misfire amid a series of bullseyes.

The culmination of ten years' fumbling in the dark: The Great Marotte and Prahec, face to face. *PENTA-GRAM LIBRARY.*

Apart from a couple of sun-drenched exterior shots on the studio's eminently adaptable European backlot streets, *Chateau* is, well, château-bound. That there is no credited art director is a pity, because the mansion's sundry foyers and chambers are all solid, imposing, and well-appointed, as per Universal's standards at the time. There are no glass shots, but none are needed. Paul's mention of the large number of rooms evokes the image of a huge, warren-like structure which would be much more conducive to nocturnal prowling than would hangar-sized public areas.

Chief Inspector Marotte should be the glue that holds the whole thing together, but as delineated by Messrs. DeMond and Behn, the officious little official is hardly more than a swaggering incompetent. It's just possible that the character was initially modeled on Agatha Christie's Belgian egocentric, Hercule Poirot; Marotte's eloquent self-indulgence (he's forever referring to himself as "The Great Marotte" and so forth) is very much in keeping with the famed Poirot temperament. And there's more than a casual physical resemblance, as well. Had Jack Pierce affixed a handlebar mustache to diminutive Ferdinand Gottschalk, the busy character man would have been the spitting image of the renowned detective, right down to his egg-shaped head. The comparison grinds to a screeching halt, however, when one considers that *Secret of the Chateau*'s little sleuth achieves his greatest triumph through serendipity, just happening to be in the right place at the right time.

Other steals by the screenwriters include not-so-oblique references to Sherlock Holmes: That decade-long cat-and-mouse business to which both Marotte and Prahec allude at the film's unexciting climax is a direct lift from Conan Doyle. Marrying the assembled suspects to the available furniture and confounding the villain into coming clean are, of course, major parts of Charlie Chan's *modus operandi*. (Even Marotte's lumpy fedora seems the twin of the lid that was gracing Warner Oland's head over on the Fox lot.) The absurd, ersatz scientific tenets the chief inspector tosses around (the nonsense about one's appetite, a comment about Prahec's drawing the blood from his own busy brain, etc.) are minor-league takes on that other great French scientific detective, Poe's C. Auguste Dupin. Leaving nothing to their possible creativity, *j'accuse* DeMond and Behn of moving the bountiful globe from Nero Wolfe's office to the château library in time for the denouement. Boy, talk about chow mein!

Despite his weighty Germanic moniker, Ferdinand Gottschalk was British-born. In his mid-sixties at the time of the filming, the perennial supporting actor was constantly in demand and was usually involved in productions whose size and scope (1932's *Grand Hotel*, or *Les Misérables*, 1935) made *Chateau* seem even more the puff piece than it was. He may never have seen his unwieldy name above the title (even here, where he's supposed to be the hero of the piece, he's billed eighth), but the little man with the sad eyes stole many a scene from much bigger names and far bulkier actors.

He's greatly hampered, though, by his character's ineptly drawn personality. However the chief inspector may have been pictured in Lawrence Blochman's original story, the screenplay has Marotte basically playing the fool. For every credible step forward he takes, the script drags him backwards moments later. When the commissioner at the Bardou investigation (Alphonse Ethier) admits to him, "I've heard of you," Marotte smugly replies, "Everyone has." That this is manifestly not the case has already been shown; in an earlier scene, Julie

escapes from his grasp by informing passersby that the detective is Prahec — and that name does draw a crowd!

Recognition apart, the Sûreté chief is made to carry some pretty wide-ranging responsibilities on his narrow shoulders. Scarcely have the gendarmes muscled Prahec off-screen when the pompous Marotte has him convicted and condemned to decapitation! Likewise, without benefit of a trial, Martin, Mrs. Martin, and the luckless Lucien are in for extravagantly heavy sentences. Either the French justice system operates on a completely autonomous plane or the crackerjack team of DeMond and Behn have chosen to overlook the differences existing among an arresting officer, a jury of one's peers, and a presiding magistrate.

Marotte has Julie in Catch-22 type circumstances, and Paul's puppy-like devotion acts as the much-needed catalyst to get her back on the road to happiness. Julie was jailed for six months for a theft which she did not commit; since then, she has been blackmailed by Lucien. Yet Marotte acknowledges that Julie might well have been innocent; the Sûreté official had had her imprisoned just so he could see what would happen with the girl out of circulation! This kind of an announcement is a two-edged sword: For all his posturing about justice and honor, the Great Marotte is revealed to be self-serving and heartless, while Julie's exoneration removes any doubt the audience may have had about her ultimately getting together with good old Paul. (Of course, she does snatch an invaluable original Molière, but the girl's under a lot of pressure.)

Top-billed Claire Dodd is quite a departure from the typical genre female lead. Tall, lovely, and without a doubt a force to be reckoned with, she gives Julie's inner struggles the touch they deserve. Universal borrowed Dodd from Warner Bros. for *Secret of the Chateau*; perhaps resident horror heroine Gloria Stuart had felt that the previous year's *Blue Room* had held quite enough secrets for her, thank you. The tall actress, who looks like she could twist Ferdinand Gottschalk into a pretzel, keeps her character tearless and treacle-free. This trait was probably due to her Warners experience, where the female leads found it difficult to collapse into tears and avoid being machine-gunned at the same time. Four years later, with scarcely any change at all, Claire as Julie became Claire as Julia in another tale of mystery, murders, secret caches, and books: MGM's *Fast Company* (1938). It's a shame that Universal would wait until the turn of the decade before recalling Dodd to meet Abbott and Costello (*in the Navy*), Don Winslow (*of the Navy*) and *The Mad Doctor of Market Street* (who had nautical problems of his own.)

Neither Clark Williams nor William Faversham made much of a mark in movieland. Faversham had been a stage actor long before he was called upon to wear the hair and the hunch of Professor Raque, and apart from a handful of silent features (like Paramount's *The Silver King* in 1919), *Chateau* seems to be his only role of consequence. His few lines as Fos are unremarkable, his woolly hairpieces as Raque are unlikely; and for a hunchback, Raque has the best posture I've ever seen. There's a perverse humor in the business about the frequent and enthusiastic death-knell coming from the tower; it's so screwily ironic that I have to concede its beauty to DeMond and Behn. For all the ominous clanging of that damned bell, virtually the only person who never goes near the bell-rope is the heavy, who is made up as a hunchback!

Young Williams is everything the juvenile lead should be — handsome, forthright, penniless — and more: Never once does he whine, pout, posture, or threaten (though DeWitt Jennings' Bardou surely could have stood a good belt in *la bouche*). Available evidence indicates that Williams shot his load at Universal City within the first six months of 1935: *Chateau* went out in January, the young actor then appeared opposite Henry Hull in *Transient Lady* (released in March), and May saw him bringing up the rear (way *behind* Hull) in *WereWolf of London*. After a couple of bits a year or two later, the personable Williams seems to have vanished entirely from the silver screen.

George E. Stone never played a part that wasn't recognizably George E. Stone. One of a select cadre of wry, weasely types, the actor was at his busiest during the early thirties, when there were zillions of bowler-hatted syndicate czars and crime kingpins whose violent ends were precipitated by the cowardly snitches and squeals of Stone, or of someone like him. His Armand may be no more French than anyone else in *Chateau*, but his low-comedy relief makes one wish that Prahec were less discriminate in his choice of victims.

Like Claire Dodd, Alice White was on loan to Universal here, and like George E. Stone, she was much more at home in the back streets of Warners' underworld. An agreeable if narrowly typed comic actress, White contributes some patented dumb-blonde/gold-digger shtick, but without the attendant hard-as-nails demeanor that most of her stylistic colleagues typically brought with them. Vastly less irritating than Stone's Armand, her Didi could have provided a couple of genuine chuckles if there had been more tension from which one had need of respite, and if she had not been merely one of a veritable crowd of comic-relief types (including the lugubrious Martin, the catty Mme. Rombiere, and the bombastic M. Bardou).

Frank Reicher was, of course, in every second movie ever made, and a couple of lines of appreciation for the ubiquitous character man can be found in this book's essay on *Mystery of the White Room*. Alphonz Ethier, espied herein as the highly unremarkable commissioner of police, had had one moment of genre glory in the little known, totally silent, and completely lost *A Message from Mars* (1921). Based on a morality play by Richard Gathoney, the Metro feature had Ethier — the messenger from Mars — clucking at man's injustice to man to Leonard Mudie, the one venerable supporting actor who could be spotted in every picture Reicher hadn't made.

Secret of the Chateau is an amusing little picture which would probably have left a more favorable impression had it not been made smack-dab in the middle of Universal's first blood-and-thunder phase. When compared with the *frisson* attained by scores of the perambulating dead, near-dead or undead, the

The great Marotte in action, with just about every still-breathing cast member marveling at his technique. *AUTHOR'S COLLECTION.*

thrill of an old-fashioned murder-for-profit is admittedly bland. The *Motion Picture Herald* cued potential exhibitors that:

> Highly theatricalized mystery motivates everything. As is necessary, however, the companionate [sic] elements of romance, drama, comedy, thrill and suspense have their sustaining function, while it makes no attempts at pretentiousness.

If *Chateau*'s mystery had only been more supernaturally oriented (à la …*the Blue Room*), or even more perversely novel or picturesque (à la …*the French Police*), the resultant film would certainly have proven itself a "secret" well worth sharing.

Secret of the Chateau

Released December 3, 1934; 68 minutes
Cast: Claire Dodd (Julie Verlaine);

Osgood Perkins (Martin); Alice White (Didi); Clark Williams (Paul); Ferdinand Gottschalk (Chief Inspector Marotte); George E. Stone (Armand); Jack LaRue (Lucien); William Faversham (M. Fos/Raque/Prahec); DeWitt Jennings (Louis Bardou); Helen Ware (Mme. Rombiere); Alphonz Ethier (Commissioner); Frank Reicher (Auctioneer); Olaf Hytten (LaFarge); Paul Nicholson (Domme); Cecile Elliott (Cook); Tony Merlo (Arthur); Frank Thornton (George)

Credits: Producer — Lou Ostrow; Director — Richard Thorpe; Screenplay — Albert DeMond and Harry Behn; Original Story — Lawrence G. Blochman; Additional Dialogue — Llewellyn Hughes; Photographer — Robert Planck; Film Editor — Harry Marker; Continuity — Harry Behn; Assistant Director — Ralph Berger; Sound — John A. Stransky, Jr. An L.L. Ostrow Production

THE MAN WHO
RECLAIMED HIS HEAD (1934)

Being production chief of a major Hollywood studio is no bed of roses, even when you get the job through the most blatant form of nepotism. Junior Laemmle, for example, had lots more on his mind than just girls, horses, and manicures. He had to cultivate product by taking options on novels, plays, and the like, by lighting a fire under the scenario department, and by keeping abreast of the latest rage or most irresistible fad. Once Junior felt a property had potential, he had to consider the nuts and bolts: budget, cast and crew, sets and properties, and incidentals (royalties, music, etc.). If he concluded that a film would have sufficient appeal (i.e., would make a profit), was economically feasible (i.e., could be constructed without breaking the bank), and didn't affront any of the studio's markets, either actual or potential, then it would receive the green light. Only then Junior could get back to his girls, horses, and manicures.

One of the properties that fell into his lap was a middling play about pacifism, *The Man Who Reclaimed His Head*, which had closed within a month of opening on Broadway in September 1932. Contemporary reviews lauded the leads (Claude Rains and Jean Arthur) but damned the drama with faint praise. Although

the horrors of the trenches at Verdun and elsewhere hadn't faded from the minds and passions of the public, more than enough theatergoers decided to pass on Jean Bart's moralistic tub-thumping to drive the work off the boards and onto Junior's desk. It would be dangerous to attempt to reconstruct what went on in Junior's mind while he perused the property (per several of the Universal survivors interviewed by Tom Weaver, it wouldn't be so much dangerous as futile), but that title must have leapt from the page and hit him right between the eyes.

Whether Junior actually read anything beyond the title is anybody's guess, but the resultant film was niche-marketed along the lines of that other great pacifistic drama, *The Black Cat*.

The story unfolds within a framing device: During the Great War, Paul Verin (Claude Rains) marches into his attorney's office bearing his little girl and a portmanteau. The bag merits some scrutiny, as it will prove to contain more than the young writer's collected works and a change of clothes for his daughter.

Verin relates how he and his wife, Adele (Joan Bennett) had enjoyed a happy (albeit desperately poor) home life until the arrival of

The calm before the storm: Paul and Adele share a moment of joy despite their poverty. Little Linette (the ghastly Baby Jane Quigley) is elsewhere. *AUTHOR'S COLLECTION.*

Henri Dumont (Lionel Atwill), a socially conscious newspaper publisher. In flashback, we see Dumont hire Verin to ghost-write some pacifistic essays for publication. Not content merely to usurp the writer's thoughts for himself, Dumont puts the moves on Adele. In his spare time, the callous publisher collaborates with warmongers and helps precipitate (at least indirectly) the assassination of Archduke Ferdinand and the Great War. To facilitate his making time with Mrs. Verin, he sees to it that her husband is drafted and sent to the front.

Verin tells his attorney (Henry O'Neill) that news of this personal treachery reached his ears, and he headed home. There he discovered Dumont pressing his advantage, and with the aid of his army-issue bayonet, the distraught writer had his biblical justice in mind. All eyes

turn toward that bag, but as Verin is escorted away by the constabulary, he is comforted by the thought that Adele is still his own, true bride, and that his legal defense is assured.

Attaining and maintaining peace in the world has been among mankind's most fervent dreams since the day after Cain killed Abel with the leg of a table. Thirties pacifism wasn't much different from the current brand, but was much more frequently the subject of heated debate. Not only were the memories of the Great War still painfully fresh, but there were (per the cliché) storm clouds gathering over Europe once again. Anyone who wasn't a hawk or a dove was essentially an isolationist who sought the national peace by ignoring the international unrest.

The Man Who Reclaimed His Head was

largely typical of the artistic take on the world situation in the early part of the decade. Playwright Jean Bart (the *nom de plume* of social activist Marie Antoinette Sarlabous) had grounded her pacifistic themes amid the ongoing chaos of the Great War and presumably had touched enough of a nerve to influence one of Junior's staff to pass the now-available work on for consideration. Sadly, what has survived on the screen is not so much a provocative study of the monumental causes and effects of global warfare, but rather an array of naïve positions and outdated solutions.

Claude Rains had Paramount's *Crime Without Passion* under his belt by the time *The Man Who Reclaimed His Head* was released, but his Paul Verin still verges on the simplistic. The actor may have insisted on following closely his Broadway interpretation, or he may have been reluctant to discard stage devices in favor of screen technique, or he may have surrendered without argument to the starkly simple delineation found in the screenplay itself. Rains' performance as the sadistic lawyer in the Paramount piece was far more multifaceted and credible than was his portrayal in *Head*. As Ben Hecht and Charles MacArthur wrote, produced, *and* directed *Crime Without Passion*, the unity of vision which they brought to the film may have been just the tonic that cinematic journeyman Rains needed.

No one but no one has ever had such a black and white world view as Rains' Verin. Blind to his wife's heartache over their poverty, blind to his patron's Machiavellian maneuvers, blind (apparently) to evil in the world, unrest in his household, and failure in his future, the idealistic writer plays right into the hands of the forces of evil. It strains credulity that this man, who seemingly cannot recognize the wolf at his own doorstep, would in fact be a keen and perceptive seer whose ruminations garner widespread acclaim.

Greeting the most disastrous of news and events with a fatalistic shrug and a philosophical axiom, Verin personifies the sigh of resignation which passed for pacifism in the eyes of many citizens in the 1930s. If Verin does anything other than write about peace, he talks about peace, and what traps the picture in the early Depression Era (rather than in the earlier time-frame depicted onscreen) is Rains' mouthing Bart's guileless prose as if it were dogmatic and irrefutable.

Rains cannot be faulted for the stasis of the story, which pigeonholes the picture as a gabby panorama of ideological exchanges. While a real-life total pacifist would supposedly meet even the most personal of threats with calm resolve, Verin makes it clear that pacifism may be the remedy for all the world's ills, but on the home-front, he much prefers the bayonet. The behavioral opposites of the framing scenes and the picture at large are quite chilling in themselves; it is almost as if Rains, screenwriters Bart and Ornitz, and director Edward Ludwig are disavowing moderation of any type and are espousing extremism as the only solution. The really depressing implication is that the heralded voice of sanity in a world gone mad is himself quite capable of mindless violence.

The usual tampering with characters occurred during the play's transition to the screen, and Rains' character, both deformed and infirm in the play, lost his physical edge when the screenplay divested him of both handicaps. Still, as Rains' only other experience at Universal had involved stifling bandages and an overwhelming need for modesty (a quality genetically denied an actor), he must have rejoiced that in the screen adaptation he'd be allowed to wallow amid the stodgy lines unencumbered by makeup or padding.

The fact that Jean Bart was partly responsible for the screen treatment doubtless accounts for the s-l-o-w fashion in which the picture unreels. With the essence of the plot's action able to be succinctly outlined in a couple of hundred words, the process of defining the *dramatis personae* takes up most of the running time. Bart may well have felt that the 80-minute movie had sacrificed much of the impact of the 2-hour-plus legitimate drama, but the picture could well stand an additional judicious pruning. The melodrama would be the longest of the studio's "shockers" to that time, and it would remain for Rains's second

The moment of truth, as Paul Verin returns from the wars to claim what is rightfully his. PENTAGRAM LIBRARY.

contractual picture, *Mystery of Edwin Drood,* to set the new record.

Lionel Atwill is less contrived here than he is customarily (at Universal, at any rate). Sidelong glances, telling tics, and underplayed reactions notwithstanding, Atwill's Henri Dumont seems the very picture of the well-intentioned patron, whose only motive in helping the financially challenged Verin is his concern for the promulgation of the antiwar message. Bart's underlying message — that living for profit rather than living for love is the cause of all injustice — is hammered at time and again, and Dumont is the avatar of such self-serving betrayal. Scenes of Atwill waxing in high conspiratorial dudgeon with such stalwarts as Edward Van Sloan and such veteran

plotters as Jameson Thomas were designed to raise Cain with the war-weary male viewers, while the actor's unwelcome attention towards Adele was all the treachery the ladies in the audience could stand.

The "horror" overtone that attracted Junior's attention (I'm hypothesizing here) — the head in the portmanteau — is the ghoulish but cute *raison d'être* for the title. As none of the ticket-buyers ever gets a gander inside the valise, the first and only eyeful, accorded attorney De Marnay, is the film's culminating moment; thence, there's nowhere to go but down. Far from maintaining the suspense, the attorney's subsequent glances askew evoke quite the opposite response.

The Realart one-sheet of *The Man Who*

Reclaimed His Head was one of the first "horror" film posters I ever bought. Replete with swirling skulls and a brunette Joan Bennett flashing some thigh, it was in and out of my collection long before I ever saw the movie itself. Needless to say, when I did get a shot at it, the film's idealistic theme was wasted on me at first; I kept waiting for all those skulls. (I was a little young for thighs in those days.)

I still don't know just who would have appreciated the picture when it was released originally; there hadn't been enough interested people in the greater New York area to keep the play open for more than a month. Then as now, pacifism had its zealous adherents, but whether the pro-peace contingency pushed the film into the black, or whether the horror fans helped out until word of mouth warned them off, or whether the hybrid production ever saw black ink at all, I've been unable to find out. *The Man Who Reclaimed His Head* was a noble failure which sought to elicit a passionate plea for sanity by pitching a brief and dramatically ineffectual portrayal of madness. Neither a competent piece of propaganda (it tries too hard) nor a valid horror picture (it tries not at all), the film does present rather ingenuous views from simpler times on how a few persons came to discover that personal contentment is a very real part of peace in the world.

The Man Who Reclaimed His Head

Released December 24, 1934; 82 minutes

Cast: Claude Rains (Paul Verin); Joan Bennett (Adele Verin); Lionel Atwill (Henri Dumont); Baby Jane Quigley (Linette Verin); Henry O'Neill (Fernand DeMarnay); Henry Armetta (Laurent); Wallace Ford (Curly); Lawrence Grant (Marchand); William B. Davidson (Charlus); Gilbert Emery (His Excellency); Ferdinand Gottschalk (Baron); Hugh O'Connell (Danglas); Rollo Lloyd (Jean, the Butler); Valerie Hobson (Mimi, the Carnival Girl); Bessie Barriscale (Louise, the Maid); G.P. Huntley (Pierre); Doris Lloyd (LuLu); Noel Francis (Chon-Chon); Carol Coombe (Clerk); Phyllis Brooks (Secretary); Walter Walker, Edward Martindel, Craufurd Kent, C. Montague Shaw (Dignitaries); Purnell Pratt, Jameson Thomas, Edward Van Sloan (Munitions Board Directors); Judith Wood (Margot); James Donlan (Man in Theater Box); Lloyd Hughes (Andre); Bryant Washburn, Sr. (Antoine); Boyd Irwin (Petty Officer); Anderson Lawler (Jack); Will Stanton (Drunken Soldier); George Davis (Truck Driver); Lionel Belmore (Train Conductor); Emerson Treacy (French Student/Attached Pacifist); John Rutherford, Hyram Hoover, Lee Phelps (Soldiers); Rudy Cameron (Maitre d'); Norman Ainsley (Steward); Russ Powell (Station Master); Harry Cording (Mechanic); Lilyan Irene (Shopper); William Ruhl (Her Husband); Rolfe Sedan (Waiter); Ben Hendricks (Chauffeur); Maurice Murphy (Leon); William Gould (Man); Carl Stockdale (Tradesman); Tom Ricketts, Josef Swickard, William West, Colin Kenny (Citizens); Ted Billings (Newsboy); Russ Clark (French Truck Driver); William Worthington (Attendant); Nell Craig, Grace Cunard (Women); Wilfred North (Man); John Ince (Speaker); Margaret Mann (Granny)

Credits: Producer — Carl Laemmle, Jr.; Executive Producer — F.R. Mastroly; Director — Edward Ludwig; Associate Producer — Henry Henigson; Screenplay — Jean Bart (Marie Antoinette Sarlabous) and Samuel Ornitz; Additional Dialogue — Barry Trivers; Director of Photography — Merritt Gerstad; Assistant Cameraman — Paul Hill; Process Photography — John P. Fulton; Musical Director — Heinz Roemheld; Art Director — Albert S. D'Agostino; Film Editor — Murray Seldeen; Supervising Editor — Maurice Pivar; Recording Engineer — Gilbert Kurland; Assistant Directors — W.J. Reiter and Fred Frank; Wardrobe — Vera West

LIFE RETURNS (1935)

A cheap smirk could probably be had by calling *Life Returns* Universal's premier *horrible* picture, but I do have my pride and wouldn't dream of sinking that low.

Neither the product of classic literature nor the result of someone's feverish imagination, *Life Returns* is unique among its celluloid contemporaries. The scenario is based on the real-life experiments of a Doctor Robert Cornish, who not only claimed to have discovered a process whereby life could indeed be returned to the breathing-impaired, but allowed his eager friends and supporters to film his revivification of an allegedly defunct dog. That these claims and experiments were all bandied about in the renowned intellectual climate of Southern California should in no way prejudice one against their gravity or portent. And, while it may not come as a surprise that Cornish's findings were quickly dismissed as spurious and his technique denounced as preposterously ineffectual, his Warhol-given right to a few minutes of celebrity cannot be denied.

Émigré filmmaker Eugen Frenke seized upon Cornish while the young doctor was still flashing in the pan, and somehow convinced Junior Laemmle that there was money to be made by shooting some story or another around that "medical" footage featuring the canine cadaver, using inexpensive contract players. It's only a guess that Cornish provided the footage at little or no cost and also agreed to bring his life-restoring expertise to the film in exchange for the invaluable publicity his experiments would receive and, most likely, a piece of the action. Frenke and a James Hogan concocted the original story (adapted for the screen by two other sinners), and the resultant plot was awkward and frustrating.

Cornish, it came to pass, would play a scientist named Cornish, but the part of the Great Man, tagged Kendrick in the frame, would be enacted by Onslow Stevens. Only a professional actor could be expected to carry off the incredible array of emotions which would mirror the ups and downs, the triumphs and disappointments associated with such a monumental discovery. Makes sense on paper.

At any rate, Kendrick, Louise Stone (Lois Wilson) and Cornish have just graduated from medical school, and while they share an interest in concocting a serum which will revive the dead, they split up: Kendrick is off to Arnold Laboratories, and his friends make for some other nameless but really dedicated place. Once this fact has been established, headache-inducing montages of Bunsen burners, hamsters, and test tubes alternate with newspaper articles detailing Kendrick's discovery of a "life-giving fluid" and his marriage to a nameless socialite

Doctors Cornish, Stone and Kendrick are all smiles in anticipation of the conquest of death, and big bucks. The role of Dr. Cornish's sweater is played by Charles Gemora. *AUTHOR'S COLLECTION.*

(Valerie Hobson). Time passes. The little couple becomes a trio, when Danny (George Breakston, sooner or later) arrives.

Things begin to go awry. Mr. Arnold despairs of ever getting his money's worth from the loopy scientist, admitting "I'm beginning to think he's entirely hopeless." When advised that he ought to be more practical, Kendrick stares off into space and whimpers, "Practical? Why, nothing more practical has ever been thought of since the beginning of time... To bring the dead back to life..." Since the boss had had something like pig bristle brushes in mind, this pretty much tears it at Arnold Research.

As the musical score tugs at one's heart, the profoundly disappointed Kendrick shuffles on home, where his private medical practice has been steadily going down the toilet. Mrs.

K sticks her head in the door to heave a couple of half-hearted sighs at her husband: "John, I understand you," she fibs, "but why can't you be a little more practical?" While a clientele consisting entirely of hypochondriacs and lunatics should be no great loss ordinarily, it does appear to be the family's only source of income. A minuscule notice in the newspaper alerts anyone who cares that Kendrick is to "Expound His Fantastic 'Lazarus' Theory Before the Medical Board." And expound he does; standing in the operating theater set from *Dracula*, he goes on semi-coherently for a couple of minutes, before really warming to the crowd:

> Now, laugh if you must. Columbus [*they laugh*], Galileo, and the wonderful Madame Curie, whose radium discovery made that

Surrounded by all sorts of scientific-looking stuff is Dr. Kendrick (Onslow Stevens); draped around his neck is Mrs. Kendrick (Valerie Hobson), who knows enough to die young and escape from *Life Returns* by the third reel. AUTHOR'S COLLECTION.

so-called incurable disease a lesser evil, were all laughed at. I say to you here and now, when I complete my experiments, I shall be able to bring the dead back to life. [*LOTS of muttering.*]

Exiting dramatically, Kendrick is greeted by Dr. Stone, who offers him a chance at getting back together with Dr. Cornish and herself. "We're your friends. We can help you," she promises. The disillusioned doctor is having none of it.

Soon the montages return and the camera begins to squander a good bit of its budgeted raw stock following Kendrick as he stares off into space, wanders aimlessly about the dime store sets, or just lies there, obviously on a higher plane than the rest of us. In a wild stab at adding some human interest to the pro-

ceedings, the story has Mrs. Kendrick die of some damn thing or another (probably spite) halfway through, but even this fails to rouse her husband.

Nor can the pathetic, attention-seeking fumblings of Danny shake the brilliant but preoccupied scientist from his stupor. Kendrick cannot, for example, bring himself to accept a job running an elevator ("But it's a *laboratory* elevator," Danny explains, hopefully.) It takes the death of Scooter, his son's faithful canine companion and confidant, and an impassioned verbal harangue by Danny to move the lethargic genius to action, which sets the stage for the clips of the dynamic Cornish *tour de force*. Not only is the dog restored to life, but Kendrick himself experiences some kind of spiritual rebirth, and we are given to understand that, from here on in, he will be a better husband (oops, too late!), father, and scientist.

Now the genuine Cornish "operation," meant to be both the dramatic reversal which vindicates Kendrick's dysfunctional behavior and also a jaw-dropping *coup de théâtre*, disappoints in more ways than one. The footage hadn't been photographed by professionals or shot under anything like optimum circumstances and fails even to match the cheesy visual standards of the rest of the film. Much more distressing, though, is its logical shortfall. When Kendrick, adrenaline surging, hefts the pooch's carcass and hies for the hospital, the natural expectation is that the erstwhile zombie himself is going to do something that no other man on earth can do. However, as a grainy Cornish is obviously the head honcho in the "medical" procedure which drags Scooter's ringer back from eternity, Kendrick's role is reduced to standing on the sidelines and commenting on the goings-on.

The cheek of all this is breathtaking. We are asked to settle for Kendrick's schlepping the late Scooter cross town and merely handing him over to Cornish as the film's much needed catharsis. (It does earn him a gratuitous "You're the swellest dad in the world!" from his bug-eyed but grateful son.) Even if one were disposed to give Kendrick any of the credit he angles for while Cornish is giving the pooch mouth-to-mouth, this is a textbook example of too little and too late. As the music swells, the visionary intones, "Dr. Cornish is the Man of the Hour; Dr. Stone and I are merely contributors to his fulfillment." Again, what's all this "I" stuff? The film has made it abundantly clear that Kendrick hasn't even seen the other doctors for more than 30 seconds in the past ten years.

Life Returns couldn't possibly have been regarded as an important production by anyone. Virtually none of the movie's technical staff had had any experience whatsoever with the Universal horror product, save for Robert Planck, who had photographed *Secret of the Chateau* the year before. Still, as it's doubtful that Junior ever considered Frenke's picture as anything other than a low-budget exploita-

tion effort (à la Dwain Esper), this certainly didn't matter. The acting apart, the film has a wretched, hang-dog look which flat lighting and simplistic direction do nothing to dispel.

Valerie Hobson gives nowhere near her best shot as Kendrick's better half, and boy, is that ever understandable; I don't think she has 20 lines in the whole picture. The lovely actress must have been grateful to discover that, per the script, Mrs. Kendrick would expire long before anyone's life-restoring processes could be perfected. As Count Dracula had pronounced, "There are far worse things awaiting man than death," and her having had to stick around until the final reel of *Life Returns* might very well have been one of them. Thankfully, the year brought Miss Hobson other, more satisfying projects and a number of worthier genre roles for which she is still warmly remembered.

It's fortunate that Onslow Stevens could also look forward to a brighter future, both in and out of the horror field. Never the stuff of which leading men were made, Stevens nonetheless might subsequently have seen his movie career restricted to selling tickets or popcorn, had his portrayal of Kendrick received more extensive press. Admittedly, it's impossible at this late date to determine whether Stevens' non-performance was an act of professional defiance, the result of amateurish character delineation and inept direction (either in the original treatment or in Arthur Horman and John Goodrich's screenplay), or merely a case of the actor letting the punishment fit the crime. No matter which might have been true, never has a character meant to represent so fierce a genius been enacted in so totally vapid and listless a fashion.

I honestly think that Cornish himself didn't make the film except for the canned footage from Berkeley. The "Cornish" who participates in odd moments of the framing device — the big cafeteria scene, the dramatic parting of the ways on mortarboard day, the little insert with Dr. Stone — might well be one of Universal's numerous uncredited contract players. I ran the tape back twice (and was *that* ever a treat) to check on the angles and found that the figure is never seen head-on: He's shot only in profile or from a three-quarter back view, or is shrouded in shadows. The real-life doctor may have been busy elsewhere, trying to snatch gerbils from Judgment Day, or he may have felt that appearing in a movie (especially *this* movie) might have compromised his professional standing. Wherever he may be, I salute the spirit of Dr. Cornish; *Life Returns* really wasn't his fault.

It's ironic that the theme of the film, so often bandied about in genuine horror and science-fiction pictures, is so pitifully mistreated as to make the whole enterprise about as interesting as a brick in a brickyard. Had the frame been constructed with ingenuity; had the dialogue been less risible and its delivery less ludicrous (his hair fetchingly arranged à la Albert Einstein, Stevens is directed to stand in a courtroom setting and declaim, "I'll do it some day; I'll bring the dead back to life!" while holding his index finger, cocked skyward next to his head); had Frenke allowed his photographer greater play with low-key lighting — all this might have resulted, if not in a *good* film, at least in a better one than exists now. For the love of Mike, Cornish was convinced he could bring the dead back to life. He was a *real-life mad scientist*!

There's little point in carrying on. Per the AFI Catalog:

> Universal pulled the film from release after a preview, and declared the film to be a "freak picture, not suitable for the regular Universal program," although the studio had invested approximately $40,000 in the production. Despite this announcement,

Universal did release the film for a special road show run.

Life Returns was such a worthless commodity that Universal passed on reissuing the movie in 1938 and sold it outright to Scienart Pictures, which subsequently watched *its* investment go straight down the bunghole.

With less genre interest and fewer professional touches than the *Francis, the Talking Mule* series, *Life Returns* is a cheerless obscurity better left lying fallow in an unmarked grave.

Life Returns

Released January 2, 1935; 60 minutes

Cast: Onslow Stevens (Dr. John Kendrick); Robert Cornish (Dr. Robert Cornish); Valerie Hobson (Mrs. Mary Kendrick); Lois Wilson (Dr. Louise Stone); George Breakston (Danny Kendrick); Frank Reicher (Dr. James); Stanley Fields (Dog Catcher); Lois January (Nurse); Richard Carle (A.K. Arnold); Dean Benton (Intern); Richard Quine (Mickey); Maidel Turner (Mrs. Vandergriff); Otis Harlan (Dr. Henderson); George MacQuarrie (Judge); with Mario Margutti, Ralph Celmer, William Black, Roderic Krider (Cornish's staff)

Credits: Producer — Lou Ostrow; Director — Eugen Frenke; Screenplay — Arthur Horman and John F. Goodrich; Original Story — Eugen Frenke; Photographer — Robert Planck; Art Director — Ralph Berger; Film Editor — Harry Marker; Sound Recording — Richard Tyler; Dialogue — Mary McCarthy and L. Wolfe Gilbert; Music — Oliver Wallace and Clifford Vaughan

MYSTERY OF EDWIN DROOD (1935)

A real appreciation of Universal's *Mystery of Edwin Drood* almost requires that one view literature as an expression of the human soul and a perennially enjoyable form of entertainment. In this day and age, when the great unwashed find fulfillment in remote control channel-surfing, this may not be as easy as it seems.

People read a hell of a lot in the days before television and movies. More to the point, they actually discussed what they read and brought strong opinions to those discussions. Authors toured the hinterlands, offering dramatic readings from their works, answering questions, and participating in debates about their strengths and weaknesses. One of the most avidly touring authors who ever lived was Charles Dickens, who probably made more money gabbing about the books he wrote than he did from their being published in the first place. In addition to spending almost a decade on the circuit throughout the English provinces, the prolific author visited the United States (twice), Italy, and Switzerland.

A good number of contemporary literary critics found Dickens needlessly verbose, however, contending that the British novelist would never settle for a word when a sentence would do, or content himself with a paragraph when a chapter could be had for little extra effort.

While Dickens certainly didn't have a monopoly on long-windedness, one has only to try to wrestle *Bleak House* to a draw to appreciate the sentiments of those critics.

Dickens died before finishing *The Mystery of Edwin Drood*, a fruity novel touching on race relations, unrequited love, drug addiction, ecclesiastical sanctimony, societal intolerance, personal hypocrisy, and presumed foul play. Although an uneven work whose narrative technique a strong minority considered more a stylistic throwback than an artistic advance, the book aroused tremendous interest, not only for its potpourri of melodramatic interludes, but also because of the author's death, a regrettable but highly satisfactory move where publicity was concerned. Starting with H. Morford and his *John Jasper's Secret* (1871–72), dozens of would-be successors to the now-vacant throne published their "continuations" to solve the enigma of the eponymous character's disappearance.

It was within this framework of avid fascination that a famed group of literati gathered in Covent Garden early in 1914. The biggest men of letters (including George Bernard Shaw) held a mock trial — replete with prosecution, defense, and any number of "witnesses" — in which the officious Gilbert K. Chesterton et al. arrived at the ultimate dispo-

As with *Bride of Frankenstein*, a superfluous definite article. RONALD V. BORST/HOLLYWOOD MOVIE POSTERS.

sition of this mystery of Edwin Drood. The verdict made headlines internationally and prompted further discussion of Dickens' last work.

After a hiatus of some three or four decades, several more "continuations" appeared, including one in Forsyte's excellent study, *The Decoding of Edwin Drood*. A few years later, utilizing a gimmick reminiscent of schlockmeister William Castle (remember *Mr. Sardonicus*?), the smash musical adaptation of *The Mystery of Edwin Drood* on Broadway "solved" the mystery by drawing upon alternative endings, supposedly chosen by the audience.

As early as 1909, the infant British film industry seized on the work, and Gaumont Films released a two-reel adaptation of *The Mystery of Edwin Drood*. There is no record of how the film ended. Other of the author's novels were similarly impressed into service for the silent screen, and probably not only because the author had died in 1870, taking with him any and all annoying demands for royalties. (During a visit to the United States back in 1842, Dickens had infuriated the publishing industry by lobbying for recognition of international copyrights. This controversial issue still hadn't been resolved by the time of the novelist's demise.)

Deemed more popular and playable than the equally inexpensive Shakespeare, Dickens would doubtless have been more pleased with MGM's *David Copperfield* or *A Tale of Two Cities* than the Bard might have been with Warner Brothers' *A Midsummer Night's Dream*. As the later of these two English giants wrote in prose, dealt (for the most part) with contemporary issues, and offered characters who were colorful, recognizable types, film adaptations of *his* body of work were generally easier and more faithful. Standing sets were redressed without much trouble, and any number of Tinseltown's most versatile secondary cast members could be spotted traipsing through backlot reproductions of Dickensian English streets.

Universal still hadn't released its prestige production of *Great Expectations* when *Drood* began shooting, and that may have been just as well. Helmed by Stuart Walker (who must have been considered the studio's Dickens man, as he was also assigned to *Drood*), the earlier film was concocted to showcase the gruff talents of Henry Hull as Magwitch. The Laemmles harbored great expectations for the picture, but were disappointed with the receipts; taken together with the popular indifference to the critically acclaimed *Drood*, the studio's brief flirtation with Mr. Dickens ended quickly, allowing MGM to woo the shade of the English novelist and win big with dual blockbusters of 1935.

As no one at Universal had thought to read those murky English tea leaves at the outset, both *Expectations* and *Drood* were approached with vigor and optimism. Good old John L. Balderston put in his oar once again on the latter assignment, and together with Gladys Unger, did an excellent job at adapting for the screen the wordy and intentionally meandering narrative. Contrary to what has been reported elsewhere, Dickens had not "left behind voluminous notes indicating he was considering at least three possible alternatives." John Forster, the author's first biographer and literary executor, revealed that apart from the novel itself, there were virtually no indications — in the form of notes, sketches, or outlines — as to the direction that the book's climax was to take. The screenwriters did opt for Drood's out-and-out murder and did pin it on the transparently sinister Jasper, but this was merely a case of convenience; the overwhelming majority of all the foregoing "continuations" had arrived at exactly the same conclusions.

Surprisingly, Balderston and Unger departed from the mainstream theories concerning the true identity of Mr. Datchery and had Jack Pierce's crepe hair, putty and powder conceal Neville Landless, which it did very effectively. As logical as this may seem within the framework of the screenplay — certainly no one else appears to do other than wring hands or sputter furiously following the titular hero's disappearance — most of the ersatz Dickenses of continuation fame had fashioned their hypotheses around Datchery's being unveiled as Drood himself, as Bazzard (a character missing from the screen adaptation), as Mr. Grewgious, or as Helena Landless, in drag!

A great deal of care was given *Mystery of Edwin Drood*, and a relatively large pile of Depression-Era cash was expended, as if in tribute to the significance of the author and his final work-in-progress. Background plates were shot in and around Rochester, England, just down the road from Chatham, where Dickens spent his final years; massive set construction was undertaken; and enormous effort was made to guarantee the authenticity of the costuming, the properties, and the Victorian deportment. The horrendous storm that marks Edwin's final night on earth was courtesy of John P. Fulton, whose miniature recreations of nature at her worst had grown more varied and opulent since *The Old Dark House* and now could scarcely have been improved upon by the real things.

Visually, *Drood* is a stunning film that comes as close as you can get to those "Super-Jewel" productions of Universal's late silent days. Albert S. D'Agostino was not merely deemed a worthy successor to the still working Charles D. Hall, but an equally creative force with whom to be reckoned. Existing sets (those wonderful *Dracula* vaults saw the light of night yet again) melded seamlessly with new-builds, which in turn were perfectly matched with the location backgrounds shot in the UK. George Robinson lit the sepulchers to provide shadows worthy of any of Universal's greatest horror films, and far from reducing the dialogue exchanges to endless talking heads, saved his tight shots for dramatic revelations: Jasper's horrific

Durdles (Forrester Harvey), quicklime, and the old vaults from *Dracula* give John Jasper (Claude Rains) food for thought. *AUTHOR'S COLLECTION.*

reaction when Grewgious informs him that Ned and Rosa had called off their engagement the very night Drood disappeared, or the moment the disguised Landless, grotesque in his well-weathered Datchery makeup, confronts the choirmaster at his nephew's secret tomb.

Dramatically, the picture benefits from Walker's brisk pace and organization and from the screenwriters' streamlining of the novel; their judicious paring of secondary characters results in a film which, at 87 minutes, has little excess body fat. The ladies' seminary vignettes are occasionally singled out as grasping attempts at humor and period flavor. If anything, they are charming glimpses into the naïve and stereotypical behavior which

was expected of young maidens at the time. It was Balderston and Unger who were primarily responsible for the several bits of good-natured whimsy about the era's customs and mores. Dickens' later works, including *Drood*, eschewed the high-spirited humor and outrageous caricatures which had once set the author apart from his contemporaries and helped coin the label, "Dickensian.") In fact, each of his novels after *Bleak House* is heavy on hangdog atmosphere and light on the kind of charm which had won Dickens his reputation.

The ongoing exposition in the film is handled well. Claude Rains skulks, lurks, and peers without peer, and the splendid cast brings the townspeople of 1864 Cloisterham to picturesque (but never *precious*) life. The sole distressing elements in the film are the intentional "if onlys": if only Edwin and Rosa had decided to part a day sooner, if only they hadn't been so secretive, if only Jasper had had a tad more patience, etc. These types of tension-builders were part and parcel of the expository style of Mr. Dickens and his contemporary partners in crime, being intended to wring every iota of suspense and regret from the audience.

It's nearly impossible to single out any one of the supporting players over another for recognition, but Walter Kingsford, playing Grewgious for all the world like a benevolent Uriah Heep, and Francis L. Sullivan (Crisparkle) give their alter egos remarkable credibility. Theirs is no mean feat, in that Dickens' supporting male characters are almost always far more outlandish or one-dimensional than their female counterparts. Valerie Hobson must also be allowed her bow, for her Helena flies in the face of the author's usual tendency to categorize women either as wide-eyed innocents or as grotesque harpies.

Douglass Montgomery, billed above the title but below Claude Rains, deserves the critical acclaim he received for his Neville Landless. A Canadian, like David Manners, Montgomery had trod the boards (as Kent Douglass) before entering films in 1930, and this experience may have helped him pull off Landless's lightning-quick mood shifts. As the hot-blooded Ceylonese, Montgomery decisively wins the uphill battle of drawing and retaining the viewers' approval despite his confession to Crisparkle of having drawn a knife on Landless *père* (because he had abused Helena), and then having almost instinctively seized another blade during his and Drood's argument in Jasper's digs.

As Edwin and Rosa Bud ("They all call me Rosebud; I hate it"), David Manners and Heather Angel are at the top of their form. For once, Manner's juvenile isn't jumping about nervously, looking to protect his sweetheart from the clutches of some horror; *au contraire*, the boyish Ned is trying to unload her. A faithful composite of child-man who is totally

guileless in his faux pas about Sumatra and tea, and nearly so in his hot-headed racial slur against Landless prior to their tussle, he appears to be trying his best to conform to the requirements of a society he doesn't quite understand, and in which (by virtue of his 21st birthday) he has only recently become a full-fledged member. Edwin is consistently likable, and most viewers, knowing of the struggle he and Rosa are undergoing with regard to their feelings for each other, instantly forgive him the statements with which Neville takes exception. The uncovering of the charred outline of his lime-eaten body in the crypt is still a breathtaking moment which is made all the more powerful by the feelings Manners has managed to elicit from the audience for his admirable Edwin Drood.

His erstwhile fiancée is adorable in a straightforward, decidedly unsexy sort of way; it's easy to see how Neville would fall head over heels for her, or how the unbalanced Jasper could become so taken with her. Heather Angel conveys Rosa's strength of character, giving her a winning personality and intelligence in addition to beauty. In doing so, Miss Angel makes her character memorable but removes her to a distant kinship of the author's Rosa, who— typically for Dickens — was wont to shuffle about helplessly between instances of male attendance. Together with Miss Hobson's Helena, Miss Angel's Rosa is spiritually as much a woman of the late 20th century as she is physically the product of the mid–19th.

The couple's tragic error is their becoming caught up in Victorian society's compulsion to maintain appearances. It is this pressure which twists into a fateful series of conclusions and commitments their innocent desire to surprise Jasper and open the door to young Neville and Helena. For the inhabitants of Cloisterham, the mystery of Edwin Drood involves the young man's disappearance; for John Jasper, what remains mysterious is why his "beloved boy" didn't confide in him and thus forestall his own murder.

Excepting the Landlesses, Dickens and his redactors present a broad range of Victorian types, all of whom are perhaps more concerned with appearances than they should be. Much has been written and filmed about the social hypocrisy practiced by the moneyed class during the last quarter of the 19th century. Cinematic revisions of such classic works of Victorian repression as *Dr. Jekyll and Mr. Hyde* and *Dracula* and the popular mythos which has arisen from the factual accounts of Saucy Jack have emphasized the moral corruption which allowed psychological and physical perversion to run rampant. Peter Sasdy's *Taste the Blood of Dracula* (1969) utilized the most overt of these exposés to give the first new and really interesting slant to a formula which Hammer, among others, had reduced to predictable pap.

John Jasper, of course, is the precursor of the quartet of doomed Victorian patriarchs in the Sasdy adventure. Behind his stiff, Church of England front, the choirmaster deals with his lack of faith, his jealousy, and his lust through biweekly visits (as Mr. Horridge) to a London opium den. Even the love he professes for his nephew Edwin cannot save the younger man from being murdered in a fit of sexual desperation. Jasper's public display of moral outrage is likewise fraudulent; just as his lust for Rosa overwhelms his love for Edwin, his insistent demands for an easy and obvious "justice" are nothing more than the next steps needed to frame Neville Landless for the crime. Still, his duplicity and menace cannot be hidden from Rosa's innocent eyes; his other self may only gradually become clear to the canny Grewgious (Walter Kingsford), "Datchery," and the nameless hag from the opium den (Zeffie Tilbury), but to Edwin's dear friend and Neville's beloved, Jasper is a figure of fear right from the start.

Claude Rains is excellent as the tormented Jasper. Still not having shaken completely his theatrical habits, the actor's tremolo recitation of a couple of plummy lines taken verbatim from the source work is in perfect counterpoint to the overly deliberate delivery that many of his colleagues affect in order to embody a Dickensian character and approximate a Dickensian pronunciation. Rains even shares some shtick with Boris Karloff: During the aforementioned confrontation with Grewgious, Rains allows his lower lip to conduct a symphony of shock, disbelief, and impotence in the face of what has already transpired. Watching Karloff's Monster play a variation on this theme while being rejected by his newly created Mate makes you shake your head in admiration for two splendidly unique actors, each of whom could make a simple facial tic speak more eloquently than the screenwriters' best.

Compact and in constant motion for its comparatively lengthy running time, *Mystery of Edwin Drood* is quite the best of the pseudo-horror pictures Universal produced during the thirties. Unsure of what to expect—the film is almost always either underestimated or misunderstood—many genre fans opt to pass on it in favor of something more readily available or more easily categorized. This is as tragic as John Jasper's frantic efforts to find love and peace through murder, and equally unnecessary.

Mystery of Edwin Drood

Released February 4, 1935; 87 minutes

Cast: Claude Rains (John Jasper); Douglass Montgomery (Neville Landless/Mr. Datchery); Heather Angel (Rosa Bud); Valerie Hobson (Helena Landless); David Manners (Edwin Drood); Francis L. Sullivan (Crisparkle); Zeffie Tilbury (Opium Den Harridan); Ethel Griffies (Mrs. Twinkleton); E.E. Clive (Thomas Sapsea); Walter Kingsford (Mr. Grewgious); Forrester Harvey (Durdles); Veda Buckland (Mrs. Tope); Elsa Buchanan (Mrs. Tisher); George Ernest (Deputy); J.M. Kerrigan (Chief Verger Tope); Louise Carter (Mrs. Crisparkle); Harry Cording, D'Arcy Corrigan (Opium Fiends); Anne O'Neal (Crisparkle Maid); Will Geer (Villager)

Credits: Associate Producer—Edmund Grainger; Director—Stuart Walker; Screenplay—John L. Balderston and Gladys Unger; Based on the novel *The Mystery of Edwin Drood* by Charles Dickens; Adapted by Bradley King and Leopold Atlas; Special Effects—John P. Fulton; Director of Photography—George Robinson; Film Editor—Edward Curtiss; Musical Score—Edward Ward; Art Director—Albert S. D'Agostino; Assistant Directors—Phil Karstein and Harry Mancke; Technical Advisor—Mme. Hilda Grenier

BRIDE OF FRANKENSTEIN (1935)

For most Americans, 1935 was significant in that it signaled that they had weathered five full years since the stock market crash of 1929. Only a comparative handful had been immediately wiped out by the devastating economic reversal, but nearly everyone was affected to one degree or another. Through the ineptitude of one-term president Herbert Hoover, little had been done to keep the wolf from people's doors, save for the erection of shanty-towns that came to be called Hoovervilles, the main effect of which was merely to make those doors less easy to find. The election in 1933 of Franklin D. Roosevelt had brought a "New Deal" that would spell the beginning of the end for the Depression.

Strange as it may seem, 1935 also spelled the beginning of the end for what is now known as the "Golden Age of Horror Movies." The contemporary genre fan would have dismissed as a nut anyone who predicted that, within a year, horror pictures would be as dead as yesterday's news. When viewed from the vantage point of the year's end, 1935 had seen Columbia's *The Black Room* (with Karloff); Monogram's *Mysterious Mr. Wong* (with Lugosi); a pair of biggies from MGM, *Mad Love* (with Peter Lorre and Colin Clive) and *Mark of the Vampire* (Tod Browning's remake of *London After Midnight*, with Lugosi and crusty

Lionel Barrymore); Erich Von Stroheim's latest over at Republic, *The Crime of Dr. Crespi*; *Le Golem* (A French/Czech collaboration); *Transatlantic Tunnel* from England; and yet another German import of *Der Student von Prag*. A formidable lot in themselves, this current batch of spookers didn't even include the armful of serials and penny-dreadfuls emanating from Poverty Row, or the varied and exciting array of Universal releases. Dead within a year? Pshaw!

One might have gotten away with suggesting that from this *pinnacle*, there was nowhere to go but down, but ... down and out? The year's Laemmle crop included *WereWolf of London*, a startling picture in which Universal reintroduced lycanthropy to the movie-going public; *The Great Impersonation*, which was only marginally a horror film but featured Edmund Lowe (Chandu himself!), along with *King Kong*'s Frank Reicher and everyone's favorite goblin, Dwight Frye; *The Raven*, which reunited Karloff and Lugosi; and *Mystery of Edwin Drood*, worth a peek not only for Claude Rains, but for those well-used *Dracula* vaults that hadn't looked so good since *Frankenstein*. There was always a worm or two in a bushel of apples, though, and *Life Returns* was almost immediately dismissed as "boring and incomprehensible," two unforgivable sins in the eyes of the box-office gods.

Rising higher than any of these was James Whale's *Bride of Frankenstein*, which to this day remains the definitive horror film for scads of genre aficionados. Several years in the making, if one counts the time spent in script development, *Bride* possesses a charm which the original lacked and is generally acknowledged as that rarest of birds: a sequel superior to its source. The movie's quirky nature can be off-putting, though, especially when one views it in combination with *Frankenstein* and *Son of Frankenstein*. The macabre humor and more than normally eccentric characterizations in *Bride* strike some viewers as having a dampening effect on the horrific content of the film (it's also been said that adapter John Balderston was quite upset with Whale for having inserted all that horror in Balderston's satirical treatment), and this is nowhere more apparent than when sandwiched between the unrelenting thrust of its sire and the epic grandeur of its own sequel. If there's more than a little truth to this observation, the reason is that, as with all aspects of a James Whale production, the ratio between chuckles and chills was precisely envisioned beforehand.

The most significant reason Whale had had for originally selecting *Frankenstein* from among the other cards in Universal's deck was his professional desire to break new ground. Typing was a danger to directors and technicians as well as actors, and after *Waterloo Bridge*, Whale had felt that he was in grave danger of endlessly walking the trenches of the Great War. The Shelley piece had opened new doors for him, but by 1935, despite his every effort at varying the types of pictures with which he became involved, James Whale had instead become pegged as a horror man. In reality, he had helmed only two more thrillers since the 1931 Karloff smash — *The Old Dark House* (1932) and *The Invisible Man* (1933) — but these had almost completely overshadowed the body of his other work, which (save for 1934's *One More River*) tended toward light romantic comedy.

As it was no better to be scarred by one brand than another, Whale determined to make the new Frankenstein film as atypical of the genre as he could. If there had been elements of black humor in his other thrillers, this one would have wry situations to spare. Whereas several of his earlier grotesques had betrayed the eccentricity which had since become a Whale trademark, off-kilter behavior would now become the norm. Because they had praised the Monster's mute elegance, he'd have the Monster learn to speak. If they'd been riled by Henry Frankenstein's *talking* about being God, they'd drop dead when they came across the most daring Christus imaginable. In place of a tidy, predictable little sequel or just another spooker in a year which promised an overabundance of them, Whale would hand over the damnedest horror picture anyone had ever seen.

Plans to revive the Monster had essentially been in the works from the day the banks opened after *Frankenstein*'s New York premiere. Robert Florey, either hopelessly naïve or an eternal optimist, had even prepared a treatment detailing Frankenstein's new "adventures," but he got nowhere fast with Junior. Feelers were then put out to playwright R.C. Sherriff, who returned them with his compliments and a polite refusal. Whale may or may not have started to put some thoughts on paper in collaboration with Philip Macdonald, but there is no doubt that he spoon-fed to John Balderston and William Hurlbut what he regarded as his most crucial material (culled both from the novel and his psyche). Trade press promises that were made one day about *The Return of Frankenstein*, which was the most popular working title, would be amended, overruled, or ignored the next, when information about the *Bride of Frankenstein* would appear. Depending upon the date and edition, Lugosi was in or out; big news was that another search was being conducted, this time for the lucky actress who would play "the bride."

More enduring than the publicity-oriented quest for the actress was the fascination engendered by the identity of the titular bride; the omission of the definite article opened the door to some precious and intentional

Posters called it *The Bride of Frankenstein*, but the article was not part of the title as released. AUTHOR'S
COLLECTION.

vagueness. Only the posters refer to the film as
The Bride of Frankenstein. While most audience members had been calling the Monster
"Frankenstein" all along, though it would
remain for Basil Rathbone to clue Josephine
Hutchinson in on the misnomer officially in
the 1939 Rowland V. Lee followup, that mix-up
didn't generate a whole lot of talk. When
Ernest Thesiger struck his most flamboyant
pose and, accompanied by Franz Waxman's
stirring bridal march/leitmotif, solemnly pronounced Elsa Lanchester's shrouded Nefertiti
"The Bride of Frankenstein" to absolutely no
one in particular, the discussions began. Although a trifle presumptuous on his part, Dr.
Pretorius's formal tones did lend weight to the
opinion that the bizarrely beautiful English elf
was the bride in question. Valerie Hobson's

role, albeit larger than Mae Clarke's had been,
was basically that of a damsel in distress, so
giving the nod to the more memorable of the
two mates made greater logical and dramatic
sense. Of course, had Whale filmed the original screenplay, wherein Elizabeth's still-beating
heart was used to vitalize the Monster's intended, the virulent debate as to who was who
and all that would have had more bite.

The ambiguity about the lady in question
is in perfect counterpoint to the gentlemen
involved; because of that public confusion as
to the name, there are already two Frankensteins. Henry, if anything more neurotic on
the eve of his marriage than he'd ever been
as a bachelor, finds himself torn between two
passions: the natural and, if you will, the
supernatural. The former, symbolized by his

anxious wife-to-be, Elizabeth, includes normal sexuality, procreation, and the joy of father-hood. The latter, embodied by the epicene Pretorius, deals in a non-sexual creation of artificial life and results in his feeling more inventor than sire. Even Pretorius's assortment of miniature homunculi tends toward diamet-rically opposed pairs: King and Queen, Bishop and Devil, Mermaid and Ballerina. The ulti-mate duality reposes, of course, in Miss Lan-chester, whose Mary Shelley gives the Monster his literary life, and whose tragically fickle femme drives him to his death.

Boris Karloff and Colin Clive naturally re-peated their signature roles (with Clive taking second billing to the upper-case KARLOFF), but Mae Clarke's day in the Universal sun was over, and she was replaced by the aforementioned Miss Hobson. Talented, gorgeous, and fresh from a hefty featured role in *Mystery of Edwin Drood*, Valerie Hobson was Irish born and thus complemented Whale's home-grown cast; apart from Dwight Frye, who provided another of his stock-in-trade unstable derelicts, and the venerable O.P. Heggie, who was Australian, vir-tually every featured player in *Bride* came from the British Isles. Perhaps Whale sought to bol-ster his own tepid enthusiasm for the project by surrounding himself with fellow expatriates, but whatever his motivation, such a geograph-ically homogeneous crowd was the perfect means of bringing to life the establishing scene (even if it was firmly entrenched in good old Goldstadt) as it fell from the lovely lips of its English narrator.

One of the more daring moves made by the English director was the prologue, wherein a rococo and self-centered Lord Byron (Gavin Gordon) prompts Miss Lanchester's charming Mary Shelley to pick up her original tale and run with it. With her sparkling eyes and win-some smile, the nouveau authoress regales her two gentlemen (also present is Douglas Wal-ton's flaccid Percy Bysshe Shelley) with further particulars; the Monster didn't perish in the windmill fire, but rather... The sequence, which must have tickled a good portion of the audience while mystifying the rest, was halved in the process of revision *Bride* underwent after

a series of previews held in Hollywood during the first week of April 1935. Missing were details of the Shelley-Wollstonecraft adultery and the rest of the *mishegas* which had scan-dalized 19th century England but hadn't raised an eyebrow since.

In all, almost 15 minutes of footage were left behind when the film opened at the Pan-tages Theater on April 22 and at the Roxy (New York's premiere took a back seat to Hollywood's this time around) on May 10. Dwight Frye saw the lion's share of his part stored on cores in the Universal vaults when his Karl, who had been the key figure of an uncomfortable subplot, was deemed virtually expendable when the trim was ordered. At the outset, Frye's charac-ter was not only an unkempt assistant mad sci-entist, but also a hired knife who had taken advantage of the monster's reappearance to do in a number of relatives for their gelt ("Very convenient to have a Monster around," he had chuckled). Before the retakes, wherein he obtained the yet-unborn monsterette's heart from a street waif, he had removed it from Eliz-abeth's distraught breast.

Scenes of the Monster stalking about the countryside, pummeling extras here and there, were likewise excised. E.E. Clive's condescend-ing burgomaster received a well-deserved trouncing by the Monster in a vignette which didn't survive the recut. One disturbing rem-nant of the footage in question does remain in the extant version, however. Whether it is disquieting because it has been taken out of context, or because Whale had determined to undermine whatever sympathies Karloff's por-trayal had managed to evoke up to that point, is unclear. After the Monster tears himself free of the oversized shackles in the village jail-house, he clomps through the streets and over anyone who gets in his way. Totally contrary to the mythos which the original film had established, he apparently tramples underfoot a little first-communicant in front of the church.

Colin Clive was again denied an onscreen death scene, and, according to several accounts, was very vocal in his displeasure. Trying to please as many paying customers as possible,

In a sequence clipped from the film, the Monster looks for a little understanding from some nattily attired kids. In the film, he runs right over one of them in a tragic error in judgment. *BUDDY BARNETT/CINEMA COLLECTORS.*

either Junior or Uncle Carl decreed that Henry and his own true love were to survive the final cataclysmic explosion and assure the continuance of the line both for the house of Frankenstein and for the box office. Said edict was issued *after* the climactic blast had taken place for John J. Mescall's camera, however, and quick-eyed spectators can still catch a glimpse of the figure of Henry Frankenstein cowering against the laboratory's far wall as that wonderful lever atomizes the tower. With the budget having been blown once (the final costs of some $397,000 exceeded the initial allocation by over $100,000), the lab couldn't be blown up twice, so despite visual evidence to the contrary, Herr Baron remained hale and hearty after the cuts.

What also remained after the cuts was a 75-minute masterpiece which manipulated the viewers' emotions as surely as a virtuoso pianist would toy with the keyboard. The helpless terror felt by Reginald Barlow (*Bride*'s substitute father for 1931's little Maria, Michael Marks apparently marshaling his reserves for later encounters) at the sight of Karloff's emergence from the shadows in the flooded windmill basement is still shared by audiences everywhere. Sympathy for the Monster's tears of joy in the hermit's cottage, as his profound loneliness seems to be coming to an end; dismay at the hunters' subsequent arrival, and anger at their misguided interference; empathy with the Monster's rejection at the bandaged hands of his artificial soulmate: although reduced and trivialized by the constraints of television, the power of Boris Karloff's performance tugs at the heartstrings as effectively as it did over 60 years ago.

It would be only the mildest of exaggerations to state that everyone in the picture is grand. Elsa Lanchester does a wonderful job in keeping her two polar *personae* separate and autonomous, despite their being joined at the spiritual hip. The pert, distinctive actress executes the double role (somewhat akin to the classic Mr. Darling/Captain Hook pairing, with a dash of Jekyll & Hyde) with the proper élan, and the resultant display has rightly been praised ever since. Renowned forever after as the towering Monster's Mate, Miss Lanchester took delight in sharing her many reminiscences of the film and her fellow-players, and in modeling her swan-inspired hiss, until her death in 1986.

The other bride of the piece, Valerie Hobson, has frequently suffered the slings and arrows of too-clever criticism on the part of genre reviewers. Coming from a girl all of 17 years old when she was called upon to indulge in umpteen different degrees of histrionics, the actress's performance, while hardly seasoned, really doesn't merit the apologetic tone that has become prevalent in the recent rash of commentary on the film. Many of Elizabeth's lines, particularly the awkward, breathless "figure like Death" speech delivered amidst growing hysteria at her husband's bedside, would have taxed the credibility of a Bette Davis. Although her set-upon ingenue appears to be younger and less experienced than 1931's Elizabeth (only seven years Miss Hobson's senior, Mae Clarke had a slightly matronly air about her by comparison), she has a much more protracted proximity to the Monster. The combination of such ungainly dialogue and intense melodramatics served to reconfigure the role and demanded a much higher degree of barnstorming than the young actress could manage. Still, Miss Hobson created a mate for Henry Frankenstein who could match his high-strung outbursts with equal verve and panache.

Boris Karloff's fans need have looked no further than here to justify the actor's then-unique billing. The *Bride's* Monster wore his heart on his sleeve, and Karloff gave an Acad-

emy Award–caliber performance if ever there was one. Infused with greater emotional balance than before, Frankenstein's Monster proves that he can demonstrate mercy (how else to explain his sparing the caterwauling Minnie, played by Una O'Connor) and exercise not only remarkable self-restraint (when dealing with invasive hunters John Carradine and Robert Adair) but actual compassion, as when he braves chilly waters and bullets to rescue the frightened shepherdess (Ann Darling). He also displays the frantic hunger of a growing boy in his scene with the gnarled old gypsy woman (Elspeth Dudgeon); added after post-preview cuts had necessitated a bridge between scenes, the brief vignette is the film's only sequence to screen without any musical accompaniment whatsoever.

Grateful as ever for his signature role, Karloff still harbored some doubts about one of James Whale's latest decisions: Thanks to the efforts of the blind hermit, Frankenstein's Monster would find a voice! Boris felt that the move would destroy the childlike facet of the character he had worked so hard to delineate, and because the lumbering creature operated within the milieu of physical and emotional isolation, his inability to communicate save by the simplest of gestures had reinforced his solitude and added poignancy to the situation. The gift of gab, argued the actor, would rob the Monster of his carefully established innocence and give his occasionally violent actions the beginnings of a more rational motivation.

Karloff had bristled over one of Whale's directives from the first movie, as well; there had been no reason, he had felt, for the Monster to drown little Maria in the pond inadvertently. Couldn't the poor creature have some respite from the terrible loneliness which was always to be his? Whale had had troubles of his own with articulation here but had finally overruled Karloff and others on the grounds that the slaughter of the innocent was part of the "ritual." Representing nearly uncharted cinematic ground, the original *Frankenstein* had required strict adherence to Whale's vision as auteur, and anything inconsistent with his interpretation was sacrificed without a second

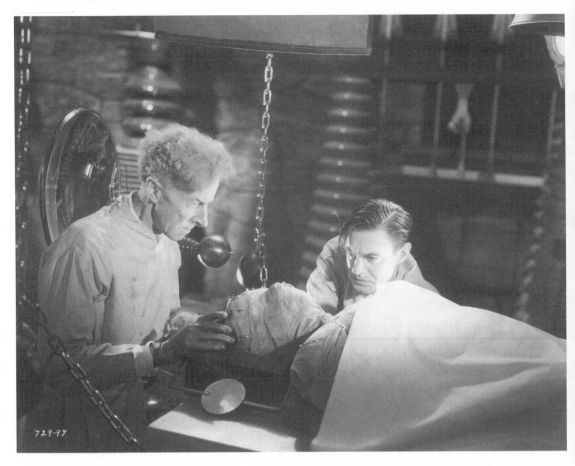

729-97

Riveted as they are on Elsa Lanchester's swaddled stand-in, neither Ernest Thesiger nor Colin Clive pays heed to the spotlight and reflector that have intruded into a poorly framed but fascinating scene. *JOHN PARNUM.*

thought. *Bride of Frankenstein* was a sequel, however, and not a work of radical innovation, so Whale kept his creative juices flowing by amusing himself with the various twists and turns he could affect on the original theme without either betraying its integrity or failing to satisfy the Laemmles.

Ernest Thesiger very nearly steals the show while everyone else save for Karloff is playing to the back row. From the moment of his first appearance amid howling winds, flickering candles, and inky shadows, Doctor Pretorius makes the darkness his own. Ill at ease in Frankenstein's brightly lit bedroom, he hastens to entice the new Baron away to his own haunts with promises of "life, as they say, in God's own image." Thesiger's ability to mirror

the nuances of Pretorius's dark soul by flaring a nostril or arching an eyebrow gives his Machiavellian heavy a substantial dramatic advantage; how better to stand out in a room full of wailing maidservants or skulking coconspirators than to lower one's voice, or narrow one's eyes? An in-joke about gin ("It's my only weakness," confesses the gaunt scientist to his curious ex-pupil) links *Bride* directly to Whale's earlier *The Old Dark House* and is attributed to the director's fondness both for Thesiger and for his character type.

Back in his own peculiar digs, the elderly doctor (Thesiger was only 56 when he played the part, yet seemed, as he always did, decades older) removes his coat and dons a skull-cap before displaying his tiny creations to the astonished Frankenstein. An interesting question: Is the odd little bit of haberdashery a scholar's cap or merely an eccentric affectation on Pretorius's part? Given Henry's comments, "This isn't science; it's more like black magic," is the scrap of black cloth more akin to the modern notion of a wizard's hat? Or is there a deeper symbolism present? Is the cap his yarmulke? Is Pretorius both an English Jew and a reincarnation of Rabbi Löwe, fixed on creating life from base clay, ersatz science, and undeniably darker forces?

On another level, the effeminate Pretorius seems to introduce a note of sexual "deviance" into the mixture, and this extended sick joke could only have existed with Whale's own imprimatur. Working with John Balderston and William Hurlbut on the script and then overseeing Hurlbut's solo screenplay, the arch director must have snickered aloud over the spate of vocal and dramatic innuendo with which he had gotten away. None of the cuts imposed by the studio heads involved any of the craftily layered suggestiveness (except Mary Shelley's clucking about her forbidden romance with paramour Percy). As for the ever-vigilant guardians of the Production Code, blatant skirtings with blasphemy had, as intended, distracted them from headier material.

As etched by Whale and played by Thesiger, Pretorius is a demonic and perverse catalyst. Leaning purposefully upon Frankenstein's already monumental sense of guilt ("It was because of you that I have been kicked out of the University," he snaps in the original script; "*booted* is the word," he sneers in the film itself), the waspish ex-doctor becomes the instigator of further, more complex, yet less savory experiments. Finding his twisted psychological arguments insufficient to seduce Frankenstein to his way of thinking, he is forced to resort to other means. Essentially expressing his preference for crypts and cadavers ("I shall stay here for a bit," he informs an uneasy fellow ghoul, referring to a tomb he has just defiled; "I rather like the place"), the mad scientist operates amidst intimations of necrophilia. Henry's similar predilections are undoubtedly clinical. Confronted by the hesitant Monster in that same crypt, the cigar-smoking Pretorius becomes the most revolting of pimps, promising the dull-witted giant a woman (constructed from the very parts over which they're sharing a meal) in exchange for his help with some proposed extortion. Karloff's subtle mastery is never more evident than at the end of this scene, where, in the course of uttering only three words, "woman, friend, wife," his vocal intonation changes from winsome to almost lustful, his facial expression mirroring his shifting emotions.

The male preoccupation with size, a significant matter only where females are concerned, is cannily alluded to in the context of shared experience: "Normal size has been my difficulty," admits the peculiar Pretorius; "You did achieve size; I need to work that out with you." Ironically, Frankenstein is as incapable of attaining normal size as is his erstwhile mentor; both Monster and Mate are somewhat larger than life. (*Young Frankenstein*'s Teri Garr, some 40 years later, wondered aloud about the size of the Monster's *schwanzstücker*.) Dramatic phallic imagery can find no greater graphic depiction than during the closing moments of *Bride of Frankenstein*. Having produced the stipulated woman on schedule, both pimp and extortion victim are aghast at her shameful behavior toward the Monster. Shedding tears at the love which will never be his, the suicidal giant allows Frankenstein his own salvation, before pulling on that significant lever to end it all. With a mighty roar, the erect tower explodes, its mighty energies, which have been contained and utilized for the creation of life, fitfully overwhelming once and for all the faithless pseudo-woman and the perverse and epicene tempter.

Sutured together by the same unsteady hand, shot through with the same electricity, and possessed of fresher parts than her male counterpart, the Monster's Mate still would not survive the cleansing eruption of the tower as would her intended. Within a few years the Monster himself would be napping comfortably on a slab of his own, but sexuality would never again rear its seductive head with Universal's Frankenstein Monster. The 1939 sequel would find the undying Monster, weakened by his brief encounter with the temptations of the flesh, safely in the hands of a male protégé. He would never again be the same product of innocence and inadvertent menace he had once been. The fulfillment he had so anxiously sought had been yet another bitter disappointment, and there were no other comparable driving forces with which he had to contend. No longer would he have the power of speech (save for a brief and interesting misfire some years later), but neither would he have any need to inquire plaintively, "Friend?" He would lose his self-sufficiency and be forced to rely upon Ygor, Frank Mannering, and the various others who would seek to "restore" him or "bring him back to full strength." No more women for him; from this point on, the Monster would headline in essence a series of buddy movies.

It has been alleged that Whale's cruel side always inevitably came to the fore. Both his smug superiority and his sexual ambivalence, which gave way to exclusive homosexuality following the end of his early engagement to Scottish designer Doris Clare Zinkeisen, contributed to his being admired professionally and despised personally by many of his coworkers. In *Frankenstein*, it has been suggested that his envy of the attention the Monster was receiving prompted him to punish the *character* for his cheek by having the *actor* carry the hefty Colin Clive uphill to the windmill at least a dozen times for their final confrontation. The needless exertion chronically worsened Karloff's already bad back. Even Whale's attempts at honest humor generally rang untrue. Numerous publicity stills taken on *Bride* sets depict him engaging in banter with the fully costumed Karloff and others; despite their apparently spontaneous, light-hearted spirit, Whale seems disapproving, stiff, or uncomfortable in every one of them.

In no way, shape, or form a lewd or sullied work, *Bride of Frankenstein* does reflect the coarse humor and sexual ambiguities of its sire.

It also encompasses his technical genius, his insistence on detail, his unparalleled knack for eliciting supercharged performances from his cast members, and timeless portrayals by Boris Karloff, Colin Clive, Elsa Lanchester, and Ernest Thesiger. A study in characterization, motivation, cause and effect, dark humor, and improbable sexuality, *Bride of Frankenstein* is the second entry in that classic sub-genre: Golden Age horror films for adults.

Bride of Frankenstein

Released May 6, 1935; 75 minutes

Cast: Boris Karloff (The Monster); Colin Clive (Baron Henry Frankenstein); Valerie Hobson (Elizabeth Frankenstein); Ernest Thesiger (Dr. Septimus Pretorius); Elsa Lanchester (Mary Wollstonecraft Shelley/The Monster's Mate); Una O'Connor (Minnie); E.E. Clive (Burgomaster); O.P. Heggie (The Hermit); Gavin Gordon (Lord Byron); Douglas Walton (Percy Shelley); Dwight Frye (Karl); Lucien Prival (Albert); Reginald Barlow (Hans); Mary Gordon (Hans' Wife); Ann Darling (Shepherdess); Ted Billings (Ludwig); Neil Fitzgerald (Rudy); John Carradine, Robert Adair, John Curtis, Frank Terry (Hunters); Walter Brennan, Rollo Lloyd, Mary Stewart (Neighbors); Helen Parrish (Communicant); Brenda Fowler (A Mother); Sarah Schwartz (Marta); Arthur S. Byron (Little King); Joan Woodbury (Little Queen); Norman Ainsley (Little Archbishop); Peter Shaw (Little Devil); Kansas DeForrest (Little Ballerina); Josephine McKim (Little Mermaid); Frank Benson, Edward Piel, Sr., Anders van Haden, John George, D'Arcy Corrigan, Grace Cunard, Peter Shaw, Maurice Black (Villagers); Helen Gibson (Woman); Elspeth Dudgeon (Old Gypsy); Murdock MacQuarrie (Sympathetic Villager); Monty Montague, Peter Shaw (Doubles for Thesiger); George DeNormand (Double for Barlow); with Harry Northrup, Joseph North

Credits: Producer — Carl Laemmle, Jr.; Director — James Whale; Screenplay — William Hurlbut; From an adaptation by William Hurlbut and John L. Balderston; Suggested by the novel *Frankenstein; or, The Modern Prometheus* by Mary Wollstonecraft Shelley;

Director of Photography — John J. Mescall; Music — Franz Waxman; Musical Director — Mischa Bakaleinikoff; Editorial Supervisor — Maurice Pivar; Film Editor — Ted Kent; Art Director — Charles D. Hall; Special Photographic Effects — John P. Fulton and David Horsley; Sound Supervisor: Gilbert Kurland (Academy Award Nomination for Best Sound Recording); Assistant Directors — Harry Menke and Joseph McDonough; Electrical Effects — Kenneth Strickfaden; Makeup — Jack P. Pierce

CHINATOWN SQUAD (1935)

From Edwin S. Porter's groundbreaking *The Great Train Robbery* through the adventures of William S. Hart — the sentimental cowboy — and up to the slicker offerings of Ken Maynard, Hoot Gibson and Buck Jones, horse operas satisfied a good bit of the yearning that audiences of the 1920s and 1930s may have had for lost innocence or the bygone days. For every thriller that set the blood rushing, there were three oaters to get the old testosterone pumping; up until the early to mid-1960s, in fact, westerns constituted some 35 percent of the domestic product.

Nevertheless, if you didn't go in much for the West, you had plenty of options available in the East. A large number of the "modern" (i.e., non-historical) features were concerned with the Orient and with Orientals. An enormous fascination with things Chinese (and, to a lesser extent, Japanese) was reflected in both the plastic arts and the performance arts of the twenties and thirties. Sessue Hayakawa enjoyed tremendous popularity in American silent films, and Kamiyama Sojin, Hayakawa's oddball countryman, bounced gleefully back and forth between villainous and heroic roles before returning to the Land of the Rising Sun in 1931. The imagined dangers of the "Yellow Peril" became as alluring to American moviegoers as they were disconcerting. Secret societies, Tong wars, evil geniuses, irresistible femmes fatales, and skulking henchmen all became part of the Oriental mystique which guaranteed gold at the box office.

Universal, strangely, didn't jump with both feet onto the Oriental bandwagon as just about everyone else did. Charlie Chan and Fu Manchu led the hit parade for the majors while Poverty Row winnowed the chaff for the less expensive also-rans. Without a big name Chinese detective or Mandarin criminal to fall back on, Universal opted to treat the trend toward the Orient as just one more monkey in a barrel-full. *Chinatown Squad* in 1935 offered ticket-buyers a whodunit/espionage meld with all the usual accoutrements done up in Cantonese style. The film made use of those same stock New Year's parades, those same undulating dragons, and those same white bread character men (Leslie Fenton, Fred Warren) who took the bread from the mouths of Asian-American actors with distressing frequency. It also made money.

Chinatown on New Year's Eve — Chinese New Year, of course — opens the film with a whirl of costumes, lights, firecrackers, and that stock-footage dragon. While the driver of a sightseeing jitney is having traffic problems, a young woman with problems of her own climbs into a cab not far away. As she reads a

Not even halfway through *Chinatown Squad*, the cops already have their doughy mitts on the guilty party. But with four reels left to go, D.D. Palmer (Bradley Page) isn't through pointing by a long shot. PENTA-GRAM LIBRARY.

telegram ("Raybold Murdered Stop Funeral Arrangements Wait Your Arrival — George Mason"), the woman, Janet Baker (Valerie Hobson), is whisked to the Pelham Arms Apartments. Meeting George Mason (Andy Devine) face to face, however, she's in for a couple of surprises: Not only does he deny sending the telegram, but he asks her to wait. "I'll only be a minute. I want to tell Mr. Raybold that he's been murdered."

While Mason and Raybold (Clay Clement) are chuckling over the strange telegram in the bedroom, Janet is ransacking the supposed victim's desk. She finds a note in his diary reading "Dinner with William Ward — Peking Café, 7:30 tonight" and then quietly lets herself out. Raybold is puzzled that she has vanished but

dresses for his dinner engagement. As he dons an ornate Chinese ring he keeps locked in the safe, his secretary wonders aloud:

> MASON: You can pick up a ring like that for ten bucks in a Chinese hock-shop. What do you want to keep it locked up for?
>
> RAYBOLD: Don't kid yourself. You can't buy this ring for $100,000. It's not what it's worth; it's what it can do for you.

Raybold heads out the door, which gives *Mason* a chance to rifle his boss's desk for a moment or two before the phone rings. It's a Mr. Palmer, looking for Raybold; he is told about the dinner plans at the Peking Café.

That's some café, that Peking Café. While couples wend their way around the floor to the melodies of an invisible orchestra, the jitney driver and his passengers show up for dinner. The driver, Ted Lacey (an incredibly young and slim Lyle Talbot), has a jovial exchange with the restaurant's owner, Mr. Yee (Fred Warren):

> LACEY: Hello there, Yee. I've got some customers for you.
>
> YEE: I am very grateful, Ted. When you were associated with the police force, you took customers out of here quite frequently. It's much better this way.

Raybold enters with sufficient verve to prompt one of Ted's customers to ask about him. "His name is Raybold," the ex-cop replies. "He's a pretty smart duck; high class confidence man, always hopping to and from China. Mixed up with the Chinese communists." All the exposition one could ever want.

Raybold meets with Yee, who expresses some concern that the $75,000 his countrymen have given the white man for the purchase of airplanes will not just disappear. Although he must be something of a wizard to buy even one airplane for a paltry 75 grand, Raybold glibly assures Yee that "in a couple of weeks, we'll have those planes in China, dropping eggs on your enemies." In addition to his worries about the money, Yee is distressed at Raybold's brazen flashing of his Chinese ring. "I caution you," he says. "Please be very careful with that ring. In strange hands, it would work irreparable harm to our cause. It may do *you* harm if its power is abused." Called to a nearby phone booth by a waiter, the airplane supplier has an awkward conversation with Mr. Palmer: "Don't be silly, Palmer. I have every intention of giving you the money. See, old man, I won't receive the money for the planes until I get to China. I'll cable you your commission. Yes … yes … you can come over here. I'll wait for you." Yee, of course, has overheard everything and is disturbed but not surprised when Raybold suddenly announces that he has to leave. Once outside the café, though, the businessman changes his mind when he sees he's being

watched by Chinese thugs on both sides of the street. After a quick one-eighty, Raybold demands his usual booth from maître d' Su Quong (Leslie Fenton). Quong notices the opulent Chinese ring and agrees to intrude on Raybold's privacy only when his dinner has arrived.

Almost immediately, Raybold is outflanked. Another middle-aged white man enters the café and plops himself down in the booth behind Raybold while Janet, who has been watching from across the room, takes the booth on the other side. Moments after Quong is chased angrily away as he serves Raybold's dinner, George Mason comes in and makes a beeline for his boss's favorite spot. "Get the police," he yells at Quong, having found Raybold face down in the noodles. Ted takes charge during the ensuing ruckus, ordering the doors to be locked until the cops arrive — which they do, a *very* few minutes later — but that's all Mason has needed to sneak out, the man in the first booth to hide, and Yee to prize the ring from Raybold's finger and exit his booth through a secret door.

The uniforms show up first, but the detectives aren't far behind, and they send Ted and his group of sightseers home. (Janet has silently positioned herself in the group, but Ted, who notices her, says nothing.) Lieut. Norris (Wallis Clark) hands the investigation over to Sgt. McLeash (Hugh O'Connell), who was apparently something of a thorn in Ted's side during his days on the force. McLeash finds the man from the first booth hiding in a linen basket in the kitchen. Named William Ward (Arthur Hoyt), he was in the restaurant to have dinner with Raybold. In walks Palmer (Bradley Page), who won't deny that he has shown up to make sure he gets the money coming to him. Unfortunately for Palmer, none of the $75,000 is anywhere to be found.

For their last scheduled tour stop, Ted takes his little group to the Chinatown Exchange of the Pacific Telephone Company, announcing, "These operators handle calls in English, Cantonese, and nine other Chinese dialects." Janet gives Ted her address, which proves to be fake, before she leaves, and Ted

Sergeant McLeash, Ted Lacey and Lieutenant Norris: So many John Yees and so little time. Peering out from the corner of this lobby card is Fred Warren, the one John Yee who counts in *Chinatown Squad*. PENTAGRAM LIBRARY.

cuts off Wanda (Toshia Mori), the head operator and Yee's daughter, when she attempts to clue him in on the phone calls Raybold made from the restaurant. A busy girl, Janet makes for Raybold's apartment and goes right for the desk but is interrupted when Mason returns. He too goes right to the desk, where he finds and pockets his own passport — and he has scarcely left when the cops turn up. Thinking quickly, Janet lies down on Raybold's bed and presents herself to Norris as Raybold's fiancée.

Norris orders the uniforms to take Miss Baker home to the Saint Francis Hotel, and then sends McLeash down to the Oriental Line, where Raybold has a cabin booked on a steamship bound for China that very night. In the cabin, the policeman finds Mason in the act of rifling Raybold's steamer trunk. Relieving Mason of his passport and his revolver, McLeash learns that the man is really an airplane mechanic; the cop has the captain hold the ship until the airplanes intended for the Fu Chow communists are unloaded. Mason spills the beans about the telegram and Janet Baker, but when the cops are told by the Saint Francis desk clerk that neither a Janet Baker nor anyone fitting her description is stopping at the hotel, McLeash goes to visit Ted Lacey.

Janet beats him to Ted's flat, arriving with the old "I'm in trouble, and I need your help" song on her lips. It seems she had been Raybold's business associate before she agreed to marry him. Nevertheless, on the day of the wedding — but police sirens interrupt the tale.

It's McLeash, looking for "the woman in black you smuggled out of the Peking Café." While Baker hides (and then leaves), Ted gives the policeman the fake address from his little black book. Later that night, a package — complete with sputtering fuse — is tossed under the ex-cop's bed. A number of small explosions awaken Ted, who finds a note on the remnants of the box: "Stay away from Janet Baker and the Raybold case or, next time, it won't be fire crackers."

With the cops still on the lookout for John Yee, Mason and Palmer decide to team up and find the $75,000. At the Peking Café, a tall Chinese woman informs the closeted Yee that "You have some letters I want." Naturally, the woman is Janet who, despite being armed and at the ready, manages to back into a storeroom from which there is no escape. Ted has noticed the tall woman entering but not exiting the café, so he follows John Yee when the elderly proprietor leaves moments later; the cop on the beat follows Ted.

When McLeash gets the call that Ted and Yee are on the Sausalito ferry, the sergeant races madly to catch the boat as it pulls away from the pier. The boat is forced to halt at the "Man Overboard" cry, and, as McLeash is fished from the water, a stealthy figure follows John Yee into an inside cabin. Ted is bringing his old rival up to date when a second "Man Overboard" cry is raised. Ted jumps into the bay, and he and McLeash pull John Yee into a lifeboat. The Chinese fugitive has been stabbed. Pointing to his finger, he expires. Ted notes, "The guy who did this is in the clear, and he's got that jade ring."

Back on land, Ted goes nosing around the café. By accident, he opens the secret door to Raybold's booth and comes upon Janet, bound and gagged, in the storeroom. Slugging a couple of highly ineffective thugs, Lee unties the plucky young woman and takes her back to his place. Janet finally gets to explain about the letters and her involvement in the whole mess:

> JANET: I gave Raybold $15,000 for an interest in his business; I thought it was honest and legitimate. On our wedding day, I learned about his crooked business methods and called the whole thing off. I demanded my money and threatened to tell the police. He only laughed and said I was his partner and therefore as guilty as he. In a fit of anger, I wrote him several letters, threatening his life.

Raybold had sent her the telegram in order to bring her back to San Francisco; despite all that had happened, he still carried a torch for the tall beauty. Ted concocts a plan which will see the whole affair through to a neat resolution. They arrange to meet Mason and Palmer at the Peking Café, and saddled with McLeash (who thinks the disguised Janet is Quong's sister), they head over there at once. Janet and Ted take Raybold's usual booth, and McLeash stakes out the booth behind it. When the testy policeman hears Janet's voice leveled at Mason, he runs over and accuses Mason of the murder. Outraged, Mason jumps to his feet, nearly knocking the table over and exposing the $75,000 and Janet's letters, which have been hidden under the table lamp all the time.

The secret door to the outside slides open, and Quong and a couple of henchmen present Palmer to the astonished sergeant. In the Black Maria, Ted's talk of the electric chair frightens Mason into fingering Palmer, who killed Raybold and Yee and stole the ring. At headquarters, Norris offers Ted his old job back — with a promotion to sergeant — and news of a riot in Chinatown interrupts a kiss from Janet. Together with his new (and newly miserable) partner, McLeash, Ted heads happily back into his turf.

Chinatown Squad isn't much more than a standard if fast-moving programmer, but it's made all the more intriguing by its Oriental settings. Admittedly, the business about the Fu Chow communists makes little difference to the unfolding of the story; references to timely issues such as this may have lent greater contemporary significance to films but also served to date them as interests changed and news items came and went. Likewise, the mysterious ring is just a MacGuffin, an ultimately meaningless device meant to provide some dramatic impetus. We're never told whence the ring came, why it has the impact that it has, or how its power can be abused. It's just another Chinese artifact, intended to add an aura of exotica to the proceedings.

The attitudes of the screenplay are typical of the times. While white audiences were undoubtedly fascinated by Oriental culture, at the same time they felt smugly superior. With very few exceptions, when they weren't portrayed as seeking the total annihilation of the white race, Chinese were servants or laundrymen, Japanese were gardeners, and other, nondescript Far Easterners were blurs in the background. There are no Chinese cops on the Chinatown squad, and a variation on the old joke about all Orientals looking alike receives the royal treatment when one of the bulls drags in a line of bland and unexcited locals: "You sent me out for John Yee," the cop brags to McLeash, "and here's nine of them."

For all this, however, *Squad* refrains from making the kind of blanket offensive statements found in many of its competitors with like themes. Raybold's haughty attitude with Quong and Norris's impatience with the staff of the Peking Café are offset by the respect Ted Lacey shows for the inhabitants of Chinatown. Nor can any of Ted's sightseeing group be taken as an exemplary model of the white race. One of the women expresses admiration that Yee "talks such good English" and admonishes her escort for not knowing any "six-cylinder" words. Another announces smugly that the chop suey they're all ordering is made from mice. And while both of the pivotal roles of John Yee and Su Quong are played by Western actors (Fred Warren was fresh from a similar portrayal in Monogram Pictures' *Mysterious Mr. Wong*), some consolation could be taken in that key information is given to Ted by Yee's daughter, played by the genuinely Oriental (though in fact Japanese) actress Toshia Mori.

Lyle Talbot's career was long if undistinguished, and the actor is usually best remembered either as the understaffed Commissioner Gordon in Columbia's 1949 serial *The Adventures of Batman and Robin*, as Luthor in *Atom*

Man vs Superman (1950), or for his participation in Ed Wood's mind-blowing *Glen or Glenda?* and *Plan Nine from Outer Space*. Born Lysle Hollywood (I kid you not!), Talbot started out as a light romantic lead in such fare as *Love Is a Racket* and *Three on a Match* (both 1932) before moving (briefly) to Universal in 1935. Always something of a free spirit — he was never under exclusive contract anywhere — Talbot moved from juveniles to supporting roles as his waistline grew and his birth certificate yellowed. Regularly coming across as a sort of second-string Morris Ankrum in his many genre appearances, he also worked in a slew of mainstream pictures and on fifties television.

Talbot's Ted Lacey is probably one of the most personable 1930s heroes. Congenial, respectful, willing to take a risk (with Janet) or run one himself (with McLeash), Ted maintains a sure-footed balance between being witty and being obnoxious that all too many of his fellow cinematic good guys fail to achieve. *Squad*'s screenplay fails to disclose why the self-styled tour guide left the police force in the first place, but considering the almost palpable friction that exists between the two men at any given point, the implication that Ted's departure had something to do with Sergeant McLeash is virtually a foregone conclusion. Talbot's character is also the most human of the *dramatis personae*; he neither embraces a cause nor embodies one, and his insistence on seeing the investigation through to the end is motivated not by some high-handed sense of duty or loyalty, but by his attraction to Janet Baker and his respect for Mr. Yee.

Valerie Hobson was rushed into *Chinatown Squad* only days after *Bride of Frankenstein* had wrapped, but the less costly Chinese mystery must have seemed like a walk in the park to her after delivering up hysterics on command for James Whale. In Janet Baker, Miss Hobson had an opportunity to play a woman who sought to regain control of her life with her own hands. Though the role was less flashy than her counterparts in the more handsomely budgeted *Bride*, *WereWolf of London*, or *The Great Impersonation*, in none of those films was the actress able to do more than react to situations in which her character found herself, due mainly to the rigors of marriage. For fans of Miss Hobson, *Squad* has its moments to savor. It's amusing to see her, in her guise as a local Chinese girl, towering above most of the male supporting cast, and it's gratifying to watch her matching her wits with someone, rather than constantly verging on losing them.

Chinatown Squad marks the first time Andy Devine's name appears in this book, but the chunky, crackly-voiced comic was to become a studio mainstay during the thirties and early forties. Having made his screen debut in the part-sound feature *We Americans* (1928), the unique Devine added his own brand of visual girth and aural depth to over six dozen Universal features before being dropped in the general housecleaning that took place when the studio merged with International Pictures in 1946. Genre fans may note the actor's presence in *Impatient Maiden*, an early and decidedly minor James Whale production of 1932, as well as his sharing the same reel (if not the same scene) with Bela and Boris in Universal's curious *The Gift of Gab* (1934). Besides enlivening loads of B westerns along the way, Devine became the partner of choice for Richard Arlen, one of the studio's most rugged and least serious action stars, and the two men were featured in a series of rough and tumble pictures in the early forties.

Chinatown Squad is an unremarkable but welcome picture which gives a little reverse English to a couple of the standard elements (resourceful hero, endangered heroine) that went with the territory. The fact that Dore Schary worked up the scenario himself indicates that the brass ranked the film a notch or two above programmer status. A departure from the studio's usual venues, the Chinatown settings are less germane to the story than they are reflective of the current fashion. The blather about planes, communists and power rings could just as easily have been adapted to Germantown or Little Italy. Still, graced with competent and likable juveniles, granted a longer running time than the normal "hour +" to tell its tale, and no more upsetting to the public consciousness than other crime dramas set elsewhere, Universal's Chinese whodunit is a pleasant little change of pace and scene.

Chinatown Squad

Released May 20, 1935; 75 minutes

Cast: Lyle Talbot (Ted Lacey); Valerie Hobson (Janet Baker); Hugh O'Connell (Sergeant McLeash); Andy Devine (George Mason); E. Alyn (Fred) Warren (John Yee); Leslie Fenton (Su Quong); Clay Clement (Earl Raybold); Bradley Page (D.D. Palmer); Arthur Hoyt (William Ward); Wallis Clark (Lieutenant Norris); Toshia Mori (Wanda Yee); Tom Dugan (Doorman); James Flavin (Desk Cop); Otis Harlan (Old Man); with Edward Earle, King Baggot, Pat Flaherty, Jack Mulhall

Credits: Associate Producer—Maurice Pivar; Director—Murray Roth; Original Story—Lawrence G. Blochman; Screenplay—Dore Schary; Additional Dialogue—Ben Ryan; Photographer—George Robinson, ASC; Art Director—Harrison Wiley; Film Editor—Maurice E. Wright

WEREWOLF OF LONDON (1935)

Transvection

Transvection from man to werewolf occurs between hours of nine and ten at the full of the moon. The essence of the mariphasa blossom squeezed into the wrist through the thorn at the base of the stem is the only preventive known to man. Unless this rare flower is used, the werewolf must kill at least one human being each night of the full moon or become permanently afflicted.*

Rodney Dangerfield is hardly alone in his claim at getting no respect. No other trend-setting, innovative picture of the 1930s Universal canon has been damned with so much faint praise as *WereWolf of London*.

Besides myself, there are possibly two others among the hundreds of horror movie buffs I've met over the years who will allow this father of lycanthrope features to rise or fall on its own merits. Everybody else, Tom said sweepingly, insists on dragging the picture some five or ten or more years into the future for the express purpose of comparing it, usually unfavorably, with like-themed movies made by other teams, under different circumstances, with improved techniques. Never have

so many produced so little substance by making so much noise.

Yes, there are flaws. Jack Pierce was raring to go in 1935 with the full treatment that Lon Chaney would receive a half-decade later, but friction from Henry Hull resulted in a second-rate makeup job. Wilfred Glendon would have been a more well-rounded figure, worthy of the audience's sympathy and his wife's love, had he been enacted by Karloff (as originally claimed by the trades). Dr. Yogami would have been a more archly drawn, singularly obsessed figure, deserving of his fate and more vigorous in his predation, had he been played by Bela Lugosi (as leaked by those same trades on alternate days). If Robert Florey had directed, there would have been less of that irritating comic relief; had James Whale been at the wheel, the humor would have been more subtle and fey; with Papa Freund's hand at the helm, there would have been none at all.

Etc., etc., etc.

I won't deny that I initially found the botanical aspect of the film's werewolf saga patently absurd and self-defeating. Nor will I argue the contention that any protagonist who starts out as a testy curmudgeon on his good days has little dramatic room in which to

Entry from a dusty old book consulted in WereWolf of London.

225

maneuver when things really get hot. If you want to stew about Hull's makeup resembling a bat far more than it does a wolf, I'll concede the point — but so what? I just wish that my enjoying the film weren't so off-putting to the less tolerant but more vocal majority, which seems determined to harangue the picture for not being something else altogether.

There have been far more horror and mystery pictures made with feline menaces than lupine, but let's face it: It's a hell of a lot easier and cheaper to round up a couple of black kitties than to lay one's hands on wolves. This fact may even serve to explain why most werewolf movies feature wolf-*persons*, and not four-legged furies. Not only are genuine wolves disinclined to take direction — especially within the edgy framework of a tight shooting schedule — but it's a darn sight easier to arrange for a domestic animal to appear ferocious than to make a wild animal act in a fashion contrary to its nature. Hence, there have never been any completely convincing hounds at Baskerville Hall, and the more successful lycanthrope films of the thirties and forties never gave more than the briefest of passing nods to non-anthropoidal creatures.

Among the array of cinematic goblins, the werewolf alone follows two paths; in addition to its own thorny way, it figures at least theoretically in the vampire mythos. The lycanthropic aspect of cinematic vampirism was downplayed during the thirties and forties, as budgetary considerations and the animal handling difficulties cited earlier saw the vampire's shape-shifting capabilities narrowly delineated by prop-room bats. Cheaper and safer even than flapping rubber bats was talk, and so horror audiences had to take Jonathan/Juan Harker's word that both the Hungarian and the Castilian Draculas were loping across the sanitarium grounds in wolf form. This facet of Dracula's persona was conveniently forgotten by Universal after the 1931 films. Had anyone given it a thought, Dracula's battle-on-the-run with the Wolf Man in 1948's *Abbott and Costello Meet Frankenstein* would have been quite a bit more exciting had the Count transformed into a wolf (rather than a cartoon bat) and met the lycanthrope on his own turf.

Likewise, there is more than a passing resemblance between your typical werewolf and the dual protagonists of Robert Louis Stevenson's nightmare. Both lycanthrope and noble scientist experience a physical and mental schizophrenia which diminishes their humanity while unleashing a far more bestial personality. Henry Jekyll, of course, is working to separate man's two natures so as to exalt his goodness; missing from these highfalutin aspirations is an effective plan of action for the baser leftovers. The good doctor is under absolutely no compulsion save his own to drive a wedge into his soul and has no one but himself to blame for the outcome. In contrast, the wolf-people, starting with Dr. Glendon here, are infected with lycanthropy by other werewolves, the condition being passed on from one to another in the saliva left in an open wound. In the main, werewolfery is represented as a contagious disease which affects one's mind (the drive to violence, the targeting of loved ones) as it disfigures one's body.

Now, in this light, the objective silliness about the *Mariphasa lupino lumino* makes a good bit of sense. The salve or nectar of the mature blossom is the antidote to an active bout with the disease, much as a good shot of penicillin is an effective counteractive to an attack of a more mundane infection. Each potent bud is good only for a few hours, and the flower's growing exclusively among the Himalayan cliffs makes it a precious commodity indeed. Dr. Yogami becomes fairly frantic, for example, when a chambermaid pokes at his purloined specimen. The fact that Yogami has followed Glendon back to London in order to get a dose from that flower indicates that there just aren't any more, in Tibet or anywhere else. And talk about irony: The hirsute Yogami's savage attempt to frighten Glendon away from the few remaining *Mariphasa*s does nothing but create yet more demand for an item already in tragically short supply. For all intents and purposes, the only remaining source of the medicinal plant in the world is the rival for its serum.

A glorious piece of poster art from a vastly underrated film: the *WereWolf of London* six-sheet. *RONALD V. BORST/HOLLYWOOD MOVIE POSTERS.*

Moonlight itself plays a Jekyll & Hyde–like role in the proceedings. The disease reaches critical intensity, triggering "transvection," during the full moon, while the antidote contained within the last Mariphasa buds attains full potency and becomes available only when exposed to those same rays, projected at their most intense during the transvecting cycle. It would therefore appear that the nurturing power of moonlight allows the essence of the wolf-flower to counteract the transforming power of moonlight; thus does the moon both bring doom and offer promise of salvation at one and the same moment. This "kiss and kill" aspect of the lunar light is an anguished tease to Yogami and Glendon. It may even be argued that the tumultuous struggle by the two shape-shifters in Glendon's laboratory results in the picture's ultimate irony: Far from allowing him even an evening's respite from torment,

A Pyrrhic victory — Dr. Yogami (Warner Oland) managed to snatch the *mariphasa* away from Dr. Glendon. JOHN PARNUM.

Yogami's stealing the antidote right out from under the snout of the transformed Glendon brings him only the peace of the grave.

The depiction of the two werewolves fighting to the death for even a temporary reprieve from their affliction is powerful and extremely moving. No other charter member of the gallery of classic monsters abhors his own essence and deplores his own existence as does the werewolf. Surviving victims of werewolf attacks seek only to regain their full humanity, to be rid of the taint that makes them different and dangerous to others. No legitimate lycanthrope (of the '30s and '40s, at any rate) actively works to prolong his own torment, or to add to the list of sufferers. Yet the werewolf's murderous instinct is the inevitable result of his curse; the creature kills because it is driven to do so, just as it is compelled to hunt down and kill the people it loves best.

It was only after viewing the film a number of times that I began to understand just what Stuart Walker, John Colton, et al. had presented to a monster-loving public. Far from being a "poor relation" of its slicker, more expensive cousin (1941's *The Wolf Man*), *Were-Wolf of London* scampers about on different territory altogether. In their haste to pour precious oils on the later Siodmak/Waggner/Chaney classic, the most effusive of film critics have failed to see that the vinegar-soaked *WereWolf of London* is not some earlier, failed attempt at depicting a creature that would finally come into its own some five years later.

The Wolf Man remains a splendid example of the 1940s-style horror film at its best. *WereWolf of London*, on the other hand, offers an illustration of that popular but less prolific side of the genre: 1930s science fiction.

As in *The Invisible Man*, there are several art-deco "scientific" contraptions in evidence in Glendon's laboratory which, despite their casual and almost understated use, nevertheless appear better suited to a Flash Gordon serial than to the more tragic vistas being examined here. The moonlight machine itself, which appears precariously flimsy when aimed and fired by Wilfred at a moon-vine, seems straight out of Dr. Zarkov's workshop; the really neat touch is that the device fools not only the plant into thinking that the moon is out, but Glendon's *hand*, as well. (Only the hand exposed to the concentrated "moonlight" sprouts hair.) On another note, the botanist monitors unwelcome visitors to his lab with a closed-circuit TV screen (accomplished via some shaky matte work), topped with a flashing light and buzzer and activated by a rotary telephone dial!

Yet I'm not talking about such gadgetry when I speak of *WereWolf of London* as science fiction, but rather about the rational approach to the theme which is only hinted at in the later film. Per Dr. Yogami, lycanthropia is a mind-altering, physical psychosis which is emotionally oriented; how else to explain the drive to kill those one loves best? Nor does the disease allow for any supernatural trappings. Despite fang and claw (and adrenalin), neither werewolf seems to gain any measure of superhuman strength, and Glendon is stopped dead in his tracks by a regulation bullet, fired by a no-nonsense police inspector.

Dr. Yogami makes no mention of otherworldly forces at work in either of his expository chats with Glendon, who still holds the werewolf to be a creature of imagination or legend. "I'm afraid, sir, that I gave up my belief in goblins, witches, personal devils, and werewolves at the age of six," Glendon maintains, even after he has goggled at his fur-sprouting arm and has experienced firsthand the restorative power of the phosphorescent wolf-flower.

So much for explaining away the deadly transformation as resulting from any strong psychosomatic influences.

The passage quoted at the outset of this chapter is taken from one of those ancient tomes which pop up handily in every mansion encountered in a Universal chiller, providing just the right information to anyone looking for an answer. The gist therein is that scientists have been looking for a cure to this rare but not unknown condition, and that the *Mariphasa* is nothing more than a piece of preventive medicine. Neither Glendon's moldy volume nor Colton's screenplay provides a full explanation of the essay's ominous final phrase: "permanently afflicted." Joined with the creature's nightly quota of kills, the words appear eager to shift the picture's rationale into the realm of myth; that there is no specific mention of this regulated aspect of lycanthropia in the body of the film may be either an oversight or an attempt at moving the exposition back on target. Belying the almost reverential tones they use when speaking about the wolf-flower is the principals' inability to get the name of the damned flower straight: Glendon informs the itinerant missionary (Egon Brecher) that he's after the *Mariphasa lupino lumino*, while Yogami later explains that he ran into Glendon in Tibet while on his own quest for the *Mariphasa lumina lupina*.)

Farther along this track, the most interesting aspect of Wilfred Glendon's wolf-man is his ability to speak. Now, this beast is far more fascinating than the snarling, ravening, essentially mindless predator the character-type would become in future incarnations. The idea here is that Glendon remains articulate, even rational, while in his bestial state, yet is powerless to stave off the driving bloodlust that accompanies the physical transformation. To metamorphose into a furry horror, pausing only to cannily don a concealing cap and scarf; to choose a victim by virtue of his or her apparent vulnerability rather than by mere happenstance; to stalk and slay through instinctual compulsion alone, yet to be fully aware of what you're doing while you're doing it — this is the portrait of a moral soul suffering the tortures of the damned. And the pain and futility are delineated with infinitely more panache than would later accompany Lon Chaney's vague sensations and vaguer memories.

The whole love-triangle thing, reflecting the growing intolerance for apprehensive female leads, can be seen coming from way down the pike. Mae Clarke (*Frankenstein*) may have brushed off John Boles, and Gloria Stuart sure cut William Harrigan off at the knees at the outset of *The Invisible Man*, but that was then and this was now. By the mid–1930s, the (mad) scientist's main squeeze was no longer in the mood merely to weep and fret while her honey was wreaking havoc on the locals. The new trend seemed to be to bail out of the relationship, take up with the secondary male, and then try to survive until the closing music. Janos Rukh (*The Invisible Ray*) would have it no easier than Wilfred Glendon, but at least his Diana (Frances Drake) would have the decency to wait until after what passed for her husband was discovered done to a turn before traipsing down the aisle with the juvenile.

Perhaps the only perceived weakness among the leading players lies with Henry Hull's interpretation of the human Wilfred Glendon. The botanist's brooding preoccupation with the mysterious *Mariphasa whatcha-macallit* has robbed him of the saving graces of both his wife and his friends. Glendon appears to be quite aloof, suspicious, and short-tempered even before things get out of control, going so far as to leave his clearly sensual young wife to her own resources ("months on end") while he and the useless Hugh Renwick (Clark Williams) cavort among the shadowy crags of Tibet. Hull delivers the standard promises to be more of this and less of that as soon as he's done with his experiments, but doesn't quite manage to convey either the underlying tenderness of Claude Rains' Jack Griffin or Colin Clive's tragically misfocused passions. Still, Hull creates moments of genuine pathos — his heartbroken prayer in his rented digs, for example — and gives Glendon a depth which would have eluded the more forthright strategies of Bela Lugosi and which was absent from the musclebound Chaney portrayal.

Of the five classic monsters created by Universal during the early and mid-thirties, three (Frankenstein's Monster, the invisible man, and the werewolf of London) were the denizens of the science fiction branch of the horror genre. Clive and Rains enacted key roles in tales of calamity and horror which followed inevitably man's attempt via "science" to extend his knowledge beyond the limits traditionally imposed by a jealous God. The movies' proscribed fate for such meddling was always death, and Henry Frankenstein's avoiding that cathartic demise, per James Whale's directive, enraged Colin Clive. In contrast, Hull and Oland are but the passive victims of another's aggression. And while nothing of substance is ever revealed about Yogami's situation, little justice can be found in the horrible fate which befalls Glendon, a man whose only sin has been his intense interest in rare flora.

WereWolf of London deserves far more respect than it has received to date. Far more subtly than its later and more celebrated successor, the picture proposes a realistic milieu and a scientific basis to a fairy-tale ogre, yet manages in the process to comment succinctly on faith, hope, and love — those traditional virtues still held in high esteem in the mid-thirties.

WereWolf of London

Released June 3, 1935; 75 minutes

Cast: Henry Hull (Wilfred Glendon); Warner Oland (Dr. Yogami); Valerie Hobson (Lisa Glendon); Lester Matthews (Paul Ames); Spring Byington (Ettie Coombes); Lawrence Grant (Col. Thomas Forsythe); Clark Williams (Hugh Renwick); J.M. Kerrigan (Hawkins); Charlotte Granville (Lady Alice Forsythe); Ethel Griffies (Mrs. Whack); Zeffie Tilbury (Mrs. Moncaster); Jeanne Bartlett (Daisy); Harry Stubbs (Jenkins); Louis Vincenot (Head Cooley); Reginald Barlow (Timothy); Eole Galli (Prima Donna); Joseph North (Plimpton); Egon Brecher (Missionary); Boyd Irwin, Sr. (Hotel Manager); Helena Grant (Mother); Noel Kennedy (Boy); William Millman (John Bull); Tempe Pigott (Drunken Woman); Maude Leslie (Mrs. Charteris); Herbert Evans

(Jenkins' Aide); David Thursby (Photographer); Gunnis Davis, George Kirby (Detectives); Jeffrey Hassel (Alf); Amber Norman (Beggarwoman); James May (Barman); Connie Leon (Yogami's Maid); Vera Buckland (Yogami's Housekeeper); Wong Chung (Cooley); Roseollo Navello (Maid); Alex Chivra (Stand-In for Oland); George DeNormand (Double for Hull); Edwin Parker (Double for Matthews)

Credits: Producer — Carl Laemmle, Jr.; Director — Stuart Walker; Associate Producer — Robert Harris; Executive Producer — Stanley Bergerman; Screenplay — John Colton; Original Story by Robert Harris; Adapted by Harvey Gates and Robert Harris; Director of Photography — Charles Stumar; Special Photographic Effects — John P. Fulton; Assistant Directors — Phil Karstein and Charles S. Gould; Film Editors — Russell Schoengarth and Milton Carruth; Art Director — Albert S. D'Agostino; Musical Score — Karl Hajos; Sound Supervisor — Gilbert Kurland; Makeup — Jack P. Pierce

THE RAVEN (1935)

If *The Black Cat* must be considered primarily as a Karloff vehicle, an honor it earns for finally giving the actor the chance to snap and snarl without the burden of acres of wax and miles of collodion, then *The Raven* has to be adjudged the ultimate Lugosi film. In no other picture do the attendant elements of dialogue, plotline and photography converge so neatly to permit the moody star to be so unremittingly himself.

A casual perusal of Lillian Lugosi Donlevy's remembrances of her first husband impresses the reader with the actor's personal aloofness, his air of contempt for projects deemed unworthy or colleagues thought inferior, his misguided insistence on maintaining an air of mystery about his person, the ease with which he took offense and the degree to which he held grudges, his habit of resting conspicuously on earlier laurels while shortsightedly nixing future possibilities, his aversion to criticism, his intolerance of differing opinions, and his short fuse. While the real-life Bela may have stopped just short of assuming the godlike qualities to which his Richard Vollin subscribes, the rest of his character's parts add up neatly to everyone's favorite Hungarian heavy.

No one can deny that Boris Karloff takes a back seat to his partner-in-crime in *The Raven*; there was just no way the soft-spoken Englishman could compete in terms of pure bombastic personality. In addition to coming in a distant second in terms of posture and blather, Karloff would also have had to admit that, for what it was worth, Lugosi was Universal's "Grand Old Man" of Edgar Allan Poe adaptations. The two masters of horror may have shared the honors in the previous year's Poe extravaganza, but it was Bela who had broken ground with 1932's *Murders in the Rue Morgue*. Whereas neither of the two films had actually had much to do with the offbeat American writer's source pieces, the royalty-free material and the cheaply-had Hungarian seemed to go arm-in-arm at Universal. In hindsight, probably only the change in corporate ownership in 1936 prevented Carl Laemmle or his studio from presaging Roger Corman and AIP as the premier exploiters of that most famous (and bizarre) of substance-abusers.

Thankfully, the bean counters somehow provided *The Raven* with a marginally larger budget than had been accorded its predecessor. The "windfall" amounting to a tad less than $20,000, was necessary because of (a) another

Opposite: One may wonder how Jack Pierce felt about Karloff's billing as "the uncanny master of make-up" in this poster for *The Raven*. RON BORST/HOLLYWOOD MOVIE POSTERS.

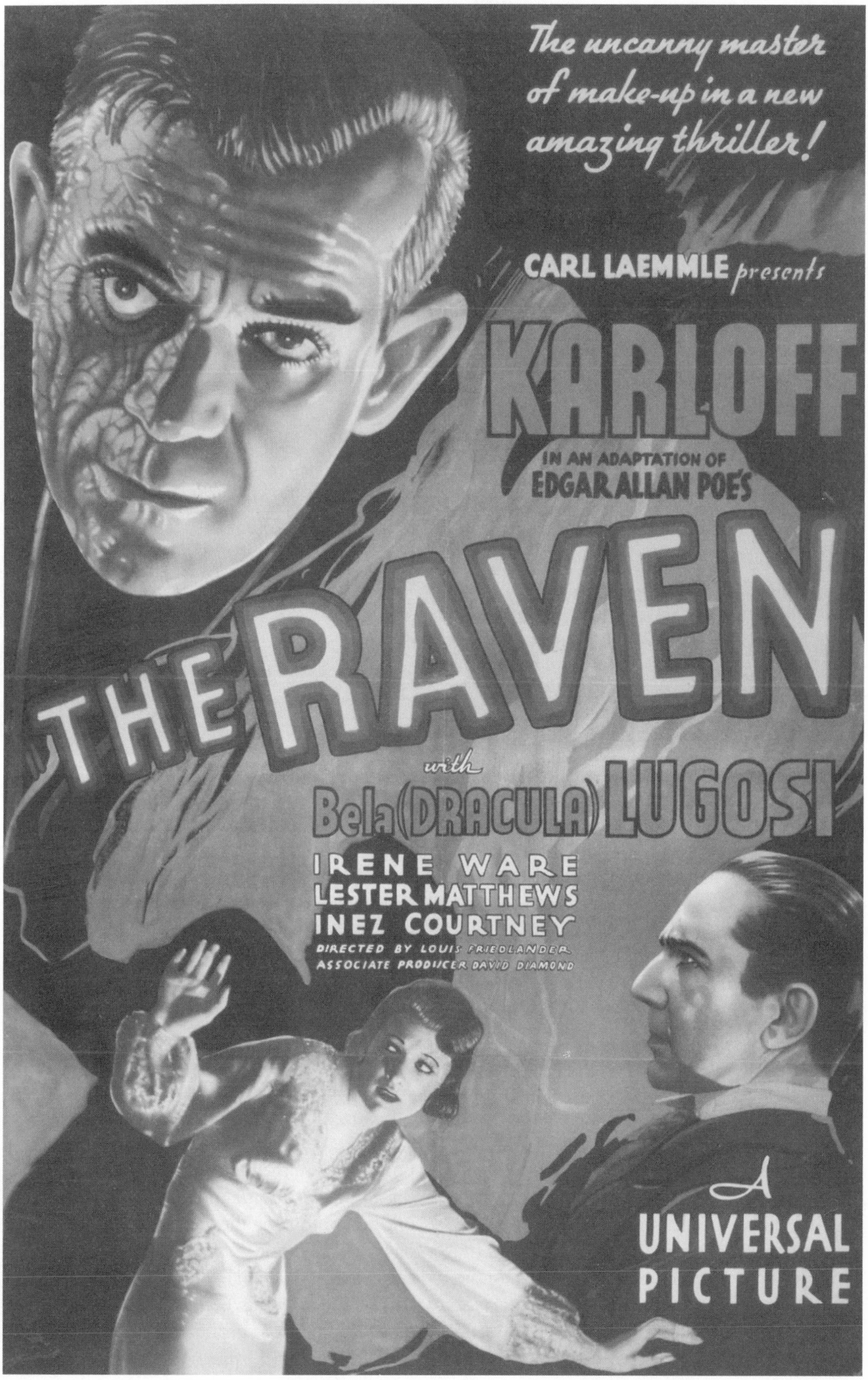
The uncanny master of make-up in a new amazing thriller!
CARL LAEMMLE presents
KARLOFF
IN AN ADAPTATION OF
EDGAR ALLAN POE'S
THE RAVEN
with
Bela (DRACULA) LUGOSI
IRENE WARE
LESTER MATTHEWS
INEZ COURTNEY
DIRECTED BY LOUIS FRIEDLANDER
ASSOCIATE PRODUCER DAVID DIAMOND
A UNIVERSAL PICTURE

In a sharp change from *The Black Cat*, Bela clearly occupies the forefront in *The Raven*. Director Louis Friedlander and director of photography Charles Stumar planned it that way and got no argument from Lugosi. *BUDDY BARNETT/CINEMA COLLECTORS.*

regularly scheduled pay raise for Karloff, who, despite a clearly supporting role, was pulling in a far heftier check than the second-billed but dramatically paramount Lugosi; (b) some healthy fees paid to various writers in their collective attempt to come up with a humdinger for the "nasty boys" (over a half-dozen were commissioned, involved, and rejected before the final nod was given to David Boehm, who had submitted three full treatments); and (c) the fact that virtually none of Vollin's instruments of torture could be jury-rigged from any of the standing Charles D. Hall sets which had been cannibalized repeatedly in the last several years. No matter. Hall realized the stunning art deco reaches of Marmaros on the pittance he'd been allotted, and Albert S. D'Agostino, now taking his shot at working some cut-rate magic, was allowed the use of

one of Hall's most recent concoctions (from *Bride of Frankenstein*) to help buoy up his budget. A few bucks were also tossed the way of studio composer Clifford Vaughan, who wove several wonderfully original leitmotifs into the body of public domain themes which had accompanied *The Black Cat*.

For every plus, there is a minus, and a perceived step backwards here was the choice of director. Up to this point in time, the classic horror renditions had been guided by directors possessed of either a personal genius or a growing familiarity with the genre. The number-one horror man on the lot, James Whale, would have visibly shuddered at any mention of being regarded as such. His *Bride of Frankenstein* had wrapped weeks before *The Raven* started production, but as part of the price for accepting the Shelley sequel, Whale had made it abundantly clear that *Bride* would be the last such film he would helm.

Karl Freund, Papa of *The Mummy*, had departed Universal when his contract ran out at the end of 1934, and was deeply involved in preproduction for the Peter Lorre–Colin Clive study in perversion, *Mad Love*, over at MGM. French-born Robert Florey, who had grudgingly led Bela Lugosi and a cast of seconds through *Murders in the Rue Morgue*, would be off the lot entirely for the next 20 years, as would Edgar Ulmer. Stuart Walker, who had supervised the chiaroscuro *Mystery of Edwin Drood* earlier that same year, had completed post-production on his *WereWolf of London* several weeks prior. The director was looking to take a breather from the darker side of life, though, and opted to guide Dorothy Page and Ricardo Cortez through *Manhattan Moon*, a semi-musical comedy.

Brought in to lead *The Raven* to the shores of profitability was Louis Friedlander, a veteran director with loads of experience, having waved his megaphone about through scores of silent features and a handful of talkie chapterplays. His familiarity with spookers, however, left something to be desired. Apart from 1934's science fiction serial *The Vanishing Shadow*, most of Friedlander's output had consisted of horse operas and mainstream "B's." Ironically, *The Raven* would actually benefit from the straightforward approach for which the director was known; with Bela Lugosi's manic protagonist swinging nonstop from *vivace* menace to overwrought hysteria with the measured pace of his basement pendulum, any attempt at creative maneuvering on the director's part would have upset the imbalance so carefully struck between the two horror greats. Charles Stumar's clever camera angles constantly provide a visual contrast between the two men — when they are together, Bela is almost always shot from below, so as to emphasize his loftier position, while Boris is rendered comparatively insignificant by being photographed from above — and any additional padding of the none-too-complex image would have been a case of cinematic overkill.

The Raven's clocking in at mere seconds over an hour is possible only because there is a tremendous compression of activity and reaction; there is simply no time for subtlety here. There is a breathless quality to *The Raven* which makes one feel that — shooting schedule apart — everyone concerned just wanted to get the damned thing over and be done with it. Other brief films such as *The Black Cat* managed to provide more detailed character studies without stinting on the horrific elements. Then again, there are many other films with similar running times, including for example Invincible's *Condemned to Live* (1935), which sacrificed virtually all of the action at the altar of gabby exposition and woefully overdrawn detail.

As with most of Friedlander's work, the picture starts off with a bang (or, more precisely, with a car crash). Inside the twisted wreckage is our heroine, Jean Thatcher (Irene Ware). In the next 59 minutes, she will be snatched from certain death by a seconds-long operation, be grateful, be awestruck, be frightened; will dance, laugh, weep, be nearly killed again; but will survive to meet the end music with a tear and a clench. The careering roadster and its horrendous fate may occupy only the film's very opening moments, but we've already missed Jean's taking leave of her many fans after another of her acclaimed dance performances. (If her later display of terpsichorean capability is any indication, she was fleeing for her life.) None of the resident surgeons at the local hospital can do much to help her. Not that they're not trying — one of them is even her sweetheart, Dr. Jerry Halden (Lester Matthews).

It seems that only Dr. Richard Vollin can prevent the sweet Jean from buying the farm. Vollin, however, is the supreme egotist of Universal horror movies; the very antithesis of Dracula, the narcissistic medico spends most of his spare time gazing into mirrors that aren't there. Jean's father, Judge Thatcher (Samuel S. Hinds), gets nowhere fast with offers of cash or appeals to humanity; Vollin won't lift a salvific finger until his ego is stroked. "So," he gobbles, "they say I am the *only* one!" In two shakes of a dead rabbit's tail, the careless young dancer is saved.

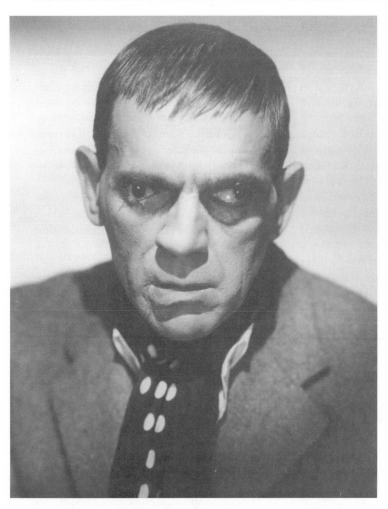

No, this is not Edmond Bateman's high school picture; it's one of Jack Pierce's early experiments. (Egad, that tie!) *BUDDY BARNETT/ CINEMA COLLECTORS.*

typical of the dialogue that made it to the screen; one can only wince at the thought of the stuff they passed on. Vollin, whose omniscience allows him to complete other people's sentences, makes a pitch for the dazzled young woman. She rebuffs him but then invites him to a special dance performance, which she has fittingly entitled "The Spirit of Poe."

It is commonly assumed that Miss Ware did her own dancing for "The Spirit of Poe." One would hate to think that Universal budgeted anything whatsoever for a *professional* dancer to leap gracelessly to Theodore Kosloff's mundane choreography, but the dancer is masked, so it's anybody's guess.* Vollin may not really be a god, but he knows good leaping when he sees it, and he rushes backstage. Judge Thatcher, disturbed by the doctor's enthusiasm, later spends a couple of minutes trying to dissuade him from seeing Jean again. Vollin grimaces and squints, sure signs that something is up.

Driven by gratitude and the ticking clock, Jean visits Vollin's home, where, this being a horror movie, he noodles (what else?) Bach's Toccata in D Minor on the organ for her. (Why don't any of these creepy types ever play the accordion?) The music sends Jean into an unlikely fit of rapture, wherein she is forced by the script to say, "You're not only a great surgeon, but a great musician, too. You're almost *not* a man. Almost..." Sadly, this is

At this point, someone on the production staff remembered that Boris Karloff was sitting around, collecting $2,500 a week for drinking tea. Mr. Karloff? On the set, please.

After a few moments of lurking and skulking (but only a few), Karloff's character, Bateman, makes a beeline for the Vollin mansion. Now, thugs and gangsters had never been Boris's forte, and Bateman promised to be the least successful of an unhappy lot, but for one

---

Brunas, Brunas and Weaver aver that there was a pro, a Nina Golden, doubling Miss Ware in the Poe "ballet." While I am second to none in my admiration for Universal Horrors, *some unknown force within me — a combination of disbelief and good taste, perhaps — renders me incapable of accepting this revelation as fact.*

thing: Karloff played the part with his tongue so far up in his cheek that his trademark lisp went all but unheard.

This attitude of his is the crux of one of the major points of interest for Karloffians and Lugosiphiles in their never-ending debate on stylistic superiority. Bela, it is argued, never saw himself as "above" his material; he always gave 110 percent. Discounting his catastrophically cavalier disregard for *Frankenstein*, this is undoubtedly true. The fact that Lugosi played the most depressingly absurd claptrap as if it were *Hamlet* points out the actor's professional sincerity and dedication to his craft. During the first part of the decade, Bela probably never noticed the humorous sparkle in the eyes of his costars or caught the inherently ludicrous tilt to some of his screenplays; this felony was compounded by his difficulties with the language and his mistrust of certain of his colleagues.

Karloff, of course, instantly saw through David Boehm's final treatment. (In fairness to Boehm, perhaps it was one of the other seven writers who should hang for the abysmally stilted dialogue.) He noticed how, within seconds of meeting Vollin, Bateman spills his guts in stereotypical gangster-speak. From his Damon Runyonesque flirtation with the fractured subjunctive ("I want that you should fix my face") to his sporadic plunges into the historical present ("Ever since I'm born, everybody looks at me and says, 'You're ugly'"), Boehm's shifty killer comes across more like Nathan Detroit from *Guys and Dolls* than as a serious menace. Karloff knew that mouthing tripe like that without cracking a smile would take a far more strait-laced actor than he, and that the man who *could* deliver the goods was already giving Vollin's equally preposterous lines the vocal weight due Holy Scripture.

Was this a case of Karloff's feeling superior to his material, or merely a slyly nuanced reading which, in his professional judgment, would offer greater rewards to actor and audience alike? The cricket-loving heavy had had "a good inning" as Hjalmar Poelzig in *The Black Cat*; spouting schoolboy Latin, relishing the clever wordplays with which Edgar Ulmer and Peter Ruric had peppered the script, and even

taking his own turn cranking out the Bach toccata at the organ — the Briton had invested his character with a dimension behind that malevolent facade. Discernible through that portrait of unwavering evil, visible to those who had eyes to see, Karloff was having a hoot. Poelzig, Marmaros, the incredible scope of the engineer's villainy — all this was *way* too far out to be taken seriously. Even under John Mescall's low lights, the twinkle in Boris's eye couldn't be missed. Bela, of course, had played Vitus Werdegast as if he were out on loan from August Strindberg.

Meanwhile, back at the mansion, Vollin has concocted an ingenious plan for revenge. Acting on Bateman's earnest desire to "look good" (surely something of a good-natured jibe at Karloff; all the talk of "ugly" going around refers to the actor's own bearded but otherwise unencumbered face), Vollin agrees to one of his 10-minute surgical specialties. (Actually, the operation lasts only long enough for Clifford Vaughan's splendid "Bateman" theme to build up a head of steam.) When the bandages are removed (where does one even find time to put bandages *on* during a 10-minute operation?), nary a soul is surprised to find that the jittery killer is now very much the worse for wear.

The makeup is not one of Jack Pierce's better efforts. Sporting a look which borrows heavily in concept from Chaney's Quasimodo, the newly unnerved Bateman exhibits only half a functional face. Apart from its alarmingly "Halloweenish" look, Pierce's handiwork robs Karloff of his most expressive feature, his eyes. In addition, a set of dental fixtures and a layer or three of facial wax now make it enormously difficult for the actor to articulate the few simplistic lines left him. If Boris had ever thought there was the remotest chance of pulling his own weight in *The Raven*, his unfortunate dialogue and debilitating, cartoonish makeup must have quickly convinced him that some discreet laughter up his sleeve was the only antidote to the effects of such "horror."

Anyhow, the enraged Bateman empties his revolver into a gallery of full-length mirrors (Ahhh, there they are), further jostles the viewers with a Monster-like growl, and then settles into an uncomfortable partnership with the beaming Vollin. In order to lure the unwary flies into his trap, the mad surgeon invites Jean, her dad, and Dr. Jerry to a sleep-over at his place. Unfathomably, he also extends the invitation to a number of comic-relief types, in from left field. While the crowd is having a rollicking good time with one of Vollin's congenial parlor games(!), the mere sight of Bateman's gargoyle-like puss elicits a scream from the sensitive Jean. This is only a setup for a later Quasimodo/Esmeralda–inspired moment when the lovely Jean will actually apologize to the misshapen brute, thus assuring that, when the guano finally hits the fan, Bateman will be her slave rather than Vollin's.

The scene of passionate rhetoric that follows was probably meant to explain why Vollin's obsession with things Poe-tic controls his every action. Unfortunately, due in part to Boehm's awkward composition and in part to Lugosi's physical inability to grow any more profoundly intense without imploding, having flirted with critical mass from our very first glimpse of him, the deep thoughts being revealed come off as little more than so much wasted time in a film that has no time to spare.

Having thus worn his heart on his sleeve for ravens to peck at, Vollin decides to shut up for a moment (but only for a moment) and allow his collection of torture devices to speak for him. Another inside joke (was Bela in on this one?) has Lugosi lead Karloff below-stairs for a virtual mirror-image replay of the celebrated cellar scene from *The Black Cat*. A second non-surprise follows immediately as Bateman predictably shackles the surprised Vollin beneath the deadly pendulum. Just as predictably, the lunatic doctor is released, unharmed; most of the viewers had seen Bateman's dilemma coming before the ink could dry on Boehm's derivative script.

In the next few minutes, all hell breaks loose. Judge Thatcher is spirited from his room, still in his jammies, and affixed to the slab beneath the pendulum. Pausing only long enough to exchange a few remarks with the judge, Vollin unveils a master control board and starts yanking at its levers with the fervor

of a frantic shopper, battling over remainders at a white sale. Jean's entire room sinks into the cellar, steel shutters close off the remaining avenues of escape, and the phone lines are automatically cut.

Besides the incredible sinking room, Vollin has outfitted his mansion with a telescoping room, whose walls close in on each other at the touch of a switch. Forcing Jean and Dr. Jerry into this last at gunpoint, the crazed Vollin then launches into a raucous litany of semi-coherent outbursts about Poe, genius, and revenge. When's he's finally ranted his way through all the appalling lines Boehm has provided (the topper being "Poe! You are avenged!"—whatever the hell that means), Lugosi tosses in some gratuitous cackling and a burst of spastic arm-waving; the only olive missing from the plate is a spontaneous mazurka.

It is now, of course, that Bateman turns on his master and shuts down the moving-wall machinery. Vollin doesn't hesitate to plug him, but the dying gangster nevertheless overpowers the lunatic and drags him to the death chamber, while Jean, Jerry, and a couple of chuckleheads rush to unfetter the judge. The walls close in on Vollin, Bateman expires, justice triumphs, and a lame wrap-up squanders the film's remaining seconds.

The Raven is a silly little movie, but despite an overload of horrific devices, it is not at all mean-spirited. The sheer volume of degradation on display was enough for the British Board of Film Censors to call it quits, and when the Brits vowed to pass on any similar future efforts, the bottom fell out of the overseas chiller market as quickly as Jean's bedroom hit the basement floor. Upon closer inspection, it would seem that the transatlantic naysayers had really picked on the wrong movie over which to take a firm stand. The excesses of *The Black Cat* had been far greater, and the adult perversions which Edgar Ulmer had sneaked past the Universal brass made the juvenile twists and shouts of Friedlander's little shocker seem like children's ghost stories told around a campfire.

Talking at length about anyone other than

Karloff or Lugosi here would be frivolous, but a few performances deserve comment. Samuel S. Hinds did his usual splendid job as Judge Thatcher, and was the most credible and coolly professional presence in the piece. Irene Ware was lovely, did what she could with the sophomoric part, and went on to other things. Lester Matthews had been better (or, at least, had appeared more manly) in *WereWolf of London*, but like Miss Ware, he now had to contend with the limitations of David Boehm's screenplay. (Note how, in simpler times, demonstrably foreign villains named Boris or Bela were continually foiled by WASPish types bearing such prosaic handles as Melvyn or Lester. Under the subsequent cloud of threatened nuclear disaster, we survived decades where far more substantial imagery was needed, and so the cinematic protectors of motherhood, homeland and the like were retitled Rip, or Rock, or Tab. Life, like most things, has come full circle, and within the last ten years, our greatest American heroes are once again guys with such schmendrick names as Arnold or Sylvester.)

For the Lugosiphiles who insist the Karloff would drift through certain of his films as if on autopilot, there is certainly enough evidence in *The Raven* to make the accusation. It's unlikely, however, that the sly Brit could be convicted — not here, at any rate. I defer to legendary film historian William K. Everson, who explained (in his *Classics of the Horror Film*):

> Karloff's screen performances generally fell into one of three categories: those where he genuinely respected the film and the role and gave of his best; those, like both versions of *The Raven* and *The Mask of Fu Manchu*, where he realized that the roles could never be taken seriously and approached them in a bravura, tongue-in-cheek style; and the *Voodoo Island* and *Frankenstein 1970* roles where he merely walked through the films without undue effort....

Mr. Everson felt that Karloff's work in *The Black Cat* fell into the first of the three categories, and while I disagree in part (the role was indeed a plum, but Karloff couldn't have failed to see the outrageousness of the entire project), I would be foolish not to allow the distinguished critic his very educated opinion. I take pride in concurring with Mr. Everson regarding the Bateman extravaganza, though. There can be no clearer indication of Karloff's view on the whole nine yards than his behavior during the wild and woolly finale. Amidst waving guns and swooping blades and creaking gears and shuddering women, Karloff stands complacently, near the supine figure of Thatcher, *pere*. As the scythe-like pendulum sways to and fro, drawing ever nearer to dissecting the tough-as-nails judge, the actor allows his one good eye to roll in rhythm with the blade. Probably humming to himself all the while, Karloff allows Bateman to become some sort of obscene metronome, marking time until called upon to perform his next bit of predictable bogey shtick.

With the house afire pace that Lugosi sets for himself from outset to the denouement, there can be little doubt that the Hungarian wouldn't have seen the absurdity of the movie if it had bitten him. Uttering his every line as if it were worthy of being etched in stone, Bela nevertheless gives a ballsy performance that has rightly been praised over the years for its no-nonsense theatricality and flamboyance. That there are far more subtle moments in the razing of an abandoned building than in his portrayal of Richard Vollin does nothing to invalidate either the wholeheartedly enthusiastic approach of the actor or the singlemindedly twisted maneuverings of his character.

Perhaps, had the pictures been made and released in reverse order, with Friedlander and Boehm's *The Raven* hitting the screens before Ulmer and Ruric's *The Black Cat*, the juvenile trappings of the former might have been regarded as nothing more than a fumbling, misguided attempt at establishing a "formula." In that light, the second film would probably have been heralded as a more successful "fine-tuning" of the formula; contemporary reviews would most likely have indicated that the Universal Poe "series" was finally hitting its stride. That wasn't the case, however, and things turned out the way they did.

For some reason, *The Raven* isn't as readily available nowadays as is *The Black Cat*; the Marmaros saga seems to turn up on late night TV (or on the Sci Fi Channel) a half-dozen times for every showing of its successor.

As Tom Weaver so astutely recognizes, *The Raven* is the only entry in the "Golden Age of Horror" in which the villains alone buy the farm. There's that wrinkle, to be sure, as well as a pendulum of which Edgar A. would have approved, and mechanical marvels worthy of Buster Keaton. In terms of subtlety and sophistication, however, the last of the studio's 1930s Poe pictures is strictly Mickey Mouse.

The Raven

Released July 22, 1935; 61 minutes

Cast: Boris Karloff (Edmond Bateman); Bela Lugosi (Dr. Richard Vollin); Lester Matthews (Dr. Jerry Halden); Irene Ware (Jean Thatcher); Samuel S. Hinds (Judge Thatcher); Spencer Charters (Col. Bertram Grant); Inez Courtney (Mary Burns); Ian Wolfe (Geoffrey "Pinky" Burns); Maidel Turner (Harriet Grant); Jonathan Hale (Dr. Cook); Arthur Hoyt (Chapman); Walter Miller (Dr. Hemingway); Cyril Thornton (Servant); Bud Osborne (Policeman); Al Ferguson (Cook); Madeline Talcott (Nurse); Monte Montague (Double for Karloff); George DeNormand (Double for Lugosi)

Credits: Associate Producer — David Diamond; Director — Louis Friedlander (Lew Landers); Screenplay — David Boehm; Suggested by the poem "The Raven" and the short story "The Pit and the Pendulum" by Edgar Allan Poe; Director of Photography — Charles Stumar; Film Editor — Albert Akst; Editorial Supervision — Maurice Pivar; Dialogue Director — Florence Enright; Art Director — Albert S. D'Agostino; Assistant Directors — Scott Beal and Victor Noerdlinger; Sound Supervisor — Gilbert Kurland; Musical Score — Clifford Vaughan, Heinz Roemheld and Y. Franke Harling; Dance Staged by Theodore Kosloff; Makeup — Jack P. Pierce

REMEMBER LAST NIGHT? (1935)

In chronologically ordered compilations such as this, Whale watchers generally pack it in after they've determined which way the wind blows on *Bride of Frankenstein*. *Remember Last Night?* seems to have a lot going for it, though: It is James Whale's first film following the Shelley sequel, the premise — the characters were all too drunk to recall who did in one of their number the night before — is intriguing, and halfway through the picture, there's a pip of an atmospheric hypnosis scene centered on one of everybody's all-time favorite goblins and culminating in his cold-blooded murder. Sound good?

I'm a fan of the film solely because of that one scene, however; the rest of Whale's "comedy mystery" I can easily live without. Some folks (like me) consider the film dated, uneven, irritating, needlessly convoluted, and overblown. Others view it as a colorful period piece (the period being the mid–1930s), a pastiche of then-popular movie types, a textbook example of formulaic filmmaking, and an exercise in ensemble acting. Still others, blind to all save the director's name, see the master's hand in the stylish but caustic touches which grace the overly intricate mystery.

The project slotted for production once *Bride* was in the can was *Show Boat*, a whole-hog remake of the company's part-talkie effort from 1928, and Whale had gone into the horror

film counting on its timely wrap, an absolute necessity if his segue into the big-budget musical was to be trouble-free. *Show Boat* had to be put on hold, though, as that perennial thorn in the Laemmle side — cash flow — got sharper as the decade wore on.

Junior immediately began to get antsy, and Whale suggested that *The Hangover Murders*, a novel which he had personally enjoyed, would make a great stopgap movie. The cast was hurriedly assembled from the contract players, Whale managed to secure the services of many of the studio's premier technicians, and shooting began in late July.

Tony (Robert Young) and Carlotta (Constance Cummings), the Milburns, are kicking off their six-month anniversary with a kiss for the record books when an invitation to a party is slipped under the door to their expansive digs. The "progressive dinner to be drunk" is as follows:

> Hors D'oeuvres and Doings at Hulings
> Sup and Such at Billy Arliss'
> Repast and Remorse at Whitridges
> Dessert and DTs at Faronea's
> Hangovers Ad Lib

Everyone in the circle the Milburns frequent has more money than God and a healthy thirst, to boot. The first two reels follow the

Gustav von Seyffertitz omitted from the title card? *Somebody* isn't remembering last night. PENTAGRAM LIBRARY.

Milburns and their married friends, Jake and Penny Whitridge (Reginald Denny, Louise Henry), Vic and Bette Huling (George Meeker, Sally Eilers), and good old bachelor Billy Arliss (Monroe Owsley), as they wend their way from mansion to mansion, quaffing up a storm, hurling invective and discretion to the wind, all to the raucous melodies of … Franz Waxman (!).

Early on, it's established that Penny has her eye out for some extramarital action and that something is going on between Bette and chauffeur Fred Flannagan (Robert Armstrong). It also becomes clear that Vic is a bit of a wastrel, having solicited "investments" in a phony oil well from his friends. Tony not-so-quietly reproaches Vic for having made threatening noises about money to Billy, but before

the words they exchange can lead to blows, the crowd is off for more merriment.

Besides delineating Vic Huling as the odds-on victim-to-be, these early reels unveil a world where people vie for each other's approval amid vulgar displays of wealth: White tie and tails and floor-length gowns are the uniforms of the evening, possessions are destroyed in direct proportion to their worth (Bette instructs Tony and Carlotta to fire a handy cannon at her home instead of shooting at the police station; "It's bigger and funnier"), servants and policemen are treated with disdain, and there's money to burn. The Hulings' butler, Phelps (Arthur Treacher), is made to wander through the story like Marley's Ghost, his lugubrious comments in counterpoint to the commands and insults flung at him by the brash moneyed set. Phelps is clearly tagged "comic relief," but there's little funny about the contempt with which he's treated.

A subplot has Faronea (Gregory Ratoff), a foreign restaurateur, planning with chauffeur Baptiste (Jack LaRue) and a burly thug who remains nameless to kidnap Vic Huling. "He's going to stay down here in the cellar, very quietly, until Mrs. Huling pays for his release," promises Faronea, as he toys with a pair of manacles.

The morning after the night before, Tony and Carlotta awaken in one of the Huling residence's cavernous guest rooms. Neither Milburn remembers much, but Carlotta foggily recalls Vic and Tony having a quarrel. When a call to the garage informs them that a bloody rag has been discovered in their car by the Hulings' resident mechanic, the worried pair is off to track down Vic. Vic, it transpires, is dead, having been shot under the arm and into the ticker. Tony runs to fetch Bette, but the lovely blonde is nowhere to be found, and her bed hasn't been slept in. They do find Penny, sans Jake and difficult to rouse. Mrs. Milburn shudders. "Steady," Tony advises her. "They can't all be dead."

Tony calls an old buddy, detective Danny Harrison (Edward Arnold), and arranges for Danny and his assistant, Maxie (Edward Brophy), to head out to the scene of the crime by train. Danny has the police photographer (E.E. Clive, in a very funny cameo) do his thing, and then assembles the survivors. "Now listen, you guys, you're a lot of crazy drunks and I like every one of you, but you're holding some things back and I want 'em." Unfortunately, no one can remember a thing. Just then, Bette and Billy turn up (raised eyebrows all around) in time to watch the morgue wagon lug off Vic's cadaver. "I'm sorry, my little playmates," announces Danny, "but it's murder. Any one of you might have killed Vic Huling."

Faronea later claims that Tony and Vic had a violent argument at his place, and that Tony had made menacing moves towards his friend, using the chef's veal knife. Danny pays no attention to such nonsense, but a card, bearing a cryptic message in Greek, sets him to wondering. The card is locked in the Huling safe, alongside some intriguing canceled checks for very large sums of money. None of the items stays put for long; everything is surreptitiously taken from the safe, but Carlotta, who happens to speak Greek, advises that the card said "Opportunity will knock twice."

Carlotta then remembers that they went for a dip in the pool the night before, and everyone runs over to hunt for clues. A set of deep footprints in shoes piques a lot of interest. Although Danny has molds made, Tony is positive the shoe prints belonged to Vic: "He had the flattest feet on Long Island." At an impasse, Tony goes to the phone once again. He announces that he is calling in Professor Karl Herman Eckhardt-Jones, a famed psychologist-cum-hypnotist. Later that evening, the crowd is dressed to the nines and nervously awaiting the arrival of the professor.

It is, of course, a dark and stormy night. Eckhardt-Jones (Gustav von Seyffertitz) wastes little time in setting the scene. Lit from below, the hypnotist informs the group, "I shall make each one of you try to remember the incidents of last night now dormant in your subconscious mind." A series of legs in pants and gowns represents the turns taken by the antsy socialites. Tony's memory is, perhaps, jogged the most. He recalls the silliness at the pool and Vic sitting there, almost comatose, with a drink being poured into his mouth. He recalls arising from his bed at 5:00 AM, watching Jake carry Vic up the stairs, and being pestered for a kiss by Penny. Eckhardt-Jones nods, and the men head back to their companions.

Eckhardt-Jones takes the floor. "The murderer of Vic Huling is in this room," he declares. "Several of you have real or imaginative motives. One of you tried to deceive me by pretended hypnosis. A link has been formed by each of you. No single story was complete, but, put together, they form a chain of evidence which proves conclusively that the murderer of Vic Huling is..."

The sound of broken glass heralds the gunshot which removes Eckhardt-Jones and his theory in one fell swoop. More footprints, this time a woman's, are found outside where the

murderer of Eckhardt-Jones had to have stood. Before anyone can note that Carlotta is missing from the group, the millionairess calls from the second story window and tells Danny that the footprint molds made earlier that day are now missing. A new Greek card has turned up, however, and, according to Carlotta, the writing means "Come at once. Wine cellar. Use back door. B.B." B.B. just may refer to Baptiste Bouclier, the chauffeur and would-be kidnapper of Vic Huling.

Tony and Carlotta zoom over to Faronea's and make for the wine cellar. Forced to hide in a musty back room when Faronea and that burly thug show up, they are discovered when Tony unwisely (but true to form) reaches out his hand for a bottle of Napoleon brandy. Faronea has the couple at gunpoint and it looks like curtains until Tony flashes the badge his wife lifted from Maxie and announces, "We got Baptiste and he confessed." Winging it for all he's worth, Tony blathers how Vic wouldn't come along quietly but put up a fight, and Baptiste killed him. Baptiste took all the money he could find, split it with Faronea, and..." While the restaurateur is in the very act of denying everything, the nameless thug lets fly with a knife, and Faronea slumps to the floor.

Tony heads back to Vic's house, where he lets a uniformed cop take Carlotta inside to safety. In the quarters over the garage, Tony finds Baptiste, dead. When Danny shows up, both men make for the apartment of Mme. Bouclier, Baptiste's mother. Bouclier, mère (Rafaela Ottiano), is already aware of her son's death and tells the police that somehow Baptist had come up with enough money to pay for the operation that restored her eyesight.

Back at Huling's, Danny and Tony catch up with Flannagan, who had bailed out during the picture's opening reel. The chauffeur, an ex-con, claims that he went into hiding because he knew that he wouldn't get a fair shake from the cops. Seething with anger, Danny does a little precipitous conclusion-jumping, and in his umpteenth extreme closeup in as many minutes, lets Flannagan have it:

> DANNY: You're gonna burn for it, Flannagan! They'll shave your head and clamp a wet sponge on it. And they'll slap you in the chair and give you the works and when the juice fries your backbone, the lights'll be dim but you won't be seeing it. And your face won't be pasty white as it is now. It'll be black! As black as your hat!

A bit anticlimactic is the fact that Flannagan, naturally, didn't do it. Bette takes her turn on the emotional merry-go-round. Flannagan, she reveals, is her brother and she, well, she's not the chic, soigné lady the world has thought; on the contrary, "I was born in the gutter, and I'm proud of it." Although not quite sure what a gutter is, Carlotta comforts Bette, as Tony and Danny — certain that they've finally got a handle on the mystery — rush over to the Whitridges'.

They couldn't be righter. Before the cops arrive, Billy Arliss informs Jake that he intends to make a clean breast of things, alluding to his own jail record under a different name. Jake overpowers the smaller man and shoves him in the gun room; within moments, Billy shoots himself out of remorse. It matters little, though, as Danny and Tony have it all figured out.

Jake had been on the receiving end of some very healthy blackmail money from Billy, who didn't want his shady past made public. In order to pay, Billy had borrowed heavily from Vic (those canceled checks), who had subsequently discovered the arrangement and come to threaten Jake with jail; Jake killed Vic in order to keep his cushy little situation quiet. After he paid Baptiste to shoot Jones (to prevent him from naming Vic's murderer), Jake plugged the chauffeur as well. Penny helped Jake pretend that Vic was still breathing at the pool party and flirted with Tony at 5:00 AM in order to keep him from noticing Vic too clearly.

Opposite: Professor Karl Herman Eckhardt-Jones (Gustav von Seyffertitz) sets ground rules for a hypnotic solution to the mystery. PENTAGRAM LIBRARY.

And believe it or not, that attempt by Faronea and the gang to kidnap Vic was merely a coincidence.

In an effort to escape, Jake pulls a small pistol from the cigarette box, but he and Penny succeed only in backing into the waiting arms of Maxie and the bulls. The socialite's smug vow that he'll beat the rap in court is undermined when he's told that Baptiste's girlfriend was hidden in the chauffeur's closet and witnessed his murder at the hands of Whitridge. The Whitridges are led off, and Danny has his crazy friends promise they'll never take another drink. Thankfully, the zany crowd can still abuse their servants.

According to Whale biographer James Curtis, the director "considered [*Remember Last Night?*] — along with *The Invisible Man* — one of his personal favorites," yet it remains a difficult film to like, for all its visual impact. The screenplay elevates every facet of Adam Hobhouse's *The Hangover Murders* to unpleasant excess, robbing the finished product of the quite definable charm that other 1930s comedy-mystery pictures had in spades. While the basic premise of the story takes an experience most people have probably had at least once in their lives (drinking to excess and being unable to remember what they did afterwards) and pushes it to a melodramatic extreme, the milieu in which it all takes place must have been as foreign to Depression-era audiences as the imperial courts of Siam or the royal necropolis of Egypt. Even now, more than six decades after the picture was first released, viewers who lived through those hardest of times shudder at the movie's depiction of the wanton behavior of the privileged, very idle rich.

Remember Last Night? is Whale's spin on the marriage of two disparate genres: the stylistically overindulgent musical comedy (à la Busby Berkeley) and the "gentleman-detective" variation on the classic whodunit. The early part of the picture unfolds to the nonstop accompaniment of a very hotcha musical score and includes a *mise-en-scène* featuring Cleopatra and her retinue, impersonated by the jolly inebriates, sporting the rich man's version of blackface: vile "Sambo" masks. The film takes off at a frenetic pace, and necessary plot details are nearly lost in the whirlwind of guzzled champagne, sexual overtures, humiliated servants, smashed crockery, and discharged cannon — all to the frothy and frivolous rhythms of an invisible orchestra.

Not one of the wealthy protagonists is admirable, and that includes Tony and Carlotta Milburn. Ostensibly the hero of the piece, Tony is as irresponsible as his friends: He willfully destroys others' property, recklessly endangers life and limb, breaks a slew of traffic laws, denigrates the police, and is demeaning and abusive to Phelps. An attempt is made to reduce the taint this behavior leaves on the young man's personality by having virtually everyone act in an equally obnoxious fashion, but this ploy reduces Tony to nothing more than a typically bad egg in a rotten dozen. Even Tony's fidelity to his wife of six months — challenged at every turn by the promiscuous Penny and regarded as truly remarkable by the rest of the drunken group — really only indicates that the millionaire hasn't sunk to that particular vice yet.

For a healthy contrast, one need only take a peek at the Thin Man movies, which proved to be far more enduring for their plausibility and proximity to reality.

Nick and Nora Charles' tremendous and timeless appeal was at least partially due to their being considerate and charming as well as usually somewhat tipsy. Nick may hobnob with a crowd of Damon Runyon types, including ex-cons, punchy fighters, race track touts, informers, enforcers, and derby-hatted comic bulls, but while he may make the occasional joke at their expense, he would never be caught dead patronizing any one of them. Nora takes as good as she gives, going so far as to down an armful of martinis — "Line them up!" — in order to catch up with her Nicky, and moves among her husband's oddball friends graciously and well. The only life Nick would occasionally endanger was his own, any laws that might receive a massaging were bent in the course of the investigation at hand, and neither partner would ever act with anything other than complete respect for those less fortunate than they. If property was to be savaged for comic effect, that duty would fall to Asta.

The charm which Robert Young would later radiate during his successful television series, however, is nowhere to be found in *Remember*, and while Cummings' Carlotta is undeniably lovely and rich, she's just not real. Clever is as clever does, and as the couple never seems to progress beyond the level of arch dialogue or cutesy interplay, the audience is left with the feeling that, Tony's sexual fidelity notwithstanding, there's less to the Milburns than meets the eye. Even if one didn't know that Whale had wanted to begin his film with the flourish others traditionally reserved for the fadeout, Tony and Carlotta's protracted initial kiss seems a stunt when compared with the shorter but somehow undeniably genuine displays of affection in which the Charleses indulge.

Edward Arnold gamely juggles the unequal halves of a poorly balanced role. His Danny Harrison is clearly a working stiff, being attached to the district attorney's office, yet he's also remarkably well acquainted with the Milburns and their ilk, who are supposedly the cream of Long Island society. The script has Danny constantly jumping vocal hurdles, and Whale has cameraman Joseph Valentine cut to extreme closeup whenever the socialite–cum–police dog barks. This constant back-and-forth is annoying, and by the picture's end, you're ready to sell your soul rather than sit through yet another ECU. The height of unreality is reached when Danny actually thanks Tony for slugging some sense back into him, admitting "I wouldn't have liked you if you hadn't. Say … You pack a hefty right."

The combination of Doris Malloy, Harry Clork and Dan Totheroth's script and James Whale's arch and insensitive helming leaves *Remember Last Night?* with not one but two bona fide grotesques: Gustav von Seyffertitz and Arthur Treacher. Treacher found a niche for himself in sound films from early on. Molded by Hollywood into a living stereotype like Franklin Pangborn, Fritz Feld, or Eric Blore, Treacher put aside for his declining years by portraying an interminable succession of gentleman's gentlemen and comic butlers, all cut of the same striped cloth. In Whale's overview, the actor is encouraged to painful excess by his dialogue and condemned to stark caricature by his delivery. During the movie's closing moments, it finally appears that the worm has turned when Phelps, blowing a verbal raspberry at the patronizing crowd, reinjects a little necessary madcap spirit into the film. Whale, again misreading the handwriting on the tapestry, has Tony and the others squirt seltzer and hurl fruit at the beleaguered butler, effectively robbing the "little man" in the audience of any kind of vicarious victory over the smugly superior millionaires.

The true delight of the picture is gaunt old Gustav von Seyffertitz as Professor Karl Herman Eckhardt-Jones, and the actor's presence in what was surely the most atypical role of his career was due solely to Whale's brilliantly eccentric eye for casting. Eckhardt-Jones is essentially a *deus ex machina*, shut down prematurely. The viewer has little doubt that the hawk-billed hypnotist has indeed systematically pared away layers of unconsciousness and deceit from the suspects and will identify the murderer. Such a revelation, however, would have mortally wounded the dramatic integrity of the picture: Neither Danny nor Tony could then be said to have done the heroic deed. More importantly, with the big scene taking place barely halfway through the movie, there's no mystery that more potent forces than Eckhardt-Jones' tendency to prattle on or Baptiste's facility with a handgun had to intervene to give the public its money's worth.

Prior to the Great War, von Seyffertitz had emigrated from the Fatherland to Britain, where his wildly angular features made him a natural-born heavy in silent films. The eponymous *Moriarty* in the 1922 thriller (based on William Gillette's play, starring John Barrymore, and released in the United States as *Sherlock Holmes*), von Seyffertitz went on to genre notoriety in such heady offerings as *The Wizard* (1927), *The Bat Whispers* (1930), and *She* (1935).

The actor never lost his heavy accent, which makes for some rough sledding during

Professor Eckhardt-Jones' lengthy recitation in *Remember Last Night?* Still, the scene in which the tired and confused survivors parade in and out of the drawing room, becoming lost in the swirling concentric circles of the hypnosis-inducing machine before submitting to Eckhardt-Jones' psychological scrutiny, is easily the best in the picture.

The critics didn't think much of *Remember Last Night?*, and, if the film's obscurity is any indication, the ticket-buyers weren't overly responsive, either. James Curtis maintains that even Junior, who had come to have absolute faith in his ace's abilities and judgment, disliked the film and the novel on which it was based.

Just as there is far too much sound and fury for the film's slim mystery element (Let's face it: we *know* Tony and Carlotta didn't do it; Billy is too obvious; Flannagan's taking a powder is too suspicious; the kidnappers are too pat; and Phelps is too funny for words — who's left?), so also is there way too little comedy to be found. Whale's vaunted humor seldom ranges beyond sophomoric limits, and even the inside jokes (Carlotta's poolside cry, "I'm Dracula's daughter," is balanced by her later confession, "I feel like the bride of Frankenstein") are too transparent to be witty. Arthur Treacher and Edward Brophy are meant to share the wealth as the comic relief, but the former is an annoying cartoon, and the latter's brutish demeanor works against his every chance at being amusing. The *bons mots* the screenwriters have popped into the mouths of Tony and Carlotta are uneven; when they do manage to wring a grin from the viewer, the credit has to go to Young's or Cummings' own sense of timing and delivery.

Those odd bits of enchantment in characterization that genre fans have come to associate with the director are nowhere in evidence. More distressingly, one comes away with the feeling that, despite his supposed affection for this picture, Whale contented himself with dusting off a handful of his most readily recognizable tricks (such as that trademark extreme closeup, which he beats into the ground here) instead of imbuing the movie

with substance as well as style. Many of the studio's best technicians did their damnedest to coax the director's vision out of the raw clay in which they worked. When the backing of these technical wizards had produced the justly renowned Frankenstein pictures, *The Old Dark House*, and *The Invisible Man*, Whale had taken the most florid of solo bows. In *Remember Last Night?*, their combined efforts can add little but visual elegance to their leader's nasty framework. Whale should be the one taking the seltzer and the fruit.

An object lesson to those who would toss around sobriquets like "genius" carelessly, *Remember Last Night?* has very few isolated moments of unfettered enjoyment, and these collapse with Gustav von Seyffertitz. Nevertheless, for those fans with more patience and greater tolerance than I, the picture is out there for perusal.

Remember Last Night?

Released November 4, 1935; 85 minutes

Cast: Edward Arnold (Danny Harrison); Constance Cummings (Carlotta Milburn); Robert Young (Tony Milburn); Sally Eilers (Bette Huling); Robert Armstrong (Fred Flannagan); Reginald Denny (Jake Whitridge); Monroe Owsley (Billy Arliss); George Meeker (Vic Huling); Edward Brophy (Maxie); Jack LaRue (Baptiste); Louise Henry (Penny Whitridge); Gregory Ratoff (Faronea); Arthur Treacher (Phelps); Gustav von Seyffertitz (Professor Eckhardt-Jones); Rafaela Ottiano (Mme. Bouclier); E.E. Clive (Police Photographer); with Frank Reicher

Credits: Producer — Carl Laemmle, Jr.; Director — James Whale; Screenplay — Doris Mallory, Harry Clork, Dan Totheroth; Based on *The Hangover Murders* by Adam Hobhouse (pseudonym); Photographer — Joseph Valentine, ASC; Additional Dialogue — Benn W. Levy; Assistant Director — Scott Beal; Film Editor — Ted Kent; Art Director — Charles D. Hall; Music Score — Franz Waxman; Musical Director — Constantin Bakaleinikoff; Make-up — Jack P. Pierce; Photographic Effects — John P. Fulton; Sound Supervisor — Gilbert Kurland; Gowns — Ernest Dryden, Vera West

THE GREAT IMPERSONATION (1935)

One thing's for sure; if you like Italian opera, you'll *love The Great Impersonation*. There's nothing remotely Italian in it, but there is a great deal about honor, betrayal, love, and revenge, as well as stupefyingly impossible coincidences which would be easier to take if they were sung by a chorus of saber-rattling baritones. There's also a minor-league "horror" sub-plot lifted bodily from Conan Doyle and featuring an unbilled Dwight Frye, sporting at least two cubic yards of dirt.

The story concerns two men — absolutely identical in form, diametrically opposite in ideology — whose paths cross not once but twice as Clotho spins their threads of life. Once students together at Oxford, Sir Everard Dominey and Baron Leopold von Ragastein (both played by Edmund Lowe) meet up again in darkest Africa, each man fleeing the consequences of a supposed crime of passion. The plot veers off toward the sort of underhanded situations which would lead to the Great War, but the audience has a few odd moments in which to savor the incalculably enormous odds against such a second chance encounter ever occurring.

Edmund Lowe never had so many of his hands so full as in *The Great Impersonation*. His initial takes on the stolid and veddy British Dominey and the stolid, haughtily Teutonic von Ragastein *had* to be one-dimensional. Again, painfully short running times do not permit deep character studies, but when the movie's title glorifies the pretense that is to follow, you had better start things off slowly. If viewers can't tell the two men apart on sight, it's absolutely crucial that they be profoundly dissimilar in terms of behavior.

Neither Dominey nor von Ragastein is particularly admirable, although the besotted Englishman somehow comes across in a more favorable light than the blatantly unwholesome German. (This subjective nod reflects sentiments which would endure long after the Second World War.) With one man clearly perceived as the innocent and unfortunate victim of circumstances and the other drawn with broad lines of arrogance and aggression, the movie itself isn't the only thing in black and white; each man virtually embodies the philosophic bent of his homeland. Lest anyone doubt, this is symbolism, overt and unnuanced. This is also the kind of character development which was old hat when hats had plumes. Fortunately, later scenes in the film will prove to be more interesting and less preposterous.

Lowe's rendering of von Ragastein's take on Dominey is much more impressive than either of his individual characterizations, and

From the wilds of the jungle to the arms of a paramour: Edmund Lowe in varying stages of sartorial splendor. *PENTAGRAM LIBRARY.*

happily so as it is the hinge upon which the whole story supposedly turns. It appears that the Baron has arranged for the Briton's death on safari, a move which will allow the duplicitous German not only to take the late baronet's place, but also his *place* (Dominey Hall). This impersonation — good, but still not great — works like a charm. The German contingent, essayed by a veritable horde of Universal's busiest minor villains, plots with the enthusiastic camaraderie of the seven dwarfs in the diamond mine. They don't doubt for a moment that it's really their boy, Leo, who's chewing the stem off that briar. The Brits, sadly headed up once again by Spring Byington (as in *WereWolf of London*, once again a sort of upper-crust ZaSu Pitts), are equally certain that that's the one and only Sir Everard bagging his tweeds at the knees.

Dominey's wife, the Lady Eleanor, isn't quite sure what she thinks, having slipped a cog or two under the constant harassment of a servant, Mrs. Unthank. (Don't you just *love* that name?) Sir Everard has reportedly murdered Unthank's son over the lovely Mrs. Dominey, after which act he took to strong drink and somehow found himself way over in Africa. All this brouhaha has caused Lady's pate to become addled by tales of ghosts and revenge from beyond. (Attention: This is the horror element insinuating itself into the story.) The newly returned Dominey/von Ragastein loves his wife, but is slow to give the matter the consideration it deserves until Lady Eleanor takes a swipe at his sleeping form with a substantial piece of cutlery. As the ghost of the murdered Unthank caterwauls on a regular basis in the nearby Black Bog, Dominey very sensibly has

That's Baron Leopold on the floor, those are a couple of Teutons (not Nazis) being held at gunpoint, and the lads in the lids are the good guys. The end is in sight. PENTAGRAM LIBRARY.

it set afire. The resultant blaze brings the raucous, very dirty, but undoubtedly still breathing Roger Unthank (Dwight Frye) into the midst of things on the double. Mrs. Unthank shoots her boy before he can finish choking Eleanor (who will recover her *compos mentis* as quickly as she regains her breath), and the story's horror element is not heard from again. Had the film given credit where it was due, the cast would have turned back to the door and waited for Basil Rathbone and Nigel Bruce to arrive.

Lowe's truly *great* impersonation becomes apparent a scant reel before the end music. Von Ragastein's erstwhile honey, the Princess Stephanie (Wera Engels), who has been dragged along to Dominey Hall by the bad guys so as not to blow the whistle that Dominey is

not Dominey, follows up on a suspicion she has and arranges for the truth to out: Dominey *is* Dominey! For most of the picture, Edmund Lowe has been playing Dominey playing von Ragastein playing Dominey! Now, Frank Wead and Eve Greene's script had settled on stark, nationalistic stereotypes for the movie's early introductions of the two individuals; Lowe could have phoned in stuff like that. More technique was required, however (as was the greater subtlety the first couple of reels eschewed), if the actor was to present different vistas of the same face to the opposing forces, and the generally underestimated Lowe dug deeply into his nearly 20 years' experience and pulled it off. As the Messrs. Brunas, Brunas and Weaver have correctly stated, Edmund Lowe was basically from "the Waxed Mustache school of acting" (Don't you just love that phrase?), but if he or his lip-fuzz ever had a finer hour (and four minutes), I haven't come upon it yet.

The Great Impersonation was Valerie Hobson's last dance at Universal, and given the hokey and amateurish turn the wildly old-fashioned screenplay compels her to give — her Lady Eleanor Dominey is reminiscent of Lucia di Lammermoor as interpreted by Lucille Ball — the decision to pass on future projects for the Laemmles was probably anything but a Hobson's choice for her. With 1935 her busiest year at Universal City, Miss Hobson could at least take consolation in the fact that the worst circumstances in which she had found herself (see also Life Returns) bracketed a body of respectable, if not quite timeless, work. The lovely actress would return to her native England where, prior to finding herself more deeply embarrassed by political scandal than she had ever been by Frank Wead and Eve Greene, she achieved a homespun celebrity in Great Expectations (1946), Kind Hearts and Coronets (1949) and such.

The idea that Dominey and von Ragastein are absolutely identical physically is nothing new. Weeks after Thespis cut his teeth on dirty limericks, the dramatic possibilities revolving around mistaken identity were already coming into their own. As literature and theater matured, there were innumerable variations on the theme of twins separated at birth only to be reunited via happenstance or the Fates, against either a comic or tragic backdrop. Shakespeare, for example, got lots of mileage out of the long-lost twin brother shtick with The Comedy of Errors (featuring two sets of identical twins), before fashioning quite an interesting variation on it (Sebastian and Viola in Twelfth Night). Alexandre Dumas made a nice pile by adapting the basic idea as The Man in the Iron Mask, and Dostoevsky gave the whole thing a Russian bent with The Brothers Karamazov. Moving down the scale of sophistication, the story was eventually updated with the stress being laid on the psychic bond between siblings — the physical dissimilarity was played for big laughs — as Arnold

Schwarzenegger and Danny DeVito joined forces as Twins.

The common thread running through these works was the blood relationship between the protagonists. Running a parallel but much less traveled road were the tales of "other selves," wherein what was shared was not so much a bloodline as the blood itself: Stevenson's The Strange Case of Dr. Jekyll and Mr. Hyde is the best known example. A step removed from this, and closer to the goings-on in The Great Impersonation, was the concept of the doppelgänger, defined by Lotte Eisner in her The Haunted Screen as the "shadow or reflection which takes on an independent existence and turns against its model." The Germanic archetype of the concept was, of course, Der Student von Prag, in any of its several versions.

Apart from the Teutonic renditions of the theme, the good old U.S. of A. had produced a couple of masterful doppelgänger tales, and had done so quite a few years before Bioscope or H.R. Sokal-Film had put their visions onto celluloid. In 1839, Edgar Allan Poe's William Wilson, a semi-autobiographical tale of the author's demonic counterpart, first saw print. Forty years later, Mark Twain turned the Poe piece inside out and murdered his own doppelgänger — the embodiment of his Calvinist conscience — in his offbeat and hilarious The Facts Concerning a Recent Carnival of Crime in Connecticut (1876). Only thus could he do away with his enemies, philander shamelessly, and have the rip-roaring time he had always been denied by that most severe of inner voices.

As Dominey and von Ragastein share no common ancestry, they can be nothing other than doppelgänger freaks of nature united as much by bitterly adverse emotions as by identical appearances. The absurdity of having the men meet a second time under the most far-fetched of conditions can only be constrained by having it be the mythic moment of truth, when the more human "original" slays his more demonic double. That this usually also results in the death of the original is neatly handled by the belief, encouraged by the storyline, that it is, in fact, Dominey who has been eradicated.

The Great Impersonation was remade by Universal some seven years later and updated to incorporate the Second World War. The double mantle of Dominey/von Ragastein was inherited by perennial second lead Ralph Bellamy, but neither his presence nor that of Evelyn Ankers (his costar in both *The Wolf Man* and *The Ghost of Frankenstein*) helped infuse the tepid spy story with sorely needed thrills. The 1942 version was thus much closer to the 1921 silent original (which had been directed for Paramount by *Drácula* veteran "Uncle" George Melford) than to the 1935 Lowe epic.

Still another of Universal's near-horrors and itself a remake, *The Great Impersonation* really is something of a misfit, cranked out as it was during the genre's most fecund and innovative period. For all this, it's not a bad film and is enjoyable in spite of its creaky underpinnings. Nevertheless, one can't help wondering which of the many succulent titles, announced for Karloff or Lugosi but never filmed, would have made better use of the time, money, and talent expended on what was essentially a sound rehash of a dated and forgettable story.

The Great Impersonation

Released December 9, 1935; 64 minutes

Cast: Edmund Lowe (Sir Everard Dominey/ Baron Leopold von Ragastein); Valerie Hobson (Lady Eleanor Dominey); Wera Engels (Princess Stephanie); Murray Kinnell (Seaman); Henry Mollison (Eddie Pelham); Esther Dale (Mrs. Unthank); Dwight Frye (Roger Unthank); Brandon Hurst (Middleton); Ivor Simpson (Dr. Harrison); Spring Byington (Duchess Caroline); Lumsden Hare (Duke Henry); Charles Waldron (Sir Ivan Brunn); Leonard Mudie (Mangan); Claude King (Sir Gerald Hume); Frank Reicher (Dr. Trenk); Harry Allen (Parkins); Nan Grey (Middleton's Daughter, the Maid); Willy Castello (Duval); Priscilla Lawson (Maid); Pat O'Hara (Chauffeur); Virginia Hammond (Lady Hume); Thomas R. Mills (Bartender); Tom Ricketts, Frank Terry, Robert Bolder (Villagers); Lowden Adams (Waiter); Violet Seaton (Nurse); David Dunbar, Frank Benson (English Farmers); John Powers (English Policeman); Leonid Snegoff (Wolff); Harry Worth (Hugo); Larry Steers (Army Officer); Doublas Wood (Nobleman); with Adolph Milar

Credits: Producer — Edmund Grainger; Director — Alan Crosland; Screenplay — Frank Wead and Eve Greene; Based on the novel by E. Phillips Oppenheim; Photographer — Milton Krasner; Art Director — Charles D. Hall; Special Cinematography — John P. Fulton; Film Editor — Philip Cahn; Sound Supervisor — Gilbert Kurland; Gowns — Brymer; Makeup — Jack P. Pierce

THE INVISIBLE RAY (1936)

Rays have got to be the neatest, cleanest catch-alls in science fiction. Stuck for a source of unimaginable power? Need to come up with a primal cause and don't want to drag in the deity? Jabbering about some ray or another is the easy way out.

Henry Frankenstein brought rays well-merited respectability when he eschewed lesser beams for the folderol they were and ranted smugly about the "Great Ray" which first brought life into the world. Wilfred Glendon created a quasi-lunar illumination machine in *WereWolf of London*, but the ray produced by the striking contraption simulated the nurturing power of moonlight and encouraged life and growth. That flash of blinding light from Isis' ankh at the end of *The Mummy* was arguably a death ray, albeit of the fantastic, ersatz-religious type. Roxor the Flamboyant (Bela, natch) had one hell of a death ray over at Fox in *Chandu the Magician*, and Sax Rohmer's mad mandarin (Karloff) was cut down mere moments before the good guys unleashed another handy death ray on the heavies during the climax of MGM's *Mask of Fu Manchu*. Even Gene Autry caught death ray fever and jump-started an atom-smashing beam which sealed forever the portals of the underground kingdom of Murania and melted

Queen Tika, her minions, and her extensive palace complex in Mascot's cheap but cheerful *Phantom Empire*.

With all these rays shooting this way and that, it remained for Universal to come up with the *pièce de résistance*, much as it had done for a different chestnut with 1932's *The Old Dark House*. And so it was that John Colton, who had injected that peculiar botanical angle into the movies' developing werewolf mythos, was called to pen the screen's definitive death ray treatment. Working from an episodic original idea by Howard Higgin and Douglas Hodges, the quirky author was at once instructed to observe several guidelines, laid down by management not so much from any artistic integrity as from a desperate desire to placate the touchy overseas market. The restrictions included a ban on heavily made-up grotesques; such physical horrors had proven offensive to prim foreign sensibilities. There were to be no gruesome murders committed onscreen; better yet would be the avoidance of any violent actions at all. Also to be axed were situations which might taint the dramatic thrust of the story with sexual innuendo or alarmingly overt displays of dementia.

In effect, Colton was given the unenviable assignment of drafting a screenplay which

Opposite: A vivid one-sheet for *The Invisible Ray*. RONALD V. BORST/HOLLYWOOD MOVIE POSTERS.

would ensnare all those shiver-loving, cash-paying ticket buyers on both sides of the Atlantic without disturbing, offending, or horrifying anyone. Contemporary fans were taken aback by the movie's somewhat tame content and execution, having been conditioned by *The Black Cat* and *The Raven* to expect a Karloff-Lugosi extravaganza to be rather more of an all-out barnstorming effort, long on energy and short on exposition. Colton's science fiction piece enjoyed a leisurely pace which its predecessors had not shared, and with all of the requisite malevolence safely taking place off screen, only John P. Fulton's phosphorescent touches gave any sort of cinematic cutting edge to the story.

Although Universal was on its best behavior in *The Invisible Ray*, it couldn't help giving in to several of its more traditional impulses. Karloff's Janos Rukh may be an egg or two shy of a dozen, but it's obvious that he's been saving his *pfennigs* or whatever for a rainy day; just feast your eyes on the castle that he, his breathtaking and sumptuously attired Diana (Frances Drake, whose gown and floor-length cloak for once make the "Gowns by..." credit a viable entry), and his crusty old mom (Violet Kemble Cooper) have to keep clean. Albert D'Agostino raided the warehouses, and bits and pieces of Universal's most celebrated haunts were brought in for alterations and pressed into service once again. As most of the production was studio-bound, Fulton's wizardry at glass shots made the approach to the castle an awesome stretch and provided the seemingly immense structure with vaulted ceilings and nigh-impossible expanses.

Fulton also did that voodoo that he did so well with the futuristic planetarium show, wherein Rukh takes Benet (Bela) and company on a fifty-cent tour of the universe. The panorama the special effects genius came up with is light-years ahead of the similar but cheesier vistas the boys over at the *Flash Gordon* wing created. I've always found Fulton's intergalactic light show to be the most charming, most distinctively thirties element of the film, and I still maintain that, for all its demonstrable scientific naïveté, *The Invisible Ray* is far less dated than many of its supposedly more timeless colleagues.

Although I'm not sure what, it says something about the gullibility of the usually skeptical scientific community that Sir Francis Stevens (Walter Kingsford) is so easily convinced that the show he's just seen hasn't been concocted — say, via motion picture film — for the express purpose of pulling the wool over his venerable eyes. "A trick?" he asks of the dapper Dr. Benet; "No, a reality," opines the French astrochemist, although how he knows for sure is never explained. And that's that. For what it's worth, this sort of casual approbation is more the rule than the exception in these early sound genre films. A loudly harrumphed "Preposterous!" may emerge at some point in the proceedings, but this is strictly *pro forma*, and such accusations are never followed up. Whenever confronted with supposedly irrefutable proof of some heretofore harebrained theory on the part of a maverick researcher, the closed-minded grousers of the movies' scientific communities never seriously question the renegade's honesty, only his sanity.

In an effort to keep them from being reduced to pawns in a battle of special effects, the screenplay schleps Karloff and Lugosi back and forth from Transylvania to such romantic climes as Gay Paree and Bornu, Nigeria. All this globe-trotting really doesn't add anything substantial to the picture's dramatic weight, though; if anything, it serves to prevent the viewer from participating fully in the development of the rhythm of the piece. With statues being melted behind one's back and innocent people being murdered just around the corner, the constant shuffling of locales makes the viewer feel that, wherever he may be at the moment, things are always hopping someplace else.

Sporting a dapper Van Dyke, Bela Lugosi never looked better in his American films. His restrained, benevolent portrait ridding him of any necessity to leer or to glare hypnotically (assorted frowns and grimaces notwithstanding), the actor's handsome features are displayed while at their peak for the last time. The collapse of the genre market would lead to

763-20

Bela's Dr. Felix Benet is about to put his imprimatur on Janos Rukh's light show, and that will be all the verification anyone seems to want. *Left to right:* Frank Lawton, Frances Drake, Bela Lugosi, Walter Kingsford, Beulah Bondi. JOHN PARNUM.

anxiety and illness which, when combined with the effects of an easy refuge taken in alcohol, would result in Bela's appearing older and heavier. The Benet of *The Invisible Ray* marks the last sighting of the "lean and mean" Lugosi; the Benez of *Postal Inspector* marks the introduction of a more mature, puffier—but usually no less crafty—Hungarian heavy.

In the course of his many films over the years, Bela had more than his share of what have come to be regarded as memorable lines, but it is doubtful that most of them would have been so memorable were it not for the actor's unique flair and delivery. Lines dripping with portent were somehow made even more dignified and mournful when given the Lugosi touch: Witness the litany of the Law in *Island of Lost Souls*. Even the simply awful stuff, like the "superstitious baloney" exchange from *The*

Black Cat, became eagerly awaited highlights when mouthed by the man from Lugos. Bela's calm assessment of the situation for the Chief of the Sûreté (Georges Renavent) in *The Invisible Ray* remains my all-time favorite.

> LUGOSI: If your men fail to capture him at the gate, then at midnight, we bolt all doors and darken the entire house. His hands and face will appear like phosphorous.
> Renavent: And, uhh, if he touches anyone...?
> Lugosi [with a shrug, a resigned smile, and the best timing in the world]: They die.

Karloff's turn as Janos Rukh is splendid, but the role, unlike Lugosi's, hardly requires the actor to play against type. The hypertense astronomer is another of the moody brooders who had of late supplanted the more well-balanced of the misguided genre protagonists on the Universal lot. As impressive as it is, the paranoid scientist's awesome discovery from the Andromeda Nebula is the only evidence we have of his ability to correctly assimilate information; every other conclusion he jumps to is (if you'll pardon me) dead wrong.

Gorgeous Frances Drake may start running around with Frank Lawton after a fair number of spousal snubs, but she doesn't totally bail out on Boris until a charred cadaver (which she has every reason to believe is his) puts new meaning in "until death do us part." Although she carefully sidesteps the issue of her love for her husband ("My father idolized him," she admits to Ronald Drake [Lawton]; "When he died, I promised him that I'd marry Janos"), she is devoted to him, and is uncomfortable with the feelings she has for Lady Arabella's nephew. Her gradual falling for Ronald is handled well, too. Lawton gets top marks for giving a virile edge to what might well have been just another tedious love-struck juvenile, and his winning Diana away from the mopey and preoccupied Janos is never in doubt to the veteran element of the audience. As with the announcement by Stevens of Radium X to a startled world, Diana's defection is brought on by Janos's own erratic behavior.

The understanding that his research will lead Rukh into madness (Benet confesses ignorance as to what "violent effect of poison and antidote will have upon the brain") is, of course, purloined from R.C. Sherriff's screenplay of *The Invisible Man*. Both monocane and Radium X (or, more properly, the combination of Radium X and its antidote) induce paranoia and megalomania, and trend-setters Griffin and Rukh are each described as meddlers in forbidden knowledge. In the case of the latter, it is his mother, played by Madame Kemble Cooper with all the solemnity her unblinking eyes can muster, who maintains that "The universe is very large, and there are some secrets we are not meant to probe."

The mouthful about Mme. Rukh appears to be the only bite taken from the Howard Higgin–Douglas Hodges "original" story. Just about everything else is stolen from a source closer to home: Colton's own *WereWolf of London*. Much like journalist John K. Balderston's going to the *Dracula* well to draw *aqua vitae* for *The Mummy*, Colton's paean to meteorites and madness is a cleverly disguised remake of his lycanthrope adaptation.

Consider: Obsessed with his experiments, the not-so-young scientist journeys into a little-known and virtually unexplored area of the world, in search of concrete proof for his theories. Ignoring his young and frustrated wife in order to track to earth whatever it is he is seeking, he is infected with an awful malignancy which will ultimately bring about his own death after causing the deaths of innocents about him. He is most readily recognizable for the horror he has become through a trick of the light — full moonlight in Glendon's case, and the absence of light in Rukh's. As extreme and unlikely as his condition may be, it is couched in terms which make it not only feasible but *likely* that a scientific counteractive would be the protagonist's ticket back to normalcy. (Colton insists on allowing the hero's tragic state to be forestalled temporarily with timely injections via hypodermics or lancet-like *Mariphasa* stems.) The doomed scientist is essentially handed the antidote by a man who may be perceived as something of a professional rival. The rival is, in turn, slain by the mutated hero in the heat of the moment of betrayal. The tormented soul finds peace in death only after he has confronted his wife — whom he still loves, despite perceived infidelities — and revealed the monstrosity he has become. Of course, the errant husband does no physical harm to his spouse, who lives on to enjoy life in the arms of another.

Released some seven months apart, the Colton films were obviously never intended to fill the opposite halves of the same double bill. Of course, as many viewers don't catch the similarities between *Dracula* and *The Mummy* unless they're pointed out, it is doubtful whether the casual horror fan would notice Colton's more adroit reconstruction even if *WereWolf* and *Ray* were shown back to back.

The Invisible Ray has enough going for it to assure audience satisfaction for decades to come. Apart from old potted ferns standing in for the Dark Continent, the sets are notable and the special effects impressive if uneven and sporadic. As mentioned above, Bela is a joy, clearly relishing what would prove to be his last classic foray on the side of the angels. Karloff's well-intentioned warnings ("You should go away at once, do you hear? This is no place for you") and misguided accusations ("You come like thieves in the night and steal everything from me") are as welcome as flowers in spring both for their familiarity and their speaker's lisp. This would be the last time the gentle Brit would be billed by his surname only, and his marvelous eyes, whether glaring defiantly from within the art-deco welder's mask or goggling in horror behind an optically rendered glow, suffuse the picture with a force more potent than the ray itself.

From here, the Bogey King would head over to Warners, where he would reign once more in *The Walking Dead*. A top-quality chiller featuring Strickfadenesque electrical life restorers, a lumbering yet angelically innocent "menace," and inserts of those magnificent eyes, *Dead* would have done the whirling globe proud. Karloff's next appearance at Universal would be in the mundane crime meller *Night Key*, whose smorgasbord of petty criminals, double-crossing industrialists, pistol-whippings, and gunplay was typical of the formulaic gats-and-gangsters product ground out over at Warners. Compounding this felony and spitting in the face of common sense, Lloyd Corrigan then robbed the actor of the greatest weapon in his arsenal by directing that his eyes were to remain obscured by Coke-bottle glasses or by being scrunched into full squint.

This dramatic reversal represented far more than momentary confusion between two of Hollywood's more niche-oriented studios. It signaled the end of an era.

The Invisible Ray

Released January 20, 1936; 79 minutes

Cast: Boris Karloff (Janos Rukh); Bela Lugosi (Felix Benet); Frances Drake (Diana Rukh); Frank Lawton (Ronald Drake); Walter Kingsford (Sir Francis Stevens); Beulah Bondi (Lady Arabella Stevens); Violet Kemble Cooper (Mother Rukh); Nydia Westman (Briggs); Daniel Haines (Headman); Georges Revenant (Sûreté Chief); Paul Wiegel (Noyer); Adele St. Maur (Mme. Noyer); Frank Reicher (Prof. Meiklejohn); Lawrence Stewart (Number One Native Boy); Etta McDaniel (Zulu Woman); Inez Seabury (Celeste); Winter Hall (Minister); Fred Toones (Safari Boy); Hans Schumm (Clinic Aide); Lloyd Whitlock, Edwards Davis, Edward Reinach (Scientists); Clarence Gordon (Boy); Daisy Bufford (Mother); Jean DeBriac, Robert Moran, Francisco Maran (Gendarmes); Ricca Allen, Isabella LaMal (Bystanders); Alex Chivar (Cook); Lucio Villegas (Butler); Mae Beatty (Mrs. Legendre); Paul McAllister (Papa LaCosta); Helen Brown (Mother); Anna Marie Conte (Blind Girl); Walter Miller (Derelict); Charles Fallon (Gentleman); Ernest Bowern, Charles Bastin (Newsboys); Andre Cheron, Alphonse Martell (Sûreté Officials); Dudley Dickerson (Native); with Ernie Adams, Raymond Turner, Jules Raucourt

Credits: Producer — Edmund Grainger; Director — Lambert Hillyer; Screenplay — John Colton; Original Story by Howard Higgin and Douglas Hodges; Director of Photography — George Robinson; Special Photography — John P. Fulton; Art Director — Albert S. D'Agostino; Film Editor — Bernard Burton; Music — Franz Waxman; Assistant Director — Alfred Stern; Sound Supervisor — Gilbert Kurland; Technical Advisor — Ted Behr; Gowns — Brymer

DRACULA'S DAUGHTER (1936)

Vampires may not be the absolute gabbiest of grotesques, for that honor probably goes to the myriad invisible persons, without whose incessant yapping one might well forget that they were about. But next to Forry Ackerman, vampires spend the most time talking about themselves. While they don't appear overly concerned with the veracity of their introductions, this might be part of the master plan: Letting on that they are Baron Latos, Count Alucard, or Doctor Lejos allows this narcissistic crowd (how *do* they get by without mirrors?) the opportunity for a reintroduction later. In the end each and every one of the aforementioned bloodsuckers turns out to be the Count himself. For an entity given to bragadoccio about his honor, his lineage, and his prowess in battle, Dracula proves to be strangely reticent about tipping his hand up front.

In *Dracula's Daughter*, the Count's only child (Alucard is an alias, not an offspring) demonstrates that the wolfsbane doesn't fall far from the bush when she takes up the practice and introduces herself as Countess Marya Zaleska. With "Von" Helsing up to his own neck in trouble with the law and no sign of collaboration from Seward, Mina or Harker (in fact, no sign at all of Seward, Mina or Harker), that old saw about the vampire's greatest

strength being a lack of belief in his existence takes on renewed vitality. Apart from the Dutchman, no one within spitting distance has the slightest notion of who or what a "dracula" really is, so the Countess need fear no whistleblowers. Hence, there's no real reason to assume an alias here, save to make the exorcism complete; with the destruction of the father's corpse comes the abjuration of the family name. Ironically, though, the vampiress's desperate attempt at burying her past by denying her own name just places her deeper within the patterns of deception her dad will trace in the sequels to follow.

Dracula's Daughter is the very antithesis of the original movie, reversing just about every element and characterization found in the source. Whereas the Count starts out in Transylvania and heads west, the Countess is in London at the outset and flees back home when things start cooking. While the father utilizes the services of a quasi-vampiric loon whom he slays in a fit of pique, the daughter employs a semi-vampiric goon who does *her* in while in mid-hissy fit. Dracula's pervasive mental powers prove the undoing of Renfield, while — despite her preoccupation with "overpowering commands" from beyond the grave — Marya Zaleska's psychic nemesis is the ghoulish Sandor, who does his best to

An early trade ad. Note the likenesses of Bela Lugosi and Jeraldine Dvorak (one of the three brides from the 1931 original) and the presence of James Whale's name. *Ronald V. Borst/Hollywood Movie Posters.*

keep his mistress on the dead side of life. The climax of the 1931 movie finds the Count, the loon, the professor, the hero, and the hypnotized heroine waltzing about the ruins of Carfax Abbey. The 1936 sequel has the Countess, the goon, the professor, the somewhat aged hero, and the hypnotized heroine maneuvering among the dilapidated quarters of Castle Dracula.

Apart from the interesting plot reversals, a number of salient bits echo the earlier film and underscore the ties between Count and Countess. Whether examining the corpse of Zaleska's first onscreen victim or the lifeless body of Lucy Weston, the forensic specialists mouth the same repartee: "When did (s)he have the last transfusion?" "About four hours before his/her death." As this entire scene is copied from the original, one has to ask how many such queries have to be posed before the English medical community catches on to what's happening in and around London. And Von Helsing repeats the caveat he had used with Dr. Seward, in nearly the same words, when he informs Sir Basil Humphrey that "The strength of the vampire lies in the fact that he *is* unbelievable." Most potent is Marya's adopt-

ing one of her father's most famous *bons mots*. When asked whether she'd care for a sherry, the lovely Countess replies, with just the right hesitation, "I never drink ... wine."

Improvements on the earlier film include an effective and comprehensive musical score, a number of hitherto unseen or redressed Castle Dracula sets, a quick gander at those infamous stairs (at the foot of which Dwight Frye's double is discovered at the outset), and some snappy give-and-take between Marguerite Churchill and both Otto Kruger (who gets a tad nastier in delivery than he ought, especially for someone so inevitably in love) and Gloria Holden.

As with the source film, some logical puzzlers intrude. All that flapping noise emanating from the holding cell: bats? Or that ominous burrowing under the floor, or the earth eerily moving on its own, prompting assorted gulps and gasps from the officious Sergeant Hawkins: rats? Apparently, the phenomena are merely odd coincidences, for when the Countess does make her eagerly awaited entrance, she does so conventionally, via the police station door. Still, the first sight the audience has of the titular femme fatale is breathtaking; imposingly tall, shrouded in black from head to toe, with only her beautiful eyes visible against the lush velvet background, Marya Zaleska cuts a lovely figure which is at once Byzantine and opulently bizarre.

Von Helsing reveals that Dracula and his daughter died 500 and 100 years ago, respectively, yet in the course of one of his sundry explanations, he indicates that vampires are "creatures who have never died." This confusion of terms and meanings — How can anyone argue what "undead" means with anything like scientific precision? — harks back to the earlier films. Carlos Villar's *Conde* articulates Drácula's death-in-life status poetically when he sighs, with an almost wistful look on his face, "To die, to be really dead. That must be sublime!" Also, Von Helsing is aghast at the news that the Vampire King had had a daughter. Both his words and his facial reaction betray the fact that this is an enormous surprise to him. How, then, can his curtain line to Sir Basil be the complacent statement that the Countess died "a hundred years ago?" Where did he get that information? Who's been giving him the skinny behind everyone's back?

Late in the picture, as Jeffrey Garth hops off the coach in Transylvania, he is warned that the peasants have espied a light in the Castle and thus have determined that "The vampire … she walks tonight with her unhallowed father." Since Zaleska has been in London long enough to build an artistic reputation, why do the locals all of a sudden feel that *she's* back home, based on a light in a window? Her dad shlepped candles up and down steps, and even had a roaring fire from time to time (there was one very much in evidence when Renfield hit town). What's all this "she" stuff?

It is subsequently revealed that Zaleska has a flat in Russell Square and a studio in Chelsea, and has obviously been in London for some time. Why has there been no brouhaha concerning her victims before this? When Von Helsing tells Sir Basil that "Dracula had many victims … into whose veins he infused his own tainted blood, making them creatures like him," he is speaking of the Voivode's experiences in England. With all of this hereto undisclosed vampiric activity due to Dracula, who apparently was going great guns in the same city where his daughter was holed up for God knows how long, why doesn't anyone apart from an aged Dutch paranormalist notice the spate of punctured necks or the plethora of wandering corpses? How dense is that team of coroners who continually anguish over "last transfusions?"

The Countess's noodling the "cradle song" on her Steinway likewise gives pause for thought. She remembers the song her mother sang to her "long, long ago, rocking me to sleep as she sang in the twilight." A vampire going to sleep in the twilight? Just when did this curse of Dracula take hold of the girl? If the Countess "died" a hundred years ago, she must have done so at an age close to that represented by her lovely face and figure; belonging to the family of the undead and "growing up" are, according to myth, mutually exclusive. If this is true, did she receive her fangs when she attained her majority, like a license to drive or the legal right to imbibe? If Dracula is to be proven randy as well as pestilent, lots of questions need to be answered.

The cast of *Dracula's Daughter* is a good one. Otto Kruger may be no spring chicken, but his social position and authoritarian air make short work of many of the stumbling blocks encountered by more traditional leading men, who are usually regarded by other characters and most audience members as still wet behind the ears. And in a horror fantasy such as this, only a short stretch is needed to believe that Kruger's angular features and receding hairline make him irresistible to both Janet and to Marya. Marguerite Churchill and Gloria Holden do excellent jobs in conveying their respective concerns; their brief but arch exchange in Dr. Garth's office succinctly raises the possibility of an altogether unsavory *ménage à trois*. The only weakness in Churchill's character is the rough edge to the gay banter in which Janet indulges with her honey, and that's the screenplay's fault.

Edward Van Sloan is far better here than he is in *Dracula*. Incredibly soft-spoken from

Conspicuously absent from Dracula's coffin are Bela Lugosi and the stake Van Helsing drove into his chest. *JOHN PARNUM.*

the start, as if drained emotionally by the weight of his struggles, he comes to life only when it dawns on him that his erstwhile student is in grave danger. ("Stop him! He's going to his death!") Not once does he stiffen up or fall back on vintage stage mannerisms as he did under Tod Browning's direction.

Irving Pichel is okay, I guess, as Sandor. Pasty-faced and brilliantined, he wanders through most of the movie garbed like the bell captain of the Saint Petersburg Hilton. Just what services he performs for the Countess are never made quite clear. Although he is something of a procurer (he talks the suicidal Lily into returning with him to the studio), Marya Zaleska is perfectly capable of rounding up her own dinner; she and her oversized ring easily ensnare that top-hatted gent early in the picture. Maybe we get the real lowdown on

Sandor's talents when the vampiress tips him to the fact that there's blood on her cloak again; still, as he is a constant damper to the Countess's aspirations for a new and wholesome life, can't she find someone else who'll both support her hopes *and* do her laundry?

There are even fewer special effects in *Dracula's Daughter* than in *Dracula*, if that can be imagined. With nary a bat to be seen, soft focus and optical highlighting (the hypnotic ring) provide the audience with its only supernatural sightings. The film's engrossing nature is such, though, that the dearth of special effects goes mostly unnoticed. *Daughter* is beautifully photographed by George Robinson, who had done such a wonderful job of wringing every atmospheric detail from the standing sets for *Drácula*. Apart from some unnecessary comic relief, Lambert Hillyer's direction runs its professional course and parallels the visual sumptuousness of much of the film. As most of Hillyer's assignments to this point had required him to do little more than keep the horses in focus as they galloped past his chair, he reveals an unexpected flair for the genre.

Likening vampirism to a curse which can be practiced while being deplored is a nice touch, whether Garrett Fort's or someone else's. Viewed in this light, the bloodsucker takes on the tragic lines usually associated with the werewolf. Impressive, too, is the concept of the vampire's spell, which, in itself, can result in the death of an innocent. Decidedly feminine in hue, this new "power" supplants the brute physical strength which would seem more proper to the male *nosferatu*, and of which there is no sign in the film. Smacking of black magic, the spell gives Marya the chance to disarm the smug Garth, whose own bag of tricks includes a working knowledge of hypnosis. Janet's condition is not due to any force with which he is familiar, the Countess informs him, but to "something older and more powerful.... All your skill cannot help her now. She's under a spell that can be broken only by me, or death."

There are several moments which speak volumes, either in terms of characterization or irony. The powerful exorcism scene gains poignancy when one realizes that, although the Count's staking had released Mina (just as Zaleska's death will free Janet), Marya's hopes for normalcy following the total destruction of Dracula will be dashed. Apparently, "the blood is the life" only when it is exchanged between vampire and victim, with the still-living victim being released from the taint when the vampire is slain. When that same blood is passed from father to child through whatever process of birth the undead can manage, the death of the sire offers no such relief.

Dracula's Daughter is usually one of the last of the 1930s originals that fans get around to seeing. Maybe this is due to the perception that a female vampire of the old school won't provide the titillation or acres of skin that modern mores have come to allow. Perhaps it's because of the fact that, as the last genre effort

of the Laemmle team (and essentially an impatient, half-hearted release of the Crowdin organization), it didn't receive the distribution that the earlier chillers had. The drying up of lucrative foreign markets certainly assured that it didn't garner the volume of press coverage that *Bride of Frankenstein* had the year before.

Inasmuch as Frankenstein's monster reared his ugly head for a second time, the whys and wherefores of a *Dracula* sequel sans Dracula make for an interesting discussion. In *The Monster Show*, David Skal puts forth the theory that the character of Dracula had become unacceptable to the emerging board of film censors. The Vampire King's unholy appetites, as well as their attendant sexual overtones, had made him a *monster non grata* in the eyes of the newly established custodians of public decency. The only way to capitalize on the earlier film, maintains Mr. Skal, was to fabricate a tale of vampirism without the Voivode's singular presence. While there is doubtless a good bit of truth in the contention that actions and intimations which had been permissible in the early thirties had become forbidden fruit by 1936, having censorship take all the blame seems a little too facile to me. The subtle constraints of the 1931 original picture — the absence of blood, fang, or claw; of overt acts of excessive violence; of evidence of covert acts of intimacy — argue powerfully against any theory which proposes that Lugosi's Count would have been any more repulsive than Karloff's scarred monster, or any more wanton than Lorre's obsessive Dr. Gogol.

The sequel to *Dracula* had attracted treatments featuring an (if you will) earthier vampire, whose aristocratic demeanor gave way, at times, to his frenzied lust for blood and fulfillment. Five years passed between original and follow-up, an indication that the studio ordered a good deal of rewriting before coming up with the final screenplay. It has always seemed to me, however, that Dracula's absence was due not so much to the inability of the hacks to control their throbbing lusts, but rather to the cruel hand dealt by the fates to Bela Lugosi.

Poor Bela, of course, had been on thin ice

Dracula, *père et fille*. Blur your eyes and imagine what might have been. *Buddy Barnett/Cinema Collectors*.

at Universal from the first. The Laemmles had taken gleeful note of how cheaply the actor was willing to work, and in *Dracula*, had paid him a fraction of the salary the third-billed David Manners had received. Anyone willing to work for less than he was worth couldn't be worth much.

Nor was Lugosi a team player. Universal demanded cooperation and sacrifice from its sundry casts and crews in order to bring the pictures in on time and on (or under) budget. Neither his tenuous grasp of the English language nor his haughty personality would allow Bela to roll up his sleeves and be "one of the boys." Arguments about makeup, interpretation, and the suitability of certain roles, along with an unfortunate tendency to have his critical comments see print in fan magazines, did absolutely nothing to cement the actor's status in the eyes of the studio chiefs during an era when belonging to a studio generally meant constant work and consistent income.

Compounding the felony was Bela's propensity for appearing in cheapjack efforts for the feeblest of independents. Without a long-term contract at Universal (and, after the debacle of the *Frankenstein* test reel, there was little real possibility of that), Lugosi was forced to accept assignments wherever he could, if only to put food on the table. With a perverse irony, though, the varying success of pictures made away from Universal City was viewed as a breach of loyalty by Uncle Carl, who had come to regard his staff, minions, and "discoveries" as family. With little on the burner at Universal, Bela looked elsewhere; because he worked elsewhere, little was offered by Universal.

And, naturally, his highly publicized bankruptcy declaration made it abundantly clear that, far from being able to negotiate from a position of strength, Bela Lugosi was the cheapest act in town.

But why, ultimately, a vampire follow-up without the Voivode himself? The stake in the heart posed no real problem; that which could be inserted could be removed. The paucity of special effects in the original film would have actually worked to the budgetary benefit

of *Dracula's Daughter*. Inasmuch as no effort had been made at having the impaled Dracula crumble into the dust of the ages, there would be no subsequent need to account for errant ashes, or to concoct an expensive means at recorporation. Certainly no brain cells would be strained explaining the Count's various resurrections during the forties, and one of the factors which contributed mightily to the cessation of Hammer's later Dracula series was the revelation that the only thing easier than killing the vampire was bringing him back to life. If the Frankenstein monster had weathered being crushed by a beam, being scorched by a raging fire, and falling through several levels of flaming wood, stone, and earth, the King of the Undead ought to be able to stand having that oversized splinter lodged in his chest.

Lugosi had signed on to play the Count at some point during *Dracula's Daughter*'s preproduction morass, for there was no question as to who was Dracula at Universal. There was no silly casting search for publicity reasons; Ian Keith's name never popped up in conjunction with this title. The fiery debate which was kindled from the smoldering ashes of many heated arguments was not about Dracula's identity, however, but rather about Dracula's presence.

Before circumstances had led to the myriad "monster mashes" of the forties, the original incarnations of the classic monsters for the most part carried the whole show by themselves. Dracula's three vampiric brides, for example, play so minor a part in the 1931 epic as to be virtually forgotten by mid-film. (One of the unfilmed *Dracula's Daughter* treatments did have mention of Van Helsing's returning to Transylvania for the express purpose of cleaning house. In the finished film, the doctor and the pistol-packing policeman turn up at the Castle in the nick of time, but whether they stick around to stake the harpies is anyone's guess.) As the ghastly trio are full-fledged bloodsuckers — we presume they are en route to Renfield's neck when waved off by the Count — this casual attitude towards their continued existence is hard to understand unless we realize that they are no more important to the storyline or the atmospheric backdrop of *Dracula* than those absurd armadillos.

Even tertiary goblins, such as most of the roles enacted by Dwight Frye, occupy tenuous niches. Fritz's misshapen ghastliness keeps the audiences titillated until the Monster backs through the door; after that, he's expendable. The Count may enslave Renfield, just as Imhotep bends Sir Joseph Whemple's Nubian to his will, but these are servants and not co-conspirators. The closest thing to diabolical teamwork that Universal unveiled during the early thirties was the partnering of Dr. Mirakle and Erik in *Murders in the Rue Morgue* (1932), and even then everybody regarded the man in the monkey suit as a hoot.

The fabulous *Bride of Frankenstein*, though, had rocked the boat by having a distaff horror rise from the table and briefly steal some thunder from Karloff. Two monsters was probably less of a selling point than the novelty of a female monster, and despite her limited screen time, the bride may have lured in various curious moviegoers who had passed on the earlier Karloff-only film. Interestingly, although the bride's initial cast listing (The Monster's Mate.........?) mirrors the Monster's in the first film in the series, the end credit ("A good cast is worth repeating") retains the question mark. While Elsa Lanchester's attractively distinctive features dispel the mystery, the practice relegates the title character to the kind of anonymity shared by the three vampiresses mentioned above. And again, the Monster's projected partner, created in the same fashion and utilizing the same "stuff" as the Monster himself, would prove to lack his robust constitution and would be replaced by a hardier male accomplice, Ygor, in the next two sequels. For all that, both *Son of Frankenstein* and *The Ghost of Frankenstein* (1942) are usually described as the last of the films in which the monster is featured "alone."

The proponents of the female-progeny angle may have felt that, given the Count's obvious appeal to women (although any of the various existing paeans to Bela Lugosi's sensuality by Carroll Borland will adequately illustrate how tastes have changed over the years),

the addition of a female *nosferatu* couldn't help but increase the number of male ticket buyers. For viewers who dared to become involved in the story, though, there would be little dramatic bonus in having two heavies, essentially identical save for gender. Is the sight of two bats flapping through the arras any more riveting than the sight of one? Would they compete for available jugulars or share the wealth? And just how many scenes of pin-spotted bedroom eyes would be too many?

The two horrors in *Bride of Frankenstein* ring the bell because of the undeniable poignancy and power of their reactions to each other; in her several brief moments of life, the Monster's mate sides with humankind and against her intended. This type of conflict has to exist if there is to be any dramatic thrust; otherwise, the two man-made creations are too much alike to permit the continued existence of both. In 1935's *WereWolf of London*, the snarling confrontation scene in Glendon's lab *must* end with the death of one of the lycanthropes; there's just not enough room in London (or in the film itself) for two werewolves. In 1943's *Frankenstein Meets the Wolfman* and in subsequent monster mashes, the formula worked as long as it did because the viewers were treated to an array of monstrosities who battled humanity when not tussling with each other. This wave of the future would prove what the mid-thirties experiments only proffered: that variety was the spice not only of life, but of pseudo-life and afterlife, as well.

It seems, then, that the Count was written out of *Dracula's Daughter* because he was superfluous.

Of course, Lugosi had to be paid off. The $4,000 he received, which exceeded his entire salary for *Dracula*, must have seemed quite a windfall. All that money for a few still photos, a handshake or two, and maybe a curious chuckle at the sight of the wax dummy which so little resembled him. (Dwight Frye got not so much as a brass farthing in compensation for the nameless double who took his place at the foot of the stairs.) The payoff may have made Bela feel a tad more charitable towards the Laemmles. Maybe they were honorable men, making good on a deal that couldn't be closed as everyone had originally hoped. The Hungarian had no idea that the quick cash he pocketed stood for much more than services sold, though unrequired; it represented the sale of his birthright as Dracula.

"In all the annals of living horror, one name stands out as the epitome of evil—Dracula!" Thus trumpeted a lurid rerelease trailer, struck by an overjoyed studio late in 1938. Two years earlier, when *Dracula's Daughter* was on "selected" screens, Universal had discovered that the requisite magic was, in fact, lodged in the vampire's name, and not in his person. Little disappointment had greeted the appearance of the Count's daughter, just as little protest had been made concerning the Count's absence. *Dracula* had been a sensation, yet the Vampire King's being upstaged by another bloodsucker wielding the same name had caused scarcely anyone to (ahem) bat an eye. Son, daughter, progenitor—it made little difference to the bottom line who was swooping, glaring or nibbling, so long as the infamous and copyrighted name was emblazoned for all to see.

In the end, a well-aimed arrow would bring her peace, and Dracula's only true daughter would never rise again. Hardly a hot enough number to lure in the more susceptible menfolk, she had had a mere 70 minutes of immortality. The *recherché* lesbian overtones had proven to be too subtle to result in any controversial (and thus invaluable) publicity. Marya Zaleska would have to wait decades before emerging from her coffin, falling out of her bodice, and transmogrifying into any of the interchangeable buxom *succubi* being pimped by England's desperate Hammer Films. The design of several of her gowns, none of which was even remotely low-cut, rather tastefully emphasized Ms. Holden's generous endowments. It is doubtful whether the actress, who had made her mark in dance and classical song before turning to movies, would even have remotely appreciated being noticed—as were many of the later Hammer heroines—more for her mammaries than for her talent.

Temporarily flush, Bela Lugosi would soon discover that the next time the name of Dracula graced a marquee, he would be just another spectator. The second coming of the gods of horror would find him relegated to sidekick status or worse at Universal. That $4,000 check had transformed the Hungarian from the one-and-only redoubtable Voivode to a waxen second banana faster than John P. Fulton would later morph John Carradine's shadow into a prop-room bat. Anyone could be Dracula now, so long as he was under contract to Universal Pictures. The legally registered name would empower a performer as surely as the swirling black cloak would enshroud his form.

In 1930, Bela had left no stone unturned, no feeling unspoken, no thought unpublished, in his quest to win the right to portray on film the role he had virtually claimed as his own on Broadway. When he was finally awarded the part, he was paid a pittance, considering the years of experience he had brought with him. In 1936, Bela was paid off with a pittance, his identity usurped by a mannequin, his future association with the role undermined, and—after the vapid *Postal Inspector*, a contractual obligation—his employment at Universal terminated.

There is no record that the proud actor opened his mouth once.

Dracula's Daughter

Released May 11, 1936; 70 minutes

Cast: Gloria Holden (Countess Marya Zaleska/Dracula's Daughter); Otto Kruger (Jeffrey Garth); Marguerite Churchill (Janet Blake); Irving Pichel (Sandor); Edward Van Sloan (Von Helsing); Nan Grey (Lili); Gilbert Emery (Sir Basil Humphrey); E.E. Clive (Sergeant Wilkes); Hedda Hopper (Lady Esme Hammond); Billy Bevan (Albert); Halliwell Hobbes (Sergeant Hawkins); Edgar Norton (Hobbs); Claude McAllister (Sir Aubrey Bedford); Eily Malyon (Miss Peabody); George Kirby (Bookstore Owner); Christian Rub (Coachman); Guy Kingsford (Radio Announcer); David Dunbar (Motor Bobby); Joseph E. Tozer (Dr. Angus Graham); Gordon Hart (Host); Douglas Wood (Dr. Townsend);

Fred Walton (Dr. Bemish); Paul Weigel (Innkeeper); Douglas Gordon (Attendant); William von Brincken, George Sorel (Policemen); Eric Walton (Butler); Agnes Anderson (Bride); William Schramm (Groom); Owen Gorin (Friend); Else Janssen, Bert Sprotte (Guests); John Blood (Bobby); Clive Morgan (Desk Sergeant); Hedwigg Reicher (Wife); John Power (Police Official)

Credits: Associate Producer — E.M. Asher; Director — Lambert Hillyer; Screenplay — Garrett Fort; Based on the story *Dracula's Guest* by Bram Stoker; Suggested by Oliver Jeffries; Director of Photography — George Robinson, ASC; Art Director — Albert S. D'Agostino; Special Photography — John P. Fulton; Film Editor — Milton Carruth; Music — Edward Ward; Supervising Film Editor — Maurice Pivar; Sound Supervisor — Gilbert Kurland; Makeup — Jack P. Pierce; Gowns — Brymer

POSTAL INSPECTOR (1936)

Neither a horror film nor one of TV's Shock Theater titles, *Postal Inspector* is included herein primarily because it was Bela Lugosi's last Universal picture on his *Black Cat* contract, and because it's probably one of the most rarely seen of his fifty-odd features. A tepid paean to the post office, the film not only wastes Lugosi's talents, but squanders the popular Ricardo Cortez in a poorly written yet overdrawn part.

A stock footage montage of mail-handlers and letter carriers segues to a postal office, wherein the assembled muckety-mucks listen avidly as FDR sings the praises of postal inspectors via the radio. Following the glowing testimonial, Inspector Bill Davis (Cortez), by far the youngest and most animated of the stuffy group, heads for the airport and home. Aboard the plane, Bill notices the passengers are tense and concerned about the thick fog surrounding them. Sitting opposite Connie Larrimore (Patricia Ellis), a singer of some repute (although he has never heard of her), Bill convinces the young woman that her singing a song while accompanied by a kid playing a harmonica will somehow calm their anxious cabin-mates. While Connie launches into something about "bluebirds on the wallpaper" and "decorating dreams," the pilot is communicating with an air traffic controller about landing in the fog. The technician, who barks

his crucial information through a telephone, of all things, and can see the plane through the fog even though the plane can't see the airport, passes on news of the musical crowd control technique to a bystander.

The bystander is Mr. Benez (Bela), an entrepreneur who has booked the blonde songbird to appear in his Golden Eagle Club that very evening. Benez spreads the word to waiting reporters, and the quaint-yet-crucial deed is on the front page the next day. While everyone fawns over Larrimore, Bill is met by his brother, Charley (Michael Loring), who turns out to be Connie's old (but innocent) childhood flame. Charley and Connie waste no time in arranging a luncheon date, but big brother Bill is less than enthusiastic about the girl (Why?), and is unequivocally down on Benez (Why?).

Charley and Connie meet at Bill's office, where they and the audience witness firsthand how postal inspectors spend countless hours retrieving monies lost in scams and on shabby goods offered through the mails. The film is laced with scenes of plodding postal investigators trying on electric hair-growth hats, modeling height enhancers, and experimenting with radical growth pills on errant guinea pigs. Lest anyone think that such comically convoluted fraud is taken lightly by the federal men,

Bill pontificates on the awesome charge he and others of his ken have willingly assumed: "You know, there's something pretty comforting about the thought that, with no more insurance than a mere postage stamp, a man may entrust his entire life's savings, or his most personal secrets into the hands of absolute strangers."

At the Golden Eagle that night, a supremely glamorous Connie repeats her famous wallpaper anthem, backed this time by a full orchestra and the kid with the harmonica, and then joins Bill and Charley for coffee. Benez stops by the table: "Everything is all right?" Bill: "Everything." Benez: "Everything … but me."

There's no time to sulk, however; the nightclub owner receives a cryptic telegram, inviting him to check the racing column from the previous day's newspaper. The current newspaper serves quite as well, though; mention of the murder of *another* night-club owner prompts Benez to own up to owing $50,000 to a singularly unpleasant Mr. Carter. "And," he adds, "I'm two months behind."

Connie is summoned to Benez's office, where the beleaguered owner asks her to mingle with the crowd ("Do you mind helping me a little?"). Among assorted *bons mots* and jibes, the singer lets it slip that Charley Davis will be accompanying 3 million bucks' worth of worn-out currency that is earmarked for the furnace to the post office later that week; the younger brother, it seems, performs this errand regularly as part of his duties at the Federal Reserve. Benez's interest is piqued, but nothing further is said.

The next morning, Bill's newspaper reveals that the entire northern part of the state is covered by flood waters, which are heading his way. In an instant, the postal inspector is on a plane, headed for the besieged town of Yarborough; there, he will assist the postmaster in keeping the post office open and will rescue the bundled mail himself. From this point on, actual newsreel footage of recent devastating floods in New England and Pennsylvania will occupy a large share of the running time. As the waters continue their inexorable

approach, there are constant interruptions to radio broadcasts, as executive orders mobilize police, volunteer firemen, National Guardsmen, and virtually anyone with an honorary commission or half a lung.

Charley belongs to the National Guard, so Connie drops him at the armory and drives his car to work. The beautiful blonde, clad in a very low-cut gown, calms the club's flood-conscious audience with an upbeat rendition of "How Dry I Am" and then heads over to the local Volunteer Relief Workers headquarters, where she signs up as a hospital worker. Flood victims queue up at radio station KWZZ to broadcast news of their condition to anxious relatives in other climes, but Benez is not listening. The distraught entrepreneur has been given 24 hours by Carter to come up with the cash, or else! Confused and upset, Benez is convinced by his associates that snatching the $3 million delivery would be a piece of cake, especially since most everyone else is preoccupied with impending doom.

Cut to shots of the three desperate men in a car; cut to a street scene, wherein Bill interviews a dying postal worker; cut to shots of the three desperate men and large postal bags in a car; cut to a police dispatcher; cut to a radio broadcaster: "…held up a United States mail truck, killed the driver, and escaped with three million dollars in cash"; cut to more newsreel footage of rising waters, swimming cattle, and flooded cars.

Bill is investigating. Strike one: Only three people knew the money was being shipped, and one of them was young Charley. Strike two: A torn postal bag was discovered in the flooded remains of a car, said car belonging to young Charley. When questioned by his big brother, Charley clams up; he's protecting someone. Bill gives the younger man two hours to make good, and only a moment or two over the allotted time, Charley returns with Connie. Connie recalls mentioning the money shipment to Benez and admits that Charley's car was stolen while in her care.

Bill heads over to the flooded Golden Eagle Club, in search of Benez's whereabouts. Connie and Charley, however, take a National

Lobby card for *Postal Inspector*. PENTAGRAM LIBRARY.

Guard speedboat and head for an address that Benez had once provided to the singer, "on the other side of town." While Bill and his partners find the same address by poking through the water-logged nightclub office, Connie has already arrived and has discovered Benez's complicity. The postal inspector shows up moments later, only to find his kid brother shaking off the effects of a pistol-whipping, the young woman sequestered in the closet, and the National Guard boat missing. Natty speed-boats supplanting the more customary sedans, the good guys chase the bad guys throughout the flood-ravaged streets. When the villains ditch their boat and head for the rooftops, Bill follows, and gun shots are exchanged. Charley and Connie finally topple the heavies into the water, when they plow their boat into the sup-port beam beneath the roof.

The half-drowned criminals are rounded up, and a succession of newspaper headlines announces arrests, convictions, sentences, and recessing flood waters. During a picnic in a hotel room, the lovebirds phone Bill, invite him to their wedding, and regale him with a bluebird wallpaper reprise, sung as a duet.

Preachy (although entertainingly so be-cause of Ricardo Cortez's rat-a-tat delivery) and episodic, *Postal Inspector* is a patchwork quilt of newsreel coverage, musical interludes, comic relief (à la Rube Goldberg), and the occasional dramatic puff. Just as there doesn't appear to be much structural integrity *to* the film, there seems to be very little actual reason for it, either. The picture was shot on the coat-tails of Warner Bros.' many successes with the government-agents-versus-organized-crime formula. Of course, Warners had pretty much exhausted the more romantic arms of government service by 1936: treasury agents (T-Men), the drug and alcohol crowd (G-Men), the FBI, and customs and immigration had all received filmed tributes to the perils of their chosen line of work. By the time Horace McCoy and Robert Presnall got around to penning a like story, all that remained for consideration were the mailmen and the chicken inspectors.

Throughout his decades-long career, Cortez continually played leapfrog with the law, upholding it rigorously in one film, thumbing his nose at it in another. Always glib and enjoyable, the performer (who was not your typical Latino, having been born Jacob Krantz) mouths his lengthy aphorisms here with the shadow of his tongue in his cheek, but otherwise enacts Bill Davis's commitment to principle with the remorseless energy it deserves. His eponymous character is not well drawn, however. Bill's hesitancy with regard to Connie Larrimore is hard to understand (especially in light of her heroic action on the plane), is never explained, and ultimately is unjustified. Equally puzzling is his dismissal of Benez at a point in the story where the nightclub owner is guilty of nothing more than professional exuberance.

Also disturbing is his blind adherence to the letter of the law, while seemingly flipping the bird to its spirit. Just prior to the breaking news story on the flood, Bill spars with Lieutenant Ordway (Paul Harvey) over a fine point: "It's a murder case," pleads the looey; "all I need to crack this case wide open is to get a look at that letter!" Sanctimonious Bill turns thumbs down, replying, "Nobody can touch the mail except the person to whom it's addressed," but he does offer another crime-fighting option: "Why don't you have one of your men tail the carrier and nab the letter after it's delivered?" No mention of the possibility of court orders dates the picture; the cop's proposed maneuver leading to an acquittal on a legal technicality is very '90s. Prior to throwing the exasperated cop out of his office, he tosses him an insurance scam as a bone. Yet the postal inspector's demeanor indicates that he normally wouldn't even give the police

department that consideration, but for the fact that the perpetrators "made just one little mistake; receiving insurance checks by mail."

Patricia Ellis's Connie Larrimore may be a tad hard-boiled, but her soft spot for her home town and her enlisting as a hospital worker during the crisis peg her as an okay gal. As apt to break into song as she is to crack wise (there are five musical interludes in the 58-minute film, three involving that mediocre dream-decorating tune), Connie undergoes an instant conversion when she's dressed down by Bill for having spilled the beans to the nightclub owner. The singer is still less judgmental than the postal man, though, and refuses to accuse Benez out of hand.

Michael Loring was a local singer when hired to essay Charley Davis in *Postal Inspector.* The personable Loring appeared in three more in-house efforts, including *Yellowstone* and a couple of William Gargan epics (*Flying Hostess* and *Breezing Home,* the latter released early in 1937), before disappearing from the scene. He appears to have amassed no other credits in film. The ebullient Hattie McDaniel plays another of her trademark maids. Miss Daniels rued her typecasting but admitted it was far more profitable for her to *play* a maid at $700 a week than to *be* a maid for $7.00 weekly. Despite her being stuck in the domestic rut, the outgoing actress appeared in many of the decade's most prestigious pictures.

If anything, *Postal Inspector* is notable for featuring the quintessential atypical Bela Lugosi performance. More than any Universal offering to date, the picture affords us a rare glimpse of a smiling, laughing, happy Lugosi, even if only for the first reel. The set-upon Mr. Benez is as equally removed from the actor's disappointing red herrings as from his operatic monsters; he is, before all else, a tragic victim of circumstances. Initially on top of the world, thanks to the safe arrival — amidst excellent publicity — of his latest featured attraction, Benez's collapse begins with Bill Davis's unwarranted criticism and ends with murder. Along the way, the nightclub owner moves from self-deprecating irony (as with that arcane telegram: "Perhaps I don't know

That's William Hall with the money and Bela with his ubiquitous cigar; Guy Usher is left holding the bag. *PENTAGRAM LIBRARY.*

English. Read it," he jokes with an associate) to mild anxiety (as when he gently pleads with Connie to spend some time with more important customers than Charley) to despair (the 24-hour ultimatum). More pointedly and less typically, the entrepreneur has to be talked into attempting the robbery, a striking departure from one of the Hungarian's notorious criminal masterminds.

With most of the movie's less-than-choice dialogue divided between Cortez's huffing about postal abuse and Ellis's musical odes to bluebirds and such, Bela doesn't have too many extended opportunities to push his vocal weight around. Nevertheless, his short scenes, presented at intervals, give a realistic if disjointed view of a rather simple businessman who is sliding into the pit through no fault of his own. Benez's early conversation is all business, and never once does the character succumb to the actor's genetic code and begin chewing Connie's wallpaper. In fact, as he's neither the instigator of the planned robbery nor even an enthusiastic participant, the beleaguered club owner operates light-years away from the non-stop cackling in which many of his dramatic blood-relatives usually indulged. Rather, several of his brief moments catch him reacting either to an associate's advice or to the latest in a series of bad breaks.

Between the healthy infusion of stock and newsreel footage, the various musical numbers, Bill Davis's post office propaganda, and the comic relief shtick with sock-sewing machines and assorted other scams, most of the running time has been accounted for. That still leaves, however, the action finale, which Richard Bojarski refers to as "an exciting chase sequence through rising flood waters." I view it as a second-rate mix of rear-projection, obvious miniatures, and rickety standing sets. The best moment of the sequence precedes the chase itself and takes place in Benez's hideout, where his impatient henchmen are egging on the impresario to escape. Looking out the window, from which no signs of life are apparent and only the water-filled channels between abandoned buildings can be seen, the accomplices suggest that they swim for it. With the casual air of a man about town hailing a cab at a busy intersection, Benez waves away the idea: "We'll get a speedboat," he explains, "and leave like gentlemen."

Released in August 1936, *Postal Inspector* doubtless saw its last days in production caught up in the painful economic crunch of Charles Rogers' new austerity plan. Director Otto Brower, a veteran of Paramount's silent Zane Grey horse operas and Mascot's Western serials, was nevertheless adjudged suitable for the feds and floods picture. George Turner and Michael Price (*Forgotten Horrors*) maintain that Brower was noted for his "spectacular second-unit sequences in epic productions," and it may have been felt that this expertise would help meld the newsreel footage with the big chase scene. For all intents and purposes, the movie's entire dramatic flow was focused on that damned flood footage. One has to question the wisdom of Universal's even attempting an authentic view of an inundated city on a shoestring when, less than three years earlier, RKO had spent a fortune credibly destroying New York City in *The Deluge*. As *Postal Inspector* turned out to be his only feature for Universal, it's clear that Brower, hired as an inexpensive replacement for Louis Friedlander, just couldn't deliver the goods.

So long as the story unfolded on dry land, the studio's standing sets could be re-outfitted and pressed into service. The most ambitious of the film's static backgrounds, the Golden Eagle Club, is a typical if somewhat spartan cinematic nightclub of the thirties. Once the flood hit the hometown, however, the special effects people were in over their heads. The climax was shot in the studio tank and looks it, while flats meant to represent the facades of the partially submerged buildings are so totally devoid of detail as to be unrealistic. Background perspective is essentially nonexistent, and Ricardo Cortez's stunt double leaps into the water against a gray and featureless backdrop.

The miniature work at either end of the movie (remember that plane ride?) is adequate at best, and the heavies take their final plunge among a series of closeups and cuts; nary a villainous body is seen hitting the broth. Nor does either of the picture's two live "action elements" — the shooting of the postal employee or the daring daylight robbery — occur onscreen. We don't even get to see Charley brained by a henchman; the cut-to action starts with his fall to the floor. At any rate, the climactic special effects are but pale ghosts of the sterling displays which the studio could still accomplish, given the time and the money. Sadly, neither was available.

It's a crying shame that neither a larger budget nor a stylish hand on the reins was available for *Postal Inspector*. Bela's sympathetic portrayal is novel enough that it might have opened a door or two during the horror film famine had the part been more substantial, or had the movie received a wider distribution. As it stands, the picture is devilishly hard to track down in viewable condition. I've never seen a 16mm original print offered for sale, and the video companies listing the public domain title inevitably apologize for the poor condition of their source material.

Postal Inspector offers a new take on the old Lugosi and some fun with Ricardo Cortez's reading of his character. So far as excitement goes, however, you're better off collecting stamps.

Postal Inspector

Released August 16, 1936; 58 minutes

Cast: Ricardo Cortez (Bill Davis); Patricia Ellis (Connie Larrimore); Michael Loring (Charley Davis); Bela Lugosi (Benez); Wallis Clark (Pottie); David Oliver (Butch); Arthur Loft (Richards); Guy Usher (Evans); William Hall (Roach); Spencer Charters (Grumpy); Hattie McDaniel (Deborah); Marla Shelton (Air Hostess); Robert Davis (Pilot); Henry

Hunter (Co-Pilot); Billy Barrud (Boy with Harmonica); Harry Beresford (Ritter); Paul Harvey (Lieut. Ordway); Anne Gillis (Little Girl); Russell Wade (Man); Anne O'Neal (Woman with Nose Machine); Gertrude Astor (Woman with Drumsticks); Flora Finch (Mrs. Armbruster); Margaret McWade (Old Maid); Jerry Mandy (Henchman)

Credits: Associate Producer — Robert Presnell; Director — Otto Brower; Screenplay — Horace McCoy; Based on an original story by Robert Presnell and Horace McCoy; Photographer — George Robinson; Art Director — Jack Otterson; Special Effects — John P. Fulton; Musical Director — Charles Previn; Film Editor — Phil Cahn

NIGHT KEY (1937)

By mid–January 1937, the new Universal, now under Charles Rogers and J. Cheever Crowdin, was making inroads only into mediocrity, and if anything, money was tighter than it had been under the Laemmles. Having haughtily dismissed horror pictures in their initial game plan that they announced with great hoopla to an indifferent public, the new owners were stuck for ideas. With the overseas market still intolerant where thrillers were concerned, Rogers found himself in a bit of a quandary.

In the midst of sacking dozens of Laemmles, pruning the contract player roster, and passing on the options of untold throngs of starlets and hopefuls, the new production chief came upon the name of Boris Karloff. Mr. Karloff, it transpired, not only had one picture left on the contract he had signed with the former management, but would continue to collect a *very* handsome salary of more than $3,000 weekly until that last picture was in the can. The quandary? How to bring that irksome contractual payment to a speedy halt, while exploiting Karloff's notoriety without creating another "monster" movie and incurring the enmity of the European community while backstepping vis-à-vis the game plan. The studio couldn't allow its resident Horror King to sit idle for all the tea in Hollywood.

In its own way, Karloff's portrayal of David Mallory in *Night Key* was as memorable as any of the assorted grotesques he had thus far created. Although the self-effacing Englishman would probably have confessed to being little more than the willing canvas to Jack Pierce's magic palette, he had been unofficially crowned successor to the Man of a Thousand Faces by innumerable fans of both men.

Playing the nearly blind inventor didn't merely afford the actor a break from villainy, it gave him a healthy taste of his own medicine. At once spectacularly brilliant and hopelessly naïve, his Mallory is bullied, manhandled, menaced, exploited, insulted, deceived, dismissed, betrayed, accused of hearsay, all but convicted on circumstantial evidence, and coerced into criminal activity through the threat of violence to his daughter. Apart from tossing a helpless kid into the river and trying to revive the dead, that's a pretty comprehensive rundown of Karloff's cinematic activity to that point.

His David Mallory is as physically unimposing as the Monster is overwhelming. When you consider that Karloff was literally midway between two appearances as the seven-foot-tall, electrical behemoth, the actor's swing in the diametrically opposite direction is noteworthy. The credibility of his near-blindness varies

A white and woolly Boris Karloff as David Mallory, a blonde and blue-eyed Jean Rogers as the virginal Joan Mallory, and a piece of Flash Gordonesque hardware as the eponymous night key. *PENTAGRAM LIBRARY.*

from scene to scene, on the other hand, and more than once Karloff wanders into silent movie territory, groping about with eyes at half-mast.

Night Key is a picture which very much gets by on the personalities of its major participants. Along with Boris the chameleon, the cast takes the succinctly but effectively drawn roles in stride. For Samuel S. Hinds, the part of Steve Ranger is payback time; Hinds sees that Karloff gets a psychological working-over which more than compensates for the earlier and more physical role reversal in *The Raven.* Ranger regards his theft of Mallory's original alarm system and his acquiring the rights to the inventor's latest brainstorm (and then shelving it) as little more than good business sense. Then, perhaps a little too conveniently,

he has a conversion experience at the wrap-up. (And Karloff's Mallory, having already been shafted twice by this man, immediately smashes his night key on the pavement, gushing "I won't need *this* anymore.") Still, Hinds adds some nice touches to what could have been a one-dimensional character; he peppers his dishonesty with an occasional dash of genuine concern (even if only for his own interests), and we need to believe if we are to accept his last-minute change of heart.

Jean Rogers and Warren Hull expend an awful lot of energy locking horns before locking lips in the closing moments. Jean's Dale Arden had given legions of young lads their first glimpse of authorized female midriff in the first *Flash Gordon* serial, and her feisty Joan Mallory proves she could display the requisite flashes of emotion even when clad in mufti. Warren Hull's Jim Travers, a jackbooted member of Ranger Protective Services before seeing the error of his ways and turning in his badge and whistle, puts in a pile of overtime on the job. Between sleeping in the hallway of Joan's boardinghouse, hounding her steps all over town, chowing down (on the company's money, no doubt) at the restaurant where she works, and frivolously tailing her back home in a taxi-cab, he also finds time to uncover what Ranger did to his sweetie's old man and to lay the foundations for a happy ending. Handsome, personable, and sincere, Jim convinces Joan and the audience to hang in there.

Edward Arnold clone Edwin Maxwell is suitably two-faced as the lawyer Kruger. The dramatics he promises Ranger — the shyster will have to put on a show of outrage while he and the crooked executive are giving poor old Mallory a hosing — should serve as a timely reminder that some of the most effective play-acting one can witness occurs not on the screen, but in the courtroom. The part is small but showy, and Maxwell demonstrates that he had come a long way from 1933's *Night of Terror*, in which he seemed very much more a Wallace Beery clone.

I just can't stomach Hobart Cavanaugh's Petty Louie, and it's not Hobart Cavanaugh's fault. Most '30s thrillers, no matter whether murder mysteries or out-and-out horror pictures, are saddled with comic relief characters who must have been amusing to Depression-era audiences, but who are merely depressing nowadays. Contemporary moviegoers looked to comic commentators to put a wry and occasionally vulgar spin on the deplorable situation, and these were usually reporters, played by a Lee Tracy or a Wallace Ford. Highly vocal, if not overly articulate, in their contempt for the establishment, they were brash and clever enough to win audience approval when doing what they did best: sticking it to society. I still enjoy the barbs that fly among the ancient plot-lines when they're genuinely acerbic and are delivered with the panache of a Glenda Farrell. When either substance or style is missing, however, you're stuck with a Petty Louie.

Cavanaugh's language-fracturing small-time crook, who owes a tremendous debt to George E. Stone, does advance the story, if only by betraying Mallory to "The Kid" (Alan Baxter's take on a patented Richard Widmark psychotic gangster) more than once. To the intense relief of the viewers (Mallory is far too polite to do other than grieve), Louie is drilled about a half-dozen times while helping the inventor escape from The Kid's clutches.

Cavanaugh is guilty only of contributory malice, however. Director Lloyd Corrigan, whose other hat was inscribed "jovial comedian," had manifested a distressing tendency to inject comic relief into the veins of the otherwise healthy projects placed in his care. Best remembered (and this is upsetting enough) for his various roles in the Bowery Boys epics of the early fifties, Corrigan began directing in the early '30s (1931's humorless *Daughter of the Dragon* is the earliest pertinent credit I can find) and stopped working behind the camera with *Night Key*. Reviews of several of his in-between efforts (like 1935's *Murder on a Honeymoon* and 1936's *The Dancing Pirate*) make mention of intrusive or unneeded comic types. Corrigan the actor would later get his in spades while on call in *She-Wolf of London*.

There's a good deal of action in *Night Key*, but most of it is either ludicrous (some knee-slapping shtick with alarm clocks, and that open-umbrella business), painful to watch (the nearly-blind genius relieved of his specs and slapped or pushed around time and again), or telegraphed (one look at the "big board" in Ranger's headquarters, and you just know you're in for a light-show before long). Still, Mallory's breaking out of The Kid's warehouse involves some jury-rigged and colorful electrical nonsense, and the cops and the Ranger rangers converging on the bad guys during the final heist is good for a couple of tame thrills.

I guess Mallory's new system, a sort of electric-eye prototype, intruded only slightly into 1937's science fiction domain, but I'm including *Night Key* as Karloff's equivalent of *Postal Inspector*. Both films were made during horror films' enforced hiatus, and both gave their colorful protagonists the chance of working against type. Even among these circumstances, the Brit still got a better shake than did his Hungarian counterpart. As silly or predictable as much of *Night Key* is, it was all first-unit stuff. Isolated shots of careering prowl cars and the like were, of course, lifted from the stock footage library, but unlike the stock material in the Lugosi film, these took only a fraction of the running time.

George Robinson photographed both pictures, yet his work on *Night Key* is inarguably superior in every way. His camera is far more mobile, and Karloff et al. were treated to the meticulous lighting patterns that had earmarked the studio's classic horror movies. To be completely fair, though, there was little anyone could have done with the overabundance of newsreel footage in the post office film. With low-budget pictures such as these, Robinson had no time to waste on tests, experimental angles, or creative camera placements. The Karloff film gets the nod largely because of Corrigan's savvy with the material. For all his leanings toward the silly side of life, the actor-director had a firmer grasp on the more mainstream movie themes than did Otto Brower, whose chief expertise lay in keeping from stepping in the horseshit which littered his more customary digs.

It's obvious that the movers and shakers at Universal regarded *Night Key* with greater favor than they did *Postal Inspector*. It's evident that the former picture enjoyed a larger budget from the moment the credits hit the screen. *Night Key* continues to show up on TV and is more readily available both on film and on quality videotape than its "rival," attesting to its status with collectors, exhibitors, and picky preservationists. It wouldn't surprise me one bit to discover that the Lugosi film received far less press attention, was given a less compre-hensive publicity campaign, or even had fewer 35mm positive prints struck for release. When all is said and done, *Postal Inspector* is an uneven rarity, of interest only to Ricardo Cortez completists and Lugosiphiles. *Night Key* remains a guilty pleasure, offering decent production values, a largely excellent cast, and a refreshing change of pace for Boris Karloff.

Night Key

Released May 2, 1937; 67 minutes

Cast: Boris Karloff (Dr. David Mallory); Jean Rogers (Joan Mallory); Warren Hull (Jimmy Travers); Hobart Cavanaugh (Petty Louie); Samuel S. Hinds (Stephen Ranger); Edwin Maxwell (Kruger); Alan Baxter (The Kid); David Oliver (Mike); Ward Bond (Fingers); Frank Reicher (Carl); George Humbert (Spinelli); Charles Wilson (Chief of Police); Michael Fitzmaurice (Ranger's Secretary); George Cleveland (Adams); Emmett Vogan, Charlie Sherlock (Reporters); Ethan Laidlaw, Monte Montague, Jack Cheatham, George Magrill, Frank Hagney, Ralph Dunn (Henchmen); Henry Rocquemore (Boarder); Roy Barcroft (Office Worker); Ruth Fallows (Waitress); Hal Cooke (Manager); Tom Hanlon (Radio Announcer); Nina Campana (Mrs. Spinelli); Charlie Sullivan (Taxi Driver); Johnnie Morris (Tailor)

Credits: Associate Producer — Robert Presnell; Director — Lloyd Corrigan; Screenplay — Tristram Tupper and John C. Moffitt; Original Story — William Pierce; Director of Photography — George Robinson; Art Director — Jack Otterson; Associate Art Director — Loren Patrick; Film Editor — Otis Garrett; Musical Director — Lou Forbes; Special Photographic Effects — John P. Fulton; Sound — Jess Moulin and Jesse T. Bastian

REPORTED MISSING (1937)

Say what you may about their capacity to frighten nowadays, but Universal's classic horror pictures are as timeless now as they were when they were first released. Either set in a deliberately nebulous time and place or planned to be as much period pieces as thrillers, they presented something of an alternate world, similar to ours but featuring enough departures from the reality we were experiencing to tip its being out of sync. The problems they presented were unlike any of the problems we had to face; their heroes were more operatic than ours; their villains, more dread. Such tales could never be thought of as dated because they were never rooted in any kind of identifiable milieu to begin with.

If the geographical locale was comparatively realistic — many more people would traipse through a sleepy English village like Iping than would career down the Borgo Pass at midnight — the scientific framework would be the key to the parallel dimension. When the research being done was of the fantastic variety, or when those crucial experiments demonstrated more an ersatz than an earnest hypothesis, we were being painlessly removed from the realm of real possibility and projected into this other world, where reviving the dead was possible even if dealing with global famine and pestilence still was beyond the ken. There is no

statute of limitations in the lunatic fringe, and a process which never existed in the first place never becomes dated.

This all helps explain why older "realistic" thrillers like *Reported Missing*, which were many times fabricated around the latest scientific discoveries, seem antiquated nowadays. The technology which they highlighted was real, did make a difference, and is now passé. Vintage mysteries grounded in that timeless universe unreel at an incredible clip; our psyche accepts those airless tombs, musty mummies, and poison-filled violins of *Charlie Chan in Egypt* as forever interesting and forever (un)likely. No matter how riveting the enigmas of *Charlie Chan at the Race Track*, however, for all save the most gadget-oriented viewers, the lengthy disquisition on electric eyes grinds the feature to a halt and stamps "1936" on its lower hind quarter.

And so, into the fray...

Tomorrow should be the big day for Steve Browning (William Gargan); his "Browning Drift Indicator" will receive its acid test during a regularly scheduled flight for Continental Air Lines. For the sake of his friends Brad Martin (Joseph [Joe] Sawyer), Ab Steele (Hobart Cavanaugh), and Paul Wayne (Dick Purcell) and the audience, Steve gives the lowdown on the device:

STEVE: My drift indicator takes the guess-work out of blind flying, especially if the pilot loses his radio beam. If this happens, he simply takes his reading from the top of this dial, which shows his side drift in the green. This enables him to keep a true course, even though his compass course may be several degrees in deviation.

With the gizmo's success all but assured, Paul proposes a little spontaneous celebration down at Tony's restaurant. Besides the folk already mentioned, we meet Steve's girlfriend, air hostess Jean Clayton (Jean Rogers), and her brother, Jack (Michael Fitzmaurice), a pilot for Continental. At Tony's, Paul, who is a semi-serious rival for Jean's affections, is happy enough for his friend to buy drinks for the house. Even the patron who snatches the glass from under Paul's nose can't spoil the fun.

The next evening, Jack Clayton is ready to take the "Skyline Flyer" to New York and Steve's drift indicator to the aviation Hall of Fame. Continental's vice president, H.M. Hastings (Charles Trowbridge), is all smiles, busily rubbing elbows with some army brass, who represent the War Department's interest in Steve's brainchild. Everything looks rosy as the plane lifts off and is tracked via shortwave radio from Paulton Airport. The Skyline Flyer makes it through a raging thunderstorm with no problem, thanks to the Browning Drift Indicator, but, 40 miles from the New Mark landing field, trouble arises. "Wait a minute!" Jack Clayton is heard to yell, and then silence.

The local paper gets a hell of a headline out of the mishap: "Skyline Flyer Missing: Passengers Guinea Pigs for Experiment!" Other banners indicate that army planes have joined the search; stock footage of biplanes bears this out. But it takes Steve Browning and Paul Wayne, in Paul's plane, to find the wreckage of the Continental aircraft. On his radio, Steve alerts the airport that "They hit Indian Mountain and slid into a ravine. No signs of life."

At the Bureau of Aeronautics, an inquiry into the cause of the plane's crash is being held. Hastings maintains that four months of rigorous testing made his company well satisfied with the performance of the drift indicator. An unidentified airline pilot avers, "The most striking circumstance is that the ship was headed *away* from the airport when she hit!" A federal inspector claims that "there are quite a few things [he] can't figure out," but is able to remember only two: that the copilot was found strapped to his seat while pilot Jack Clayton was not, and that all the money and valuables had been removed from the victims. This last eye-opener is casually attributed to "souvenir hunters."

Jean is reduced to tears when called to remember whether Jack had done any drinking at the party for Steve, and Steve is put on the spot when asked whether he felt that pilot error ("unseemly behavior") might have caused the crash. Not at all happy with Steve's noncommittal answer, Jean lets him have it: "You were so anxious to clear yourself you let them put all the blame on Jack!" To throw salt in the wound, she allows Paul to take her home.

Soon, a second plane disappears en route to Denver when only minutes from the airport. This cuts it with Continental, and Steve gets more bad news:

> Although we are still convinced that the Browning Drift Indicator is a valuable asset to aviation, the Denver wreck, following so closely after the Skyline disaster, has created a public prejudice against anything new in flying equipment and makes it impossible for us to give your invention any further consideration.

Steve is for chucking it all, but friend Paul "buys" the invention for $2500 ("When I get the $2500 back, we're partners") and takes Steve out for a few drinks. At Tony's bar, Brad catches up with the men and informs them that the Denver wreckage has been found, and was "practically a duplicate of the Skyline crash." The searchers found a certain passenger onboard, but not the $100,000 worth of negotiable securities he had been carrying. No souvenir hunters this time; the state troopers showed up first, "and they even searched the

Title lobby card for *Reported Missing*. PENTAGRAM LIBRARY.

troopers!" Desperate to do something to help, Steve takes off.

Things are starting to pick up. Jean and her fella get back together, and Steve theorizes that too many coincidences between the crashes mean robbery was the motive. Mr. Van Der Borg, a Dutch diamond merchant, is going to fly out from Paulton to Los Angeles with a fortune in gems, and Steve hopes the crooks will make an attempt on the plane when the story hits the papers; he and Brad will be onboard and will, they hope, stop the robbery. Moments before takeoff, the two men are informed that Van Der Borg canceled his reservations a half-hour earlier. He had received a phone call warning him off the original flight, and was now set to take the 4:00 departure. A traffic jam prevents Steve and Brad from boarding that plane, and Hastings refuses to

have the aircraft recalled to Paulton on Steve's suspicions.

As with the others, the Los Angeles–bound flight crashes, only minutes before approaching the airport. The newspaper tells it all: "Continental Limited Is Wrecked Near Logantown; Phantom Robber Gets Fortune in Diamonds; Officials at Paulton Airport Refused to Hold Plane When Warned of Theft Plot." Later, Steve meets with Paul, Ab, and Brad at his workshop. He has news. With the help of the police, he has found that the control wheel of the Skyline Flyer bore three sets of fingerprints! Someone was in the cockpit beside Jack and his copilot! Next morning, he and Brad will fly to Washington to have the prints matched against those of all the registered pilots in the country in hopes of identifying the "phantom robber."

Jean is working the Washington flight, so

The biggest surprise — in more ways than one — is Dick Purcell (being unmasked) as the heavy. *PENTA-GRAM LIBRARY.*

Steve alerts her to keep an eye open for anything suspicious. Good old Ab has pulled strings to serve as copilot for the important mission, and Brad is seated near the cockpit door, ready to slug anyone who might try anything funny. Two men enter separately, but begin conferring with each other during the flight. Jean says one, a Mr. Duffy, booked the flight at the last moment; she's sure she's seen him someplace. Some turbulence in mid-flight causes Jean to spill coffee on the lap of the first man, and when he and Duffy jump to their feet, Brad comes out swinging. A mighty right sends Duffy to the floor. Before a mighty left can follow, the fellow still standing identifies himself as Senator Harbuck and says that Duffy is a member of the FBI!

In the chaos that ensues, no one notices the door to the cargo hold open or a strange figure clad in helmet, goggles and muffler, and wearing a parachute, enter the cabin. At gunpoint, he makes his way up to the front of the plane and demands the incriminating fingerprints. Steve tosses the envelope on a seat and manages to unmask the figure (as Paul!) before he is slugged. A ring of the hostess's call button lures Ab out of the cockpit and into the cabin, where Paul decks him and shoots the pilot. Setting the autopilot on a crash course, Paul locks the cockpit door and makes for the exit. As he strains to push the door open, however, the recovered G-Man Duffy shoots a hole in him; Paul plummets like a stone.

But the plane is set to crash at any moment. While Duffy and the senator struggle to pry open the door to the control deck, Jean rouses Steve. Finding duplicate keys to the door in Ab's pocket, Steve regains control of the plane in time to avoid a seriously unpleasant landing. After a cut, we find Steve explaining very tersely about Paul's standard operating procedure: "Wayne owned a plane which gave him access to the airport. He depended on the fact that the employees were too busy to search for stowaways, and he was right!" Duffy had boarded to keep an eye on Steve, but had always felt that Paul was the number one suspect; the drunk at the party had been Duffy, who took Paul's glass to get a set of fingerprints! As Steve was bluffing all along about that third set of prints — the envelope he tossed to Paul in the plane contained his letter of rejection from Continental — the heart-stopping dramatics onboard had, thankfully, paid off.

There are many aspects about *Reported Missing* which could be termed quaint; others are merely dated. We are in the time before the term "flight attendant" or even "stewardess" made its bow; coffee is poured by "hostesses of the air." Nor does anyone call a plane a plane. Maybe the word didn't convey the romance or intrigue of flight in 1937, for viewers are assailed with terms like "ship" and "flyer." With real-life airplane hijackings and terrorist bombings in our own time, it's alarming to see gun-wielding figures creep out of the cargo hold, or passengers (even G-men) whipping pistols out from within their suit jackets. Luckily pressurized cabins were still in the future. On the more hysterical side is the procedure for dealing with an impending crash: seat belts be damned, Jean commands the terrified passengers to "Move to the back of the ship!" where, incredibly, they *stand* while the wildly erratic aircraft wends its way toward oblivion.

The idea that Steve's drift indicator has spooked the public also seems hopelessly naïve in this day and age. The consumers' presumption that the safety device is somehow responsible for both the deaths of the passengers and the disappearance of their wristwatches and wallets is the ultimate paranoid witch hunt. We're only a step away from an intriguing visual metaphor of the successive Universal regimes: the torch-wielding mob storming the airport.

As the budget required that all those spectacular crashes be wrought off screen, the heinousness of the crime spree in *Reported Missing* generally goes unnoticed. The ruthless Wayne arranges the cold-blooded murder of planeloads of people to eliminate their giving witness to how he robbed them in mid-air! Such a callous modus operandi gives the unmasking scene of the "phantom robber" a particularly chilling edge. The audience has been maneuvered into regarding Paul Wayne as such a decent sort that finding him ultimately responsible for all these savage catastrophes is a real gut-wrenching blow.

A chuckle can be had by noting that the same plane and its miniature counterpart fills in for all those fancily named fleet aircraft. Given the nature of the film, most of the stock footage actually seems to suit the action without the usual seams showing. The only jarring note, and it's inconsequential, is the sight of the army planes flying in formation while conducting their search for the wreckage.

At the wrap-up, there's a moment when logic seems to have bailed out along with Dick Purcell. G-man Duffy (Bill Wayne) reveals how he took Paul Wayne's glass from that impromptu party in order to get the suspect's fingerprints. You have to ask just how omniscient the FBI is, considering that no one could have known that Paul would propose a party or that Steve would go along with it. Is the Bureau so well-staffed that it can put agents in all the local bars just in case some customer's prints might happen to be needed? Equally confusing is the timing: Why would the FBI have wanted Paul Wayne's fingerprints before any of the airplane catastrophes occurred?

William Gargan's Steve Browning is his usual dependable job. Gargan is a more credible hero than most, partly thanks to the novel touch of the good guy's having his lights put out in the climactic crisis, and he is capable of the more tender end of business, too. Lovely Jean Rogers, who was between assignments as the blonde Dale Arden in two of Buster Crabbe's Flash Gordon serials, gets to give her own brunette tresses a good airing. The role of Jean Clayton requires the actress to etch a principled heroine who has faith and hope in her man, comes to realize how much she loves him, yet isn't above exercising her woman's prerogative by turning on her heel when he needs her most.

Bickering buddies (Wayne tells them they act more like brothers than friends) Ab Steele and Brad Martin provide the picture's lighter side, and they're really not bad. Joe Sawyer and Hobart Cavanaugh aren't given that much material with which to work — they switch back and forth between comic hypochondria and insult humor — but their sparring is expertly done. The biggest surprise in more ways than one is Dick Purcell as the heavy. A serviceable actor-stuntman, Purcell is absolutely top-shelf as Paul Wayne. Compassionate (that offer to get Steve back on his feet), good-naturedly resigned (Jean calls him "a darling" for not pressing his advantage when her boyfriend is momentarily off the scene), yet totally unscrupulous and immoral, Wayne is Jekyll and Hyde in 1937 small-town America. His grotesque mask and muffler get-up signal the metamorphosis from amiable philanthropist to cold-blooded killer, but Wayne hasn't even the nobility of Stevenson's tragic hero. Not victim to any mind-altering drug while metamorphosing into his baser self, Wayne is driven by avarice; perhaps this is how the "darling" came into money. The part is a doozy, and Dick Purcell cops the brass ring far more definitively than he had with any of his "B" cowboys or even his Captain America.

Reported Missing marked one of only a handful of features Milton Carruth directed for Universal. Following a quartet of 1937 programmers, Carruth returned to his first love, editing. The fact that none of his films is appreciably better or worse than the output of people like Al Rogell, Otis Garrett or John Rawlins seems to indicate that Charlie Rogers' studio was geared to crank out a demonstrably adequate product no matter who was at the wheel.

Definitely better suited to the popular understanding of the *Shock Theater* program than *The Spy Ring, Reported Missing* has a ghoulish premise and a colorful villain. Along with a better than average cast and a painless application of the requisite stock footage (John P. Fulton got credit for the nigh invisible special effects), the quasi-genre elements result in a tale which is sufficiently interesting to warrant more attention than it has received to date.

Reported Missing

Released August 18, 1937; 63 minutes

Cast: William Gargan (Steve Browning); Jean Rogers (Jean Clayton); Dick Purcell (Paul Wayne); Joseph Sawyer (Brad Martin); Hobart Cavanaugh (Ab Steele); Michael Fitzmaurice (Jack Clayton); Bill Wayne (John Duffy); Charles Trowbridge (H.M. Hastings); Edward Keane (Reinhardt); Frederick Vogeding (Van Der Borg); Pierre Watkin (Reynolds); William Royle (Senator Harbuck); Sam McDaniel (Inquiry Witness); Milburn Stone (1st Radio Operator); Jack Carson (2nd Radio Operator); with Eddie "Rochester" Anderson, Ernie Adams, Bobby Barber

Credits: Associate Producer — E.M. Asher; Director — Milton Carruth; Based on the story *Channel Crossing* by Verne Whitehead; Screenplay — Jerome Chodorov & Joseph Fields; Film Editor — Phil Landres; Photography — George Robinson, ASC; Sound — William Hedgcock & Jesse T. Bastian; Musical Director — Charles Previn; Production Designed by John Harkrider; Associate/Sets — Fred Brooks, Jr.; Special Effects — John P. Fulton; Dialogue Director — John Rawlins; Gowns — Vera West

THE MAN WHO CRIED WOLF (1937)

For many old movie buffs, Lewis Stone will forever be Judge Hardy, strict but wise and loving paterfamilias of the Hardy clan and guiding light to son Andy (Mickey Rooney). For genre fans, however, Stone's most significant role remains that of Sir Dennis Nayland Smith in MGM's campy hoot *The Mask of Fu Manchu* (1932). In the course of a lengthy Hollywood career that placed him in some twelve dozen films, beginning in 1915, the distinguished actor sailed almost exclusively on the mainstream. Apart from the Karloff classic, Stone appeared in only a very few features of special interest to us: *The Lost World* (1925), *The Phantom of Paris* (1931), and the second remake of *The Thirteenth Chair* (1937).

The Man Who Cried Wolf was released the same year as this last film and represents one of Stone's rare appearances away from Metro. Based on Arthur Rothafel's story, *Too Clever to Live*, the picture has the advantage of being set in and around the theater, a milieu which — along with the worlds of opera, radio broadcasting, and the movies themselves — used to draw audiences like moths to a flame. Boasting a lineup of some of the decade's most recognizable supporting players, *Wolf* also appealed to those '30s film buffs who not only loved to spot their favorite character people scooting about a movie's underpinnings, but

knew their names and followed their helter-skelter appearances as avidly as most other fans followed Clark Gable or Jimmy Cagney. There are even two future Perry Whites (Pierre Watkin and John Hamilton) fueling the fire here.

Of course, the picture's adroit treatment of a clever story didn't hurt, either.

Emerging from a night club, Chet Carter is shot dead by a mysterious gunman. Some time later, as we know when a cop at the Homicide Division alerts the lingering reporters that "The case is colder than jailhouse coffee," a soft-spoken man startles Captain Walter Reid (Robert Gleckler) by confessing to the crime. "I did it. I killed Chet Carter," avers the elderly Lawrence Fontaine (Lewis Stone). An actor appearing in *The Death Cry* on Broadway, Fontaine can offer no motive for the killing. Worse, the right-handed actor adamantly refuses a cigarette, though eyewitnesses had established that the killer had been a lefthanded chainsmoker. When Reid is informed that the real murderer has just been apprehended, that tears it. "Fontaine, if I had my way, you would be in jail," he thunders, "Not for murder but for being a publicity hound! You didn't kill Chet Carter any more than I did.... Now get out of here before I hang you for being an actor!"

Title lobby card for *The Man Who Cried Wolf*. PENTAGRAM LIBRARY.

The Lawrence Fontaine who enters the Temple Theater by the stage door, however, is a more vibrant and dynamic figure than the befuddled impostor at the station house, seemingly years younger than minutes before. The false confession to the police is part of his master plan: By claiming responsibility for any of the city's many homicides which fit a certain profile, he hopes to be dismissed from consideration when he actually does kill George Bradley (Jameson Thomas), the man who married and then murdered Fontaine's ex-wife, Margaret.

Privy to his plans is Jocko Jenkins (Forrester Harvey), the actor's Cockney dresser and longtime friend. In the film's ultimately tragic running gag, Jocko is constantly moving from rooming house to rooming house because his harmonica playing inevitably leads to speedy evictions. Jocko has been with his employer since Fontaine toured Australia under his real name, Eric Steele, and is very much aware of a special box containing old letters and yellowed newspaper clippings about Margaret's death. When the actor cuts his nemesis's picture from that day's paper ("Financier George Bradley Returns to Penthouse Home Atop the Adler Hotel"), Jocko realizes that the end is in sight.

The plot begins to wrinkle. Nan (Barbara Read), the company ingenue, introduces Fontaine to Tom Bradley (Tom Brown), a young man she feels could easily replace a cast member who has quit. Fontaine is all for it when he realizes that Tom is not just George Bradley's stepson, but in fact *his own* son, by his dear ex-wife Margaret. Without spilling the beans, the old actor takes the younger man under his wing and becomes a guardian angel to him and to Nan. Another coincidence: Adjoining the theater is the same Adler Hotel where George

Bradley and his sister, Amelia (Marjorie Main), are even now discussing Tom's career in the theater, his growing suspicions about George's handling of his finances, and the need for his imminent demise. "We were lucky the first time, George," Amelia warns. "I wouldn't push our luck too far."

While having a bite with Tom and Nan at the Club Basque, Fontaine overhears a radio report of another murder: "Francis Forman, head of the Cosmetics Corporation, was shot and killed at the corner of 57th and Madison by an unknown assailant, who escaped after firing three shots into the victim's body." Off rushes the actor to Captain Reid's where, once again in his guise as a milquetoast, he proceeds according to plan. "But I tell you, I killed her," he claims. Reid replies, "Francis Forman wasn't a her; he was a him!" and throws the actor out, then begs the reporters not "to encourage this nut by printing anything about this."

Naturally, the papers are full of it the next morning, and *The Death Cry* becomes the hottest ticket in town. That night, George and Amelia Bradley are in two very-hard-to-come-by orchestra seats, ostensibly showing their support for Tom. The couple leaves the performance early, however, when George recognizes Fontaine's voice as that of Eric Steele. Unaware of the irony of his statement, Tom later explains that his step-father "has a strong aversion to anything pertaining to death. I guess the play was a little heavy for him." Up in the penthouse, the Bradleys are ordering that the yacht be made ready. Not only are they looking to get out of town until things cool down, but as they did with Tom's mother years earlier, the sinister siblings are planning to heave the young man overboard.

Happily, Fontaine convinces Tom not to leave the show in order to go to Venezuela "on business" with his stepfather ("It would be *very* difficult to replace you"), but rather to take a long, hard look into the current state of his inheritance. Tom angrily confronts Bradley in the penthouse and demands a look at "that set of books you've got locked in your office." As the eavesdropping butler and maid smile to each other in the hall, Tom repays George's

bitchy slap with a good shot in the chops. "And that's not *all* you'll get, unless I see those books here tonight!" the young man thunders, as he barrels past the help.

That night, clad in slouch hat and Inverness cape, Fontaine takes advantage of the play's intermission to climb the fire escape leading to the hotel roof. He enters the penthouse, where Bradley is meticulously erasing entries in a ledger.

> BRADLEY: "Steele! Let's talk!"
> FONTAINE: "Can you talk Margaret back to life? Tommy was to be next, wasn't he?"

Realizing that there's not much he can say, the embezzler fumbles for the pistol in his desk drawer. Shots ring out, and while Bradley's body begins to grow cold, Fontaine races back to his dressing room, arriving there in time to answer Jocko's insistent knocks and to ready himself for the second act. The Cockney dresser watches balefully as his master burns his old mementos and correspondence and hides the revolver in his special box.

First in line to confess to killing George Bradley is, naturally, Lawrence Fontaine. When he is contemptuously tossed out again by Reid, it appears that the actor has indeed gotten away with murder. When Nan runs to inform him that the police have arrested Tom for the crime, however, everything begins to crumble. Although he hires the best defense attorney money can buy, Fontaine watches helplessly as the servants' statements and Amelia Bradley's calculated testimony imperil his son. He implores Reid to believe him this time, but the captain is suspicious of yet another "publicity stunt" and insists on being given the murder weapon before he'll so much as hear any more talk. Taking the detective with him to his dressing room, Fontaine produces his special box — but it is empty! As Reid leaves in disgust, the actor correctly surmises that Jocko has hidden the gun out of loyalty to him. But where is Jocko?

That question isn't difficult to answer. The cab in which Jocko is riding has just been

Lawrence Fontaine's master plan almost leads to personal catastrophe. An example of Universal's beautiful montage cards of the 1930s. *PENTAGRAM LIBRARY.*

involved in an accident outside the Temple Theater, and the faithful dresser is terribly injured. Gasping for breath, he tells the actor, "Don't worry. Guv'nor. It's at my room. They'll never find it." Jocko dies, however, before he can answer Fontaine's most crucial questions: "Where *is* your room, Jocko? *Where* did you live?"

When the jury returns a guilty verdict that afternoon, Fontaine leaps to his feet in the courtroom: "He didn't do it! I did! I'm the guilty one! I killed George Bradley!" Acting on Captain Reid's recommendation, the court has the actor remanded to the custody of the Bureau of Psychopathic Investigation for observation. During the next few days, Tom is denied a retrial, and the governor refuses to grant a stay of execution; "Tom Bradley Must Go to Chair Friday," blare the headlines.

Desperate, his father escapes from his cell and works against time to find the murder weapon which will sway Captain Reid.

A call to the taxi company reveals that the meter in Jocko's fateful cab had reached 45 cents at the time of the accident, so Fontaine hails a cab at the theater and strikes out in every which direction, stopping when the meter hits the correct amount and checking all the rooming houses in that area. A splendid montage by John P. Fulton depicts his repeated attempts to track down the location of the gun, while recording the passing of the hours remaining until his son's execution. After an eternity and a half, paydirt!

The dragnet the cops have mobilized has been futile, so it's an angry and frustrated Captain Reid who barks, "All I want is Fontaine." As if on cue, the actor walks into the police

LEWIS STONE

the man who has never been starred but who makes the tiniest rôle interesting. His latest films include "Service," released next week, and "Queen Christina," with Greta Garbo.

Suave, masterful, and almost never found away from MGM, Lewis Stone brought his talents to Universal for the inventive *The Man Who Cried Wolf*. AUTHOR'S COLLECTION.

station with the gun, and following a check with the ballistics expert, the district attorney is called. Fontaine's arrest, trial, and conviction are accounted for as quickly as newspaper banners can flash across the screen. The film closes with Tom and Nan headed toward a brighter tomorrow, and Lawrence Fontaine, who never can bring himself to reveal his true identity to his son, faced with prison walls for the rest of his life.

The Man Who Cried Wolf is almost pure psychological melodrama. The story builds and twists and turns until it seems that everything in human nature has conspired to lead to Fontaine's downfall. Even if we can spot that first curve coming — Tom's violent argument with his stepfather will, of course, put him in danger — it's followed by a succession of sliders and screwballs thrown right across the plate. When Fontaine pins all his hopes in a "brilliant" defense attorney (Selmer Jackson), he can only watch glumly as the man's every objection is overruled by the judge. (The frequency and terseness with which John Hamilton shoots the lawyer down makes the vignette almost pathetically comic.) Later, and to his horror, the actor sees the attorney and his courtroom opponent (Russell Hicks) joking jovially with each other as they leave for the recess.

Any hopes the scenarists (Charles Grayson and Sy Bartlett) giveth, the scenarists taketh away. All Fontaine has to do to get Tom off the hook is to produce the gun used to kill Bradley, but the gun has disappeared. To find it, the actor must only speak with Jocko Jenkins, but the dresser's once comic foible of changing addresses as others change their shirts now takes a deadly serious turn. When Tom's only chance is his father's enterprise, his father is institutionalized. And the actor's subsequent escape reeks of a further irony: In order to present the police with the evidence they demand so that he can be arrested, Fontaine must avoid the police at all costs.

Under Lewis Foster's capable direction, the large cast acquits itself well, with Lewis Stone naturally copping top honors. When making himself an unwelcome nuisance,

Stone's Fontaine appears aged, uncertain, and inches from being feeble. Evicted from the station house after the Francis Forman fiasco, the actor visibly metamorphoses from this rickety old man into the supremely confident master planner, and all by standing erect and adjusting his clothing. Stone pulls off the transformation as he handles all of the wildly varying emotions the role demands: coolly, professionally and with absolute credibility. It's a shame that the actor didn't take a shot at Jekyll and Hyde while in his salad days, for he might have given Jack Barrymore a run for his money.

Jocko Jenkins is one of Forrester Harvey's studied eccentrics, cut of the same cloth as the Irish actor's sodden cathedral caretaker Durdles (*Mystery of Edwin Drood*, 1935), or Glaswegian snoop Alistair MacNab from 1939's *The Witness Vanishes*. Jocko provides good comic counterpoint to Fontaine's intensity, and the brutal end to which he comes is as shocking to the audience as it is to his old employer.

The sight of a lean, mean, and reasonably attractive Marjorie Main takes some getting used to. Although now as firmly entrenched in the American pop consciousness as the exasperated Ma Kettle as Lewis Stone is as Judge Hardy, the actress spent most of the thirties after her 1933 debut tugging at hearts and jerking tears in everything from *Stella Dallas* (1937) to *The Women* (1939). For anyone unfamiliar with this side of her résumé, Main's sinister Amelia Harding is a real eye-opener.

Russell Gausman must have been otherwise occupied during *The Man Who Cried Wolf*, and he is sorely missed. Apart from an intriguing, almost science fictionish scenery for some brief snatches of *The Death Cry*, Louis Ballou's sets are purely functional and totally pedestrian. George Robinson had already had extensive experience photographing the Universal horror product, but he seems to have checked his know-how at the stage door, with Pops. Missing from *Wolf* is the key lighting savvy which could have both brought out a more vivid texture from those dreary sets and given greater visual dimension to the story. As it stands, the actors tell their tale against a flat and lifeless backdrop.

Because *The Man Who Cried Wolf* concerns the protagonist's spiraling ever downward into his own private hell — despite the audience's regarding his actions as justifiable — there is a driving need for catharsis before the fade-out, and this is where the film lets you down. Despite Tom's essentially desperate plea for truth from the horse's mouth, Fontaine inexplicably (and most unsatisfactorily) opts to keep the younger man in the dark:

> TOM: "But, the way you told Nan you were my father, and then denied it at the trial...?"
>
> FONTAINE: "The wish caused the thought, I suppose."
>
> TOM: "Well, I was a little startled when I heard it."
>
> FONTAINE: "Yes. It must have seemed quite ridiculous to you."
>
> TOM: "Oh, no! No, honestly. I wish it were true."
>
> FONTAINE: "*I* wish it were true, Tommy."

Either author Arthur Rothafel knows a great deal more about psychology and bonding than do most fathers, or his Lawrence Fontaine is the greatest fool who ever trod the face of the earth.

Although a well-structured, entertaining picture, *Wolf* could have stood a bit more attention to detail and technique by Messrs. Ballou and Robinson and by Charles Previn, who it seems never actually composed anything for those pictures in which he received credit as musical director. Still and all, the film is more subtly unnerving than most of its *Shock Theater* colleagues, even if it doesn't begin to get really interesting until after the big murder has taken place. Not for everyone (What is?),

The Man Who Cried Wolf remains a splendid, if flawed, exercise in suspense.

The Man Who Cried Wolf

Released August 25, 1937; 68 minutes

Cast: Lewis Stone (Lawrence Fontaine); Tom Brown (Tom Bradley); Barbara Read (Nan); Forrester Harvey (Jocko Jenkins); Marjorie Main (Amelia Bradley); Robert Gleckler (Captain Walter Reid); Jameson Thomas (George Bradley); Robert Spencer (Reporter); Billy Wayne (Halligan); Pierre Watkin (Governor); Selmer Jackson (Defense Attorney); Russell Hicks (Prosecutor); Howard Hickman (Doctor in Play); Stanley Andrews, John Hamilton (Judges); Matt McHugh (Desk Sergeant); Fredrik Vogeding (Resident Doctor); Rev. Neal Dodd (Prison Chaplain); Anne O'Neal (Landlady); Ben Taggart (Plainclothes Policeman); Jack Daley (Policeman); Jason Robards, Sr. (Doctor); Walter Miller (Gunman); William Castle, Hal Cook (Customers at Box Office); Eddie Fetherston (Box Office Cashier); Russ Clark (Prison Guard); Ernie Adams (Reporter); Charles Bennett (Taxi Manager); James Blaine (Doorman); Wilson Benge (Butler); Arthur Yeoman (Court Clerk); Gertrude Astor (Landlady); Harry Boman (Lodger)

Credits: Associate Producer — E.M. Asher; Director — Lewis R. Foster; Screenplay — Charles Grayson, Sy Bartlett; Based on the story *Too Clever to Live* by Arthur Rothafel; Photographer — George Robinson, ASC; Musical Director — Charles Previn; Sets — Louis Ballou; Film Editor — Frank Gross; Special Effects — John P. Fulton; Production Designer — John Harkrider; Sound — Charles Carroll, Edwin Wetzel; Gowns — Vera West

THE WESTLAND CASE (1937)

For lovers of vintage *frisson*, the years 1937 and 1938 represent the nadir of the romance between the horror–science fiction field and the cinema. Those years found the Brits and the Europeans working desperately to maintain the status quo with wildly divided energies, and hindsight allows us the grace to admit how understandable was their insistence that they would purchase only the more supportive, uplifting, and positive product that Hollywood had to offer. When a good portion of Western Civilization conspires to overthrow a movie type, it would be unfair to try to pin the blame on the policy of any one studio, so let's lighten up a bit on Messrs. Crowdin and Rogers.

Not about to give up all the gelt that was still to be had, though, Universal cast a hungry eye about for a substitute. Just about every other film company had made wise investments in the film rights for some of fiction's brightest and most idiosyncratic sleuths. We're not talking raucous, non-stop, shoot-'em-up police or G-Men tornadoes — Warners had a lock on those — but rather the more sophisticated (but no less deadly) exercises in ratiocination as performed by the "gentleman" detective. Philo Vance, Charlie Chan, and Nick and Nora Charles had all been making money — for someone else — since the earliest days of the decade. The Laemmles had never seen the need

to travel this route. The family business had produced the occasional mystery, some successful (like 1935's *Rendezvous at Midnight*), others not (*Remember Last Night?*), but it had never really jumped into the pool where swam all the competition. Who would have thought anyone would tire of horror movies?

In 1937, the Crowdin organization approached the Crime Club, an American publishing concern modeled after England's own Collins' Crime Club. Both literary houses were totally devoted to the production and preservation of the whodunit in any and all of its myriad guises, and the British company is still extant. Opting to select a number of novels from the club's prodigious output was a good move on Universal's part. The frugal Crowdin would avoid both paying high royalties for established characters and "getting burned" by an exclusive on any given fictional gumshoe to whom the public didn't take. On the down side, apart from hard-core mystery buffs, virtually no one would have ever heard of these titles or their featured sleuths.

Nevertheless, the Crime Club series was a good move and had reasonable success at the box office. Drawing heavily on the awareness most people had of the publisher, Universal concocted a stylized logo for the series entries and advertised the films' literary sources as readily as the films themselves. The series lasted until the tail end of 1939 and encompassed a total of eight features, none of which would seriously impinge on the horror or science fiction fields. Several of the pictures seemed to skirt supernatural or super-scientific territory, however, and for that reason the series is included herein, *in toto*.

The Westland Case was the first of the Crime Club novels to be adapted to the screen. There are virtually no genre elements involved in the story, which is a pity, considering that the whodunit was released on Halloween 1937.

Happy-go-lucky New York private eyes Bill Crane (Preston Foster) and Doc Williams (Frank Jenks) are called to Chicago by attorney Frazee (Clarence Wilson), to investigate the mysterious circumstances of the death of the wife of rich broker Robert Westland (Theodore Von Eltz). The detectives, merry inebriates both, are told that Westland will be executed on October 9 at 12:02 AM, unless they can prove his innocence. An alibi note telling Westland to look up a man with the initials "MG" is the only new lead.

Bill and Doc watch a film made by the prosecution team as a recreation of the discovery of the body. They are in the company of Westland's business partners, Woodbury (Russell Hicks) and Bolston (George Meeker); his lovely and love-struck secretary Brentino (Astrid Allwyn); his fiancée, Emily Lou Martin (Carol Hughes), whom he had hoped to marry following a divorce from his wife; and his accountant, Sprague (Rollo Lloyd). The film shows the body of Mrs. Westland being found within her apartment; all doors and windows were locked from the inside, and only Mr. Westland had another key.

Westland had been at the apartment earlier that night, but had claimed to have been summoned there by a voice very much like Emily Lou Martin's. Worse, the victim had been killed by a vintage Webley automatic, and both Woodbury and Westland owned such a gun. Bleaker still, the condemned man's pistol has since mysteriously disappeared!

Bill and Doc take Emily and Miss Brentino out for dinner at Joe Petro's Palace Garden,

hoping for a shot at "MG." As it turns out, a couple of gunmen locate "MG"—Manny Grant—at the restaurant first and take more than one shot at him, forcing Bill and Doc to look elsewhere for help in getting Westland his reprieve. Back at the warden's office, some promising news: Sprague announces that he has crucial information to deliver but will wait until the next day to do so. (Of course, Sprague is run down on the street and doesn't last out the reel.)

Better (and, for once, usable) news has a prosecution witness, Mrs. Westland's neighbor Doctor Shuttle (Arthur Hoyt), remember that the morning of the murder had marked the start of Daylight Savings Time in Chicago. This means that the woman was murdered at 1:10 AM, and that Westland's claim to have left his wife, alive and well, at 12:40 AM now has some teeth.

The sleuths and Frazee check out Mrs. Westland's apartment, which has been let to Miss Agatha Hogan (Barbara Pepper), a Mae West wannabe who allows them a look around. Westland's butler, Simmons, later admits he never left his master's apartment during any of the commotion, except to bring some personal items down to Westland at the jail. The lovely Miss Brentino, not a little jealous of her boss's situation with Miss Martin, suggests to Bill that, as for that unlikely and duplicitous summons to the dead woman's apartment, "Who could imitate a person's voice better than that person herself?" A trip over to Miss Martin's house reveals that the young woman's phone wires had, indeed, been tampered with. Who could have made the call which set up Mr. Westland?

After stopping in a local watering hole, Bill and Doc end up back at Agatha Hogan's place, where, come the dawn, Bill takes a shower and determines that running water could have been the "sound like Niagara Falls" Westland heard when the fatal phone call came through. The detectives hop a cab and travel three times from Mrs. Westland's apartment to her husband's office. Clocking the progress with his stopwatch, Bill has the cabbie stop in the middle of a bridge in "the underground,"

First of the series, and Barbara Pepper to boot. Title lobby card for *The Westland Case*. PENTAGRAM LIBRARY.

a section of highway crossing the river below street level. A monkey wrench is tossed into the river at a spot where the outside world is visible from the underground. Marking the spot, Bill and Doc hire a diver to search the river bed at and around the area; sure enough, the monkey wrench and the missing Westland Webley are retrieved in the search.

Time is running out for Westland, yet Bill takes off to visit the Washington Arms Company of Peoria. The detective has discovered that a vintage Webley was sold to a Mr. P.T. Brown not long before the murder, and he has no trouble in having Mr. Havemeyer, the clerk who had sold the gun, pick out Brown from photographs brought over from Chicago. Bill also has the bullets Brown fired at the company's test range on the day he had made the purchase dug out and studied.

Doc and Frazee read the cable from Bill: "Have everybody including the murderer in the warden's office at 9:00 PM." Sounds good, except that it's already 11:42 PM, and Westland is due to die in 20 minutes. In walks Bill, who begins to unfold the case for State Attorney Ross (Bryant Washburn), the one man who can grant a stay of execution if Bill's evidence is strong enough. As the clock ticks, Bill proceeds.

Westland was lured to his estranged wife's apartment by a phone call from Emily Lou Martin, who not only didn't love him, but was married to his partner, Bolston! Emily made the phone call from her bathroom, letting the water run to help disguise her voice; for all that, the smitten Westland recognized her, and obeyed. The broker met briefly with his wife and left at 12:40 AM, but the witness to

A MURDER MYSTERY CHILLER-DILLER!

Preston FOSTER in *The* **Westland Case** *A Crime Club* PRODUCTION

At the wrap, Bill and Doc get their man (as everyone knew they would). Frazee (Clarence Wilson) ends up with Agatha Hogan (Barbara Pepper)— now, who would have thunk it? *PENTAGRAM LIBRARY.*

his departure, Manny Grant, was successfully removed on Bolston's say-so.

Bolston had used Emily Lou's intimacy with Westland to swap phony stocks and bonds for his partner's genuine articles. To prevent either of the Westlands from discovering the fake securities, Bolston killed the woman and framed her husband for the murder. The frantic broker shot Mrs. Westland with the Webley he had purchased as P.T. Brown and got rid of the gun somewhere. He then called Simmons and told him to bring Westland some personal items at the jail; this gave the murderer the chance to slip into the unguarded apartment (using Emily Lou's key) and to steal his partner's pistol, which he threw into the Chicago River from the spot Bill and Doc had discovered during their cab rides.

Ballistics tests, states Bill, prove that Westland's gun was not the murder weapon, and also that the bullets fired out on the Peoria range matched the bullet which had taken Mrs. Westland's life. Enter Mr. Havemeyer, who dramatically points to Bolston as P.T. Brown. Attorney Ross is convinced, Bill's and Doc's case is clenched, and Westland is given his freedom, only seconds before his scheduled execution.

The Westland Case may be no masterpiece, but it really wasn't a bad jumping-off point for the Universal–Crime Club collaboration. Bill and Doc's race against the clock is a good gimmick, although the film's closing moments offer an absurd situation: Bill has to talk quickly enough and convincingly enough to close the case against Bolston before 12:02 AM.

The payoff—that the state will execute Westland, come what may, if Bill doesn't speak faster—is too much for even the most hopeless naïf to swallow whole.

Preston Foster and Frank Jenks really don't fit the term "gentleman detectives," but they do share the propensity to tipple while sleuthing with most of their contemporary cinematic colleagues. The men are a likable pair, trading quips and insults, sharing an appreciation for pretty girls, lying and swearing to it in tandem, and contributing to minor scams and frauds. (We first meet the two as they're impressing a trio of swozzled patrons with Bill's reputedly unerring sense of smell. When asked whether his nose helped him solve the "Slaughterhouse Murders," Bill admits that it did, but that "The testimony of five eyewitnesses and a man's confession helped.")

In an effort to allow the theater-seat patrons to try their hands at being armchair detectives, the screenplay has Bill keep a couple of his deductions to himself, a tactic which elicits not terribly unfunny remarks from his partner. The revelation that Emily Lou is Bolston's wife is the only real cheat, but the Effie Perine syndrome, which states that gorgeous young secretaries might fall in love with older bosses or even with two-timing, four-flushing bosses, but never with guilty bosses, should provide an effective counterweight to those in the know.

The cast is filled with names we know and faces we know, even if the names and faces don't always go together. Preston Foster, of course, will always be remembered by genre aficionados as the moon-killer in *Doctor X*, and by fans of early fifties television as Captain Herrick in the 1953 series *Waterfront*. Frank Jenks had made a career out of Damon Runyon–type gangsters or cops' sidekicks before he, too, popped up on early television (as Alan Mowbray's larcenous aide in *Colonel Flack*, also of 1953.) Jenks' big genre contribution was made in AIP's *The She-Creature* (1956).

Carol Hughes had been Jean Rogers' successor to the role of Dale Arden in *Flash Gordon Conquers the Universe*; that role and this one pretty much capped her genre assignments. George Meeker was a contract player at Universal until the early forties, and he was almost always the murderer or the murderee in fare such as this. Film editor Otis Garrett would be promoted to full-fledged director with the fourth Crime Club entry, *Danger on the Air*, and would stay on for each of the remaining features.

All things being relative, the biggest name left on the cast/credits lists of *The Westland Case* is that of Christy Cabanne, and there's more infamy than fame attached to that one. An industry veteran since 1915 and a coworker of D.W. Griffith and Douglas Fairbanks, Cabanne is remembered best for helming *The Mummy's Hand* (1940), first and oh-my-God-yes best of the forties follow-ups to the 1932 Karloff classic. Sadly, he is best remembered for *Scared to Death*, an incomprehensible (and worse, boring) 1947 independent effort which is notable for the presence of Bela Lugosi, George Zucco, and Cinecolor. A practitioner (but not a master) of the second feature, Cabanne died in 1950; *Scared to Death* probably had little to do with it.

The Westland Case is not without several illogical moments, beginning with the film of the "reconstruction" of the discovery of the body. Without pausing to comment on legal precedent or why anyone would think a 16mm film clip of people going through the motions they claim they underwent once before would prove anything whatsoever, one can imagine a smart lawyer objecting that the camera is anything but disinterested. Outside the apartment, the photographer follows the action dispassionately; he precedes the others inside, however, and from that point on, the jury sees only those things which the photographer has chosen to film. Certainly not admissible as it stands.

Likewise, the whole affair of the fraudulent securities — the reason why Mrs. Westland was slain and Mr. Westland framed for the crime — is just too pat. The screenplay maintains that Sprague himself had just discovered the fraud and that this had resulted in his death. If the defendant's will and chattels were investigated during the trial, why wasn't the property of the deceased examined until so much later? If even the butler is suspected (briefly) due to his being in for a small legacy when Westland is fried, why didn't anyone go over the late Mrs. Westland's stuff with a fine-tooth comb and try to establish motive there?

The whole notion of retaining a second attorney (Frazee) to prove that the convicted and condemned Westland is innocent is laughable. Assuming that a salaried attorney and investigative staff would do so with the blessings of the prison warden demands a far heftier suspension of disbelief than does a man metamorphosing into a wolf during the cycle of the full moon.

The Westland Case introduces a couple of enjoyable dicks, a cast more than decent at conveying indecency, and a fair enough whodunit to satisfy all but the most enlightened. While it might not ever have generated goosebumps, it may still elicit a chuckle or even outfox a few of this current generation's most blasé viewers. It and its Crime Club consorts represent the best that Universal had to offer folk such as us back in 1937 and 1938.

The Westland Case

Released October 31, 1937; 64 minutes

Cast: Preston Foster (Bill Crane); Carol Hughes (Emily Lou Martin); Barbara Pepper (Agatha Hogan); Astrid Allwyn (Brentino); Frank Jenks (Doc Williams); George Meeker (Richard Bolston); Theodore Von Eltz (Robert Westland); Russell Hicks (Woodbury); Clarence Wilson (Frazee); Rollo Lloyd (Sprague); Arthur Hoyt (Dr. Shuttle); Selmer Jackson (Warden); Bryant Washburn (State Attorney Ross); Ward Bond (Death-Row Inmate)

Credits: Producers — Larry Fox, Irving Starr; Director — Christy Cabanne; Screenplay — Robertson White; From the novel *Headed for a Hearse* by Jonathan Latimer; Cinematographer — Ira Morgan, ASC; Film Editor — Otis Garrett; Special Effects — John P. Fulton; Art Director — Ralph Berger; Associate Art Director — Emile Kuri; Gowns — Vera West; Musical Director — Charles Previn; Sound — Robert Pritchard, Jesse T. Bastian; Production Manager — Ben Hersh; Through Arrangements with Walter Futter. A Crime Club Production

THE SPY RING (1938)

For Baby Boomers, born too late to experience all of these Universal treasures when they were first released, salvation came in 1957. It was as if zillions of kids were roused from their lethargy and given a peek at the Promised Land. They were bowled over, helplessly enthralled, forever transformed by the irresistible force. I know I was. By *Shock Theater*, of course.

To a wide-eyed seven-year-old, it was like striking gold. I had no clue where all these goodies had come from, but it was obvious that I couldn't go on living without them. Unbeknownst to me, the exact same sentiments were being felt all across the country; children of all ages cheerfully submitted to *Shock* treatments on a weekly basis. Many of the grown-ups had seen these pictures when they had first come out, but who among us kids would have dared imagine that there was anything like this anywhere? It was the Eisenhower era, and our idea of excitement was having the Good Humor man show up with a fully stocked truck. As those wonderful films were shown and reshown; as horror hosts proliferated regionally; as *Famous Monsters* and *Castle of Frankenstein* replaced *Children's Digest* and *Boy's Life*; as Aurora's series of Universal's classic goblins outsold models of tanks and battleships; a hefty portion of America's youth went into a monster frenzy.

Therein lies the rub.

Hidden among all those tales of werewolves, vampires and mummies were a few films which dealt with murder or intrigue as practiced by mere mortals. These were the movies which merited the contempt of the horror hosts, the pictures they were loath to screen. The tremendous monster rush had caused those cool ghouls to overlook a very basic fact about the program from which they were earning their keep: The name of the game was *Shock Theater*, not *Horror Theater*. Presumably, there were members of the TV audience (although I certainly didn't know any) for whom the walking dead and their ilk had little appeal. These viewers would get their shocks from the more realistic elements in the series. In the interest of attracting as large an audience share as possible, then, *Shock Theater* passed on a couple of decidedly minor monster forays (like *Jungle Woman*, in which the cosmically untalented Aquanetta appears to be in shock) in favor of *The Man Who Cried Wolf*, *Chinatown Squad*, and *Reported Missing*.

And *The Spy Ring*.

It's nearly impossible to accept the above rationalization for the selection of a picture like *The Spy Ring*, wherein the forces of righteousness are a bunch of polo-playing U.S. cavalrymen, and the suspense generated is not so

300

Tension abounds in the title lobby card for *The Spy Ring*. Pentagram Library.

much along the lines of "Whodunit?" as "When is this going to end?" Justifying *Spy*'s inclusion in the package when stuff like 1939's *The House of Fear* was left out requires a more adept apologist than I. Nonetheless, it was as much a charter member of *Shock Theater* as *Bride of Frankenstein*, so let's take a look.

At the U.S. Army Proving Grounds, Captain Scott (Philip Trent) has come within inches of adapting a machine gun to fire accurately from either a stationary or mobile position. Colonel Bowen (Egon Brecher) hails Scott's invention, a device which looks like a metallic cigar, and says that once the bugs have been removed, it "will revolutionize anti-aircraft defense." Dropped off at the Bachelor Officers' Quarters by his good buddy (and co-inventor) Captain Todd Hayden (William Hall), Scott comes upon a beautiful blonde

steaming open his top secret orders. A heartbeat later, when Hayden stops by to return a briefcase Scott left in the car, he finds his friend's body in the kitchen and the window to the fire escape open.

A day or so later, Bowen gives Hayden his take on espionage.

> BOWEN: There's some excuse for a wartime spy; at least he's working for his country. But those freelance agents, they're a despicable lot. Washington — every capital — is infested with them, selling secrets to the highest bidder.

Who should walk into his office, mid-speech, but Mrs. Bruce (Jean Carleton), the doyenne of local charities and (Ta-Dah!) the woman

Steely-eyed Captain Todd Hayden wraps up one of the many despicable freelance agents who have infested Washington and other locales. No mention of Nazis made it to the screen in *The Spy Ring*. PENTAGRAM LIBRARY.

who killed Captain Scott! Mrs. Bruce departs after a moment or two, and Hayden is told to report back to his regular command (with the 19th Cavalry at Monterey, California), where he will perfect the invention.

Military matters take a back seat to polo at the Monterey installation, though; the officers of the 19th Cavalry have bet their last dollar that they will defeat their rivals, the Rainbows, in the "big match" to be held within days. Among his many accomplishments, Hayden is a crackerjack polo player, and a couple of frantic non-coms (including a silent Glenn Strange, mugging grimly as "The Champ") assign him a combination orderly and guardian angel in the person of PFC Timothy O'Reilly (Don Barclay). Hayden meets the captain of the

rival team, handsome playboy Frank Denton (Leon Ames). In reality, Denton is a member of the spy ring along with Mrs. Bruce, who to no one's surprise turns up in Monterey for the festivities. Mrs. Bruce tries to use her wiles on the young captain in an effort to obtain information about the device, but fortunately for the U.S.A. and for his old girl-friend, Elaine (Jane Wyman), Hayden is aware of the woman's true purpose and resists her every ploy.

The night before the big match, Denton is discovered at the project site by Hayden and Captain Mayhew (Ben Alexander), but the spy escapes by switching cars with Mrs. Bruce, who orders her chauffeur (Paul Sutton) to give them time to get away by allowing himself to be captured. The following day, Hayden is told that Mrs. Bruce and her friends have bet against Denton, fearing that should he win, the handsome spy would take the money and flee across the border. Interested in seeing what transpires, Hayden holds back and Denton's team is victorious.

All hell breaks loose. Having been informed that Denton escaped from Leavenworth Prison in 1924 and is still wanted in connection with "Kansas City killings," Hayden heads over to the spy's apartment. He finds Denton lifeless in the bathtub and Mrs. Bruce, breathing fire and armed to the teeth, standing in the doorway. "Interesting, isn't it?" she asks. "His troubles are over; yours are just beginning. I want the plans of the CQ machine gun, especially the new firing pin." Hayden laughs in her face, but Mrs. Bruce has snatched his honey, Elaine, and things are looking pretty bleak.

Back at the barracks, Captain Mayhew has tricked Charley, the chauffeur, into a full confession which reveals that Mrs. Bruce and her gang have an airplane standing by, and they're going to leave the country with Captain Scott's invention. A cut brings us to the airport, where Hayden, Elaine, and the heavies are piling into the plane. As they taxi towards takeoff, Mayhew and Private O'Reilly save the day by blowing out the plane's tires, using a CQ machine gun mounted on their motorcycle.

Time has accorded *The Spy Ring* a certain charm which it certainly could not have had when it was released back in 1938. While their European relatives were busy gearing up for what threatened to be Armageddon, Americans were still indulging in nervous self-hypnosis, trying desperately to convince themselves that nothing of import had actually changed and that events in the offing a few thousand miles away were none of their concern. In light of such delusions, U.S. cavalrymen could be preoccupied with polo matches and not receive a hazing from the citizenry.

The Spy Ring reflects the naïveté of that mindset and takes it a step further: It reduces the deadly serious business of espionage to a *Boy's Own* level of thrusts, parries, and hits, much like the pattern of a compacted movie

serial. God only knows how machine guns were fired prior to Captain Scott's inventing his incredible cigar, the doodad that shifts the plot into fourth gear, just as only He can explain how villains always manage to keep surplus aircraft close by for emergency escapes. There's not sufficient running time to allow the bad guys to gain and lose the gun, and then gain and lose the plans, and then ditto ditto with the device, itself, the way a 15-episode chapterplay would have it, but there's enough running around to kill a good part of the hour. The rest is filled with polo stock footage and the perennial hero's dilemma: Hayden may know with whom he's dealing and how they operate, but, being an American Army officer (and a gentleman), he must bide his time until enough concrete evidence can be gathered to legally warrant his taking action.

Spy's rather facile screenplay was by George Waggner, who turned in his fair share of both original stories and adaptations of other people's work (here, Frank VanWyck Mason's) when he wasn't helming B westerns for the studio. Waggner would turn his back on horse operas with the coming of the new decade, when he began to assume the producer's responsibilities for some of Universal's more prestigious efforts (like 1943's *Phantom of the Opera*). Monogram's own Trem Carr, who had supervised his last feature for his own company back in 1935, took on the assignment of producing *The Spy Ring*. Carr had been production head at Monogram since 1931 and would remain the executive director of production for the company after its reorganization in 1936-37, but he moonlighted at Universal and elsewhere for a number of years in order to keep his hand in the creative end of the business.

You'd never guess from looking at *The Spy Ring*, but director Joseph H. Lewis would go on to acclaim as a master of the economical thriller. His flair for paring away extraneous bullshit from a narrative and then marrying the result with well-defined and credible characters would result in such cult favorites as *Gun Crazy* (1950), *The Big Combo* (1955), and *Terror in a Texas Town* (1958). Someone more perspicacious than myself might find that technique here in embryonic form, but all I can sense is a simplistic story, involving one-dimensional characters, told in a bland and predictable fashion. To be fair, up to this point Lewis's career at Universal consisted in his directing any of the Bob Baker B westerns that George Waggner couldn't fit into his schedule. On top of that, he's given zilch in terms of help from Harry Neumann's sophomoric lighting (the big nighttime car chase involving Denton and Hayden is far too monochromatic) and flat, lackluster photography.

A slender, animated Ben Alexander, decades before his signature role as *Dragnet*'s Frank Smith, is fun to catch, and Egon Brecher's Teutonic accent lends Colonel Bowen's jingoistic speeches an amusingly incongruous touch. The rest of the cast is serviceable, with Jane Wyman exhibiting a pretty, if too frequent, pout, but Todd Hayden represents William Hall's last hurrah at Universal. Back in 1936, the actor had held his own opposite Victor McLaglen in *The Magnificent Brute* and had kept William Gargan honest (an equally impressive feat) in *Flying Hostess*. *The Spy Ring* was his only lead at the House That Carl Built, though, and Hall's granite-jawed phiz was soon relegated to bits, billed or otherwise.

When a chuckle over the presence of a mute Glenn Strange is the greatest reward a film can offer, it's time to bail out. Not much

to look at and far less memorable than just about anything else that shared the *Shock Theater* slate, *The Spy Ring* is a dated and inconsequential waste of time.

The Spy Ring

Released January 9, 1938; 61 minutes

Cast: William Hall (Capt. Todd Hayden); Leon Ames (Frank Denton); Jane Wyman (Elaine Burdette); Jane Carleton (Jean Bruce); Ben Alexander (Capt. Don Mayhew); Don Barclay (PFC Timothy O'Reilly); Robert Warwick (Col. Burdette); Paul Sutton (Chauffeur [Charley]); Jack Mulhall (Tex Randolph); Egon Brecher (Col. Bowen); Philip Trent (Capt. Scott); LeRoy Mason (Paul Douglas); Harry Woods (Capt. Holden); Glenn Strange (The Champ); Lester Dorr (Radio Operator); Eddie Gribbon, Forrest Taylor (Sergeants); Harry Harvey, Eddie Parker, Pat Gleason (Reporters)

Credits: Producer — Trem Carr; Director — Joseph Lewis; Associate Producer — Paul Malvern; Screenplay — George Waggner; From a story by Frank VanWyck Mason; Assistant Director — Glen Cook; Cinematographer — Harry Neumann, ASC; Art Director — Charles Clague; Set Dressings — Albert Greenwood; Sound Technicians — Robert Pritchard and Jesse Bastian; Musical Director — Charles Previn; Film Editor — Charles Craft

THE BLACK DOLL (1938)

A great deal of 19th century romantic literature revolved around tontines, and so did a healthy number of silent westerns and swashbucklers. Tontines were a kind of annuity designed so that participants would receive the shares of other members as they died, leaving the entire nest egg to whichever lucky (or canny) devil managed to survive the rest. One needn't belong to a cult to join a tontine; adventurers, soldiers of fortune, rebellious youths, and ruthless businessmen were all known to start one up and then get down and dirty among themselves in order to finish it off.

It's never completely clear whether the precipitous force in *The Black Doll* is a tontine or merely a studied act of revenge, but it is doubtless a MacGuffin and so makes little difference. C. Henry Gordon plays Nelson Rood, a grasping businessman, tyrant to his own household, and murderer. Some years earlier, Rood and his partners, Barrows, Walling (John Wray), and Mallison (Addison Richards), became rich through underhanded dealings in Mexico. Uneasy allies at best, Rood then killed Barrows, whose share of the loot then devolved upon the survivors, and tossed his body and a black doll — the harbinger of death, per local Mexican traditions — into a handy gorge. Unable to act without exposing themselves to prosecution, Mallison and Walling kept silent about the crime.

During the 15 years which have passed since then, Rood has been one busy villain. In addition to defrauding his partners so that he now has control of all of the ill-gotten gains from their Mexican endeavors, he has denied his penniless sister, Laura Leland (Doris Lloyd), permission to marry her beau, Dr. Giddings (Holmes Herbert); he has continually berated and threatened with jail Laura's son, Rex (William Lundigan), a young wastrel with a gambling problem; and he has put the fear of something other than God into his Mexican servants, Esteban (Fred Malatesta) and Rosita (Inez Palange). Rood has even managed to come within an inch of alienating the affections of his daughter, Marian (Nan Grey), by refusing to allow her fella, Nick Halstead (Donald Woods), to come a courting.

Rood has troubles of his own, however. A black doll much like the one he once hurled after Knox Barrows' corpse lies ominously on his desk. Unnerved by the portent of death, he confronts Mallison and Walling with it when they arrive at the Rood home during a driving thunderstorm later that evening. Esteban takes the two men to their rooms upstairs, while Rood stops in to speak with his daughter, whom he chewed out earlier for picnicking on

THE CRIME CLUB ON THE SCREEN AGAIN! IN BAFFLING SPLIT-SECOND MURDER MYSTERY!

The BLACK DOLL

NAN GREY · DONALD WOODS
EDGAR KENNEDY WILLIAM LUNDIGAN · DORIS LLOYD
SYD SAYLOR · C. HENRY GORDON
SCREEN PLAY BY HAROLD BUCKLEY
FROM THE NOVEL "THE BLACK DOLL" by WILLIAM EDWARD HAYES
Directed by Otis Garrett   Produced by Irving Starr
A New UNIVERSAL PICTURE   A Crime Club Production

What's really baffling is how the mystery is felt to take but a "split-second." PENTAGRAM LIBRARY.

the grounds with Nick. Weeping on her bed, Marian fails to see her father collapse in a heap at the doorway. Rood has been knifed, and his body, like that of Knox Barrows, is graced with a black doll.

Grabbing the doll, Marian heads downstairs, but the sight of the front door opening on its own — compounded by some pretty impressive lightning and the sudden power outage — causes her to lose control. Running out into the storm through the side door, she is seized by a man in a black hat and knocked senseless. Luckily for her, Nick's dog has heard the commotion, and Nick shows up on the scene before the mystery man can do more damage. Nick carries the unconscious girl back to the Rood house, where Rex, in a classic red herring setup, walks in with his wet jacket still askew from his jaunt outside. Brought upstairs

by Esteban, Nick leaves Rood to decorate the carpet and checks out Marian's room. Through her window he witnesses the arrival of the police.

Fortunately for Marian and other of the innocents, Nick was once a detective. His spearheading the investigation will cinch the unraveling of the mystery, despite the contributions of Sheriff Renick (Edgar Kennedy), whose appearance in rain garb more proper to a Gloucester lobsterman than a serious lawman heralds his primary responsibility as comic relief. While the sheriff is padding the running time, Mallison is found strangled in his closet, a black doll lying on the floor. When a black doll is tossed at Marian from behind the curtains of her room (good old loyal Esteban tries to dispatch the killer with a knife, but takes a bullet instead), things start to come together for Nick.

The annoying Sheriff Renick may have the black doll, but Nick Halstead has both the scrambled eggs and the solution to the mystery. *PENTAGRAM LIBRARY*.

The homey feeling of the denouement, which gathers the whole household round the kitchen table as Nick whips up a batch of scrambled eggs and potatoes, lends a slightly incongruous air to the detective's presentation of the evidence. Obviously, he explains, the black doll was meant to throw suspicion on the two ex-partners for Rood's death, just as it should have moved the spotlight onto Walling when Mallison was found murdered. As the last of the four rogues, Walling should have come into all of the erstwhile friends' holdings, but Rood's old double-cross had put the kibosh on that; Marian now stood to inherit the works.

Rood, it seems, killed Barrows not only for his fortune, but also for his wife, though no one knew of this except the doctor who treated the murderer for jungle fever, and to whom Rood had mumbled all in his delirium. Marian, then, was Knox Barrows' daughter, not Rood's, and Giddings was that doctor! Over the plates of hashbrowns, Nick recounts how Giddings intended to do away with Marian in order to come into the money (and marry Laura, of course), and had meant to frame Walling for the dirty work. Cornered, Giddings fires his revolver from under the checkered tablecloth, but Renick's men finally do something right and nab the physician before any more harm can be done.

The truth having been revealed, the murderer is led away. Rex will not go to jail for forging his uncle's name to checks to cover gambling debts, Marian finally has her Nick, and Laura at least has her health, if not someone to scratch where she can't reach.

The Black Doll is the only one of the Crime Club adaptations to intimate (at least initially) supernatural activity. Though the doll is revealed in fairly short order to be nothing but a sinister ploy, its turning up out of nowhere adds a bit of a tingle that other entries in the series could have used. A scratch of the head, though, as to why Giddings would go to all the trouble of fabricating a load of dolls (he can scarcely have used the same one more than once) and schlepping them all over the place when he could have pulled off his scheme more efficiently without them. The little mannequins really do nothing but call attention to the murder of Knox Barrows and all of its attendant baggage; Rood, Mallison and Marian could have easily been dispatched — and Walling framed — without ever having raised the specter of that first partner, his wife, or his daughter.

Sheriff Renick puts the skids to anyone's attempts at taking this stuff seriously, and scenarist Harold Buckley should have been crowned with a black doll himself for concocting such a painfully irritating character. Comedian Edgar Kennedy had been polishing his trademark "slow burn" since the silent days and had enriched many a film for the Marx Brothers or Laurel and Hardy when he wasn't behind the scenes, directing them. Kennedy also starred for RKO in his own popular series of shorts, which lasted from the early thirties up until his death in 1948.

The problem here, as elsewhere in the mystery or horror genres throughout the decade and later, is the perceived need for comic relief. It is not known who first decided that audiences needed a break from the mind-numbing stresses of thrilling motion pictures, but surely even the most sensitive of souls would have recommended retiring the custom in 1934 or so, after all those impressionable viewers had become inured by a half-dozen good jolts under their belts. As the horror/mystery formulae became more familiar, the practice became counter-productive. A certifiable idiot who is oblivious to tragic or terrifying circumstances does not lessen the audience's tension but does increase its resentment.

For this reason, no matter how good the comedian — and Edgar Kennedy was among the very best in his field — a screenplay which dictates that there must be a fool to balance others' more rational behavior is setting that person and the story up for a big fall.

Familiar faces going through familiar paces give *The Black Doll* an added edge. That prince of blackguards, C. Henry Gordon, succeeds in having Nelson Rood despised by the viewers before they've even settled in their seats. The actor, who would be dead of heart failure within two years, was so seldom cast against type that audiences would no more accept him as an upholder of law and order than they would Bela Lugosi on the side of the angels.

Adroit at playing professional men with a penchant for impropriety, Addison Richards makes the first of his three appearances in a Crime Club adaptations. His record would be matched only by the team of Preston Foster and Frank Jenks, who were recurring characters in the series, and by Roland Drew, a specialist in oily, spineless types. Neither Richards nor John Wray, whose stock had taken a nosedive since his starring days in *All Quiet on the Western Front*, has much to do in *Doll*, but they and grand old Holmes Herbert give the solid support to which their fans had become accustomed. It is distressing to see how John Wray had apparently deteriorated; less than eight years earlier, the actor had been considered — on paper, anyway — for the title role in *Dracula*.

Nan Grey and Donald Woods make a nice couple, and they would again make a nice couple in Crime Club's July follow-up, *Danger on the Air*. William Lundigan would share the bill with them then, too; the handsome young man played his share of hangers-on and red herrings (and, at least once, the actual trigger-man) before he was promoted to the guy who usually got the girl.

For those who insist on a hint of the supernatural in their whodunits, *The Black Doll* is the only title to come close in the Crime Club series. If you can survive the disappointment of yet another thrill explained away and overlook Sheriff Renick, the picture remains an enjoyable outing with lots of old friends.

The Black Doll

Released January 30, 1938; 66 minutes

Cast: C. Henry Gordon (Nelson Rood); Donald Woods (Nick Halstead); Nan Grey (Marian Rood); Edgar Kennedy (Sheriff Renick); Doris Lloyd (Laura Leland); William Lundigan (Rex Leland); Holmes Herbert (Dr. Giddings); Addison Richards (Mallison); John Wray (Walling); Fred Malatesta (Esteban); Inez Palange (Rosita); Sid Saylor (Red); Arthur Hoyt (Coroner); John Harmon (Cabbie)

Credits: Producer — Irving Starr; Director — Otis Garrett; Screenplay — Harold Buckley; Based on the novel *The Black Doll* by William Edward Hayes; Photography — Stanley Cortez, ASC & Ira Morgan, ASC; Film Editor — Maurice Wright; Assistant Director — Phil Karstein; Art Director — Ralph Berger; Settings — Emile Kuri; Musical Director — Charles Previn; Sound — Charles Carroll; Production Manager — Ben Hersh; Gowns — Vera West. Walter Futter presents: A Crime Club Production

THE LADY IN THE MORGUE (1938)

Back by popular demand are those madcap detecting fools, Bill Crane and Doc Williams. Having stolen the show in *The Westland Case*, the tippling sleuths (Preston Foster and Frank Jenks, respectively) were now officially Universal's premier recurring detectives. This wasn't a signal honor, of course, as the studio had expended literally no effort in creating the team — they were the product of author Jonathan Latimer, whose source novels framed out the screenplays — and had incurred virtually no expense in promoting them. As Universal picked and chose which of the Crime Club novels would hit the screen, however, the fact that three of Latimer's were selected (his *The Dead Don't Care* would be released as *The Last Warning* in January) may have indicated the studio was somewhat taken with the author's quirky plots and adroit handling, or that the appeal might have rested with the characters of Bill and Doc themselves.

The film opens as a woman is found hanging in her hotel bathroom and removed to the morgue. A column heading, "Blond Beauty Ends Life in Darlow Hotel: Police Seek Identity," sums it up neatly. The lady had registered under the phony name of Alice Ross and now, it seems, has more interested gentlemen callers than ever she did in life. Gangster Steve Collins (Joseph Downing) sends his goon, Spitzy (Al Hill), down to check whether the woman is Arlene, Collins' ex-wife who left his arms for those of professional rival Frankie French. If it is Arlene, Spitzy is instructed to "take her out of there." Over at his own digs, Frankie (James Robbins) is aghast to read that only four dollars were found in the woman's purse. "I gave her three grand a week ago," he crows, also figuring the deceased to be Arlene. Accompanied by a stooge of his own, Frankie makes for the morgue, promising himself, "If it's Arlene, we'll take her out."

While Steve is figuring Frankie as the killer and Frankie is thinking just the opposite, Colonel Black (Gordon Hart) is sending the Black Detective Agency's ace Bill Crane to see whether he can identify the body as Catherine Courtland, the daughter of their client. "Mrs. Courtland is money and doesn't want to be seen looking in the morgue for her daughter," he is told. Morgue attendant Al Horn (Byron Foulger) hasn't had so much curious company in years; neither Bill nor a couple of reporters can identify the cadaver on their own, but there's always the chance that Spitzy, who glowers his way into the morgue moments later, can. The problem is, when Spitzy accompanies Crane and the newshounds back into the viewing room, the body is gone, and Al Horn is lying dead on the floor!

A title lobby card for *The Lady in the Morgue*: That's Preston Foster, looking very Bela Lugosi–ish, in the upper corner. PENTAGRAM LIBRARY.

Spitzy takes off in a hurry and the reporters phone in their stories; Bill noses around the facility. In walks Lieut. Strom (Thomas Jackson) with a couple of uniforms and a man who might be able to identify the body: "From her description, she could be my cousin … Edna Brown." Bill is tossed out after he gives his account of the incident, and he promises to show up for the inquest the next morning. Leaving by the ambulance entrance, Bill bumps into Gus the cabbie (Don Brodie), who tells him of the two fellows in the black sedan who sped away moments earlier. Bill hires Gus, and en route to the Darlow Hotel, Bill figures out that the guy who hit and killed Al Horn was left-handed.

At the Darlow, Bill bribes the elevator man to let him take a gander at room 418, where "Alice Ross" was found. The woman's body was

hanging from just inside the bathroom door, which bears wet heel-marks. "She'd taken a bath first before she did it," the employee explains; "water's still in the tub." "Alice" had had one visitor that night — a musician, who had carried his horn case in with him. Strom and the cops show up, forcing Bill to move (via the window ledge) into the adjoining room. Before she opens her door to the police, who have noticed the open window, the occupant of that adjoining room hides a small bundle in the closet inches from where Bill is standing. It's a wad of bills, coincidentally totaling $3,000, and Bill and the woman (Patricia Ellis) settle down to chat about Alice Ross until the cops leave room 418.

The next morning, Strom is apoplectic that Bill hasn't shown up at the inquest. A quick cut to the hotel shows the detective holding his head; apparently the woman had used a liquor bottle in a way far different from what Crane had hoped. Halfway through the inquest proceedings, Bill turns up and is promptly accused by Mrs. Horn of killing Mr. Horn. No one save the reporters takes the accusation seriously, and Bill is accosted by Frankie French, who offers the detective $5,000 for Arlene Vincent's body! Just as it seems that things can't get any screwier, Doc finally appears on the scene and Bill tells him to check out all the undertaker supply houses until he finds one who knows a redheaded, left-handed undertaker.

While Doc is puzzling this out, a visitor arrives. It's Chauncey Courtland (Gordon Elliott), who sought earlier to identify the dead woman as Edna Brown. "I use the name Brown to avoid publicity," he explains. Courtland fears that the missing body is that of his sister, as Catherine had sent a distressing note to their mother:

> Dear Mother: By the time you read this, I will be in a different, perhaps a better, world. I have taken a great deal of trouble to lose myself, so that what I am about to do won't bring disgrace to you and Chance. Goodbye, Kit.

Courtland (Chance is a nickname for Chauncey) admits that his mother and sister quarreled most of the time, but not about money. Catherine withdrew $6,000 from her own account when she left home. He later bumped into his sister at the Roost, a nightclub with a "hot band." Catherine was "a little swing crazy," he says. "And the last bird who called on Alice Ross was a musician," remembers Bill.

Through the door come a gun-wielding Spitzy and Steve Collins, but it doesn't take too long for the two detectives and Courtland to disarm the thugs. Steve offers Bill $10,000 for the body, maintaining, "She's my wife." Actually turning down an offer to go for a drink with Courtland, Bill has Doc chase after that undertaker, while he plans on going dancing "wherever the band that used to be at the Roost is playing."

Both sleuths have success. At the club that night (Doc: "A couple of whiskey and sodas." Bill: "Make mine the same."), Doc informs his partner that he has tracked down the redheaded, left-handed accomplice, but that he's an undertaker's assistant at the Haslan Funeral Parlor. When he spots the anonymous woman from the hotel out on the floor, where she works as a hostess, Bill tells Doc to dance with her for a few minutes, and then to let her know that the police have been asking questions. Doc does as he's told, and the woman leaves the club immediately. Bill follows her to her apartment. The woman is surprised when Bill addresses her as "Miss Courtland." Bill is surprised when the musician, Sam Taylor (Roland Drew), shows up moments later. Taylor is surprised when Crane informs him that the elevator man at the Darlow Hotel identified the trumpet player as the last person to see Alice Ross alive.

Taylor says that Alice Ross wanted Mrs. Taylor, the woman Bill had called "Miss Courtland," to agree to a divorce so that the musician and his blonde lover could be married. His wife's constant spying finally drove Alice Ross to suicide. Leaving the "Taylors," Bill joins Doc and the two drive over to the Haslan mortuary, where they find the red-headed undertaker's assistant shot behind the ear. "Must have been someone that knew him pretty well to get that close," offers Doc. Latching on to the book of burial records, Bill rips out the last entry: Agnes Christie, 54-54 Parnwell Avenue. Sending Doc to check out the woman's address and gravesite at Edgemoor Cemetery, Crane alerts the press to the murder at the funeral home.

Far from going well, things collapse all around Crane. Doc returns with news: Christie's address was a fake, but the grave is right where it should be. However, the paper's account of the mortuary killing notes fingerprints all over the establishment's back door. "They're mine," moans Bill. Colonel Black has gone on record denying that he sent Crane to the funeral home on business, and Chauncey Courtland doesn't make it any better with the news that his mother has received a second letter from Kit, who realized how

A typical shot from *The Lady in the Morgue*: Bill giving it out, Doc taking it in. Neither man is absolutely sure, but Bill is more comfortable with it. *Pentagram Library.*

tragic the first must have sounded. Bill is on the spot.

> BILL: I'm in this thing up to my neck. If I stand still for five minutes, Spitzy and Collins start shooting at me, Frankie French is gonna kill me on sight, Lehman and Strom are on my heels like a couple of bloodhounds, and the D.A. says I'm practically in the Death House right now! Get me Alice Ross or Arlene Vincent!

Providentially, Courtland can help. "I know Arlene Vincent. She calls herself Kay Renshaw now, and she's going to be at a party at Martin's penthouse tonight!" With nothing to lose, Bill and Doc crash that party at Martin's penthouse and kidnap Kay Renshaw (Barbara Pepper).

Giving the brassy blonde the choice of being dropped off at Collins' or French's, she opts for the former. With one blonde accounted for, the partners grab some tools and head out to Edgemoor Cemetery. Bill isn't terribly optimistic, for "Everything depends on what's in the grave now."

There's *nothing* in the grave, but the cemetery is full of cops, and in looking to hide out, Bill and Doc stumble upon an old mausoleum with a shiny new lock. Inside is the lady from the morgue. With Courtland's help, they bring the body down to the morgue, where the attendant balks at accepting it, objecting, "It's been embalmed!" It gets worse: Collins is no longer an interested party, and when called to identify the corpse, Frankie French swears, "I never saw this girl before in my life." Sam Taylor finally admits that "Mrs. Taylor" is actually Alice Ross, and Doc is sent out to locate Mrs. Taylor. Bill and Courtland agree to stand guard that night, not wanting the body to disappear again. In the wee hours, the shadow of a man wielding a pipe approaches the sleeping Crane, but Doc grabs him from behind before any attack can be made. It is Courtland! "I'm sorry, Crane, but I couldn't let her be identified." Now wise to the situation, Bill has Doc round up Strom, the Coroner, and Mr. and Mrs. Taylor. The solution to the mystery is at hand.

Courtland admits to killing Al Horn ("I only meant to stun him") and the undertaker, and to having stolen and secreted his sister's body to prevent "the disgrace" from killing his mother. It seems to fit, but Bill is anything but satisfied. Only when the detective threatens to put Mrs. Taylor's hair into a basin of hydrogen tetroxide does the truth come out. She is revealed as Catherine Courtland; the dead woman is the real Mrs. Taylor. Her husband killed her because she wouldn't give her a divorce to marry the rich, "swing-crazy" Miss Courtland. There *had* been endless spying and harassment, but on the part of the lady in the morgue.

> BILL: When you found her occupying a room next to Miss Courtland, you killed her while she was taking a bath and you dragged her through the connecting door into Miss Courtland's room. When you got through, you discovered her body had left water marks on the door, so you filled the tub to explain them.

As per most cornered villains, Taylor pulls a pistol. "That's the gun he killed the undertaker with, if you can get it!" yells the helpful Bill. They do.

Courtland admits to knowing his sister was alive from the very first. "When Taylor told her his wife had killed herself, it frightened her, and she wired me." In his misguided attempt to prevent scandal, Courtland took the body from the morgue, hitting Horn — too hard — in the process. The district attorney advises Courtland to turn state's evidence; Taylor will

hang, and the D.A. will try to get Courtland off with a light sentence. This sits well with everyone concerned, and Doc and Bill head off to wet their whistles.

The Lady in the Morgue is the kind of title that generates lurid vistas of the city ice house and its cold, silent population with the titular cadaver nestled comfortably among kindred corpses. I mean, this was a Universal picture, right? Released by the people who had made "monster" a household word? Well, there's not so much as a peek at Alice Ross or Mrs. Taylor or whoever in blazes the lady really is. Only Courtland and the detectives get a gander in the mausoleum, and even Agnes Christie's coffin is empty.

The disparity between my expectations and what the film delivers just points out one of the differences between '30s horror films and '30s detective pictures: turf. Each genre has its own unique parameters and niceties, and each approaches the dominant, common theme of death in a different way. The rationale given for most occurrences in a horror film is irrational in real life; screwing around with impossible science or the supernatural results in death and destruction.

Mysteries, on the other hand, approach that same death and destruction from an entirely different angle. The answers to who done it and why are grounded in readily appreciable human motivations: greed, lust, fear, revenge and the like. A hotcha redhead with a poison ring is just as deadly as a seven-foot automaton whose head-bones are connected to his neck-bones with bolts, and a darn sight easier to swallow. Solutions to sundry puzzles are found by studying motive and opportunity, psychology, relationships, canceled checks, blood stains, and the level to which the knife sank in the butter. *De rigueur* venues include the back room at the police station, Art Deco nightclubs, outlandishly spacious apartments, cheap hotels, alleyways, and hospital bedsides. Morgues are a necessary evil in the world of the '30s private eye, but one neither dawdles nor gawks unnecessarily therein.

Sure, there was the occasional crossover. Charlie Chan's Honolulu buzzer must have been good in Cairo; otherwise, how could he forage among mummies and musty tombs in search of clues? Sherlock Holmes also went hell bent for leather — several times, in fact — to help the Baskervilles rein in their hound. Still, most of the time, the twain never did meet.

Despite its rather frightless unreeling (incidentally, it does feature the *Bride of Frankenstein* fanfare under the main titles), *The Lady in the Morgue* is a smart, if confusing, example of this latter school. Crooks Steve Collins and Frankie French are willing to pay some serious money for Arlene Vincent's corpse, but not a thin dime for the pleasure of her company. This escapes me. Bill claims that Taylor killed his wife in her own bathroom and then dragged her over and strung her up in Miss Courtland's, but the murder site is room 418, and there's never any evidence given that Miss Courtland lived in any room other than 420. Huh? In fact, why would Taylor bother with the move in the first place? Would Alice Ross be any less (or more) Alice Ross somewhere else? And why would Taylor kill the redheaded you-know-what? He couldn't put a name on the missing blonde any faster than the others could.

I can only assume that Eric Taylor's efforts at adapting Jonathan Latimer's source novel for the screen resulted in the derailment of Bill Crane's train of thought. Co-scenarist Robertson White had done a top-notch job dealing with Latimer's *Headed for a Hearse* (*The Westland Case*) the year before, and Edmund L. Hartmann would prove more than equal to the task when the prolific author's *The Dead Don't Care* reached movie houses as *The Last Warning* in December of 1938. Taylor's contributions to Universal's genre product were much more extensive and rather more impressive during the forties. His screenplay for *Son of Dracula* probably won him the most huzzahs from horror fans, but even it gets a bit bogged down with chatter. Dialogue does not seem to have been Mr. Taylor's strong suit.

Preston Foster and Frank Jenks continue on their merry way, but this time around the pair are slightly more sober and alert than they were in *The Westland Case*. As before, Bill is pretty much the brains of the operation, with Doc the gofer, but Doc's examination of the redheaded, left-handed mortician's aide hints at a medical background behind his nickname. He's quick on the draw with the approximate time of death, too. Another nice touch is having Bill frantic about where the case is taking him, a delightful departure from the usual concern of movie private eyes: coming up with enough double entendres for the blondes and insults for the cops to last out the picture.

Patricia Ellis did virtually all of her "important" screen work during the thirties. Adept but hardly outstanding in musicals (such as *42nd Street*), screwball comedies (*Here Comes the Groom*, Laurel and Hardy's *Block-Heads*) or "light" dramas (*The Case of the Lucky Legs* or *Postal Inspector*), the lovely young actress made the rounds of the majors in leads and featured roles before descending into bits and disappearing from the scene.

Miss Ellis gives the essentially thankless role of Catherine Courtland a decent shot, but the character comes off a mile shy of credibility. With her family's money and influence and the brawny Chauncey watching over her, why would she continue to live with Taylor, especially when she has admitted that he frightens her? And how can any female character worth her salt expect to retain the audience's sympathy when she passively sits by and watches her brother put his head in a noose for a murder he didn't commit? Miss Ellis was an attractive, if limited, actress for whose course *The Lady in the Morgue* was pretty much par.

A bit of an eye-opener is the casting of Gordon Elliott as Chauncey Courtland. Later a full-fledged cowboy star ("Wild Bill" Elliott), earlier a leading man during the waning days of silent film, the rough and ready actor is charmingly soft-spoken and all smiles until he tries to brain Bill with a lead pipe — after which, he apologizes! During the thirties, Elliott's versatility led to his being cast in pictures like *Love Takes Flight* (Grand National, 1937) or *A Boy of the Streets* (1938, for Monogram) as often as his manly backside would end up in a saddle. Quite dapper in his pencil-line mustache and not at all out of place in a silk hat, Elliott's presence in *The Lady in the Morgue* is one of the film's genuine pleasures.

The lovely Barbara Pepper — here so chilly that butter wouldn't melt in her succulent, ruby-lipped mouth — is always a treat for the sensory nerves. Role-wise, she was always a bridesmaid, never a bride, though she was seldom allowed to be as moral as all that. She specialized in tarts, molls, "other women," and flirts, as in *The Westland Case*, in a career that spanned from the early thirties until the year before her death. Thomas Jackson — Lieutenant Strom here — can be espied flashing his badge in other Universal genre entries of the period. Almost always a cop, from *Little Caesar* to *Mystery of the Wax Museum* to *The Mystery of the White Room*, the crusty character man was also active in films almost until his death in 1967.

Director Otis Garrett keeps *The Lady* moving at a good clip, which may be the reason Bill Crane's logic doesn't cause more headscratching in the film. This was Stanley Cortez's third of four Crime Clubs pictures (*The Last Express* was up next), and although the cinematographer's masterpieces (*The Magnificent Ambersons, The Night of the Hunter*) were still ahead of him, he could take justifiable pride in his contribution to the mystery series' success.

Batting about .500 in relation to its team-mates, with its constant motion and interesting cast offset by the story's illogical and unsatisfactory solution, *The Lady in the Morgue* warrants a look from armchair detectives and couch potatoes alike.

The Lady in the Morgue

Released April 22, 1938; 67 minutes

Cast: Preston Foster (Bill Crane); Frank Jenks (Doc Williams); Patricia Ellis (Catherine Courtland); Thomas Jackson (Lieut. Strom); Barbara Pepper (Kay Renshaw); Gordon Elliott (Chauncey Courtland); Byron Foulger (Al Horn); Rollo Lloyd (Coroner); Roland Drew (Sam Taylor); Joseph Downing (Steve Collins); Al Hill (Spitzy); James Robbins (Frankie French); Morgan Wallace (Inspector Lehman); Brian Burke (Johnson); Donald Kerr (Greening); Don Brodie (Gus, the Cabbie); Gordon Hart (Colonel Black)

Credits: Producer — Irving Starr; Director — Otis Garrett; Based on the novel *The Lady in the Morgue* by Jonathan Latimer; Screenplay — Eric Taylor and Robertson White; Cinematography — Stanley Cortez, ASC: Art Director — Jack Otterson; Associate Art Director — Charles H. Clark; Film Editor — Ted Kent; Sound — Charles Carroll & Edwin Wetzel; Production Manager — Ben Hersh; Gowns — Vera West. A Crime Club Production

DANGER ON THE AIR (1938)

Another installment in the popular Crime Club series, *Danger on the Air* boasts a number of clever touches, an interesting and lively crime scene, and several bright performances. If the murderer's *modus operandi* doesn't quite cross the border into science fiction, it does dance on the fringe of the unpredictable and overdone techniques of the most madcap of serial villains.

From almost the moment he enters the elevator at station WGAB, sponsor Caesar Kluck (Berton Churchill) might as well wear a clock for a hat; it's obvious to even the most casual of mystery buffs that the soft drink mogul's time is running out fast. The "Popola" king has used rumor and innuendo to drive several of his competitors to ruin or suicide, and as if that weren't enough to paint a bullseye on his brow, he's also a lustful and abrasive bully. In addition, within the first 20 minutes, he manages to enrage almost everyone in sight. Anyone that obnoxious can't be expected to survive the third reel unmurdered, and he doesn't.

In the course of the introductory footage, we meet Steenie MacCorkle (Nan Grey) and her brother, Mac (Frank Milan); along with Vinnie Fish (Skeets Gallagher), they perform any number of jobs at the station from an office whose door proclaims "Radio Productions and Advertising." Usher-cum-impressionist Harry Lake ([Peter] Lind Hayes) finds himself on the receiving end of Kluck's sharp tongue, while Maria (Louise Stanley), one of the young, pretty receptionists, receives a gift and a promise of "a little bite together after the broadcast" from the elderly lothario. This last business is overheard by Tony the janitor (Lee J. Cobb), who's not about to let Kluck put the moves on Maria, his daughter.

The rest of the first cast are introduced during the *Kluck's Popola Hour* broadcast. Dave Chapman (William Lundigan) is the handsome announcer and soda pitch man. Mr. Tuttle (no Christian name, played by George Meeker) has been at the studio for two weeks now and it's still anybody's guess as to why. Further into the story, the sound engineer (Donald Woods) is unveiled as Benjamin Franklin Botts ("It's a good thing I wasn't born on Saint Swithin's Day"), incipient love interest and hero of the piece.

Having demonstrated Kluck's distasteful proclivities, the screenplay pauses only to establish his high blood pressure and his sensitivity to the stuffy conditions of soundproof booths before maneuvering him, via the insistence of any number of the people we've just met, into "Sponsor Room X," whence he can observe the broadcast and hit on Steenie without driving the rest of the characters to

Danger on the Air was the second Crime Club adventure for Nan Grey and Donald Woods. PENTAGRAM LIBRARY.

distraction. He's scarcely in the room, however, before another county is heard from. It's Carney, a thug who represents "the best little group of whisperers in this business." The boys want a bonus ("say … a hundred grand") for having succeeded in driving rival soda man Nelson to suicide. Kluck waves off the threat, informing the little weasel that there are enough incriminating records safely hidden to put Carney and his boys away for good.

At any rate, it doesn't take long for Steenie to haul off and belt the amorous sponsor right in his presumption, and she storms down the spiral stairs and into the sound room. When Mac heads upstairs to tell Kluck where to get off, he misses seeing Carney leave the sponsor room, but can't fail to find the soda king's body on the floor. Steenie reappears,

and the siblings are joined by Fish and Botts, who finds a diamond brooch (the gift Maria received earlier) in Kluck's lifeless hand. Botts sends the men away on various errands, and Steenie promptly faints.

When she is revived, Steenie is told that "the air in that room had been tampered with by someone who knew Kluck's phobia about ventilation." It seems that Botts is no slouch when it comes to scientific detection, having studied at five colleges and having done postgraduate work in chemistry, physics, biology, bacteriology, etc. His finely attuned ears allow him to notice something peculiar about the sound of the orchestra on the sponsor room's radio. "You can't smell reduced pressure, but you *can* hear it," he explains, and later deduces that someone introduced gas into the room.

Asking Steenie to stay put for a moment, the young genius heads for the sound room, but is nearly killed by a fall from the spiral staircase. Steenie, meanwhile, is chased from the scene of the crime by a stentorian threat from the radio: "Keep out of this! Keep out if you don't want death to call again! Ha ha ha ha ha ha..."

Returning cautiously to the sponsor room, they manage to discover a broken balloon fragment before answering a summons to the office of the station's president, Mr. Jones (Jed Prouty). Jones warns the entire staff not to speak to the press and introduces Dr. Sylvester (Edward Van Sloan), Kluck's personal physician, who claims he was with the soda magnate at the time of his death. When said press arrives at the office mere seconds later, Dr. Sylvester announces that Kluck expired from natural causes; "[He] suffered for years from coronary sclerosis." Botts contributes his own theory: The ventilating system was tampered with, and Kluck's death was nothing short of murder. That smells like a scoop to the press but angers Jones, who sacks his brilliant employee.

Steenie catches up with Botts, and as the two—who by now have begun to hit it off—head for a convenient cab, Carny and an accomplice stage a slow-motion, ineffectual, drive-by rub-out attempt. Without bothering to report the near-homicide to the police, the starry-eyed couple rides off into the night. That evening's *New York Star* features Botts' theory as gospel on the front page, and Jones and Sylvester are at their wits' end as to how to get the press off their necks. Mr. Tuttle shows up with the answer to their dilemma: Steenie's purse, which contains a very suspicious letter about deadly poisons. Now that he thinks about it, Sylvester concludes that Kluck *was* poisoned, and Steenie is hauled into the studio president's *sanctum sanctorum*.

The letter doesn't faze Miss MacCorkle; it was, she explains, just an answer to a research inquiry for some crime stories she was writing. Undeterred, Sylvester tells Steenie that "this box of tablets was found in your purse. The contents would kill several people." The tables are turned again, however; Botts saw Kluck take one of those pills himself just before his death, and the smarmy doctor is reminded that "the label on the box had *your* name as prescribing physician." After thinking some more about it, Sylvester is now sure that Kluck did not die of poison. Botts gets 24 hours' leeway from Jones, promising, "I'll find out who did this thing and prove that there isn't anything wrong with your ventilating system!"

Steenie and her boyfriend break into Kluck's apartment, where Botts survives a booby-trapped safe to discover all those incriminating documents Kluck had earlier mentioned to Carney. Between a lengthy account of Carney's police record and a couple of mentions of heavy cash payments to Dr. Sylvester, Steenie and Botts feel that the end is in sight. Another tragedy intervenes, however, when Tony is found dead in a janitor's closet, poisoned by one of those balloons. Botts tells Steenie that only some of the balloons—marked ones—are filled with the toxic gas, and that he's going to flush out the killer by waving the balloon under his nose.

The District Attorney and the cops finally show up, and they allow Botts to amass the station staff and guests in Jones' private office. Tuttle is exposed as an FCC officer, sent from Washington to look into ties between Sylvester and Kluck. Mac admits that he blocked the ventilating system in the sponsor's room, but did so only to frighten the phobic Kluck. Botts then reveals how a straight pin, balanced with paper wadding, could be blown through an ordinary soda straw to burst the deadly balloon in the intended victim's face. As he begins his demonstration, Dave Chapman caves in and confesses.

"All right. I killed him. He ruined my father, who was president of Johnson's Beverage.... With our business gone and nothing left, I came to work here." Ironically, Kluck had liked the new announcer's voice and had insisted on Dave's handling all of the Popola spots. Poor Tony, it seems, bought the farm by accident, as Dave "put the balloons everywhere [he] thought Kluck would go." Jones offers the triumphant Botts an enormous promotion and raise, but the engineer demurs for the time

A couple of gauges, some plate glass, and a microphone or two, and voila! Instant radio station! *PENTA-GRAM LIBRARY.*

being, as he and his honey have a lengthy session ahead of them at Niagara Falls.

During the earliest days of Universal City's existence, Uncle Carl had cadged quarters from a public anxious to get a backstage gander at how movies were made. Twenty-five cents bought a spot in the grandstand, guaranteed a view at an actual silent-movie filming, and even included a box lunch. It couldn't have been much later that Laemmle or one of his like-minded fellow moguls had a brainstorm: If the people were willing to pay to see a movie, and were willing to pay to see a movie being made, wouldn't it follow that they'd also pay to see a movie about how movies are made? Of course they would, and they'd also spring to get the lowdown on life in the thea-ay-ter, and the insider's dope on radio (and this new television thing, too). The Golden and Silver Age

horror canon pretty much bypassed movie palaces when it came to recurring haunts for twisted killers, but like that notorious opera house, both theater and radio station would prove to be suitable stomping grounds for ersatz ghosts and mysterious murderers.

The radio milieu was probably the cheapest of these show business locales to concoct. Radio stations could be jury-rigged from standing office sets, a microphone or two, a few sheets of plate glass, and some stock shots of a rooftop antenna. When radio was in its heyday, sitting in as part of the studio audience of a popular broadcast was among the favorite pastimes of local fans, big-city radio buffs, and visitors on bus tours. Still, the percentage of moviegoers who could nay-say any studio's version of a radio station was infinitesimal, and potted ferns, switchboards, and vintage headsets could camouflage a multitude of stylistic sins.

Danger on the Air looks good. The plethora of overstuffed furniture and art deco sconces gives the film a thirties feel which was undoubtedly authentic at the time, and which is delightfully fruity nowadays. The spiral staircase is a fabulous touch. Sure, there's all that plate glass and those standing mikes and general-purpose offices, but the less-is-more treatment works like a charm, particularly when the necessary apparatus for the purely aural medium is so plain and simple.

The story itself, adapted from the novel *Death Catches Up with Mr. Kluck* by "Xantippe," is strictly formulaic, right down to the well-deserving victim who goes out of his way to provide a motive for everyone down to the janitor. This sets the stage for a couple of other time-honored devices: the programming of the audience to view the crime as justifiable homicide, and the encouragement of sympathy for the murderer. When Dave Chapman spills his guts, it would take a harder heart than most to want to see him fry, and if the local judiciary system is as lax as is the police department, the personable tragic hero stands a good chance of getting off.

For the most part, the novelty and charm of the picture reside in the innovative if unwieldy method employed by the killer and in the scientific investigation conducted by Steenie (who's level-headed and appealing from the outset) and Botts (who grows on you). The *Kluck's Popola Hour* balloons are very much in evidence from the opening reel, where they cleverly provide a bit of exposition and signal the time-frame for the alert viewer. After it has been made clear that some of the balloons are really floating carriers of sudden death, we become aware that the film's title has been pulling double duty all along; danger isn't only *on* the air, it's *in* it, as well.

There are loads of scientific axioms kicked around by the super-educated Botts, and more than once the pedantic flow strays into overkill. (For all mavens of fifties television, Botts and Steenie's discussion on the whys and wherefores of a partial vacuum plays like an episode

of *Ask Mr. Wizard*.) The sometimes dry recitation of the principles of physics and such are offset to an extent by Donald Woods' and Nan Grey's endearing personalities. Woods' character is introduced in an adroit fashion: The second-billed actor, who will (per the formula) be either the hero or the heavy, just sits there through one of Kluck's extended snit-fits, before getting to his feet and physically tossing the obnoxious sponsor out of the sound room. Between his good looks and his gumption, it's a foregone conclusion that Botts will soon be working in tandem with Steenie, especially when it is revealed that the other MacCorkle on the office door is the pretty blonde's brother.

Given that a good bit of the technical stuff the young couple mulls over is beyond the ken of the average viewer (although Ben advises Steenie that high school students are routinely warned by their chemistry teacher not to make the type of poison gas used to kill Kluck), frequent changes of setting help to keep the scholarly chats endurable, if not completely engrossing. Nan Grey is a doll as Steenie MacCorkle, and during Ben's last reel grilling of the assembled cast, her writing down variations of *Mrs. Christina Botts* is a cute (but not cloying) testimony to her faith in her feller. It's nice to see the lovely actress in a part which asks her to express a greater range of emotion than did her wimpy vampiric victim in *Dracula's Daughter*.

Edward Van Sloan is always welcome, and his Dr. Sylvester is alternately amiable and oily, domineering and submissive. Given a chance for once to handle relatively normal dialogue rather than dire warnings or weighty pronouncements, the actor is enjoyable to watch as he ducks and dodges any bursts of truth fired his way. It must have been a relief for him to be allowed down from his pedestal of iron-clad rectitude and to wallow in human frailty for a couple of reels. Van Sloan makes Dr. Sylvester's weaknesses where veracity is concerned wryly amusing without dragging the character, mugging and posturing, into the comic relief swamp.

Yes, that is *the* Lee J. Cobb schlepping brooms and balloons as Tony the janitor. The actor can be excused for the mopey, stereotypical portrayal, as *Danger on the Air* came very early in his screen career (following only *Ali Baba Goes to Town* and a couple of westerns). Like that other whirlwind theatrical force and mediocre impersonator of Italians named Tony, Charles Laughton, Cobb would soon begin to appear only in Significant Productions, leaving folderol like Tony Lisante to other actors on their way up (or down).

Released midway through the Crime Club series, *Danger on the Air* isn't so much a dead-ringer for any of its antecedents or successors as it is a guideline for a couple of maniacally entertaining and far more popular comedy-thrillers of the early forties. The colorful murder at the radio station slipped easily into the next decade as background for the antics of Abbott and Costello. *Who Done It?* (1942) borrowed the locale, jazzed up the final unmasking scene, and replaced the more mundane tale of revenge with a timely story of fifth column agents at work in America. And, in terms of their characterization, their burgeoning relationship, and even their physical appearance, the enjoyable and slightly off-kilter Richard Carlson and Evelyn Ankers of 1941's satirical spooker *Hold That Ghost* are presaged by Donald Woods and Nan Grey.

Common sense dictates that there have to be a few drawbacks, or *Danger on the Air* would be a far more popular title than it is. As it only wins inclusion in this volume courtesy of its official association with the more full-blooded Universal genre titles (via the *Shock Theater* television package), we can be forgiven our unfamiliarity with what is essentially a standardized mystery film. Probably its greatest weakness is no longer apparent: Quirky murder method apart, the picture is but one more of a series of similar whodunits which staked out the lower halves of double bills during the latter part of the thirties. "B" movies were double-feature fodder, and double features were the movies' answer to the free allure of radio.

Low budget mysteries, weepers, horse operas, comedies, and third-rate musicals featuring legions of fourth-rate talents were tossed in the hopper and combined almost haphazardly in order to attract as wide an audience share as possible. With very few exceptions, the several years separating the death of horror movies from their resurrection witnessed an industry-wide slacking off in quality, in style, and in exuberance. There was no dearth of product, merely a cosmic shortage of class. Within a given genre, one picture would follow hot on the heels of another, and distinctions among films and actors blurred. When better stuff came back, however, it came back big; 1939 is probably *the* golden year of cinema, no matter what your taste or propensity.

Like countless other drill-pressed whodunits, *Danger on the Air* was slave to an established mystery formula which was so familiar to fans as to be almost second-nature. The careful arrangement of suspicious movement among the red herrings, having the deck stacked against the profoundly obstreperous victim, the second (and usually secondary) murder, the cutesy boy-girl ritual: All of these elements may have been as comfortable as an old (gum)shoe, but they did nothing to help distinguish the movie from any of a dozen clones. Interestingly, now that black and white films have all but vanished from the small screen (save for the classics, which have been colorized), and now that the most creative of the thirties and forties productions have all been remade, updated, and technologically "improved," this perceived fault of *Danger on the Air* is not so readily apparent. The picture nowadays seems to offer a naïve charm, displaying, as it does, facile motives, less overtly complex relationships, and downright picturesque behavior. Of course, this can be said of virtually any of the dozens of similar films cranked out during those lean years, as well.

The lack of a musical score also serves both to date and to diminish the picture. It may have been felt that the sundry pieces of aired broadcasts, the musical excerpts played by the pathetically adequate studio orchestra, or the varying Lind Hayes impressions would contribute enough background noise to balance the chatter up front. But, no. Despite a couple of deftly humorous touches (Kluck crabs about Rossini's *Una voce poco fa*, as warbled by soprano Miss Bello[w]), there are just too many long stretches where a viewer might enjoy more the hard facts about air pressure if they were only discussed in counterpoint to some stock musical themes. Musical director Charles Previn's credit seems to apply only to the mediocre snatches of melody that accompany the title and credits.

Ultimately, *Danger on the Air* strays off-rhythm for me because of all those science-class gabfests. Ben's omniscience is too pat for real life (I know; this is *not* real life). His hypothesis that the villain has had to create a partial vacuum (by somehow sucking the atmosphere out of the room) so as to introduce by nefarious means an instantly fatal, odorless, poisonous gas (of a type forbidden to underclassmen), to be triggered by the inequalities existing within and without the deadly balloon ... well, it gets to be a bit much. Hell's bells, horror movies' most certifiably mad scientists employ far less cumbersome processes to raise the dead than this fershlugginer announcer does to bump off the encroaching old bastard. As far-fetched as it is, though, Dave's convoluted procedure is not without interest, but if only Ben and Steenie had lightened up on the technical jargon, the picture would have been a delight.

Nonetheless, as these last few paragraphs indicate, none of the obstacles to enjoying *Danger on the Air* is insurmountable. Like its other Crime Club cronies, the picture offers a harmless little thriller with a slight twist and asks only that you go along for the ride. A deep breath may be necessary when the heavy pedagogy starts, but these passages are few, and lots of charm and silliness lie in between.

Danger on the Air

Released July 1, 1938; 67 minutes

Cast: Nan Grey (Steenie MacCorkle); Donald Woods (Benjamin Franklin Botts); Jed Prouty (Harry Jones); Berton Churchill (Cesar Kluck); William Lundigan (Dave Chapman); Skeets Gallagher (Vincent Fish); Edward Van Sloan (Dr. Sylvester); George Meeker (Tuttle); Lee J. Cobb (Tony); Johnny Arthur (Aiken); (Peter) Lind Hayes (Harry Lake); Louise Stanley (Marian); Eloise Rawitzer (Miss Bello); Joseph Downing (Carney); with Frank Milan

Credits: Producer — Irving Starr; Director — Otis Garrett; Screenplay — Betty Laidlow and Robert Lively; Based on *Death Catches Up With Mr. Kluck* by "Xantippe"; Director of Photography — Stanley Cortez, ASC; Art Director — Jack Otterson; Film Editor — Maurice Wright; Musical Director — Charles Previn; Associate Director — N.V. Timchenko; Sound — William H. Hedgcock and Edwin Wetzel; Production Manager — Ben Hersh; Gowns — Ira West. A Crime Club Production

THE MISSING GUEST (1938)

The *Missing Guest* is an unnecessary remake of *Secret of the Blue Room*, which itself had been released scarcely half a decade earlier. To this day, I can't understand why Universal didn't just reissue the earlier picture and be done with it. The cast members were all still working and still popular — some more than they had been in 1933, in fact. The barely dusty Lionel Atwill chiller had been a talkie, and not a primitive one, either, so there was no question of "recreating its original magic with sound." True, 1938 was one of those interim years when genre elements were few and far between. Maybe it was felt that the Erich Philippi piece could be stripped of its several "supernatural" overtones and farmed out as a straight comic whodunit. If that was the case, then why all the attempts at atmosphere? Why the (rather well done) haunted house milieu? Why the costumes? Why the Halloween-ish sound effects? Why intimate about the mysterious deaths of other owners?

The *Missing Guest* does move the plotline from Central Europe to Long Island, reflecting Universal's new tendency to set more of its thrillers in the States than it had earlier in the decade. Pictures like *Remember Last Night?* and *The House of Fear* are also set in New York, and a few of the forties monster shows would have their bugbears cavorting among the comforts of the New World, having eschewed the war-torn ruins of the Old. As with *Blue Room*, there's a Blue Room, wherein lies the mystery. As with *Blue Room*, the unsuccessful suitor for the hand of the heroine (here, Stephanie "Steve" Kirkland, played by Constance Moore) will prove to be both daring enough to sleep alone in the dread chamber and brash enough to plug other cast members and think he can get away with it.

After some protracted nonsense involving nincompoop newspaper editor Frank Kendall (Harlan Briggs) and his search for "the next Edison" for his New Inventors column in *The Daily Blade*, Scoop Hanlon (Paul Kelly) is assigned to crash Stephanie Kirkland's masquerade party at "the old Baldrich estate" and to get the lowdown on the mansion's infamous Blue Room. Scoop takes the assignment literally and runs his car into the gate to the estate; he is carried "injured" into the house. Following a spell when the lights go out and the piano plays by itself, Steve begins to open up to the reporter, thinking he is Ronald Ranger, a "psychic researcher." Between creepy old Edwards the butler (Patrick J. Kelly) and Frank Baldrich (Selmer Jackson), however, Scoop's camera is confiscated, his cover blown, and his abrupt departure from the house speedily arranged.

Later, during the wee hours, guest Larry

The old pipe organ in the musty cellar is the source of some of the film's eerie music. Comic relief duo Vic and Jake (sporting the hats) are the source of most (but not all) of *The Missing Guest*'s irritation factor. PENTAGRAM LIBRARY.

Dearden (William Lundigan) proposes to spend the night in the Blue Room, the supposedly cursed chamber where Steve's father, Sam, was murdered 20 years before. Steve doesn't take to this proposal of Larry's any more than she did to his earlier one, concerning marriage, but she can't dissuade him from his plan; neither can Steve's stepfather, Mr. Baldrich, nor family physician Dr. Carroll (Edwin Stanley). (At different times during the film, Dr. Carroll takes Larry and Steve aside separately and speaks to each of Sam Kirkland's youthful love affair, a dalliance which resulted in Larry's being Steve's half-brother; it is therefore providential that Steve cares not a fig romantically for young Mr. Dearden.) It appears that it takes

more than pluck to overcome the secret of the Blue Room, though; a check at first light finds Larry gone!

Counterbalancing Larry's disappearance is Scoop's buzzing the butler's pantry for orange juice and coffee. Having gotten the chauffeur drunk ("As a matter of fact, *none* of your servants are very trustworthy"), Hanlon slipped back into the mansion and spent the night in the guest room. Baldrich thinks twice about calling in the cops, dreading all that nasty publicity, and hires two private eyes instead. The two dicks are Vic (Billy Wayne) and Jake (George Cooper), both of whom are just out of stir ("for impersonating officers, and not very well at that") and old cronies of

Scoop's. After a good bit of running time is squandered on their "comic" byplay and Hanlon's attempts at convincing Steve that he's true-blue, Dr. Carroll's cadaver is discovered in the Blue Room. Like Sam Kirkland, two decades earlier, the family physician has been murdered amid mysterious circumstances.

Baldrich calls the cops. As in the 1933 original, they nose around, but it's left to one of the guests (Scoop, natch) to come up with clues, evidence, and solution. Steve discloses to him that Dr. Carroll was a suspect in her father's murder, but that he couldn't have left the room where he was playing cards and reached the Blue Room without being seen. In the course of poking about, Scoop discovers that the doctor was paying Edwards to engineer the self-playing piano, the timely power outages, and other eerie effects. Later, Scoop comes upon a secret passageway connecting a garden bench with the Blue Room and finds himself in a shootout with a mysterious figure. Scoop survives the encounter, but Larry Dearden does not. With his dying breath, Larry reveals why he became the missing guest:

> LARRY: Steve … maybe you can understand. When I went up to sleep that night, it was really to find out who killed your father — *my* father. I discovered the staircase. I knew that was how the murderer got up the stairs without being discovered. I always had an idea that Dr. Carroll had done it…

Hanlon fills in the details as the vengeful Larry dies, and it is abundantly clear that Scoop will straighten out and fly right, with the lovely Steve by his side.

In the course of updating, or improving, or whatever it was that screenwriters Charles Martin and Paul Perez felt they were doing to *Blue Room*, they apparently regarded it as their sworn duty to confuse the issues by populating the cast with idiots. The big party scene boasts a truckload of moneyed scatterbrains, all baroquely costumed without the slightest awareness of incongruity. If this weren't enough, weaving through the film like a pair of busy ants on a sugar cube are the two low comics, whose antics are purely a sop to 1938's house rules on comedy-mystery convention. None of the "humor" is remotely amusing nowadays, and I won't try to guess the odds on any of this getting much of a reaction from the people sitting in the theater.

The story's more dramatic side doesn't sit well, either. We are asked to believe that, having murdered Steve's father some two decades before the opening titles, Doctor Carroll has somehow installed and tested all of the ghostly paraphernalia within the last four weeks and has lured Edwards, the double-dipping butler, into his scheme just to make sure no one ever tumbles onto the secret passage to the Blue Room! The elaborate lengths to which the two scoundrels have gone to keep daredevils and "psychic researchers" away from the Blue Room are nearly as unwieldy and far-fetched as the visual rigamarole Lionel Barrymore set up to catch Jean Hersholt in MGM's *Mark of the Vampire*. If Dr. Carroll had the time and opportunity to turn the old building into a funhouse, why didn't he just wall up the entrances to the passage and get on with his life?

Equally upsetting is the persona of the movie's "hero": As played by Paul Kelly, Scoop Hanlon is a shallow, deceitful jerk. Quick with a quip (insult humor seems to be his forte), Scoop apologizes time and again to Steve for the way he's behaved "up till now." In spite of this, the reassurances he gives her and her family are dashed (due mainly to the dictates of his simple-minded editor), his word is worthless, and his impetuosity goes unchecked. He is even sufficiently graceless to butt in on Larry's dying explanations to his sister. The picture's biggest mystery is how the level-headed Steve would fall for a three-dollar bill like Scoop Hanlon.

Again, attention to detail suffered in the race to bring the film in on time and at budget. According to Brunas, Brunas and Weaver's *Universal Horrors*, *Guest* came in at some $8,000 *under* budget, and so was approximately equivalent to *Blue Room*. Strange, indeed, are the ways of talent: The same $70,000 applied to basically the same story brought in one picture which still maintains its flavor, charm and mystery, and a second which consistently misses the mark. We exit the theater, for example, still completely in the dark as to why Dr. Carroll dispatched his old friend a lifetime ago. And, while Larry's romantic interest in Steve gets the ball rolling, the revelation that the couple shares Kirkland's genes takes us nowhere. Even if he had a dozen sisters, the young man couldn't have killed Dr. Carroll any more completely, and Steve's not reciprocating Larry's feelings pretty much precludes other, more complex motives. And again, although the film closes with light shed on the Kirkland murder, there remains the question of all those other unfortunate owners, who found that buying the estate usually meant buying the farm, too.

John Rawlins' direction is adequate only insofar as it allows Jack Otterson's intriguing sets a few unencumbered moments in front of Milton Krasner's perceptive camera. As for the thespians, save for Constance Moore and William Lundigan, who would both go on to better things, the cast is no better than the spiritless picture warrants. Low on chills and chuckles, high on chutzpah, and profoundly unnecessary as a remake, *The Missing Guest* has nothing to offer to anyone save the completist.

The Missing Guest

Released August 12, 1938; 68 minutes

Cast: Paul Kelly (Scoop Hanlon); Constance Moore (Stephanie [Steve] Kirkland); William Lundigan (Larry Dearden); Selmer Jackson (Frank Baldrich); Edwin Stanley (Dr. Carroll); Billy Wayne (Vic); George Cooper (Jake); Patrick J. Kelly (Edwards); Florence Wix (Linda Baldrich); Harlan Briggs (Frank Kendall); Guy Usher (Inspector McDonald); Pat C. Flick (Inventor); Margo Yoder (Maid); Hooper Atchley (Business Manager); Michael Slade (Kendall's Aide); Frank McCarroll (Oscar); Leonard Sues (Office Boy); Ray Parker (Wolf); John Harmon, George Ovey (Gatekeepers); with Thomas Carr, Myrtis Crinley, Allen Fox, Billy Engle

Credits: Associate Producer — Barney A. Sarecky; Director — John Rawlins; Screenplay — Charles Martin and Paul Perez; Based on *The Secret of the Blue Room* by Erich Philippi; Film Editor — Frank Gross; Director of Photography — Milton Krasner, ASC; Art Director — Jack Otterson; Musical Director — Charles Previn; Assistant Directors — Charles Gould and Jack Bernhard; Sound Supervisor — Bernard B. Brown; Camera Operator — Maury Gertsman; Sound Mixer — Joe Lapis; Technician — Robert Pritchard

THE LAST EXPRESS (1938)

Not the last Crime Club drama, an honor that falls to *The Witness Vanishes*, but the "lost" Crime Club drama (probably as a result of legal complications), *The Last Express* is the eighth entry in what is usually touted as a series of seven motion pictures.

Based on Baynard Kendrick's novel of the same name, the film was brought to the screen with about the same ballyhoo the others received (not much), only to vanish from view soon after its first run. A pet theory is that Kendrick was apoplectic at Universal's cavalier treatment of his detective and exercised his contractual prerogative to pull the plug. This is worth a look, but everything will set more easily if we've got the plot (as outlined in Universal's copyright packet) under our belts first.

Frank Hoefle (Addison Richards), underworld chief indicted for murder by special prosecutor Paul Zarinka (Edward Raquello) returns to New York City despite the warnings of his henchmen, including Pinky (Henry Brandon) and Marshall (Al Hill). Hoefle tells his men that he has a contact planted in the district attorney's office to steal an affidavit signed by his murder victim concerning his underworld activities.

The evidence is stolen but is, in turn, hijacked from Pinky and held by unknown parties for $300,000 ransom.

Following the instructions on the ransom note, Hoefle goes to the William Barton Detective Agency, where Spud Savage (Don Brodie), a private detective, is told to take a bag containing the money and deposit it in a locker at the subway station, and then proceed to the 96th Street station.

With Duncan MacLain (Kent Taylor), another Barton detective, following him, Spud leaves the money and boards the crowded subway. On the car, a pickpocket, Eddie Miller (John Milier), lifts the locker key from Spud's pocket. MacLain follows Miller off the car, while Spud is met at the 96th Street station by Marshall. MacLain follows Miller to an apartment house and is met by two sharpers, Trilby (Samuel Lee) and Shane (Albert Shaw). He roughs his way past the two, then overpowers Miller after the latter has sent the key up a dumbwaiter.

MacLain goes up in the dumbwaiter and finds blonde Amy Arden (Dorothea Kent) in the apartment. The locker key is on the table, but Amy puts it in her bodice. Zarinka walks in, finds MacLain with Amy, and walks out angrily. Amy goes into another room and when MacLain follows her, he is knocked unconscious. When MacLain revives, Hoefle and Spud are there. Hoefle tells them to retrieve the evidence "or else," and then leaves before Assistant

THE
LAST
EXPRESS

A NEW UNIVERSAL PICTURE

Special prosecutor Paul Zarinka shoots an icy glance at the unflappable Duncan MacLain as semi-wholesome Amy Arden fidgets fetchingly in *The Last Express*. PENTAGRAM LIBRARY.

District Attorney Springer (Paul Hurst), who has been tipped off to a murder in the apartment—breaks in to find MacLain pulling up the dumbwaiter, which contains the dead body of Miller.

MacLain and Spud are taken to headquarters, questioned, and jailed, before being released and assigned to the case by the district attorney (Charles Trowbridge), who suspects Zarinka. While the two detectives are watching the subway locker, an attractive woman takes the money out of it, then disappears. MacLain tricks Trilby, who is acting as a private detective, into disclosing that his client is the chief city engineer, Howard Hewitt (Robert Emmett Keane). MacLain concludes that Hewitt suspects his wife of having an affair with Zarinka. At Zarinka's apartment, MacLain

and Spud see Springer also waiting; then they see the same woman who got the money from the locker enter the apartment house. MacLain rightly guesses that she is Mrs. Hewitt (Greta Granstedt).

Gladys Hewitt finds Amy with Zarinka, and after Amy leaves, an argument ensues, ending only when Zarinka breaks off the affair. Trilby and Shane are in the next apartment, listening through a dictaphone. Back on the street, Zarinka dismisses Springer, then drives off. Mrs. Hewitt draws a gun and shoots at him, and Zarinka's car swerves and crashes with a terrific explosion. MacLain and Spud arrive at the wreck in time to hear Zarinka's dying words: "Sea Beach subway ... last ... express." They also find on the sidewalk a cage containing two dead white mice.

THE LAST EXPRESS

A NEW UNIVERSAL PICTURE

The big denouement. The derby at which Duncan MacLain is pointing sits on the head of underworld boss Frank Hoefle. Pointing the gun at MacLain is Pinky, played by Henry (Fu Manchu) Brandon. *PENTAGRAM LIBRARY.*

In a talk with Hewitt, MacLain finds out that Zarinka questioned the engineer about subway construction. Meanwhile, Amy Arden is taken off the Sea Beach subway and arrested on suspicion of Zarinka's murder. But MacLain learns that Zarinka wasn't shot, but killed by a bomb attached to the brakes of his car. Everything points to the subways as a hiding place for the ransom money and the Hoefle evidence, but the Sea Beach subway is miles long. Knowing that Zarinka expected to return to his apartment, MacLain and Spud go there to seek evidence. Spud runs across a 1914 newspaper containing a story about New York's first underground railway, the Beach Subway, which was one block long before it was abandoned. MacLain interprets Zarinka's last words as "See Beach Subway."

While the detectives are on their way to meet the district attorney, they are shot at in the street. Pinky, Hoefle's man, is following them, so they know it was not Hoefle that planned their deaths. MacLain, Spud, the district attorney, Hewitt and Springer visit the old Beach Subway, which is entered through a regular subway tunnel. There they find the evidence and the ransom money, and MacLain is nearly killed by a train when Springer drops the evidence on the tracks. MacLain concludes that Zarinka's words, "last ... express," meant that it was not safe to enter the Beach Subway until the last express had gone by in the adjoining tunnel.

MacLain gathers all the suspects in the Barton office, then waits for Hoefle to come in and identify the one who originally stole the evidence, murdered Miller and Zarinka, and attempted to kill MacLain and Spud. But Hoefle betrays no sign, and MacLain is turning over the evidence and the money to him when the district attorney, Springer, and the police break in. Hoefle takes a swing at Springer, crying, "They may get me, but they'll get you too."

MacLain then proves that Springer was the one hired by Hoefle to steal the evidence, that he killed Miller to get the key, and that he murdered Zarinka to prevent the prosecutor's disclosing the evidence. Amy worked for Hoefle, but loved Zarinka. She tipped him off and the prosecutor had the evidence hijacked from Pinky; then Amy hit MacLain over the head and gave Zarinka the key. Mrs. Hewitt, who also loved Zarinka, picked up the money for him. Amy, who is freed from suspicion of Zarinka's murder, walks out on the arms of MacLain and Spud as Hoefle and Springer are take into custody by the district attorney.

The Last Express gave mystery buffs their first look at Baynard Kendrick's stellar creation, Duncan MacLain, and that may have been the trouble in the first place. A prolific writer, Kendrick had hit upon a winner: Duncan Maclain (lowercase l), quirky master detective. What the novelist may have perceived as being Universal's purposeful tearing out of his heart was not the minor misspelling promulgated by the scenarists — heck, it was a cause for celebration when all the actors' and technicians' names made it to the screen without error. What moved Kendrick to yank the rights to further of his renowned character's adventures — and to this movie — was the studio's complete disregard for Maclain's most interesting characteristic. In the film, Duncan MacLain would look you in the eye and call you Mary; in the novels, he was blind.

The smart money says that the outraged Kendrick, who was one of the founders of the Mystery Writers of America, threatened to take Universal in general and everyone whose name appeared on the cast and credits scroll in particular, and involve them in a lawsuit which would garner the kind of publicity that the film

could not with its newly unremarkable and flaccid hero. In lieu of legal action, the theory goes, Universal agreed to withdraw *The Last Express* from circulation, completely relinquished any and all negotiated rights to the character, and waived all future claim to Duncan MacLain or Maclain or whomever.

In the early forties, MGM approached Kendrick, looking to utilize his blind sleuth in a series of films to star Edward Arnold. Arnold was certainly no stranger to playing eccentric investigators; he had puzzled through *The Secret of the Blue Room* and *Remember Last Night?* for Universal, had doggedly trailed Peter Lorre's Raskolnikov in 1935's *Crime and Punishment*, and had created the role of Rex Stout's stout and fanatically homebound detective in *Meet Nero Wolfe* (1936). The Maclain "series" dwindled to only a couple of offerings, but the first, *Eyes in the Night* (1942), was helmed by future world-class director Fred Zinnemann (*High Noon*, *From Here to Eternity*, *A Man for All Seasons*) and became more notable in retrospect than it was during its initial release. Just for the record, the second film *The Hidden Eye* (1944), was no slouch, either.

Harrison's Reports could take *The Last Express* or leave it:

> Just a moderately entertaining program murder mystery melodrama, with comedy. In its favor is the comedy, which is good.... But the story is so muddled that it is difficult for the spectator to follow it; one has no idea how the hero gets his information to unravel the mystery, or why certain characters are mixed up in the case.

Although I'm always suspect of reviews that save the best phrases for clods like Don Brodie, the cast is another reason I'd give your eyeteeth to see *The Last Express*. Equally at home in white or black hats, adept in both ten-gallon jobs or snap-brims, Kent Taylor always had the knack for giving the heroine a look which would warm the cockles of her loins, and then, with scarcely any effort at all, adjusting his gaze at the heavy so as to freeze the marrow in his bones. Of course, his ability to look any way at anyone is what effectively killed off his Duncan MacLain as a series regular for Universal, but the fault was hardly Taylor's.

Good old Charles Trowbridge is here, a few years before achieving genre immortality as *The Mummy's Hand*'s Dr. Petrie, the original man in the wrong place at the wrong time. Just about midway between his most famous mainstream assignment (Barnaby in Laurel and Hardy's *Babes in Toyland*, 1934) and his most acclaimed genre role (the title character in Republic's 1940 serial *Drums of Fu Manchu*), is Henry Brandon. Like Karloff, Brandon's onscreen villainy belied a remarkable real-life congeniality. As noted elsewhere in this volume, Addison Richards was one of the Crime Club's keystones, and *The Last Express* would not be the popular actor's last stop in the series. Dorothea Kent, only 21 years old when *Express* was released, promised to be one of Universal's brightest ingenues, though the promise never materialized. Starting out as a lead in stuff like this in 1937, Kent was reduced to playing second banana to Deanna Durbin (*It Started with Eve*, 1941) when the doors closed on her career.

The Last Express didn't receive any more publicity than any of the "New" Universal's other mediocre programmers, but the excerpt from Vance King's review for the *Motion Picture Herald* makes one wish that some other entry in the series had been the one to slip into the cracks:

> This *Crime Club* production, for Universal release, raises itself over the entertainment levels of its predecessors in the series because of its closely-woven story, the crisp direction which sustains suspense until the final fade-out, the well adapted comedy relief in dialogue, and the craftsmanship of its players. And, as in all the predecessors, it uses the formula of bringing all suspects together at the finale for the denouement. At the preview it was evident from the audience reaction that the entertainment rating was high.

Why do only the good die young, and why do lost films always sound so much better than the stuff that manages to survive?

The Last Express

Released October 28, 1938; 63 minutes

Cast: (capsule tags from Universal's own publicity mill): Kent Taylor (Duncan MacLain: Happy-go-lucky detective, equally fearless at solving murder cases and flirting with beautiful blondes); Dorothea Kent (Amy Arden: Mystery woman who welcomed the detective's attentions by socking him over the head with a chair); Don Brodie (Spud Savage: A daring sleuth as long as he's doing the shooting, but allergic to bullets); Greta Granstedt (Gladys Hewitt: Beautiful redhead who disappeared with $300,000 in ransom money); Paul Hurst (Springer: Assistant District Attorney, an expert at nabbing the wrong suspects); Samuel Lee (Trilby: Sometimes a private detective, sometimes a crook, but a success in neither line); Albert Shaw (Shane: Trilby's mimicking sidekick, carried along merely for emphasis); Edward Raquello (Paul Zarinka: Special Prosecutor whose own affairs could stand official investigation); Robert Emmett Keane (Howard Hewitt: One jealous husband who had sound reasons for his suspicions); Charles Trowbridge (District Attorney Meredith: He had to hire private detectives because he couldn't even trust his own men); Addison Richards (Frank Hoefle: King of the underworld, whose crown got too hot to handle); with Henry Brandon (Pinky); Al Hill (Marshall); John Milier (Eddie Miller)

Credits: Producer — Irving Starr; Director — Otis Garrett; Based on the novel *The Last Express* by Baynard Kendrick; Screenplay — Edmund L. Hartmann; Photography — Stanley Cortez, ASC; Art Director — Jack Otterson; Film Editor — Maurice Wright; Sound Supervisor — Bernard B. Brown; Technician — Jess Bastian; Assistant Director — Phil Karstein; Publicity Unit Writer — George Thomas, Jr.; Costumes — Vera West. A Crime Club Production

THE LAST WARNING (1939)

The Crime Club's antepenultimate presentation, 1939's *The Last Warning* is the best of the lot in terms of sheer customer satisfaction. The mystery anthology concept had proved slow to catch on and difficult to refine, but in this, the third (and, regrettably, the last) of the adventures of Bill Crane and Doc Williams, the formula finally jelled. The tippling teammates' swan song boasts genuinely clever dialogue, a heavy with seemingly preternatural powers, unlikely characters (but likable character actors), and an adequate if not terribly puzzling mystery, all packed tightly into 63 of the fastest minutes ever to come down the pike.

John Essex (Raymond Parker) has hired detectives Bill Crane (Preston Foster) and Doc Williams (Frank Jenks) to protect him from "The Eye," a mysterious figure seeking to dun the young man for $50,000. Leaving behind their familiar New York haunts, the partners against crime head out to Essex's California mansion, where only the young man's sister, Linda (Frances Robinson), and his uncle, Major Barclay (E.E. Clive), know the men to be sleuths. The guests — Linda's "brand new fiancé" Tony Henderson (Robert Paige), aspiring actress Dawn Day (Joyce Compton), and South American beauty Carla Rodriguez (Kay Linaker) — are to be fooled into thinking that the two New Yorkers are present merely to hobnob.

Also on site is Higgs, the Cockney butler (Albert Dekker), who is throwing fortune hunter Paul Gomez (Roland Drew) off the premises just as Bill and Doc are arriving. Essex wastes no time in showing his protectors a note he has received:

> Essex,
>   You have a debt to pay. That first shot was a warning. The second won't miss.
>   The Eye

Together with "that first shot," discovering the note beside his bed at the crack of dawn has put Essex off his champagne. After flirting with Dawn and Carla in the Olympic-sized pool, Bill discovers from Linda that her brother is in hock to Steve Felson, owner of the Plantation casino, for gambling debts. Everyone plans to visit the casino later that night, and as Bill and Doc already know Felson, having run him out of New York some years earlier, the idea seems a good one. But Linda finds a note in the pocket of her beach robe:

> Linda,
>   This is my last warning. If you love your brother, get that money!
>   The Eye

333

Having been there less than 15 minutes, and having already met three girls and read two notes, Doc and Bill are summoned to meet Linda and John's uncle, Major Barclay, who, says Linda, "won't let us have a cent over our allowance." Despite Bill's reminder that not paying his debts could get John seriously killed, Barclay—late of His Majesty's 16th Punjab Regiment—refuses to part with a dime. What's more, having already caught Bill with his head in the portable bar, the pompous Brit feels little confidence in Johnny's hired men. "Calm down, Colonel," Bill advises. "Crane and Williams are on the job, and you got nothing to worry about!" "Sure," agrees Doc, "look at what we did on the Westland case. We got the killer before he killed his fifth victim!"

Pausing only to observe that Higgs is disrespectful to the major when he thinks no one is looking, the men head up to their room to dress for dinner. Showered and resplendent in their tuxes, they discover a new note intended for them on their bed in the center of the room.

Listen, coppers!
Get out while you can.
The Eye

Checking that all of the doors and windows of their room are still locked from the inside, Bill is impressed: "This guy's gonna be tough." Doc couldn't agree more: "Tough? He's a lunatic! He's so crazy he don't even know this is impossible!"

At the casino, Gomez and Major Barclay mix it up a little in the men's room, with the Major getting a punch right in his stiff upper lip. Bill elbows his way into Felson's private office after overhearing Carla put the terrified casino boss in his place with a veiled threat: "For a long time, you work for me; now maybe you like to quit, no?" Bill's presence causes Carla to transform instantly into the very picture of a polite tourist, as Felson reverts to form as a loud-mouthed thug. "I just want to find out how badly you need the money Essex owes you," Crane asks him. Having Bill thrown out of his office—Carla leaves on her own after a very pointed parting shot—Felson lights a much-needed cigarette before being plugged three times by someone standing just outside the frameline.

The shots are heard outside, of course, and pandemonium ensues. Doc, who has lost Gomez in the brouhaha, joins Bill, who has just come upon Essex; Linda, however, can't be found, and Major Barclay runs in telling of the girl's forceful abduction. With Essex at the wheel of his convertible, the partners and Tony chase the gray sedan which, says the doorman, contains the two men who slugged him, and Miss Essex! As the good guys pull close to the careering sedan, Bill lets fly at its tires with a couple of bullets. The heavies fire back, and the convertible wildly screeches off to the side of the road. Essex has not been shot, thankfully, but has passed out momentarily. "He always had a bad heart," advises Tony. The villains get away.

At breakfast, Bill announces that he had alerted the cops to the mess the night before, and Essex turns up, wide-eyed. When he awoke, he found another note, right in his hand.

Essex,
Get 50 grand in old bills, and wait for further instructions.
The Eye

The boys think that the oily Gomez has engineered the snatch to get money to finance a revolution in South America. Carla knows where Gomez is holed up, and takes Bill and Doc to his apartment. Behind a pistol, the would-be revolutionary is tough as nails; he accuses Carla of the murder of his brother, also a freedom fighter. Once disarmed by Bill and nearly skewered by a knife thrown by Carla, however, he's a bit more compliant, but not terribly helpful. He knows *nada* about Linda's situation.

On the stairwell outside the apartment, the detectives' plan of action takes a much-needed step

Doc: Well, Brains, what do we do now?"
Bill: We walk to the nearest bar and get a drink.
Doc: Well, why walk? Let's run!

Linda Essex restrains Tony Henderson's mighty arm in *The Last Warning*; Bill Crane appears grateful. PENTAGRAM LIBRARY.

This maneuver is their most successful to date. Over lots of scotch, they register the fact that Carla once worked for the Secret Service, and that Higgs, the bullying lout of a butler, is observing them at this very moment.

The next morning, Doc has recovered enough from Higgs' outrage the night before to flirt a bit with Dawn, who is seated in one of the estate's arboreal dells and is practicing her lines as Scarlett O'Hara, just in case the worldwide search for the actress to play the belle should ever reach her. For the first time in three films, it appears that Doc's line of baloney is getting him somewhere with a woman until a pair of men shooting semi-automatic rifles at some quail chase him and Dawn from the spot. More's the pity that Doc doesn't catch a glimpse of Linda Essex, peer-ing worriedly from a window in the shack behind those men.

Bill's attempt at getting to know Carla better at poolside is also interrupted, but by the wildly drunken John Essex's fall into the pool. The lady and the detective set a date for a later hour and, at the stroke of 12:20 AM, Bill is knocking on her door. Carla's wide-eyed damsel in distress routine doesn't cut it with the skeptical Crane: "Secret Service, political murderer, knife-thrower, racketeer — now what?" As she's busy spilling the beans, a noise in the bathroom demands the attention of Bill and his gun. When he returns to the bedroom, he finds that, rather ironically, Carla has been knifed, while the doors and windows to her suite remain locked from the inside. Rushing into the hall, he bellows a

The LAST WARNING

A New Universal Picture

Major Barclay (E.E. Clive) scowls with disapproval at the goings-on at his phone. What do you expect of a man who keeps a framed portrait of himself on his desk? *PENTAGRAM LIBRARY.*

stentorian "Doc!" that is enough to rouse the household.

Bill rushes down the main staircase and out the front door, passing an imperturbable Higgs, a quizzical Major Barclay, and a severely unsteady John Essex. In Bill's absence, Doc entertains the local constabulary and presents them with the note that was affixed by the stiletto to Carla's lovely back.

> Essex,
> Wrap the money in a waterproof package and take it to the bridge foundation on the south side of San Barto creek. Place the package on the shelf of the center piling at 10:30 tonight. No tricks or police if you want to see your sister.
> The Eye

Another noise in the bathroom sends everyone packing therein, and, when they return, Doc finds a note where there was no note moments earlier:

> You poor, dumb, two-for-a-nickel suckers:
> Guess how this note got here.
> The near-sighted Eye

Crane drops from a ventilation duct opening in the ceiling, having demonstrated how mysterious notes could be left and assassinations affected through the use of the pruning stick the sleuth has found outside on the grounds. "I even found the typewriter up here The Eye's been using." Bill has narrowed it down: The Eye "has to be someone who could stab Carla and replace the pruning stick before

I could get to the gardener's shed." While that may be so, John Essex decides to go ahead with the ransom payment. He receives no argument from the chastened Major Barclay. With Higgs providing a waterproof cardboard box, Essex packs up the cash and, followed by Bill and Doc, makes for the pilings.

After the young heir has planted the money, the two detectives settle in for a long night. Having been perched in a tree for hours, Doc has his partner investigate a suspicious movement in the bush. Bill finds the action was due to a skunk, but that's not all that smells: The money is gone, and there are no footprints on the sandy reaches under the bridge. The only clue is a torn piece of cardboard, bearing the letters LIFO. Red-faced and Eye-less, Bill and Doc return to Essex Manor. "You've bungled this job ever since you've been here," Essex snarls. "If The Eye saw you, he'll never return Linda. You're fired! Now pack up and get out!"

The cops move in *en masse*. While the partners are packing, Doc's tale of the "hunters" with "semi-automatic rifles" finally gets through Bill's thick skull. Out in their car they go, with Bill confident they'll run into Linda any minute now. Son of a gun if Linda isn't wandering around on the darkened road! Back at the house, Bill fires a couple of shots into the air in order to alert the cops by the bridge. When the gunfire is returned, Doc rushes outside and nabs Major Barclay, who naturally has a cock and bull story explaining his actions. Back to the house come the police, Essex, and Tony. Bill is now in his element.

Despite Doc's beliefs, Major Barclay is not The Eye. The major was cashiered from the 16th Punjab regiment for continued cowardice in action and Higgs, who was his orderly in India, has been blackmailing Barclay for a job ever since. The whole kidnapping was a hoax; Linda agreed to go along with her brother's idea in order to use the "ransom" money to pay off Felson. Essex, however, killed Felson and Carla and kept the money, which he still has on him in a money belt. Essex never put it under the bridge, but secreted it on his person, having torn up and disposed of the CaLIFOrnia Prune box — all save for the fragment Bill

found. Essex "murdered Felson to get back his IOU's, but Felson didn't have them." Bill summarizes, "The real gambling boss was Carla, and she demanded payment. So, after one murder, the second came easy. I showed you how he killed her with the pruning stick." An attempt at making a break for it goes nowhere, and the murderer is led away to justice. Happiness reigns, and Doc snuggles up to Dawn. Nevertheless, before the couple can sneak off together, Bill "finds" a note in Doc's pocket:

> Dear Doc,
>   Don't look now, but somebody's running off with your girl. You can trust me
>   In a pig's eye!

No explanation, I think, is necessary.

Come 1942, the studio's fog machine would begin dampening the brogues of Basil Rathbone and Nigel Bruce, but I assume the not-too-distant arrival of a far more renowned team of sleuths had nothing to do with the sudden departure of Bill Crane and Doc Williams.

It had taken three episodes in release to cement the team in the public's consciousness; by *The Last Warning*, audiences had come to expect the partners' give and take, their occasional need for a pick-me-up, and Bill's assuming the top spot in unraveling the puzzle in the closing reel. Despite Frank Jenks' perceived subordinate status (Preston Foster was still, by far, the bigger name of the two), with *Warning* the men shared the action and the wisecracks more or less equally. By now, the characters had been established as refreshingly fallible; following a drubbing by Higgs, for example, Doc moans to his partner how the pugnacious butler obviously hadn't heard how the detective was supposed to win!

Why did such a winning combination — the Bill and Doc entries came to be among the highest grossers of the series — up and disappear? The Crime Club lost its appeal for Universal with the resurgence of interest in the horror film, and someone (the buck always stopped with Charles Rogers) failed to discriminate between the series as a whole and the subseries within it. It's a safe bet that the studio could have come to terms with Jonathan Latimer for rights to the team and other of their published adventures apart from the Crime Club publishing empire. If push came to shove and the organization refused to relinquish novels already in print, Universal's scenario department could always have fabricated treatments around the characters. (However, this practice always contained the seeds of its own peril. The experience of *The Last Express* demonstrates how the studio's crackerjack writers could take a proven literary commodity and screw it into the ground.)

Nonetheless, in relegating its mystery series to the scrap heap, Universal had thrown out the baby with the bath water. Perhaps the production chief had been unable to appreciate the sleuths' readily identifiable charms. William K. Everson, as always, put the matter succinctly in his *The Detective in Film*:

> In Bill Crane, writer Jonathan Latimer created a cynical and liquor-fancying detective who, especially in his sleazy clients, seemed to predate Philip Marlowe.... On film Crane was a little more conventional, but the plots were intelligently worked out and the casts above average. However, since Preston Foster made so many crime "B"s in that period — either as official detective, private eye, or newspaper reporter turned amateur sleuth — at both Universal and Fox, it was difficult for the Crane series to retain much of an identity of its own [p. 222].

Notwithstanding Foster and Jenks, the cast of *The Last Warning* is wildly uneven. While Bill and Doc have a ball with the material, Kay Linaker's Carla Rodriguez is a mixed bag. Her "Spanish" accent fades in and out (at first, you figure she's leveling with Bill and is dropping all facades; second time, though, there is no rationale), and she switches from femme fatale to ungainly virago almost with the breeze. Granted, the woman's a sideshow unto herself — knife-thrower, political murderer, etc.— but the feeling one comes away with is less that Carla has a many-sided personality than that Kay doesn't have a grip on the role.

Joyce Compton as semi-airhead Dawn Day does a more competent job than Linaker but she's playing a one-dimensional character. Frances Robinson's Linda is adequate in her brief scenes; Raymond Parker as brother John, however, is way over his head in both goods and delivery. Even with his supposedly righteous indignation showing, Parker seems such a pantywaist that you can't believe he could summon the nerve to raise his voice, let alone kill two people. Not for a second is his poolside "drunk" scene believable, nor is it amusing.

The two veterans of His Majesty's 16th Punjab Regiment almost conspire to walk out the door sideways with the picture between them. Albert Dekker's Sgt. Hibbs is alternately ominous and comical, with an added dash of low-class brazenness. He gets away with confessing that "Personally now, Oy loik the Major!" while blackmailing the older man over his cowardice in action; this takes a special kind of two-edged credibility which Dekker has in spades. A lesser actor might have found it difficult to switch hats with such facility or panache.

Definitely up there in the top ten targets for vintage genre impersonators (along with Karloff and Lugosi) is E.E. Clive. From the moment PC Jaffers opened his walrus-mustache-festooned mouth in *The Invisible Man* (1933), a distinct and hitherto unimagined veneer of pompous officiousness coated the fascinated audiences via a slow drizzle of painstakingly precise, plum-shaped tones. Clive's motion picture career would last only for another seven years until the actor died in 1940, but his unique take on bureaucrats, law enforcement officers, appointed *or* elected minor officials, judicial types, and hucksters would be considered among the high points of over 75 films. While roles the size of Major Barclay were much more the exception than the rule, as Clive specialized in cameo-sized displays of eccentricity and appeared in a good number of unbilled bits, a little of the actor went a long way.

The Last Warning's Major Barclay was somewhat unusual for the British expatriate. Far more grimly strait-laced than the figures

Clive usually impersonated, Barclay is a coward, a bully, a liar, and, most likely, an embezzler. I don't know whether the business about the Punjab regiment was added by the studio to accommodate the casting of the popular Clive, or whether the acutely English character man was thrust into circumstances held to be unalterable by Latimer's novel. In either instance, although undeniably welcome, Clive and his vocal affectations are as out of place in this tale of South American Secret Service persons and California prune boxes as Gabby Hayes would be in a musical remake of *Tea and Sympathy*. Yet, despite this, it's practically impossible to take your eyes from the quintessential British curmudgeon, as he manages to accomplish with an uplifted eyebrow what all the Raymond Parkers and Kay Linakers in this world could not do with a John Philip Sousa march and a keg of gunpowder.

Most of the fun in the movie is to be had watching the two American semi–con men joust with their scurrilous opposites from the U.K. The entire scene wherein Bill and Doc first meet the Major and then interact with Higgs is a wonderful study in contrasts: Bill and Doc conspire to aggravate the old boy through underplaying (for them) their hand, while Barclay's anger and disbelief mount to the point of apoplexy. Of course, no one ever came close to reaching apoplexy in such measured increments as E.E. Clive, and in the moment he needs to steady his boat, the boys are matching long vowels with the gentility-challenged Higgs. The give and take continues as Higgs drops all pretense to social status when he demands that the major tell him what the two new guests are up to, and then almost successfully reverses himself again to deal with further hazing from Bill and Doc. Such acrobatics may not follow the Stanislavsky method, but they do add up to a delightful few minutes.

As with *The Westland Case*, *The Black Doll*, and *The Witness Vanishes*, *The Last Warning* goes in to the three-quarter turn with a quasi-inexplicable element to ponder: How does The Eye manage to deliver his voluminous correspondence to rooms which are locked from the inside? And, likewise, how could Carla be done in behind Bill Crane's back, when both were in a similarly locked room? The solution proved to be as mundane in this instance as it had been in the other three titles mentioned above, but the rundown indicates that fully half of the Crime Club features had some kind of hook—*possibly supernatural*—which was used to catch any errant fans of horror film who were still cruising for thrills, just below the surface of the mainstream.

The Last Warning

Released January 6, 1939; 63 minutes

Cast: Preston Foster (Bill Crane); Frank Jenks (Doc Williams); Kay Linaker (Carla Rodriguez); E.E. Clive (Major Barclay); Albert Dekker (Higgs); Raymond Parker (John Essex); Frances Robinson (Linda Essex); Joyce Compton (Dawn Day); Roland Drew (Paul Gomez); Robert Paige (Tony Henderson); Orville Caldwell (Wilson); Glen Wilenchick (Slocumbe); with Richard Lane

Credits: Producer—Irving Starr; Director—Al Rogell; Based on the novel *The Dead Don't Care* by Jonathan Latimer; Screenplay—Edmund L. Hartmann; Director of Photography—George Meehan, ASC; Film Editor—Maurice Wright; Art Director—Jack Otterson; Associate Art Director—Charles H. Clarke; Musical Director—Charles Previn; Sound Supervisor—Bernard B. Brown; Technician—Robert Pritchard; Gowns—Vera West; Production Manager—Ben Hersh. A Crime Club Production

SON OF FRANKENSTEIN (1939)

Whereas *Frankenstein* had materialized in *Dracula*'s profit-making wake, and *Bride of Frankenstein* had capitalized on its predecessor's popularity and financial return, 1939's *Son of Frankenstein* traced its genesis to a neighborhood movie house's last-ditch attempt at staving off bankruptcy. In late summer 1938, Los Angeles' Regina Theater was as close to shutting its doors forever as it had ever been when its manager, desperate for bottoms in his seats, leased inexpensive prints of *Frankenstein*, *Dracula*, and *Son of Kong*. Hoping to entice monster movie fans, bargain hunters, and anyone looking to get in out of the rain, that nameless entrepreneur almost singlehandedly jumpstarted the "Silver Age" of horror films. The triple-feature revival broke all house records and sent Universal a wake-up call it wouldn't forget. Lurid new trailers paved the way for brand-new prints, as the two early-thirties war horses returned with a vengeance. By gum, there still *was* "gold in them thar thrills!" What to do next?

No one would have had to ask the Laemmles what to do next. Uncle Carl may not have cared much for horror films, but he had been quite capable, thank you, of taking the pulse of the average audience. It had been Junior's job to make sure that the family business was providing enough of a "quality product"—and that included horror pictures—to hold its own with the big boys. But then, Universal had basically invented monster movies; what *was* there to ask?

How about, where were the Laemmles now that we needed them?

Gone. Junior may have been the compulsive gambler, but it was Uncle Carl who lost the big bet. In November 1935, Universal had been more than normally strapped for cash. Trying to keep up with the cinematic Joneses, Junior had been okaying expenditures and approving budgets that the incoming revenues couldn't cover. *Sutter's Gold*, for example, a prestige "A" biography released that very year, didn't come close to covering its own costs, let alone offering financial relief from some other turkeys. The usual belt-tightening measures wouldn't cut it; there were only so many non–Laemmles to lay off. Fedora in hand, Uncle Carl approached a financial syndicate headed by Charles Rogers and J. Cheever Crowdin and cut what he thought was a good deal.

As security against $750,000 in cash, Laemmle offered Universal's entire up-and-coming slate and controlling interest in the studio; terms included a codicil on buying out current ownership within a specified time. Risky? Sure, but Uncle Carl had his ace relief man, James Whale, warming up with *Show Boat*, and there were a number of other productions on the hopper which, if not genuine blockbusters, would turn a bit of a profit and help retrieve the note. But even the best laid schemes of mice and moguls occasionally gang a-gley, and on March 14, 1936, Rogers and Crowdin exercised their option and took over control of the company Laemmle had started almost a quarter-century before. At the new Universal, financier Crowdin would ensure that there were no more impossible budgets, while film man Rogers would make sure that all new productions reflected an acceptable quality for the money. Horror pictures were struck from the menu; the blue plate special for some time to come would be that wholesome young warbler, Deanna Durbin.

Miss Durbin did as much to keep the New Universal solvent at the end of the decade as Abbott and Costello would a half-dozen years later. The young singer's appealing personality and undeniable talent brought audiences to the theaters again and again, but she received little support from the mediocre efforts being ground out under Charles Rogers' austerity plan. Appalled by the financial reports and depressed by the stream of dreck that complemented Miss Durbin's regular successes, the stockholders reacted, and for the second time in as many years, there was a corporate shake-up. Imported from RKO were Nate J. Blumberg and Cliff Work, who replaced nominal president Robert H. Cochrane and Rogers, respectively. By 1941, the new team would dramatically reverse the company's fortunes, converting a million dollar loss into a $2.4 million profit. Much of the welcome cash would come from horror pictures, and those horror pictures owed a great debt to *Son of Frankenstein*.

There was very little controversy this time around as to whom the title concerned, since the Monster had blasted his "bride" to kingdom come in the earlier film and remained only a shadow of his former self. The titular son is Wolf von Frankenstein (Basil Rathbone), whose presence is evidence that his father finally married Elizabeth, and whose high-

strung temperament is proof of the theory of genetic heredity. Returning to his ancestral home with Wolf are his charming wife, Elsa (Josephine Hutchinson), and his precocious son, Peter (Donnie Dunagan). In whatever time has passed since Wolf left home, the village has been renamed (from Goldstadt to Frankenstein). Universal's insistence on rendering vague both the locale(s) and the date(s) in question still holds fast; there aren't many tangible clues as to precisely where or when we are.

This policy of refusing to pin down the unfolding of the Frankenstein saga either chronologically or geographically does have its charms. While the films have long lost their capacity to frighten anyone other than very small children, happily that loss has been more than offset by their acquisition of a patina of cultural respectability. As Tom Weaver has suggested, they have been readily accepted into the world of fairy tales, with the Monster and sundry of his classical horrific compeers taking their places alongside such childhood mainstays as the Giant from *Jack and the Beanstalk* and the Evil Queen from *Snow White*. Although surely not the intention of the original filmmakers, the hazy mist which surrounds the Frankenstein canon makes this transition a piece of cake; how better to start a fairy tale than with "Once upon a time..."?

The vagaries of time and space also conspire to create a dimension which contains recognizable elements while still being removed from reality. The array of names and titles, the prevailing architectural style, and those ludicrous comic-opera costumes worn by the townspeople all serve to position the goings-on somewhere in Teutonic Central Europe. The vintage costumes and a singular lack of motorized technology seem to indicate that the first two films in the ongoing saga take place at the end of the nineteenth or on the cusp of the twentieth century. (As modern clothing is worn by that crowd of giggling medical students at Dr. Waldman's lecture, apparently only the *hoi polloi* are too busy playing the accordion, dancing in circles, and quaffing the local brew to get decent jobs and dress better.)

"Of course, when we give supper parties, we use the *big* dining room." Those shadows on the wall in the made-over Frankenstein castle must come from the largest venetian blinds in the world. *JOHN PARNUM.*

The von Frankensteins blow into town on a train, however, and are whisked to the castle in a beauty of a touring car. When taken together with Wolf's age (perhaps 40), the style of the car puts us around the mid–1930s. Continuing the logical progression from this point, however, is not recommended. The peregrinations of the Monster will soon involve Henry's other son, Ludwig, his granddaughter Elsa, and a number of brilliant scientists who are a brick or two short of a full hod. As most of the action remains confined within rather narrow geographical boundaries, were the time frame not purposefully left obscure, one of the latter titles

in the series would have to be *Frankenstein Meets the Luftwaffe.*

Another discrepancy to which we should turn a blind eye is the shape-shifting propensity of the Château/Castle Frankenstein. Having pulled double duty in the original film (wherein its intriguing angles and internal flying buttresses also served as home to poor-little-rich-girl Elizabeth), the mansion totally metamorphoses in *Bride*; only vaguely glimpsed from without, its interior has been reshuffled to attain cavernous proportions. The one fixed point in this rapidly changing locale, however, is the old watchtower, which

Frankenstein uses as his base of operations in both Whale films. (A scripted *faux pas* falls from Frederick Kerr's lips when, in a scene in the 1931 original, the crusty old Baron wonders why his son is "messing around a ruined old windmill," foreshadowing the climactic battle-ground, but giving the lie to Henry's own words.) We are given to understand that the crumbling structure is situated some distance from the highly unstable contours of the Château.

In *Son of Frankenstein*, the venerable family manse, once replete with stodgy pseudo-Victorian wallpaper and conventional if enormous rooms, is now a faded medieval fortress. Entering through the oversized portals, one moves into a grand hall which, even in broad daylight (and the daylight never gets *too* broad hereabouts) casts ominous shadows through twisting staircases which must ultimately lead upstairs, although only God knows how.

(Art director Jack Otterson's sets are magnificent, giving the best that *Das Kabinett des Dr. Caligari* could offer a close race to the finish.) The twisted corridors do more than indicate the film's roots in German Expressionism, though; they mirror the perverse turn the fortunes of the house of Frankenstein have taken due to the bent of its most notorious member. As for the desolate watchtower-laboratory: another miracle. Reduced to rubble (via a splendid miniature) in the closing moments of *Bride*, the laboratory has now reappeared on the grounds adjacent to Wolf's castle, and save for the loss of its roof and its original shape, seems none the worse for wear. In its abrupt move from the other side of town, in fact, the edifice has also acquired a bubbling sulfur pit (dating back to the Roman Empire!) and an adjunct to the family crypt.

It is within this crypt that Wolf is let in for a surprise: the Frankenstein Monster, lying dormant atop a stone sarcophagus like some *alto-rilievo* sculpted nobleman. (The audience receives a second jolt moments later when it is revealed that Wolf's dad was christened "Heinrich von Frankenstein.") The shock value of the first disclosure (despite a wonderfully dramatic, almost regal, backwards tracking shot)

is dubious, however, as the inevitable appearance of the Monster in the proceedings is never in doubt, and the second revelation is really more a matter of pretentiousness or disregard than an object of concern. A beaut of a surprise, though, and one that is warmly welcomed and will be ever celebrated, is the identity of the now-requisite secondary villain. His prominent features completely altered by masterful makeup and his distinctive voice artfully disguised, Bela Lugosi has a field day as that scoundrel of a shepherd whom the townspeople would just love to hang (again): crafty old Ygor.

Bela does such a grand job with Ygor ("God, he was cute," the Hungarian actor would later crow of his shaggy alter-ego), that it's totally unfair to refer to the broken-necked catalyst as a secondary anything. Having submitted daily to four hours of Jack Pierce's prosthetics, yak hair, putty, and self-satisfied smirks, Bela would head out onto the set and steal the show. With Karloff's baby reduced to henchman status, for it is the Monster and not Ygor who is the sidekick in the ghastly pair, and with Basil Rathbone's basically one-note character courting hysteria for the bulk of the running time, the frequently underestimated Lugosi took stock of the situation, consulted his artistic palette, and acted his way to the top.

Sharing the above-the-title billing with Boris and Basil (partial compensation for the financial screwing Universal was giving him), Bela makes it clear that, in terms of caring for the Monster, protecting him from treachery, and insisting upon his receiving the required pseudo-scientific/medical treatment, it is Ygor who is the proper son of Frankenstein. Hence, having triumphed over the malice of the studio bosses who insisted that his part be shot within a week's time and a sketchily conceived part (director Rowland V. Lee had chucked the approved script and — where Lugosi was concerned, at any rate — winged it), by dint of his bravura portrayal, Bela was once again the big cheese.

A surprise of a different sort was the absence of James Whale. Although the director's emphatic refusal to do sequels was a matter of

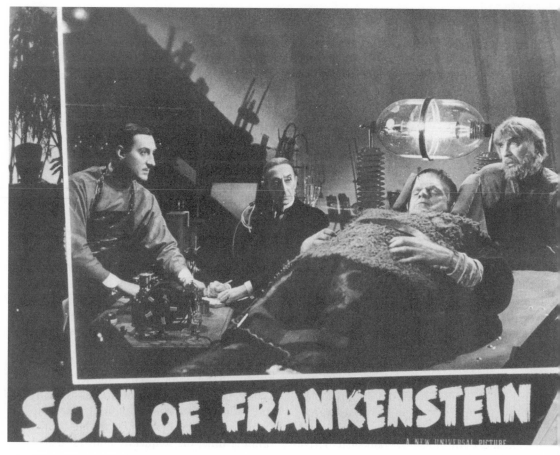

He may have been billed third and paid least, but Bela Lugosi landed where he belonged in *Son of Franken-stein*— at the head of the table. *AUTHOR'S COLLECTION.*

record, he had made an exception with the offbeat *Bride of Frankenstein*. According to his chief biographer, James Curtis, following the less than stupendous opening of *The Road Back* (Universal's antiwar follow-up to *All Quiet on the Western Front*) and an out-and-out bomb (*The Great Garrick*) at Warner Bros., Whale was in no position to pick and choose. Why didn't he take *Son of Frankenstein*? Most likely, because it was never offered to him. Instead, the former favorite son was assigned to two "punishment pictures": *Sinners in Paradise*, hokum about air-crash survivors on an un-charted island, and *Suspicion*, a quasi-remake of Whale's own *The Kiss Before the Mirror*. This latter film, retitled *Wives Under Suspicion*, hit (but scarcely dented) the screens while *Son of Frankenstein* was in preproduction. For all this,

I share Curtis's opinion that the haughty direc-tor would have nixed the second sequel even had it been presented on a silver platter. Hav-ing not only cut the path but having plowed it in the sequel, Whale would have undoubtedly regarded the third trip as having nothing to offer save ennui.

As he had in both of the earlier films, Boris Karloff groused about a facet of the Monster's persona which he felt didn't fit in with the orig-inal concept. This time around, he found fault with the giant's clothing. Gone was the black suit which the Monster had worn from the day after his creation to the scenes of both of his violent demises, and in its place was a shape-less woolly vest-like garment which covered what appeared to be a sweatshirt. The black suit, argued the Briton, was part and parcel of the icon; it ought to be as indestructible as the Monster himself. Given the fact that Dracula's starched collar was never seen to wilt, nor his trousers to bag at the knees despite countless metamorphoses and graceless maneuverings in and out of caskets, it would seem only fair that the sartorially challenged Monster be allowed his one good suit.

There was more to Karloff's lament this time, though, than just "furs and muck." The actor had determined that this was to be his swan song as the Monster; he was hanging up his neck bolts for good. An intelligent and articulate man — the diametric opposite of many of the bogeys he had created — Karloff was aware of the inherent constraints of the character. The Monster's hole card had always been his awesome physical presence. Unbridled strength, unpredictable behavior, unnatural stamina: There were a sheaf of "uns" that went into making him the frightening yet fascinating figure that he was. After his initial appearance upon any scene, however, the Monster could hold one's interest only by virtue of his reactions to other characters or situations. Karloff appreciated the fact that the Monster's limited intellect precluded him from initiating anything other than simple (and thus quickly repetitious) physical actions; so far as the actor was concerned, this was the handwriting on the wall. If there were to be additional "chapters" in the saga of the Monster (and the returns on *Son* assured that there would be), there would have to be a succession of geniuses (misguided or just downright evil) to provide motivation for him and to get the melodramatic ball rolling.

Karloff's farewell performance is clearly not the equal of his two earlier portrayals, but despite the opinion of many, this is not due to the absence of the patented Whale imagination. With this his third appearance in his trademark role, the savvy actor needed no one's advice on the niceties of monster behavior. Nor was the script unable to take the heat because, essentially, there was no script. In his effort to make Bela Lugosi's part more substantial (and to stick it to those front office "God-damned sons of bitches" who had cut the Hungarian's

traditional salary in half), Rowland Lee jettisoned Willis Cooper's original screenplay, and in the now-necessary process of on-site plot development, had relegated Karloff's Monster to playing a subsidiary role. Willis Cooper would still receive onscreen credit for his work, but he must have been hard put to recognize the surviving elements.

Time and James Whale's sense of the absurd had taken their toll, and a couple of changes were wrought to compensate. The Monster was mute once again, as Karloff had persuaded Rowland Lee that speech had not made the giant figure more human, only less formidable. And since the actor had filled out somewhat since the days of *Bride*, Jack Pierce crafted a larger headpiece in order to maintain his cadaverous facial lines.

Another change proved to be more subtle but more distressing. No longer driven by his own autonomy, the Monster in *Son* exhibits fewer truly human traits; his pathetic devotion to his rascally friend and his heartrending cry of remorse upon finding Ygor's lifeless body stand out amid the series of reactive moves that comprise the role as filmed. It was the curtailing of this humanity which finally moved Karloff to resign his commission. It would be the lack of this humanity which, among other things, would separate the definitive Monster from any and all of his subsequent incarnations.

An earlier comment concerning Basil Rathbone's "one-note character" demands modification; it would be grossly unfair to allow Boris Karloff consideration for the scriptless chaos and not afford Rathbone the same. The dashing, top-billed actor had become, of late, one of the cinema's great "elegant" villains, while also demonstrating a flair for meaty character parts (such as his Oscar-nominated performance as the eccentric Louis XI in Paramount's *If I Were King*). Just prior to signing on as Wolf von Frankenstein, the aquiline leading man had won superlative notices as Major Brand in Warner Bros.' remake of *The Dawn Patrol*. It's obvious, then, that the dramatic baggage Rathbone brought with him to Universal in late 1938 included a facility with over-the-top performances, geared to grabbing complacent viewers by their lapels and shaking some life into them.

Rathbone's paterfamilias in *Son of Frankenstein* is yet another of these performances. The part of Wolf demands an actor who can dash madly among locations while demonstrably shifting emotional gears, and whose range of expression must allow him to maintain a more or less even front while hiding nothing from the viewer, a good deal from the wily Inspector Krogh, and virtually everything from his wife. As whipped up on the spot ("as a housewife would whip up an omelet!") by Lee et al., Wolf is a role whose "comfort level" borders on hysteria and whose impersonator must be equal to the task. Rathbone performs magnificently and infuses Wolf's every statement with a nigh-irrepressible energy. Whether persuading the ambivalent Elsa that there's more to their future than dead trees and desolation, braving the rain and the chilly reception to express his personal (if naïve) opinions, or snarling desperate lies between clenched teeth, Frankenstein is incapable of operating at less than a fever pitch. Only in this sense can Basil Rathbone's bravura portrayal of the edgy Wolf be characterized as "one-note."

Lionel Atwill enjoyed some good lines and some better notices in conjunction with the first genre film he'd worked on at Universal since 1933's *Secret of the Blue Room*. Krogh would be the largest and most bizarre of the roles he would play opposite future Monsters, and his pained recollection of his childhood meeting with the current Monster not only takes the haughty Wolf down a peg, but makes his steely resolve to end the charade perfectly understandable:

> KROGH: I was but a child at the time — about the age of your own son, Herr Baron. The Monster had escaped and was ravaging the countryside — killing, maiming, terrorizing. One night he burst into our house. My father took a gun and fired at him, but the savage brute sent him crashing into a corner. Then he grabbed me by the arm. One doesn't easily forget, Herr Baron, an arm torn out by the roots.

If Krogh invests the speech with enough self-satisfaction to make a Jehovah's Witness cringe, he likewise has the grace to accept Wolf's apologetic stroke moments later, when little Peter has put his young foot in it:

> KROGH: I only have one real arm. This one isn't mine.
> PETER: Well, whose is it?
> WOLF: You see, Inspector Krogh lost his other real arm in the war. He's a soldier.
> PETER: Oh? Are you a general?
> WOLF: No. He's something more than a general. He's an Inspector.

Atwill had spent over 20 years in films prior to *Son of Frankenstein* and had had more than his share of parts through which he could run on automatic pilot. Krogh was not one of these; actually, "Pinky" had to monitor the false-arm business extremely carefully to keep it from stealing the more legitimate thunder from the portrayal. (The ease with which shtick can usurp reality — no matter how tenuous that reality is — can be seen in Kenneth Mars' dead-on imitation of Atwill/Krogh in the aforementioned silly treasure, *Young Frankenstein*.) Inspector Krogh is also a one-note character: he is singlemindedly attentive to his duty and genuinely possessed with a concern for his charges. Whereas much of Wolf's fiery rhetoric is bravado, Krogh stands coldly and implacably behind his statements; the several scenes the erstwhile chums share add a psychological power that balances the more conventional contrast between obvious heroes and equally obvious villains. The test of both men's mettle — the confrontation with the Monster at the brink of that peculiar sulfur pit — finds them equally worthy, with the frantic Frankenstein placing himself at risk as never before to rescue his son and Krogh reliving the most traumatic experience of his life, yet firing away even while confronted by the sight of the Monster brandishing his false arm.

Josephine Hutchinson has gone on record

931-10

Wolf von Frankenstein may be the titular master of the house, but Ygor knows where the bodies are buried. *John Parnum.*

(with Greg Mank) as stating that "doing a Frankenstein is kind of a phony bit." The lovely actress could hardly have thought that it would be for the "phony bit" that she would be best remembered. By far the least of the three Karloff Frankenstein heroines — she doesn't confront the Monster once — Hutchinson adds a realistic albeit mundane touch to the proceedings. Available whenever Wolf needs a squeeze or Krogh a kind word, her most dramatic scene involves some hyperventilating when informed that Peter's been taken from his room. A classic screamer she's not.

Son of Frankenstein is the last of the "epic" Frankenstein movies, and "epic" describes it to a tee. Grand in scale, costing some $420,000 (as compared to an original estimate of $250,000), and grand in execution, Rowland V. Lee's 94-minute summation was met with enthusiasm, joy, and not a little relief. The New Universal had broken the ice a second time with a classic party, involving almost every resident bogey of Tinseltown, wherein no expense had been spared and all stops had been pulled. For the third time, the Frankenstein Monster had demonstrated that his baleful presence could guarantee an impressive number of occupied seats in participating theaters; presumably, this would happen again (and again, and again).

Even without Karloff, the Frankenstein saga would continue. The Monster would gradually lose his humanity, moving from little real personality to none, but the series' attendant sound and fury (and "guest stars") would briefly compensate. The "monster rallies" would not be an indictment of Frankenstein's Monster, any more than they would be accusations of inadequacy leveled at Dracula or the Wolf Man; entertainment value apart, they would be testaments to the regrettable creative stagnation of Universal's (and everybody else's) scenario department, as well as to the growing cynicism and impatience of 1940s America. The pervasive spirit of innocence, so necessary to appreciate the Monster's childlike guilelessness, and the naïveté that had been required to follow the movies' simplistic

morals were lost as the world fragmented and fought.

Already germinating in 1939 were the seeds of a global paranoia which, a decade or so later, would emerge from a tainted earth in all its malformed, mutated glory. The Universal of the fifties, as anxious to discern the financial pulse of the contemporary American public as its founder had been decades earlier, would abandon its classic monsters for a series of gargantuan arachnids, insects, and crystals. The humanity the studio's horrors had sought to emulate in the thirties would be replaced by the humanity it would seek to intimidate. Having virtually created the popular representations of Frankenstein, Dracula, the Mummy, and others, Universal would soon share a rather cramped seat with the crude monstrosities of its domestic competitors and the garish trend-resetting of England's Hammer studios.

But that's another story altogether.

Son of Frankenstein

Released January 13, 1939; 94 minutes

Cast: Basil Rathbone (Baron Wolf von Frankenstein); Boris Karloff (The Monster); Bela Lugosi (Ygor); Lionel Atwill (Inspector Krogh); Josephine Hutchinson (Baroness Elsa von Frankenstein); Donnie Dunagan (Peter); Emma Dunn (Amelia); Edgar Norton (Benson); Perry Ivins (Fritz); Lawrence Grant (Burgomeister); Michael Mark (Ewald Neumüller); Lionel Belmore (Emil Lang); Gustav von Seyffertitz, Lorimer Johnson, Tom Ricketts (Burghers); Caroline Cooke (Frau Neumüller); Clarence Wilson (Dr. Berger); Ward Bond, Harry Cording (Policemen at the Gate); Bud Wolfe (Double for Karloff); with Betty Chay, Jack Harris

Credits: Producer and Director — Rowland V. Lee; Original Screenplay — Willis Cooper; Suggested by the novel *Frankenstein; or, The Modern Prometheus* by Mary Wollstonecraft Shelley; Director of Photography — George Robinson; Film Editor — Ted Kent; Assistant Director — Fred Frank; Art Director — Jack Otterson; Associate Art Director — Richard H. Reidel; Musical Score — Frank Skinner; Musical Director — Charles Previn;

Musical Arrangements — Hans J. Salter; Special Photographic Effects — John P. Fulton; Set Decorator — Russell A. Gausman; Sound Director — Bernard B. Brown; Technician — William Hedgcock; Makeup — Jack P. Pierce; Gowns — Vera West

MYSTERY OF
THE WHITE ROOM (1939)

Consider, if you will, the pervasive presence of the doctor in the genre during the thirties and forties. Although frequently overshadowed by the monster he's created, the vampire he's destroyed, or the maniacal fiend whose patterns he's studied, Doctor — embodies the knowledge and authority to overcome whatever scourge of God the picture's title may be promoting. The Doctor may be a trifle misguided, overzealous, paranoid, pigheaded, or offensive, but these are forgivable lapses, due to temporary setbacks, dead-end experiments, constant interruptions, disappointments, and betrayals; soon he will again demonstrate that he is canny, tireless, intuitive, resilient, and dedicated.

Occasionally, he might even be a physician.

Universal was hardly the only purveyor of mayhem to front-load its movies with practitioners of some esoteric science or other or with occupants of the lunatic fringe, and call them "doctor," but a quick flip through these pages will certainly leave that impression. For every pipe-smoking "doc" of a country medico, there are a half-dozen quirky nerve-bundles who "studied at University" long enough to establish a reputation for being a flake before being expelled. For every grouchy coroner with a medical degree, there are scads of literary types (whose voluminous personal libraries always contain the exact piece of arcane information needed to answer the enigma at hand), research scientists (ranging from absent-minded near-cartoons to cackling retort-bearers who are usually lighted from below), and life-long devotees of Egyptology, Nosferatu, botany, astronomy, astrology, ethereal vapors, the revivification of corpses, etc., who will insist upon being addressed as "Doctor."

Universal had a couple of Doctor Frankensteins (their father, Henry, doesn't seem to have officially copped the title at any point in his checkered career), a Dr. Seward (Van Helsing was a *Professor*, which was merely a synonym for Doctor), Doctor Mirakle (so help me!), Dr. Muller, Drs. Griffin, Kemp, and Cranley, Dr. Vitus Werdegast, and that truckload of "doctors" in *Life Returns*. These were gathered from the studio's genre output from 1931 to 1935 and don't include such '40s aberrations as Dr. Paul (scientific detective) Dupin, Richard Carlson's Dr. Jackson, or wily old Dr. Rx, who turns out to be a lawyer!

Confronted by doctors of questionable

ability and spurious credentials at every turn, it must have been something of a relief for audiences to check into the hospital in *Mystery of the White Room*. At least the murderous goings-on therein involved "real" medical personnel and not starched-collared dabblers in the academic end of the Black Arts.

When a madly careening ambulance brings a little boy straight from the scene of an accident, the surgeon on duty, Dr. Norman Kennedy (Roland Drew), refuses to operate, despite an X-ray revealing a potentially terminal skull fracture. Kennedy is refused help from his uncle, Dr. Morton (Addison Richards), who happens also to be chief of staff at the hospital. Morton is on his way out to an "important board meeting" (his nurse, Lila Haines [Joan Woodbury], knows better: "I remember when *I* was your board meeting"), and tells his nephew to use his own judgment. Nurse Carole Dale (Helen Mack), recognizing that Kennedy's opting to wait until morning will result in the boy's death, convinces her boyfriend, Dr. Bob Clayton (Bruce Cabot), and his mentor, Dr. Amos Thornton (Frank Reicher), to do the job.

The men's decision is a big deal. Overruling the findings of the man on duty and operating in his stead are considered to be serious violations of the hospital's code of ethics, and Bob — who, along with Kennedy, is up for the post of assistant to the chief of staff — will probably lose his chance by performing the life-saving operation. The earnest Dr. Clayton doesn't give this a second thought, and the boy is saved. Back in the pharmacy, the three celebrate their success with coffee, and as Tony the janitor (Frank Puglia), who Thornton notes has been "stone-deaf for ten years," comes in to clean up. Bob admires a case containing some of the older man's custom-made scalpels.

Next morning, Dr. Morton has awkward confrontations with Kennedy and Clayton, and Lila is witness to both. The chief of staff denies the assistancy to both men, with Kennedy's indecisiveness and Clayton's ethics violation cited as the causes. Neither man responds well, but Bob uses some unfortunate words which, like Dr. Thornton's scalpels, will come back to haunt him.

Later that day, as deaf Tony tries once again to tidy up the pharmacy, he is knocked unconscious and blinded by a container of acid hurled into his face. Almost simultaneously, a very important operation gets underway, one which demands not only all of the staff already introduced, but also the hospital's anesthesiologist, Dr. Donald Fox (Don Porter, making his movie debut), and Nurse Ann Stokes, Kennedy's girlfriend. The lights go out momentarily, and when the emergency generator kicks in, Dr. Morton falls to the floor with one of Amos Thornton's scalpels in his back! Bob takes over the operation when Kennedy freezes, and Carole goes for the superintendent while Dora (Mabel Todd), the female comic relief character, calls the police.

The superintendent (Holmes Herbert) isn't good for much save sputtering about scandal, but the police turn out in force. As the O.R. is brought under control, the doctors tread lightly around Sgt. MacIntosh Spencer (Thomas Jackson), the coroner (Byron Foulger) and the fingerprint expert (John Harmon). When it is determined that Morton was skewered by a left-hander, Lila out and out lies, telling the cops that Morton had promised the left-handed Kennedy the much-coveted assistancy; hence, the bewildered surgeon would have had no reason to kill his uncle. Carole tells Sgt. Spencer that Morton was not slain with one of the operating room scalpels: She counted them before the surgery had started, and "they're all here." Oddly enough, though everyone in the surgery was wearing rubber gloves, there are several clear fingerprints on the knife.

Dr. Thornton identifies the murder weapon as belonging to him, and offers to show the police an entire case full, back in the pharmacy. While everyone else heads thataway, Lila admits to having her own reasons for covering for Norman: "I'm not in the habit of helping murderers, but in this case, I thought it might pay me." Evidently, the canny nurse wants to remain the head nurse (and whatever else) to the new man in charge. In the pharmacy, one of Thornton's scalpels is found to be missing from the case, and Tony's prostrate form is discovered on the floor. Bob ascertains that most

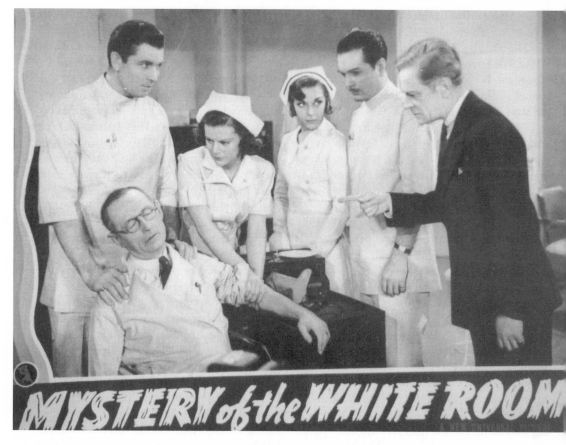

"I didn't know it was loaded." Goaded insufferably by Sgt. Spencer's index finger and big mouth in *Mystery of the White Room*, Dr. Thornton requires the aid of Dr. Bob Clayton and nurse Carole Dale. Nurse Lila Haines and resident weasel Dr. Norman Kennedy look on. PENTAGRAM LIBRARY.

of the acid hit the poor janitor in the mouth and the eyes, effectively rendering the deaf man mute and blind as well. Spencer sums it up: "It looks like Tony came in here to clean up and whoever was stealing the knife tossed acid in his face when he saw him."

A trip to the basement has the sergeant, Bob and Carole find the timing device which turned out the O.R. lights at precisely the right moment. Spencer is all for lugging everyone downtown and plugging them into a lie detector, but Bob allows the grouchy cop the use of the hospital's sphygmomanometer, an instrument for measuring arterial blood pressure. Using the device as an ad-hoc lie detector, Spencer finds Kennedy "as cool as ice," but works Dr. Thornton into a lather with accusations of grudges against Morton, who

succeeded Thornton as chief surgeon when the older man had to step down for health reasons. Thornton stumbles off "to get a stimulant" to counteract his wildly pounding heart, as Bob explains to Spencer that his mentor has a bad heart and his arterial pulse readings therefore have no validity.

Although Bob goes off to check on the young accident victim he operated on the night before, a scream from Dr. Morton's office brings him and the sergeant together again within seconds. They find Lila, who claims that someone flung a scalpel—which they find imbedded in the wall next to the door—at her when she entered the office. Sgt. Spencer finds "a nice set of fingerprints on this knife, too." The prints on both scalpels are identified as Bob's, and Lila admits that he and Dr. Morton

Dr. Thornton is dead, and it remains for Dr. Clayton to do some quick thinking to keep the case open.
PENTAGRAM LIBRARY.

had some angry words that morning. It looks bad for Bob, but Carole remembers that her beau handled those scalpels in the pharmacy the previous night, at Dr. Thornton's invitation. Seeking collaboration from the old doctor, the frustrated cop hies himself to the pharmacy, where he finds Thornton slumped over at his desk, with an admission to murdering Morton still stuck in the carriage of his typewriter!

Bob shoots down Spencer's theory of suicide by producing a syringe filled with adrenaline next to Thornton's body. The old physician died of a heart attack before he could give himself a shot of the drug. The confession was obviously typed by the murderer himself, who thought to take advantage of Thornton's death in order to tie up all the loose ends. When

Spencer discovers that a third scalpel is now missing from the case, he makes a beeline for Tony's room. "Come on," he barks at Bob. "I wanna talk to Tony before that killer does."

With only his nose exposed from the bandages encircling his head, Tony is of little help to the police. "The shock has caused complete, temporary paralysis," reveals the nurse. "His mouth is so badly scarred, he won't be able to speak for weeks." Bob hatches a plan which will both help the deaf, dumb, blind and immobile janitor and serve to finger the murderer: he will transplant Morton's corneas onto Tony's acid-scarred eyes. "The murdered man's own eyes will identify his murderer," Bob exalts. Permission of Morton's next of kin is needed, of course, and Spencer's interest is piqued when he finds that this means Dr. Kennedy. Bob announces he will perform the recently perfected operation first thing in the morning.

That night, Carole replaces Ann Stokes as night nurse in Tony's room, and Sgt. Spencer bunks down across the hall. During the wee hours, a caped figure quietly opens the window of the sickroom and hurls a scalpel right into the sleeping figure. Carole screams, and Spencer runs in to her aid. Carole discloses that the scalpel has skewered only the nursing school dummy, and that Tony is under police guard in the adjoining room.

The delicate operation is performed by a specialist the next morning, and despite the lights in the O.R. being extinguished several times, the procedure is successful. Bob and Sgt. Spencer fail to prevent the tampering with the basement fuse box, but the resourceful Dr. Clayton has anticipated the murderer's move and alerted the surgeon to await an all-clear signal before starting the transplant: "The killer figured Dr. Towne would puncture Tony's eyes when the lights went off."

Everyone is assembled as Tony's bandages are removed. When the frazzled janitor can't focus on anyone from a distance, Bob wheels him closer to Kennedy, Ann, the superintendent, and the others but to no avail. Bob is instructed to move into the injured man's line of vision, and immediately the mute patient shakes, groans, and points. He's not pointing at Bob, though, but at a mirror behind Bob, wherein he espies the reflection of Lila! Defiantly, the head nurse owns up to everything: "Yes, I killed Dr. Morton. I said no other woman would have him for long, and I kept my word. That's more than he did." The mystery of the white room having been solved, the murderess is removed, and the energies of the doctors and nurses turn once again to their traditional battle against injury and disease.

Shortest of the Crime Club features, *Mystery of the White Room* is also right up there among the most dynamic of the series. Sure, it's got your typical pigeonholing: As soon as Addison Richards exchanges snarls with two of the male leads, is caught arranging an assignation by his girlfriend, and stands accused of placing abstract principles above human

decency by irreproachable Frank Reicher, we know he's being set up for a fall. Sure, it's got a half-ton too much "comic relief"; I thoughtfully mentioned the painful Mabel Todd only in passing, and I didn't even allude to her male counterpart, Tom Dugan. Didn't miss him, did you? Sure, the resident cop is clueless, and his every deduction is quickly shattered by observations or information forthcoming from the hero. Sure, the structure of the plot is as close to a Charlie Chan picture as you can legally get without hiring Sidney Toler. That doesn't mean it's a bad movie.

Mystery of the White Room is a tight little mystery wherein every statement and every action, no matter how seemingly trivial, demands attention if the armchair or movie seat detective plans on beating Bruce Cabot to the solution. Alex Gottlieb's lean, mean screenplay is devoid of distracting special effects but chock full of atmospheric gimcracks. In a locale where everyone wears a mask, the need for further disguise is nil; as everyone also wears gloves, the existence of pristine sets of fingerprints on the scalpels rather neatly points to genius rather than ingenuousness. That brief view of the mystery killer wearing a cape is no mere sop to the genre's more flamboyant side, either; when we finally discover the murderer's true identity, we realize that a cape goes with the territory.

Drawn from Dr. James G. Edwards' novel *Murder in the Surgery* and benefiting from Universal's springing for a medico to act as technical advisor, *White Room* allows its whodunit to unfold before a backdrop of the era's most current and authentic techniques. Corneal transplants had only recently become possible, and it must have been something of a coup to highlight the procedure's playing a plausible role in the mystery's solution. Prior to this breakthrough, the naïve (and totally fictional) insistence that the image of the murderer would be retained on the lens of the victim's eyes took many otherwise erudite mystery buffs down the road to Mandalay. The supplanting of the lie detector by the sphygmomanometer is another painless instance of adapting the medium to suit the mystery. In

1939, polygraph readings were considered admissible evidence, and the adroit substitution of one instrument for the other helps keep the hospital milieu from being just another ploy.

Frank Reicher takes top honors in the thespic department, his Amos Thornton flashing greater depth in his few scenes than Bruce Cabot's Bob Clayton unveils throughout the whole movie. Those who insist on cementing Reicher to his foggy Captain Englehorn persona are doing him a great disservice. The veteran actor and silent film director was damn near ubiquitous in and out of the genre during the '30s and early '40s, and his supporting roles and bits were usually among the more vivid characterizations those films had to offer.

Helen Mack is Reicher's only real competition in terms of credibility and intensity. *White Room* was the second film in which the pair had appeared together, and both profit from the mystery's more realistic bent. Carole Dale and Dr. Thornton epitomize the best of the medical profession, sharing a passion to heal and an outrage with anyone who does not share their passion; allowing for the difference in their ages and the prevailing sexual stereotypes, their characters are mirror images of each other. It may be her makeup or a trick of the light, but Miss Mack's eyes photograph here with a subtly exotic cast, giving the former child star an allure that was purposefully missing from her more famous portrayal of Hilda Peterson in *Son of Kong*.

I wish I could honestly note a greater depth to Bruce Cabot since his John Driscoll grunted his way through the original *King Kong*, but the intervening six years seem to have made little impact on the actor's technique. Even when his old friend and mentor lies dead in a heap by his side, Cabot's Bob Clayton doesn't betray the slightest reaction. Laid back to the point of being nearly oblivious to the implications surrounding him, the young physician continuously provides information which the script would otherwise deny Sgt. Spencer, and does so as if solving murders were nothing compared with taking temperatures rectally. In trying to delineate a figure whose obvious innocence dictates his apparent lack of concern, Cabot comes dangerously close to making Clayton a disinterested party and an uninteresting character.

Joan Woodbury is a beautiful woman first and an articulate actress only thereafter. Her several little speeches, including that all-important confession, are inordinately difficult to understand. Roland Drew does an admirable job of making Norman Kennedy a less than admirable person, and Addison Richards always plays Addison Richards as if he were born to the role. Frank Puglia is a decent Tony the janitor and manages to survive until the end credits, a feat which Lee J. Cobb (as another Tony the janitor) had been unable to perform the year before in *Danger on the Air*.

Released between *Son of Frankenstein* and *The House of Fear*, *Mystery of the White Room* didn't make much noise at the box office, a fact that could hardly be attributed solely to the film itself. Shot on a handful of indoor (but effective) sets, and requiring only a limited cast, its minuscule budget guaranteed a profit. (Per Blackie Seymour, Don Porter remembered getting paid "only a hundred bucks — for the whole thing!") It's just that only one Crime Club feature remained, that being October's *The Witness Vanishes*, and neither it nor its medical predecessor received anything near the promotional funds earlier club entries had enjoyed. With horror pictures back in vogue, Universal opted to go with its strengths, and increased advertising dollars for Karloff, Lugosi and Rathbone meant less publicity for Cabot, Mack and Reicher. Nowadays hardly anyone but the most fanatical of whodunit buffs can name more than a couple of the studio's nonfantastic murder mysteries; while this is obviously the effect of such a budgetary policy, that a knee-jerk association of horror pictures with Universal Pictures still exists indicates the underlying wisdom of the decision.

Mystery of the White Room

Released March 17, 1939; 57 minutes

Cast: Bruce Cabot (Dr. Bob Clayton); Helen Mack (Nurse Carole Dale); Joan Woodbury (Nurse Lila Haines); Constance North

(Nurse Ann Stokes); Mabel Todd (Nurse Dora Stanley); Thomas Jackson (Sgt. MacIntosh Spencer); Frank Reicher (Dr. Amos Thornton); Addison Richards (Dr. Finley Morton); Roland Drew (Dr. Norman Kennedy); Tom Dugan (Hank Manley); Don Porter (Dr. Donald Fox); Frank Puglia (Tony, the Janitor); Holmes Herbert (Superintendent); Byron Foulger (Coroner); John Harmon (Fingerprint Man)

Credits: Producer — Irving Starr; Director — Otis Garrett; Screenplay — Alex Gottlieb; Based on the novel *Murder in the Surgery* by James G. Edwards, M.D.; Technical Advisor — Dr. Thomas MacLaughlin; Director of Photography — John Boyle, ASC; Musical Director — Charles Previn; Art Director — Jack Otterson; Sound — Bernard B. Brown; Technician — Jess Moulin; Associate Art Director — Ralph DeLacey; Film Editor — Harry Keller; Production Manager — Ben Hersh. A Crime Club Production

THE HOUSE OF FEAR (1939)

Crime Club adaptations apart, the studio's three 1939 chillers were each as different from the others as different can be. *Son of Frankenstein*, the most forthright item in the year's genre catalogue, was the second sequel to the original Whale classic, was never marketed as anything other than a horror film, and was soon to take on special status as being the vehicle for Karloff's last performance as the Monster. *Tower of London* was a hybrid: part epic history (related *cum grano salis*) and part melodrama colored with Karloff; the picture was profitable bologna no matter how you sliced it, and the title laid it on the table. Series picture, autonomous feature ... the only genus missing was remake, and *The House of Fear* filled the bill with panache.

In this case, however, the curious moviegoer was pretty much driving blind. Until the reviews came out or word of mouth hit the streets, who in blazes knew what to expect from a title like *The House of Fear*?* Joe May's little thriller was a rehash of one of Junior's early talkies, *The Last Warning* (the first film detailed in this volume), which had been the last film helmed by German genre master Paul Leni. In December of '38, Universal had released

another film entitled *The Last Warning*, which may well have confused the hell out of the studio's most staunch advocates as it bore absolutely no relation to the 1929 Leni thriller or to this new film. Adding yet another wrinkle to the uncertainty, the "house" of the title referred to a theater and not to any kind of a dwelling place (as in the 1945 Sherlock Holmes mystery *The House of Fear*).

The house we're concerned with is Broadway's Woodford Theater, and within minutes of the film's spunky opening music, an actor named John Woodford is murdered right in front of a capacity crowd. The curtain is wrung down, and most of the principals—theater owners Joe and Robert Morton (Alan Dinehart, Robert Coote), director Dick Pierce (Harvey Stevens), and leading lady Alice Tabor (Irene Hervey)—mill about, confused and upset. The two comic relief stagehands, Mike (Tom Dugan) and Jeff (the always unwelcome El Brendel), carry Woodford's cadaver into his dressing room and place it on a chaise lounge, beneath a life mask of the actor. Things perk up when the coroner arrives and can't find the body!

A succession of those good old newspaper

"Bearing such a title, it would be contrary to expectations if the picture were not full of weirdly spooky stuff. It is, but for every bit of business, situation, dialogue line and stage trick that sends chills chasing up and down the spine, there's a comedy counteraction"—Motion Picture Herald, June 10, 1939.

headlines informs us that a year has passed and that stories have been circulating about the theater's being haunted by Woodford's restless ghost. The Morton brothers are approached by Arthur McHugh (William Gargan), a Midwestern impresario who not only doesn't mind the notoriety, but tells the owners, "It's *because* of the ghost stories that I want your theater." McHugh tells the men that he plans on opening with *Dangerous Currents,* the play in which John Woodford was killed onstage, and that he's bent on reassembling the same cast. The moment the lease is signed, a phone rings, and McHugh is regaled by an eerie voice: "You must not open this theater. This is a warning. This is John Woodford speaking." The three men regard the call as a grim prank until they're told the phone is "dead as a graveyard" by the installer, come to restart the service.

A cut establishes McHugh as a detective working undercover on the Woodford case, which the police have never officially closed. Another cut, and both Alice and Dick turn up at the theater where they agree (after some minor exposition) to sign on with the show. The next thespian on the scene is Gloria DeVere (Dorothy Arnold), a saucy actress-cum-gold-digger if ever there was one. Without so much as reading a line ("I can act any part any lug can write"), she is given the part of the secretary. The last two of the original cast members, Carleton (Walter Woolf King) and Sarah Henderson (Jan Duggan), arrive moments later, and a read-through is arranged for eight o'clock that night.

Problems ensue. It seems that the full script is nothing but blank pages, and each actor's individual part contains a note: "Warning. Don't play this part. John Woodford." It doesn't get any easier when Dick confirms that the handwriting is, indeed, that of the dead actor. Rehearsal at two the next afternoon brings news of another posthumous note received by Carleton, who has been promoted to play the role of Clarke, the part Woodford was playing when he was murdered. The run-through is interrupted by Woodford's voice, reading the lines in lieu of the stunned Carleton; a quick search of the theater reveals that

dim-witted Jeff found a record of Woodford's performance "between 'Flat-Foot Floogie' and 'My Heart Belongs to Daddy'" and put it out over the house audio system inadvertently. Everyone has a good laugh, but it only takes a piece of falling scenery to give them the jitters again.

McHugh convinces Dick to sit up all night with him in the orchestra boxes after the producer gets another note, "Warning. Abandon this theater before twelve tonight!" At 2:00 AM, McHugh is startled by a ghastly sight: Floating toward him, eerily aglow, is the disembodied face of John Woodford! The detective pumps a couple of shots into the face, which immediately disappears. Turning on the house lights, McHugh discovers Dick unconscious in his box, his head bloodied from a blow — or a graze by a bullet. The men run into Woodford's dressing room, where they find the life mask in pieces and discover a secret passage, linking Woodford's dressing room with Alice's. McHugh also discovers Alice in her room, and spilling who he is and why he's there to the couple, the policeman warns them to keep mum and keep showing up for rehearsal. When Dick and Alice leave, McHugh moves back into the tunnel where, behind the ineffectively mortared wall, he finds the year-old corpse of John Woodford!

The day of the dress rehearsal begins promisingly but ends tragically: Carleton is spirited from his dressing room during a blackout and is found dead in a piece of scenery which was hanging in the flies. McHugh buoys up the cast and promotes Dick to that deadly leading role, promising him and everyone else lots of hand-picked policemen at the performance. With only hours to go before *Dangerous Currents* reopens in the haunted theater, the detective finally gets a few breaks. He finds out that Carleton was killed by "a poison ... out of some South American snake," although the cops still don't know how it got into his bloodstream. From a handwriting expert, he learns that all of the Woodford notes were clever forgeries, as was a check the actor cashed on the day he was killed. The expert has his own theory: "Woodford found out about the

Title lobby card for *The House of Fear*, Universal's 1939 remake of 1929's *The Last Warning*. Pentagram Library.

forged check, confronted the guilty party, and probably gave him a chance to make good. The guy couldn't and killed Woodford."

At the opening there are so many cops visible that they, and not the ghost, are the topic of everyone's comments. All is quiet until Act II, which takes place in a radio studio; this is where Woodford had met his fate. Providentially, two bits of information fall into place and lead to the beginning of the end. A cop tells McHugh that the coroner found "a very small needle of invisible glass in Carleton's body … it had been poisoned and shot into him with a special gun." Alice then adds, "It was in this scene, at the microphone, that he died."

McHugh wonders why there's a wire leading from the floor into the phony microphone.

A cop sent beneath the stage to investigate is overpowered by a masked man, but McHugh kicks over the microphone before the wire can be pulled and another poisoned needle fired. A blast on his whistle musters all of the cops, and the masked man is flushed from below-ground to the scaffolding up near the ceiling. Despite a good bit of acrobatics on the curtains and guy-wires, the mysterious figure is captured and unmasked. It is Mike the stagehand, known to McHugh as Mike Hanlon, ex-convict. "Someone threatened to expose you, forced you into committing those murders! Who was it?" Mike clams up, but the threat of the chair has him pointing at Robert Morton and singing like a canary.

Morton was caught by Woodford with the forged check, so the owner had the ex-convict

Foreground, left to right: Alan Dinehart, William Gargan, El Brendel. The heroics of William Gargan have weathered the years far better than the studied imbecility of El Brendel. *PENTAGRAM LIBRARY.*

do his worst. As for the rumors about the hauntings, the theater had become a key property in a construction promotion, and Morton hoped that by delivering it at a low price, he could get a piece of the action. According to McHugh (and his wife, the undercover policewoman who has been impersonating Gloria DeVere!), "Robert invented the ghost stories, and with the help of Mike, kept them going." The gag at the wrap is that McHugh is resigning from the force to be a theatrical producer. "The show must go on," he tells his astonished ex-boss.

Sure, you've got to check a few of your wits at the cloak room when you enter the theater, but *The House of Fear* is neater and less cluttered than any of the other offbeat whodunits examined within these pages. The picture sets itself up as if it were being shot under

Jack L. Warner's baleful glare; the viewer scarcely has time to digest the fact that he's watching a play and not a radio broadcast when the coroner — who must have been chasing ambulances a block away — stomps out of the corpseless dressing room in a huff. Nor does that newspaper montage really deserve the playful slap it was given above. One has to go back to Paul Leni's fascinating effect in *The Last Warning* to come up with another instance wherein the hoary old device accomplishes its various ends — denoting the passage of time, reporting the extent of the local legends — as efficiently as it does here.

The picture's "supernatural" elements are stunning in their simplicity. The idea that Woodford's corpse could essentially vanish right out from under the noses of a theater full of people is a grabber and a welcome change from the likewise clever but more widely seen murder-committed-within-a-locked-room gambit. There are a few too many ghostly notes for my taste, and the tripe involving Jeff and the phonograph record shtick is overly precious, but the scene involving the luminescent life-mask is really well done. The amorphous image seems to focus and cohere as it moves ominously onward, and its silent journey produces a moment of genuine unease. And, when all is said and done, no one ever does get around to explaining how Tom (or Robert) could have gotten that first threat to McHugh over a dead telephone. (But it's a great idea, spooky as all get-out, and was lifted from Universal's own 1917 15-chapter serial *The Voice on the Wire*.)

One thing the novice will gain from reading about these movies is an appreciation for the rules governing red herrings during the 1930s. Rule number one: Never look where you're supposed to look. Mysteries are like magic tricks; the audience is guided through the thrill of it all by the *mis*director, whose job it is to create the appearance of fair play while using subtleties and gimmicks to keep your attention away from the solution. Rule number two: Always plumb the depths of the cast list and troll among the cowards, whiners, milquetoasts, cripples, and morons. Films like *Night Monster* and *Doctor X* have been entertaining legions of fans for years, but they've succeeded in fooling only those who forget that the impossible is a given in our genre, and that the wildly improbable is usually the way to go in the mystery field.

Whether or not you assumed Tom Dugan's villainous leanings early on or managed to tie him in with silly ass Robert Coote, you can't deny that *The House of Fear* is the fast-moving and genial experience that it is mainly because of the considerable talent of the cast members. The biggest names were William Gargan and Irene Hervey, and while they would never be considered among the brightest of Hollywood's stars, they each brought realism and appeal to their roles, and both enjoyed careers spanning nearly four decades.

Gargan's contract with Universal began with 1936's *Flying Hostess*, an ode to airline stewardesses which featured the actor as an instructor of same. A succession of similar material followed (including three other features scrutinized herein for their inclusion in the 1957 *Shock Theater* milestone), but amidst the low-budget morass, Gargan managed to cop an Academy Award nomination for his participation in *They Knew What They Wanted*. If Universal felt that the signal honor received by the actor's performance in the RKO release should entitle him to a promotion from the programmers in which he was mired, they certainly didn't act on it; Gargan would continue to be ensconced in the same predictable stuff until he and a host of other "outdated" forties personalities were let go by the studio in 1946.

Miss Hervey likewise had a nonexclusive contract with Universal, where her most memorable film might have been *Destry Rides Again*, but where her bread and butter came from formulaic pap very similar to Mr. Gargan's. Robert Coote's amiably silly Briton sauntered through dozens of big features (like *Gunga Din*, 1939, and *The Prisoner of Zenda*, 1952), little features (like *Sally in Our Alley*, 1931), and television (1964's *The Rogues*). Coote will perhaps be forever associated with the role of Colonel Pickering in Lerner and Loewe's musical triumph *My Fair Lady*.

No matter how hard I try, I can never think of Walter Woolf King as anyone other than Lassparri, the lecherous tenor in The Marx Brothers' *A Night at the Opera* (1935).

Director Joe May (Josef Mandel) had been part of the German invasion of the Laemmle homestead earlier in the decade, and the émigré does a capable, journeyman job of holding off those dull moments which ought never to be found in a picture such as this. Milton Krasner's camera doesn't sit in any one place long enough to gather dust, and his sole *faux pas* is his over-lighting of the climactic chase up in the flies: McHugh's barking directions gives us the only clue we have as to where anyone is at any given moment. The Phantom stage is looking good, and all that activity would keep it in shape for the 1943 remake of the Chaney triumph.

Given the wide range of classic horrors

from which to choose and the somewhat confusing circumstances of its own title, *The House of Fear* is seldom among the first dozen or two (or three) Universal chillers one sees. Once that hurdle has been jumped, however, the little mystery usually wins favor. Not quite vintage, perhaps, but it does leave a very nice taste in one's mouth.

The House of Fear

Released June 30, 1939; 65 minutes

Cast: William Gargan (Arthur McHugh); Irene Hervey (Alice Tabor); Alan Dinehart (Joseph Morton); Walter Woolf King (Carleton); Dorothy Arnold (Gloria DeVere); Harvey Stephens (Dick Pierce); Robert Coote (Robert Morton); Jan Duggan (Sarah Henderson); Tom Dugan (Mike Hanlon); El Brendel (Jeff); Donald Douglas (John Woodford); Charles C. Wilson (Police Chief); Harry Hayden (Coroner); Milton Kibbee (Telephone Man); Emory Parnell, William Gould (Cops); Ben Lewis (Tommy); Stanley Hughes (Cameraman); Eddie Parker (Watson); Donald Kerr (Cab Driver); Tom Steele (Stagehand); with Raymond Parker

Credits: Associate Producer — Edmund Grainger; Director — Joe May; Screenplay — Peter Milne; Based on the play *The Last Warning* by Thomas Fallon; Adapted from the novel *The House of Fear* by Wadsworth Camp; Working Title — *Backstage Phantom*; Photographer — Milton Krasner, ASC; Film Editor — Frank Gross; Art Directors — Jack Otterson and John Ewing; Musical Director — Charles Previn; Sound Supervisor — Bernard B. Brown; Technician — Joe Lapis; Set Decorations — Russell A. Gausman; Gowns — Vera West

THE WITNESS VANISHES (1939)

Of all of the Crime Club adaptations, *The Witness Vanishes* is the most cleverly titled. The film itself is an enjoyable enough exercise in the *Ten Little Indians* vein, wherein the members of a certain group are knocked off one by one, but the significance of the title doesn't become apparent until the denouement. Based on the novel *They Can't Hang Me* by James Ronald, *The Witness Vanishes* features a cast chock-a-block with infamous character people, a series of puzzling assassinations, and a decent enough massaging of the red-herring regulations to keep most people guessing until the end.

Lucius Marplay (Barlowe Borland), erstwhile owner of the *London Evening Sun* and a longtime resident of Hillsdale Sanitorium, has compiled four notebooks, each brimming with "ingenious schemes for the destruction of four people." Marplay's solicitor, Sir John Digby (Reginald Barlow), has come to arrange for the inmate to meet with his daughter, Joan (Wendy Barrie), who has not seen her father for years and believes him dead. Before this subject can be broached, however, Marplay shows Sir John the notebooks and vows to murder "those four scoundrels who stole my newspaper!" He muses, "I've been thinking, as I'm not in my right mind ... I could commit murder, and they can't hang me for it, can they?"

Locking the solicitor in the closet, the newspaper man escapes, and the camera lingers on a Marplay notebook titled "The Fortunate Finish to Ambrose Craven."

For the record, Craven (Walter Kingsford) is the associate editor of the "new" *London Evening Sun*, and the other scoundrels are his colleagues Sinclair Ellis (Boyd Irwin), Nigel Partridge (Vernon Steele), and Mark Peters (Edmund Lowe), the newspaper's publisher and editor-in-chief. Some years before, the cads connived to cause Lucius Marplay to lose financial control of the paper. This disaster unhinged the old man, necessitating his institutionalization. News of his escape brings the quartet together for a powwow, and all of these past sins are laid on the table. In addition to his being cowardly (his surname is singularly apt), Craven is depicted as being something of a womanizer; he has a difficult time keeping his hands off his secretaries.

While the scoundrels are watching their collective arse, we learn that Marplay has holed up in a secret room in the old *London Evening Sun* building, which has been abandoned and is fortuitously situated right next door. In addition, Joan has met Sir Noel Stretton (Bruce Lester), a baronet reduced to writing gossip columns. As Noel and Joan spar incessantly, we're certain that they're just made for each

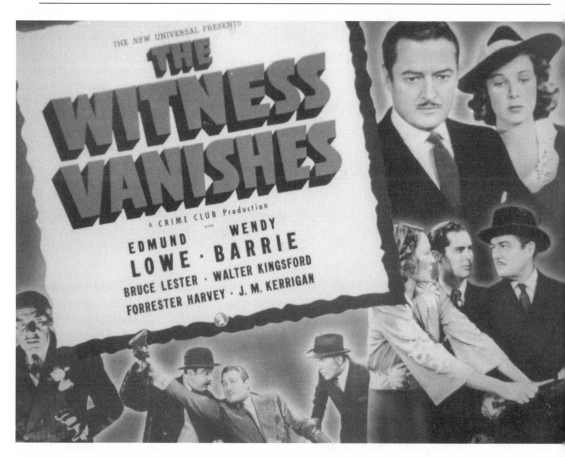

Bowlers, fedoras, and clipped mustaches: We must be in Britain. Title lobby card for *The Witness Vanishes*. PENTAGRAM LIBRARY.

other. In an effort to locate her father, Joan takes a job under an alias as Ambrose Craven's new secretary. A conniving old newspaperman and a former associate of Lucius Marplay, Flinters (J.M. Kerrigan), begins to wend his way through the matters at hand and furnishes Joan and her beau with the occasional clue as to what in hell's going on.

The guano hits the fan when the romantic leads discover a disturbing item in the current *Sun*'s obituary column: "ELLIS, on the 17th of September at his office at 3 PM. Sinclair Ellis, news editor of the *Evening Sun*, aged 53, of severe head injuries." Joan asks, "What time is it now?" Noel replies, "Just after three o'clock." The couple hurry down the stairs to Ellis's office and enter with editor-in-chief Peters. There they find the *very* recently deceased Ellis and one of Marplay's notebooks. Scotland Yard

is called in, and Peters is aghast to discover a rival paper has scooped the *Sun* with a special edition on the murder that has just been committed!

Through Flinters, Joan learns of the secret room in the old *Sun* building, but the young woman braves the dark and stormy night for nothing; the room is empty. Joan has been followed, however, by Sergeant Dade (Leyland Hodgson), who takes credit for the discovery of the cache when he reports in to Inspector Wren (Robert Noble) the next day. Of greater interest to the audience is the introduction of Alistair MacNab (Forrester Harvey), a picturesque little man who claims to be a tracer of lost persons. "When you're dealing with lunatics, you've got to put yourself in their shoes," he explains, "and I've got the neck to do it." Peters hires MacNab to conduct an independent investigation, but no sooner has the diminutive Scotsman left than a distraught Nigel Partridge appears. There's another obituary notice: "PARTRIDGE, on the 19th of September at his office in Fleet Street. Nigel Partridge was poisoned. "Although four of the fugitive's fingerprints are found on the insertion, Peters manages to calm Partridge down: "Marplay would have to walk through a concrete wall to reach you, and no living man can do that."

Somewhat mollified, and under police guard, Partridge goes to his private lavatory "to freshen up a bit." The edgy editor makes it through a couple of swipes with an electric shaver, but the application of aftershave lotion fells him dead on the spot. In checking out the lotion atomizer, Peters finds a second notebook: "The Strange Demise of Nigel Partridge." Within moments, the rival newspaper has hit the streets with another extra (this time, with photographs!). Despite a smell of acid, the atomizer is subsequently found to contain nothing harmful, but a strange button is found on the floor of the crime scene. Of course, Scotland Yard is "completely baffled."

By now, Craven is an absolute mess, and his finding a third obituary (in his cigarette case!) just about tears it: "CRAVEN, on the 20th of September, at 9 PM. Ambrose Craven, aged fifty-one. Associate Editor *London Evening Sun*." Making things much worse, Craven has been hiding out in the flat of his new secretary, and he's just discovered that she's Lucius Marplay's daughter! Joan hits a switch with her foot, alerting Noel (who's in an adjoining room) to engage a recording machine; the frantic Craven comes clean:

> CRAVEN: It wasn't my fault. 'Twasn't mine at all. It was Peters' idea from the start.... He wanted the *Evening Sun* for himself. He couldn't work it alone, so he talked us into going in with him. He said Marplay was preoccupied and distraught over his sick little daughter. When he came back, Peters had tangled things up so much, Marplay almost had a nervous breakdown trying to save his paper.

Craven reveals how Peters had Marplay declared insane and then took control himself. The confession has been overheard by Peters, though, who has quietly entered the apartment. Noel is slugged from behind, and when Peters and Joan rush in to investigate, the editor wastes no time in smashing the record containing Craven's statement. Noel reveals that Peters has broken "a dummy. The fellow who hit me on the head has got the good one." The assailant's shadow is spotted on the wall, whence it eerily moves out and into the next room. The trio is locked in, and Craven is apparently alone with Marplay! "Dad!" cries Joan. "Don't do it!" The door is broken down, the shadow has vanished, and the three watch as Craven collapses onto the floor, a fatal notebook at his side.

Putting first things first, Peters fires Noel and then orders the *Sun* to publish an extra immediately. Too late; the *Tribune* has beaten its rival to the punch once again. As Joan helps Noel clean out his desk, a note arrives, addressed to her: "Notice of Auction: One used dictaphone record. 10 PM at 13 Haggard Place. Room 12 off first landing."

The couple has barely arrived when in walks MacNab: "'Tis a bonnie place for a murder." Brief snatches of the Monster's theme from *Son of Frankenstein* are heard as a body with a knife between its shoulder blades tumbles out of the cupboard. It's Flinters, and the crucial dictaphone record lies in pieces beneath him. Capping the scene, a triumphant Peters enters.

The next morning, Peters finds MacNab going through his desk (the Scot having put a little something away for safekeeping in his pocket before being discovered), and is regaled by Inspector Wren's reading of the latest obituary: "PETERS, on the 21st of September at 9 PM At his country home." Peters agrees to open his country place in order to force Marplay's hand. That night, Wren and Sgt. Dade take up their posts outside the editor's digs, as Peters studies "The Eerie End of Mark Peters," the notebook supposedly containing the plans for his own demise. Down the stairs creeps Marplay, ever closer, until Peters draws his revolver on the older man. "You're too cowardly to shoot," Marplay sneers. "You wouldn't dare, unless my back was turned."

A shot does ring out, but it comes from behind a curtain as MacNab shoots the gun from Peters' hand. Instantly the police rush in and seize Peters! Marplay has been held prisoner at the country home until this evening, when he was to have been killed "in self-defense," effectively wrapping up the loose ends in what was a monumental frame-up by Peters. MacNab produces Partridge's atomizer, the item he found in Peters' desk; the editor-in-chief switched it for a harmless duplicate after he arranged for Partridge to poison himself.

Joan is aghast: "You killed them! All of them! And you kept my father prisoner here after he saw you kill Ellis!" Suavely lighting a cigarette, Peters admits to the plot:

> PETERS: I caught [your father] leaning over Ellis with a truncheon, but Marplay couldn't strike him…. It was too fine an opportunity with those four black books of deadly detail. I hit Ellis and then knocked out Marplay and brought him to this house…

As Craven mentioned, the fanatical Peters has always wanted the *Sun* "for himself." The poison in his cigarette does the trick, and Peters escapes His Majesty's justice through suicide. Marplay pledges to give a job to MacNab (an ace reporter for the *Glasgow News*), and Joan is reunited with both father and boyfriend at the fadeout.

Making the escaped madman himself the witness to the first murder and then removing him from the scene lends integrity to Robertson White's adroit title, while allowing a little sidearm snookery. By having Lucius Marplay play an equivocal role — it is taken for granted by everyone, including his daughter, that he is the killer, whereas it devolves that he has *witnessed* the killing — White and original novelist, James Ronald, pull an Agatha Christie–like fast one, à la *The Murder of Roger Ackroyd*. That particularly admirable aspect apart, *The Witness Vanishes* is a decent if slightly protracted

thriller with an overabundance of eccentric characters and a tendency to become too mysterious for its own good. The *Motion Picture Herald* of October 28, 1939, opined that "the picture has four murders to handle and so must keep to a mayhem schedule of offering a victim every 15 minutes. As to the identity of the witness, that may prove to be a bigger puzzler than the action."

In keeping with that perverse title tease, virtually no one plays according to Hoyle. Joan wanders through the body of the film using a fake name, while the screenplay doesn't begin to explain how *Lord* Stretton came to be grinding out trashy hearsay for a daily newspaper. In addition, Flinters' enacting the role of seedy double agent leads to his own murder, and one is never quite certain just who MacNab is in the first place. Even Scotland Yard plays it close to the vest, with the detectives working against Peters' interests while going through the motions of protecting him. With a lineup like this one, Lucius Marplay's own peculiar identity crisis is just one more float in the parade.

Amidst all the cleverness, there's some obvious stuff. Although calling on Marplay in late afternoon, Sir John sports a top hat, has a voluminous opera cape draped over his business suit, and is toting a gold-headed cane! It wouldn't take Charlie Chan to predict that Sir John's flamboyant garb will soon be waltzing out through the gates on someone else's frame. Likewise, Craven's propensity for putting the moves on his female aides ("Sometimes they call you Amorous Ambrose," Peters chides) is more a transparent device to get Wendy Barrie's character situated in the nest of journalistic vipers than an honest effort at fleshing out the scoundrel's personality.

There's also more intrigue than a 66-minute movie can comfortably carry. Flinters' insistence on making his every disclosure the end product of a wearying series of cloak and dagger maneuvers seems motivated only by the necessity to pad the running time. When Joan asks him where Marplay might be found, Flinters arranges to meet her at a certain pub at eight o'clock that night. At the pub, she pays him 20 pounds and receives verbal instructions

To the ominous tones of the Monster's leitmotif from *Son of Frankenstein*, what's left of J.M. Kerrigan's Flinters comes out of the closet. *From left to right:* Bruce Lester, Forrester Harvey, J. M. Kerrigan, Wendy Barrie. PENTAGRAM LIBRARY.

to return home to await an envelope that will arrive at nine o'clock. The appointed hour brings a knock at the door; no one's there, naturally, but an envelope left behind contains a note advising her, "In his office in the *old* Sun building Lucius Marlay had a fireplace. Look behind it." Having to deal with time-consuming tactics such as these makes Joan's finding her aged father much before his centenary celebration seem less and less likely.

The same sort of enigmatic behavior occurs while Craven is spilling the beans to Joan's and Noel's recorder. Despite its somewhat supernatural capabilities — it moves out of the room without revealing its human source — that shadow on Noel's wall has to belong to Flinters. Why does he go to the trouble of stealing the record and then announce an

"auction" with one of his needlessly mysterious notes when he already knows the heroes don't have enough cash to make a winning bid and that Peters will never let him live to spend the money?

Although the film is ostensibly set in and around London, director Otis Garrett doesn't seem to have gone out of his way to spread around much of a British veneer. There's very little vocal consistency. Irish actors Forrester Harvey and J. M. Kerrigan do their bit, contributing Scottish and whiskey-burnished Cockney accents, and South African–born Bruce Lester has his Lord Stretton sounding properly upper-crust. British expatriate Wendy Barrie, however, has the flat pronunciation of a TV anchorman — she was also "out-Englished" by Basil Rathbone, Nigel Bruce, and Richard Greene in *The Hound of the Baskervilles*, released by Fox that same year — while Edmund Lowe's Peters appears to have arrived at Fleet Street by way of Hoboken, New Jersey. A canny bit of verisimilitude is having the news-hawkers hang posters announcing the day's headlines from their stands; apart from this, however, shelling out "pounds" in "pubs" and hiding out in "flats" is as close as we get to English soil.

While other Crime Club entries (like *The Westland Case* or *The Last Warning*) are quintessential thirties whodunits — fast-moving, reasonably witty, undeniably "up to date" — *The Witness Vanishes* seems like a throwback to the more studied and leisurely approach that had started off the decade. As Otis Garrett had also directed the spunkier *Danger on the Air*, the blame isn't entirely his. Arthur Martinelli's camera work can't really be faulted either. The cinematographer's practiced eye, along with Bela Lugosi's performance, had generally been acknowledged as the saving grace of the Halperin brothers' cheesy classic *White Zombie*, and the camera dispassionately records much more than it artfully conceals. The film's English milieu probably accounts for some of this effect; after all, most people would expect more dramatic tension in the air from a thriller set in a New York City radio station than they would from a tale centered on a newspaper office in London. Still, for a film released in the last months of 1939, within spitting distance of the forties and the era of slick programmers, its measured pacing makes it seem positively old-fashioned and out of its league.

Some mention has to be made of the fact that Mark Peters commits suicide at the end of the movie. Since the inception of the Hays Office in 1921, Hollywood had found itself scrutinized by a self-imposed industry censorship board, the responsibility of which was to insure that public morality went uncompromised. In 1930, the first Production Code was implemented, featuring among other dicta a steadfast prohibition against suicide as a means of plot resolution. I can't fathom how or why Edmund Lowe was allowed to suck death into his lungs from that coffin nail, but his doing

himself in is the only instance of out-and-out suicide (apart from *Cleopatra* and her asp in 1934, and stuff like the noble voluntary self-starvation in 1937's *The Outcasts of Poker Flat*) that I can recall in pictures of this era.

The Witness Vanishes was the last of Universal's Crime Club features. The year 1939, the film industry's *annus mirabilis*, had seen the rebirth of the horror film, a genre to which the studio felt a special affinity and owed a special allegiance. The public's clamoring for the grand old monsters assured that Boris Karloff and Bela Lugosi would be kept busy, that popular players like Basil Rathbone and Lionel Atwill now had other irons in their fires, and that new personalities, like Lon Chaney's son, would have to be introduced in order to keep up with the demand. With the full-blooded fare scheduled with names such as these, there would be little room left on the plate for more mundane mysteries or formulaic whodunits.

The Crime Club disappeared from the screen as surely as Lucius Marplay had dropped from sight, but its legacy returned during the early forties, when Sherlock Holmes busied himself over missing eccentrics (*The House of Fear*) or radio's murderous potential (*Sherlock Holmes and the Voice of Terror*). The *Inner Sanctum* series would demonstrate that there had always been a spot on the glitzy globe for tepid chillers of varying quality, but the foolhardy decision to top-bill Lon Chaney (in an assortment of roles as artists, doctors, and scientists whose genius was matched only by their Machiavellian tendencies) made audiences yearn mightily for the less stellar but conspicuously better suited leading men of the best of the Crime Club films.

Taken on its own, the final picture of the series is an adequate reshuffling of familiar material and a lesser installment in the Crime Club anthology. Considered in context, it represents the lower end of the gamut Universal was forced to offer mystery fanciers during the monsters' holiday. *The Witness Vanishes* might well prove to be a pleasant surprise if it crosses your path on late night TV, but I can't really recommend going to heroic lengths to track it down.

The Witness Vanishes

Released September 22, 1939; 66 minutes

Cast: Edmund Lowe (Mark Peters); Wendy Barrie (Joan Marplay); Bruce Lester (Noel Stretton); Walter Kingsford (Ambrose Craven); Barlowe Borland (Lucius Marplay); Forrester Harvey (Alistair MacNab); J.M. Kerrigan (Flinters); Vernon Steele (Nigel Partridge); Boyd Irwin (Sinclair Ellis); Reginald Barlow (Sir John Digby); Leyland Hodgson (Sergeant Dade); Robert Noble (Inspector Wren); Denis Green (Leets)

Credits: Producer — Irving Starr; Director — Otis Garrett; Screenplay — Robertson White; Based on the novel *They Can't Hang Me* by James Ronald; Director of Photography — Arthur Martinelli, ASC; Art Director — Jack Otterson; Film Editor — Harry Keller; Associate Art Director — Richard H. Riedel; Musical Director — Charles Previn; Sound Supervisor — Bernard B. Brown; Technician — Robert Pritchard; Production Manager — Ben Hersh; Gowns — Vera West. A Crime Club Production

TOWER OF LONDON (1939)

No one was happier with the phenomenal comeback of the horror film than the Universal brass, who rushed to locate the genre veterans who had moved off into other directions with the death of the first horror "cycle" and to acquire new personnel with similar talents and new properties with similar themes. If that fabled triple bill at the Regina (see page 340) had made anything clear to the suits, it was that the incredible appeal of the classic Laemmle creatures (apologies to little Kong) had put the lie to the Rogers/Crowdin philosophy that what the people wanted was cheap but wholesome pap.

Projects which had been earmarked in the early thirties but then abandoned (like *The Wolf Man*) were resurrected, lubricated, and given a new lease on life. *Son of Frankenstein* had proved beyond an Expressionistic shadow of a doubt that there was still plenty of what passed for life in the old monsters. As the new decade dawned, however, it appeared that the ticket-buyers were less particular about the fictional *frissons* with which they could temporarily escape the all-too-factual horrors of Fascism and Nazism. As the viewers' "needs" changed, the movie factories reacted so that product quantity took precedence over product quality. Soon, there would never be enough time or money (a sob story for which the war effort would take the heat), creativity for its own sake

would become *passé*, and the drive for innovation would diminish; remakes, sequels, and series entries would become the genre norm.

Before all this came to pass, though, events conspired to produce *Tower of London*, a unique member of the studio's collection of thrillers. A handful of budgetary and judgmental concessions aside, the picture is a successful blend of English history (taken *cum grano salis*), political intrigue, and the studio's patented bogey baloney.

Universal didn't turn to Shakespeare for help with its English magnum opus, a decision which, given the studio's tendency to suck the literary blood of long-dead authors, goes against what we've come to view as the corporate grain. Not only was Shakespeare the original "free ride," but even the most obtuse schoolboy alive at the time associated Richard III with the Bard, and a few choice quotes might have given an air of legitimacy to Robert Lee's screenplay. Considering that his cast included a good handful of players (like Leo G. Carroll and Miles Mander) with experience at juggling Shakespeare's brilliant dialogue, Rowland Lee could have thumbed his nose at Warner Bros., whose insistence on casting either from its studio rosters or through frugally arranged trade-outs made *A Midsummer Night's Dream* seem more like *A Nightmare in Speech Class*.

Basil got the largest type, but Boris made the poster twice. Title lobby card for Universal's 1939 foray into British history, ***Tower of London***. PENTAGRAM LIBRARY.

How could it have hurt to have plopped the juicy "Now is the winter of our discontent" soliloquy into the eager mouth of Basil Rathbone? Already a seasoned Shakespearean veteran, Rathbone's facility with lyrical language and his association with the blackest of cinematic blackguards would have made the speech as natural as a foggy day in Londontown. Its inclusion could also have allowed justifiable pandering to that more intellectually oriented branch of the public which usually passed on Universal horror shows as a matter of routine.

The film was probably tagged *Tower of London* because the famed structure and its bloody history were pretty notorious, even to folk who knew little else about England or its past. Apart from something like *Mord, the Mad Executioner*, about the only other title which

would have made sense would have been *Richard III*, but that would have led most people right back to Shakespeare. Actually, *Tower of London* is a quite good title, as the dreaded redoubt is the focal point of the action throughout the picture: Henry VI (Miles Mander) et al. are stored there for less-than-safe-keeping, Mord earns his living in the keep's nether regions, and Richard does his best plotting while comfortably ensconced within its dank and rough-hewn walls.

For the most part, the movie revolves around Richard's ruthless self-maneuvering toward the throne of England. In fact, his canny schemes to remove those who stand between him and the crown are the most engaging aspects of the film. They become all the more fascinating when one realizes that, according to Shakespeare and his sources, they are the same means to the same end that the real-life Richard III had used some five centuries ago.

Robert Lee's account of the saga was the first to hit the screen if we don't count the recently rediscovered 1912 American feature-length version starring Frederick Warde, the preeminent Shakespearean interpreter of his day (in the Colonies, at least), or Frank Benson's earlier effort for Britain's Cooperative Cinematograph Company (1911). As Benson was not only the father of British Actors' Equity and the founder of the Stratford-Upon-Avon Shakespeare Festival but also Basil Rathbone's cousin, we might want to take a moment and marvel how well everything fits into the cosmic scheme of things. Benson had given his young cousin his first featured role in a Shakespearean play (Hortensio in *The Taming of the Shrew*) barely a month before his own filmed *Richard III* appeared on bedsheets throughout England. (The Benson opus had yet another interesting connection with Basil the kinsman: Dead last in the existing cast scroll of the silent adaptation is Queen Margaret, played by a Marion Rathbone.)

It's strange, but most people who like *Tower of London* (and there's a great deal there to like) do so dispassionately; they don't become involved with the characters or "get into" the situations to the extent that they do with Universal's more traditional shudderfests. This may, in part, be due to the average person's lack of familiarity with 15th century English history. Even that most faithful of expository devices, the explanatory crawl, has its task cut out for it. *Tower*'s crawl is first rate, but it's a rare viewer who can ingest enough background information in 30 seconds to carry him through 92 minutes of undiluted political intrigue.

Nor does *Tower of London* allow for much requisite audience identification. Apart from the clusters of sword-waving footsoldiers and the hundred or so rag-pickers (half of whom work for Mord!) who seem to comprise the population of London, we're up to our arses in nobles and royalty. By way of contrast, one of the main strengths of Warner Bros.' The

Adventures of Robin Hood is its depiction of the common folks' part in the action. Audiences cheered when a hundred hooded friars transformed into a hundred men of Sherwood at what was to have been Prince John's coronation; the scene still produces chills, even when squeezed onto a 21-inch TV screen. In *Robin Hood*, it's Good King Richard and his loyal English subjects against the bad, power-hungry, oppressive nobles. Identifiable sides are drawn, there being no doubt as to whom we would pay our fealty were we to be involved — and we're in there, rooting and carrying on and perched on the edges of our seats.

In *Tower of London*, we essentially remain untouched by all this jockeying for the throne because we never get any indication of how good a king this one was, or how kind and just that one was, or what possible difference having Richard on the throne rather than young Prince Edward would have made to the English people. The only evidence we receive is hearsay, and the only opinion we hear is touted by yet another interested party. How can the viewer differentiate among characters who are all alien to him? If he can't identify with anyone, then everyone becomes blurry. As Sir William Gilbert summed it up in his (and Sir Arthur Sullivan's) operetta *The Gondoliers*, "When everyone is somebody, then no one's anybody."

Henry Tudor and his pedestrian swordplay may carry the day at Bosworth Field, but the 90 minutes preceding his triumph never once escape the grasping clutches of Richard and Mord. Rathbone and Karloff have a scoundrels' field day, and their bravura performances are the nuclei of the film. The two veteran heavies (and Ian Hunter, for his Edward VI is a less obvious but no less conniving knave) relish every move in this insidious struggle for power as much as they relish each other's company and admire each other's particular skills. In an early scene, Mord confesses that Richard is more than a man or a king to him; he is almost a god. The paean is more than casually similar to an exchange between Irene Ware and Bela Lugosi in *The Raven*. That it plays rather more convincingly here is due not only to less awkward circumstances —

unlike Dr. Vollin, the crook-back forswears any pretensions to deity, much preferring an earthly crown—but also to the ability of the *Tower of London* costars to breathe life even into such unlikely dialogue.

Our first view of Richard finds him and Edward hammering away at each other with halberds. "Hard to believe they're brothers," muses a nearby soldier, impressed with the ballsy full-throttle workout by the royals. Our last glimpse of Richard also includes halberds, thrust under the armpits of his corpse as it is dragged in ignominy across the bloody stretches of Bosworth Field. In between is sandwiched one of Basil Rathbone's finest screen performances; even clad in cardboard and denied the chance to offer his kingdom for a horse, Rathbone's Richard III was worthy of everyone's serious consideration for an Academy Award. He wasn't even nominated; horror picture, you know.

With the exception of the genuine respect and admiration he has for his brother, Edward, Richard operates with clearly ulterior motives on every level he can reach. Yet despite the fact that Elyzabeth, Wyatt, and Lady Alice are not taken in by him for even a moment, Rathbone's master villain is drawn with meticulous care and fine brushstrokes, as were most of his other classic rogues. (Several of his more heroic figures, on the other hand, were laid on with a trowel.) He manages to get through the silly business of the cupboard full of dolls without breaking his tight-lipped resolve, and his ruthlessness is pocked with conflicting emotions. A nice touch (kudos to Robert Lee) has his ordering the double murder of the young princes more to break the Queen's spirit than to hasten the move of his own mannequin onto the toy throne. And, unlike Hamlet's refusal to slay Claudius while his uncle is at prayer, the thoughtful Duke has Mord assassinate the senile Henry VI in the midst of his devotions, as much for the sake of the old king's soul as for his (Richard's) own convenience.

Boris Karloff also appears to be having a hell of a good time in *Tower of London*. Imbuing Mord's daily routine with (literally) gallows humor—on his way to fling water in the face of a man dying of thirst, he takes a moment to add another heavy weight to the chest of an incipient asphyxiation victim—Boris plays his executioner as a demonic workaholic, constantly in search of new ways to bedevil the locals. Whether crushing a cute-as-a-button page under his clubfoot, threatening to tear the tongues from a pair of elderly commoners, or jiggling his iron maiden a bit so that the perforated victim within will collapse in a heap just so, Mord is the quintessential brawny heavy. Balancing all this physical exuberance, however, are a couple of wildly disparate vignettes which reveal other facets of Gloucester's crippled henchman. Creeping stealthily into the "bloody tower" to do away with the young princes, Mord reacts briefly to an unfamiliar sensation when the sleeping figure of young Prince Richard drapes his arm around the assassin's neck. The mixed thoughts and contrary feelings running through the heretofore imperturbable Mord are as vivid on Karloff's face as his shaggy eyebrows and hawksbill nose.

Earlier, a different side of the grim headsman is displayed for its comedic value. Recognizing the importance of having the solid support of the citizenry while he and his brother are off battling the troops of the newly landed Prince of Wales, Richard commissions Mord to spread the word throughout London that the "Paper Crown" King Henry has switched allegiance and now supports Edward's claim to the throne. With the measured cadence of a schoolteacher patiently droning a lesson over and over again for the benefit of his slower students, Mord leads his band of scurvy street spies in a rote rendition of "Henry is renouncing the throne...." Absurd as it may be, the scene becomes an eagerly anticipated and enormously enjoyable highlight, thanks to Boris Karloff's puckish sense of humor and Rowland Lee's perfect composition.

Just watching Ian Hunter's King Edward can make one tired, but it's a joy to see the actor chewing up a worthier and more diversified role than his ho-hum, goody-goody Richard the Lionheart over at Warners. For what it's worth, Edward is more principled than either

Richard or Clarence, but his ambition to found the staunchest of dynasties ever to occupy the English throne leads him to cut ethical corners, arrange marriages for profit, and lop off treasonous heads. By explaining away these less than forthright proclivities as part and parcel of the business of being king, Hunter not only keeps his Edward from falling into the pit with Richard, he actually makes the king seem noble. A bout of verbal sparring (and snuggling) with his spirited queen shows him to have a lovable side, as well.

As the Duke of Clarence, the young Vincent Price spends so much time squinting suspiciously through bloodshot eyes that he resembles the old José Ferrer in drag. With his character a dynastic featherweight (albeit a bounder, a drunkard, and a coward), Price has neither the right material nor enough screen time to sketch the whiny duke with other than the broadest of lines. Intolerable to just about everyone, Clarence is such a weasel that when Edward is awakened with the news of his half-brother's death, his only reactions are to order that the bell not be tolled until a decent hour and then to head back to sleep!

To hold their own against such a heady assemblage of cads, the forces of righteousness must consist of men and women of singular strength and character. Unfortunately, here they do not. Nan Grey is lovely and straightforward as Lady Alice, and Rose Hobart's Anne Neville is beautiful and semi-straightforward: she cops a plea and agrees to wed Richard, but her instinct for self-preservation is readily understandable. Everybody else is several shades of *blah*.

Barbara O'Neil has her moments as Queen Elyzabeth, but these do not include her various looks (à la Oliver Hardy) directly at the camera. Miss O'Neil handles her big scene, wherein the queen anguishes over sending little Richard (her second son, not the rock and roll legend) to the tower, with precisely the right mix of dignity, maternal concern, and downright hostility. Any good impression this might make is dashed on the rocks, though, just prior to the Battle of Bosworth Field. Caught up in the spirit of patriotic sacrifice, the queen pays tribute to her dear, dead boys with all the heartfelt emotion of a woman ordering the extra crispy at the fried chicken takeout.

And it gets worse. Basil Rathbone's son, John Rodion (Lord DeVere), is execrable; don't tell me he won the part on his own, God-given talent. G.P. Huntley's cocky Prince of Wales looks like such an inept butterball that he might as well wear a bullseye on his chain mail instead of an heraldic insignia. Ralph Forbes' Henry Tudor, spoken of throughout the film in the sort of awed tones usually reserved for the second coming of Christ, really does little more than sit pensively by the French seaside. Granted, he manages to hack his way clumsily through Richard's expert parries and thrusts at Bosworth Field, but his absence during the picture's closing moments speaks volumes as to just how important the new king is in Robert Lee's cinematic overview.

The movie's denouement centers on the marriage of John Wyatt (the immaculately coiffured John Sutton) and Lady Alice as if that were the cause for which the flower of English manhood has fought and died for 92 minutes. Such an abrupt finale is typical of Universal's horror films, which regularly saw the bogey's destruction segue into (mercifully brief) glimpses of the juveniles enjoying each other's presence, but surely a closing shot of Henry Tudor regally wielding a quill pen or sashaying about in his ermine breeches would have made a more satisfactory wrap-up for an historic saga such as this.

Both of the big battle scenes fail to impress. At least the historically challenged in the audience are tipped to which battle is which by a couple of place markers which announce Tewkesbury and Bosworth Field much in the same way a side-stage easel announced *Burns and Allen* in vaudeville. Amid all the rear-screen projection, the most memorable image of Tewkesbury is that of the hopelessly befuddled Henry VI, looking for all the world like an old man in distress searching anxiously for the gents' at the library. And one does have to wonder what happened to all of those mounted knights who paraded so proudly out through the city gates on their way to battle. During the height of the melee, we are treated to the sight of a single horse, led this way and that among the crowds of saturated extras, and this casts a pall on the already dreary proceedings for which even their speedy resolution cannot compensate.

Things are marginally better at Bosworth Field. Cardboard doesn't react as violently to fog as it does to rainfall, and the energy level evidenced here is several notches higher than the earlier conflict, if only for the presence of the hyperactive Mord. Karloff may have been elsewhere when the technical advisor was showing the lads how to wield their antique arms; otherwise it is hard to explain why Mord runs in tight circles, fervently punching people in the face with the fist which holds his mace, rather than with the mace itself. Despite the boundless energy Mord exhibits as he's finally allowed to kill in "hot blood," the deciding fall goes to the good guys after Richard takes a lucky shot from Henry Tudor, and the mad executioner is half-stabbed, half-shoved over a cliff by the sartorially impeccable Wyatt.

Tower of London may well have marked one of the first instances in which the ambitious heavy's *modus operandi* would prove as enthralling to audiences as his endgame (if not more so), but it certainly wouldn't be the last. For many, Laurence Olivier's definitive adaptation of the Shakespeare opus was the absolute last word on the subject. Sir Larry shared the screen with a carload of other actual and potential "Sirs" (including Gielgud, Richardson, and Hardwicke), and restored to the Duke of Gloucester the more pronounced disfigurement Basil Rathbone had rejected. The majority of scholarly opinion does not view Richard's deformity as pure myth, but opines that the prince was rather more a dwarf than a hunchback. Contemporary cynicism has its way where surviving portraits of a hale monarch are concerned. Nowadays, an artist expecting to collect a fee for a portrait will always tend, even if subconsciously, to flatter his subject. In bygone days, when an artist's hopes of winning an influential patronage were balanced by the very real chance of his losing his life, toning down a physical impairment or

Fortunately the young Vincent Price would go on to far greater things. *JOHN PARNUM.*

eliminating it altogether made good business sense.

Other Anglophiles found an earlier, more contemporary variation on the theme equally rewarding and easier on the psyche. Britain's Ealing Studios, site of many of what have come to be regarded as the "classic English comedies" of the fifties, successfully reworked *Richard III* into the more sardonically humorous *Kind Hearts and Coronets* (1949). The black comic masterpiece had Sir Alec Guinness, himself no slouch as a Shakespearean, impersonate no fewer than eight unfortunates who dared to separate Louis Mazzini (Dennis Price) from the title to which he aspired.

No great shakes as a horror picture and nearly requiring a scorecard to tell the dukes from the earls, *Tower of London* is still a first class piece of entertainment. The Lee brothers' historic saga-cum-melodrama is a splendid showcase for Basil Rathbone's and Boris Karloff's appreciable talents. Fans preferring *Son of Frankenstein*'s more blatant genre qualities would have to admit honestly that, by his doing the honorable thing for Bela Lugosi in this third of the Monster's adventures, Rowland Lee left the Hungarian's two costars bereft of any real characterization. By allowing the pair of British scoundrels to pool their menace and interact with greater depth, Lee makes amends for the inadvertent disparity of the earlier picture.

For the viewer with a flagon, a mutton joint, and the right predisposition, *Tower of London* is a noble way to slay some time.

Tower of London

Released November 17, 1939; 92 minutes

Cast: Basil Rathbone (Duke of Gloucester/King Richard III); Ian Hunter (King Edward IV); Boris Karloff (Mord); Barbara O'Neil (Queen Elyzabeth); Vincent Price (Duke of Clarence); Nan Grey (Lady Alice Barton); John Sutton (John Wyatt); Ernest Cossart (Tom Clink); Rose Hobart (Anne Neville); Leo G. Carroll (Hastings); Miles Mander (King Henry VI); Lionel Belmore (Beacon Chiruegeon); Ralph Forbes (Henry Tudor); G.P. Huntley (Wales); Ronald Sinclair (Boy King Edward); John Rodion (DeVere); Frances Robinson (Duchess Isobel); Donnie Dunagan (Baby Prince Richard); John Herbert-Bond (Young Prince Richard); Georgia Caine (Dowager Duchess); Walter Tetley (Chimney Sweep); Nigel de Brulier (Archbishop); C. Montague Shaw (Majordomo); Ivor Simpson (Retainer); Ernie Adams (Thirsty Prisoner); Venecia and Yvonne Severn (Princesses); Michael Mark (Servant to Henry VI); Donald Stuart (Bunch); Holmes Herbert and Charles Miller (Nobles); Louise Brian and Jean Fenwick (Ladies in Waiting); Charles Peck (Page); Reginald Barlow (Sheriff at DeVere's Execution); Robert Grieg (Father Olmstead); Jack C. Smith (Forrest); Ivo Henderson (Haberdeer); Evelyn Selbie, Denis Tankard, Dave Thursby (Beggars); Harry Cording (Tyrell); Russ Powell (Sexton/Bell Ringer); Claire Whitney (Woman); Ann Todd (One of Queen Elyzabeth's Daughters); with Murdock MacQuarrie, Ed Brady, Arthur Mulliner, Marty Faust, Caroline Cooke, Edgar Sherrod, Francis Powers, Richard Alexander, Stanley Blystone, Claude Payton

Credits: Producer and Director — Rowland V. Lee; Screenplay — Robert N. Lee; Director of Photography — George Robinson; Art Director — Jack Otterson; Associate Art Director — Richard H. Riedel; Musical Director — Charles Previn; Orchestrations — Frank Skinner (from *Son of Frankenstein*); Assistant Director — Fred Frank; Technical Advisors — Major G.O.T. Bagley and Sir Gerald Grove; Film Editor — Edward Curtiss; Set Decorator — Russell A. Gausman; Sound Supervisor — Bernard B. Brown; Makeup — Jack P. Pierce; Technician — William Hedgcock; Gowns — Vera West

APPENDIX 1:
THE SHADOW DETECTIVE SHORTS

<hr>

In and around the Great Depression, even those wonderful old pulps had to make ends meet, and a brainstorm the folks over at Street and Smith Publications had in 1930 was a real godsend. In order to buoy up sales of their *Detective Story Magazine*, the publishers created a half-hour weekly radio show, introduced by a mysterious figure called the Shadow. Initially, the programs were adaptations of *Detective Story* novellas, and the character was little more than an announcer. When Orson Welles became involved, the popularity of *The Shadow* took off; author Maxwell Grant (pen-name of Walter Gibson, a prolific writer, and like Welles, a magician) began a series of novels and short stories which endured for years. The cackling crimefighter soon received his own periodical (*The Shadow Magazine*), headed the cast lists of the radio adaptations, and made for the movies.

The year 1931 saw Grant's first novel, *The Living Shadow*, reach print, and Universal Pictures arranged the Shadow's first appearance(s) on the screen, via a series of six two-reel mystery shorts. His participation in the two-reelers, however, was a throwback, essentially limiting him to the role of narrator he had played during that first year of radio dramas. Information on this series of shorts is sketchy at best; the plot synopses are courtesy of Universal's copyright listings at the Library of Congress, and all quaint phraseology and outright grammatical mistakes are as on file. I know of no one who has actually seen any of these short films.

A Burglar to the Rescue
Released July 1931; 20 minutes

First entry in the series; original story by Herman Landon. Adaptation and direction — George Cochrane

> Conscience is a task-master no crook can escape. It is a jeering shadow even in the blackest lives.

Steve Canley, president of a small town bank, finds himself in great difficulty. He phones his sweetheart (an extravagant young actress) to meet him late at night in his office at the bank. When she arrives, he confesses that, in order to provide her with the jewels and money which she demanded, he had appropriated the bank funds. He sees no way out of his difficulties and pleads with her to go away with him immediately, suggesting that she

377

bring her jewels, and that he will take the $14,000 in cash remaining at the bank, which will help them to start life in some other community. The heartless young woman reviles him for allowing her to think that he was wealthy, and leaves him flat, threatening to expose him if he, in any way, discloses the fact that she has been at his office.

She has no sooner disappeared than he is terrified by the arrival of a man who appears to be Jack Dunning, a former cashier of the bank. Because of Canley's false testimony, Dunning had been sent up to serve a prison sentence for robbery. He tells Canley that he has escaped and has returned to the bank for the sole purpose of killing him. Canley pleads with him to spare his life, and finally agrees to give Dunning the $14,000 in the vault if he will spare him. When Dunning has disappeared with the money, Canley phones for the local police inspector. The inspector listens to Canley's story of the return of Dunning to rob the bank with little patience and accuses him of lying. Canley insists that he call the State Penitentiary to verify his story that Jack Dunning has escaped. When the inspector gets the prison, the warden tells him that Jack Dunning is still in stir, and that it is his cell-mate who has escaped. Canley finally realizes that he can cheat justice no longer, and the Shadow jeers as the handcuffs are snapped about Canley's wrists by the inspector.

Trapped

Released September 1931; 20 minutes

Original story (*The Cat's Paw*) by Ray Humphries; Adaptation by Kurt Neumann & Robert F. Hill; direction by Kurt Neumann. No relation to the Daphne Pollard short comedy, *The Cat's Paw*, released in June 1931.

When Mr. Van Moore was shot down by a burglar, detective machinery was immediately set into motion. Jack the detective, put on the assignment, brings back a pistol which the experts' testimony proves to belong to Jim Dare, a henchman of Tony Volissimo.

In an effort to get evidence, Joan, who is employed as a private detective, has gone through a fake marriage with Jim and asserts that, in this particular instance, Jim must have been framed as she had been with him at the time the murder was committed. Convinced she can prove this, she returns to Jim's apartment.

A telephone call from Tony invites her to come at once with Jim to Tony's apartment so that he can congratulate them. They have no sooner arrived than Tony, who has an eye for a pretty woman, makes advances to Joan which so infuriate Jim that a fierce argument ensues during which it develops that Joan's surmise as to the framing of Jim is correct.

Tony forces Jim to leave and then unconsciously gives his hand away by offering Joan jewels which she is confident are part of the Moore loot. While she is trying to stave off Volissimo's unwanted attentions, the closet door swings open and Jack, who has been bound and gagged, falls to the floor. Joan is horrified since she had no idea that Jack had preceded her to the apartment in an effort to get the "low down" on Volissimo. The tenseness of the situation is augmented by the arrival of detectives who promptly handcuff Volissimo — proving that the shadow of the law is ever present and cannot be violated with impunity.

Sealed Lips

Released October 1931 — 20 minutes

Original story (*Dying Lips*) by Donald Van Riper; Adaptation by Samuel Freedman; direction by Kurt Neumann. No relation to the 1941 feature of the same name which was part of the original *Shock* package.

"Crime never pays," says the Shadow Detective. "For instance, take the case of Buzz Stanwyck." Stanwyck is in love with Enid. He is intensely jealous. He suspects her of being in love with Anderson, the manager of the theater in which Enid is the cashier. He swears to get even with Anderson. Stanwyck has made Quinn, an actor on the bill, do things for him because he had something on Quinn. Quinn is a wonderful make-up artist. Stanwyck orders him to make himself up like Stanwyck and to make him, Stanwyck, look like Quinn.

Later that evening, Anderson is killed

backstage. The stage manager darts after the murderers and wounds one of them as he is getting into the car. This man is picked up later mortally wounded, but is able to whisper the name of Stanwyck to DeVine, the city detective who is working on the case. The Chief of Police and DeVine take Stanwyck to the City Hospital, where the wounded crook was taken.

They conduct Stanwyck into the ward, where the wounded man's face is entirely covered with gauze. "That's the man," exclaimed the crook. "He framed me. I thought it was going to be a hold-up. He shot Anderson." "It's a lie," cried Stanwyck. "You did it. I saw you." And right there, he busted into smithereens his beautifully built up alibi. Of course, the figure on the bed was DeVine and not the crook.

Cast: Josephine Dunn (Enid); Carl Miller (Stanwyck); Walter Miller (DeVine); E.H. Calvert (Kramer); Lew Harvey (Quinn); Willard Hall (Korwin); Robert Littlefield (Bresline); William Bailey (Anderson); Hal Price (The Watchman); Vance Carol (The Girl)

House of Mystery

Released December 1931; 20 minutes

Original story (*The House of Death*) by Judson Phillips; Adapted for the screen by Samuel Freedman, and directed by Kurt Neumann.

On a dark, stormy night, the scream of a woman was intermingled with the howl of the wind as two hunters, caught in the storm, decided to take refuge in Mr. Craig's summer cabin. Opening the door, they were horrified to encounter the body of Sharon Craig, who, to all intents and purposes, had been killed. The hunters, one of whom was a member of the district attorney's office, rushed to Mr. Craig's townhouse to break the horrifying news. The finger of suspicion was pointed at Mr. Craig's son, Douglas, and the butler, Higgins, both of whom had been acting in a peculiar manner.

Confronted with the threat of their arrest, Mr. Craig, Sr. is forced to relate to the questioners the story of his son's unfortunate marriage which reached its climax of unhappiness when an actor named Truesdale appeared in town and lured Sharon Craig, his former

sweetheart, from her husband. Discovering that they were at the cabin, Higgins, knowing that young Craig (who had become suspicious) was hunting for Truesdale, tried to warn them. By an unfortunate circumstance, Sharon fell to her death through a trap door. Wishing to save young Craig further agony, the father and butler had contrived together to have Truesdale leave town, little realizing that this procedure would throw suspicion on them all.

Cast: James Durkin (John Craig); Wilfred Lucas (Sheriff Franklin); Leland Hodgson (Phil Moore); Frank Auslin (Higgins); Geneva Mitchell (Sharon); Eddie Phillips (Truesdale); Bernard Stone (Douglas Craig)

The Circus Show-Up

Released January 1932; 20 minutes

Leslie T. White's original story was adapted by Harold Tarshis and directed by Lou Seiler.

Irene, the daredevil trapeze worker, was instantly killed through the mysterious throwing of a switch which controlled the lights in the circus tent. Because of professional jealousy which she openly admitted, May, another performer, was accused, together with her fiancé, the switch-man [*sic*], of the crime. The manager of the circus had his own ideas on the subject, particularly when Irene's little boy showed terror in his sleep and mentioned the name of Al Wallace, a former team-mate of Irene's.

On looking over old press notices, the manager found that Wallace had been implicated in various disreputable undertakings and that Irene had taken him into court because of his cruelty to her child. He arranged to have various members of the circus brought before the little boy who, in spite of his disguise, identified the sandwich-man [*sic*] as Al Wallace, who had been so neat in his arranging of the crime that the blame appeared to fit on the shoulders of May and her sweetheart.

The Red Shadow

Released January 1932; 20 minutes

Original story (*The Red Scare*) by Ronald Everson; adaptation and dialogue by Frank Bowers; directed by Mr. Neumann.

Andrew Cross, a wealthy but somewhat dissipated character, planned to dismiss his housekeeper, Olga, whom he had employed for some 20 years, since he expected to marry a young and charming woman and would no longer need her. He arranged with a man named Hamilton to have a second great Dane added to his kennels to protect a valuable necklace, which he was indiscreet enough to show to show to his servants and Hamilton before he put it away in his safe. The next morning, Cross was found murdered.

His butler, chauffeur, and housekeeper, each one under a cross-examination, admitted his murder since each felt one of the other two was guilty and wished to protect the murderer from the dire results of the crime. This made the detectives suspicious, particularly as the victim had been knifed, not shot, as all three suspects declared he had been. As Hamilton returned for his dog and approached the kennel, a detective saw him secrete [*sic*] a small package. This led to his arrest and conviction when he admitted, under duress, that he had not only murdered Cross but had stolen the necklace from the safe.

Cast: Walter Miller (Detective Fowler); Walter McGrail (Andrew Cross); Harriet Lorraine (Olga); Ernie Adams (Hamilton); Norman Stewart (The Chauffeur); Thomas McGuire (Chief Lynch); Sidney Bracey (The Butler)

APPENDIX 2:
THE RADIO MURDER MYSTERY

It's depressing to think that such a dynamic personality as the Shadow, the man who knew what evil lurked in the hearts of men, would be displaced as host of a series of two-reel shorts by someone like columnist Louis Sobol — the man who *printed* what evil lurked there — but he was. A syndicated journalist, Sobol offered his adoring public a mixture of show business fluff, gossip, and nostalgia. Much as the Shadow had done in '31 and '32, in 1933 the newspaperman provided the framework for several two-reel novelties, listed officially as "Louis Sobol shorts" and introduced by the dreary novelty song "Down Memory Lane."

Second of the Sobol shorts, *The Radio Murder Mystery* opens in the columnist's office, where we meet him and his two guests: radio actor Richard Gordon and radio announcer James Wallington. Gordon, known as "The Sherlock Holmes of the Air," regales Sobol with the tale of the murder of Theodore Anson, the elderly inventor of a deadly "war gas."

In a flashback, Anson's four servants are listening to a radio broadcast of Gordon as Holmes. They are an ungainly group: two men, two women, and all wearing enough makeup to paint a barn. Anson storms in, mid-broad-cast, and sacks the lot of them; he's warned them before about standing around, listening to the radio while he's busy upstairs, trying his damnedest to concoct more war gas. Cut to the radio station, where Wallington is congratulating Gordon on a job well done, and then back to the Anson estate; in deep shadow, someone is using an eye-dropper to load up a cigarette lighter.

At the studio microphone, chanteuse Alice Joyce is warbling "I'm a Dreamer." As she intones, "I'm a fool, but aren't we all?," Anson, who has just that moment set his cigar on fire with the fateful lighter, keels over. This being a two-reeler, there's time for only one headline: *Theodore Anson Found Mysteriously Murdered*. In a flash, three dicks are seated in the late inventor's parlor and are grilling that group of servants. When he's informed that Richard Gordon was on the radio playing Sherlock Holmes at the time of the murder, Inspector Farrell instructs another cop to "have him come down here at once." The wisdom of this unorthodox move will soon be evident.

A cut to Sobol reminds us just who the star is around here, and then — *Voila!* — we're back at the Anson mansion with Richard Gordon. Farrell clues Gordon in on what's

Cinched uncomfortably into his tweeds, Richard Gordon demonstrates why he was merely the radio Sherlock Holmes. Hearing him voice his lines in *The Radio Murder Mystery* reduces one to a state of baffled bemusement. *PHOTOFEST*.

happened—the cigar in the policeman's hand shrinks to a butt as the passage of time is cleverly handled—and the actor informs the servants that he's going to unmask Anson's murderer at that night's broadcast! At the studio, Gordon tells Wallington to await his signal; when it's given, the announcer is to turn out all the lights in the studio. Before justice can be served, however, America is treated to Peggy Healy's rendition of "Fit as a Fiddle."

Wearing a deerstalker hat and a muffler, Gordon approaches the mike. He elucidates:

> I have become personally interested in this case. This is just another case of where a perfect crime was planned, but the old saying, "Murder will out," is still infallible. This murder is what is known as an inside job. The guilt can only rest on one of four persons. I have made a careful analysis of the characteristics of these four people and have been led to conclude that the person who foully murdered Theodore Anson was...

Of course, Gordon motions for the lights, and pandemonium breaks out. A gunshot is sandwiched between a pair of screams, and a close-up of hands wiping clean a pistol (before dropping it to the floor) precedes the lights coming up again. Richard Gordon is also on the floor, but no harm has been done. Out of nowhere, the actor produces a couple of cigars, and hands one to Farrell (who takes it without a word). As rude as can be, Gordon turns on his heel and attempts to light the cigar of the man standing *behind* him. The man, whose cigar is surrounded by a beard as patently phony as a campaign promise, lets out a shriek when he sees Gordon flailing away with the deadly cigarette lighter. The bulls take the villain and his whiskers away. When asked by the awestruck Farrell how he knew, Gordon suavely replies: "The beard wasn't big enough to cover those butler's elbows!"

Finis.

Of interest only to the Baker Street Irregulars, surviving relatives of any of the picture's principals, or fanatics such as ourselves, *The Radio Murder Mystery* is as painful as it is dated. Hearing Richard Gordon mutilate "Elementary, my dear Watson" in his nasal whine is bad enough, but sitting through three songs (I spared you details on Jack Fulton's ghastly "A Boy and a Girl Were Dancing") before he gets around to "solving" this thing is *worse* than murder. Neither Frank M. Thomas, who plays the murderer, nor any of his fellow skulking servants received credit in the film itself. Leigh Lovell, the "Dr. Watson of the Air," is absent from the short; he was doubtless afoot elsewhere.

The Radio Murder Mystery

Released February 1933; 20 minutes

Credits: Producers—William Rowland, Monte Brice; Director—Monte Brice; Original Story—H.O. Kusell; Film Editor—Robert Snody; Photography—William Steiner, George Webber; Supervisor—William Rowland

BIBLIOGRAPHY

Allen, J.C. *Conrad Veidt: From* Caligari *to* Casablanca. Pacific Grove, CA: The Boxwood Press, 1987.

The American Film Institute Catalogue: Feature Films 1911–1920; 1921–1930; 1931–1940. Berkeley: University of California Press.

Anderson, Robert G. *Faces, Forms, Films: The Artistry of Lon Chaney.* New York: Castle Books, 1971.

Bansak, Edmund G. *Fearing the Dark: The Val Lewton Career.* Jefferson, NC: McFarland, 1995.

Belford, Barbara. *Bram Stoker: A Biography of the Author of Dracula.* New York: Alfred A. Knopf, 1996.

Blake, Michael F. *Lon Chaney: The Man Behind the Thousand Faces.* Vestal, NY: The Vestal Press, 1990.

_____. *A Thousand Faces: Lon Chaney's Unique Artistry in Motion Pictures.* Vestal, NY: The Vestal Press, 1995.

Bojarski, Richard. *The Films of Bela Lugosi.* Secaucus, NJ: Citadel, 1980.

_____, and Kenneth Beals. *The Films of Boris Karloff.* Secaucus, NJ: Citadel, 1974.

Brunas, Michael, John Brunas, and Tom Weaver. *Universal Horrors: The Studio's Classic Films, 1931–1946.* Jefferson, NC; McFarland, 1990.

Bucher, Felix. *Screen Series: Germany.* New York: A.S. Barnes, 1970.

Callow, Simon. *Charles Laughton: A Difficult Actor.* New York: Grove Press, 1987.

Clarens, Carlos. *An Illustrated History of the Horror Film.* New York: G.P. Putnam's Sons, 1967.

Cremer, Robert. *Lugosi: The Man Behind the Cape.* Chicago: Henry Regnery, 1976.

Curtis, James. *James Whale.* Metuchen, NJ: Scarecrow, 1982.

Drinkwater, John. *The Life and Times of Carl Laemmle.* New York: G.P. Putnam's Sons, 1931.

Druxman, Michael B. *Basil Rathbone: His Life and His Films.* New York: A.S. Barnes, 1975.

Edmonds, I.G. *Big U: Universal in the Silent Days.* New York: A.S. Barnes, 1977.

Eisner, Lotte H. *The Haunted Screen.* Berkeley: University of California Press, 1969.

_____. *Fritz Lang.* New York: Da Capo, 1976.

_____. *Murnau.* London: Secker and Warburg, 1973.

Everson, William K. *Classics of the Horror Film.* Secaucus, NJ: Citadel, 1974.

_____. *The Detective in Film.* Secaucus, NJ: Citadel, 1972.

_____. *More Classics of the Horror Film.* Secaucus, NJ: Citadel, 1986.

Eyman, Scott. *The Speed of Sound: Hollywood and the Talkie Revolution; 1926-1930.* New York: Simon and Schuster, 1997.

Fitzgerald, Michael G. *Universal Pictures: A Panoramic History in Words, Pictures, and Filmographies.* New Rochelle, NY: Arlington House, 1977.

Florescu, Radu. *In Search of Frankenstein.* Greenwich, CT: New York Graphic Society, 1975.

Franklin, Joe. *Classics of the Silent Screen.* New York: Citadel, 1959.

Gifford, Denis. *The British Film Catalogue: 1895–1985*. New York: Facts on File Publications, 1986.

_____. *Karloff: The Man, the Monster, the Movies*. New York: Curtis Books, 1973.

Halliwell, Leslie. *The Dead That Walk*. New York: The Continuum, 1988.

_____. *The Filmgoer's Companion*, 4th ed. New York: Hill and Wang, 1974.

Hanke, Ken. *Charlie Chan at the Movies: History, Filmography, and Criticism*. Jefferson, NC: McFarland, 1989.

Hardy, Phil, ed. *The Encyclopedia of Horror Movies*. New York: Harper & Row, 1986.

_____. *The Encyclopedia of Science Fiction Movies*. Minneapolis, MN: The Woodbury Press, 1986.

Heinink, Juan B., and Robert G. Dickson. *Cita en Hollywood*. Bilbao: Ediciones Mensajero, 1990.

Hernández Girbal, Florentino, and Juan B. Heinink, eds. *Los que pasaron por HOLLYWOOD*. Madrid: Verdoux, undated.

Hirschhorn, Clive. *The Universal Story*. New York: Crown, 1983.

Hurst, Richard Maurice. *Republic Studios: Between Poverty Row and the Majors*. Metuchen, NJ: Scarecrow, 1979.

Jones, Ken D., Arthur F. McClure, and Alfred E. Twomey. *Character People: The Stalwarts of the Cinema*. New York: A.S. Barnes, 1976.

Juran, Robert A. *Old Familiar Faces: The Great Character Actors and Actresses of Hollywood's Golden Era*. Sarasota, FL: Movie Memories, 1995.

Kendrick, Walter. *The Thrill of Fear: 250 Years of Scary Entertainment*. New York: Grove Press, 1991.

Kinnard, Roy. *Horror in Silent Films: A Filmography, 1896–1929*. Jefferson, NC: McFarland, 1995.

Kracauer, Siegfried. *From Caligari to Hitler: A Psychological History of the German Film*. Princeton, NJ: Princeton University Press, 1947.

Kreimeier, Klaus. *The Ufa Story: A History of Germany's Greatest Film Company, 1918–1945*. New York: Hill and Wang, 1996.

Lennig, Arthur. *The Count: The Life and Films of Bela "Dracula" Lugosi*. New York: Putnam, 1974.

Lindsay, Cynthia. *Dear Boris: The Life of William Henry Pratt a.k.a. Boris Karloff*. New York: Alfred A. Knopf, 1975.

Littman, Bill. "Dracula Espanol: The 1930 Spanish-Language Version of *Dracula*," in *Midnight Marquee* no. 37 (fall 1988). Albany, NY: Fantaco Enterprises.

Mank, Gregory William. *Hollywood Cauldron: Thirteen Horror Films from the Genre's Golden Age*. Jefferson, NC: McFarland, 1994.

_____. *It's Alive! The Classic Cinema Saga of Frankenstein*. San Diego: A.S. Barnes, 1981.

_____. *Karloff and Lugosi: The Story of a Haunting Collaboration*. Jefferson, NC: McFarland, 1990.

_____, James T. Coughlin, and Dwight D. Frye. *Dwight Frye's Last Laugh: An Authorized Biography*. Baltimore: Midnight Marquee Press, 1997.

McNally, Raymond T., and Radu Florescu. *In Search of Dracula: A True History of Dracula and Vampire Legends*. Greenwich, CT: New York Graphic Society, 1972.

Meyrink, Gustav. *The Golem*. Boston: Houghton Mifflin, 1928.

Okuda, Ted. *Grand National, Producers Releasing Corporation, and Screen Guild/Lippert: Complete Filmographies with Studio Histories*. Jefferson, NC: McFarland, 1989.

_____. *The Monogram Checklist: The Films of Monogram Pictures Corporation, 1931–1952*. Jefferson, NC: McFarland, 1987.

Perry, George. *The Complete Phantom of the Opera*. New York: Henry Holt, 1987.

Pratt, George C. *Spellbound in Darkness: A History of the Silent Film*. Greenwich, CT: New York Graphic Society, 1966.

Rainsberger, Todd. *James Wong Howe: Cinematographer*. New York: A.S. Barnes, 1981.

Rathbone, Basil. *In and Out of Character*. New York: Limelight Editions, 1991.

Rhodes, Gary Don. *Lugosi: His Life in Films, on Stage, and in the Hearts of Horror Lovers*. Jefferson, NC: McFarland, 1997.

Riley, Philip J. *The Bride of Frankenstein: Universal Filmscripts Series, Volume 2*. Absecon, NJ: MagicImage Filmbooks, 1989.

_____. *Dracula: Universal Filmscripts Series, Volume 13*. Absecon, NJ: MagicImage Filmbooks, 1990.

_____. *Frankenstein: Universal Filmscripts Series, Volume 1*. Absecon, NJ: MagicImage Filmbooks, 1989.

_____. *The Hunchback of Notre Dame: Ackerman Archives Series, Volume III*. Hollywood, CA: Magic-Image Filmbooks, 1988.

_____. *The Mummy: Universal Filmscripts Series, Volume 7*. Absecon, NJ: MagicImage Filmbooks, 1989.

_____. *Son of Frankenstein: Universal Filmscripts Series, Volume 3*. Absecon, NJ: MagicImage Film-books, 1990.

Robertson, James C. *The Casablanca Man: The Cinema of Michael Curtiz*. London: Routledge, 1993.

Sennett, Ted. *Great Movie Directors*. New York: Harry N. Abrams, 1986.

Singer, Kurt. *The Laughton Story: An Intimate Story of Charles Laughton*. Philadelphia: The John C. Winston Company, 1954.

Skal, David J. *Hollywood Gothic: The Tangled Web of* Dracula *from Novel to Stage to Screen*. New York: W.W. Norton, 1990.

_____. *The Monster Show: A Cultural History of Horror*. New York: Norton, 1993.

_____, and Elias Savada. *Dark Carnival: The Secret World of Tod Browning, Hollywood's Master of the Macabre*. New York: Anchor Books, 1995.

Svehla, Gary J., and Susan Svehla, eds. *Bela Lugosi/Midnight Marquee Actors Series*. Baltimore: Mid-night Marquee Press, 1995.

_____. *Boris Karloff/Midnight Marquee Actors Series*. Baltimore: Midnight Marquee Press, 1996.

Taves, Brian. *Robert Florey: The French Expressionist*. Metuchen, NJ: Scarecrow, 1987.

Tropp, Martin. *Mary Shelley's Monster: The Story of FRANKENSTEIN*. Boston: Houghton Mifflin, 1976.

Turner, George E., and Michael H. Price. *Forgotten Horrors: Early Talkie Chillers from Poverty Row*. New York: A.S. Barnes, 1979.

Weaver, Tom. *Poverty Row HORRORS! Monogram, PRC and Republic Horror Films of the Forties*. Jeffer-son, NC: McFarland, 1993.

Wolf, Leonard, ed. *The Essential Dracula: The Definitive Annotated Edition of Bram Stoker's Classic Novel*. New York: Plume, 1993.

Young, Jordan R. *Reel Characters: Great Movie Character Actors*. Beverly Hills, CA: Moonstone Press, 1986.

INDEX

Page numbers in **boldface** indicate photographs.

387